THE LANGUAGE OF
PSYCHO-ANALYSIS

Books by SIGMUND FREUD

AN AUTOBIOGRAPHICAL STUDY

CIVILIZATION AND ITS DISCONTENTS

THE COMPLETE INTRODUCTORY LECTURES ON PSYCHOANALYSIS

THE EGO AND THE ID

JOKES AND THEIR RELATION TO THE UNCONSCIOUS

LEONARDO DA VINCI AND A MEMORY OF HIS CHILDHOOD

NEW INTRODUCTORY LECTURES ON PSYCHOANALYSIS

ON DREAMS

ON THE HISTORY OF THE PSYCHO-ANALYTIC MOVEMENT

AN OUTLINE OF PSYCHO-ANALYSIS

THE PROBLEM OF ANXIETY

THE PSYCHOPATHOLOGY OF EVERYDAY LIFE

THE QUESTION OF LAY ANALYSIS

TOTEM AND TABOO

THE LANGUAGE OF
PSYCHO-ANALYSIS

By

J. LAPLANCHE AND J.-B. PONTALIS

Translated by
DONALD NICHOLSON-SMITH

With an Introduction by
DANIEL LAGACHE

W · W · NORTON & COMPANY · INC ·

NEW YORK

Library of Congress Cataloging in Publication Data
Laplanche, Jean.
    The language of psycho-analysis.

    Translation of Vocabulaire de la psychanalyse.
    1. Psychoanalysis—Dictionaries. 2. Freud,
Sigmund, 1856-1939. I. Pontalis, J. B., 1924-
joint author. II. Title.   DNLM: 1. Psychoanalysis—
Dictionaries. WM13 L314v 1973
RC437.L313 1974   616.8'917'03   73-18418
ISBN 0-393-01105-4

The orignal French edition of the book, written by
Jean Laplanche and J.-B. Pontalis, was published
under the title *Vocabulaire de la Psychanalyse* by
Presses Universitaires de France.

PRINTED IN THE UNITED STATES OF AMERICA

1 2 3 4 5 6 7 8 9 0

Editorial Preface

'I would not have believed ... that psychoanalysis could mean so much to someone else or that anyone would be able to read so much in my words.'

Freud's letter to Lou Andreas-Salomé, 9 Nov. 1915

Since Socrates, in European cultures one would be hard put to find a thinker and a scientist more humble, more self-questioning and more self-convinced than Sigmund Freud. From the very beginning, as his correspondence with Wilhelm Fliess testifies, Freud had no doubt that he had through an act of heroic and unique courage undertaken to understand in himself, and others, what humans had always sought to repress, mythologise, or rationalise in terms other than the truth of the experience itself. To say what he was discovering, Freud was compelled to borrow the vocabulary of the language as it existed; but Freud had to distort and extend it to yield the meanings and insights he meant it to communicate. Hence a completely new *language* gradually crystallised in Freud's hermeneutics of human epistemology. Freud himself was fully and painfully aware that in time the concepts he had so diligently created to establish a new instrument of self-discovery, would get taken over by the vulgar zeal of shallow familiarity.

What Freud in affection had attributed to Lou Andreas–Salomé, Laplanche and Pontalis have with singular devotion and industry turned into an instrument of research and discovery of what Freud's concepts really entail. It was a daunting task that they have accomplished with an authentic veracity and exactitude.

March, 1973   M. MASUD R. KHAN

Introduction

BY
DANIEL LAGACHE

THE ORIGINS AND HISTORY OF THIS WORK

Aversion to psycho-analysis sometimes takes the form of disparaging comments about its terminology. Naturally, psycho-analysts do not endorse the abuse or over-hasty use of technical words as a way of covering up woolly thinking. But psycho-analysis–like any trade or science–needs a special vocabulary of its own. It is hard to see how the novelty of the discoveries and conceptualisations of this discipline, which is a method of investigation and treatment and a theory of the normal and pathological operation of the mental apparatus, could ever have been formulated without resorting to new terms. Moreover, it is true of any scientific discovery that it takes shape not by following the dictates of common sense but by flying in the face of it. The shocking thing about psycho-analysis is less its emphasis on sexuality than its introduction of unconscious phantasy into the theory of the mental functioning of man in his struggle with the world and with himself. Now ordinary language has no words to evoke mental structures and tendencies that do not exist for common sense. It has therefore been necessary to invent a number of terms–somewhere between two and three hundred, depending on the strictness of one's reading of the texts and one's criteria of technicality. Apart from direct examination of psycho-analytical writings we have few aids in attempting to grasp the meaning of these expressions: glossaries appended to expository works, definitions proposed by the lexicons and dictionaries that have been published over the last twenty or thirty years–but, to all intents and purposes, no real specialised and complete reference work (1). The nearest approach to the present work to date is Dr Richard F. Sterba's *Handwörterbuch der Psychoanalyse*; circumstances brought the composition of this work to a halt at the letter L, and its publication at the entry '*Grössenwahn*'. 'I cannot say,' Dr Sterba has written to me, 'whether this was due to my megalomania or to Hitler's.' Dr Sterba has been kind enough to send me the five published instalments of his work, which are very hard if not impossible to find (Internationaler Psychoanalytischer Verlag, 1936–37).

A work quite different in conception may also be mentioned, an alphabetically arranged collection of Freudian texts translated into English: N. Fodor and

(1) *Translator's note:* This situation has been modified recently, with the publication, in particular, of the following works: Charles Rycroft, *A Critical Dictionary of Psychoanalysis* (London and New York, 1968); Humberto Nagera (ed.), *Basic Psychoanalytic Concepts on the Libido Theory, Basic Psychoanalytic Concepts on the Theory of Dreams, Basic Psychoanalytic Concepts on the Theory of Instincts, Basic Psychoanalytic Concepts on Metapsychology, Conflicts, Anxiety and Other Subjects* (London and New York, 1969, 1971); Burness E. Moore and Bernard D. Fine, *A Glossary of Psychoanalytic Terms and Concepts* (New York: American Psychoanalytic Association, second edition, 1968).

Introduction

F. Gaynor, *Freud: Dictionary of Psychoanalysis*, prefaced by Theodor Reik (New York: Philosophical Library, 1950).

The technical terminology of psycho-analysis is for the most part the work of Freud; its evolution proceeds in step with the elaboration of his discoveries and his thinking. By contrast with the development of classical psychopathology, Freud borrowed little from Latin and Greek. Of course he did draw from the psychology, psychopathology and neurophysiology of his time, but by and large his words and expressions come from German common usage, for Freud relied on the resources of his own language. Sometimes a faithful translation is difficult and the analytic terminology gives an esoteric impression that the original German text does not, while sometimes the resources of the translator's language are not fully exploited; in other cases, the very simplicity of Freud's wording tends to conceal its technicality. But this linguistic problem is only of secondary importance, the real difficulty lies elsewhere. His inventiveness as a writer notwithstanding, Freud showed scant interest in perfecting his vocabulary. We shall not here enumerate the types of difficulties encountered – suffice it to say that the same goes for psycho-analytic phraseology as for many another language: multiplicity of meaning and semantic overlapping are to be found, while different words may not have very different connotations.

We are fighting, then, with words – but not *for* words. Behind the words we have to find facts, ideas, and the conceptual organisation of psycho-analysis. A task made laborious both by the long and fruitful evolution of Freud's own thought and by the size of a literature which, in catalogue, already fills the nine volumes of Grinstein's bibliography. Moreover, words, like ideas (and together with ideas), are not merely created – they have a fate: they may fall into disuse or lose their currency, giving way to others which are better suited to the needs of fresh orientations in research and theory. The core of Freud's terminology has nevertheless stood the test of time: the few new departures that have been made have been assimilated without modifying its organisation or general tone. Consequently, a lexicon such as the present one cannot confine itself to definitions distinguishing between the various meanings that psycho-analytic terms have taken on: the propositions arrived at have to be backed up by a commentary complete with references and quotations.

This commentary requires an extensive perusal of the literature, it is true, but what is needed above all is knowledge of the Freudian texts themselves, for all conceptual and terminological development is undoubtedly grounded in them; and moreover the dimensions of the literature will defy the efforts of an invidual researcher or even a small team of coworkers. Next, a work of the kind envisaged cannot be based on erudition alone – it calls for specialists with first-hand knowledge of the psycho-analytic experience. At the same time, though setting our sights beyond words, on the facts and ideas that lie behind them, we must yet avoid the pitfall of producing an encyclopaedia or 'dictionary of knowledge'. Finally, the task is to take stock of usages, to see what light they cast upon one another, and to highlight the problems they raise without attempting to provide solutions. The need for actual innovation is small, limited to such things as proposing more faithful translations.

The method appropriate here is above all a historical-critical one, after the fashion of André Lalande's *Vocabulaire technique et critique de la philosophie*.

Such was our perspective when the notion of a 'vocabulary of psycho-analysis' first began taking concrete form around 1937–39. But the data assembled at that time were lost; the circumstances, other tasks, lack of documentation–all meant that the idea lay fallow if not forgotten. Our aims were not completely abandoned, however, in that a variety of projects went forward that dealt to some extent with questions of terminology. Only in 1958 was the original proposal revived; the perspective was still the historical-critical one of Lalande's *Vocabulaire*, but the *form* suggested now was somewhat modified.

After some hesitation, the demands of the task and the desire to carry it through both found an apt response in the collaboration of Jean Laplanche and J.-B. Pontalis. They were to devote almost eight years of work to consulting the psycho-analytical literature, reflecting on the basic texts, drafting, revising and polishing articles; obviously, this has been a fruitful labour, but it has also been a demanding and at times even a wearisome one. We read and discussed most of the draft articles together, and I clearly remember the liveliness of those exchanges, whose cordiality did not stop us expressing divergent opinions and adhering to the rule of uncompromising intellectual rigour. Without the pioneering effort of Laplanche and Pontalis the plan formed twenty years ago would never have been realised in this book.

During these years of labour, especially the last ones, the work's orientation has altered somewhat–a mark not of hesitance but of vitality. Thus Laplanche and Pontalis increasingly centred their research and reflection on Freud's own writings, referring readily to the earliest psycho-analytic texts including the 'Project for a Scientific Psychology' of 1895, which had only just been published (1950a). This added emphasis on the *origins* of ideas and terms has not, however, reduced the importance accorded to their vicissitudes and their range. So the present work, while it bears the personal stamp of Laplanche and Pontalis, does not betray the principles which inspired the original project.

The aim was and remains the answering of a need–a necessity felt by us, acknowledged by others, and hardly ever denied. Our wish is that it may be *useful*, serving as a work-tool for researchers and students in psycho-analysis as well as for other specialists and for the curious reader. However great the care and conscientiousness which have gone into its compilation, the informed, attentive and demanding reader will doubtless come upon gaps and errors of fact or of interpretation; if such readers communicate their criticisms these will not be set aside but warmly welcomed and studied with interest. Furthermore, neither the object, nor the content, nor the form of the work would appear to stand in the way of its translation. Comments, criticisms and translations will help fulfil a second ambition, which is that this book should become not only a tool but also a record of work in progress.

Foreword

This work deals with the chief concepts of psycho-analysis. It is based on a number of premisses:

a. Inasmuch as psycho-analysis has reshaped our view of most psychological and psychopathological phenomena, and even of man in general, an alphabetic manual aiming to cover all of its contributions might justifiably include not only libido and transference but also love and dreams, delinquency or surrealism. Our goal has been a quite different one: we have deliberately chosen to analyse the conceptual equipment of psycho-analysis–i.e. the whole set of concepts which it has gradually evolved in order to account for its own discoveries. This book deals, not with everything that psycho-analysis seeks to explain, but with the tools it uses in doing so.

b. It is now almost three-quarters of a century since psycho-analysis came into being. The psycho-analytical 'movement' has had a long and stormy history. Groups of analysts have been formed in many countries where the specificity of cultural factors could hardly have failed to exert an influence upon the actual concepts of the science. Rather than attempt to catalogue what seems, at any rate, to be a great multiplicity of usages, depending on place and time, we have sought to recapture the pristine novelty of Freud's concepts, now often obscured or lost; consequently we have paid especial attention to their *genesis*.

c. This emphasis has led us to take Sigmund Freud's pioneering work as our basic frame of reference. Any sample, any good cross-section of the massive literature of psycho-analysis clearly reveals how the great majority of its concepts originate in Freud's own writings. This then is another respect in which this book differs from works of an encyclopaedic nature.

The same concern to rediscover the fundamental conceptual contributions of psycho-analysis has meant that some authors other than Freud have had to be considered. Thus – to cite but one instance – we have included a number of concepts introduced by Melanie Klein.

d. In the area of psychopathology our choices have been governed by three principles:

(i) The definition of terms coined by psycho-analysis, whether they are still in use (e.g. *anxiety neurosis*) or not (e.g. *retention hysteria*).

(ii) The definition of terms used by psycho-analysis in a way that differs, or which may at times have differed, from the generally accepted psychiatric usage (e.g. *paranoia, paraphrenia*).

(iii) The definition of terms which, though doubtless having the same sense for psycho-analysis as for clinical psychiatry, constitute the main axes of analytic nosology (e.g. *neurosis, psychosis, perversion*). Our aim was in fact to provide at least some points of reference for readers unfamiliar with clinical psychopathology.

*   *   *

The articles are arranged in alphabetical order. In order to indicate the connections between different concepts we have adopted two conventions: an explicit cross-reference to another entry or a q.v. means that the topic under discussion is also broached – and often more thoroughly treated – in the article referred to; an asterisk indicates merely that a term or expression is itself the subject of an article. The reader is thus encouraged to identify for himself the significant links between concepts, and to find his own bearings in the associative networks of the language of psycho-analysis. We hope by this means to have avoided two pitfalls: on the one hand, the arbitrariness that threatens a purely alphabetical classification and, on the other hand, the danger of dogmatism that so often besets expositions of the hypothetical-deductive type. It should thus be possible to discover groupings, internal relationships, and 'nodal points' which differ from those upon which systematic presentations of Freud's teaching are based.

Each entry comprises a definition and a commentary. The *definition* seeks to sum up the concept's accepted meaning as it emerges from its strict usage in psycho-analytic theory. The *commentary* constitutes the critical portion and the essence of our own work. The method we have applied here might be described under three headings – historical, structural and problematic. As to the *historical*, we have sought, without restricting ourselves to a strictly chronological presentation, to indicate the origins of each concept and the chief stages in its evolution. In our opinion this search for origins is more than an academic exercise: it is striking to see how the basic concepts are illuminated, how they regain their living contours, their definition, and how the links between them become clear, once they are shown in relation to the experiences which originally brought them into being, and to the problems that have punctuated and shaped their development.

Though presented separately in the case of each concept, this historical research naturally brings us back to the history of psycho-analytic thought as a whole. Such research must therefore consider the position of each particular element *vis-à-vis* the overall *structure*. In some cases this position seems easily ascertained, and is explicitly acknowledged in the psycho-analytical literature. Often, however, similarities, differences and connections, no matter how indispensable they may be if we are to grasp a concept's originality, are merely implicit. To take some especially eloquent examples: the difference between 'Trieb' and 'Instinkt', which is vital in understanding psycho-analytic theory, is nowhere formulated by Freud. The contrast between the 'anaclitic type of object-choice' and the 'narcissistic' type, though adopted by most authors, is often considered without reference to Freud's assertion which makes its meaning clear – namely, the thesis of the 'anaclitic' dependence of the 'sexual instincts' upon the 'self-preservative' functions. The relationships between 'narcissism' and 'auto-erotism', without reference to which we can tie down neither of these notions, quickly became obscured even within Freud's work itself. Lastly, there are a number of structural phenomena which are much more disconcerting: it is not unusual in psycho-analytic theory for the function of specific concepts or groups of concepts to re-emerge at a later stage, transferred on to other components of the system. Only by offering an *interpretation* can we hope to trace certain constant structures of psycho-analytical thought and experience as they pass through transformations of this kind.

Our commentary has striven to dispel or at any rate to make plain the ambiguities of the principal notions, to expose their contradictory aspects. Usually these contradictions lead us to a *problematic* area that can be recognised in actual experience as well as on the level of terminology.

Less ambitiously, this discussion has also enabled us to air a number of purely semantic problems and to make a number of proposals designed to increase the coherence of psycho-analytical usage.

*   *   *

At the head of each entry we have listed the German (D.), Spanish (Es.), French (Fr.), Italian (I.) and Portuguese (P.) equivalents of the term in question.

Notes and references are placed at the end of each article. Notes are indicated by Greek letters, references by Arabic numerals.

Acknowledgements

We wish to thank all those who have expressed their interest in this work and contributed to its production.

The *New German–English Psycho-Analytical Vocabulary* republished by Alix Strachey in 1943 has long been for us, despite its brevity, one of the most useful of reference works. As for the *Standard Edition of the Complete Psychological Works of Sigmund Freud*, translated and published under the editorship of James Strachey, in collaboration with Anna Freud and with the assistance of Alix Strachey and Alan Tyson, there is no way of expressing our indebtedness. It must suffice to evoke the eagerness with which we awaited the appearance of each volume. Its translations, editorial commentary, critical apparatus and indexes make this great enterprise an unrivalled source of references for the scholar.

As regards the choice of foreign-language equivalents, the present work owes another debt to Dr Angel Garma, Dr Fidias R. Cesio and Dr Marie Langer for the Spanish; to Dr Elvio Fachinelli of Milan, the Italian translator of Freud, assisted by M. Michel David, Reader in French at the University of Padua, for the Italian; and to Madame Elza Ribeiro Hawelka and Dr Durval Marcondes for the Portuguese.

From beginning to end, Madame Elza Ribeiro Hawelka, Collaboratrice Technique près la Chaire de Psychologie Pathologique (Faculté des Lettres et Sciences Humaines, Paris-Sorbonne), has been a devoted assistant, indefatigable, meticulous and multilingual. A similar devotion has been shown since the Spring of 1965 by Mlle Françoise Laplanche and, since January 1966, by Mlle Évelyne Chatellier, Collaboratrice Technique at the Centre National de la Recherche Scientifique (Laboratoire de Psychologie Pathologique).

The work has thus benefited directly and, above all, indirectly from the aid of the Faculté des Lettres et Sciences Humaines, Paris-Sorbonne, and of the Centre National de la Recherche Scientifique.

We cannot omit to mention the heartening reception given to our project by our publishers at the Presses Universitaires de France, beginning in 1959. This welcome was in no way tempered even when the dimensions of the work expanded to almost double what had been planned initially.

THE LANGUAGE OF
PSYCHO-ANALYSIS

A

Abreaction

= *D.*: Abreagieren. – *Es.*: abreacción. – *Fr.*: abréaction. – *I.*: abreazione. – *P.*: ab-reação.

Emotional discharge whereby the subject liberates himself from the affect* attached to the memory of a traumatic event in such a way that this affect is not able to become (or to remain) pathogenic. Abreaction may be provoked in the course of psychotherapy, especially under hypnosis, and produce a cathartic* effect. It may also come about spontaneously, either a short or a long interval after the original trauma*.

The notion of abreaction can only be understood by reference to Freud's theory of the genesis of the hysterical symptom, as set out in his paper 'On the Psychical Mechanism of Hysterical Phenomena' (1893*a*) (1*a*, α). The persistence of the affect attached to a memory depends on several factors, of which the most important is related to the way in which the subject has reacted to a particular event. Such a *reaction* may be composed of voluntary or involuntary responses, and may range in nature from tears to acts of revenge. Where this reaction is of sufficient intensity a large part of the affect associated with the event disappears; it is when the reaction is suppressed* (*unterdrückt*) that the affect remains bound* to the memory.

Abreaction is thus the normal way for the subject to react to an event and to ensure that it does not keep too great a *quota of affect**. For the reaction to be cathartic, however, it has to be 'adequate'.

Abreaction may be spontaneous; in other words, it may come about fairly shortly after the event and prevent the memory from being so burdened with a great quota of affect that it becomes pathogenic. Alternatively, it may be secondary, precipitated by a cathartic psychotherapy which enables the patient to recall the traumatic event, to put it into words and so deliver himself from the weight of affect which has been the cause of his pathological condition. As early as 1895, in fact, Freud noted that 'language serves as a substitute for action; by its help, an affect can be "abreacted" almost as effectively' (1*b*).

A massive abreaction is not the only way for a subject to get rid of the memory of a traumatic event; the memory may be integrated into a series of associations which allows the event to be corrected – to be put in its proper place. From the *Studies on Hysteria* (1895*d*) onwards, we find Freud speaking on occasion of the actual effort of recollection and mental working out* as a process of abreaction in which the same affect is revived at the memory of each of the different events which have given rise to it (1*c*).

The effect of an absence of abreaction is the persistence of the groups of ideas* which lie at the root of neurotic symptoms; they remain unconscious and isolated from the normal course of thought: '. . . the ideas which have become

1

pathological have persisted with such freshness and affective strength because they have been denied the normal wearing-away processes by means of abreaction and reproduction in states of uninhibited association' (1*d*).

Breuer and Freud were concerned to identify the different sets of conditions which *prevent* the subject from abreacting. They felt that in certain cases these sets of conditions were related not to the nature of the event, but rather to the mental state of the subject at the moment of its occurrence: fright*, autohypnosis or hypnoid state*. Alternatively, their origin was sometimes to be found in the circumstances–usually of a social nature–which oblige the subject to restrain his reactions. A final possibility was that there were 'things which the patient wished to forget, and therefore intentionally repressed from his conscious thought and inhibited and suppressed' (1*e*). These three different sets of conditions defined the three types of hysteria: hypnoid hysteria*, retention hysteria* and defence hysteria*. It was immediately after the publication of the *Studies on Hysteria* that Freud abandoned the first two of these three types.

*   *   *

The exclusive emphasis on abreaction as the key to psychotherapeutic effectiveness is above all typical of the period in Freud's work which is known as the period of the cathartic method. Yet the notion is retained in the later theory of psycho-analytic treatment. There are empirical reasons for its survival, for every cure involves manifest emotional discharge, though to varying degrees according to the type of patient. There are theoretical reasons too, in so far as every theory of the cure must take into account *repetition** as well as *recollection*. Concepts such as *transference**, *working-through** and *acting out** all imply some reference to the theory of abreaction, even though they also lead us to more complex conceptions of treatment than the idea of a pure and simple elimination of the traumatising affect.

(α) The neologism *'abreagieren'* seems to have been coined by Freud and Breuer from the verb *reagieren* in its transitive use and the prefix *ab*-, which has several meanings, particularly distance in time, the fact of separation, diminishment, suppression etc.

(1) BREUER, J. and FREUD, S.: a) Cf. G.W., I, 81–9; S.E., II, 3–10. b) G.W., I, 87; S.E., II, 8. c) G.W., I, 223–4; S.E., II, 158. d) G.W., I, 90; S.E., II, 11. e) G.W., I, 89; S.E., II, 10.

Abstinence (Rule of)

= *D*.: Abstinenz (Grundsatz der).–*Es*.: abstinencia (regla de).–*Fr*.: abstinence (règle d').– *I*.: astinenza (regola di).–*P*.: abstinência (regra de).

Rule according to which the analytic treatment should be so organised as to ensure that the patient finds as few substitutive satisfactions for his symptoms as possible. The implication for the analyst is that he should refuse on principle to satisfy the patient's demands and to fulfil the roles which the patient tends to impose upon him. In certain cases, and at certain moments during the treatment, the rule of abstinence may be given explicit expression in the form of advice about the

patient's repetitive behaviour which is hindering the work of recollection and the working out*.

The justification for the rule of abstinence is of an essentially economic* order. The analyst must make sure that the quantities of libido released by the treatment are not immediately redirected towards a fresh cathexis of external objects; they must so far as possible be transferred into the analytic situation. The libidinal energy is thus monopolised by the transference* and deprived of any occasion for discharge other than through verbal expression.

From the dynamic* point of view, the treatment relies basically on the existence of suffering brought about by frustration – a suffering which tends to decrease as the symptoms are replaced by more satisfying substitutive behaviour. The important thing, therefore, is to maintain or to re-establish the frustration so as to assure the progress of the treatment.

Implicitly, the notion of abstinence is linked to the whole principle of the analytic method, in that interpretation* is its fundamental aim – not the gratification of the patient's libidinal demands. It should come as no surprise that when Freud tackles the question of abstinence directly, in 1915, it is apropos of a particularly pressing demand – the one inevitably associated with transference-love: 'I shall state it as a fundamental principle that the patient's need and longing should be allowed to persist in her, in order that they may serve as forces impelling her to do work and to make changes, and that we must beware of appeasing these forces by means of surrogates' (1).

It was with Ferenczi that the technical problems posed by the observance of the rule of abstinence were to come to the forefront of psycho-analytic debate. In certain cases, Freud maintained, measures should be taken which tend to drive away the surrogate satisfactions which the patient finds both within the treatment and outside it. In his concluding address to the Budapest Congress of 1918, Freud approved such measures on principle and offered a theoretical justification for them: 'Cruel though it may sound, we must see to it that the patient's suffering, to a degree that is in some way or other effective, does not come to an end prematurely. If, owing to the symptoms having been taken apart, and having lost their value, his suffering becomes mitigated, we must re-instate it elsewhere in the form of some appreciable privation' (2).

The notion of abstinence is still the subject of debate. In our opinion, it is worth while drawing a clear distinction here between abstinence as a rule to be followed by the analyst – a simple consequence of his *neutrality**-and those *active measures** which he takes in order to get the patient to abstain from certain things of his own accord. Such measures range from interpretations whose persistent repetition makes them tantamount to injunctions, to categorical prohibitions. The latter, when they are not designed to forbid the patient all sexual relations, are usually directed against specific forms of sexual activity (perversions) or specific manœuvres of a repetitive character which seem to be paralysing the work of analysis. The majority of analysts have serious reservations about recourse to active measures of this type – notably on the grounds that in this way the analyst may with justice be accused of expressing repressive authority.

3

Acting Out

(1) FREUD, S., G.W., X, 313; S.E., XII, 165.

(2) FREUD, S. 'Lines of Advance in Psycho-Analytic Therapy' (1919a [1918]), G.W., XII, 188; S.E., XVII, 163.

Acting Out

= *D.*: Agieren.–*Es.*: actuar.–*Fr.*: mise en acte; acting out.–*I.*: agire.–*P.*: agir.

According to Freud, action in which the subject, in the grip of his unconscious wishes and phantasies, relives these in the present with a sensation of immediacy which is heightened by his refusal to recognise their source and their repetitive character.

Such action generally displays an impulsive aspect relatively out of harmony with the subject's usual motivational patterns, and fairly easy to isolate from the overall trends of his activity. Acting out often takes the form of aggressive behaviour directed either at the self or at others. When it occurs in the course of analysis – whether during the actual session or not – acting out should be understood in its relationship to the transference*, and often as a basic refusal to acknowledge this transference.

'*Agieren*', a term of Latin origin which Freud uses both verbally and substantivally, is not a part of German common usage. For referring to action or acting German prefers such words as '*die Tat*', '*tun*', '*die Wirkung*', etc. Freud employs '*agieren*' transitively – as he does '*abreagieren*', which has the same root (see 'Abreaction'); its object (i.e. what is 'acted out') is instincts, phantasies, wishes, etc.

'*Agieren*' is nearly always coupled with '*erinnern*', to remember, the two being contrasting ways of bringing the past into the present.

Freud observed this contrast essentially in the context of the treatment, with the result that it is repetition in the transference that he most often refers to as 'acting out': the patient 'acts it before us, as it were, instead of reporting it to us' (1a). Acting out extends beyond the transference proper, however: 'We must be prepared to find, therefore, that the patient yields to the compulsion to repeat*, which now replaces the compulsion to remember, not only in his personal attitude to his doctor but also in every other activity and relationship which may occupy his life at the time–if, for instance, he falls in love or undertakes a task or starts an enterprise during the treatment' (2).

The term 'acting out' enshrines an ambiguity that is actually intrinsic to Freud's thinking here: he fails to distinguish the element of *actualisation* in the transference from the resort to *motor action*–which the transference (q.v.) does not necessarily entail. It is hard to see, for example, how Freud was able to go on being satisfied, as a way of accounting for repetition in the transference, with the metapsychological model of motility he had put forward as early as *The Interpretation of Dreams* (1900a): '. . . the fact of transference, as well as the psychoses, show us that [unconscious wishes] endeavour to force their way by

4

way of the preconscious system into consciousness and to obtain control of the power of movement' (3).

The confusion may be further illustrated by the following definition of acting out, offered by English and English in their *Comprehensive Dictionary of Psychological and Psychoanalytical Terms*: 'manifesting the purposive behaviour appropriate to an older situation in a new situation which symbolically represents it. Cf. *transference*, which is a form of acting out.' This definition conflicts with the most commonly held psycho-analytic view, which treats the domain of the transference and recourse to acting out as distinct if not actually opposed to one another, the latter being looked upon as an attempt to *break off* the analytic relationship.

*   *   *

From the descriptive point of view, the range of actions ordinarily classified as acting out is very wide. At one pole are violent, aggressive and criminal acts–murder, suicide, sexual assault, etc.–where the subject is deemed to proceed from an *idea* or *tendency* to the corresponding *act* (the *passage à l'acte* of French clinical psychiatry); at the other extreme we find much more subdued forms–although the impulsive aspect must still be evident: the act is ill-motivated even in the subject's own eyes, constituting a radical departure from his usual behaviour even if he rationalises it after the fact. For the psycho-analyst indications such as these betoken the *return of the repressed**. Also placed under the rubric of acting out are certain accidents which befall subjects who feel they have no part in bringing them about. Giving such a broad connotation to 'acting out' naturally makes a problem of the concept's delimitation: it has only been marked off from* other concepts forged by Freud (notably from parapraxis* and so-called repetition phenomena) in a manner which tends to be vague and to vary from one author to the next (α). Parapraxes too are sharply distinct and isolated, but–at any rate in the most prototypical form–their nature as compromise formations* is patent. By contrast, in lived-out repetition phenomena (e.g. 'fate compulsions'), the repressed contents often return in a scenario of great fidelity whose authorship the subject fails to recognise as his own.

*   *   *

One of the achievements of psycho-analysis has been to bring the occurrence of specific impulsive acts into relation with the dynamics of the treatment and the transference. This line of advance was clearly indicated by Freud when he underscored the tendency of certain patients to 'act out' the instinctual impulses aroused *during* the analytic session *outside* the consulting room. But inasmuch as Freud, as we have seen, describes even transference on to the analyst as a modality of acting out, he fails either to differentiate clearly or to show the interconnections between repetition phenomena in the transference on the one hand and manifestations of acting out on the other. The distinction he does propose is apparently meant as a solution to problems of a predominantly technical nature: the subject who acts out conflicts outside the treatment has less chance of becoming aware of their repetitive character and he is in a position, since he is free of any control or interpretation by the analyst, to satisfy his repressed instincts to the limit–i.e. to complete the act in question: 'We think it

5

most undesirable if the patient *acts* (*agiert*) outside the transference instead of remembering. The ideal conduct for our purposes would be that he should behave as normally as possible outside the treatment and express his abnormal reactions only in the transference' (1*b*).

One of the outstanding tasks of psycho-analysis is to ground the distinction between transference and acting out on criteria other than purely technical ones – or even mere considerations of locale (does something happen within the consulting room or not?). This task presupposes a reformulation of the concepts of *action* and *actualisation* and a fresh definition of the different modalities of *communication*.

Only when the relations between acting out and the analytic transference have been theoretically clarified will it be possible to see whether the structures thus exposed can be extrapolated from the frame of reference of the treatment – to decide, in other words, whether light can be shed on the impulsive acts of everyday life by linking them to relationships of the transference type.

(α) Such a demarcation has to be made if the notion of acting out is to preserve any specificity and escape assimilation into a generalised conception which does no more than point up the more or less close relationship that exists between any human project and unconscious phantasies.

(1) FREUD, S. *An Outline of Psycho-Analysis* (1940*a* [1938]): a) G.W., XVII, 101; S.E., XXIII, 176. b) G.W., XVII, 103; S.E., XXIII, 177.

(2) FREUD, S. 'Remembering, Repeating and Working-Through' (1914*g*), G.W., X, 130; S.E., XII, 151.

(3) FREUD, S., G.W., II–III, 573; S.E., V, 567.

Active Technique

= *D*.: aktive Technik.–*Es*.: técnica activa.–*Fr*.: technique active.–*I*.: tecnica attiva.–*P*.: técnica ativa.

Set of technical procedures recommended by Ferenczi: the analyst ceases to confine his action to interpretation* and formulates injunctions and prohibitions with regard to certain repetitive behaviour by the analysand, which may occur within the treatment or outside it, whenever such behaviour is procuring satisfactions for him of a kind likely to block recollection and hold up the treatment's progress.

In the history of psycho-analysis the idea of active technique and the term itself are associated with the name of Sandor Ferenczi. Ferenczi first raised the topic in connection with larval forms of masturbation which are encountered in the analysis of cases of hysteria and which it is desirable to prohibit; indeed the patient may 'attach all his pathogenic phantasies to them, short-circuit them constantly by motor discharge, and thus save himself the irksome and unpleasant task of bringing them to consciousness' (1*a*). Ferenczi stresses that recourse to prohibitions of this kind is intended solely to help get out of dead ends in the work of analysis; and he invokes the precedent set by Freud when he enjoined phobic patients, at a certain point in their analysis, to confront the phobia-producing situation (1*b*, 2).

At the 1920 Congress in The Hague, encouraged by approval from Freud, who had formulated the rule of abstinence* at the Budapest Congress the year before, Ferenczi presented an overview of his active therapy. This comprises two phases which are supposed to permit the activation and control of erotic tendencies–even where these have been sublimated. The first of these phases consists of *injunctions* designed to transform repressed instinctual impulses into a manifest satisfaction, so making them into fully conscious formations. The second one consists of *prohibitions* regarding these same formations; by this time the analyst is able to relate the activities and affects brought out by the first phase to infantile situations.

Theoretically speaking, the resort to active measures is justified as follows: in contrast to the cathartic method*, where the emergence of a memory brings on an emotional reaction, the active method, by provoking acting out* and the manifestation of the affect*, facilitates the return of the repressed*. 'It is [...] possible that certain early infantile [...] contents [...] can not be simply remembered at all, but can only be reproduced by a re-living' (3).

From a technical point of view, Ferenczi considers that one should resort to active measures only in exceptional cases, for a very limited time, solely if the transference has become a compulsion, and mainly towards the end of the treatment. Finally, he stresses that he intends no modification of the fundamental rule*: instead, the 'artifices' he suggests are meant to make it easier to observe the rule.

Later on, Ferenczi considerably broadened the scope of active measures (4). In a short work written in collaboration with Otto Rank, *The Development of Psycho-Analysis* (1924), he offers an interpretation of the progress of the treatment in terms of the libido which makes a resort to active measures (the laying down of a deadline for the ending of the treatment) a necessity, especially in the final stage (the stage of 'weaning from the libido').

Ferenczi was eventually to reverse himself on this point. His final view was that active measures considerably increase the patient's resistances; by formulating injunctions and prohibitions the analyst plays the part of a parental super-ego, or even of a schoolmaster; as for fixing a deadline for bringing the treatment to a close, the setbacks met with here show that this procedure is rarely called for, and only if the patient agrees with it and if the possibility of revoking the deadline is left open (this goes too for any active measures envisaged) (5). Ferenczi finally abandoned the promotion of active measures entirely: '. . . we must content ourselves with interpreting the patient's concealed tendencies to action and supporting his feeble attempts to overcome the neurotic inhibitions to which he had hitherto been subject, without pressing or even advising him to take violent measures. If we are patient enough, the patient will himself sooner or later come up with the question whether he should risk making some effort, for example to defy a phobic avoidance. [...] In other words, it is the patient himself who must decide the timing of activity, or at any rate give unmistakable indications that the time is ripe for it' (6).

The active technique is often contrasted with the purely expectant and passive attitude supposedly required by the analytic method. Actually this opposition is forced: for one thing, Ferenczi persistently treated the techniques he proposed as auxiliary to analysis, not as a variant form of it; and further, the analytic method itself does not rule out a certain amount of activity on the part of the analyst (questions, spacing out of the sessions, etc.), and interpretation is active inasmuch as it inevitably has an effect on the flow of associations. The hallmark of active technique is the stress it lays on *repetition** in the sense in which Freud contrasted it to *remembering*: in order to overcome the compulsion to repeat and at last make recollection possible—or at least let the treatment proceed—Ferenczi judged it needful not merely to permit but actually to encourage repetition. This is the basis of the active technique (α).

(α) For a fuller discussion of the subject the reader is referred to Glover's *Technique of Psychoanalysis* (1955) (7), which shows that the questions opened by Ferenczi are not yet resolved.

(1) FERENCZI, S. 'Technical Difficulties in the Analysis of a Case of Hysteria' (1919), in *Further Contributions*: a) 193. b) Cf. 196.
(2) Cf. FREUD, S. 'The Future Prospects of Psycho-Analytic Therapy' (1910*d*), G.W., VIII, 108–9; S.E., XI, 145.
(3) FERENCZI, S. 'The Further Development of an Active Therapy in Psycho-Analysis' (1920), in *Further Contributions*, 217.
(4) Cf. notably FERENCZI, S. 'Psycho-Analysis of Sexual Habits' (1925) and 'On Forced Phantasies' (1924), both in *Further Contributions*, cf. 259–97 and 68–77.
(5). FERENCZI, S. 'Contra-Indications to the "Active" Psycho-Analytical Technique' (1925), in *Further Contributions*, 217–30.
(6) FERENCZI, S. 'The Elasticity of Psycho-Analytic Technique' (1928), in *Final Contributions*, 96–97.
(7) Cf. Chapter IV.

Activity/Passivity

= *D*.: Aktivität/Passivität.—*Es*.: actividad/pasividad.—*Fr*.: activité/passivité.—
I.: attività/passività.—*P*.: atividade/passividade.

One of the pairs of opposites* which are fundamental to mental life. Activity and passivity are the defining characteristics of specific types of *instinctual aims**. From the genetic point of view the active-passive dichotomy is prior to the subsequent oppositions between phallic and castrated, masculine and feminine*, which eventually subsume it.

Although activity and passivity are principally seen in Freud's terms as attributes of the modalities of instinctual life, it does not follow that there is a corollary distinction to be made between active and passive instincts. On the contrary, Freud was concerned to emphasise—particularly on the occasion of his polemic with Adler (see 'Aggressive Instinct')—that *being active* was itself a defining quality of the instincts: 'Every instinct is a piece of activity; if we speak loosely of passive instincts, we can only mean instincts whose *aim* is passive' (1*a*).

Psycho-analysts may observe this passivity of the aim in the special instances of people who want to be ill-treated (masochism) or to be seen (exhibitionism). If we are to understand what is meant by passivity here, we should distinguish between two levels: the level of explicit behaviour and the level of the underlying phantasies. It is certain that the masochist's behaviour, for example, is the expression of a response to instinctual demands – in other words, it is an activity aiming to get him into a situation which provides satisfaction. Yet the final stage of this behaviour is not attained unless the subject manages to take up a position in which he is at the mercy of the other. It can be shown how, at the phantasy level, every passive position is in fact inseparable from its opposite; thus, in masochism, 'the passive ego places itself back in phantasy in its first role, which has now in fact been taken over by the extraneous subject' (1b). In a similar way it is always possible to discover the simultaneous or alternating presence, at the phantasy level, of the two poles of activity and passivity. All the same, when we are considering the type of satisfaction looked for, just as when we turn our attention to the position sought in phantasy, this complementarity must not be allowed to obscure the real measure of ineradicable attachment which may be present in the subject's fixation to an active or a passive sexual role.

As far as the development of the subject is concerned, Freud assigns an important part to the opposition of activity and passivity, which precedes two other oppositions – those between phallic and castrated and between masculinity and femininity. At the anal stage*, Freud maintains, 'the opposition between two currents, which runs through all sexual life, is already developed [...]. The *activity* is put into operation by the instinct for mastery* through the agency of the somatic musculature; the organ which, more than any other, represents the *passive* sexual aim is the erotogenic mucous membrane' (2). This does not mean that activity and passivity do not coexist during the oral phase*, but simply that they have not yet emerged as antagonistic poles.

Ruth Mack Brunswick, in her description of 'The Preoedipal Phase of the Libido Development' (1940), has this to say: 'Three great pairs of antitheses exist throughout the entire libido development, mingling, overlapping and combining, never wholly coinciding, and ultimately replacing one another. Infancy and childhood are characterised by the first two, and adolescence by the third' (3a). She shows how the child starts by being totally passive in its role towards a mother who satisfies its needs, and how, gradually, 'each bit of activity is based to some extent on an identification with the active mother' (3b).

(1) FREUD, S. 'Instincts and their Vicissitudes' (1915c): a) G.W., X, 214–15; S.E., XIV, 122. b) G.W., X, 220; S.E., XIV, 128.

(2) FREUD, S. *Three Essays on the Theory of Sexuality* (1905d), G.W., V, 99; S.E., VII, 198.

(3) BRUNSWICK, R. MACK, in *Psa. Read.*: a) 234. b) 234–45.

Actual Neurosis

= *D*.: Aktualneurose.–*Es*.: neurosis actual.–*Fr*.: névrose actuelle.–*I*.: nevrosi attuale.–
P.: neurose atual.

A type of neurosis which Freud distinguishes from the psychoneuroses*:

a. The origin of the actual neuroses is not to be found in infantile conflicts, but in the present.

b. The symptoms here, instead of being a symbolic and overdetermined form of expression, are the direct outcome of the absence or inadequacy of sexual satisfaction.

At first Freud considered that anxiety neurosis* and neurasthenia* made up the actual neuroses, but he later proposed that hypochondria should be counted among them.

The term 'actual neurosis' appears for the first time in Freud's work in 1898, when it is used to denote anxiety neurosis and neurasthenia (1*a*). The idea that these conditions were to be set apart from the other neuroses had been developed much earlier, however, during his researches into the aetiology of the neuroses, as can be seen from both the correspondence with Fliess (2) and the writings of 1894–96 (3).

a. The opposition between the actual neuroses and the psychoneuroses is essentially aetiological and pathogenic: the cause is definitely sexual in both these types of neurosis, but in the former case it must be sought in 'a disorder of [the subject's] contemporary sexual life' and not in 'important events in his past life' (4). The adjective 'actual' is therefore to be understood first and foremost in the sense of *temporal* 'actuality' (1*b*) [a sense which has largely been abandoned by modern English usage – *tr*.]. In addition, this aetiology is somatic rather than psychical: '. . . the source of excitation, the precipitating cause of the disturbance, lies in the somatic field instead of the psychical one, as is the case in hysteria and obsessional neurosis' (5). In anxiety neurosis, this precipitating cause is considered to be the non-discharge of sexual excitation, while in neurasthenia it is the incomplete satisfaction of it, as in masturbation, which is held to be responsible.

Lastly, the mechanism of symptom-formation* is taken to be somatic in the actual neuroses (as when there is a direct transformation of the excitation into anxiety); so that 'actual' connotes the absence of the mediations which are to be encountered in the symptom-formation of the psychoneuroses (displacement, condensation, etc.).

From the therapeutic standpoint, the upshot of these views is that the actual neuroses cannot be treated psycho-analytically because their symptoms do not have a meaning that can be elucidated (6).

Freud never abandons this position in respect of the actual neuroses. He puts it forward on a number of occasions, remarking that the explanation of the mechanism of symptom-formation in these cases can be left to the chemical sciences (intoxication of the sexual substances by products of the metabolism) (7).

b. There is, in Freud's view, more than an overall antithesis opposing the psychoneuroses to the actual neuroses: he attempts several times to establish a thoroughgoing isomorphism between neurasthenia and anxiety neurosis on the one hand and the various transference neuroses* on the other. When he later introduces hypochondria into the class of the actual neuroses (8), he sees it as corresponding to the paraphrenias* or narcissistic neuroses* (schizophrenia and paranoia). These parallels are not justified only by structural analogies, but also by the fact that 'a symptom of an "actual" neurosis is often the nucleus and first stage of a psychoneurotic symptom' (9). The idea that psychoneurosis is precipitated by frustration leading to the damming-up of the libido serves in effect to emphasize the presence of the 'actual' element (10).

*   *   *

The concept of actual neurosis is tending to disappear from present-day nosography. This is due to the fact that it is always possible–however important the actual factors may be as precipitating causes–to detect the symbolic expression of older conflicts in the symptoms. Which said, the idea of actual conflicts and symptoms has conserved its utility; it is an idea which calls for some comment:

a. Psycho-analytic practice brings out the necessity to distinguish between those conflicts of infantile origin which are reactualised, and those which are principally determined by an actual (present) situation: the existence of an acute actual conflict can often present an obstacle to progress in the course of the psycho-analytic treatment.

b. In every psychoneurosis a longer or shorter catalogue of symptoms will be met with, alongside those with an explicable significance, which are of the type described by Freud in the context of the actual neuroses: unjustifiable fatigue, vague pains and so on. Where the defensive conflict is preventing the fulfilment of unconscious wishes, it is conceivable that this libido which has not been satisfied is at the root of a certain number of non-specific symptoms.

c. To pursue this line of thought, it may be remarked that according to Freud's view of the matter 'actual' symptoms are chiefly somatic in character, so that the old idea of actual neurosis leads directly to the present-day conception of psychosomatic troubles.

d. As a last point, it is worth noting that it is only the lack of satisfaction of the *sexual* instincts which is taken into consideration by Freud's theory. In attempting to understand the genesis of actual and psychosomatic symptoms, we should be well advised to pay some attention too to the suppression of aggressiveness.

(1) Cf. FREUD, S. 'Sexuality in the Aetiology of the Neuroses' (1898a): a) G.W., I, 509; S.E., III, 279. b) G.W., I, 496–97; S.E., III, 267–67.

(2) Cf. FREUD, S. Fliess papers, Drafts B and E, *Anf.*, 76–82 and 98–103; S.E., I, 179–84 and 189–95.

(3) Cf. for example FREUD, S.: 'The Psychotherapy of Hysteria', in *Studies on Hysteria* (1895d); 'On the Grounds for Detaching a Particular Syndrome from Neurasthenia under the Description "Anxiety Neurosis"' (1895b); 'Heredity and the Aetiology of the Neuroses' (1896a).

(4) FREUD, S. 'Heredity and the Aetiology of the Neuroses' (1896a), G.W., I, 414; S.E., III, 149.

Adhesiveness of the Libido

(5) FREUD, S. 'On the Grounds for Detaching a Particular Syndrome from Neurasthenia under the Description "Anxiety Neurosis" ' (1895b), G.W., I, 341; S.E., III, 114.

(6) Cf. FREUD, S. 'The Psychotherapy of Hysteria', in Studies on Hysteria (1895d), G.W., I, 259; S.E., II, 261.

(7) Cf. for example FREUD, S. 'Contributions to a Discussion on Masturbation' (1912f), G.W., VIII, 337; S.E., XII, 248. And Introductory Lectures on Psycho-Analysis (1916-17), G.W., XI, 400-4; S.E., XVI, 385-89.

(8) Cf. FREUD, S. 'On Narcissism: An Introduction' (1914c), G.W., X, 149-51; S.E., XIV, 82-85.

(9) FREUD, S. Introductory Lectures on Psycho-Analysis (1916-17), G.W., XI, 405; S.E., XVI, 390.

(10) 'Types of Onset of Neurosis' (1912c), G.W., VIII, 322-30; S.E., XII, 231-38.

Adhesiveness of the Libido

= D.: Klebrigkeit der Libido.–Es. adherencia de la libido.–Fr.: viscosité de la libido.–I.: vischiosità della libido.–P.: viscosidade da libido.

Property postulated by Freud to account for the libido's variable capacity for fixation* to an object or at a stage, and for the variable facility with which it can shift its cathexes once these have become established. Adhesiveness is said to vary from individual to individual.

In Freud's writings several kindred terms are used to designate this property of the libido: *Haftbarkeit* (adhesiveness) or *Fähigkeit zur Fixierung* (susceptibility to fixation), *Zähigkeit* (pertinacity), *Klebrigkeit* (viscosity), *Trägheit* (inertia).

The last two terms in this list are those most readily called upon by Freud. It is noteworthy that words like 'viscosity' and 'adhesiveness' evoke the Freudian image of the libido as a flow of liquid. In introducing the idea of the fixation of libido in the *Three Essays on the Theory of Sexuality* (1905d), Freud assumes the existence of a factor which, taken in conjunction with an accidental experience, is able to explain the intensity of a fixation (see 'Complemental Series'): 'a psychical factor of unknown origin', 'an increased pertinacity or susceptibility to fixation' which is characteristic of 'these early impressions of sexual life' (1).

Freud maintains this view all the way through his work. There are two contexts in particular where he sets it forth:

a. On the theoretical level, when the evolution of childhood sexuality and its fixations has to be traced–notably in 'From the History of an Infantile Neurosis' (1918b [1914]): 'Any position of the libido which [the Wolf Man] had once taken up was obstinately defended by him from fear of what he would lose by giving it up and from distrust of the probability of a complete substitute being afforded by the new position that was in view. This is an important and fundamental psychological peculiarity, which I described in my *Three Essays on the Theory of Sexuality* as susceptibility to "fixation" ' (2a).

b. In the theory of the treatment, where it connotes one of the limits of therapeutic action: 'The processes which the treatment sets in motion in [certain

12

subjects] are so much slower than in other people because, apparently, they cannot make up their minds to detach libidinal cathexes from one object and displace them on to another, although we can discover no special reason for this cathectic loyalty' (3).

Freud further notes that an excessive libidinal mobility may create just the reverse problem, in which event the achievements of the treatment may be very precarious.

In the last analysis, then, how does Freud conceive of this viscosity, this susceptibility to fixation which can be a major obstacle in therapy? He sees it as in some way irreducible, as 'a prime number' (2b), an element which is unanalysable and which it is impossible to change; for the most part he defines it as a constitutional factor which the process of ageing tends to accentuate.

The adhesiveness of libido seems to bear witness to a sort of psychical inertia analogous to entropy in a physical system: in transformations of psychical energy there is apparently never any way of mobilising a whole quantity of energy that has once become fixated. It is in this sense that Freud uses the Jungian expression 'psychical inertia' on occasion, in spite of his stated reservations about the excessive explanatory value accorded this notion by Jung in his account of the aetiology of the neuroses.

(1) FREUD, S., G.W., V, 144; S.E., VII, 242.

(2) FREUD, S., a) G.W., XII, 151; S.E., XVII, 115. b) G.W., XII, 151; S.E., XVII, 116.

(3) FREUD, S. 'Analysis Terminable and Interminable' (1937c), G.W., XVI, 87; S.E., XXIII, 241.

Affect

= D.: Affekt.–Es.: afecto.–Fr.: affect.–I.: affetto.–P.: afeto.

Term borrowed by psycho-analysis from German psychological usage. It connotes any affective state, whether painful or pleasant, whether vague or well defined, and whether it is manifested in the form of a massive discharge or in the form of a general mood. According to Freud, each instinct expresses itself in terms of affect and in terms of ideas* (*Vorstellungen*). The affect is the qualitative expression of the quantity of instinctual energy and of its fluctuations.

The notion of affect takes on a great deal of importance as early as Breuer's and Freud's first research into the psychotherapy of hysteria, and their discovery of the therapeutic value of abreaction* (*Studies on Hysteria* [1895d]). The origin of the hysterical symptom, they asserted, was to be found in a traumatic event which has been met with no corresponding and proportionate discharge of affect (the affect, in other words, remains 'strangulated').

It is only when the recall of the memory brings about the revival of the affect which was originally attached to it that recollection can be effective as therapy.

Freud therefore drew the conclusion from his consideration of hysteria that

Affect

the affect is not necessarily bound* to the idea; indeed, their separation–an affect without an idea or an idea without an affect–makes them sure to follow different paths. Freud lists three possible lines of development of the affect: 'I know three mechanisms: transformation of affect (conversion hysteria), displacement of affect (obsessions) and (iii) exchange of affect (anxiety neurosis and melancholia)' (1).

From this period on, the concept of affect is applied in two different ways. At times it has a purely descriptive value, designating the emotional repercussions of an experience–usually a powerful one. Most often, however, its use presupposes a quantitative theory of cathexis–the only theory which can account for the affect's independence of its various manifestations.

Freud deals with the question systematically in his metapsychological writings –in 'Repression' (1915d) and in 'The Unconscious' (1915e). The affect is defined as the subjective transposition of the quantity of instinctual energy. Freud makes a clear distinction at this point between the subjective aspect of the affect and the energy-processes which determine it. It will be noticed that, besides the term 'affect', he makes use of the expression 'quota of affect'* (*Affektbetrag*) when wanting to place emphasis on the strictly economic aspect: thus the quota of affect 'corresponds to the instinct in so far as the latter has become detached from the idea and finds expression, proportionate to its quantity, in processes which are sensed as affects' (2a, α).

It is hard to see how the term affect could remain intelligible without some reference to self-consciousness. Freud poses the question whether it is legitimate to speak of 'unconscious affect' (3a). He rejects any parallel between the supposedly 'unconscious' affect–as in unconscious guilt feelings, for example–and unconscious ideas; and he establishes that there is a considerable difference between unconscious ideas and unconscious emotions: '. . . unconscious ideas continue to exist after repression as actual structures in the system *Ucs.*, whereas all that corresponds in that system to unconscious affects is a potential beginning which is prevented from developing' (3b) (see 'Repression' and 'Suppression').

Finally, it is worth noting that Freud formulated a genetic hypothesis intended to account for that aspect of the affect which is directly experienced. Affects, he suggests, are 'reproductions of very early, perhaps even pre-individual, experiences of vital importance' comparable to 'universal, typical and innate hysterical attacks' (4).

(α) In other passages Freud overlooks this distinction: apropos of conversion hysteria*, he does not speak of a conversion of the quota of affect determining the disappearance of the subjective affect, but simply of a 'total disappearance of the quota of affect' (2b).

(1) FREUD, S., *Anf.*, 95; S.E., I, 188.

(2) FREUD, S. 'Repression' (1915d): a) G.W., X, 255; S.E., XIV, 152. b) G.W., X, 258; S.E., XIV, 155.

(3) FREUD, S. 'The Unconscious' (1915e): a) Cf. G.W., X, 276–77; S.E., XIV, 178. (b) G.W., X, 277; S.E., XIV, 178.

(4) FREUD, S. *Inhibitions, Symptoms and Anxiety* (1926d), G.W., XIV, 163; S.E., XX, 133.

Affection (or Tenderness)

= *D.*: Zärtlichkeit.–*Es.*: ternura.–*Fr.*: tendresse.–*I.*: tenerezza.–*P.*: ternura.

In the specific sense which Freud gives to this term, it means an attitude towards the other person which, as opposed to 'sensuality' (*Sinnlichkeit*), perpetuates or reproduces the earliest mode of the child's love-relationship, where sexual pleasure is not attained independently but always stands in an anaclitic relation to the satisfaction of the instincts of self-preservation.

It was in analysing one particular type of amorous behaviour (in 'On the Universal Tendency to Debasement in the Sphere of Love' [1912*d*]) that Freud came to make a distinction between a 'sensual trend' and an 'affectionate trend' in so far as they appeared in clinical experience as separated from one another (see 'Genital Love').

Freud is less concerned with describing the manifestations of affection than with tracing its origin. This he situates in the primary object-choice of the child in its love for the person who tends and feeds it. This type of love has erotic components from the outset, but to begin with these are not separable from the satisfaction obtained from nourishment and care of the body (see 'Anaclisis').

On the other hand, the 'sensual' or, properly speaking, the sexual trend may be defined, in childhood, by the fact that erotic pleasure is at first diverted from the object laid down for it by the vital needs and becomes auto-erotic (see 'Sexuality').

During the latency period*, owing to repression, the sexual aims undergo a sort of softening effect, and this serves to reinforce the affectionate trend. With the instinctual pressure of puberty, 'the powerful "sensual" current [...] no longer mistakes its aims'. Only gradually will the sexual objects be able to 'attract to themselves the affection that was tied to earlier ones' (1).

(1) FREUD, S., G.W., VIII, 80–81; S.E., XI, 181.

Agency

= *D.*: Instanz.–*Es.*: instancia.–*Fr.*: instance.–*I.*: instanza.–*P.*: instância.

In the context of a view of the psychical apparatus* that is topographical and dynamic, one or other of the various substructures of this apparatus. Examples would be: the agency of the censorship* (first topography), the agency of the super-ego* (second topography).

Freud's different expositions of his conception of the psychical apparatus generally use the terms 'system' (*System*) and 'agency' to designate the parts or substructures of this apparatus. More rarely, we find the words 'organisation' (*Organisation*), 'formation' (*Bildung*) and 'province' (*Provinz*).

Aggression Instinct

The earliest of these terms used by Freud was 'system' (1): it referred to an essentially topographical* plan of the psyche, which was pictured as a series of devices through which excitations passed just as light passes through the different 'systems' of an optical apparatus. The term 'agency' appears for the first time in *The Interpretation of Dreams* (1900a) as a synonym for 'system' (2a); Freud was still using it in his last works (3).

Although these two terms are often used interchangeably, it is worth noting that while 'system' refers to a more exclusively topographical approach, 'agency' has both a topographical and a dynamic* meaning. Freud speaks for example of mnemic *systems* (2b), of the perception-consciousness *system*-and not, in such cases, of agencies. Conversely, he speaks more readily of agencies when dealing with the super-ego or the censorship, in that they exert a positive action and are not defined simply as the points through which excitations pass; thus the super-ego, for example, is looked upon as the heir of the 'parental agency' (4). It is further of note that when Freud introduces the term 'agency'–literally 'instance', understood in a sense, as Strachey notes, 'similar to that in which the word occurs in the phrase "a Court of the First Instance" '–he introduces it by analogy with tribunals or authorities which judge what may or may not pass (2c).

In so far as such a fine distinction is legitimate, the term 'system' is closer to the spirit of the first Freudian topography, while 'agency' is better fitted to the needs of the second model of the psychical apparatus, which is at once more structural and more dynamic.

(1) Cf. FREUD, S. *Anf.*, 373–466; S.E., I, 295.

(2) Cf. FREUD, S.: a) G.W., II–III, 542; S.E., V, 536–37. b) G.W., II–III, 544; S.E. V, 539. c) G.W., II–III, 147–50; S.E., IV, 141–45.

(3) Cf. for example FREUD, S. *An Outline of Psycho-Analysis* (1940a [1938]), G.W., XVII, 67; S.E., XXIII, 145.

(4) FREUD, S. *New Introductory Lectures on Psycho-Analysis* (1933a [1932]), G.W., XV, 68, 70; S.E., XXII, 62–64.

Aggressive Instinct

= *D.*: Aggressionstrieb.–*Es.*: instinto agresivo.–*Fr.*: pulsion d'agression.– *I.*: istinto *or* pulsione d'aggressione.–*P.*: impulso agressivo *or* pulsão agressiva, *or* de agressão.

Term used by Freud to designate the death instincts in so far as they are turned towards the outside world. The aim of the aggressive instinct is the destruction of the object.

It was Alfred Adler who introduced the idea of an aggressive instinct in 1908 (1), along with the notion of *Triebverschränkung* or 'instinctual confluence' (see 'Fusion/Defusion'). Although the analysis of 'Little Hans' had at that time just displayed the importance and extent of aggressive tendencies and behaviour, Freud declined to make these a function of a specific 'aggressive instinct': 'I cannot bring myself to assume the existence of a special aggressive instinct

16

alongside of the familiar instincts of self-preservation and sex, and on an equal footing with them' (2). The concept of an aggressive instinct, Freud felt, would tend without justification to monopolise the essential character of instinct in general (see 'Aggressiveness').

Freud's later adoption of the term '*Aggressionstrieb*', starting with *Beyond the Pleasure Principle* (1920g), comes in the context of his dualistic theory of the life and death instincts.

A textual examination of Freud's writings, though it cannot establish an absolutely unequivocal sense of this term, nor precise lines of demarcation between the death instinct*, the destructive instinct* and the aggressive instinct, does confirm that Freud rarely speaks of an aggressive instinct except in a restricted sense: for the most part, the term designates the death instincts *directed outwards*.

(1) Cf. ADLER, A. 'Der Aggressionstrieb im Leben und in der Neurose' (The aggressive instinct in life and in neurosis), in *Fortschritte der Medizin*, 1908.

(2) FREUD, S. 'Analysis of a Phobia in a Five-Year-Old Boy' (1909b), G.W., VII, 371; S.E., X, 140.

Aggressiveness (or Aggression or Aggressivity)

= *D*.: Aggression, Aggressivität.–*Es*.: agresividad.–*Fr*.: agressivité.–*I*.: aggressività.– *P*.: agressividade.

Tendency or cluster of tendencies finding expression in real or phantasy behaviour intended to harm other people, or to destroy, humiliate or constrain them, etc. Violent, destructive motor action is not the only form that aggressiveness can take: indeed there is no kind of behaviour that may not have an aggressive function, be it negative – the refusal to lend assistance, for example – or positive; be it symbolic (e.g. irony) or actually carried out. Psycho-analysis has gradually come to give great importance to aggressiveness, showing it to be at work in the early stages of the subject's development and bringing out the complicated ebb and flow of its fusion with, and defusion from, sexuality*. The culmination of this increasing stress on aggressiveness is the attempt to find a single and basic instinctual underpinning for it in the idea of the death instinct*.

There is a school of thought which holds that Freud admitted the importance of aggressiveness only at a very late point. Partisans of this view quote Freud himself in support of their claim: 'Why have we ourselves needed such a long time before we decided to recognise an aggressive instinct*? Why did we hesitate to make use, on behalf of our theory, of facts which were obvious and familiar to everyone?' (1a). These two questions, however, deserve to be treated separately; it is perfectly true that the hypothesis of an autonomous 'aggressive instinct' (proposed by Adler as early as 1908) was for a long time rejected by Freud, but it is nevertheless mistaken to suggest that psycho-analytic theory declined to take aggressive *behaviour* into account until the 'turning-point' of 1920.

17

Aggressiveness (or Aggression or Aggressivity)

It is easy to show just how aware of aggressiveness Freud was in a number of areas. In the first place, in the course of *treatment*, he had very soon encountered the aggressiveness which is the mark of *resistance**: '. . . what was to begin with such an excellent, honest fellow, becomes low, untruthful and defiant, and a malingerer – till I tell him so and thus make it possible to overcome this character' (2). In discussing the case of 'Dora' ('Fragment of an Analysis of a Case of Hysteria' [1905*c*]), Freud goes much further and treats the emergence of aggressiveness as an essential feature of the psycho-analytic treatment: under other forms of treatment, 'a patient will call up affectionate and friendly transferences to help towards his recovery [. . .]. In psycho-analysis, on the other hand, [. . .] all the patient's motives, including hostile ones, are aroused; they are then turned to account for the purposes of the analysis by being made conscious' (3). From the outset transference became evident to Freud in the form of resistance – a resistance largely due to what he was to call negative transference (see 'Transference').

Clinical experience leaves no doubt that in certain conditions, such as obsessional neurosis and paranoia, hostile tendencies are especially significant. Freud introduces the term 'ambivalence'* to denote the coexistence of love and hate – if not at the most fundamental metapsychological level, then at least in experience. It is worth recalling Freud's analysis of jokes, where he has this to say: 'Where a joke is not an aim in itself – that is, where it is not an innocent one – there are only two purposes that it may serve [. . .]. It is either a *hostile* joke (serving the purpose of aggressiveness, satire or defence) or an *obscene* joke' (4).

Freud speaks several times in this connection of 'hostile impulses' or of a 'hostile trend'. And the Oedipus complex*, from the moment of its introduction, is conceived of as a combination of loving and hostile wishes–indeed its first exposition, in *The Interpretation of Dreams* (1900*a*), comes under the heading of 'Dreams of the Death of Persons of whom the Dreamer is Fond'. Each step in the progressive elaboration of the Oedipus-complex theory represents an attempt to grasp more fully the interplay between these two kinds of wish within the various forms taken on by the complex.

The variety, range and importance of these phenomena called for an explanation consistent with the first instinct theory. Schematically, Freud's response to this demand may be said to have several tiers:

a. He declines to postulate a specific instinct to account for these aggressive tendencies and behaviour. It is his view that this would amount to an attribution to a single instinct of something which is in fact the essential characteristic of instinct in general–namely, the fact of its being an inescapable pressure which requires a certain amount of work from the psychical apparatus and which activates motricity. In this sense, if an instinct is to achieve its aims–even where these are 'passive' (to be loved, to be looked at, etc.)–an *activity* is required which may have to overcome obstacles: 'every instinct is a piece of activity' (5*a*).

b. In the first instinct theory, it will be recalled, the sexual instincts* stand opposed to the instincts of self-preservation*. The latter, generally speaking, have as their function the maintenance and affirmation of the individual's existence. In this theoretical context an explanation of behaviour or feelings as manifestly aggressive as sadism or hate, say, is sought in a complicated interplay between the two great classes of instincts. To read 'Instincts and their Vicissi-

18

tudes' (1915c) is to realise that Freud does have a metapsychological theory of aggressiveness at his disposal at this point. The apparent turning-round of love into hate is a mere illusion: hate is not a negative form of love, for it has its own genesis, which Frcud cxpounds in all its complexity, his central thesis being that 'the true prototypes of the relation of hate are derived not from sexual life, but from the ego's struggle to preserve and maintain itself' (5b).

c. Finally, in dealing with the self-preservative instincts Freud singles out the activity of assuring mastery over the object, sometimes as a function, sometimes as an autonomous instinct in its own right (see 'Instinct to Master' [*Bemächtigungstrieb*]). This concept is seemingly intended to cover an intermediate area lying between the simple *activity* intrinsic to any function and a trend towards destruction for the sake of destruction. The instinct to master is an independent instinct bound to a specific apparatus (the musculature) and to a specific developmental stage (the anal-sadistic stage*). But at the same time, 'injury or annihilation of the object is a matter of indifference' (5c) to this urge for mastery: the other person and his suffering will only be taken into consideration with the turning-round towards masochism, at which point the instinct to master can no longer be distinguished from the sexual excitation which it arouses (see 'Sadism/ Masochism').

*   *   *

In the final instinct theory aggressiveness plays a more considerable part and comes to occupy a different position.

Freud's explicit theoretical statements regarding aggressiveness are summed up by the following passage: 'A portion [of the death instinct] is placed directly in the service of the sexual function, where it has an important part to play. This is sadism proper. Another portion does not share in this transposition outwards; it remains inside the organism and, with the help of the accompanying sexual excitation [. . .], becomes libidinally bound there. It is in this position that we have to recognise the original, erotogenic masochism' (6).

Freud as a rule keeps the expression 'aggressive instinct' (*Aggressionstrieb*) for that portion of the death instinct which is directed outwards, with the help, in particular, of the muscular apparatus. It should be remembered that for Freud this aggressive instinct (in the same way perhaps as the tendency towards self-destruction) cannot be conceived of at all without envisaging its fusion with sexuality (see 'Fusion/Defusion of Instincts').

Psycho-analysts are given to conflating the opposition between life instincts and death instincts with that between sexuality and aggressiveness, and Freud himself occasionally endorsed this (1b). Such an assimilation calls, however, for a number of comments:

a. The facts invoked by Freud in *Beyond the Pleasure Principle* (1920g) to justify his introduction of the idea of the death instinct are phenomena which give expression to the repetition compulsion*–and this has no special affinity with aggressive behaviour.

b. Although it is true that certain phenomena which may be classed as aggressive become more and more significant in Freud's eyes, these are without exception representative of aggression directed against the self: the clinical manifestations of mourning and melancholia, 'unconscious guilt feelings*', the 'negative therapeutic reaction'*, etc.—such are the phenomena that bring Freud to talk of the 'mysterious masochistic trends of the ego' (7).

c. As for the notions involved here, the life instincts* (or Eros*) are certainly far more than just a new label for what has hitherto been referred to as sexuality*. Indeed Freud means for 'Eros' to connote the whole group of instincts which create or maintain organic unities, and this group must eventually include not only the sexual instincts in as much as they tend to preserve the species but also the self-preservative instincts, which aim to maintain and assert the existence of the individual.

d. Similarly, the idea of the death instinct* is not simply a generic concept designed to cover indiscriminately everything formerly designated as aggressiveness (and nothing else). As a matter of fact one part of what may be called the struggle for life certainly belongs to Eros. Conversely the death instinct may lay claim (no doubt in a more emphatic way) to that aspect of human sexuality which Freud had recognised as definitive of human *desire**: its ineradicability, persistence, unrealistic nature and—from the economic point of view—its tendency to reduce tensions to zero.

*   *   *

Exactly what revisions does the concept of aggressiveness undergo after 1920? The main changes may be summarised as follows:

a. The field in which aggressiveness is acknowledged to be at work is broadened. In the first place, the conception of a destructive instinct capable of directing itself first outwards and thence inwards once more allows the alternation of sadism and masochism to be treated as a highly complex reality which can account for many modalities of mental life. Secondly, aggressiveness is no longer evoked only in dealing with relationships with objects and with the self: it is now said to characterise relations between the different psychical agencies (notably the conflict between the super-ego and the ego).

b. By locating the original source of the death instinct in the subject's own self, by making self-aggression into the very essence of *all* aggressiveness, Freud explodes the traditional definition of aggressiveness as a mode of relation to others typified by the expression of violence towards them. It is perhaps appropriate in this context to draw attention to the contrast between some of Freud's declarations on the natural wickedness of man (8) and what is original in his own theory.

c. Lastly, does the final instinct theory permit us to draw a more specific distinction between aggressiveness and activity? Daniel Lagache has noted that 'on the face of it, the concept of activity would appear to have a much broader extension than that of aggressiveness; all biological or psychological processes are forms of activity, so that, in principle, aggressiveness only covers certain types of activity' (9). Now, in so far as Freud tends to place everything which can be called vital behaviour in the service of Eros, the question arises of what defines *aggressive* behaviour; the notion of fusion/defusion helps us to begin answering this question. For this conception does not merely imply that instincts may blend together in varying proportions—it further entails that defusion is basically a triumph for the destructive instinct, in that this instinct's objective is to break up those unities which it is up to Eros to create and maintain. From this point of view aggressiveness must certainly be seen as a radical force for disorganisation and fragmentation. Naturally these trends have been under-scored by those who–with Melanie Klein–insist upon the predominant part played by the aggressive instincts from earliest childhood onwards.

*   *   *

It will be noticed that Freud's attitude, as outlined above, runs directly counter to the sense acquired in psychology by the terms derived from the root-word 'aggression'. This is especially true of English usage: in their *Comprehensive Dictionary of Psychological and Psychoanalytical Terms*, English and English note that aggressiveness has come to be used in a much weakened manner, and has so lost all suggestion of hostility that it expresses nothing more than a 'tendency to be enterprising, energetic, active'; 'aggressivity', according to the same authority, has not lost so much of its force and remains closer to 'aggression', 'to aggress', etc. A final terminological point is that Freud's mother tongue is able to use the one term '*Aggression*' to refer to both aggressions in the sense of *acts* of aggression and aggressiveness as an inclination or state of mind. [Modern English psycho-analysis has of course followed this example: although the *Standard Edition* uses 'aggressiveness', 'aggression' is now almost universally accepted.–*tr.*]

(1) FREUD, S. *New Introductory Lectures on Psycho-Analysis* (1933a [1932]): a) G.W., XV, 110; S.E., XXII, 103. b) Cf. G.W., XV, 109 *ff*; S.E., XXII, 103 *ff*.

(2) FREUD, S., letter to Fliess dated October 27, 1897, *Anf.*, 241; S.E., I, 266.

(3) FREUD, S., G.W., V, 281; S.E., VII, 117.

(4) FREUD, S. *Jokes and their Relation to the Unconscious* (1905c), G.W., VI, 105; S.E., VIII, 96–97.

(5) FREUD, S. 'Instincts and their Vicissitudes' (1915c): a) G.W., X, 214; S.E., XIV, 122. b) G.W., X, 230; S.E., XIV, 138. c) G.W., X, 231; S.E., XIV, 139.

(6) FREUD, S. 'The Economic Problem of Masochism' (1924c), G.W., XIII, 376; S.E., XIX, 163–64.

(7) FREUD, S., G.W., XIII, 11; S.E., XVIII, 14.

(8) Cf. FREUD, S. *Civilization and its Discontents* (1930a).

(9) LAGACHE, D. 'Situation de l'agressivité', *Bul. Psycho.*, 1960, XIV, 1, 99–112.

Aim of the Instinct, Instinctual Aim

= *D.*: Triebziel.–*Es.*: hito *or* meta instinual.–*Fr.*: but pulsionnel.–
I.: meta istintuale *or* pulsionale.–*P.*: alvo *or* meta impulsor(a) *or* pulsional.

Activity to further which the instinct exerts pressure and whose outcome is a resolution of internal tension; such activity is sustained and orientated by phantasies*.

The notion of the instinctual aim is bound up with Freud's analysis of the concept of instinct under its different aspects: pressure*, source*, aim, object* (1a, 2a).

Aim of the Instinct, Instinctual Aim

In a broad sense, the term 'instinctual aim' might be said to be unambiguous: the aim in all cases is satisfaction – that is to say, according to Freud's economic conception, a non-qualitative discharge of energy regulated by the 'principle of constancy'*. Yet even when he speaks of the instinct's 'final aim' (*Endziel*), Freud is referring to a specific aim tied to a specific instinct (2*b*). Such a final aim may itself be reached via means (or 'intermediate aims') that are more or less interchangeable; but Freud asserted the thesis of the specificity of aim of each component instinct* as early as the *Three Essays on the Theory of Sexuality* (1905*d*): 'The sexual aim of the infantile instinct consists in obtaining satisfaction by means of an appropriate stimulation of the erotogenic zone* that has been selected in one way or another' (1*b*). This idea seems to stem from the 'Project for a Scientific Psychology' (1950*a* [1895]), where it appears in the form of the 'specific action'* which is alone capable of eliminating the internal tension. It is reiterated even more explicitly in the 1915 edition of the *Three Essays*: 'What distinguishes the instincts from one another and endows them with specific qualities is their relation to their somatic sources and to their aims' (1*c*).

By the same token these passages posit a close link between the aim and the source, which is generally represented by an erotogenic zone: in infantile sexuality, the 'sexual aim is dominated by an erotogenic zone' (1*d*). Or again: 'The aim which each of [the sexual instincts] strives for is the attainment of "organ-pleasure"* (*Organlust*)' (2*c*). Thus the aim corresponding to the oral instinct would be the satisfaction associated with the activity of sucking. Conversely, it is through the instinctual aim that we can get to know the instinctual source, in the sense of the organic process which occurs in the erotogenic organ: 'Although instincts are wholly determined by their origin in a somatic source, in mental life we know them only by their aims. [. . .] Sometimes [the source of the instinct] may be inferred from its aims' (2*d*).

The source is thus seen as the *ratio essendi* of the aim, and the aim as the *ratio cognoscendi* of the source. How are we to reconcile this strict reciprocal determination with the existence of those 'deviations in respect of the sexual aim' to which Freud devotes a whole chapter of the *Three Essays*? Freud's goal in this section is to demonstrate – against the popular view – that sexuality* covers a field very much wider than the adult sexual act which is usually looked upon as normal – i.e. limited to a sole source, namely the genital apparatus, and to a sole aim, namely 'sexual union, or at all events actions leading in that direction' (1*e*). The 'deviations' Freud lists are not modifications in the aim of one particular component instinct, but rather the varieties of sexual aims that are possible. These fall under two heads: they are either aims linked to *sources* – to erotogenic zones – other than the genital region (e.g. kissing, which is linked to the oral zone); or else they are modifications of the sexual act consequent upon a displacement of *object*. (Thus although Freud places fetishism among the 'deviations in respect of the aim', he concedes that it is in fact essentially a 'deviation in respect of the object' (1*f*).)

In 'Instincts and their Vicissitudes' (1915*c*) the angle of approach is a very different one. Freud's concern now is not to draw up an inventory of the variants of the sexual aim in general but to show instead how the aim of *one specific component instinct* can be transformed. With this as his perspective, Freud is led to draw a distinction between the auto-erotic instincts and those instincts which are directed towards the object from the start (sadism* and the 'scopophilic instinct'). For the former, 'the part played by the organic source is so decisive that, according to a plausible suggestion of Federn and Jekels, the form and function of the organ determine the activity or passivity of the instinctual aim' (2e). Only for the second type of instinct is that modification of the aim known as 'reversal into the opposite'* possible (reversal of sadism into masochism and of voyeurism into exhibitionism); but it should be pointed out that this change of aim is once again closely tied to a change of object—namely, the process of 'turning round upon the subject's own self'* (2f).

In sublimation*, the modification of the instinct consists essentially in a change of aim; yet here too this change is conditioned by a transformation of the instinct's other elements; the object is exchanged, and one instinct is supplanted by another (the replacement being an instinct of self-preservation with which the sexual instinct has been operating in anaclisis*) (1g, 2g).

Plainly, if we confine ourselves to the categories of which the Freudian theory makes explicit use, the notion of the aim must remain in a no-man's-land between the notions of the *source* and the *object* of the instinct. Defined in terms of its close link with the organic source, the instinctual aim takes on a very clear-cut but somewhat feeble meaning: the aim is sucking in the case of the mouth, vision in that of the eye, 'mastery'* in that of the muscular apparatus, etc. On the other hand, if each type of sexual activity is viewed–as the evolution of psycho-analytic theory encourages us to do–in its relation with the type of object striven after, then the notion of instinctual aim will tend to give way to that of 'object-relationship'*.

*   *   *

No doubt a clearer light will be thrown on the problems besetting the idea of the instinctual aim in Freud's work once the ambiguities in his concept of instinct itself have been brought out. For Freud places the sexual *instinct* and the *instinct* of self-preservation in the same category in spite of the fact that his whole theory of sexuality points to the profound differences which separate them in their functioning and–precisely–in their *aims*, i.e. in the path each of them follows to satisfaction.

The aim of a self-preservative instinct can only be conceived as a specific action* which puts an end to a state of tension provoked by need, which can be located in a particular somatic apparatus, and which naturally requires the carrying out of an actual task (e.g. the provision of food). The aim of the sexual instinct, by contrast, is far harder to characterise. Indeed, precisely because this instinct is at first bound up, in anaclisis, with the self-preservative function, and only comes into its own by breaking this bond, it attains satisfaction through an activity which, though it bears the stamp of the vital function that has been its support, is nonetheless deviant, and profoundly perverted, relative to it. This rift becomes the point of emergence of a phantasy-activity that may involve ideational elements often very far removed from the corporeal prototype (see 'Auto-Erotism', 'Anaclisis', 'Instinct', 'Sexuality').

(1) FREUD, S. *Three Essays on the Theory of Sexuality* (1905d): a) Cf. G.W., V, 34; S.E., VII, 135–36. b) G.W., V, 85; S.E., VII, 184. c) G.W., V, 67; S.E., VII, 168. d) G.W., V, 83;

S.E., VII, 182–83. e) G.W., V, 33; S.E., VII, 135. f) Cf. G.W., V, 52; S.E., VII, 153. g)Cf. G.W., V, 107; S.E., VII, 205–6.

(2) FREUD, S. 'Instincts and their Vicissitudes' (1915c): a) Cf. G.W., X, 214; S.E., XIV, 121. b) Cf. G.W., X, 215; S.E., XIV, 122. c) G.W., X, 218; S.E., XIV, 125–26. d) G.W., X, 216; S.E., XIV, 123. e) G.W., X, 225; S.E., XIV, 132–33. f) G.W., X, 220; S.E., XIV .127, g) Cf. G.W., X, 219; S.E., XIV, 125–26.

Aim-Inhibited

= *D*.: zielgehemmt.–*Es*.: coartado *or* inhibido en su meta.–*Fr*.: inhibé quant au but.– *I*.: inibito nella meta.–*P*.: inibido quanto ao alvo *or* à meta.

Qualifies an instinct which as a result of either external or internal obstacles fails to achieve its direct mode of satisfaction (or aim), but which obtains an attenuated satisfaction from activities or relationships that may be considered as approximations more or less far-removed from the original aim.

It is especially in order to account for the origin of feelings of affection (q.v.) or social feelings that Freud uses the concept of aim-inhibition. He himself points out the difficulty encountered in attempting to make such an account a rigorous one from the metapsychological point of view (1). How is such inhibition to be understood? Does it imply a repression of the original aim* and a return of the repressed*? And how does it stand in relation to sublimation (q.v.)? As regards this last question Freud appears to consider that inhibition is a sort of incipient sublimation, but he is nonetheless at pains to distinguish the two processes: 'The social instincts belong to a class of instinctual impulses which need not be described as sublimated, though they are closely related to these. They have not abandoned their directly sexual aims, but they are held back by internal resist-ances from attaining them; they rest content with certain approximations to satisfaction and for that very reason lead to especially firm and permanent attachments between human beings. To this class belong in particular the affectionate relations between parents and children, which were originally fully sexual, feelings of friendship, and the emotional ties in marriage which had their origin in sexual attraction' (2).

(1) Cf. FREUD, S. *Group Psychology and the Analysis of the Ego* (1921c), G.W., XIII, 155; S.E., XVIII, 138–39.

(2) FREUD, S. 'Two Encyclopaedia Articles' (1923a [1922]), G.W., XIII, 232; S.E., XVIII, 258.

Allo-Erotism

= *D.*: Alloerotismus.–*Es.*: aloerotismo.–*Fr.*: allo-érotisme.–*I.*: alloerotismo.–
P.: alo-erotismo.

**Term occasionally used as the opposite of 'auto-erotism': sexual activity which
finds satisfaction through an external object.**

When Freud used the term 'auto-erotism' (q.v.) for the first time, in 1899, he
coupled it with 'allo-erotism'–itself subdivisible into 'homo-erotism' (satisfaction attained by means of an object of the same sex: homosexuality) and 'hetero-
erotism' (satisfaction attained by means of an object of the opposite sex:
heterosexuality) (1). Though little used, this term was adopted, notably, by
Ernest Jones.

(1) Cf. FREUD, S., *Anf.*, 324; S.E., I, 280.

Alteration of the Ego

= *D.*: Ichveränderung.–*Es.*: alteración del yo.–*Fr.*: altération du moi.–
I.: modificazione dell' io.–*P.*: alteração do ego.

**All those restrictions and anachronistic attitudes which the ego adopts in the course
of the various stages of the defensive conflict, and which have an unfavourable
effect on its ability to adapt.**

This expression occurs at the very beginning and at the very end of Freud's work,
in two rather different contexts.

In 'Further Remarks on the Neuro-Psychoses of Defence' (1896*b*), Freud
draws a distinction, apropos of paranoia, between delusions as the return of the
repressed* and a secondary type, interpretative delusions, also known as
'combinatory' and (elsewhere) as 'assimilatory' delusions. Such delusions are
said to be the mark of an adaptation of the ego to the delusional idea: the
paranoic's final state of delusion is the outcome of an attempt to reduce the
contradictions between the *primary* delusional idea and the logical functioning
of thought.

'Analysis Terminable and Interminable' (1937c) makes a relatively systematic
approach to what had been 'so indefinitely termed an "alteration of the ego" '
(1*a*).

As an extension of Anna Freud's recently published work on the mechanisms
of defence (1936), Freud shows how such mechanisms, originally set up to deal
with specific internal dangers, may eventually become 'fixated in the ego',
constituting 'regular modes of reaction of [the subject's] character' (1*b*)
which he will repeat throughout his life, using them like obsolete institutions
even after the initial threat has vanished. Once ensconced, such defensive habits

Ambivalence

result in 'distortions' (*Verrenkungen*) and 'restrictions' (*Einschränkungen*). The work of therapy shows them up particularly clearly: a resistance* is encountered which militates against the uncovering of resistances.

The alteration of the ego, however, should be compared rather to those behaviour patterns which–as the ethologists have shown on the basis of instinctual behaviour–can operate *in vacuo*, as it were, and which may even create motivating situations for themselves artificially: the ego 'finds itself compelled to seek out those situations in reality which can serve as an approximate substitute for the original danger' (1c). What Freud has in mind here is something other than the direct effects of the defensive conflict upon the ego (the symptom itself could be considered as a modification of the ego–as a foreign body within it; reaction-formation* also modifies the ego).

These two texts in which Freud speaks of alteration of the ego have more than one aspect in common. In both instances such alteration is conceived of as secondary, as removed from the conflict and from whatever bears the stamp of the unconscious. Viewed in this light, it would seem to pose a particular obstacle to cure, in that the elucidation of the conflict can have little effect on modifications which affect the ego in an irreversible fashion, and which have been likened to 'lesional troubles of the organism' (2). Further, the reference to psychosis which is central to the earlier of these two texts is also to be found in the second: the ego of every human being, says Freud, 'approximates to that of the psychotic in some part or other and to a greater or lesser extent' (1d).

(1) FREUD, S.: a) G.W., XVI, 80; S.E., XXIII, 235. b) G.W., XVI, 83; S.E., XXIII, 237. c) G.W., XVI, 83; S.E., XXIII, 238. d) G.W., XVI, 80; S.E., XXIII, 235.

(2) Cf. NACHT, S. 'Causes et mécanismes des déformations névrotiques du moi', *R.F.P.*, 1958, 2, 199–200.

Ambivalence

= *D*.: Ambivalenz.–*Es*.: ambivalencia.–*Fr*.: ambivalence.–*I*.: ambivalenza.–*P*.: ambivalência.

The simultaneous existence of contradictory tendencies, attitudes or feelings in the relationship to a single object – especially the coexistence of love and hate.

The term of ambivalence was borrowed by Freud from Bleuler, who introduced it (1). Bleuler had considered ambivalence under three heads: first, ambivalence of the will (*Ambitendenz*), as when the subject wants to eat and not to eat at the same time; secondly, intellectual ambivalence, involving simultaneous adherence to contradictory propositions; and lastly, affective ambivalence, in which a single impulse contains both love and hate for the same person.

Bleuler treats ambivalence as a major symptom of schizophrenia (2), but he acknowledges its existence in normal subjects.

The novelty of the notion of ambivalence as compared to earlier evocations of the complexity of the emotions and the fluctuations of attitudes consists on the

26

one hand in the maintenance of an opposition of the yes/no type, wherein affirmation and negation are simultaneous and inseparable; and, on the other hand, in the acknowledgement that this basic opposition is to be found in different sectors of mental life. Bleuler eventually gives pride of place to ambivalence of feeling, however, and this emphasis is inherited by the Freudian usage.

The term makes its first appearance in Freud's work in 'The Dynamics of Transference' (1912*b*), where it is used to account for the phenomenon of negative transference: '. . . it is found side by side with the affectionate transference, often directed simultaneously towards the same person. [. . .] Ambivalence in the emotional trends (*Gefühlsrichtungen*) of neurotics is the best explanation of their ability to enlist their transferences in the service of resistance' (3). The idea of a conjunction of love and hate, however, can be found earlier, as for example in the analyses of 'Little Hans' (4) and the 'Rat Man': 'A battle between love and hate was raging in the lover's breast, and the object of both these feelings was one and the same person' (5).

In 'Instincts and their Vicissitudes' (1915*c*), Freud uses Bleuler's term apropos of the activity/passivity* opposition, to express the fact that, when we consider the active instinctual impulse, 'its (passive) opposite may be observed alongside of it' (6*a*). But this very extended meaning of 'ambivalence' is rare, and even in the same text it is the 'material' opposition between love and hate directed towards a single object which is able to exemplify ambivalence most clearly.

Ambivalence is exhibited above all in certain pathological conditions (psychoses, obsessional neurosis) and in certain states of mind such as jealousy and mourning. It is characteristic of certain phases of libidinal development in which love and destructive tendencies towards the object are to be found alongside each other: namely, the oral-sadistic* and anal-sadistic* stages.

It is in this sense that the concept is developed by Karl Abraham into a genetic category, able to serve as a criterion for determining the particular object-relationship* which corresponds to each stage. The primary oral stage is described as pre-ambivalent: 'Sucking at the breast is certainly an incorporation, but it is one which does not put an end to the existence of the object' (7). Ambivalence only comes into play for Abraham with the cannibalistic*, oral-sadistic stage, which brings with it a hostility towards the object. The individual next learns to spare the object, to save it from destruction, before passing into the genital (postambivalent) stage in which ambivalence can at last be overcome. In the work of Melanie Klein, which is closely related to Abraham's, the notion of ambivalence is central. For her, the instinct is ambivalent from the start: 'love' for the object is inseparable from its destruction, so that ambivalence becomes a quality of the object itself. As such an ambivalent object, perfectly benevolent and fundamentally hostile at one and the same time, would be intolerable, the subject struggles against his predicament by splitting it into a 'good' and a 'bad' object*.

*　　*　　*

Ambivalence

Psycho-analysis has often used 'ambivalence' in a very broad sense. The term has thus come at times to mean the actions and feelings resulting from a defensive conflict in which incompatible motives are involved; considering that in such cases what is pleasurable for one agency is unpleasurable for another, one might categorise every 'compromise-formation'* as ambivalent. The danger of such a procedure is that the concept may come, in a vague way, to connote all kinds of conflict-ridden attitudes. If the term is to keep all the descriptive–and even symptomatic–value that it originally possessed, it is advisable to have recourse to it only in the analysis of specific conflicts in which the positive and negative components of the emotional attitude are simultaneously in evidence and inseparable, and where they constitute a non-dialectical opposition which the subject, saying 'yes' and 'no' at the same time, is incapable of transcending.

Are we obliged, in the last analysis, to bow to the imperative of the Freudian theory of the instincts, and postulate a basic dualism in order to account for ambivalence? If we do so, the ambivalence of love and hate can then be understood in terms of the development peculiar to each of them: hate has its origin in the instincts of self-preservation ('the true prototypes of the relation of hate are derived [. . .] from the ego's struggle to preserve and maintain itself' (6b)); while love for its part originates in the sexual instincts. The opposition between life instincts* and death instincts* encountered in Freud's second theory tends to root ambivalence even more firmly in an instinctual dualism (see 'Fusion/Defusion').

It should be remembered that at the end of his work Freud tends to lend an increased significance to ambivalence in the treatment and the theory of the conflict. Oedipal conflict, in its instinctual roots, is conceived of as a conflict of ambivalence (*Ambivalenz Konflikt*), one of whose principal dimensions is 'a well-grounded love and a no less justifiable hatred towards one and the same person' (8). This approach treats the formation of neurotic symptoms as the attempt to provide a solution to such a conflict: thus phobia displaces one of the components–hate–towards a substitute object, while obsessional neurosis tries to repress the hostile impulse with a reinforcement of the libidinal one, by way of a reaction-formation*. This is a new way, in Freud's theory, of looking at conflict, and it is significant in that it anchors defensive conflict in the instinctual dynamic; also in that it encourages us to seek the contradiction which are inherent to instinctual life behind the defensive conflict, in so far as the latter sets in motion the agencies of the psychical apparatus.

(1) Cf. BLEULER, E. 'Vortrag über Ambivalenz' (1910), *Zentralblatt für Psychoanalyse*, I, 266.

(2) Cf. BLEULER, E. *Dementia praecox oder Gruppe der Schizophrenien* (Leipzig and Vienna, 1911). Trans.: *Dementia Praecox or the Group of Schizophrenias* (New York: I.U.P., 1950).

(3) FREUD, S., G.W., VIII, 372–73; S.E., XII, 106–7.

(4) Cf. FREUD, S. 'Analysis of a Phobia in a Five-Year-Old Boy' (1909b), G.W., VII, 243–377; S.E., X, 5–149.

(5) FREUD, S. 'Notes upon a Case of Obsessional Neurosis' (1909d), G.W., VII, 413; S.E., X, 191.

(6) FREUD, S. 'Instincts and their Vicissitudes' (1915c): a) G.W., X, 223–24; S.E., XIV, 131. b) G.W., X, 230; S.E., XIV, 138.

(7) ABRAHAM, K. 'A Short Study of the Development of the Libido, Viewed in the Light of Mental Disorders' (1924), in his *Selected Papers* (London: Hogarth Press, 1927), 450.

(8) FREUD, S. *Inhibitions, Symptoms and Anxiety* (1926d), G.W., XIV, 130; S.E., XX, 102.

Ambivalent; Pre-Ambivalent; Post-Ambivalent

= *D*.: ambivalent; prä-ambivalent; post-ambivalent. –
Es.: ambivalente; preambivalente; postambivalente. –
Fr.: ambivalent: préambivalent; postambivalent. –
I.: ambivalente; preambivalente; postambivalente. –
P.: ambivalente; pré-ambivalente; pós-ambivalente.

Terms introduced by Karl Abraham to qualify the evolution of the libidinal stages* viewed in the light of object-relationships*. The oral stage* in its first (sucking) phase is described as pre-ambivalent; ambivalence arises in the second (biting) phase, comes to a peak in the anal stage*, persists through the phallic stage* and disappears only after the latency period* and the corresponding institution of the genital love-object.

The reader is referred to Abraham's 'Short Study of the Development of the Libido, Viewed in the Light of Mental Disorders' (1924), included in his *Selected Papers* (London: Hogarth Press, 1927).

The ontogenetic table presented by Robert Fliess may also be consulted (1).

See 'Ambivalence', 'Libidinal Stage', and the articles on the libido's various stages.

(1) Cf. *Psa. Read.*, 254–55.

Anaclisis; Anaclitic (or Attachment)

= *D*.: Anlehnung. – *Es*.: apoyo *or* anáclisis; anaclítico. –
Fr.: étayage; par étayage (*or* anaclitique). –
I.: appoggio *or* anaclisi; per appoggio *or* anaclitico. – *P*.: anaclísia or apoio; anaclítico.

Term introduced by Freud to designate the early relationship of the sexual instincts to the self-preservative ones: the sexual instincts*, which become autonomous only secondarily, depend at first on those vital functions which furnish them with an organic source*, an orientation and an object*. By extension, 'anaclisis' is also used to refer to the fact of the subject's basing himself on the object of the self-preservative instincts* in his choice of a love-object; this is what Freud calls the anaclitic type of object-choice* (α).

The adjective 'anaclitic' (from the Greek ἀνακλίνω, to rest upon, to lean on) was introduced as a rendering of the genitive '*Anlehnungs-*' in such expressions as '*Anlehnungstypus der Objektwahl*' (anaclitic type of object-choice). But what must unavoidably escape the reader of Freud in translation is the fact that the concept of *Anlehnung* is a cornerstone of the first Freudian instinct theory. It is by no means only in dealing with the anaclitic object-choice that Freud evokes it: on many occasions he has recourse either to the substantival '*Anlehnung*' or to verbal forms such as '*sich an (etwas) anlehnen*'. These uses are translated in various ways, however, so that no clear picture of the concept emerges for the non-German reader. This terminological problem is aggravated by the fact that 'anaclisis' is a 'learned' word, artificially coined, whereas '*Anlehnung*' is in every-day use in German.

* * *

As a vital part of Freud's conception of sexuality, the idea of anaclisis is present in the first edition of the *Three Essays on the Theory of Sexuality* (1905*d*), and it never ceases to gain in importance thereafter.

In 1905, in his first theoretical exposition of the concept of instinct, Freud describes the tight relationship that exists between the sexual instinct and certain bodily functions. This relationship is particularly obvious in the oral activity of the infant at the breast: in the pleasure obtained from sucking, 'the satisfaction of the erotogenic zone is associated, in the first instance, with the satisfaction of the need for nourishment' (1*a*). The bodily function furnishes sexuality with its source or erotogenic zone; it lays down its object – the breast – from the outset; and it procures a pleasure for it which is not merely the assuaging of hunger but which includes a sort of bonus pleasure: soon, 'the need for repeating the sexual satisfaction [. . .] becomes detached from the need for taking nourishment' (1*b*). Thus sexuality becomes independent only at a second stage and, once the outside object has been abandoned, functions in accordance with the auto-erotic mode (see 'Auto-Erotism').

Anaclisis also occurs in the case of the other component instincts*: 'Like the labial zone, the anal zone is well suited by its position to act as a medium through which sexuality may attach itself to other somatic functions' (1*c*).

Lastly, it is from 1905 – throughout the section of the *Three Essays* on 'The Finding of an Object' – that Freud begins describing the genesis of object-choice in terms corresponding exactly to what will later be referred to as the 'anaclitic type of object-choice' (1*d*).

In the writings of 1910–12, where Freud brings forward the major opposition between sexual and self-preservation instincts, the notion of anaclisis is still present: the term now refers to the original relationship between the two great classes of instincts: '. . . the sexual instincts find their first objects by attaching themselves to the valuations made by the ego-instincts, precisely in the way in which the first sexual satisfactions are experienced in attachment to the bodily functions necessary for the preservation of life' (2).

The contrast which Freud introduces in 1914 between two kinds of object-choice does not entail any revision of the idea of anaclisis; it merely demarcates the anaclitic type of object-choice from another type – namely, the narcissistic one*.

Finally, in 1915, a number of Freud's additions in the third edition of the *Three Essays* shed a clearer light on the term '*Anlehnung*' and its significance for him. Thus he writes that one of 'the three essential characteristics' of in-

30

fantile sexuality lics in thc fact that 'it attaches itself to one of the vital somatic functions' (1*e*).

*   *   *

In our opinion the notion of anaclisis has not yet been fully extricated from Freud's work; for the most part, consideration has been given only to its part in the conception of object-choice*–a conception which, far from furnishing a complete definition of anaclisis, presupposes its existence at the heart of any theory of the instincts.

Its main function, in fact, is the establishment of a link and an opposition between the sexual instincts and the self-preservative ones.

a. The very idea that the sexual instincts originally borrow their source and object from the self-preservative instincts suggests that there is a basic difference in kind between the two sorts of instinct. The instincts of self-preservation have their whole functioning preconditioned by their somatic apparatus, and their object is fixed from the start, whereas the sexual instincts are defined in the first place by a certain mode of satisfaction that to begin with is nothing but a kind of fringe benefit (*Lustnebengewinn*) derived from the operation of the instincts of self-preservation. This vital differentiation is attested to in Freud's terminology by his repeated use, when referring to the self-preservative instincts, of such words as 'function' and 'need'. To pursue this further, one could suggest for the sake of a more consistent terminology that what Freud calls instincts of self-preservation be referred to simply as 'needs', the better to distinguish them from the sexual *instincts*.

b. By contributing to our understanding of the genesis of sexuality, the notion of anaclisis permits us to clarify the place of sexuality in Freud's theory as a whole. Freud has often been accused of *pansexualism*, a charge he countered by pointing out his abiding adherence to a dualistic view of the instincts; a somewhat less crude rebuttal is possible, however, if we refer to the concept of anaclisis. In one sense sexuality is indeed encountered on all sides: it arises from the very functioning of bodily activities, and also, as Freud remarks in the *Three Essays*, from all sorts of other activities–intellectual ones, for instance. Yet at the same time it only becomes detached secondarily, as we have seen, and is rarely found as a completely autonomous function.

c. A problem much debated in psycho-analysis–that of whether we must assume the existence of a 'primary object-love' or, alternatively, take it that the infant is initially in a state of auto-erotism or narcissism*–is one to which Freud offers a solution more complex than is generally claimed. The sexual instincts obtain satisfaction auto-erotically before they embark upon the evolution that leads them to object-choice. But the self-preservative instincts have a relationship to an object from the start; consequently, in so far as sexuality functions in anaclisis with these instincts, it too must be said to have a relationship to objects; only after detaching itself does sexuality become auto-erotic. 'At a time at which the first beginnings of sexual satisfaction are still linked with the taking of nourishment, the sexual instinct has a sexual object outside the infant's own body in the shape of the mother's breast. It is only later that the instinct loses that object. [...] As a rule the sexual instinct then becomes auto-erotic [...]. The finding of an object is in fact the refinding of it' (1*f*).

Anaclitic Depression

(a) The term 'anaclitic' is sometimes used in a looser sense which is not directly connected with the use of the idea in the Freudian theory, as for example in the expression 'anaclitic depression'*.

(1) FREUD, S.: a) G.W., V, 82; S.E., VII, 181–82. b) G.W., V, 82; S.E., VII, 182. c) G.W., V, 86; S.E., VII, 185. d) Cf. G.W., V, 123–30 and 123, *n*. 1 (added 1915); S.E., VII, 222–30 and 222, *n*. 1. e) G.W., V, 83; S.E., VII, 182. f) G.W., V, 193; S.E., VII, 222.

(2) FREUD, S. 'On the Universal Tendency to Debasement in the Sphere of Love' (1912*d*), G.W., VIII, 80; S.E., XI, 180–81.

Anaclitic Depression

= D.: Anlehnungsdepression.–*Es*.: depresión anaclítica.–*Fr*.: dépression anaclitique.– *I*.: depressione anaclitica.–*P*.: depressão anaclítica.

Term coined by René Spitz (1): disturbance which resembles the clinical manifestations of adult depression but which develops by degrees in children who are deprived of their mother after having had a normal relationship with her during at least the first six months of life.

For terminological comment on the adjective 'anaclitic', the reader is referred to the last article.

As regards the clinical picture presented by anaclitic depression, this is described by Spitz as follows:

'*First month:* The children become weepy, demanding, and tend to cling to the observer when he succeeds in making contact with them.

'*Second month:* The weeping often changes into wails. Weight loss sets in. There is an arrest of the developmental quotient.

'*Third month:* The children refuse contact. They lie prone in their cots most of the time, a pathognomonic sign. Insomnia sets in; loss of weight continues. There is a tendency to contract intercurrent diseases; motor retardation becomes generalized. Inception of facial rigidity.

'After the third month: facial rigidity becomes firmly established. Weeping ceases and is replaced by whimpering. Motor retardation increases and is replaced by lethargy. The developmental quotient begins to decrease' (2).

'Provided the mother is restored to the baby, or an acceptable substitute is found, before the elapse of a critical period between the end of the third month of separation and the end of the fifth, then the disturbance disappears with striking rapidity.'

Spitz considers 'the dynamic structure of anaclitic depression as fundamentally distinct from depression in adults' (3).

(1) SPITZ, R. A. 'Anaclitic Depression', *Psycho-Analytic Study of the Child*, II (New York: I.U.P., 1946), 313–42.

(2) SPITZ, R. A. *The First Year of Life* (New York: I.U.P., 1965), 270–71.

(3) SPITZ, R. A. *La première année de la vie de l'enfant* (Paris: P.U.F., 1953), cf. 119–21.

Anaclitic Type of Object-Choice

= *D*.: Anlehnungstypus der Objektwahl.–*Es*.: elección objetal anaclítica, *or* de apoyo.–
Fr.: choix d'objet par étayage (*or* anaclitique).–
I.: tipo anaclitico (*or* per appoggio) di scelta d'oggetto.–
P.: escolha anaclítica de objeto.

Object-choice* in which the love-object is selected on the model of parental figures in so far as they guarantee the child nourishment, care and protection. An object-choice of this type is based on the fact that the sexual instincts originally depend anaclitically* on the self-preservative instincts.

In 'On Narcissism: An Introduction' (1914*c*) Freud speaks of an anaclitic type of object-choice in contradistinction to the narcissistic type*.

The essential contributions of this 1914 article are the idea that there are *two* basic types of choice of love-object, and a description of the narcissistic one. The other form of object-choice had already been described as early as the *Three Essays on the Theory of Sexuality* (1905*d*), in connection with the theory of *anaclisis* (q.v.) which it presupposes. Freud had shown there how, at the beginning, the first sexual satisfactions arise out of the functioning of the mechanisms responsible for the preservation of life, and how, as a result of this initial attachment, the self-preservative functions direct sexuality to its first object–the mother's breast. Later, 'children learn to feel for other people who help them in their helplessness and satisfy their needs a love which is on the model of, and a continuation of, their relation as sucklings to their nursing mother' (1). Here is what will orientate the post-pubertal object-choice, which according to Freud is always governed, though to a greater or lesser degree, by a dependence on the images of parental figures. As Freud writes in 'On Narcissism', 'a person may love [...] according to the anaclitic (attachment) type: a. the woman who feeds him, b. the man who protects him, and the succession of substitutes who take their place' (2*a*).

It will be seen that the notion of the anaclitic object-choice carries two implications: in terms of the instincts, the sexual instincts depend on the self-preservative ones; in terms of objects, a choice of love-object is made in which it is 'the persons who are concerned with a child's feeding, care and protection' (2*b*) who supply the prototype of the sexually satisfying object.

(1) FREUD, S., G.W., V, 124; S.E., VII, 222–23.
(2) FREUD, S.: a) G.W., X, 157; S.E., XIV, 90. b) G.W., X, 153–54; S.E., XIV, 87.

Anagogic Interpretation

= *D*.: anagogische Deutung.–*Es*.: interpretación anagógica.–*Fr*.: interprétation anagogique.–
I.: interpretazione anagogica.–*P*.: interpretação anagógica.

Term used by Silberer: mode of interpretation of the products of symbolism (myths, dreams, etc.) which is said to bring out their universal ethical meaning. Since anagogic interpretation relates symbols to 'elevated ideals', it is considered to be the opposite of analytic interpretation, which supposedly reduces them to their specific and sexual content.

The idea of anagogic interpretation (from the Greek ἀνάγω, to bear upwards) belongs to the language of theology, where it implies an interpretation 'which ascends from the literal meaning to a spiritual one' (Littré). This concept represents the most evolved stage of Silberer's thinking on symbolism, as expounded in his *Probleme der Mystik und ihrer Symbolik* (1914). Silberer recognises a double determination at work in parables, rites, myths, etc.: for instance, the same symbol which stands in psycho-analysis for the death of the father may be interpreted anagogically as the 'death of the Old Adam' in us (1*a*). This contrast is brought into parallel with the one between the *material phenomenon* and the *functional phenomenon* (q.v.) in the broadened sense that Silberer eventually gave it.

The difference between 'functional' and 'anagogic' is merely that 'the true functional phenomenon characterises a present mental state or process, while the anagogic image seems to indicate a mental state or process yet to be lived through (*erlebt werden soll*)' (1*b*). Anagogic interpretation would thus tend to create new, more and more universal symbols representing the great ethical problems of the human mind. Silberer further claims that such a trend is discernible in dreams during psycho-analytic treatment (1*c*).

Freud and Jones criticised this view. Freud looks upon anagogic interpretation as merely a reversion to pre-analytic ideas which take what is actually derived from the symbol by reaction-formation, rationalisation, etc. (2) for the symbol's ultimate meaning. Jones compares the anagogic interpretation to the 'prospective' meaning that Jung attributed to symbols: 'The symbol is taken to be the striving for a high ethical ideal, one which fails to reach this ideal and halts at the symbol instead; the ultimate ideal, however, is supposed to be implicit in the symbol and to be symbolised by it' (3).

(1) Cf. SILBERER, H. *Probleme der Mystik und ihrer Symbolik* (Vienna and Leipzig: Hugo Heller, 1914): a) 168. b) 155. c) 153.

(2) Cf. FREUD, S. 'Dreams and Telepathy' (1922*a*), G.W., XIII, 187; S.E., XVIII, 216.

(3) JONES, E. 'The Theory of Symbolism' (1916), in *Papers on Psycho-Analysis*, 5th edn. (London: Baillière, Tindall & Cox, 1950), 136. (For Jones's criticism of Silberer's theory as a whole, cf. all of Chapter V.)

Anal-Sadistic Stage (or Phase)

= *D.*: sadistisch-anale Stufe (*or* Phase).–*Es.*: fase analsádica.–*Fr.*: stade sadique-anal.–
I.: fase sadico-anale.–*P.*: fase anal-sádica.

Freud's second stage of libidinal development, occurring approximately between the ages of two and four. The stage is characterised by an organisation* of the libido under the primacy of the anal erotogenic zone*. The object-relationship* at this time is invested with meanings having to do with the function of defecation (expulsion/retention) and with the symbolic value of faeces. The anal-sadistic stage sees the strengthening of sado-masochism in correlation with the development of muscular control.

Freud began by identifying the characteristics of an anal erotism in adults and by describing its operation in childhood in defecation and in the retention of faecal matter (1).

It was on the basis of anal erotism that the idea of a pregenital* organisation of the libido was evolved. In his article on 'Character and Anal Erotism' (1908*b*) (2), Freud had already linked character-traits surviving in the adult–the triad constituted by orderliness, parsimony and obstinacy–with anal erotism in the child.

The notion of a pregenital organisation where sadistic and anal-erotic instincts predominate appears for the first time in 'The Disposition to Obsessional Neurosis' (1913*i*); here, as in the genital stage*, there is a relationship with the outside object. 'And now we see the need for yet another stage to be inserted before the final shape is reached–a stage in which the component instincts have already come together for the choice of an object and that object is already something extraneous in contrast to the subject's own self, but in which the primacy of the genital zones has not yet been established' (3).

In the later revisions of the *Three Essays on the Theory of Sexuality* (1905*d*), in 1915 and 1924, the anal stage appears as one of the pregenital organisations lying between the oral organisation and the phallic one. It is the first stage in which there is a polarity between activity* and passivity: Freud has activity coincide with sadism and passivity with anal erotism, assigning distinct sources to each of the corresponding component instincts–namely, the *musculature* (for the instinct to master*) and the *anal mucous membrane*.

In 1924 Karl Abraham suggested that the anal-sadistic stage should be broken down into two phases on the basis of two contrasted types of behaviour *vis-à-vis* the object (4). In the first of these phases anal erotism is linked to evacuation and the sadistic instinct to the destruction of the object; in the second, by contrast, anal erotism is connected to retention and the sadistic instinct to possessive control. On Abraham's view, the transition from the first to the second of these phases constitutes a decisive step on the way to object-love, as is borne out by the fact that the dividing-line between neurotic regressions and psychotic ones runs between the two periods in question.

How should the link between sadism and anal erotism be understood? The suggestion is that sadism, being essentially bipolar (since its self-contradictory

35

aim is to destroy the object but also, by mastering it, to preserve it) corresponds *par excellence* to the biphasic functioning of the anal sphincter (evacuation/ retention) and its control.

At the anal stage, the symbolic meanings of giving and witholding are ascribed to the activity of defecation; in this connection, Freud brings out the symbolic equation: faeces = gift = money (5).

(1) FREUD, S. *Three Essays on the Theory of Sexuality* (1905*d*), G.W., V, 86–88; S.E., VII, 185–87.

(2) Cf. FREUD, S., G.W., VII, 203–9; S.E., IX, 169–75.

(3) FREUD, S., G.W., VIII, 446–47; S.E., XII, 321.

(4) Cf. ABRAHAM, K. 'A Short Study of the Development of the Libido, Viewed in the Light of Mental Disorders', *Selected Papers* (London: Hogarth, 1927), 422–33.

(5) Cf. FREUD, S. 'On Transformations of Instinct as Exemplified in Anal Erotism' (1917*c*), G.W., X, 402–10; S.E., XVII, 127–33.

Anticathexis, Countercathexis

= *D*.: Gegenbesetzung.–*Es*.: contracarga.–*Fr*.: contre-investissement.– *I*.: controcarica *or* controinvestimento.–*P*.: contra-carga *or* contra-investimento.

Economic process postulated by Freud as the underpinning of numerous defensive activities of the ego. It consists in the ego's cathexis* of ideas, systems of ideas, attitudes, etc., which are capable of impeding the access to consciousness and motility of unconscious ideas and wishes.

The term may also designate the more or less permanent result of such a process.

The notion of anticathexis is mainly utilised by Freud in the context of his economic theory of repression*. In so far as the ideas to be repressed are permanently cathected by the instinct and constantly seeking to break through into consciousness, they can only be kept in the unconscious if an equally constant force is operating in the opposite direction. In general, therefore, repression presupposes two economic processes each of which implies the other:

a. Withdrawal, by the system *Pcs.*, of the cathexis hitherto attached to a particular unpleasurable idea.

b. Anticathexis, using the energy rendered available by this withdrawal.

Here the question arises: what is it that is chosen as the object of anticathexis? It should be noted that this process results in an idea being kept within the system from which the instinctual energy originates. Anticathexis is therefore the cathexis of an element of the preconscious-conscious system, a cathexis which prevents the repressed idea from emerging in the place of this element. The anticathected element may be of several kinds: it may be simply a derivative* of the unconscious idea (a substitutive formation*, as in the case, for example, of those animals which in phobia become the object of an unremitting awareness and of which the function is to keep the unconscious wish and its related phantasies repressed). Or it may be an element directly opposed to the unconscious idea (a reaction-formation*–for example, the exaggerated concern of a mother for her children masking aggressive wishes, or a preoccupation with cleanliness representing a struggle against anal tendencies).

Furthermore, a situation, a particular form of behaviour, a character trait, etc., may as easily be anticathected as an idea–the aim always being to maintain the repression in as constant a way as possible. To this extent the notion of anticathexis connotes the economic aspect of the dynamic concept of ego defence; it accounts for the stability of the symptom, which, as Freud puts it, 'is supported from both sides'. The indestructibility of unconscious desire is countered by the relative rigidity of the ego's defensive structures, which require a permanent expenditure of energy.

The notion of anticathexis is not only applicable in the context of the frontier between the unconscious system on the one hand and the preconscious one on the other. Though initially invoked by Freud in his theory of repression (1), anticathexis is also to be met with in a large number of defensive operations: isolation*, undoing*, defence by reality, etc. In such operations–just as in the mechanism of attention and discriminating thought–we see that this process also plays a part *within* the preconscious-conscious system.

Lastly Freud invokes the idea, in connection with the organism's relationship to the environment, to account for the defensive reactions to an inflow of external energy which has broken through the protective shield* (pain, trauma). In such an event the organism sets internal energy in motion at the expense of its own activities (which are correspondingly deprived) in order to create a sort of barrier for staunching or reducing the influx of external excitations (2).

(1) Cf. FREUD, S. *The Interpretation of Dreams* (1900a), G.W., II–III. 610; S.E., V, 604–5.

(2) Cf., for example, FREUD, S. *Beyond the Pleasure Principle* (1920g), G.W., XIII, 30–31; S.E., XVIII, 30–31.

Anxiety Hysteria

= *D.*: Angsthysterie.–*Es.*: histeria de angustia.–*Fr.*: hystérie d'angoisse.– *I.*: isteria d'angoscia.–*P.*: histeria de angústia.

Term introduced by Freud to distinguish a neurosis whose central symptom is phobia, and to emphasise its structural resemblance to conversion hysteria*.

It was Wilhelm Stekel who, following a suggestion of Freud's (1), brought the term 'anxiety hysteria' into psycho-analytical usage in his *Nervöse Angstzustände und ihre Behandlung* (*Neurotic Anxiety-States and their Treatment*), published in 1908.

This terminological innovation has the following justification:

a. Phobic symptoms are to be met with in a variety of neurotic and psychotic conditions. They may be observed in obsessional neurosis as in schizophrenia;

and even in anxiety neurosis*, according to Freud, certain apparently phobic symptoms can be encountered.

This is the reason why Freud, in his account of the case of 'Little Hans', considers that phobias can not be held to be an 'independent pathological process' (2*a*).

b. There does exist, nonetheless, a neurosis whose principal symptom is phobia. Freud did not isolate it straight away and, as first conceived, phobias were associated with obsessional neurosis or with anxiety neurosis *qua* actual neurosis* (3). It was the analysis of little Hans which gave Freud occasion to propose a phobic neurosis as a specific entity, and to point out the structural similarity between this neurosis and conversion hysteria. The basis of this analogy is that the job of repression in both cases is essentially to separate affects from ideas. There is nevertheless an essential difference between the two conditions, which Freud emphasizes: in anxiety hysteria, 'the libido which has been liberated from the pathogenic material by repression is not *converted* [...] but is set free in the shape of anxiety' (2*b*). The formation of phobic symptoms comes about because 'From the outset in anxiety-hysteria the mind is constantly at work in the direction of once more psychically binding the anxiety which has become liberated' (2*c*). 'An anxiety-hysteria tends to develop more and more into a "phobia" ' (2*d*).

As this text shows, 'anxiety hysteria' and 'phobic neurosis' cannot, strictly speaking, be treated as completely synonymous terms. 'Anxiety hysteria' is used less descriptively, concentrates attention on the constitutive mechanism of the neurosis in question and stresses the fact that displacement on to a phobic object is secondary to the emergence of a liberated anxiety which is not bound to an object.

(1) Cf. FREUD, S., G.W., VII, 467; S.E., IX, 250–51.

(2) FREUD, S. 'Analysis of a Phobia in a Five-Year-Old Boy' (1909*b*): a) G.W., VII, 349; S.E., X, 115. b) G.W., VII, 349; S.E., X, 115. c) G.W., VII, 350; S.E., X, 117. d) G.W., VII, 350; S.E., X, 116.

(3) Cf. FREUD, S. 'On the Grounds for Detaching a Particular Syndrome from Neurasthenia under the Description "Anxiety Neurosis" ' (1895*b*); 'The Neuro-Psychoses of Defence' (1894*a*); 'Obsessions and Phobias' (1895*c*).

Anxiety Neurosis

= *D*.: Angstneurose.–*Es*.: neurosis de angustia.–*Fr*.: névrose d'angoisse.–
I.: nevrosi d'angoscia.–*P*.: neurose de angústia.

A type of illness which Freud isolated, distinguishing it:

a. symptomatically speaking, from *neurasthenia*, because of the predominance here of anxiety (chronic anxious expectation; attacks of anxiety or of its somatic equivalents);

b. aetiologically, from *hysteria*: anxiety neurosis is an actual neurosis* characterised more particularly by the accumulation of sexual excitation which is held to be transformed directly into symptoms without any psychical mediation.

The problem of the origin of anxiety and its relation to sexual excitation and the libido had become a preoccupation of Freud's as early as 1893, a fact to which the correspondence with Fliess bears witness. He gave the matter systematic treatment in his article 'On the Grounds for Detaching a Particular Syndrome from Neurasthenia under the Description "Anxiety Neurosis"' (1895*b* [1894]).

The nosographical revision proposed by Freud was to separate a condition basically defined by the major symptom of anxiety from the syndrome classically described as neurasthenia. It is against a background of 'general irritability', he suggests, that different kinds of anxiety appear: chronic anxiousness or anxious expectation apt to become bound* to any ideational content which is able to lend it support; pure anxiety attacks (e.g. *pavor nocturnus*) accompanied or replaced by various somatic equivalents such as vertigo, dyspnoea, cardiac troubles, sweating, etc.; and phobic symptoms where the affect*–anxiety–is bound to an idea*, but to an idea which it is impossible to identify as a symbolic substitute for another, repressed, idea.

Freud associates anxiety neurosis with highly specific aetiologies, whose common basis is:

a. The accumulation of sexual tension.

b. The absence or insufficiency of a 'psychical working-over'* of the somatic sexual excitation, which can only be transformed into 'psychical libido' (see 'Libido') on condition that it be connected to pre-established groups of sexual ideas. When the sexual excitation is not controlled in this way it is deflected directly on to the somatic plane, where it manifests itself in the form of anxiety (α).

Freud considers that the psychical working-over is inadequate in such cases either 'because of insufficient development of psychical sexuality or because of the attempted suppression of the latter (defence), or of its falling into decay, or because of habitual alienation between physical and psychical sexuality' (1*a*).

He attempts to show how these mechanisms operate in the differing aetiologies which he lists–virginal anxiety, anxiety as a result of abstinence, of *coitus interruptus*, and so forth.

Freud draws attention to the common features in the symptomatology–and to some extent too in the functioning–of anxiety neurosis and hysteria; in both cases, 'there is a kind of *conversion* [...]; but in hysteria it is a *psychical* excitation that takes a wrong path exclusively into the somatic field, whereas [in anxiety neurosis] it is a *physical* tension, which cannot enter the psychical field and therefore remains on the physical path. The two are combined extremely often' (1*b*).

It can thus be seen that Freud is conscious of the psychical element which may be present in the preconditions of the appearance of anxiety neurosis; and he emphasizes the affinity between this neurosis and hysteria, evoking the possibility of their combination in a 'mixed neurosis'*. All the same, he never abandons his position on the specificity of anxiety neurosis as an actual neurosis.

Psycho-analysts today do not accept the concept of actual neurosis unreservedly, yet the clinical picture of anxiety neurosis, which Freud was the first to differentiate from neurasthenia (a fact, incidentally, which is often forgotten), has conserved its nosographical value in clinical practice as a neurosis

Aphanisis

characterised by the predominance of a massive anxiety, by the absence of any obviously privileged object, and by the manifest role of actual factors.

Thus understood, anxiety neurosis is to be clearly distinguished from *anxiety hysteria** or phobic neurosis, in which anxiety attaches itself to a substitute object.

(α) It should be mentioned that these are not Freud's very earliest views on the subject of anxiety. He remarks himself that his conception of an *actual*, somatic functioning of anxiety came as a stricture on his previous, completely psychogenic theory of hysteria. Cf. a note apropos of Emmy in the *Studies on Hysteria* (1895d): 'At the time I wrote this [i.e. 1889] I was inclined to look for a *psychical* origin for all symptoms in cases of hysteria. I should now [1895] explain this sexually abstinent woman's tendency to anxiety as being due to *neurosis* (i.e. anxiety neurosis)' (2). ('Neurosis' is here used in its primary sense of disturbance in the working of the nervous system.)

(1) FREUD, S.: a) *Anf.*, 103; S.E., I, 194. b) *Anf.*, 104; S.E., I, 195.
(2) FREUD, S., G.W., I, 118; S.E., II, 65.

Aphanisis

= *D.*: Aphanisis.–*Es.*: afánisis.–*Fr.*: aphanisis.–*I.*: afânisi.–*P.*: afânise.

Term introduced by Ernest Jones: the disappearance of sexual desire. According to Jones aphanisis is the object, in both sexes, of a fear more profound than the fear of castration.

Jones introduced the Greek term ἀφάνισις in connection with the question of the castration complex* (1a). He argues that, even in the man, abolition of sexuality and castration are not identical (for example, 'many men wish to be castrated for, among others, erotic reasons, so that their sexuality certainly does not disappear with the surrender of the penis' (1b)); if they seem indistinguishable, this is because the fear of castration (along with ideas of death) is the concrete expression of the more general fear of *aphanisis*.

In women it is in the fear of separation from the loved object that the fear of aphanisis is to be discerned.

Jones evokes the notion of aphanisis in the context of his enquiries into feminine sexuality. Whereas Freud had centred the development of the little girl –just like that of the boy–on the castration complex and the predominance of the phallus, Jones attempts to describe the girl's development in more specific terms, laying the stress on a sexuality that has its own aims and activity from the outset.

For Jones, therefore, the common denominator in the sexuality of the boy and the girl has to be sought at a more fundamental level than the castration complex, that level being the fear of aphanisis.

(1) JONES, E. 'Early Development of Female Sexuality' (1927), in *Papers on Psycho-Analysis*, 5th edn. (London: Baillière, Tindall & Cox, 1950): a) cf. 438–51. b)439–40.

Association

= *D*.: Assoziation.–*Es*.: asociación.–*Fr*.: association.–*I*.: associazione.–*P*.: associação.

Term borrowed from associationism designating any *bond* between two or more psychical elements which, in series, form an associative chain.

Sometimes the term is used to denote the *elements* that are associated in this way. This is what is meant when one speaks, in connection with the treatment, of the 'associations' of such and such a dream—i.e. whatever is associated with the dream in the subject's statements. 'Associations' may even connote all the material verbalized in the course of the psycho-analytic session.

A thorough commentary on the term 'association' would require an historical and critical investigation tracing the spread of the associationist doctrine in nineteenth-century Germany, its influence upon the thinking of the 'young Freud', and above all the way in which it was integrated and transformed by the Freudian discovery of the laws of the unconscious.

In the remarks that follow, we have restricted ourselves to the last point.

I. It is impossible to grasp the meaning and importance of the concept of association in psycho-analysis without reference to the clinical experience on the basis of which the method of free association was evolved. The *Studies on Hysteria* (1895*d*) show how Freud was brought more and more to follow up the free associations of his patients, who pointed out this line of enquiry for themselves (see our commentary on 'Free Association'). As far as the theory of association is concerned, what emerges from Freud's experience during these pioneering years of psycho-analysis may be summarized as follows:

a. An 'idea which comes' (*Einfall*) to the subject in an apparently isolated way is invariably an element referring back in reality–whether consciously or not–to other elements. In order to describe the series of associations that are uncovered in this way Freud uses a number of figurative terms: line (*Linie*), thread (*Faden*), chain (*Verkettung*), train (*Zug*), etc. These lines run into each other so as to form veritable networks, with 'nodal points' (*Knotenpunkte*) where several lines intersect.

b. Associations, as linked together in the subject's discourse, correspond in Freud's view to a complex organization of memory. This he compared to a system of archives set up according to various methods of classification, which may be consulted via different routes (chronological order, subject order, etc.) (1*a*). The postulation of this type of organization assumes that the idea* (*Vorstellung*) or the memory-trace* (*Erinnerungsspur*) of a single event may be found in several of those groups which Freud was still referring to as 'mnemic systems'.

c. This organisation into systems is borne out by clinical experience: there exist veritable 'separate psychical groups' (1*b*)–complexes of ideas split off from the associative pathways: 'It may sometimes happen,' as Breuer noted, 'that every one of the individual ideas comprised in such a complex of ideas is thought of consciously, and that what is exiled from consciousness is only the particular combination of them' (1*c*). In contrast with Breuer, Freud does not

41

Association

see hypnoid states* as the ultimate explanation of this fact, but he holds none-theless to the notion of a split* (*Spaltung*) within the psyche. The idea of a separate group of associations underlies the topographical conception of the unconscious.

d. The 'force' of an element in a complex of associations does not remain irrevocably attached to this element. The interplay of associations depends on *economic* factors: the cathectic energy is displaced from one element to another, condenses upon the nodal points, and so on (independence of affects* *vis-à-vis* ideas).

e. In short, the associative discourse is not the passive object of general laws such as those described by associationism: the subject is not a 'polypary of images'. The groupings of associations, their possible isolation, their 'false con-nections', their chances of acceding to consciousness–all play a part in the *dynamics* of the defensive conflict specific to each person.

II. The 'Project for a Scientific Psychology' (1950a [1895]) sheds light on the Freudian use of the idea of association by showing how, from a speculative viewpoint, the psycho-analytic discovery of the unconscious gave new meaning to those associationist assumptions upon which Freud had leaned:

a. The way associations function is pictured as a circulation of energy within a 'neuronal apparatus' with a complex structure consisting of layers of successive bifurcations. At each intersection, each excitation takes one particular path in preference to another, according to the 'facilitations' left by preceding excita-tions. The notion of facilitation* (*Bahnung*) should not be understood primarily as referring to ease of passage from one image to the next, but rather as a process of differential opposition: a given pathway is only facilitated in proportion as the alternative one is not.

b. In Freud's initial hypotheses there is no question of images in the sense of mental or neuronal impressions bearing a resemblance to the actual object: to begin with, everything is seen in terms of 'neurones' and 'quantity' (2).

This conception, with its mechanistic character and neurophysiological language, might seem very far removed from real experience, but it must clearly be compared with that antagonism between ideas and quota of affect* which is a constant of Freudian psychology. Like neurones, ideas are discrete, discon-tinuous elements in a chain. The significance of ideas, like that of neurones, depends upon the complex which, along with other elements, they help con-stitute. From this point of view, the operation of the 'neuronal apparatus' might be compared to the operation of language as analysed by structural linguistics: in both cases discontinuous units are organized into binary oppositions.

(1) BREUER, J. and FREUD, S.: a) Cf. G.W., I, 291 *ff.*; S.E., II, 233 *ff.* b) Cf., for example, G.W., I, 92 and 289; S.E., II, 12 and 286. c) G.W., I, 187*n*.; S.E., II, 214–15*n*.
(2) Cf. FREUD, S., *Anf.*, 379–86; S.E., I, 295–302.

Attention, (Evenly) Suspended or Poised

= *D.*: gleichschwebende Aufmerksamkeit.–*Es.*: atención (parejamente) flotante.–
Fr.: attention (également) flottante.–*I.*: attenzione (ugualmente) fluttuante.–
P.: atenção equiflutuante.

**Manner in which, according to Freud, the analyst should listen to the analysand:
he must give no special, *a priori* importance to any aspect of the subject's discourse; this implies that he should allow his own unconscious activity to operate
as freely as possible and suspend the motives which usually direct his attention.
This technical recommendation to the analyst complements the rule of free
association* laid down for the subject being analysed.**

It is above all in his 'Recommendations to Physicians Practising Psycho-
Analysis' (1912*e*) that Freud formulates and comments upon this essential
injunction which lays down the subjective attitude to be adopted by the psycho-
analyst when listening to his patient. This consists in as complete a suspension as
possible of everything which usually focusses the attention: personal inclinations, prejudices, and theoretical assumptions however well grounded they
might be. 'Just as the patient must relate everything that his self-observation can
detect, and keep back all the logical and affective objections that seek to induce
him to make a selection from among them, so the doctor must put himself in a
position to make use of everything he is told for the purposes of interpretation
and of recognizing the concealed unconscious material without substituting a
censorship of his own for the selection that the patient has foregone' (1*a*).

It is this rule which in Freud's view allows the analyst to discover the unconscious connections in what the patient says. Thanks to it the analyst is able to
keep in mind a multitude of apparently insignificant elements whose correlations
are only to emerge later on.

Suspended attention poses theoretical and practical problems which the term
itself, in its apparent self-contradiction, already suggests.

a. The theoretical basis of this idea is obvious if the question is viewed in
relation to the analysand: unconscious structures as described by Freud come
to light via multiple distortions, as is the case, for example, in that 'transvaluation of all psychical values' (2*a*) as a consequence of which the most insignificant
details often turn out to be concealing very important unconscious thoughts.
Thus suspended attention is the only truly objective attitude in that it is suited
to an essentially distorted object. It is worth noting that Freud, without as yet
using the term 'suspended attention', did describe an analogous mental attitude
in *The Interpretation of Dreams* (1900*a*)–an attitude which he looked upon as the
prerequisite for the analysis of one's own dreams (2*b*).

b. From the analyst's standpoint, by contrast, the theory of suspended attention raises difficult questions. It is conceivable that the analyst, like his patients,
should try to eliminate the influence of his conscious prejudices, and even of his
unconscious defences, upon his attention. Indeed, it was in order to get rid of
the latter as far as possible that Freud counselled the training analysis*, for
'every unresolved repression in [the analyst] constitutes what has been aptly
described by Stekel as a "blind spot" in his analytic perception' (1*b*).

43

Attention, (Evenly) Suspended or Poised

Freud demands more than this, however: the desired goal would appear to be actual direct communication between one unconscious and another (α): the analyst's unconscious has to relate to the emerging unconscious of the patient 'as a telephone receiver is adjusted to the transmitting microphone' (1c). This is what Theodor Reik was later to describe figuratively as 'listening with the third ear' (3).

Now, as Freud points out himself when speaking of free association, the suspension of conscious 'purposive ideas'* can only result in their replacement by unconscious ones (2c). The analyst who adopts the attitude of suspended attention is therefore faced with a particular problem: how can his attention *not* be orientated by his own unconscious motives? The answer would no doubt be that the personal makeup of the psycho-analyst is not only reduced as a factor by virtue of his training analysis but also subjected to evaluation and control by his own analysis of the counter-transference.

Generally speaking, the rule of suspended attention must be understood as an *ideal* which in practice comes up against requirements that are incompatible with it: how is it conceivable, for example, that the transition from interpretation* to construction* could be made without the analyst, at some point, giving especial attention to particular material, without his comparing it, schematising it and so on?

*   *   *

In the present-day psycho-analytic movement, various orientations towards the question of suspended attention (which Freud omitted to reformulate in the context of his second topography) may be distinguished:

a. Following Theodor Reik (*loc. cit.*), some authors tend to interpret the idea of one unconscious tuning in to another unconscious in terms of an empathy (*Einfühlung*) expressed essentially at a subverbal level. On this view the counter-transference does not stand in the way of communication – on the contrary, it becomes the mark of the depth of the communication, which is looked upon here as a form of perception.

b. For other writers, the technical rule of suspended attention calls for a relaxation of the inhibitory and selective functions of the ego; it implies no increased emphasis on what is felt rather than spoken, but merely that the analyst should 'open himself up' to the exhortations of his own psychical apparatus with a view to avoiding the interference of his defensive compulsions. The essential part of the psycho-analytic dialogue continues to take place, however, on an ego-to-ego level.

c. Lastly, from a theoretical standpoint that accentuates the analogy between the mechanisms of the unconscious and those of language (Lacan), it is to this structural similarity between all unconscious phenomena that the psycho-analyst's listening posture must aim to give as free a play as possible.

(α) Two passages from Freud may be quoted in this connection: '. . . everyone possesses in his own unconscious an instrument with which he can interpret the utterances of the unconscious in other people' (4); '. . . the *Ucs.* of one human being can react upon that of another, without passing through the *Cs.* This deserves closer investigation, especially with a view to finding out whether preconscious activity can be excluded as playing a part in it; but, descriptively speaking, the fact is incontestable' (5).

44

(1) FREUD, S.: a) G.W., VIII, 381; S.E. XII, 115. b) G.W., VIII, 382; S.E., XII, 116. c) G.W., VIII, 381; S.E., XII, 115–16.

(2) FREUD, S. *The Interpretation of Dreams* (1900a): a) G.W., II–III, 335; S.E., IV, 330. b) Cf. G.W., II–III, 108; S.E., IV, 103. c) Cf. G.W., II–III, 533; S.E., V, 528–29.

(3) Cf. REIK, T. *Listening with the Third Ear. The Inner Experience of a Psycho-Analyst* (New York: Grove Press, 1948).

(4) FREUD, S. 'The Disposition to Obsessional Neurosis' (1913i), G.W., VIII, 445; S.E., XII, 320.

(5) FREUD, S. 'The Unconscious' (1915e), G.W., X, 293; S.E., XIV, 194.

Auto-Erotism

= *D.*: Autoerotismus. – *Es.*: autoerotisme. – *Fr.*: auto-érotisme. – *I.*: autoerotismo. – *P.*: auto-erotismo.

I. In a broad sense: a form of sexual behaviour in which the subject obtains satisfaction solely through recourse to his own body, needing no outside object; in this sense masturbation is referred to as auto-erotic behaviour.

II. More specifically: a form of early infantile sexual behaviour whereby a component instinct*, bound to the operation of an organ or to the stimulation of an erotogenic zone*, attains satisfaction *in situ* – i.e:

a. without resorting to an external object;

b. without depending on an image of a unified body, or on an embryonic ego such as that which characterises narcissism*.

It was Havelock Ellis who introduced the term 'auto-erotism' (α), using it in a wide sense close to our sense I above: 'By "auto-erotism" I mean the phenomena of spontaneous sexual emotion generated in the absence of an external stimulus proceeding, directly or indirectly, from another person' (1a).

It should be observed, however, that Ellis had already distinguished an 'extreme form' of auto-erotism: narcissism, or 'the tendency for the sexual emotion to be absorbed and often entirely lost in self-admiration' (1b).

Freud adopts the term in the *Three Essays on the Theory of Sexuality* (1905d), essentially in order to describe infantile sexuality. He considers Ellis's use of it too broad (2a) and defines auto-erotism by the instinct's relationship to its object: '. . . the instinct is not directed towards other people, but obtains satisfaction from the subject's own body' (2b). This definition is to be understood by reference to the distinction Freud established between the instinct's different aspects: pressure*, source*, aim*, object*. In auto-erotism the object of the sexual instincts 'is negligible in comparison with the organ which is their source, and as a rule coincides with that organ' (3a).

I. The theory of auto-erotism is based on the fundamental thesis of the *Three Essays* which holds that the object of the sexual instinct* is *contingent*. Showing how satisfaction may be obtained at the beginnings of sexual life without recourse to an object amounts to a demonstration that there is no ready-made path to carry the subject towards a predetermined object.

45

Auto-Erotism

This theory does not assume the existence of a primitive, 'objectless' state. The action of sucking, which Freud takes as the model of auto-erotism, is in fact preceded by a first stage during which the sexual instinct obtains satisfaction through an anaclitic* relationship with the self-preservative instinct* (hunger), and by virtue of an object–namely, the mother's breast (2c). Only when it becomes detached from hunger does the oral sexual instinct lose its object and, by the same token, become auto-erotic.

Thus although it is possible to describe auto-erotism as objectless, this is by no means because this state occurs prior to any relationship with an object, nor yet because with its advent all objects cease to be present in the search for satisfaction. The statement is only true in that in auto-erotism the natural mode of apprehending the object is split: the sexual instinct now detaches itself from the non-sexual functions (e.g. nutrition) upon which it has heretofore depended anaclitically and which have laid down its aim and object.

The 'origin' of auto-erotism is thus considered to be that moment–recurring constantly rather than fixed at a certain point in development–when sexuality draws away from its natural object, finds itself delivered over to phantasy* and in this very process is constituted *qua* sexuality.

II. At the same time, starting with Freud's earliest evocation of it, the notion of auto-erotism implies a different frame of reference from that of the relation to the object: it implies a reference to that state of the organism in which each of the instincts seeks satisfaction on its own account and in which no overall organisation exists. From the *Three Essays* onwards auto-erotism is invariably defined as the activity of the different 'component instincts'*; it is to be understood as a sexual excitation which is generated and gratified at the same site in the case of each individual erotogenic zone (organ-pleasure*). Granted, auto-erotic activity generally requires the erotogenic zone's contact with another part of the body (thumb-sucking, masturbation, etc.), yet its ideal prototype is that of the lips kissing themselves (2d).

The introduction of the notion of narcissism furnishes a retrospective clarification of the notion of auto-erotism: in narcissism it is the ego, as a unified image of the body, which is the object of narcissistic libido, while auto-erotism, by way of contrast, is defined as the anarchic stage preceding this convergence of the component instincts upon a common object: '. . . we are bound to suppose that a unity comparable to the ego cannot exist in the individual from the start; the ego has to be developed. The auto-erotic instincts, however, are there from the very first; so there must be something added in auto-erotism–a new psychical action–in order to bring about narcissism' (4).

Freud upholds this idea quite clearly in many places: in the transition from auto-erotism to narcissism, he argues, 'the hitherto isolated sexual instincts have already come together into a single whole and have also found an object' (5a); this object is the ego. Later on, however, this distinction tends to disappear–especially in those passages where Freud comes to recognise the existence of a state of 'primary narcissism' from the beginning of life, perhaps within the womb itself. Auto-erotism is no longer defined as anything more than 'the sexual activity of the narcissistic stage of allocation of the libido' (6, 3b).

*   *   *

In short, it is clear from the foregoing that the idea the term 'auto-erotism' seeks to connote may be defined fairly consistently if we assume a primal state of fragmentation of the sexual instinct. So far as the relationship to the object is concerned, such a state of affairs does indeed imply the absence of a total object (ego or other person), but it in no way implies the absence of a phantasied part-object*.

Is auto-erotism a developmental notion? May we speak of an auto-erotic libidinal stage*?

This is a point on which Freud's opinion varied: in 1905 he tends to place the whole of infantile sexuality under the head of auto-erotism, the better to contrast it with adult sexual activity, which involves an object-choice*. Subsequently he moderated this view, commenting: 'I was [...] made aware of a defect in the account I have given in the text, which, in the interests of lucidity, describes the conceptual distinction between the two phases of auto-erotism and object-love as though it were also a separation in time' (2e).

Freud certainly does not abandon the idea of a genetic transition from auto-erotism to object-love, however, and when he introduces narcissism he interpolates it into this temporal sequence (5b). All the same, this succession of periods should not be taken too literally, and it should be borne in mind particularly that it is complemented by a structural distinction: auto-erotism is not the attribute of a specific instinctual activity (oral, anal, etc.), but is rather to be found in each such activity, both as an early phase and, in later development, as the component factor of *organ-pleasure*.

The tendency to treat auto-erotism as a stage sharply demarcated in time was carried to an extreme by Karl Abraham, who conflates the auto-erotic stage and one particular stage of libidinal organisation: the early oral (sucking) stage*.

(α) The word 'auto-erotism' was first used by Havelock Ellis in an article published in 1898: 'Auto-Erotism: A Psychological Study', *Alien. Neurol.*, 19, 260. Freud employs it for the first time in a letter to Fliess dated December 9, 1899.

(1) ELLIS, H. *Studies in the Psychology of Sex*, vol. I: 'The Evolution of Modesty, etc.' (Philadelphia: F. A. Davis Company, 1901): a) 110. b) 3rd edn. (1910), 206.

(2) FREUD, S. *Three Essays on the Theory of Sexuality* (1905d): a) Cf. G.W., V, 82, *n*. 1; S.E., VII, 181, *n*. 2. N.B. German editions before 1920 contain the following comment, deleted thereafter: 'Havelock Ellis, however, has spoilt the meaning of the term he invented by including the whole of hysteria and all the manifestations of masturbation among the phenomena of auto-erotism.' b) G.W., V, 81–82; S.E., VII, 181. c) Cf. G.W., V, 87–83; S.E., VII, 98–99. d) Cf. G.W., V, 83; S.E., VII, 182. e) G.W., V, 94, note added 1910; S.E., VII, 194.

(3) FREUD, S. 'Instincts and their Vicissitudes' (1915c): a) G.W., X, 225; S.E., XIV, 132. b) G.W., X, 227; S.E., XIV, 134.

(4) FREUD, S. 'On Narcissism: An Introduction' (1914c), G.W., X, 142; S.E., XIV, 76–77.

(5) FREUD, S. *Totem and Taboo* (1912–13): a) G.W., IX, 109; S.E., XIII, 88–89. b) G.W., IX, 109; S.E., XIII, 88.

(6) FREUD, S. *Introductory Lectures on Psycho-Analysis* (1916–17), G.W., XI, 431; S.E., XVI, 416.

Automatic Anxiety

= *D.*: automatische Angst.–*Es.*: angustia automática.–*Fr.*: angoisse automatique.–
I.: angoscia automatica.–*P.*: angústia automática.

Subject's reaction each time he finds himself in a traumatic situation–that is to say, each time he is confronted by an inflow of excitations, whether of external or internal origin, which he is unable to master. Automatic anxiety is opposed in Freud's view to *anxiety as signal**.

This expression is introduced as part of Freud's revision of his theory of anxiety in *Inhibitions, Symptoms and Anxiety* (1926*d*); it may be understood by comparison with the notion of *anxiety as signal*.

In both cases, 'as an automatic phenomenon and as a rescuing signal, anxiety is seen to be a product of the infant's mental helplessness which is a natural counterpart of its biological helplessness*' (1). Automatic anxiety is a spontaneous response by the organism to this traumatic situation or to a reproduction of it.

By 'traumatic situation' is meant an incontrollable influx of excitations that are too numerous or too intense; this is a very old idea of Freud's, found in his earliest writings on anxiety, which is there defined as the result of an accumulated, undischarged libidinal tension.

The term 'automatic anxiety' denotes a type of reaction; it implies no prejudgement as to the internal or external origin of the traumatogenic stimuli.

(1) FREUD, S., G.W., XIV, 168; S.E., XX, 138.

Autoplastic / Alloplastic

= *D.*: autoplastisch/alloplastisch.–*Es.*: autoplástico/aloplástico.–
Fr.: autoplastique/alloplastique.–*I.*: autoplastico/alloplastico.–
P.: autoplástico/aloplástico.

Terms qualifying two types of reaction or adaptation: autoplastic modification affects the organism alone; alloplastic modification affects the surroundings.

These terms are sometimes employed in psycho-analysis, within the framework of a theory which defines the field of psychology by the interaction of organism and environment, to distinguish between two kinds of operation, one directed towards the subject himself, the other directed towards the outside world. Daniel Lagache (1) utilises these notions in working out his conception of behaviour (α).

Ferenczi speaks of autoplastic adaptation in a more specifically genetic sense. What he is referring to is a very primitive method of adaptation which corresponds to an onto- and phylogenetic stage of development (the stage of the 'protopsyche') at which the organism has control over nothing but itself and

48

can bring about only somatic changes. To this method Ferenczi attributes hysterical conversion and, more specifically, what he calls a 'materialization phenomenon', whose 'essence consists in the realization of a wish, as though by magic, out of the material in the body at its disposal and–even if in primitive fashion–by a plastic representation' (2). We are here concerned with a deeper regression than in dreams, for the unconscious wish is incarnated not in visual images but in bodily states or actions.

Ferenczi sometimes speaks also–by way of contrast–of alloplastic adaptation, by which he means all those actions directed towards the outside world which allow the ego to maintain its equilibrium (3).

(α) Cf. the following table:

Operations

	Autoplastic	Alloplastic
Concrete	Physiological	Material actions
Symbolic	Mental activity, conscious and unconscious	Communications, languages

(1) Cf. LAGACHE, D. 'Éléments de psychologie médicale', in *Encyclopédie médico chirurgicale: Psychiatrie*, 37030 A 10.

(2) FERENCZI, S. 'The Phenomena of Hysterical Materialization. Thoughts on the Conception of Hysterical Conversion and Symbolism' (1919), in *Further Contributions*, 96.

(3) Cf. also FREUD, S. 'The Loss of Reality in Neurosis and Psychosis' (1924e), G.W., XIII, 366; S.E., XIX, 185. And ALEXANDER, F. 'Der neurotische Charakter', *Internat. Zeit.*, 1928.

B

Binding

= *D*.: Bindung.—*Es*.: ligazón.—*Fr*.: liaison.—*I*.: legame.—*P*.: ligação.

Term used by Freud in a very general way and on comparatively distinct levels (as much on the biological level as on that of the psychical apparatus) to denote an operation tending to restrict the free flow of excitations, to link ideas to one another and to constitute and maintain relatively stable forms.

Although the term 'binding' ought to be seen in connection with the contrast between free energy and bound energy*, its meaning is not exhausted by this purely economic connotation. Beyond its strictly technical use, the expression—which occurs at different points in Freud's work—answers a permanent conceptual need.

Rather than enumerate its uses, we have chosen to outline its importance at three stages of Freud's metapsychology where it plays a cardinal role:

I. In the 'Project for a Scientific Psychology' (1950*a* [1895]), *Bindung* denotes primarily the fact that the energy of the neuronal apparatus proceeds from the free to the bound state, or else that it is already in the bound state. For Freud, this binding implies the existence of a mass of neurones which are well connected and which have good facilitations between them—in other words, the ego: '. . . the ego itself is a mass like this of neurones which hold fast to their cathexis —are, that is, in a bound state; and this, surely, can only happen as a result of the effect they have on one another' (1*a*).

This bound mass itself exerts an inhibitory or binding effect on other processes. When Freud concerns himself, for example, with the fate of certain memories relating to painful experiences (*Schmerzerlebnisse*) which upon recollection 'arouse affect and also unpleasure', he describes them as 'untamed' (*ungebändigt*): 'If a passage of thought comes up against a still *untamed mnemic* image of this kind, then its indications of quality, often of a sensory kind, are generated, with a feeling of unpleasure and an inclination to discharge, the combination of which characterizes a particular affect, and the passage of thought is interrupted.' Before such a memory can be tamed, a 'relation to the ego or to ego-cathexes' must be established; 'particularly large and repeated binding from the ego is required before this facilitation to unpleasure can be counterbalanced' (1*b*).

Two ideas seem to need emphasis here:

a. The binding of energy presupposes the establishment of relations, of facilitations, with an already cathected system which forms a whole: in other words, 'fresh neurones' are drawn into the ego (1*c*).

b. Throughout the 'Project', *Bindung* has its opposite pole: *Entbindung* (literally, 'unbinding'); this term denotes a trigger mechanism involving the sudden release of energy, such as that which occurs in muscles or glands, where the effect, measured quantitatively, far surpasses the quantity of energy that provokes it. The term is generally found in the composite forms: *Unlustentbindung* (release of unpleasure), *Lustentbindung* (release of pleasure), *Sexualentbindung* (sexual release [of excitation]), *Affektentbindung* (release of affect) and, in other texts, *Angstentbindung* (release of anxiety). In all these cases what is referred to is a sudden emergence of a free energy tending irresistably towards discharge.

When we bring these terms together we are inevitably surprised by the economic approach that they imply: that the same term should be used to describe both the release of pleasure and the release of unpleasure would seem to run counter to the basic idea that pleasure and unpleasure are antagonistic processes affecting a single energy–involving the reduction of tension in the former case and the increase of it in the latter; it would be quite inconsistent with the Freudian thesis were we to suppose that pleasure and unpleasure correspond to qualitatively distinct forms of energy.

The *Entbindung-Bindung* opposition seems particularly useful for getting out of this difficulty. In its antagonism to the bound state of the ego, every release of primary-process energy–no matter whether it tends to increase or to diminish the *absolute* level of tension–poses a threat to the ego's relatively constant level. We may suppose that it is the release of sexual excitation, in particular, which in Freud's view checks the ego's binding function in this way (see 'Deferred Action', 'Seduction').

II. With *Beyond the Pleasure Principle* (1920g) the problem of binding is not only brought to the forefront of Freud's thought–it is also posed in a more complex fashion. It is apropos of the subject's repetition of the trauma, taken as the model of the repetition of all unpleasurable experiences, that Freud has recourse once again to the notion of binding. He returns to the idea, present in his work from the 'Project' onwards, that it is an already heavily cathected system that is capable of psychically binding an influx of energy. But the case of the trauma, seen as an extensive breach of the ego's boundaries, allows us to perceive this binding capacity at the very moment when it is threatened. As a result the binding process stands in an unusual relationship to the pleasure principle and the primary process. Whereas binding is usually looked upon as an influence exerted by the ego upon the primary process–namely, the introduction of the inhibition which characterizes the secondary process and the reality principle–Freud is led in this instance to ask himself whether in certain cases the very 'dominance of the pleasure principle' does not depend upon the prior accomplishment of 'the task of mastering or binding excitations', a task which 'would have precedence–not, indeed, in *opposition* to the pleasure principle, but independently of it and to some extent in disregard of it' (2).

Even if this binding process works ultimately for the benefit of the ego, Freud seems nevertheless to accord it an independent significance, in that he sees it as the basis of the repetition compulsion*, and in that he makes this compulsion, in the last reckoning, into the very mark of the instinctual as such. Thus the question remains open whether there exist two types of binding: one, long-recognised, which correlates with the notion of the ego, and another, closer to the laws governing unconscious desire and the organisation of phantasy

–the laws, in others words, of the primary process–where the free energy itself, as identified by psycho-analysis, is not a massive discharge of excitation but rather an energy which flows along chains of ideas and implies associative 'links'.

III. Lastly, in the framework of Freud's final theory of instincts, binding becomes the major characteristic of the life as opposed to the death instincts: 'The aim of [Eros] is to establish even greater unities and to preserve them thus –in short, to bind together; the aim of [the destructive instinct] is, on the contrary, to undo connections and so to destroy things' (3).

In the ultimate formulation of the theory, the agency of the ego and the instinctual energy which this has at its command are essentially located on the side of the life instincts: this energy 'would still retain the main purpose of Eros–that of uniting and binding–in so far as it helps towards establishing the unity, or tendency to unity, which is particularly characteristic of the ego' (4).

*   *   *

In conclusion, it seems to us that the psycho-analytic problematic of binding can be approached from three semantic directions which are suggested by the word itself: the idea of a relation between several terms which are linked up, for example, by an associative chain (*Verbindung*); the idea of a whole in which a certain cohesion is maintained, a form demarcated by specific limits or *bound*aries; and the idea of a fixation in one place of a certain quantity of energy which can no longer flow freely.

(1) FREUD, S.: a) *Anf.*, 447; S.E., I, 368. b) *Anf.*, 459; S.E., I, 380–81. c) *Anf.*, 448; S.E., I, 369.

(2) FREUD, S., G.W., XIII, 36; S.E., XVIII, 34–35.

(3) FREUD, S. *An Outline of Psycho-Analysis* (1940*a* [1938]), G.W., XVII, 71; S.E., XXIII, 148.

(4) FREUD, S. *The Ego and the Id* (1923*b*), G.W., XIII, 274; S.E., XIX, 45.

Bisexuality

= *D.*: Bisexualität.–*Es.*: bisexualidad.–*Fr.*: bisexualité.–*I.*: bisessualità.–*P.*: bissexualidade.

Notion introduced into psycho-analysis by Freud, under the influence of Wilhelm Fliess, according to which every human being is endowed constitutionally with both masculine and feminine sexual dispositions; these can be identified in the conflicts which the subject experiences in assuming his own sex.

As far as the history of the psycho-analytic movement is concerned, the notion of bisexuality must without doubt be attributed to the influence of Wilhelm Fliess. It was to be encountered in the philosophical and psychiatric literature of the 1890's (1*a*), but it was Fliess who advocated it to Freud, a fact to which their correspondence testifies (2).

The theory of bisexuality is based in the first instance on the data of anatomy and embryology (α): '. . . a certain degree of anatomical hermaphroditism occurs normally. In every normal male or female individual, traces are found of the apparatus of the opposite sex. [...] These long-familiar facts of anatomy lead us to suppose that an originally bisexual physical disposition has, in the course of evolution, become modified into a unisexual one, leaving behind only a few traces of the sex that has become atrophied' (1*b*).

Fliess attached considerable importance to those facts which point to a biological bisexuality. For him, bisexuality is a universal human phenomenon which is not restricted, for example, to the pathological case of homosexuality, and it has essential psychological consequences. Thus Fliess, interpreting the Freudian theory of repression, invokes the conflict which exists in every human individual between the masculine and feminine tendencies; Freud sums up Fliess's interpretation in these terms: 'The dominant sex of the person [...] has repressed the mental representation of the subordinate sex into the unconscious' (3*a*).

Freud never thoroughly defined his position with respect to the problem of bisexuality; in 1930 he himself admitted that 'The theory of bisexuality is still surrounded by many obscurities and we cannot but feel it as a serious impediment in psycho-analysis that it has not yet found any link with the theory of the instincts' (4). Although the psychological importance of bisexuality was never in doubt for him, Freud's thinking about the problem includes a number of reservations and doubts which may be summarised as follows:

a. The concept of bisexuality presupposes a clear grasp of the antithesis between masculinity and femininity. As Freud remarked, however, these notions have different meanings for biology, psychology and sociology–meanings which are often confused and which do not allow us to establish any terminological correlations between these various levels (1*c*).

b. Freud criticises Fliess's approach for sexualising the psychological mechanism of repression–'to sexualise' here meaning 'to explain it on biological grounds' (5*a*). Such an approach leads in fact to an *a priori* definition of the modality of the defensive conflict according to which the repressing force is on the side of the sex of the subject's manifest sexual characteristics, and the repressed on the side of the opposite sex. To this contention Freud objects 'that both in male and female individuals masculine as well as feminine instinctual impulses are found, and that each can equally well undergo repression and so become unconscious' (3*b*).

It is true that in 'Analysis Terminable and Interminable' (1937*c*) Freud appears nonetheless to be following Fliess's line when he admits that 'it is the attitude proper to the opposite sex which has succumbed to repression' (5*b*) (penis envy in women, the feminine attitude in men); this is a work, however, which emphasizes the importance of the castration complex*, and for this the biological data can provide no sufficient explanation.

c. It is clear that Freud's acceptance of the idea of *biological* bisexuality created a major difficulty for him; the same goes for the notion of the primacy of the phallus* in women as well as in men–an idea which is maintained throughout his work with ever-increasing conviction.

53

Borderline Case

(α) In the 1920 edition of the *Three Essays on the Theory of Sexuality* (1905d), Freud further draws attention to physiological experiments on the hormonal determination of sexual characteristics.

(1) Cf. FREUD, S. *Three Essays on the Theory of Sexuality* (1905d): a) G.W., V, 42n; S.E., VII, 143n. b) G.W., V, 40; S.E., VII, 141. c) G.W., V, 121n; S.E., VII, 219n.

(2) FREUD. S. *The Origins of Psycho-Analysis* (1950a [1887–1902]), *passim.*

(3) FREUD, S. ' "A Child is Being Beaten" ' (1919e): a) G.W., XII, 222; S.E., XVII, 200–201. b) G.W., XII, 224; S.E., XVII, 224.

(4) FREUD, S. *Civilization and its Discontents* (1930a), G.W., XIV, 466n; S.E., XXI, 106n.

(5) FREUD, S. 'Analysis Terminable and Interminable' (1937c): a) G.W., XVI, 98; S.E., XXIII, 251. b) G.W., XVI, 98; S.E., XXIII, 251.

Borderline Case

= *D.*: Grenzfall.–*Es.*: caso limítrofe.–*Fr.*: cas-limite.–*I.*: caso limite.–*P.*: caso limítrofe.

Term most often used to designate psychopathological troubles lying on the frontier between neurosis and psychosis, particularly latent schizophrenias presenting an apparently neurotic set of symptoms.

This term has no strict nosographical definition. The variations in its use reflect the real uncertainty concerning the area to which it is applied. Different writers, according to their diverse approaches, have extended the category to psychopathic, perverted and delinquent personalities, and to severe cases of character neurosis. Current usage is apparently tending to reserve the term for cases of schizophrenia whose symptoms have a neurotic aspect.

The spread of psycho-analysis has had a good deal to do with the coming to prominence of the so-called borderline case. Psycho-analytic investigation is indeed able to uncover the psychotic structure of cases that would formerly have been treated as neurotic disturbances. Theoretically speaking, it is generally felt that in such cases the neurotic symptoms carry out a defensive function against the outbreak of the psychosis.

C

Cannibalistic

= *D.*: kannibalisch. – *Es.*: canibalístico. – *Fr.*: cannibalique. – *I.*: cannibalico. – *P.*: canibalesco.

Term used, by analogy with the cannibalism practised by certain peoples, to qualify object-relationships and phantasies correlated with oral activity. It is a figurative description of the various dimensions of oral incorporation*: love, destruction, preservation within the self of the object and the appropriation of its qualities. The name 'cannibalistic stage' is sometimes given to the oral stage* – or, more specifically, to Abraham's second oral stage (oral-sadistic stage*).

Although the first edition of the *Three Essays on the Theory of Sexuality* (1905*d*) does contain one allusion to cannibalism, it is not until *Totem and Taboo* (1912–13) that this idea is developed. Freud brings out the belief that is implicit in this practice of 'primitive races': 'By incorporating parts of a person's body through the act of eating, one at the same time acquires the qualities possessed by him' (1*a*). The Freudian conception of the 'murder of the father' and of the 'totem meal' invests this idea with great importance: 'One day the brothers [...] came together, killed and devoured their father and so made an end of the patriarchal horde. [...] In the act of devouring him they accomplished their identification with him, and each one of them acquired a portion of his strength' (1*b*).

Whatever the validity of Freud's anthropological views, the term 'cannibalistic' has attained a well-defined meaning in psycho-analytic psychology. In the 1915 edition of the *Three Essays*, where Freud introduces the idea of an oral organisation, cannibalism is seen as a characteristic of this stage of psychosexual development. Writers since Freud have often spoken of a cannibalistic stage when referring to the oral stage. Karl Abraham, when he subdivides the oral stage into two phases – a preambivalent sucking phase and an ambivalent* biting phase – treats only the second one as cannibalistic.

This epithet underlines certain characteristics of the oral object-relationship: fusion* of libido and aggressiveness, incorporation and appropriation of the object and its properties. The notion of cannibalism itself implies the close connections that exist between the oral object-relationship and the earliest modes of identification (see 'Primary Identification').

(1) FREUD, S.: a) G.W., IX, 101; S.E., XIII, 82. b) G.W., IX, 171–72; S.E., XIII, 141–42.

Castration Complex

= *D*.: Kastrationskomplex.–*Es*.: complejo de castración.–*Fr*.: complexe de castration.– *I*.: complesso di castrazione.–*P*.: complexo de castração.

Complex centring on the phantasy of castration which is produced in response to the child's puzzlement over the anatomical difference between the sexes (presence or absence of the penis): the child attributes this difference to the fact of the girl's penis having been cut off.

The structure and consequences of the castration complex are different in the boy and in the girl. The boy fears castration, which he sees as the carrying out of a paternal *threat* made in reply to his sexual activities; the result for him is an intense *castration anxiety*. In the girl, the absence of a penis is experienced as a wrong suffered which she attempts to deny, to compensate for or to remedy.

The castration complex is closely linked with the Oedipus complex, and especially with the latter's prohibitive and normative function.

The analysis of Little Hans was decisive in Freud's discovery of the castration complex (α).

The complex is first described in 1908; it is associated with that 'sexual theory of children' which, since it attributes a penis to all human beings, can only explain the anatomical difference between the sexes by a castration. Although Freud does not claim at this point that the complex is universal, he seems to make this assumption implicitly. The castration complex is explained by the primacy of the penis in both sexes, and there is already a hint of its narcissistic significance: '. . . already in childhood the penis is the leading erotogenic zone and the chief auto-erotic object; and the boy's estimate of its value is logically reflected in his inability to imagine a person like himself who is without this essential constituent' (1).

From this point onwards in Freud's work the castration phantasy is identified behind a variety of symbols: the threatened object can be displaced (the blinding of Oedipus, extraction of teeth, etc.); the act may be distorted or replaced by other types of attack upon the wholeness of the body (accidents, syphilis, surgical operations) or even of the mind (madness as the result of masturbation); and the agency of the father lends itself to a great variety of substitutions (the anxiety-inducing animals of phobic subjects, for example). The castration complex is also held to account for a wide range of clinical consequences: penis envy*, the taboo of virginity, feelings of inferiority* and so on; and its modalities are deemed to be observable in all psychopathological structures, though especially in perversions (homosexuality, fetishism) (β). It is only comparatively late on, however, that Freud proceeds to assign this complex to its fundamental position in the development of infantile sexuality in both sexes, to outline its relationship to the Oedipus complex in detail and to posit its complete universality. This theoretical elaboration by Freud is a corollary of his identification of a phallic stage*: at this 'stage of infantile genital organisation [...] *maleness* exists, but not femaleness. The antithesis here is

56

between having *a male genital* and being *castrated*' (2). The unity of the complex in the two sexes is inconceivable without this common foundation: the object of castration–the phallus–enjoys an equal significance at this stage for the little girl and for the boy, and the question which arises is identical–to possess a phallus (*q.v.*) or not to possess one. The castration complex is encountered in every single analysis (3*a*).

A second theoretical characteristic of the castration complex is its impact upon *narcissism*: the phallus is an essential component of the child's self-image, so any threat to the phallus is a radical danger to this image; this explains the efficacity of the threat, which derives from the conjunction of two factors, namely, the primacy of the phallus and the narcissistic wound.

Empirically, there are two concrete facts which have a part to play in the genesis of the castration complex as described by Freud. The emergence of the complex depends entirely upon the child's *discovery* of the anatomical distinction between the sexes. This discovery actualises and validates a *threat* of castration which may have been real or phantasied. For the little boy, the castrating agent is the father–the authority to whom, in the last resort, he attributes all threats made by other people. The situation is not so clear-cut in the case of the girl, who perhaps feels herself to have been deprived of a penis by the mother rather than actually castrated by the father.

With respect to the Oedipus complex, the castration complex has a different role in the two sexes. For the little girl, it initiates the research which leads her to desire the paternal penis; it thus constitutes the point of entry into the Oedipal phase. In the boy, on the other hand, it marks the terminal crisis of the Oedipus complex in that it has the effect of placing a prohibition upon the child's maternal object; for him, castration anxiety inaugurates the period of latency* and precipitates the formation of the super-ego* (4).

*   *   *

The castration complex is met with constantly in analytic experience. The problem is how to account for its all but universal presence in human beings when the real threats from which it supposedly derives are far from being always evident (and even more rarely carried out!). It is quite obvious, moreover, that the girl could hardly for her part experience as serious a threat to deprive her of what she has not got. This ambiguity has naturally led psycho-analysts to look for alternatives to the threat of castration as the castration complex's concrete basis in reality. We may enumerate a variety of approaches among the resulting lines of theoretical development.

It is possible to put castration anxiety in the context of a series of traumatic experiences which are also characterised by an element of loss of or separation from an object: the loss of the breast in the routine of feeding; weaning; defecation. The validity of this assimilation is confirmed by the symbolic equivalences which psycho-analysis has brought out between the various part-objects* from which the subject is separated in this way: penis, breast, faeces and even the infant in childbirth. In 1917 Freud devoted a particularly suggestive paper to the equation penis = faeces = child, the transformations of the wish which this equation facilitates, and its relationship to the castration complex and the claims of narcissism: the little boy 'concludes that the penis must be a detachable part of the body, something analogous to faeces, the first piece of bodily substance the child had to part with' (5).

A. Stärcke, following the same line of research, was the first to put the whole emphasis on the experience of suckling and on the withdrawal of the breast as the prototype of castration: '. . . a penis-like part of the body is taken from another person, given to the child as his own (a situation with which are associated pleasurable sensations), and then taken away from the child causing "pain" (*Unlust*)' (6a). This *primary castration*, which is repeated at every feed and culminates with the weaning of the child, is considered to be the only real experience capable of accounting for the universal presence of the castration complex: the withdrawal of the mother's nipple, it is argued, is the ultimate unconscious meaning to be found behind the thoughts, fears and wishes which go to make up this complex.

Rank also attempts to found the castration complex on an actual primal experience. His thesis is that the separation from the mother in the birth trauma, together with the physical reactions which this occasions, provide the prototype for all subsequent anxiety. He concludes that castration anxiety is the echo–mediated through a long series of traumatic experiences–of the anxiety of birth.

Freud adopts a reserved attitude towards these different ways of tackling the problem. Even where he acknowledges that experiences of oral and anal separation are 'roots' of the castration complex, he nevertheless upholds the principle that 'the term "castration complex" ought to be confined to those excitations and consequences which are bound up with the loss of the *penis*' (3b). It is reasonable to assume that Freud is concerned here with more than mere considerations of terminological rigour. In the course of his long discussion of Rank's thesis in his *Inhibitions, Symptoms and Anxiety* (1926d), he clearly states his interest in attempts to trace the sources of castration anxiety as far back as possible and to discover the working of the category of separation–that is, of narcissistically invested object-loss–both in the earliest infancy and in a great variety of lived experiences (as, for example, in the case of moral anxiety interpreted as anxiety associated with separation from the super-ego). On the other hand, however, every page of *Inhibitions, Symptoms and Anxiety* bears witness to Freud's wish to disassociate himself from Rank's argument, and his constant concern in this work of synthesis is to replace the castration complex in its literal sense at the very centre of clinical psycho-analysis.

There are profounder reasons, however, for Freud's reluctance to commit himself completely to this sort of approach, for it runs counter to a basic theoretical demand which is illustrated by a number of Freudian notions. One example is the concept of deferred action*: this idea is incompatible with the thesis that it is necessary to delve further and further in order to find an experience able to assume a full prototypic function. But the category of *primal phantasies**–under which Freud subsumes the act of castration–provides the best illustration; both terms of this expression serve to point up what is at issue here: 'phantasy', because it indicates that the effects of castration are felt without it being carried out–and without it even becoming the subject of express formulations on the part of the parents; and 'primal', because it signifies that castration is one of the aspects of that complex of interpersonal relationships in which the sexual desires of the human being have their origin, develop their structure and become specific–and this despite the fact that castration anxiety, which arises only at the phallic stage, is far from being the first in the series of anxiety-producing experiences. The fact is that the part assigned by psycho-analysis to the castration complex cannot be understood if it is not related to the basic–and constantly restated–Freudian thesis of the nuclear nature and structuring function of the Oedipus complex.

The paradox of the Freudian theory of the castration complex might be put as follows (to restrict ourselves to the instance of the boy): the child cannot transcend the Oedipus complex and achieve identification with the father without first having overcome the castration crisis; in other words, he must have confronted the rejection of his demand to use his penis as an instrument of his desire for his mother. The castration complex has to be understood in terms of the cultural order, where the right to a particular practice is invariably associated with a prohibition. The 'threat of castration' which sets the seal on the prohibition against incest is the embodiment of the Law that founds the human order; this is illustrated, in a mythical form, by the 'theory' put forward in *Totem and Taboo* (1912–13) of the primal father who, by threatening his sons with castration, reserves the exclusive sexual use of the women of the horde for himself.

It is precisely because the castration complex is the *a priori* condition governing interhuman exchange in the form of exchange of sexual objects that it can appear to concrete experience under several aspects, that it can be expressed in ways that are at once different and complementary–as in the formulations proposed by Stärcke, which combine the categories of subject and other, of losing and receiving:

'1. I am castrated (sexually deprived, slighted), I shall be castrated.

'2. I will (wish to) receive a penis.

'3. Another person is castrated, has to (will) be castrated.

'4. Another person will receive a penis (has a penis)' (6b).

(α) All the passages concerning castration in *The Interpretation of Dreams* (1900a) were added in 1911 or in even later editions; the sole exception is an allusion–which is in fact erroneous–to Zeus's castration of Kronos.

(β) It is possible, from this standpoint, to imagine a psycho-analytical nosography taking the modalities and transformations of the castration complex as a major axis of its frame of reference; the suggestions made by Freud, towards the end of his work, concerning the neuroses (7), fetishism and the psychoses would lend support to such an approach.

(1) FREUD, S. 'On the Sexual Theories of Children' (1908c), G.W., VII, 178; S.E., IX, 215–16.

(2) FREUD, S. 'The Infantile Genital Organization' (1923e), G.W., XIII, 297; S.E., XIX, 145.

(3) FREUD, S. 'Analysis of a Phobia in a Five-Year-Old Boy' (1909b): a) Cf. G.W., VII, 246, note 1 added in 1923; S.E., X, 8, note 2. b) G.W., VII, 246, note 1 added in 1923; S.E., X, 8, note 2.

(4) Cf. FREUD, S. 'The Dissolution of the Oedipus Complex' (1924d), G.W., XIII, 395; S.E., XIX, 173.

(5) FREUD, S. 'On the Transformations of Instinct, as Exemplified in Anal Erotism' (1917c), G.W., X, 409; S.E., XVII, 133.

(6) STÄRCKE, A. 'The Castration Complex', *I.J.P.*, 1921, II: a) 182. b) 180.

(7) Cf. FREUD, S. *Inhibitions, Symptoms and Anxiety* (1926*d*), G.W., XIV, 129–39; S.E., XX, 101–10.

Cathartic Method (or Therapy)

= *D.*: kathartisches Heilverfahren *or* kathartische Methode.–
Es.: terapia carártica *or* método catártico.–*Fr.*: méthode cathartique.–*I.*: metodo catartico.–
P.: terapêutica *or* terapia catártica, método catártico.

Method of psychotherapy in which the therapeutic effect sought is 'purgative': an adequate discharge of pathogenic affects. The treatment allows the patient to evoke and even to relive the traumatic events to which these affects are bound, and to abreact them.

Historically, the cathartic method belongs to a period (1880–95) during which psycho-analytic therapeutics were gradually emerging from a type of treatment carried out under hypnosis.

'Catharsis' is a Greek word meaning purification or purging. Aristotle used it to denote the effect tragedy produces on the spectator: 'A tragedy [...] is the imitation of an action that is serious and also [...] complete in itself [...] with incidents arousing pity and fear, wherewith to accomplish its catharsis of such emotions' (1).

Breuer and then Freud adopted this term and used it to mean the desired result of an adequate abreaction* of a trauma* (2*a*). According to the theory worked out in the *Studies on Hysteria* (1895*a*), as we know, those affects that do not succeed in finding a pathway to discharge remain 'strangulated' (*eingeklemmt*) and bring about pathogenic results. In a later *résumé* of the theory of catharsis, Freud was to write: 'According to that hypothesis, hysterical symptoms originate through the energy of a mental process being withheld from conscious influence and being diverted into bodily innervation ("conversion"). [...] recovery would be a result of the liberation of the affect that had gone astray and of its discharge along a normal path ("abreaction")' (3).

The beginnings of the cathartic method are closely bound up with hypnosis. But Freud soon stopped using hypnotism as a procedure aimed at suppressing the symptom directly by suggesting to the patient that it did not exist; instead, he employed it merely to provoke recollection by bringing back into the field of consciousness the experiences which underlie the symptoms but which the subject has forgotten–i.e. 'repressed' (α). The fresh evocation, or even the reliving with dramatic intensity, of these memories gives the subject a chance to express and discharge those affects which were originally tied to the traumatic experience but which have undergone repression immediately.

Freud quickly rejected hypnosis proper and replaced it with simple suggestion (backed up by a technical artifice: the application with the hand of pressure to the patient's forehead) as a means of convincing the sick person that he is going to recover the pathogenic memory. Eventually he gave up suggestion too, and relied merely on the patient's free associations*. The purpose of the treatment might seem to have remained unchanged throughout this evolution in technique: the patient is to be cured of his symptoms by the restoration of the normal path of discharge of the affects. In point of fact, however–as Freud's chapter in the *Studies* on 'The Psychotherapy of Hysteria' attests–this technical evolution goes hand in hand with a change in perspective as regards the theory of the treatment: namely, the taking into consideration of the resistances* and the transference*, and the ever-increasing emphasis placed upon the efficacy of psychical working out* and of working-through*. To this extent, therefore, the cathartic effect associated with abreaction ceases to be the main foundation of the treatment.

Nevertheless, catharsis remains one of the dimensions of any analytic psychotherapy. For one thing–although this will vary according to the psychopathological structures in question–many treatments present us with intense revivals of certain memories, accompanied by a more or less tempestuous emotional discharge. Furthermore, it would be an easy matter to show that the cathartic effect is visible in the various modalities of repetition displayed during the treatment, and particularly in transferential actualization. Similarly, working-through and symbolisation by language were already prefigured in the cathartic force that Breuer and Freud attributed to verbal expression: '. . . language serves as a substitute for action; by its help, an affect can be "abreacted" almost as effectively. In other cases speaking is itself an adequate reflex, when, for instance, it is a lamentation or giving utterance to a tormenting secret, e.g. a confession' (2*b*).

Apart from those cathartic aspects that may be recognised in every psychoanalysis, it should be pointed out that there are certain types of psychotherapy which are orientated above all around catharsis: narco-analysis, which is applied especially in cases of traumatic neurosis, uses medicinal means to bring about effects akin to those obtained by Breuer and Freud through hypnosis. And the psychodrama, according to Moreno, is defined as a release from internal conflicts by means of play-acting.

(α) On this evolution in Freud's use of hypnosis, cf. for example 'A Case of Successful Treatment by Hypnotism' (1892–93*b*).

(1) *Poetics*, 1449*b*.

(2) Cf. FREUD, S. *Studies on Hysteria* (1895*d*): a) G.W., I, 87; S.E., II, 8. b) G.W., I, 87; S.E., II, 8.

(3) FREUD, S. 'Psycho-Analysis' (1926*f*), G.W., XIV, 300; S.E., XX, 263–64.

Cathectic Energy

= *D.*: Besetzungsenergie.–*Es.*: energía de carga.–*Fr.*: énergie d'investissement.–
I.: energia di carica *or* d'investimento.–*P.*: energia de carga *or* de investimento.

Substratum of energy postulated as the quantitative factor in the working of the psychical apparatus.

This notion is discussed under 'Economic', 'Cathexis', 'Free Energy/Bound Energy' and 'Libido'.

Cathexis

= *D.*: Besetzung.–*Es.*: carga.–*Fr.*: investissement.–*I.*: carica *or* investimento.–
P.: carga *or* investimento.

Economic* concept: the fact that a certain amount of psychical energy is attached to an idea or to a group of ideas, to a part of the body, to an object, etc.

The term '*Besetzung*' is encountered throughout Freud's writings: although its connotation and significance may vary, he makes use of it at every stage in his thought (α).

It first makes its appearance in 1895, in the *Studies on Hysteria* and in the 'Project for a Scientific Psychology' but related terms like 'sum of excitation' and 'quota of affect' were employed even earlier, and as early as his Introduction to his translation of Bernheim's *De la Suggestion et de ses applications à la thérapeutique* (*Die Suggestion und ihre Heilwirkung*, 1888–9) Freud speaks of displacements of excitability in the nervous system (*Verschiebungen von Erregbarkeit im Nervensystem*). The hypothesis in question is founded on both clinical and theoretical considerations.

Clinically, the treatment of neurotics–and particularly hysterics–obliged Freud to postulate a basic distinction between 'ideas'* and the 'quota of affect'* by which they are cathected. Such a distinction explains how a subject can evoke an important event in his own history with indifference, while the unpleasant or intolerable nature of an experience may be associated with a harmless event rather than with the one which originally brought about the unpleasure (displacement, 'false connection'). As described in the *Studies on Hysteria*, the cure re-establishes the relation between the memory of the traumatic event and its affect by restoring the connection between the different ideas involved and so facilitating the discharge of the affect (abreaction*). Furthermore, the disappearance of the somatic symptoms of hysteria is parallel to the bringing out into the open of the repressed emotional experiences; this implies, conversely, that the symptoms are brought into being by the conversion of a psychical energy into an 'innervation' energy.

These phenomena–and especially the phenomenon of conversion*–appear to be based on an actual principle of conservation of a nervous energy which is capable of taking different forms. Freud does in fact formulate such a notion systematically in the 'Project for a Scientific Psychology', in which the working of the nervous apparatus is described exclusively in terms of variations of energy within a system of neurones. In this text, the term '*Besetzung*' denotes both the action of cathecting a neurone (i.e. loading it with energy) and the quantity of energy (especially quiescent energy) with which it is cathected (1).

Freud subsequently abandoned these neurological schemata and transposed the notion of cathectic energy into the framework of a 'psychical apparatus'*. Thus in *The Interpretation of Dreams* (1900a) he shows how the cathectic energy is shared out between the different systems. The functioning of the unconscious system is subordinated to the principle of the discharge of quantities of excitation; the preconscious system attempts to inhibit this immediate discharge while simultaneously devoting a small amount of energy to the thought-activity needed for the exploration of the outside world: 'I therefore postulate that for the sake of efficiency the second system succeeds in retaining the major part of its cathexes of energy in a state of quiescence and in employing only a small part on displacement' (2a) (see 'Free Energy/Bound Energy').

It should nevertheless be borne in mind that this transposition of the hypotheses of the 'Project' does not imply that all reference to the idea of a nervous energy has been dropped. Freud remarks that 'anyone who wished to take these ideas seriously would have to look for physical analogies for them and find a means of picturing the movements that accompany excitation of neurones' (2b).

The elaboration of the idea of instinct furnished a reply to a question which the development of the economic concepts of *The Interpretation of Dreams* had left in abeyance: cathected energy is now identified as the instinctual energy which originates from internal sources, exerting a continual pressure and obliging the psychical apparatus to take on the job of transforming it. Consequently, such an expression as 'libidinal cathexis' means cathexis by the energy of the sexual instincts. In the second theory of the psychical apparatus, it is the id, as the instinctual pole of the personality, which is seen as the origin of all cathexes, and the other agencies* draw their energy from this primary source.

*   *   *

The notion of cathexis–like most of the economic notions–plays a part in Freud's conceptual apparatus without his ever having given a rigorous theoretical definition of it.

These economic concepts, moreover, were in part inherited by 'the young Freud' from the neurophysiologists under whose influence he had come, such as Brücke and Meynert. This state of affairs goes some way towards explaining the uncertainty of Freud's readers when faced with a number of questions:

a. The use of the term 'cathexis' never escapes a certain ambiguity which analytic theory has nowhere managed to dispel. The concept is generally taken in a metaphorical sense, in which case it does no more than express an analogy between psychical operations and the working of a nervous apparatus conceived of in terms of energy.

63

Cathexis

To speak of the cathexis of an *idea* is to define a psychological operation in terms which merely evoke a physiological mechanism analogically, as a possible parallel to psychical cathexis (the model being the cathexis of a neurone, say, or of an engram). But when mention is made of a cathexis of *objects*, as opposed to that of ideas, the appeal to a psychical apparatus understood as a closed system analogous to the nervous system can no longer be upheld. It may make sense to say that an idea is loaded and that its fate is determined by the variations in this load, but the cathexis of a material, independent object cannot be envisaged in the same 'realist' sense. This ambiguity is well shown up by a notion such as that of introversion—meaning the transition from the cathexis of a real object to the cathexis of an imaginary intrapsychical object—for the idea of a conservation of energy during this withdrawal is extremely hard to picture.

Some psycho-analysts seem to feel that using a term like 'cathexis' provides objective proof that their dynamic psychology is—in principle at least—related to neurophysiology. It is true that by employing such formulations as cathexis of parts of the body, cathexis of the perceptual apparatus, and so on, one may get the impression that one is speaking in a neurological language, and so building a real link between psycho-analytic theory and neurophysiology. In reality, a neurophysiology so conceived could not be anything more than a reflection of psycho-analysis.

b. A further problem arises over the integration of the notion of cathexis with the topographical conceptions of Freud. On the one hand, all cathectic energy is supposed to have its source in the instincts, while on the other hand a specific cathexis is ascribed to each of the psychical agencies. The difficulty becomes acute in the case of unconscious cathexis, so-called. If we consider this type of cathexis to be libidinal in origin, we are bound to see it as responsible for constantly impelling the ideas which have been cathected towards consciousness and motility; yet Freud often speaks of unconscious cathexis as though it were a cohesive force belonging specifically to the unconscious system and capable of attracting ideas into that system; to this force, what is more, he assigns a major part in repression. It is therefore legitimate to ask whether 'cathexis' is not being used to connote essentially heterogeneous ideas (3).

c. Can the notion of cathexis be restricted to its economic sense? Freud certainly equates it with the notion of a positive load attributed to an object or an idea. It would seem, however, that it takes on a broader meaning both clinically and descriptively. In the subject's personal world, objects and ideas are affected by certain *values* which organise the fields of perception and behaviour. Now, in the first place these values may appear to differ qualitatively among themselves to such an extent that it becomes difficult to imagine equivalences or substitutions between them. A further consideration is that it is observable that certain objects which are pregnant with value for the subject are affected by a negative rather than a positive load: in phobia, for example, cathexis is not withdrawn from the object—on the contrary, the object is heavily 'cathected' as an object-to-be-avoided.

There is thus a temptation to abandon the economic terminology and to translate the Freudian conception of cathexis into a language inspired by phenomenological thinking and based on such concepts as intentionality and value object. This line of approach, furthermore, finds some support in the language used by Freud himself. For example: in his article, 'Some Points for a Comparative Study of Organic and Hysterical Motor Paralyses' (1893c), which was originally published in French, Freud adopts the term '*valeur affective*' as the equivalent of '*Affektbetrag*' (quota of affect) (4). In other places, cathexis seems to mean less a measurable load of libidinal energy than qualitatively differentiated emotional intentions, so that the maternal object–missed by the infant–can be said to have a 'cathexis of longing' concentrated upon it (*Sehnsuchtbesetzung*) (5).

*　　*　　*

Whatever the difficulties presented by the concept of cathexis, psycho-analysts would certainly find it hard to do without it, essential as it is in accounting for a large number of clinical data, and in assessing the progress of the treatment. There are certain pathological conditions which seem to leave us no alternative but to postulate that the subject draws on a specific quantity of energy which he distributes in variable proportions in his relationships with objects and with himself. In a state such as mourning, for example, the manifest impoverishment of the subject's relational life is to be explained by a hypercathexis of the lost object, and from this we can only infer that a veritable balance of energy holds sway over the distribution of the various cathexes of external or phantasied objects, of the subject's own body, of his ego, and so on.

(α) *Translator's note:* 'Cathexis' is the generally accepted rendering of '*Besetzung*'. James Strachey coined the word in 1922 from the Greek κατέχειν, to occupy. He records in the *Standard Edition* that Freud was unhappy with this choice because of his dislike of technical terms (S.E., III, 63, *n.* 2). The German verb '*besetzen*' is indeed part of everyday usage; it has a variety of senses, the chief one being *to occupy* (e.g. in a military context, to occupy a town, a territory). An alternative English translation, used occasionally, is 'investment', 'to invest'.

(1) Cf. FREUD, S. *Anf.*, 382; S.E., I, 298.

(2) FREUD, S.: a) G.W., II–III, 605; S.E., V, 599. b) G.W., II–III, 605; S.E., V, 599.

(3) For a more thorough treatment of this topic, cf. LAPLANCHE, J. and LECLAIRE, S. 'L'inconscient', *Les Temps Modernes*, 1961, No. 183, chap. II.

(4) Cf. FREUD, S., G.W., I, 54; S.E., I, 171.

(5) Cf. FREUD, S. *Inhibitions, Symptoms and Anxiety* (1926d), G.W., XIV, 205; S.E., XX, 171.

Censorship

= *D.*: Zensur.–*Es.*: censura.–*Fr.*: censure.–*I.*: censura.–*P.*: censura.

Function tending to prohibit unconscious wishes and the formations deriving from them from gaining access to the preconscious-conscious system.

This term is encountered chiefly in those texts of Freud's that deal with the 'first topography'. Freud uses it for the first time in a letter to Fliess dated December 22, 1897, in order to account for the apparently absurd character of certain delusions: 'Have you ever seen a foreign newspaper which has passed the Russian censorship at the frontier? Words, whole clauses and sentences are blacked out so that what is left becomes unintelligible' (1). This idea is further developed in *The Interpretation of Dreams* (1900a), where it is proposed as an explanation of the different mechanisms of distortion* (*Enstellung*) in dreams.

Freud holds the censorship to be a permanent function: it constitutes a selective barrier between the unconscious* system on the one hand and the preconscious*-conscious* one on the other, and it is thus placed at the point of origin or repression*. Its effects are more clearly discernible when it is partially relaxed, as it is in dreaming: the sleeping state prevents the contents of the unconscious from breaking through on to the level of motor activity; since they are liable to come into conflict with the wish for sleep, however, the censorship continues to operate in an attenuated way.

Freud does not see the censorship as working only between the unconscious and the preconscious, but also between the preconscious and consciousness. He assumes 'that to every transition from one system to that immediately above it (that is, every advance to a higher stage of psychical organisation) there corresponds a new censorship' (2a). Indeed, Freud notes, we would do better, instead of picturing two censorships, to imagine just one which 'takes a step forward' (2b).

In the context of his second theory of the psychical apparatus, Freud is brought in the first place to include the censorship in the vaster field of defence*; and secondly, he poses the question of what agency should have the censoring function attributed to it.

It has often been remarked that the idea of the censorship prefigures that of the super-ego*, whose 'anthropomorphic' character is already discernible in certain of Freud's descriptions of the censorship: between the 'entrance hall' where unconscious desires jostle one another and the 'drawing-room' where consciousness resides, a guardian keeps watch with a greater or lesser amount of vigilance; this guardian is the censorship (3a). When the notion of the super-ego emerges, Freud explicitly relates it to what he had formerly described as the censorship: 'We know the self-observing agency as the ego-censor, the conscience; it is this that exercises the dream-censorship during the night, from which the repressions of inadmissible wishful impulses proceed' (3b).

Later in Freud's work, though the question is never raised explicitly, the functions of the censorship, particularly the distortion of dreams, are assigned to the ego* (4).

It should be noted that, wherever this term is employed, its literal sense is always present: those passages within an articulate discourse that are deemed unacceptable are suppressed, and this suppression is revealed by blanks or alterations.

(1) FREUD, S., *Anf.*, 255; S.E., I, 273.

(2) FREUD, S. 'The Unconscious' (1915e): a) Cf. G.W., X, 290–91; S.E., XIV, 192. b) G.W., X. 292; S.E., XIV, 193.

(3) Cf. FREUD, S. *Introductory Lectures on Psycho-Analysis* (1916–17): a) G.W., XI, 305–6; S.E., XVI, 295–96. b) G.W., XI, 444; S.E., XVI, 429.

(4) Cf. FREUD, S. *An Outline of Psycho-Analysis* (1940a [1938]), G.W., XVII, chap. IV; S.E., XXIII, chap. IV.

Character Neurosis

= *D.*: Charakterneurose. – *Es.*: neurosis de carácter. – *Fr.*: névrose de caractère. –
I.: nevrosi del carattere. – *P.*: neurose de caráter.

Type of neurosis in which the defensive conflict, instead of being manifested by the formation of clearly identifiable symptoms, appears in the shape of character-traits, modes of behaviour or even a pathological organisation of the whole of the personality.

The term 'character neurosis' has achieved currency in contemporary psycho-analytical usage without ever having been given a very exact meaning.

That the notion remains so ill-defined is no doubt due to the fact that it raises not only *nosographical* problems (what are the specific attributes of character neurosis?) but also both *psychological* questions regarding the origin, basis and function of character and the *technical* question of what place ought to be given to the analysis of so-called 'character' defences.

The precedents for the use of the concept are, in fact, to be found in psycho-analytic works of differing orientations:

a. In studies of certain traits or certain types of character, particularly in relation to libidinal development (1).

b. In Wilhelm Reich's theoretical and technical conceptions of 'character armour' and of the need, especially in cases which are resistant to classical analysis, to bring out and interpret those defensive attitudes which are repeated whatever the verbalised content (2).

*   *   *

Even if we confine ourselves to strictly nosographical considerations – which the term 'character neurosis' itself inevitably evokes – confusion immediately arises over the multiplicity of possible meanings:

a. The term is often used in a not very rigorous way to refer to any clinical picture which does not at first sight exhibit symptoms but merely modes of behaviour leading to recurrent or permanent difficulty in the patient's relation to his environment.

b. There is a psycho-analytically orientated characterology which correlates different character types either with the major psychoneurotic conditions (speaking of obsessional, phobic, paranoiac characters and so on) or else with the various stages of libidinal development (which are said to correspond to oral, anal, urethral, phallic-narcissistic and genital character types – sometimes reclassified in terms of the major opposition between genital and pre-genital characters). According to this approach it is legitimate to talk of character neurosis when referring to any apparently asymptomatic neurosis where it is the type of character which betrays a pathogenic organisation.

In going further than this, however, and appealing – as is done today with increasing frequency – to the concept of structure, one tends to transcend the distinction between neuroses with symptoms and neuroses without symptoms: the emphasis is placed on the way desire and defence are organised rather than on the explicit manifestations of the conflict (i.e. symptoms or character-traits) (α).

c. The mechanisms most usually invoked to account for the formation of character are sublimation* and reaction-formations*. The latter 'avoid second-ary repressions by making a "once-and-for-all", definitive change of the person-ality' (3). In so far as it is the reaction-formations which predominate, the character itself may appear as an essentially defensive formation intended to protect the individual against the emergence of symptoms as well as against the instinctual threat.

From the descriptive standpoint, character defence is to be distinguished from the symptom particularly by its relative integration into the ego: there is a failure to recognise the pathological aspect of the character-trait; rationalisation; and a defence originally directed against a specific threat is generalised into a pattern of behaviour. It is possible to see such mechanisms as so many charac-teristics of the obsessional structure (4), in which case character neurosis would mean, first and foremost, a particularly common form of obsessional neurosis typified by a predominance of the mechanism of reaction-formation and by the discrete or sporadic nature of its symptoms.

d. Lastly, in contradistinction to the heterogeneity of 'neurotic characters', there has been an attempt to apply the term 'character neurosis' to a unique psychopathological structure: thus Henri Sauguet reserves the category 'for cases where the infiltration of the ego is so considerable that it determines an organisation reminiscent of a pre-psychotic structure' (5).

Such a conception echoes a tradition of psycho-analytic work which has tried to place anomalies of character in between neurotic symptoms and psychotic disorders (Alexander, Ferenczi, Glover) (6).

(α) In the context of a structural conception of the psychical apparatus, it is worth establish-ing a very clear distinction between the notions of *structure* and *character*. The latter could be defined–to adopt a formula of Daniel Lagache's–as the projection of the relations between and within the various systems on to the ego system. In dealing with a particular character-trait which appears as an intrinsic personal disposition, this approach would attempt to discover a corresponding dominance of one or another of the psychical agencies (e.g. the ideal ego*).

(1) Cf. particularly: FREUD, S. 'Character and Anal Erotism' (1908b); 'Some Character-Types Met with in Psycho-Analytic Work' (1916d); 'Libidinal Types' (1931a). ABRAHAM, K. 'Ergänzung zur Lehre vom Analcharakter' (1921); 'Beiträge der Oralerotik zur Charakter-bildung' (1924); 'Zur Charakterbildung auf der "genitalen" Entwicklungsstufe' (1924). GLOVER, E. 'Notes on Oral Character-Formation' (1925).

(2) Cf. REICH, W. *Charakteranalyse* (Berlin, 1933). English translation: *Character-Analysis*, third edn. (New York: Noonday, 1949).

(3) FENICHEL, O. *The Psychoanalytic Theory of Neurosis* (New York: Norton, 1945), 151.

(4) Cf. FREUD, S. *Inhibitions, Symptoms and Anxiety* (1926d), G.W., XIV, 190; S.E., XX, 157–58.

(5) EY, H. *Encyclopédie médico-chirurgicale (Psychiatrie)* (1955), 37320 A 20, 1.

(6) Cf. particularly: GLOVER, E. 'The Neurotic Character', *I.J.P.*, 1926, VII, 11–30.

Choice of Neurosis

= *D.*: Neurosenwahl.–*Es.*: elección de la neurosis.–*Fr.*: choix de la névrose.–
I.: scelta della nevrosi.–*P.*: escolha da neurose.

The whole group of processes whereby the subject embarks upon the formation of one particular type of psychoneurosis as opposed to any other.

The problem raised by the expression 'choice of neurosis' is a fundamental one for any analytic psychpathology: how and why is it that the general processes which account for the formation of neurosis (e.g. the defensive conflict) assume specific shape in neurotic organisations so diverse that a nosography can be established?

This is a question that had Freud's attention throughout his work; it cannot be divorced from any profound elucidation of neurotic structures. Freud suggested a variety of solutions to this problem, the history of which there can be no question of our following up here since it is inseparable from the history of the notions of trauma*, of fixation*, of predisposition, of unevenness of development between libido and ego, etc. The ramifications of this problem are such as to place it beyond the scope of the present work.

Restricting ourselves to the terminological side of the matter, therefore, we may ask why Freud selected and stood by the word 'choice' (1). His intention is clearly not to put stress on the role of the intellect–it is not a matter of one of a number of equally available possibilities being opted for; the same is true, moreover, in the case of the notion of *object-choice**. All the same, it is certainly not without significance, in an approach which appeals otherwise to an absolute determinism, that this word should appear, suggesting as it does that an act on the subject's part is required if the various historical and constitutional determinants which psycho-analysis brings out are to become meaningful and attain the force of motivating factors.

(1) Cf., for example, FREUD, S., letter to Fliess of May 5, 1896, in *Anf.* and S.E., I; and 'The Disposition to Obsessional Neurosis' (1913*i*), G.W., VIII, 442; S.E., XII, 317.

Cloacal (or Cloaca) Theory

= *D.*: Kloakentheorie.–*Es.*: teoría cloacal.–*Fr.*: théorie cloacale.–*I.*: teoria cloacale.–
P.: teoria cloacal.

A sexual theory of children which ignores the distinction between vagina and anus. The woman is pictured as having only one cavity and only one orifice, which is confused with the anus. This orifice is thought to serve for both parturition and coitus.

It is in his article 'On the Sexual Theories of Children' (1908*c*) that Freud described what he called the cloacal theory as a typical infantile theory, one

69

connected in his view with ignorance of the vagina in children of both sexes. This ignorance gives rise to the conviction that 'The baby must be evacuated like a piece of excrement, like a stool. [...] The cloacal theory, which, after all, is valid for so many animals, was the most natural theory, and it alone could obtrude upon the child as being a probable one' (1). The notion that only one orifice exists also entrains a 'cloacal' image of coition (2).

According to Freud, a theory of this kind is formed very early on. It will be noted that it corresponds to certain observations made by psycho-analysis, particularly in connection with the evolution of feminine sexuality: 'The clear-cut distinction between anal and genital processes which is later insisted upon is contradicted by the close anatomical and functional analogies and relations which hold between them. The genital apparatus remains the neighbour of the cloaca, and actually "in the case of women is only taken from it on lease"' (3, α). For Freud, it is starting from this sort of undifferentiated state of affairs that 'the vagina, an organ derived from the cloaca, has to be raised into the dominant erotogenic zone' (4).

(α) Freud is quoting here from Lou Andreas-Salomé's article, ' "Anal" and "Sexual" ' (1916).

(1) FREUD, S., G.W., VII, 181; S.E., IX, 219.

(2) FREUD, S. 'From the History of an Infantile Neurosis' (1918b [1914]), G.W., XII, 111; S.E., XVII, 79.

(3) FREUD, S. *Three Essays on the Theory of Sexuality* (1905d), G.W., V, 88n; S.E., VII, 187n.

(4) FREUD, S. 'The Disposition to Obsessional Neurosis' (1913i), G.W., VII, 452; S.E., XII, 325–26.

Combined Parent(s), Combined Parent-Figure

= *D.*: vereinigte Eltern, vereinigte Eltern-Imago. –
  Es.: pareja combinada, imago de la pareja combinada. – *Fr.*: parent(s) combiné(s). –
  I.: figura parentale combinata. – *P.*: pais unificados, imago de pais unificados.

Term introduced by Melanie Klein to denote an infantile sexual theory expressed in various phantasies representing the parents as united in an everlasting sexual embrace: the mother contains the father's penis or the whole father; the father contains the mother's breast or the whole mother; the parents are inseparably fused in an act of coition.

Such phantasies are said to be very primitive and highly anxiogenic.

The idea of the 'combined parent' is intrinsic to the Kleinian conception of the Oedipus complex (1): what is involved here is 'a sexual theory, formed at a very early stage of development, to the effect that the mother incorporates the father's penis in the act of coitus, so that in the last resort the woman with a penis signifies the two parents joined together' (2a).

The phantasy of the 'woman with a penis'* is not a discovery of Klein's (3): Freud brings it to light as early as his article 'On the Sexual Theories of Children' (1908c). For Freud, however, this phantasy is embodied in the childhood sexual theory that refuses to accept the difference between the sexes and the castration of women. Melanie Klein proposes a very different genesis for it in *The Psycho-Analysis of Children* (1932), where it is said to derive from very early phantasies: a primal scene* heavily marked by sadism, the internalisation* of the father's penis, the picturing of the mother's body as a receptacle for *'good'* and (particularly) *'bad' objects**. 'The child's belief that its mother's body contains the penis of its father leads [...] to the idea of "the woman with a penis". The sexual theory that the mother has a female penis of her own is, I think, the result of a modification by displacement of more deeply seated fears of her body as a place which is filled with a number of dangerous penises and of the two parents engaged in dangerous copulation. "The woman with a penis" always means, I should say, the woman with the father's penis' (2b). The phantasy of the 'combined parent', allied with archaic infantile sadism, commands great anxiogenic force.

In a later article Klein links the notion of the 'combined parent' with a fundamental attitude of the child's: 'It is characteristic of the young infant's intense emotions and greed that he should attribute to the parents a constant state of mutual gratification of an oral, anal and genital nature' (4).

(1) Cf. KLEIN, M. 'Early Stages of the Oedipus Conflict' (1928), in *Contributions*, 202–14.

(2) KLEIN, M. *The Psycho-Analysis of Children* (1932): a) 103–4. b) 333.

(3) Cf. FREUD, S., G.W., VII, 171–88; S.E., IX, 209–26.

(4) KLEIN, M. 'The Emotional Life of the Infant' (1952), in *Developments*, 219.

Complemental Series

= *D*.: Ergänzungsreihe.–*Es*.: serie complementaria.–*Fr*.: série complémentaire.– *I*.: serie complementare.–*P*.: série complementar.

Term used by Freud in order to account for the aetiology of neurosis without making a hard-and-fast choice between exogenous or endogenous factors. For Freud these two kinds of factors are actually complementary–the weaker the one, the stronger the other–so that any group of cases can in theory be distributed along a scale with the two types of factors varying in inverse ratio. Only at the two extremities of such a serial arrangement would it be possible to find instances where only one kind of factor is present.

The idea of the complemental series is most clearly expressed in the *Introductory Lectures on Psycho-Analysis* (1916–17). The initial context is the causation of neurosis (1a): from the aetiological point of view, we have no need to choose between the endogenous factor represented by the fixation* and the exogenous one represented by frustration*. The two vary in inverse ratio to each other: for

71

neurosis to develop in the case of a strong fixation only a minimal trauma* is required–and vice versa.

In addition the fixation may itself be broken down into two complemental factors: hereditary constitution and childhood experiences (1b). The concept of a complemental series allows us to ascribe any given case to a position on a scale according to the relative significance of constitutional factors, childhood experiences and later traumas.

Freud's main use of this notion is in accounting for the aetiology of neurosis, but we may speak of complemental series in other areas where a multiplicity of factors is in play and where these factors vary inversely to one another.

(1) Cf. FREUD, S.: a) G.W., XI, 359–60; S.E., XVI, 346–47. b) G.W., XI, 376: S.E., XVI, 362.

Complex

= D.: Komplex.–Es.: complejo.–Fr.: complexe.–I.: complesso.–P.: complexo.

Organised group of ideas and memories of great affective force which are either partly or totally unconscious. Complexes are constituted on the basis of the inter-personal relationships of childhood history; they may serve to structure all levels of the psyche: emotions, attitudes, adapted behaviour.

Common usage has received the term 'complex' with open arms (cf. 'having complexes', etc.). Psycho-analysts, by contrast, have progressively abandoned it except for its use in the expressions 'Oedipus complex'* and 'castration complex'*.

Most authors–Freud included–claim that psycho-analysis owes the term 'complex' to the Zurich psycho-analytic school (Bleuler, Jung). In point of fact it is to be met with as early as the *Studies on Hysteria* (1895d)–when Breuer is expounding Janet's views on hysteria (α), for example, or when he invokes the existence of 'ideas that are currently present and operative but yet unconscious': 'It is almost always a question of *complexes* of ideas, of recollections of external events and trains of thought of the subject's own. It may sometimes happen that every one of the individual ideas comprised in such a complex of ideas is thought of consciously, and that what is exiled from consciousness is only the particular combination of them' (1a).

Jung's 'association experiments' (2) were to provide this hypothesis of the complex, formulated apropos of cases of hysteria, with a basis at once empirical and more inclusive. In his first commentary upon this topic Freud writes: '. . . the reaction to the stimulus-word could not be a chance one but must be determined by an ideational content present in the mind of the reacting subject. It has become customary to speak of an ideational content of this kind, which is able to influence the reaction to the stimulus-word, as a "complex". This influence works either by the stimulus-word touching the complex directly or by the complex succeeding in making a connection with the word through inter-mediate links' (3).

Although Freud acknowledged the worth of the association experiments he very soon expressed misgivings about the use of the word 'complex'. He writes that 'it is a convenient and often indispensable term for summing up a psycho-logical state descriptively. None of the other terms coined by psycho-analysis for its own needs has achieved such widespread popularity or been so mis-applied to the detriment of the construction of clearer concepts' (4). The same judgement is found in a letter to Ernest Jones: the complex is an unsatisfactory theoretical notion (5a); and again in a letter to Ferenczi: there is a Jungian 'complex-mythology' (5b).

Thus for Freud the term may serve the demonstrative and descriptive purpose of singling out certain 'groups of strongly emotional thoughts and interests' (6) from amongst apparently discrete and contingent elements; but its theoretical contribution is nil. The fact is that Freud, unlike many authors claiming alle-giance to psycho-analysis, makes very little use of the term (β).

Several motives may be found for Freud's holding back on this point. He always shrank from a certain kind of psychological typing (e.g. 'failure complex') which runs the double risk of concealing the specificity of individual cases and of passing off a statement of the problem as an explanation of it. Furthermore, the notion of complex tends to be confused with the idea of a purely pathological nucleus which it is supposedly necessary to destroy (γ); this is to lose sight of the structuring function of complexes—especially the Oedipus complex—at certain points in human development.

*   *   *

It may help clear up the confusion that still attaches to the use of 'complex' if we distinguish three senses of the term:

a. The original sense: a relatively stable arrangement of chains of association (see 'Association'). At this level the existence of the complex is an assumption made in order to account for the particular way in which associations originate.

b. A more general sense: a collection of personal characteristics—including the best integrated ones—which is organised to a greater or lesser degree, the emphasis here being on emotional reactions. At this level the existence of the complex is inferred chiefly from the fact that new situations are unconsciously identified with infantile ones; behaviour thus appears to be shaped by a latent, unchanging structure. But such a use of 'complex' is liable to give rise to un-founded generalisation in that we may be tempted to invent as many complexes as there are conceivable psychological types—if not more. In our opinion it was this deviation towards psychologism that aroused first the reservations and then the dissent of Freud in respect of the term 'complex'.

c. The stricter sense which is embodied in the expression 'Oedipus complex' and which Freud never relinquished: a basic structure of interpersonal relation-ships and the way in which the individual finds and appropriates his place in it (see 'Oedipus Complex').

Terms belonging to Freud's own language such as 'castration complex', 'father complex', and the more rarely found 'mother complex', 'brother com-plex', 'parental complex', rightly belong to this last frame of reference. It will be noticed that the seeming diversity of the qualifications 'mother', 'father', etc., only refers in each case to a different dimension of the same Oedipal structure, either because the aspect in question is especially marked in a particular subject or because Freud is at pains, at some stage in his analysis, to view things from a particular angle. Thus he speaks of a father complex when he wishes to accentuate the ambivalent relationship with the father. The castration complex, even though its theme may be somewhat isolated, is wholly integrated into the dialectic of the Oedipus complex.

(α) On the restriction of the field of consciousness: 'For the most part the sense-impressions that are not apperceived and the ideas that are aroused but do not enter consciousness cease without producing further consequences. Sometimes, however, they accumulate and form complexes' (1b).

(β) In the *Dictionnaire de Psychanalyse et Psychotechnique* published under the editorship of Maryse Choisy in the review *Psyché*, fifty or so complexes are described. In the words of one of the contributors, 'We have tried to present as complete a nomenclature as possible of those complexes known at present. But every day new ones are being discovered.'

(γ) Cf. the letter to Ferenczi already cited: 'A man should not strive to eliminate his complexes but to get into accord with them: they are legitimately what directs his conduct in the world' (5c).

(1) BREUER, J. 'Theoretical' chapter in *Studies on Hysteria* (1895d): a) 1st German edn., 187, *n.* 1; S.E., II, 214–15, *n.* 2. b) 1st German edn., 202; S.E., II, 231.

(2) Cf. JUNG, C. G. *Diagnostische Assoziationsstudien* (Leipzig: J. A. Barth, 1906).

(3) FREUD, S. 'Psycho-Analysis and the Establishment of the Facts in Legal Proceedings' (1906c), G.W., VII, 4; S.E., IX, 104.

(4) FREUD, S. 'On the History of the Psycho-Analytic Movement' (1914d), G.W., X, 68–69; S.E., XIV, 29–30.

(5) JONES, E. *Sigmund Freud: Life and Work*, II (London: Hogarth Press, 1955): a) 496. b) 188. c) 188.

(6) FREUD, S. *Introductory Lectures on Psycho-Analysis* (1916–17), G.W., XI ,106–7; S.E. XV, 109.

Component (or Partial) Instinct

= *D.*: Partialtrieb.–*Es.*: instinto parcial.–*Fr.*: pulsion partielle.–
I.: instinto *or* pulsione parziale.–*P.*: impulso *or* pulsão parcial.

Term designating the most fundamental elements that psycho-analysis is able to identify in breaking down sexuality. Each such element is specified by a source* (e.g. oral instinct, anal instinct) and by an aim* (e.g. scopophilic instinct, instinct to master*).

The qualification 'component' does not simply mean that these instincts are individual types within the class of the sexual instincts–it is to be taken above all in a developmental and structural sense: the component instincts function independently to begin with, tending to fuse together in the various libidinal organisations.

Freud was always critical of any theory of the instincts resembling a catalogue, postulating as many instincts as there are types of activity–invoking a 'herd instinct', for instance, to account for the fact of communal life. For his part he only distinguishes two major classes of instincts: the sexual* and the self-preservative* instincts or–in his second scheme–the life* and death* instincts.

Freud nevertheless introduces the notion of the component instinct as early as the first edition of the *Three Essays on the Theory of Sexuality* (1905d). His motive for establishing such a differentiation of sexual activity is the concern to isolate *constituents* attributable to organic sources and definable in terms of specific aims.

Thus the sexual instinct as a whole can be broken down into a number of component instincts. Most of these are readily assigned to particular erotogenic zones* (α); others tend rather to be defined by their aim (e.g. the instinct to master), although in such cases it is still possible to identify a somatic source (the musculature, in the case of the instinct to master).

The action of the component instincts can be observed in the fragmented sexual activities of children (polymorphous perversity) and–in the adult–in forepleasure and in the perversions.

The concept of the component instinct is correlated with that of organisation*. Analysis of a given sexual organisation brings out the instincts which are an integral part of it. There is also a genetic differentiation, however, for Freudian theory assumes that the instincts function anarchically at first and only become organised secondarily (β).

In the first edition of the *Three Essays* Freud had accepted the idea that sexuality only achieves organisation with the onset of puberty; consequently the whole of infantile sexual activity is seen as being shaped by the unorganised interplay of the component instincts.

The introduction of the notion of infantile pregenital organisations has the effect of pushing this phase of free play between the component instincts back to an earlier point–to the auto-erotic period 'during which the subject's component instincts, each on its own account, seek for the satisfaction of their desires' (1) (see 'Auto-Erotism').

(α) 'Don't you see that the multiplicity of instincts goes back to the multiplicity of erotogenic organs?'–Freud, letter to Oskar Pfister dated October 9, 1918 (2).

(β) Cf., for example, the following passage from Freud's encyclopaedia article on 'Psycho-Analysis' (1923a [1922]): 'The sexual instinct, the dynamic manifestation of which in mental life we shall call "*libido*", is made up of component instincts into which it may once more break up and which are only gradually united into well-defined organizations. [. . .] At first the individual component instincts strive for satisfaction independently of one another, but in the course of development they become more and more convergent and concentrated. The first (pregenital) stage of organization to be discerned is the *oral* one' (3).

(1) 'The Disposition to Obsessional Neurosis' (1913i), G.W., VIII, 446; S.E., XII, 321.

(2) Quoted in JONES, E. *Sigmund Freud: Life and Work*, II (London: Hogarth Press, 1955), 506.

(3) FREUD, S., G.W., XIII, 220; S.E., XVIII, 244.

Compromise-Formation

= *D*.: Kompromissbildung.–*Es*.: transacción *or* formación transaccional.–
Fr.: formation de compromis.–*I*.: formazione di compromesso.–
P.: transação *or* formação de compromisso.

Form taken by the repressed memory so as to be admitted to consciousness when it returns in symptoms, in dreams and, more generally, in all products of the unconscious: in the process the repressed ideas are distorted by defence to the point of being unrecognisable. Thus both the unconscious wish and the demands of defence may be satisfied by the same formation–in a single compromise.

It was on the basis of his study of the mechanism of obsessional neurosis that Freud developed the idea that symptoms themselves bear the imprint of the defensive conflict* from which they result. In 'Further Remarks on the Neuro-Psychoses of Defence' (1896*b*), he points out that the return of the repressed memory comes about in distorted form in obsessive ideas which constitute 'structures in the nature of a *compromise* between the repressed ideas and the repressing ones' (1).

This notion of compromise is rapidly extended to apply to any symptom, to dreams and to all products of the unconscious. An exposition of it will be found in Chapter XXIII of the *Introductory Lectures on Psycho-Analysis* (1916–17). Freud underlines the fact that neurotic symptoms 'are the outcome of a conflict [...]. The two forces which have fallen out meet once again in the symptom and are reconciled, as it were, by the compromise of the symptom that has been constructed. It is for that reason, too, that the symptom is so resistant: it is supported from both sides' (2*a*).

Are all symptomatic phenomena compromises? The value of such an assumption is indisputable, but cases are encountered in clinical experience where either the defence or the wish appears to predominate to such an extent that we seem–at any rate at first glance–to be dealing either with defences that are in no way infected by what they are working against, or else, conversely, with a return of the repressed memory in which the wish finds expression without any compromise. We may take it that such cases constitute the two extremes of a range of compromises that ought to be looked upon as a complemental series *: '. . . symptoms aim either at a sexual satisfaction or at fending it off, and [...] on the whole the positive, wish-fulfilling character prevails in hysteria and the negative, ascetic one in obsessional neurosis' (2*b*).

(1) Freud, S., G.W., I, 387; S.E., III, 170.
(2) Freud, S.: a) G.W., XI, 373; S.E., XV–XVI, 358–59. b) G.W., XI, 311; XV–XVI, 301.

Compulsion, Compulsive

= *D*.: Zwang, Zwangs-.–*Es*.: compulsión, compulsivo.–*Fr*.: compulsion, compulsionnel.–
I.: coazione, coattivo.–*P*.: compulsão, compulsivo.

Clinically, a form of behaviour to which the subject is obliged by an internal constraint. Thoughts (obsessions), actions, defensive operations or even complex patterns of behaviour may be termed compulsive where their not being accomplished is felt as inevitably giving rise to anxiety.

In the Freudian vocabulary, '*Zwang*' is used to denote a constraining internal force. It is most frequently employed in the context of obsessional neurosis*, where it implies that the subject feels himself obliged by this force to act or think in a particular way, and that he struggles against it.

Occasionally, where it is not a question of obsessional neurosis, this implication is not present: the subject in this case does not have any feeling of conscious dissent from his actions, which are nonetheless carried out in accordance with unconscious prototypes. This happens particularly in what Freud calls *Wiederholungszwang* (the compulsion to repeat*) and *Schicksalszwang* (see 'Fate Neurosis').

In a general way, Freud's conception of *Zwang*, taken in a broader and more basic sense than the one it has in the clinical treatment of obsessional neurosis, implies that compulsion holds the key to the most profound aspect of the instincts: '. . . it is possible to recognize the dominance in the unconscious mind of a "compulsion to repeat" proceeding from the instinctual impulses and probably inherent in the very nature of the instincts–a compulsion powerful enough to overrule the pleasure principle, lending to certain aspects of the mind their daemonic character' (1).

This basic meaning of '*Zwang*', which makes it analogous to a sort of *fatum*, is met with again when Freud speaks of the Oedipus myth; in the following passage from *An Outline of Psycho-Analysis* (1940*a* [1938]), he even goes so far as to apply the term to the words of the oracle: '. . . the coercive power [*Zwang*] of the oracle, which should make the hero innocent, is a recognition of the inevitability of the fate which has condemned every son to live through the Oedipus complex' (2, α).

*   *   *

['*Zwang*' is not invariably rendered in English by 'compulsion' and 'compulsive': in certain cases the equivalent is 'obsession' and 'obsessional' (or 'obsessive'), this being the traditional psychiatric designation for *thoughts* which the subject feels himself obliged to have–by which he feels literally besieged. Thus the usual translation of '*Zwangsneurose*' is 'obsessional neurosis' (β), while '*Zwangsvorstellung*' is rendered by 'obsessional idea', and so on. On the other hand, when it is *behaviour* that is involved, one speaks of compulsions, of compulsive acts (*Zwangshandlungen*), of the compulsion to repeat, etc.—*tr*.]

77

Compulsion to Repeat (Repetition Compulsion)

(α) Cf. the thought expressed as early as a letter to Wilhelm Fliess dated October 15, 1897: '. . . the Greek legend seizes on a compulsion which everyone recognizes because he feels its existence within himself' (3).

(β) Cf. the commentary on 'Obsessional Neurosis', particularly note α.

(1) FREUD, S. 'The "Uncanny"' (1919*h*), G.W., XII, 251; S.E., XVII, 238.

(2) FREUD, S., G.W., XVII, 119; S.E., XXIII, 192.

(3) FREUD, S., *Anf.*, 238; S.E., I, 265.

Compulsion to Repeat (Repetition Compulsion)

= *D*.: Wiederholungszwang.–*Es*.: compulsión a la repetición.–
Fr.: compulsion de répétition. –*I*.: coazione a ripetere.–*P*.: compulsão à repetição.

I. At the level of concrete psychopathology, the compulsion to repeat is an ungovernable process originating in the unconscious. As a result of its action, the subject deliberately places himself in distressing situations, thereby repeating an old experience, but he does not recall this prototype; on the contrary, he has the strong impression that the situation is fully determined by the circumstances of the moment.

II. In elaborating the theory of the compulsion to repeat, Freud treats it as an autonomous factor which cannot ultimately be reduced to a conflictual dynamic entirely circumscribed by the interplay between the pleasure principle and the reality principle. It is seen, in the final analysis, as the expression of the most general character of the instincts, namely, their conservatism.

The notion of the compulsion to repeat is at the centre of *Beyond the Pleasure Principle* (1920*g*), an essay in which Freud reappraises the most fundamental concepts of his theory. So important is the part played by this idea at this crucial moment that it is difficult either to lay down its strict meaning or to define its own particular problematic: the concept reflects all the hesitations, the dead ends and even the contradictions of Freud's speculative hypotheses. This is one of the reasons why the discussion of the repetition compulsion is so confused – and so often resumed–in psycho-analytic literature. The debate inevitably involves fundamental options regarding the most vital notions of Freud's work, such as the pleasure principle*, instinct*, the death instincts* and binding*.

*　　*　　*

It is quite obvious that psycho-analysis was confronted from the very beginning by repetition *phenomena*. In particular, any consideration of *symptoms* reveals that a certain number of them–obsessional rituals for instance–are repetitive in character; furthermore, the defining property of the symptom is the very fact that it reproduces, in a more or less disguised way, certain elements of a past conflict (it is in this sense that Freud, at the beginning of his work, described symptoms as mnemic symbols*). In a general way, the repressed seeks to 're-turn' in the present, whether in the form of dreams, symptoms or acting-out*:

'. . . a thing which has not been understood inevitably reappears; like an unlaid ghost, it cannot rest until the mystery has been solved and the spell broken' (1).

Transference phenomena emerging during the treatment serve to confirm this necessity for the repressed conflict to be re-enacted in the relationship with the analyst. In fact it was the ever-increasing consideration demanded by these phenomena, and the technical problems they gave rise to, which led Freud to complete his theoretical model of the cure by introducing transference repetition and working-through*, alongside recollection, as major stages of the therapeutic process (see 'Transference'). When, in *Beyond the Pleasure Principle*, Freud brought the notion of the repetition compulsion (which dated from his paper on 'Remembering, Repeating and Working-Through' [1914g]) to the fore, he grouped together a certain number of examples of repetition which had already been recognised, while further identifying other cases where it is to be observed in the forefront of the clinical picture (as, for example, in fate neurosis* and traumatic neurosis*). These were phenomena which in Freud's view warranted a new theoretical analysis. The fact is that when what are clearly unpleasant experiences are repeated, it is hard to see at first glance just what agency of the mind could attain satisfaction by this means. Although these are obviously irresistible forms of behaviour, having that compulsive character which is the mark of all that emanates from the unconscious, it is nonetheless difficult to show anything in them which could be construed – even if it were seen as a compromise – as the fulfilment of a repressed wish.

*   *   *

The set of Freud's thinking in the first chapters of *Beyond the Pleasure Principle* does not come down to a simple rejection of the basic hypothesis according to which what is sought under the cloak of apparent suffering – as in the symptom – is the realisation of desire. He goes much farther, for it is in these pages that he puts forward the well-known thesis that what is unpleasure for one agency of the psychical apparatus is pleasure for another one. Such attempts at an explanation, however, still fail to account in Freud's opinion for certain residual facts. To make use of a terminology proposed by Daniel Lagache, we may sum up the question raised here as follows: must we postulate the existence, alongside the *repetition of needs*, of a *need for repetition*, the latter being both radically distinct from and more basic than the former? Although Freud acknowledged that the repetition compulsion is never to be encountered in a pure state, but that it is invariably reinforced by factors which are under the sway of the pleasure principle, he nevertheless continued to invest the notion with an increasing significance right up to the end of his work (2, 3). In *Inhibitions, Symptoms and Anxiety* (1926d) he deems the repetition compulsion to be the very epitome of that resistance* which is peculiar to the unconscious: it is described as 'the attraction exerted by the unconscious prototypes upon the repressed instinctual process' (4).

*   *   *

Although the compulsive repetition of what is unpleasant and even painful is acknowledged to be an irrefutable *datum* of analytic experience, there is disagreement among psycho-analysts as to the correct theoretical explanation of it. Schematically speaking, the debate may be said to turn on two questions.

Compulsion to Repeat (Repetition Compulsion)

First, what is the tendency towards repetition a function of? Is it a matter of attempts made by the ego, in a piecemeal fashion, to master and abreact excessive tensions? Repetitive dreams following mental traumas would especially tend to bear this out. Or must we accept the idea that repetition has, in the last analysis, to be related to the most 'instinctual' part – the 'daemonic' aspect – of every instinct – to that tendency towards absolute discharge which is implied by the notion of the death instinct?

Secondly, does the compulsion to repeat really cast doubt on the dominance of the pleasure principle, as Freud contended? The contradictoriness of Freud's own pronouncements, together with the diversity of the solutions attempted by other psycho-analysts, would best be cleared up, in our view, by a preliminary discussion of the ambiguity surrounding terms such as 'pleasure principle', 'principle of constancy'* and 'binding'. To take just one case in point, it is obvious that if the place of the pleasure principle is 'to serve the death instincts' (5), then the compulsion to repeat – even understood in the most extreme sense proposed by Freud – can not be situated 'beyond the pleasure principle'.

These two questions, moreover, are intimately connected: a particular type of reply to the one implies a corresponding answer to the other. A whole gamut of possible solutions have been put forward, ranging from the thesis which treats the repetition compulsion as a unique factor to attempts to reduce it to previously recognised mechanisms or functions.

The approach adopted by Edward Bibring furnishes a good illustration of an attempt to find a *via media*. Bibring proposes a distinction between a *repetitive tendency* defining the id and a *restitutive tendency* which is a function of the ego. The former can certainly be said to be 'beyond the pleasure principle' in so far as the repeated experiences are as painful as they are pleasant, yet it does not constitute a principle antagonistic to the pleasure principle. The restitutive tendency is a function working by various means to re-establish the situation which had existed prior to the trauma; it exploits repetitive phenomena in the interests of the ego. From this standpoint, Bibring differentiates between the *defence mechanisms*, where the ego remains under the domination of the repetition compulsion without any resolution of the internal tension; the *abreactive processes* (see 'Abreaction') which discharge the excitation, whether in an immediate or a deferred way; and finally what he calls '*working-off*' *mechanisms** whose 'function is to dissolve the tension gradually by changing the internal conditions which give rise to it' (6).

(1) FREUD, S. 'Analysis of a Phobia in a Five-Year-Old Boy' (1909*b*), G.W., VII, 355; S.E., X, 122.

(2) Cf. FREUD, S. 'The Economic Problem of Masochism' (1924*c*), *passim*.

(3) Cf. FREUD, S. 'Analysis Terminable and Interminable' (1937*c*), *passim*.

(4) FREUD, S., G.W., XIV, 192; S.E., XX, 159.

(5) FREUD, S. *Beyond the Pleasure Principle* (1920*g*), G.W., XIII, 69; S.E., XVIII, 63.

(6) BIBRING, E. 'The Conception of the Repetition Compulsion', *Psychoanalytic Quarterly*, 1943, XII, 502.

Condemnation (Judgement of)

= *D.*: Verurteilung *or* Urteilsverwerfung.–*Es.*: juicio de condenación.–
Fr.: jugement de condamnation.–*I.*: rifiuto da parte del giudizio *or* condamna.–
P.: julgamento de condenação.

Operation or attitude whereby the subject becomes conscious of a wish but forbids himself to fulfil it, as a rule either on ethical grounds or for reasons of propitious-ness. Freud considers condemnation to be a more developed and appropriate mode of defence than repression. Daniel Lagache has proposed that it be conceived of as a process of 'working-off' of the ego–in action particularly in psycho-analytic treatment.

The terms '*Verurteilung*' and '*Urteilsverwerfung*', which Freud himself treats as synonyms (1*a*), are to be met with on several occasions in his work. Freud sees condemnation as occupying one rung in a hierarchy of forms of defence which goes from the most primitive to the most elaborate modes: from the flight reflex (in the case of an external danger), through repression (in the case of an internal threat) to condemnation (1*b*). This last, when compared with repression, seems at times to share the same aims: condemnation 'will be found to be a good method to adopt against an instinctual impulse' (1*c*). At other moments, the condemning judgement is defined as a successful modification of repression: 'The subject only succeeded in the past in repressing the unserviceable instinct because he himself was at that time still imperfectly organized and feeble. In his present-day maturity and strength, he will perhaps be able to master what is hostile to him with complete success' (2).

It is this positive side of the judgement of condemnation which Freud stresses in the closing pages of his 'Analysis of a Phobia in a Five-Year-Old Boy' (1909*b*). He poses the question of the possible effects of Little Hans's becoming conscious of his Oedipal, incestuous and aggressive desires. The reason analysis does not have the effect of impelling Hans towards the immediate satisfaction of his wishes is that it 'replaces the process of repression, which is an automatic and excessive one, by a temperate and purposeful control on the part of the highest agencies of the mind. In a word, *analysis replaces repression by con-demnation*' (3).

It may be remarked here that condemnation is all the more valuable in Freud's eyes on this occasion in that it coincides at this stage of Hans's life with the structuring function of the prohibition against incest and with the entry into the latency period.

At all events, condemnation is never more than a transform of *negation** for Freud, and it still bears the mark of the repression which it replaces: 'A negative judgement is the intellectual substitute for repression; its "no" is the hall-mark of repression, a certificate of origin–like, let us say, "Made in Germany" ' (4*a*). What is expressed above all in the condemning judgement according to Freud is the contradiction which is inherent to the function of judgement itself, which 'is not made possible until the creation of the symbol of negation has endowed thinking with a first measure of freedom from the consequences of repression and, with it, from the compulsion of the pleasure principle' (4*b*); yet judgement,

81

Condensation

especially when it is negative, has an essentially defensive role to play: '. . . negation is the successor to expulsion' (4c).

* * *

According to Daniel Lagache, we may use the idea of the condemning judgement in order to solve the intrinsic difficulty of the Freudian conception of defence, and to clarify the distinction between defensive compulsions and working-off mechanisms*–in which the judgement of condemnation can play a part. In the case of Little Hans, the hope of growing bigger, which he expresses from the start with the idea that his penis–which is 'fixed in'–will get bigger, should be seen as a concrete example of one of the mechanisms whereby the ego works off the Oedipal conflict and the fear of castration. More generally, Lagache sees this kind of process as part of the outcome of the psycho-analytic cure, bringing about the postponement of satisfaction, the modification of aims and objects, the consideration of the possibilities which reality offers the subject, the taking into account of the different priorities which have been put into play, and the assessment of the compatibility of these with the subject's overall requirements.

(1) Freud, S. 'Repression' (1915d): a) Cf. G.W., X, 248; S.E., XIV, 146. b) Cf. G.W., X, 248; S.E., XIV, 146. c) G.W., X, 248; S.E., XIV, 146.

(2) Freud, S. 'Five Lectures on Psycho-Analysis' (1910a [1909]). G.W., VIII, 58; S.E., XI, 53.

(3) Freud, S., G.W., VII, 375; S.E., X, 145.

(4) Freud, S. 'Negation' (1925h): a) G.W., XIV, 12; S.E., XIX, 236. b) G.W., XIV, 15; S.E., XIX, 239. c) G.W., XIV, 15; S.E., XIX, 239.

Condensation

= D.: Verdichtung.–Es.: condensación.–Fr.: condensation.–I.: condensazione.– P.: condensação.

One of the essential modes of the functioning of the unconscious processes: a sole idea represents several associative chains at whose point of intersection it is located. From the economic point of view, what happens is that this idea is cathected by the sum of those energies which are concentrated upon it by virtue of the fact that they are attached to these different chains.

Condensation can be seen at work in the symptom and, generally speaking, in the various formations of the unconscious. But it is in dreams that its action has been most clearly brought out.

It is shown up here by the fact that the manifest account is laconic in comparison with the latent content of the dream: it constitutes an abridged translation of the dream. Condensation should not, however, be looked upon as a summary: although each manifest element is determined by several latent meanings, each one of these, inversely, may be identified in several elements; what is more, manifest elements do not stand in the same relationship to each of the meanings from which they derive, and so they do not subsume them after the fashion of a concept.

Condensation was first described by Freud in *The Interpretation of Dreams* (1900*a*) as one of the fundamental mechanisms by means of which the 'dream-work'* is carried out. It may operate in various different ways: sometimes one element (theme, person, etc.) is alone preserved because it occurs several times in different dream-thoughts ('nodal point'); alternatively, various elements may be combined into a disparate unity (as in the case of a composite figure); or again, the condensation of several images may result in the blurring of those traits which do not coincide so as to maintain and reinforce only those which are common (1).

Though analysed on the basis of dreams, the condensation mechanism is not exclusive to them. In *The Psychopathology of Everyday Life* (1901*b*) and *Jokes and their Relation to the Unconscious* (1905*c*), Freud demonstrates that condensation is one of the essential factors in the technique of joking, in *faux pas*, in the forgetting of words, etc.; in *The Interpretation of Dreams*, he notes that the process is particularly striking when it affects words (neologisms).

How is condensation to be explained? It can be seen as a consequence of the censorship *and* as a means of avoiding it. As Freud pointed out himself, if one inclines towards the view that it is not an effect of the censorship*, the fact remains that 'in any case the censorship profits from it' (2); and indeed condensation makes interpretation of the manifest account more complicated.

At all events, if dreams operate by condensation, it is not *only* in order to outwit the censorship, for condensation is a propensity of unconscious thought. The primary process enshrines those preconditions (free, unbound energy*; the tendency towards perceptual identity*) which permit and facilitate condensation. Unconscious wishes are thus subjected to it from the start, while preconscious thoughts–which are 'drawn into the unconscious'–are liable to condensation subsequent to the action of the censorship. Is it possible to determine at what stage condensation occurs? It 'must probably be pictured as a process stretching over the whole course of events till the perceptual region is reached. But in general we must be content to assume that all the forces which take part in the formation of dreams operate simultaneously' (3).

Like displacement, condensation is a process which Freud accounts for by means of the economic hypothesis: the energies which have been displaced along different associative chains accumulate upon the idea which stands at their point of intersection. If certain images–especially in dreams–acquire a truly exceptional intensity, this is by virtue of the fact that, being products of condensation, they are highly cathected.

(1) Cf. FREUD, S., G.W., V, 299–300; S.E., IV, 293–95.

(2) FREUD, S. *Introductory Lectures on Psycho-Analysis* (1916–17), G.W., XI, 176; S.E., XV, 191.

(3) FREUD, S. *Jokes and their Relation to the Unconscious* (1905*c*), G.W., V, 187–88; S.E., VIII, 164.

Consciousness

= I.; *D.*: Bewusstheit (the attribute or fact of being conscious).–*Es.*: el estar consciente.–
Fr.: le fait d'être conscient.–*I.*: consapevolezza.–*P.*: o estar consciente.
II. *D.*: Bewusstsein.–*Es.*: conciencia psicológica.–*Fr.*: conscience (psychologique).–
I.: coscienza.–*P.*: consciência psicológica.

I. In the descriptive sense: a transient property which distinguishes external and internal perceptions from psychical phenomena as a whole.

II. According to Freud's metapsychological theory, consciousness is the function of a system – the perception-consciousness system (*Pcpt.-Cs.*).

From the *topographical** point of view, the perception-consciousness system lies on the periphery of the psychical apparatus* and receives information both from the outside world and from internal sources: this information is composed of sensations, which impress themselves at some point on the pleasure-unpleasure scale, and of revived memories. Freud often ascribes the function of perception-consciousness to the preconscious system, in which case this is referred to as the preconscious-conscious system (*Pcs.-Cs.*).

From the *functional* standpoint, the perception-consciousness system stands opposed to the unconscious and preconscious as systems of mnemic traces*: here no lasting trace of any excitation remains. From the *economic* point of view, the system is characterised by the fact that it has at its disposal a freely mobile energy capable of hypercathecting a given element (the mechanism of attention).

Consciousness plays an important part in the *dynamics* of the conflict (conscious avoidance of what is disagreeable; a more selective control over the pleasure principle) and of the treatment (function and limitations of the *prise de conscience*); yet it cannot be defined as one of the *poles* of the defensive conflict (α).

Although the theory of psycho-analysis emerged from a refusal to define the psychical field in terms of consciousness, this does not mean that it treats consciousness as a non-essential phenomenon. Indeed Freud ridiculed such a claim, which was sometimes made in psychology: 'One extreme line of thought, exemplified in the American doctrine of behaviourism, thinks it possible to construct a psychology which disregards this fundamental fact' (1*a*).

Freud holds consciousness to be a fact of individual experience lying open to immediate intuition, and he makes no attempt to define it beyond this. It is 'a fact without parallel, which defies all explanation or description [. . .]. Nevertheless, if anyone speaks of consciousness we know immediately and from our most personal experience what is meant by it' (1*b*).

This dual thesis – which holds, in the first place, that consciousness provides us with but a sketchy picture of our mental processes, since these are for the most part unconscious, and, secondly, that it is by no means an indifferent matter whether a phenomenon is conscious or not – calls for a theory of consciousness that makes its function and position clear.

As early as Freud's first metapsychological model two vital claims are made. First, Freud brackets together consciousness and perception and deems the essence of the latter to be the ability to receive sensible *qualities*. Secondly, he assigns this function of perception-consciousness to a system – the system ω or

W–that is autonomous *vis-à-vis* the psyche as a whole, which operates for its part according to purely quantitative principles: 'Consciousness gives us what are called *qualities*–sensations which are *different* in a great multiplicity of ways and whose *difference* is distinguished according to its relations with the external world. Within this difference there are series, similarities and so on, but there are in fact no quantities in it' (2*a*).

The first of these two propositions was to be maintained right the way through Freud's work: '. . . consciousness is the subjective side of one part of the physical processes in the nervous system, namely of the ω processes' (2*b*). This view gives priority in the phenomenon to *perception*–and chiefly to the perception of the outside world: 'The process of something becoming conscious is above all linked with the perceptions which our sense organs receive from the external world' (1*c*). In the theory of reality-testing* a significant synonymity can be noticed between the terms 'indication of quality', 'indication of perception' and 'indication of reality' (2*c*). At the beginning of life the 'equation "perception = reality (external world)" ' is said to apply (1*d*). *Consciousness of psychical phenomena* is also inseparable from the perception of qualities: consciousness is nothing but 'a sense-organ for the perception of psychical qualities' (3*a*). It perceives states of instinctual tension and discharges of excitation in the qualitative form of the pleasure-unpleasure series. But the most difficult problem is posed by consciousness of what Freud calls 'thought-processes', by which he means not only reasoning but also the revival of memories and, generally speaking, all processes where 'ideas'* play a part. Throughout his work Freud upheld a theory which has the bringing of thought-processes to consciousness depend on the association of these processes with *Wortreste*–'verbal residues' (see 'Thing-Presentation/Word-Presentation'). Since the reactivation of such residues has the character of a fresh perception–the remembered words are, initially at any rate, repronounced (2*d*)–consciousness is enabled to find a kind of anchorage whence its hypercathectic* energy may radiate: 'In order that thought-processes may acquire quality, they are associated in human beings with verbal memories, whose residues of quality are sufficient to draw the attention of consciousness to them and to endow the process of thinking with a new mobile cathexis from consciousness' (3*b*).

This association of consciousness with perception leads Freud to combine them most of the time in a single system, which he refers to in the 'Project for a Scientific Psychology' (1950*a* [1895]) as the system ω, and from the metapsychological works of 1915 onwards as 'perception-consciousness' (*Pcpt.-Cs.*). The separation of such a system from all systems where memory-traces* can be inscribed (*Pcs.* and *Ucs.*) is based, through a kind of logical deduction, on an idea already worked out by Breuer in his 'Theoretical' contribution to the *Studies on Hysteria* (1895*d*): 'It is impossible for one and the same organ to fulfil these two contradictory conditions'–namely, the speediest possible restoration of the *status quo ante* so that no new perceptions can be received, and the storing-up of impressions so that they can be reproduced (4). Later, Freud rounded out this conception in a formulation which attempts to account for the 'inexplicable' emergence of consciousness: it 'arises in the perceptual system *instead of* the permanent traces' (5*a*).

*   *   *

Consciousness

The *topographical* position of consciousness is not easy to tie down: although the 'Project' locates it in 'the upper storeys' of the system, its close link to perception soon causes Freud to place it on the frontier between the outside world and the mnemic systems: '. . . the perceptual apparatus of our mind consists of two layers, of an external protective shield against stimuli whose task it is to diminish the strength of excitations coming in, and of a surface behind it which receives the stimuli, namely the system *Pcpt.-Cs.*' (5b) (see 'Protective Shield'). This peripheral position prefigures the one later assigned to the ego: in *The Ego and the Id* (1923b) Freud looks upon the system *Pcpt.-Cs.* as the 'nucleus' of the ego (6a): '. . . the ego is that part of the id which has been modified by the direct influence of the external world through the medium of the *Pcpt.-Cs.*; in a sense it is an extension of the surface-differentiation' (6b) (see 'Ego').

From the economic point of view also, consciousness inevitably presented Freud with a specific problem. For consciousness is a qualitative phenomenon – it is aroused by the perception of sensory qualities; quantitative phenomena only become conscious in qualitative form. Yet at the same time a function such as attention, which, despite the apparent assumption that it is *more* or *less* intense, is manifestly bound up with consciousness, or a process such as the accession to consciousness, which plays such an important role in the treatment, obviously need explaining in economic terms. Freud hypothesises that the energy for attention, which is said, for example, to 'hypercathect' perceptions, is derived from the ego ('Project'), or from the system *Pcs.* (*Interpretation of Dreams*), and that it is directed by the qualitative indications furnished by consciousness: 'For the ego, then, *the biological rule of attention* runs: *If an indication of reality appears, then the perceptual cathexis which is simultaneously present is to be hypercathected*' (2e).

By the same token the attention which is attached to thought-processes allows for a more sensitive control of these processes than that achieved by the pleasure principle alone: 'We know that perception by our sense-organs has the result of directing a cathexis of attention to the paths along which the in-coming sensory excitation is spreading: the qualitative excitation of the *Pcpt.* system acts as a regulator of the discharge of the mobile quantity in the psychical apparatus. We can attribute the same function to the overlying sense-organ of the *Cs.* system. By perceiving new qualities, it makes a new contribution to directing the mobile quantities of cathexis and distributing them in an expedient fashion' (3c) (see 'Free Energy/Bound Energy', 'Hypercathexis').

Lastly, from the *dynamic* perspective, we may note a certain evolution in Freud's position on the importance of consciousness as a factor in the defensive process as well as in the effectiveness of the treatment. We cannot retrace the whole course of this evolution here, but we can point out a few aspects of it:

a. A mechanism such as repression is conceived of in the early period of psycho-analysis as a voluntary rejection still akin to the mechanism of attention: 'The splitting of consciousness in these cases of acquired hysteria is [. . .] a deliberate and intentional one. At least it is often *introduced* by an act of volition' (7).

As we know, it was the gradually increasing emphasis laid on the at any rate partially unconscious character of defences and resistances, as expressed in the treatment, which prompted Freud to revise the notion of the ego and to introduce his second theory of the psychical apparatus.

b. An important stage in this development is marked by the metapsychological writings of 1915, where Freud states that 'the attribute of being conscious, which is the only characteristic of psychical processes that is directly presented to us, is in no way suited to serve as a criterion for the differentiation of systems' (8a). Freud does not mean by this that consciousness is no longer to be attributed to a system – to an actual specialised 'organ' – but he points out that the capacity of a given content to gain access to consciousness does not suffice to determine its position in the preconscious or in the unconscious system: 'The more we seek to win our way to a metapsychological view of mental life, the more we must learn to emancipate ourselves from the importance of the symptom of "being conscious" ' (8b, β).

c. In the theory of the treatment the difficult question of the *prise de conscience* and its curative value has always been a major concern. What is called for here is an evaluation of the relative importance, and of the combined action, of the different factors that play a part in the treatment: remembering and constructions*, repetition in the transference* and working-through*, and finally interpretation*– whose impact, in so far as it induces structural reorganisation, is not confined to conscious communication; '. . . psycho-analytic treatment is based upon an influencing of the *Ucs.* from the direction of the *Cs.*, and at any rate shows that this, though a laborious task, is not impossible' (8c). Yet at the same time Freud constantly increased his stress on the fact that communicating the interpretation of a particular unconscious phantasy to the patient, no matter how apt it may be, does not suffice to bring about structural changes: 'If we communicate to a patient some idea which he has at one time repressed but which we have discovered in him, our telling him makes at first no change in his mental condition. Above all, it does not remove the repression nor undo its effects' (8d).

The transposition to consciousness does not of itself imply a real integration of the repressed into the preconscious system: it has to be complemented by a whole effort which is capable of overcoming the resistances that impede communication between the unconscious and preconscious systems, and capable too of binding the memory-traces and their verbalisation closer and closer together. Only at the end of this work can what has been heard and what has been experienced come together: 'To have heard something and to have experienced it are in their psychological nature two quite different things, even though the content of both is the same' (8e). The period of working-through is said to be the one during which this gradual integration into the preconscious takes place.

(α) The adjective *'bewusst'* means conscious in both the active sense (conscious of) and the passive one (the quality of whatever is an object of consciousness). German can call upon several substantival forms based on *'bewusst'*. *Bewusstheit* = the quality of being an object of consciousness, the fact or attribute of being conscious. *Bewusstsein* = consciousness *qua* psychological reality; this tends to mean the activity or function of consciousness. *Das Bewusste* = the conscious – used especially to designate a type of content distinct from preconscious or unconscious contents. *Das Bewusstwerden* = the 'becoming conscious' of a particular idea, accession to consciousness. *Das Bewusstmachen* = the fact of making a given content conscious.

Construction

(β) It is worth noting in this connection that the nomenclature of the systems of the first theory of the psychical apparatus takes consciousness as its axis: un*conscious*, pre*conscious*, *conscious*.

(1) FREUD, S. *An Outline of Psycho-Analysis* (1940a [1938]): a) G.W., XVII, 79n.; S.E., XXIII, 157n. b) G.W., XVII, 79; S.E., XXIII, 157. c) G.W., XVII, 83; S.E., XXIII, 161. d) G.W., XVII, 84; S.E., XXIII, 162.

(2) FREUD, S. 'Project for a Scientific Psychology'(1950a [1895]): a) *Anf.*, 393; S.E., I, 308. b) *Anf.*, 396; S.E., I, 311. c) *passim.* d) Cf. *Anf.*, 443–44; S.E., I, 365. e) *Anf.*, 451; S.E., I, 371.

(3) FREUD, S. *The Interpretation of Dreams* (1900a): a) G.W., II–III, 620; S.E., V, 615. b) G.W., II–III, 622; S.E., V, 617. c) G.W., II–III, 621; S.E., V, 616.

(4) Cf. BREUER, J. 'Theoretical' chapter of *Studies on Hysteria* (1895d), German edn., 164; S.E., II, 188–89n.

(5) FREUD, S. 'A Note upon the "Mystic Writing-Pad" ' (1925a): a) G.W., XIV, 4–5; S.E., XIX, 228. b) G.W., XIV, 6; S.E., XIX, 230.

(6) FREUD, S.: a) G.W., XII, 251; S.E., XIX, 24. b) G.W., XIII, 252; S.E., XIX, 25.

(7) FREUD, S. *Studies on Hysteria* (1895d), G.W., I, 182; S.E., II, 123.

(8) FREUD, S. 'The Unconscious' (1915e): a) G.W., X, 291; S.E., XIV, 192. b) G.W., X, 291; S.E., XIV, 193. c) G.W., X, 293; S.E., XIV, 194. d) G.W., X, 274; S.E., XIV, 175. e) G.W., X, 275; S.E., XIV, 175–76.

Construction

= D.: Konstruktion.–*Es.*: construcción.–*Fr.*: construction.–*I.*: costruzione.–*P.*: construção.

Term proposed by Freud to designate an explanation by the analyst which is more extensive and further removed from the material* than an interpretation*, and which aims essentially at the reconstitution of a part of the subject's childhood history in both its real and its phantasy aspects.

It is hard – and possibly even undesirable – to restrict the term 'construction' to the comparatively narrow sense that Freud assigns to it in 'Constructions in Analysis' (1937d). Freud's main purpose in this article is to emphasise how difficult it is to achieve the ideal goal of the treatment – to bring about complete recollection including the eradication of infantile amnesia*: the analyst is obliged to build up veritable 'constructions' and to put them to the patient – and, indeed, in favourable cases (where the construction is accurate and made known at a moment when the subject is ready to receive it) this procedure may be rewarded by the emergence of the repressed memory or fragments of memories (1). Even in the absence of such a result, the construction, according to Freud, still has a therapeutic effect: 'Quite often we do not succeed in bringing the patient to recollect what has been repressed. Instead of that, if the analysis is carried out correctly, we produce in him an assured conviction of the truth of the construction which achieves the same therapeutic result as a recaptured memory' (2).

*　　*　　*

The particularly interesting idea connoted by the term 'construction' cannot be reduced to the quasi-technical notion of this article of Freud's of 1937. It would be no difficult matter, moreover, to find ample evidence in Freud's work attesting to the fact that the theme of a construction or organisation of the material was present in it from the outset, and in more than one form. At the moment when he discovers the unconscious, Freud describes it as an organisation that the treatment ought to allow us to reconstruct. In the patient's discourse, in fact, 'the whole spatially-extended mass of psychogenic material is in this way drawn through a narrow cleft and thus arrives in consciousness cut up, as it were, into pieces or strips. It is the psychotherapist's business to put these together once more into the organization which he presumes to have existed. Anyone who has a craving for further similes may think at this point of a Chinese puzzle' (3).

In ' "A Child is Being Beaten" ' (1919e), Freud endeavours to reconstitute the whole evolution of a phantasy: it is seemingly in the nature of certain stages in this evolution that they are inaccessible to memory, yet there is a real internal logic here which obliges us to postulate their existence and to reconstruct them.

In a more general way, we cannot speak only of construction by the analyst or during the treatment: the Freudian conception of phantasy assumes that this is itself a form of construction by the subject – a construction that is partly grounded in reality, as is clearly illustrated by the existence of infantile sexual 'theories'. In the last reckoning, the term 'construction' raises the whole problem of unconscious structures and of the structuring role of the treatment.

(1) Cf. FREUD, S. *An Outline of Psycho-Analysis* (1940a [1938]), G.W., XVII, 103–4; S.E., XXIII, 178.

(2) FREUD, S. 'Constructions in Analysis' (1937d), G.W., XVI, 53; S.E., XXIII, 265–66.

(3) FREUD, S. 'The Psychotherapy of Hysteria', in *Studies on Hysteria* (1895d), G.W., I, 296; S.E., II, 291.

Control Analysis (or Supervised or Supervisory Analysis)

= *D*.: Kontrollanalyse.–*Es*.: análisis de control *or* supervisión.–
Fr.: psychanalyse contrôlée *or* sous contrôle.–*I*.: analisi di controllo *or* sotto controllo.–
P.: análise sob contrôle *or* supervisão.

Psycho-analysis carried out by an analyst in the course of his training: the student must report back at intervals to an expert analyst who guides him in his understanding and direction of the treatment and helps him become aware of his counter-transference. This form of training is designed in particular to aid the student's grasp of those peculiar aspects of psycho-analytic treatment that mark it off from other modes of psychotherapeutic* action (suggestions, advice, directives, clarifications, support, etc.).

The practice of control analyses, instituted around 1920 (1), has gradually become a major component of the psycho-analyst's technical training and a prerequisite of his accession to the status of practitioner. Today the various psycho-analytic societies lay down that no student analyst may undertake control

analyses (he will generally carry out at least two) until his own *training analysis**
is far enough advanced (α).

(α) It is worth noting that it has been proposed that we distinguish between the two main
aspects of control by using the terms '*Kontrollanalyse*' and '*Analysenkontrolle*': the suggestion
is that the former term should denote the analysis of the candidate's counter-transference
vis-à-vis his patient, and the latter the supervision of his analysis of the patient.

(1) Cf. Eitingon's report on the Berlin psycho-analytical polyclinic given at the International Psycho-Analytical Congress of 1922, *I.J.P.*, 1923, 4, 254–69.

Conversion

= *D.*: Konversion.–*Es.*: conversión.–*Fr.*: conversion.–*I.*: conversione.–*P.*: conversão.

**Mechanism of symptom-formation which operates in hysteria and, more specifically,
in conversion hysteria** (q.v.).
 **Conversion consists in a transposition of a psychical conflict into, and its at-
tempted resolution through, somatic symptoms which may be either of a motor
nature (e.g. paralyses) or of a sensory one (e.g. localised anaesthesias or pains).**
 **Freud's sense of conversion is tied to an *economic* approach: the libido
detached from the repressed idea* is transformed into an innervational* energy.
But what specifies conversion symptoms is their *symbolic* meaning: they express
repressed ideas through the medium of the body.**

Freud introduced the term 'conversion' into psychopathology in order to
account for that 'leap from a mental process to a somatic innervation' which he
himself considered difficult to comprehend (1). As we know, this idea, which was
new at the end of the nineteenth century, has since acquired a very broad
extension, especially with the development of psychosomatic research. This
makes it all the more necessary to decide what may be more properly ascribed
to conversion within this field which has become so wide. We may note, moreover, that Freud was already at pains to do this–notably with his distinction
between the hysterical and the somatic symptoms of the actual* neuroses.
 The introduction of the term is contemporaneous with Freud's earliest
researches on hysteria: it occurs first in the case-history of Frau Emmy von N.
in the *Studies on Hysteria* (1895*d*), and in 'The Neuro-Psychoses of Defence'
(1894*a*). Its initial meaning is an economic one: a libidinal energy is transformed
or *converted* into a somatic innervation. Conversion goes hand in hand with the
detachment of the libido from the idea in the process of repression; the libidinal
energy is then 'transformed into something somatic' (2*a*).
 This economic interpretation of conversion is inseparable for Freud from a
a symbolic conception: through bodily symptoms, repressed ideas 'join in the
conversation' (3), although they are distorted by the mechanisms of condensa-
tion* and displacement*. Freud notes that the symbolic relation linking symptom and meaning is such that a single symptom may express several meanings,

not only at once but also one after the other: 'In the course of years a symptom can change its meaning or its chief meaning [. . .]. The production of a symptom of this kind is so difficult, the translation of a purely psychical excitation into physical terms–the process which I have described as 'conversion'–depends on the concurrence of so many favourable conditions, the somatic compliance necessary for conversion is so seldom forthcoming, that an impulsion towards the discharge of an unconscious excitation will so far as possible make use of any channel for discharge which may already be in existence' (4).

As to the reasons why conversion symptoms form rather than other kinds, such as phobic or obsessional ones, Freud at first invokes a 'capacity for conversion' (2b) and later takes up the same idea when he uses the expression 'somatic compliance'*, meaning a constitutional or acquired factor which, in a general sense, predisposes a particular subject to conversion, or which–more specifically –makes a specific organ or apparatus suitable for the purposes of conversion. Thus this question leads us back to the question of the 'choice of neurosis'* and of the specificity of neurotic structures.

What place are we to assign to conversion in a nosographical perspective?

a. *In the field of hysteria.* Conversion at first appeared to Freud as a mechanism invariably–though in varying degrees–present in hysteria. Subsequently a deeper understanding of the structure of hysteria brought him to subsume under this category a form of neurosis that does not manifest conversion symptoms: this was essentially a phobic syndrome that he isolated as anxiety hysteria*; conversely, this allowed him to circumscribe a conversion hysteria.

This tendency to stop treating hysteria and conversion as coextensive is to be met with today whenever we speak of hysteria, or of the hysterical structure, in the absence of conversion symptoms.

b. *In the more general field of the neuroses.* Somatic symptoms having a symbolic relationship to the subject's unconscious phantasies are to be encountered in neuroses other than hysteria (consider, for example, the intestinal troubles of the 'Wolf Man'). Must we therefore treat conversion as so basic a mechanism in the formation of symptoms that it may be found in varying degrees in different classes of neuroses, or, alternatively, should we continue to look upon it as specific to hysteria, invoking an 'hysterical nucleus' or talking of 'mixed neurosis' when we come across it in other types of affection? This is not merely a verbal problem, for it brings us to differentiate neuroses in terms of their structure and not just in terms of their symptoms.

c. *In the field now called 'psychosomatic'.* Without wishing to prejudge an issue that is still being debated, we may note the current tendency to distinguish hysterical conversion from other processes of symptom-formation; the name 'somatisation', for example, has been suggested for these processes. According to this approach, the hysterical conversion-symptom has a more precise symbolic relationship to the subject's history, it is less easily identifiable as a somatic clinical entity (e.g. stomach ulcer, hypertension), it is less stable, etc. If in many cases this distinction is unavoidable for the clinician, the theoretical distinction that ought to correspond to it remains problematic.

(1) FREUD, S. 'Some General Remarks on Hysterical Attacks' (1909a), G.W., VII, 382; S.E., X, 157.

Conversion Hysteria

(2) Cf. FREUD, S. 'The Neuro-Psychoses of Defence' (1894a): a) G.W., I, 63; S.E., III, 49. b) G.W., I, 65; S.E., III, 50.

(3) Cf., for example, FREUD, S. Studies on Hysteria (1895d), G.W., I, 212; S.E., II, 148.

(4) FREUD, S. 'Fragment of an Analysis of a Case of Hysteria' (1905e [1901]), G.W., V, 213; S.E., VII, 53.

Conversion Hysteria

= D.: Konversionshysterie. – Es.: histeria de conversión. – Fr.: hystérie de conversión. – I.: isteria di conversione. – P.: histeria de conversão.

Type of hysteria characterised by the prevalence of conversion symptoms.

This term is not used in Freud's early work, where the mechanism of conversion* is treated as a characteristic of hysteria in general. When Freud decides, with the analysis of 'Little Hans', to treat a phobic syndrome as a subdivision of hysteria under the name of 'anxiety hysteria'*, the term 'conversion hysteria' is introduced in order to distinguish what is now just one of the forms of hysteria: 'There exist cases of pure conversion-hysteria, without any trace of anxiety, just as there are cases of simple anxiety-hysteria, which exhibit feelings of anxiety and phobias, but have no admixture of conversions' (1).

(1) FREUD, S. 'Analysis of a Phobia in a Five-Year-Old Boy' (1909b), G.W., VII, 349; S.E., X, 116.

Counter-Transference

= D.: Gegenübertragung. – Es.: contratransferencia. – Fr.: contre-transfert. – I.: controtransfert. – P.: contratransferência.

The whole of the analyst's unconscious reactions to the individual analysand – especially to the analysand's own transference*.

Only on very rare occasions did Freud allude to what he called the counter-transference. He sees this as 'a result of the patient's influence on [the physician's] unconscious feelings', and stresses the fact that 'no psycho-analyst goes further than his own complexes and internal resistances permit' (1); consequently, the analyst must absolutely submit to a personal analysis.

Since Freud's time, the counter-transference has received increasing attention from psycho-analysts, notably because the treatment has come more and more to be understood and described as a *relationship*, but also as a result of the penetration of psycho-analysis into new fields (the analysis of children and psychotics) where reactions from the anlyst may be more in demand. We shall only deal with two aspects of the matter here:

I. A large measure of disagreement exists regarding the extension of the concept: some authors take the counter-transference to include everything in the analyst's personality liable to affect the treatment, while others restrict it to those unconscious processes which are brought about in the analyst by the transference of the analysand.

Daniel Lagache adopts the latter, more restricted definition, and he clarifies it by pointing out that the counter-transference understood in this sense – i.e. as the reaction to the other's transference – is not found only in the analyst but also in the subject. On this view, therefore, transference and counter-transference are no longer seen as processes specific to the analyst and the analysand respectively. In considering the analysis as a whole, we have to ascertain the part of transference and the part of counter-transference in *each* of the two people present (2).

II. So far as technique is concerned, a schematic distinction may be drawn between three orientations:

a. To reduce manifestations of counter-transference as far as possible by means of personal analysis so that the analytic situation may ideally be structured exclusively by the patient's transference.

b. To exploit the counter-transference manifestations in a controlled fashion for the purposes of the work of analysis. This approach takes its cue from Freud's remark that 'everyone possesses in his own unconscious an instrument with which he can interpret the utterances of the unconscious in other people' (3) (see 'Suspended Attention').

c. To allow oneself to be guided, in the actual *interpretation*, by one's own counter-transference reactions, which in this perspective are often not distinguished from emotions felt. This approach is based on the tenet that resonance 'from unconscious to unconscious' constitutes the only authentically psycho-analytic form of communication.

(1) FREUD, S. 'The Future Prospects of Psycho-Analytic Therapy' (1910*d*), G.W., VIII 108; S.E., XI, 144–45.

(2) Cf. LAGACHE, D. 'La méthode psychanalytique', in MICHAUX, L. *et al.*, *Psychiatrie*, (Paris: 1964), 1036–66.

(3) FREUD, S. 'The Disposition to Obsessional Neurosis' (1913*i*), G.W., VIII, 445; S.E., XII, 320.

D

Damming up of Libido

= *D*.: Libidostauung.–*Es*.: estancamiento de la libido.–*Fr*.: stase libidinale.–
I.: stasi della libido.–*P*.: estase da libido.

Economic process which according to a hypothesis of Freud's may underlie the subject's lapse into neurosis or psychosis: deprived of an outlet towards discharge, libido collects on intrapsychic formations; the energy thus accumulated is put to use in the constitution of symptoms.

The economic notion of the damming up of libido originates in the theory of the actual neuroses* as expounded by Freud in his earliest writings: he deems the aetiological factor in these neuroses to be an accumulation (*Anhäufung*) of sexual excitations which, in the absence of an adequate specific action*, arc unable to find any path towards discharge.

In 'Types of Onset of Neurosis' (1912*c*) the notion of the damming up of libido becomes very broad in that the process is said to take place in all the various forms of entry into neurosis that Freud distinguishes; these forms are 'different ways of establishing a particular pathogenic constellation in the mental economy–namely the damming up of libidio, which the ego cannot, with the means at its command, ward off without danger' (1). All the same, important reservations are made about the aetiological function of damming up:

a. Freud does not make the damming up of libido a *primary* factor in all the types of onset; it is apparently in the cases nearest to actual neurosis–those involving *reale Versagung* or real frustration–that it plays the decisive role. Elsewhere, it is merely a consequence of the psychical conflict.

b. Damming up is not in itself pathogenic. It may lead to normal behaviour: sublimation, or the transformation of 'actual' tension into activity that results in the acquisition of a satisfying object.

As from 'On Narcissism: An Introduction' (1914*c*) the notion of damming up is extended to the mechanism of the psychoses, which is seen as the damming of the libido cathecting the ego. 'It seems that an accumulation of narcissistic libido beyond a certain point is not tolerated' (2). Thus the hypochondria which is so often met with as a more or less transitory stage in the development of schizophrenia is an expression of this intolerable accumulation of narcissistic libido; and delusion, economically speaking, represents an attempt to redirect the libidinal energy on to a newly formed external world.

(1) FREUD, S., G.W., VIII, 329–30; S.E., XII, 237.
(2) FREUD, S. *Introductory Lectures on Psycho-Analysis* (1916–17), G.W., XI, 436; S.E., XVI, 421.

Day-Dream

= *D.*: Tagtraum.–*Es.*: sueño diurno (devaneo).–*Fr.*: rêve diurne.–*I.*: sogno diurno.–
P.': sonho diurno (devaneio).

Freud gives this name to scenarios imagined during the waking state; he does so in order to bring out the analogy between such reveries and dreams. Like nocturnal dreams, day-dreams are wish-fulfilments; both are formed by identical mechanisms, though secondary revision* is the one which predominates in day-dreams.

The *Studies on Hysteria* (1895*d*), especially the chapters written by Breuer, underline the importance taken on by day-dreams in the genesis of hysterical symptoms: according to Breuer, the habit of day-dreaming (Anna O.'s 'private theatre') facilitates the setting up of a split (*Spaltung*)* within the field of consciousness (see 'Hypnoid State').

Freud interested himself in day-dreams (especially in the context of his dream theory) from two points of view: in the first place, he compared their genesis to that of dreams proper; secondly, he studied the part they play in nocturnal dreaming.

Day-dreams have several essential characteristics in common with night-dreams: 'Like dreams, they are wish-fulfilments; like dreams, they are based to a great extent on impressions of infantile experiences; like dreams, they benefit by a certain degree of relaxation of censorship. If we examine their structure, we shall perceive the way in which the wishful purpose that is at work in their production has mixed up the material of which they are built, has re-arranged it and has formed it into a new whole. They stand in much the same relation to the childhood memories from which they are derived as do some of the Baroque palaces of Rome to the ancient ruins whose pavements and columns have provided the material for the more recent structures' (1*a*).

One trait specific to day-dreams, however, is that secondary revision has a dominant role in shaping them, with the result that their scenarios have a greater consistency than those of ordinary dreams.

Day-dreams for Freud–who uses the term in *The Interpretation of Dreams* synonymously with 'phantasy' (*Phantasie*) or 'daytime phantasy' (*Tagphantasie*) –need not always be conscious: '. . . . there are unconscious ones in great numbers, which have to remain unconscious on account of their content and of their origin from repressed material' (1*b*) (see 'Phantasy').

Day-dreams constitute an important portion of the dream-material. They may be found among the day's residues* and they are subject, just as these are, to all forms of distortion*; more specifically, they can provide the secondary revision with a ready-made story–the 'façade of the dream' (1*c*).

(1) FREUD, S. *The Interpretation of Dreams* (1900*a*): a) G.W., II–III, 496; S.E., V, 492. b) G.W., II–III, 496; S.E., V, 492. c) G.W., II–III, 497; S.E., V, 493.

Day's Residues

= *D.*: Tagesreste.−*Es.*: restos diurnos.−*Fr.*: restes diurnes.−*I.*: resti diurni.−
P.: restos diurnos.

According to the psycho-analytic theory of dreams, elements from the waking state of the day before which are found in the narrative of the dream and in the dreamer's free associations. They are connected, more or less distantly, to the unconscious wish that is fulfilled in the dream. Cases may be met with at any point between two extremes: cases where the presence of a particular day's residue appears to be motivated − in the first analysis at any rate − by a preoccupation or wish of the day before; and, at the opposite pole, cases where it is apparently insignificant daytime elements that are selected because of their being bound by association to the dream-wish.

According to a traditional view discussed at length in the first chapter of *The Interpretation of Dreams* (1900*a*), the elements found in most dreams are derived from the waking activity of the previous day. Several authors, however, had already noted that the elements retained did not always relate to important events or concerns, but instead only to apparently banal details.

Freud accepts these findings but gives them a fresh meaning by incorporating them into his theory of the dream as an unconscious wish-fulfilment. The nature and function of the various day's residues can best be circumscribed, according to Freud, by reference to the basic thesis that the energy of the dream derives from unconscious desire.

It may be a question of various wishes or worries which the subject has had during the preceding day and which reappear in the dream; as a rule such day-time problems are present in the dream in a displaced and symbolic form. The day's residues are subject to the mechanisms of the dream-work* just as all the dream-thoughts are. As a famous metaphor of Freud's has it, the day's residues here play the part of the dream's entrepreneur, and function as an instigator (bodily impressions during sleep may have an analogous role). Yet even in this case the dream can only be fully explained by the intervention of the unconscious wish which provides the instinctual force (*Triebkraft*) − or 'capital' − necessary. '*My supposition is that a conscious wish can only become a dream-instigator if it succeeds in awakening an unconscious wish with the same tenor and in obtaining reinforcement from it*' (1*a*).

In extreme instances the relationship between the day's residues and the unconscious wish may forego the mediation of a current preoccupation, with the result that the residues become nothing more than elements or signs used by the unconscious wish; and in consequence the apparent arbitrariness of their selection will be all the more striking. What then is their function? We may sum it up as follows:

a. By selecting these residues the dream deceives the censorship. Under the cover of their insignificant aspect, repressed contents are able to find expression.

b. They are better suited to connection with the unconscious wish than memories laden with interest and already integrated into rich associative complexes.

96

c. Their contemporaneous character seems to lend them a special status in Freud's view: he invokes the idea of a 'transference'* to account for the presence of the *recent* in every dream: '. . . the day's residues [. . .] not only *borrow* something from the *Ucs.* when they succeed in taking a share in the formation of a dream – namely the instinctual force which is at the disposal of the repressed wish – but they also *offer* the unconscious something indispensable – namely the necessary point of attachment for a transference' (1*b*). This importance of the present is borne out by the fact that the residues most often encountered date from the day immediately preceding the dream.

(1) FREUD, S.: a) G.W., II–III, 55&; S.E., V, 553. b) G.W., II–III, 569; S.E., V, 564.

Death Instincts

= *D.*: Todestriebe. – *Es.*: instintos de muerte. – *Fr.*: pulsions de mort. – *I.*: instinti *or* pulsioni di morte. – *P.*: impulsos *or* pulsões de morte.

In the framework of the final Freudian theory of the instincts, this is the name given to a basic category: the death instincts, which are opposed to the life instincts, strive towards the reduction of tensions to zero-point. In other words, their goal is to bring the living being back to the inorganic state.

The death instincts are to begin with directed inwards and tend towards self-destruction, but they are subsequently turned towards the outside world in the form of the aggressive or destructive instinct.

The notion of a death instinct, which Freud introduced in *Beyond the Pleasure Principle* (1920g) and which he continued to uphold right to the end of his work, has not managed to gain the acceptance of his disciples and successors in the way that the majority of his conceptual contributions have done – and it is still one of the most controversial of psycho-analytic concepts. If its meaning is to be fully grasped, it is necessary in our view to do more than refer to Freud's explicit pronouncements on the question; nor is it enough merely to identify those clinical phenomena which seem best able to justify this speculative hypothesis. It is essential, in addition, to relate the concept of the death instinct to the evolution of Freud's thought, and to discover what structural necessity its introduction answers to in the context of the more general revision known as the turning-point of the 1920's. Only with the help of such an evaluation can we hope to gain insight – over and above Freud's explicit assertions and indeed despite his conviction that he was breaking radically new ground – into the need the notion testifies to; for, under other guises, this need had already demanded attention in the earlier theoretical models.

*   *   *

We may begin with a *résumé* of Freud's theses regarding the death instinct. This instinct is held to represent the fundamental tendency of every living being to return to the inorganic state. In this context, 'If we assume that living things came later than inanimate ones and arose from them, then the death instinct fits in with the formula [...] to the effect that instincts tend towards a return to an earlier state' (1a). From this standpoint, 'all living substance is bound to die from internal causes' (2a). In multicellular organisms, 'the libido meets the instinct of death, or destruction, which is dominant in them and which seeks to disintegrate the cellular organism and to conduct each separate unicellular organism [composing it] into a state of inorganic stability [...]. The libido has the task of making the destroying instinct innocuous, and it fulfils the task by diverting that instinct to a great extent outwards–soon with the help of a special organic system, the muscular apparatus–towards objects in the external world. The instinct is then called the destructive instinct, the instinct for mastery, or the will to power. A portion of the instinct is placed directly in the service of the sexual function, where it has an important part to play. This is sadism proper. Another part does not share in this transposition outwards; it remains inside the organism and [...] becomes libidinally bound there. It is in this portion that we have to recognise the original, erotogenic masochism' (3a).

Freud was able to describe the roles of the life and death instincts as being combined in the individual's libidinal development, this under a sadistic form (2b) as well as under a masochistic one (3b).

The death instincts make up one pole of a new dualism in which they are opposed to the life instincts (or Eros*), which now come to subsume all the instincts previously enumerated by Freud (see 'Life Instincts', 'Sexual Instinct', 'Instincts of Self-Preservation', 'Ego-Instincts'). The death instincts consequently appear in the Freudian conceptual system as a completely new type of instinct which had no place in the previous classifications (sadism* and masochism*, for example, having been formerly explained in terms of a complex interplay between instincts all with a perfectly positive character) (4a). Yet at the same time Freud looks upon these new instincts as the instincts *par excellence*, in that they typify the repetitive nature of instinct in general.

*   *   *

What are the motives which most clearly led Freud to posit the existence of a death instinct?

a. First, there is the need to give some consideration to the appearance, at very different levels, of repetition phenomena (see 'Compulsion to Repeat') which are difficult to account for in terms of the search for libidinal satisfaction or as a simple attempt to overcome unpleasant experiences. Freud sees the mark of the 'daemonic' in these phenomena–the mark, in other words, of an irrepressible force which is independent of the pleasure principle and apt to enter into opposition to it. It was starting from this idea that Freud was brought to wonder whether instinct might not have a regressive character, and this hypothesis, pushed in turn to its logical conclusion, led him to see the death instinct as the very epitome of instinct.

b. Another factor was the importance attained in psycho-analytic practice by the concepts of ambivalence*, aggressiveness*, sadism and masochism–as developed, for example, from the clinical experience of obsessional neurosis and melancholia.

c. It had seemed impossible to Freud from the very beginning that hate could be derived, metapsychologically speaking, from the sexual instincts. He was never to espouse the tendency which ascribes 'whatever is dangerous and hostile in love to an original bipolarity in its own nature' (5a). In 'Instincts and their Vicissitudes' (1915c), sadism and hate are viewed in their relation to the ego-instincts: '. . . the true prototypes of the relation of hate are derived not from sexual life, but from the ego's struggle to preserve and maintain itself' (4b); Freud sees hate as a relation to objects which 'is older than love' (4c). After the introduction of the concept of narcissism*, the distinction between two kinds of instincts–the sexual instincts and the ego-instincts–tends to disappear and to be replaced by an explanation in terms of the modalities of the libido; we may suppose that at this point Freud found hate particularly hard to integrate into the framework of an instinctual monism. The idea of a *primary masochism*, mooted as early as 1915 (4d), is a first pointer to one pole of Freud's great new dualism, yet to be developed.

As is well known, the dualistic tendency is fundamental to Freudian thought: it can be seen in numerous structural aspects of his theory, and it comes out for example in the notion of 'pairs of opposites'*. The demands of this search for dualistic explanations are particularly imperious when it comes to the instincts, for these are the forces which, in the last reckoning, confront one another in psychical conflict* (2c).

*   *   *

What role does Freud assign to the notion of the death instinct? The first point to note is that Freud himself stresses that the concept is founded on speculative considerations, and that it gradually imposed itself, as it were, upon him: 'To begin with, it was only tentatively that I put forward the views I have developed here, but in the course of time they have gained such a hold upon me that I can no longer think in any other way' (5b). It was apparently above all because of the theoretical value of the concept and its concordance with a particular view of instinct that Freud was so concerned to uphold the death-instinct thesis despite the 'resistances' which it ran into in the psycho-analytical milieu, and despite the difficulty of anchoring it in concrete experience. The fact is–as Freud underlined on many occasions–that a libidinal satisfaction, whether sexual satisfaction directed towards the object or narcissistic enjoyment, can always be present, even in those cases where the tendency towards destruction of the other or of the self is most in evidence–even where the fury of destruction is at its blindest (5c). 'What we are concerned with are scarcely ever pure instinctual impulses but mixtures in various proportions of the two groups of instincts' (6a). It is in this sense that Freud was able to remark on occasion that the death instinct 'eludes our perception [...] unless it is tinged with erotism' (5d).

This is also at the root of the difficulties which Freud encountered in attempting to integrate the lessons of the new instinctual dualism into the theory of the neuroses and the models of psychical conflict: 'Over and over again we find, when we are able to trace instinctual impulses back, that they reveal themselves as derivatives of Eros. If it were not for the considerations put forward in *Beyond the Pleasure Principle*, and ultimately for the sadistic constituents which

99

have attached themselves to Eros, we should have difficulty in holding to our fundamental dualistic point of view' (7*a*). It is indeed striking to see, in a text such as *Inhibitions, Symptoms and Anxiety* (1926*d*), which reconsiders the whole problem of neurotic conflict and its various modalities, what an insignificant place is reserved by Freud for the two great antagonistic types of instinct: their opposition is not given any *dynamic* function whatsoever. When Freud gives explicit consideration (7*b*) to the question of the relation between the agencies of the personality which he has just differentiated (id, ego, super-ego) and the two instinctual categories, it is significant that he does not see conflict between agencies as able to be superimposed upon the instinctual antithesis. Although he does attempt to gauge the respective parts played by the two instincts in the constitution of each agency, when it comes to the description of the modalities of conflict the supposed antagonism between life and death instincts is not visible. In fact, 'There can be no question of restricting one or other of the basic instincts to one of the provinces of the mind. They must necessarily be met with everywhere' (1*b*). The gap between the new theory of the instincts and the new topography is at times even more sharply felt: the conflict becomes a conflict between psychical agencies in which the *id* eventually comes to represent *all* instinctual demands as opposed to the *ego*. It is in this context that Freud goes so far as to assert that empirically speaking the distinction between ego-instincts and object-instincts still retains its validity: it is only 'theoretical speculation which leads to the suspicion that there are two fundamental instincts [i.e. Eros and the destructive instinct] which lie concealed behind the manifest ego-instincts and object-instincts' (8). It is clear that Freud is here taking up once again–even on the instinctual level–a model of conflict which pre-dates *Beyond the Pleasure Principle* (see 'Ego-Libido/Object-Libido'); the assumption is simply that each of the two forces in play–the 'ego-instincts' and 'object-instincts' whose confrontation with each other is quite clearly observable–is in fact itself the expression of a fusion* between life instincts and death instincts.

Lastly, it is remarkable how little manifest change is wrought by the new theory of the instincts upon either the description of defensive conflict or the account of the instinctual stages (6*b*).

Although Freud affirms and maintains the notion of a death instinct right up until the end, he does not claim that it is implied inescapably by the theory of the neuroses. Instead, he justifies it in two ways: first, it is the product of a speculative need which he considers to be fundamental; secondly, it seems to him that such a hypothesis is inevitably suggested by the persistence of very precise and irreducible phenomena of an increasing significance, in his view, for clinical experience and for analytic treatment: 'If we take into consideration the whole picture made up of the phenomena of masochism immanent in so many people, the negative therapeutic reaction* and the sense of guilt* found in so many neurotics, we shall no longer be able to adhere to the belief that mental events are exclusively governed by the desire for pleasure. These phenomena are unmistakable indications of the presence of a power in mental life which we call the instinct of aggression or of destruction according to its aims, and which we trace back to the original death instinct of living matter' (9).

The action of the death instinct, Freud claims, can even be glimpsed in its pure state when it tends to become defused from the life instinct, as in the case of the melancholic whose super-ego appears as 'a pure culture of the death instinct' (7c).

* * *

As Freud himself acknowledges, 'Since the assumption of the existence of the instinct is mainly based on theoretical grounds, we must also admit that it is not entirely proof against theoretical objections' (5e). A good number of analysts have indeed obliged with such objections; they have maintained on the one hand that the *notion* of a death instinct is unacceptable, and on the other hand that the clinical *data* adduced by Freud must be interpreted without having recourse to such a concept. These criticisms may be classed – very schematically – according to the different levels at which they have been made:

a. On a metapsychological plane, some critics have refused to look upon the reduction of tensions as the work of a specific group of instincts.

b. Others have attempted dissenting accounts of the genesis of aggression. They sometimes treat it as a factor which is in conjunction with every instinct from the start, in so far as this instinct finds expression through an activity of the subject which is imposed upon the object. Alternatively, aggressiveness has even been seen as a secondary reaction to the frustration caused by the object.

c. Others again have acknowledged the importance and autonomy of aggressive instincts, but rejected the hypothesis according to which they are reducible to a *self*-aggressive tendency; there is a refusal in this case to hypostasise, within every living organism, the pair of opposites constituted by the life instincts and the self-destructive instinct. On this view an instinctual ambivalence may certainly be said to exist from the start, but the love-hate opposition, as manifested straight away in oral incorporation*, can only be understood in terms of the relation to an external object.

In contrast to these critics, a school such as the Kleinian one reasserts the dualism of death and life instincts in all its force: Melanie Klein and her followers go so far as to assign a major role to the death instincts from the beginning of human existence, and not only inasmuch as these instincts are orientated towards external objects, but also in that they work within the organism and induce anxiety about disintegration and annihilation. We are justified in asking, however, whether the Kleinian manichaeism accepts the full implications of Freud's dualism: there can be no doubt that the two types of instinct invoked by Melanie Klein are antagonistic to each other as regards their aims, yet she postulates no basic difference in the principle of their functioning.

* * *

The difficulty encountered by Freud's heirs in integrating the notion of the death instinct leads to the question of what exactly Freud meant by the term 'Trieb' in his final theory (see 'Instinct'). In fact it is very jarring to find the same name, 'instinct', applied, on the one hand, to that factor which Freud described and whose operation he demonstrated in the complex functioning of human sexuality (*Three Essays on the Theory of Sexuality* [1905d]); and, at the same time, to those 'mythical forces' whose confrontation he postulates not so

101

much at the level of clinically observable conflict as in a combat which transcends the human individual in that it can be identified in veiled form in all living things – including the most primitive ones: 'The instinctual forces which seek to conduct life into death may also be operating in protozoa from the first, and yet their effects may be so completely concealed by the life-preserving forces that it may be very hard to find any direct evidence of their presence' (2d).

The opposition between the two basic instincts is apparently to be compared to the great vital processes of assimilation and dissimilation, and in its most extreme form this analogy extends even 'to the pair of opposing forces – attraction and repulsion – which rule the inorganic world (1c). This fundamental aspect of the death instinct, moreover, is stressed by Freud in a multitude of ways; it is brought out particularly by the reference to philosophic conceptions such as those of Empedocles and Schopenhauer.

In fact what Freud was explicitly seeking to express by the term 'death instinct' was the most fundamental aspect of instinctual life: the return to an earlier state and, in the last reckoning, the return to the absolute repose of the inorganic. What is designated here is more than any particular *type* of instinct – it is rather that factor which determines the actual *principle* of all instinct.

It is interesting, with these considerations in mind, to observe how difficult Freud found it to situate the death instinct in relation to those 'principles of mental functioning' which he had laid down long before – and especially in relation to the pleasure principle. Thus in *Beyond the Pleasure Principle* – as the title itself suggests – the death instinct is postulated on the basis of facts which supposedly run counter to the principle in question; and yet Freud is able to conclude by asserting that 'The pleasure principle seems actually to serve the death instincts' (2e).

He was not unaware of this contradiction, however, and this led him subsequently to differentiate the Nirvana principle* from the pleasure principle*; the latter, as an economic principle working towards the reduction of tensions to nil, 'would be entirely in the service of the death instincts' (3c). As to the pleasure principle, which is now defined more in qualitative than in economic terms, it 'represents the demands of the libido' (3d).

It might be asked whether the introduction of the Nirvana principle, which 'expresses the trend of the death instinct', constitutes a radical innovation. It would be an easy matter to show how the formulations of the pleasure principle proposed by Freud throughout his work confuse two tendencies: a tendency towards the complete discharge of excitation and a tendency towards the maintenance of a constant level (homoeostasis). But it is noteworthy too that Freud had distinguished these two tendencies in the very first stage of his metapsychological constructions ('Project for a Scientific Psychology' [1895]), by speaking of a principle of inertia* and by showing how this is modified into a tendency to keep the level of tension constant (10).

What is more, Freud continued to distinguish these two trends inasmuch as they can be said to correspond to two kinds of energy – free and bound* – and to two modes of mental functioning – primary and secondary processes*. In this sense one can look upon the death-instinct thesis as a reaffirmation of what Freud had always held to be the very essence of the unconscious in its indestructible and unrealistic aspect. This reassertion of the most radical part

102

of unconscious desire can be correlated with a change in the ultimate function which Freud assigns to sexuality; under the name of Eros, the latter is no longer defined as a disruptive force, as an eminently perturbatory factor, but rather as a principle of cohesion: 'The aim of [Eros] is to establish even greater unities and to preserve them thus – in short, to bind together; the aim of [the destructive instinct] is, on the contrary, to undo connections and so to destroy things' (1*d*) (see Life Instincts').

* * *

Nonetheless, even though it is possible to recognise the death instinct as a new guise for a basic and constant *sine qua non* of Freudian thought, it must be emphasised that its introduction does embody a new conceptual departure: the death instinct makes the destructive tendency, as revealed for example in sado-masochism, into an irreducible *datum*; it is furthermore the chosen expression of the most fundamental principle or psychical functioning; and lastly, in so far as it is 'the essence of the instinctual', it binds every wish, whether aggressive or sexual, to the wish for death.

(1) FREUD, S. *An Outline of Psycho-Analysis* (1940*a* [1938]): a) G.W., XVII, 71; S.E., XXIII, 148–49. b) G.W., XVII, 71–72; S.E., XXIII, 149. c) G.W., XVII, 71; S.E., XXIII, 149. d) G.W., XVII, 71; S.E., XXIII, 148.

(2) FREUD, S. *Beyond the Pleasure Principle* (1920*g*): a) G.W., XIII, 47; S.E., XVIII, 44. b) G.W., XIII, 58; S.E., XVIII, 54. c) G.W., XIII, 57; S.E., XVIII, 54. d) G.W., XIII, 52; S.E., XVIII, 49. e) G.W., XIII, 69; S.E., XVIII, 63.

(3) FREUD, S. 'The Economic Problem of Masochism' (1924*c*): a) G.W., XIII, 376; S.E., XIX, 163. b) G.W., XIII, 377; S.E., XIX, 164. c) G.W., XIII, 372; S.E., XIX, 160. d) G.W. XIII, 273; S.E., XIX, 160.

(4) FREUD, S. 'Instincts and their Vicissitudes' (1915*c*): a) G.W., X, 220 *ff*; S.E., XIV, 127 *ff*. b) G.W., X, 230; S.E., XIV, 138. c) G.W., X, 231; S.E., XIV, 139. d) G.W., X, 220–21; S.E., XIV, 128.

(5) FREUD, S. *Civilization and its Discontents* (1930*a*): a) G.W., XIV, 478; S.E., XXI, 119. b) G.W., XIV, 478–79; S.E., XXI, 119. c) G.W., XIV, 480; S.E., XXI, 121. d) G.W., XIV, 479; S.E., XXI, 120. e) G.W., XIV, 480–81; S.E., XXI, 121–22.

(6) FREUD, S. *Inhibitions, Symptoms and Anxiety* (1926*d*): a) G.W., XIV, 155; S.E., XX, 125. b) Cf. G.W., XIV, 155; S.E., XX, 124–25.

(7) FREUD, S. *The Ego and the Id* (1923*b*): a) G.W., XIII, 275; S.E., XIX, 46. b) Chapter IV, *passim.* c) G.W., XIII, 283; S.E., XIX, 53.

(8) FREUD, S. 'Psycho-Analysis' (1926 *f* [1925]), G.W., XIV, 302; S.E., XX, 265.

(9) FREUD, S. 'Analysis Terminable and Interminable' (1937*c*), G.W., XVI, 88; S.E., XXIII, 243.

(10) FREUD, S., *Anf.*, 380–81; S.E., I, 295–97.

Defence

= *D.*: Abwehr. – *Es.*: defensa. – *Fr.*: défense. – *I.*: difesa. – *P.*: defesa.

Group of operations *aimed at* the reduction and elimination of any change liable to threaten the integrity and stability of the bio-psychological individual. Inasmuch as the ego is constituted as an agency which embodies this stability and strives

to maintain it, it may be considered as both the *stake* and the *agent* of these operations.

Generally speaking, defence is *directed towards* internal excitation (instinct); in practice, its action is extended to whatever representations* (memories, phantasies) this excitation is bound to; and to any situation that is unpleasurable for the ego as a result of its incompatibility with the individual's equilibrium and, to that extent, liable to spark off the excitation. Unpleasurable affects*, which serve as *motives* or *signals* for defence, may also become its object.

The defensive process is expressed concretely in *mechanisms* of defence which are more or less integrated into the ego.

Defence is marked and infiltrated by its ultimate object–instinct–and consequently it often takes on a compulsive aspect, and works at least in part in an unconscious way.

It was by bringing the notion of defence to the fore in dealing with hysteria–and, soon afterwards, with the other psychoneuroses*–that Freud developed his own conception of mental life in contrast to the views of his contemporaries (see 'Defence Hysteria'). The *Studies on Hysteria* (1895*d*) demonstrate all the complexity of the relations between defence and the ego which is made responsible for it. The ego in question is that area of the personality–that 'space'–which seeks freedom from all forms of disturbance–from conflicts between contradictory wishes for instance. It is further a 'group of ideas' at variance with an idea* deemed 'incompatible' with itself; the sign of this incompatibility is an unpleasurable affect. Lastly, it is the agent of the defensive operation (see 'Ego'). In the works in which he evolves the concept of defence neuro-psychosis*, Freud invariably places the emphasis on the notion of the incompatibility of an idea with the ego; the different forms of defence are seen as corresponding to the different *ways* in which this idea is dealt with, particularly in so far as these procedures make use of the separation of the idea from the affect which was originally bound to it. At the same time, it will be recalled that Freud very soon opposed the neuro-psychoses of defence to the actual neuroses*, these being a group of neuroses where an intolerable increase in internal tension, due to an undischarged sexual excitation, finds an outlet in a variety of somatic symptoms. It is significant that Freud refuses to speak of defence in the case of the actual neuroses, despite the fact that they do involve a form of self-protection on the part of the organism and the attempt to restore a certain equilibrium. From the moment of its discovery, then, defence is implicitly distinguished from those measures which an organism takes to reduce any increase in tension whatsoever.

At the same time as trying to specify the different modalities of the defensive process according to the various mental illnesses, and while his clinical experience was enabling him–in the *Studies on Hysteria*–to give a more accurate account of the steps in this process (the re-emergence of the unpleasurable affects which have served as motives for defence, the layering of resistances, the stratification of the pathogenic material, etc.), Freud was also attempting to construct a metapsychological model of defence. This theory refers from the outset to a distinction that Freud was always to maintain subsequently: that between *external* excitations on the one hand, from which flight is possible or against which a damming mechanism is set up for the purpose of filtering them (see 'Protective Shield') and, on the other hand, *internal* excitations which it is impossible to evade. It is in answer to this aggression from the inside–in other words, against instinct–that the different defensive procedures are instigated. The 'Project for a Scientific Psychology' (1950a [1895]) tackles the problem of defence in two ways:

a. Freud seeks the origin of what he calls 'primary defence' in an 'experience of pain', just as he had found the model of desire and its inhibition by the ego in an 'experience of satisfaction'*. This conception, however, is not expounded with the same clarity, in the 'Project' itself, as that of the experience of satisfaction (α).

b. Freud attempts to differentiate a pathological form of defence from a normal form. The latter occurs in the case of the revival of a distressing experience; in normal defence, the ego must have been able to begin inhibiting the unpleasure on the occasion of the initial experience by means of 'side-cathexes': 'If the cathexis of the memory is repeated, the unpleasure is repeated too, but the ego-facilitations are there already as well; experience shows that the release [of unpleasure] is less the second time, until, after further repetition, it shrivels up to the intensity of a signal acceptable to the ego' (1a).

This kind of defence enables the ego to avoid the danger of being overwhelmed and infiltrated by the primary process*; in pathological defence, on the other hand, this is precisely what does happen. As we know, Freud considers that this latter operation only comes into play as a consequence of a sexual scene which, at the time, did not give rise to normal defence but whose memory, once reactivated, triggers off a rise in excitation from the inside. 'Attention is [normally] adjusted towards perceptions, which are what ordinarily give occasion for a release of unpleasure. Here [however, what has appeared] is no perception but a memory, which unexpectedly releases unpleasure, and the ego only discovers this too late' (1b). Which explains 'the fact that in the case of an *ego-process* consequences follow to which we are accustomed only with primary processes' (1c).

Pathological defence is thus conditional upon the setting in motion of an excitation of internal origin which brings about unpleasure, and against which no defensive procedure has been learnt. Its coming into play is not therefore motivated by the intensity of the affect *per se*, but rather by quite specific conditions which are to be found neither in the case of a distressing perception, nor even on the occasion of the recollection of such a perception. For Freud, these conditions are only fulfilled in the sexual realm (see 'Deferred Action', 'Seduction').

*   *   *

However great the differences may be between the various modalities of the defensive process in hysteria, obsessional neurosis, paranoia, etc. (see 'Defence Mechanisms'), the two poles of the conflict are invariably the ego and the instinct: it is against an internal threat that the ego seeks to defend itself. This conception, though validated constantly by clinical experience, poses a theoretical problem which was never far from Freud's attention: how does it

105

come about that instinctual discharge, which is given over by definition to the attainment of pleasure, can be perceived as unpleasure or as the threat of unpleasure to the point of occasioning a defensive operation? It is true that the topographical diversification of the psychical apparatus clears the way for the thesis that what is pleasure for one system is unpleasure for another (i.e. the ego), but this distribution of roles still leaves one question unanswered: what exactly leads certain instinctual demands into opposition with the ego? Freud rejects a theoretical solution along the lines that defence arises '. . . in cases where the tension produced by lack of satisfaction of an instinctual impulse is raised to an unbearable degree' (2). Unsatisfied hunger, for example, is not repressed; whatever the 'methods of defence' may be which are open to the organism for dealing with a threat of this type, they certainly have nothing to do with defence as it is known to psycho-analysis. And defence cannot be adequately accounted for by *homoeostasis of the organism*.

So what is the ultimate basis of the defence of the ego? Why does the ego experience a certain instinctual impulse an unpleasure? The question is fundamental to psycho-analysis, and there are a variety of answers to it which are not necessarily mutually exclusive. An initial distinction is often made as regards the fundamental source of the danger which is inseparable from instinctual satisfaction: the instinct itself may be deemed dangerous to the ego, and seen purely as an attack upon it from the inside. Alternatively, all danger can be attributed, in the last reckoning, to the individual's relations with the outside world: in this sense, the instinct is only dangerous because of the real harm which its satisfaction might bring in its wake. It is the latter option, for example, which informs the thesis adopted by Freud in *Inhibitions, Symptoms and Anxiety* (1926d) and, in particular, his new interpretation of phobia; consequently, he promotes 'realistic anxiety'* (*Realangst*) to a special status and –carrying this tendency to the extreme– he treats neurotic anxiety, or anxiety in the face of the instinct, as purely derivative.

If the problem is approached from the standpoint of the way the ego is conceived of, the solution will naturally vary according to whether the stress is laid upon its function as the agent of reality and the representative of the reality principle; or whether the main emphasis is placed instead on its 'compulsion to synthesis'; or, again, whether the ego is seen above all as a *gestalt*–a sort of intrasubjective replica of the organism–governed, like the organism, by a principle of homoeostasis. Lastly, from the dynamic point of view, it is tempting to account for the difficulty raised by unpleasure of instinctual origin by positing an antagonism not just between the instincts and the agency of the ego but also between two kinds of instinct with differing aims. Freud embarked upon just such a course in the years 1910–15, when he set up an opposition between the sexual instincts and the instincts of self-preservation or ego-instincts. In his final theory, of course, this instinctual pair of opposites was to be replaced by the antithesis between the life and death instincts–an opposition which no longer coincided directly with the disposition of forces in the dynamics of the conflict*.

*   *   *

The term 'defence' itself, especially when used in its absolute sense, is full of ambiguity and necessitates the introduction of notional distinctions. It connotes both the action of *defending*–in the sense of fighting to protect something–and that of *defending oneself*. It might be of use therefore to distinguish between different parameters of defence, even if these coincide with one another to some extent, viz. *the stake of defence*: the 'psychical space' which is threatened; *the agent of defence*: whatever supports the defensive action; *the aims of defence*: an example would be the tendency to maintain and re-establish the integrity and the constancy of the ego, and to avoid all perturbing factors liable to be transposed into subjective unpleasure; *the motives of defence*: whatever heralds the danger and sets the defensive process in motion (affects reduced to the function of signals, anxiety as signal*); and *the mechanisms of defence*.

A final point: the distinction between *defence*, in the virtually strategic sense that it has acquired in psycho-analysis, and *prohibition*, particularly as it is understood in the context of the Oedipus complex, underlines the discrepancy which exists between the two levels of the structuring of the psychical apparatus and the structure of the most fundamental wishes and phantasies; the question of the articulation of these two levels in the theory and practice of the psycho-analytic cure remains an open one.

(α) The thesis of an 'experience of pain' taken to be the diametrical opposite of the experience of satisfaction is paradoxical from the outset, for why would the neuronal apparatus repeat a pain–which is defined by an increased charge–to the point of hallucinating it, when the function of this apparatus is, precisely, the avoidance of any rise in tension? This paradox can be explained if one takes into consideration the many passages in Freud's work in which he tackles the economic problem of pain. Any such examination, in our opinion, reveals that physical pain, as a breach of the confines of the body, ought rather to be taken as a model of that internal aggression which the instinct constitutes for the ego. The 'experience of pain' should therefore be understood not as an hallucinatory repetition of an actually experienced pain but rather as the emergence, with the revival of an experience which may not have been painful in itself, of that 'pain' which anxiety consists of from the ego's point of view.

(1) FREUD, S.: a) *Anf.*, 438; S.E., I, 359. b) *Anf.*, 438; S.E., I, 358, c) *Anf.*, 432; S.E., I, 353.
(2) FREUD, S. 'Repression' (1915*d*), G.W., X, 249; S.E., XIV, 147.

Defence Hysteria

= *D.*: Abwehrhysterie.–*Es.*: histeria de defensa.–*Fr.*: hystérie de défense.–
I.: isteria da difesa.–*P.*: histeria de defesa.

Type of hysteria distinguished by Freud in 1894-95 from two other forms, namely, hypnoid hysteria* and retention hysteria*.

Defence hysteria is characterised by the defensive activity of the subject against ideas liable to provoke unpleasant affects.

As soon as Freud recognises the fact that defence has a part to play in every hysteria, he drops the term 'defence hysteria' along with the distinction which it implies.

Defence Hysteria

It was in 'The Neuro-Psychoses of Defence' (1894a) that Freud first made a distinction, from a pathogenic point of view, between three forms of hysteria (hypnoid, retention, defence), claiming defence hysteria as his personal discovery and treating it as the prototype of the neuro-psychoses of defence (1).

It may be noted that from Breuer and Freud's 'Preliminary Communication' (1893a) onwards the impossibility of abreaction*–which is characteristic of hysteria–is associated with two sets of conditions: on the one hand, a specific state in which the subject must be at the moment of the trauma's occurrence (hypnoid state*); and on the other hand, conditions relating to the nature of the trauma* itself–whether external conditions or intentional (absichtlich) action by the subject in defending himself against 'distressing' (2a) contents of consciousness. At this first theoretical stage, defence, retention and the hypnoid state appear as aetiological factors which work together to produce hysteria. In so far as any of these is accorded a predominant role, it is the hypnoid state which Freud, under the influence of Breuer, calls 'the basic phenomenon of this neurosis' (2b).

In 'The Neuro-Psychoses of Defence', as we have seen, Freud focusses on this ensemble of symptoms to the point of differentiating between three corresponding types of hysteria; he is only really preoccupied, however, with defence hysteria.

The Studies on Hysteria (1895d) represent a third development in Freud's attitude: although the former distinction is maintained, its main purpose seems to be to direct attention to the notion of defence, and the assertion of the hypnoid state's predominance is abandoned. Freud notes: 'Strangely enough, I have never in my own experience met with a genuine hypnoid hysteria. Any that I took in hand has turned into a defence hysteria' (2c). Similarly, he questions the existence of an independent retention hysteria, putting forward the hypothesis that 'at the basis of retention hysteria, too, an element of defence is to be found which has forced the whole process in the direction of hysteria' (2d).

The expression 'defence hysteria' disappears after the Studies on Hysteria. It is almost as though it was only introduced in order to establish the primacy of the idea of defence over the idea of the hypnoid state. Once this had been achieved–once defence could be treated confidently as the basic process of hysteria and the model of the defensive conflict extended to the other neuroses –the term 'defence hysteria' was obviously deprived of any raison d'être.

(1) Cf. FREUD, S., G.W., I, 60–61; S.E., III, 45–47.

(2) FREUD, S. Studies on Hysteria (1895d): a) Cf. G.W., I, 89; S.E., II, 10–11. b) Cf. G.W., I, 91; S.E., II, 12. c) G.W., I, 289; S.E., II, 286. d) G.W., I, 290; S.E., II, 286.

Defence Mechanisms

= *D.*: Abwehrmechanismen.–*Es.*: mecanismos de defensa.–*Fr.*: mécanismes de défense.–
I.: meccanismi di difesa.–*P.*: mecanismos de defesa.

Different types of operations through which defence may be given specific expression. Which of these mechanisms predominate in a given case depends upon the type of illness under consideration, upon the developmental stage reached, upon the extent to which the defensive conflict has been worked out, and so on.

It is generally agreed that the ego puts the defence mechanisms to use, but the theoretical question of whether their mobilisation always presupposes the existence of an organised ego capable of sustaining them is an open one.

Freud's choice of the word 'mechanism' is intended, from the outset, to indicate the fact that psychical phenomena are so organised as to permit of scientific observation and analysis; adequate confirmation of this is provided by the mere title of Breuer and Freud's 'Preliminary Communication' (1893a): 'On the Psychical Mechanism of Hysterical Phenomena'.

At a time when Freud was engaged in developing the concept of defence, making it the defining principle of hysterical phenomena (see 'Defence Hysteria'), he was simultaneously seeking to specify other psychoneurotic illnesses in terms of the mode of operation of defence peculiar to each: '. . . different neurotic disturbances arise from the different methods adopted by the "ego" in order to escape from [its] incompatibility [with an idea]' (1).

Thus, in his 'Further Remarks on the Neuro-Psychoses of Defence' (1896b), Freud distinguishes between the mechanisms of hysterical conversion, obsessional substitution and paranoiac projection.

The term 'mechanism' appears sporadically throughout Freud's work. As for 'mechanism of defence', it is to be met with for example in the metapsychological writings of 1915, and this in two rather different senses: it is used either to denote the *whole* of that defensive process which is characteristic of a given neurosis (2), or else to mean the defensive employment of a *particular* 'instinctual vicissitude' (repression, turning round upon the subject's own self, reversal into the opposite) (3).

In *Inhibitions, Symptoms and Anxiety* (1926d), Freud justifies what he calls his 're-introduction of the old concept of *defence*' (4a) on the grounds that it is necessary to have an inclusive category under which other 'methods of defence', aside from repression, may be subsumed. He stresses the possibility of establishing 'an intimate connection between special forms of defence and particular illnesses', and concludes by putting forward the hypothesis that 'before its sharp cleavage into an ego and an id, and before the formation of a super-ego, the mental apparatus makes use of different methods of defence from those which it employs after it has reached these stages of organization' (4b).

Although Freud appears, in this passage, to underestimate the extent to which such ideas have been constantly discernible in his work up to this point, there is no doubt that from 1926 onwards the study of the defence mechanisms is to

109

become a major theme of psycho-analytic research. This development was spearheaded by Anna Freud's book devoted to the topic, in which, basing herself on concrete examples, she attempts to describe the variety, complexity and compass of the mechanisms of defence. In particular, she shows how defensive aims may make use of the most varied activities (phantasy, intellectual activity) and how defence can be directed not only against instinctual claims but also against everything which is liable to give rise to the development of anxiety: emotions, situations, super-ego demands, etc. It may be noted that Anna Freud does not claim that her approach is either exhaustive or systematic – a reservation which applies especially to her incidental enumeration of the defence mechanisms. Her list includes: repression*, regression*, reaction-formation*, isolation*, undoing*, projection*, introjection*, turning against the self*, reversal into the opposite*, sublimation*.

Many other defensive procedures have been described. Anna Freud herself further brings under this heading the processes of denial in phantasy, idealisation*, identification with the aggressor*, etc. Melanie Klein describes what she considers to be very primitive defences: splitting of the object*, projective identification*, denial of psychic reality, omnipotent control over objects, etc.

*   *   *

Inevitably, the blanket use of the concept of the defence mechanism raises a number of problems. When operations as diverse as, say, rationalisation*, which brings complex intellectual mechanisms into play, and turning against the self, which is a 'vicissitude' of the instinctual aim, are attributed to a single function, and when the same term 'defence' connotes such a truly compulsive operation as 'undoing what has been done' as well as the search for a form of 'working-off' after the fashion of certain kinds of sublimation (see 'Working-Off Mechanisms'), then it may well be asked whether the concept in question is a really operational one.

Many authors, while speaking of 'ego defence-mechanisms', do not hesitate to distinguish between different sub-categories: 'Methods such as that of undoing and isolation stand side by side with genuine instinctual processes, such as regression, reversal and turning against the self' (5a). At this point, however, it becomes necessary to show how the same process can function on different levels; for instance, introjection, which is first and foremost a mode of the instinct's relation to its object, having its somatic prototype in the act of incorporation, can be made use of *secondarily* by the ego for the purposes of defence (particularly manic defence).

Another fundamental theoretical distinction ought not to be overlooked – namely, the distinction which marks off repression from all other defensive processes. Freud had no qualms about recalling this specificity even after having said that repression was merely a special case of defence (6). This uniqueness of repression is not due so much to the fact – invoked by Anna Freud – that it may be defined, in essence, as a permanent anticathexis*, and that it is at once 'the most efficacious and the most dangerous' of the mechanisms of defence: its special function derives rather from its role in the constitution of the unconscious as such (see 'Repression').

Lastly, there is a danger that by basing the theory on the idea of the defence *of the ego* one may easily be brought to set this against a supposedly pure instinctual demand which, by definition, is devoid of any dialectic of its own: 'Were it not for the intervention of the ego, or of those external forces which the ego represents, every instinct would know only one fate–that of gratification' (5*b*).

The upshot of this line of reasoning is that the instinct comes to be seen as a completely positive force, bearing the traces of no prohibition. But do not the *mechanisms* of the primary process itself–displacement, condensation, etc. –with their implication that the interplay of instincts is structured, stand in contradiction to this approach?

(1) BREUER, J. and FREUD, S. *Studies on Hysteria* (1895*d*), G.W., I, 181; S.E., II, 122.

(2) FREUD, S. 'The Unconscious' (1915*e*), G.W., X, 283; S.E., XIV, 184.

(3) FREUD, S. 'Repression' (1915*d*), G.W., X, 249–50; S.E., XIV, 147.

(4) FREUD, S.: a) G.W., XIV, 197; S.E., XX, 164. b) G.W., XIV, 197; S.E., XX, 164.

(5) FREUD, A. *Das Ich und die Abwehrmechanismen* (1936). English translation: *The Ego and the Mechanisms of Defence* (London: Hogarth, 1937; New York: International Universities Press, 1946): a) 54. b) 47.

(6) Cf. for example FREUD, S. 'Analysis Terminable and Interminable' (1937*c*), G.W., XVI, 80; S.E., XXIII, 235.

Deferred Action; Deferred

= *D.*: Nachträglichkeit (sb.); nachträglich (adj. & adv.).–
Es.: posterioridad; posterior; posteriormente.–*Fr.*: après-coup (sb., adj. & adv.).–
I.: posteriore (adj.); posteriormente (adv.).–*P.*: posterioridade; posterior; posteriormente.

Term frequently used by Freud in connection with his view of psychical temporality and causality: experiences, impressions and memory-traces* may be revised at a later date to fit in with fresh experiences or with the attainment of a new stage of development. They may in that event be endowed not only with a new meaning but also with psychical effectiveness.

Freud uses the term '*nachträglich*' repeatedly and constantly, often underlining it. The substantival form '*Nachträglichkeit*' also keeps cropping up, and this from very early on. Thus, although he never offered a definition, much less a general theory, of the notion of deferred action, it was indisputably looked upon by Freud as part of his conceptual equipment. The credit for drawing attention to the importance of this term must go to Jacques Lacan. It should be pointed out that by failing to adopt a single rendering both the English and the French translators of Freud have made it impossible to trace its use.

We do not propose to set forth any theory of deferred action here; we shall merely give a brief indication of its meaning and import in the context of Freud's conception of psychical temporality and causality.

a. The first thing the introduction of the notion does is to rule out the

111

summary interpretation which reduces the psycho-analytic view of the subject's history to a linear determinism envisaging nothing but the action of the past upon the present. Psycho-analysis is often rebuked for its alleged reduction of all human actions and desires to the level of the infantile past; this tendency is said to get progressively worse as psycho-analysis evolves: delving further and further back, analysts supposedly end up maintaining that the entire destiny of the human individual is played out in the first months of his life—perhaps even during his sojourn in the womb . . .

In actuality Freud had pointed out from the beginning that the subject revises past events at a later date (*nachträglich*), and that it is this revision which invests them with significance and even with efficacy or pathogenic force. On December 6, 1896, he wrote to Wilhelm Fliess: 'I am working on the assumption that our psychical mechanism has come into being by a process of stratification: the material present in the form of memory-traces being subjected from time to time to a *re-arrangement* in accordance with fresh circumstances —to a *re-transcription*' (1a).

b. This idea might lead one to the view that all phenomena met with in psycho-analysis are placed under the sign of retroactivity, or even of retroactive *illusion*. This is what Jung means when he talks of retrospective phantasies (*Zurückphantasieren*): according to Jung, the adult reinterprets his past in his phantasies, which constitute so many symbolic expressions of his current problems. On this view reinterpretation is a way for the subject to escape from the present 'demands of reality' into an imaginary past.

Seen from another angle, the idea of deferred action may also suggest a conception of temporality which was brought to the fore by philosophers and later adopted by the various tendencies of existential psycho-analysis: consciousness constitutes its own past, constantly subjecting its meaning to revision in conformity with its 'project'.

*　　*　　*

The Freudian conception, however, would seem to be a much more precise one. In our opinion it may be characterised as follows:

a. It is not lived experience in general that undergoes a deferred revision but, specifically, whatever it has been impossible in the first instance to incorporate fully into a meaningful context. The traumatic event is the epitome of such unassimilated experience.

b. Deferred revision is occasioned by events and situations, or by an organic maturation, which allow the subject to gain access to a new level of meaning and to rework his earlier experiences.

c. Human sexuality, with the peculiar unevenness of its temporal development, provides an eminently suitable field for the phenomenon of deferred action.

These views of Freud's are attested to by numerous texts where the term '*nachträglich*' is used. Two among them, however, seem to us particularly illuminating.

In the 'Project for a Scientific Psychology' (1950a [1895]), in dealing with hysterical repression, Freud asks himself why repression falls especially upon the sexual realm. He gives an example to show how repression presupposes two events clearly separated from one another in their time sequence. The first of these events consists in a scene (seduction* by an adult) which is of a sexual nature but which at the time of its occurrence has no sexual significance for the child. The second event presents certain points of similarity with the first, though they may be superficial. This time, however, having reached puberty meanwhile, the subject is capable of sexual feeling–a feeling which he will associate consciously with the second event although it has actually been provoked by the memory of the earlier one. The ego in such a case is unable to mobilise its normal defences against this unpleasurable sexual affect (e.g. avoidance by means of the mechanism of attention): 'Attention is [normally] adjusted towards perceptions, which are what ordinarily give occasion for a release of unpleasure. Here, [however, what has appeared] is no perception but a memory, which unexpectedly releases unpleasure, and the ego only discovers this too late' (1b). The ego therefore calls upon repression, a mode of 'pathological defence' in which it operates in accordance with the primary process*.

The general precondition of repression is thus clearly deemed to lie in the 'delaying of puberty' which is characteristic, according to Freud, of human sexuality: 'Every adolescent individual has memory-traces which can only be understood with the emergence of sexual feelings of his own' (1c). *'The retardation of puberty makes possible posthumous primary processes*' (1d).

From this point of view, only the occurrence of the second scene can endow the first one with pathogenic force: '. . . a memory is repressed which has only become a trauma by *deferred action*' (1e). Thus the notion of deferred action is intimately bound up with the earliest Freudian formulation of the notion of defence*: the theory of seduction.

It might be objected that Freud's discovery of infantile sexuality shortly afterwards stripped this conception of any validity. The most effective rebuttal of this charge is furnished by Freud's account of the 'Wolf Man' case (1918b [1914]), where this same process of deferred action is evoked time and time again–although it is now said to take place in the earliest years of childhood. It lies at the core of Freud's analysis of the pathogenic dream in its relation to the primal scene*: the Wolf Man only understood his parents' coitus 'at the time of the dream when he was four years old, not at the time of the observation. He received the impressions when he was one and a half; his understanding of them was deferred, but became possible at the time of the dream owing to his development, his sexual excitations and his sexual researches' (2a). As Freud shows, in the history of this infantile neurosis it was the dream that precipitated the phobia: the dream 'brought into deferred operation his observation of intercourse' (2b).

In 1917 Freud added two lengthy discussions to the Wolf Man case-history in which he is evidently disconcerted by Jung's thesis of retrospective phantasies. He concedes that the primal scene, since it is the outcome of a reconstruction during the analysis, might indeed have been manufactured by the subject himself. But he emphatically maintains, nonetheless, that perception must have provided at least some indication–albeit nothing more than dogs copulating. . . . Furthermore–and most importantly–when apparently on the very point of abandoning his search for a solid basis in a reality that has turned out upon inspection to be so shaky, Freud introduces a new idea–that of *primal*

Depressive Position

phantasies: the idea of a substrate, a structure which is the phantasy's ultimate foundation, and which transcends both the individual's lived experience and his imaginings (see 'Primal Phantasy').

* * *

As these texts show, the Freudian conception of *nachträglich* cannot be understood in terms of a variable time-lapse, due to some kind of storing procedure, between stimuli and response. The *Standard Edition* translation 'deferred action' could be taken to imply such a reading. The editors of the *S.E.* cite (2c) a passage in the *Studies on Hysteria* (1895d) where Freud speaks, apropos of the so-called retention hysteria*, of 'traumas accumulated during sick-nursing being dealt with subsequently' (3a). The deferred action here might at first sight be construed as a delayed discharge, but we should notice that for Freud a real working over is involved – a 'work of recollection' which is not the mere discharge of accumulated tension but a complex set of psychological operations: 'Every day [the patient] would go through each impression once more, would weep over it and console herself – at her leisure, one might say' (3b). It is preferable, in our view, to illuminate the concept of abreaction* by reference to the concept of *nachträglich* than to confine 'deferred action' to the status of a narrowly economic theory of abreaction.

(1) FREUD, S.: a) *Anf.*, 185; S.E., I, 233. b) *Anf.*, 438; S.E., I, 358. c) *Anf.*, 435; S.E., I, 356. d) *Anf.*, 438; S.E., I, 359. e) *Anf.*, 435; S.E., I, 356.

(2) FREUD, S. 'From the History of an Infantile Neurosis' (1918b [1914]): a) G.W., XII 64, *n.* 4; S.E., XVII, 37–38, *n.* 6. b) Cf. G.W., XII, 144; S.E., XVII, 109. c) G.W., XII, 72*n.* S.E., XVII, 45*n.*

(3) FREUD, S.: a) G.W., I, 229; S.E., II, 162. b) G.W., I, 229; S.E., II, 162.

Depressive Position

= *D.*: depressive Einstellung. – *Es.*: posición depresiva. – *Fr.*: position dépressive. – *I.*: posizione depressiva. – *P.*: posição depressiva.

According to Melanie Klein, a modality of object-relations which is established after the paranoid position*. The depressive position is reached around the fourth month of life and is gradually overcome in the course of the first year, though it may recur during childhood and can be reactivated in the adult, notably in states of mourning and depression.

The depressive position is characterised as follows: from this point onwards the child is able to apprehend the mother as a whole object*; the splitting of the object into a 'good' object and a 'bad' object is attenuated, with libidinal and hostile instincts now tending to focus on the same object; anxiety, described here as depressive, is associated with the phantasied danger of the subject's destroying and losing the mother as the result of his sadism; this anxiety is combated by various modes of defence (manic defences, or, more appropriately, the distribution or inhibition of aggressiveness), and it is overcome when the loved object is introjected in a stable way that guarantees security.

As regards Melanie Klein's choice of the word 'position', the reader is referred to our commentary at 'Paranoid Position'.

The Kleinian theory of the depressive position is in the tradition of works by Freud—namely, 'Mourning and Melancholia' (1917e)—and by Abraham—namely, 'A Short Study of the Development of the Libido Viewed in the Light of Mental Disorders. Part 1: Manic-Depressive States and the Pre-Genital Levels of the Libido' (1924). Both authors had highlighted the notions of loss of the loved object and introjection in melancholic depression, sought points of fixation in psychosexual development which could be correleated with this disturbance (Abraham's second oral stage*), and underscored the kinship between depression and normal processes like mourning.

Klein's first original contribution here was to describe a phase of infantile development as fundamentally analogous to the clinical picture of depression.

The notion of the depressive position is introduced in 1934 in 'A Contribution to the Psychogenesis of Manic-Depressive States' (1). Klein had previously drawn attention to the frequency with which depressive symptoms occur in children: '. . . the change between excessive high spirits and extreme wretchedness, which is a characteristic of melancholic disorders, is regularly found in children' (2). Her most systematic exposition of the depressive position is found in 'Some Theoretical Conclusions regarding the Emotional Life of the Infant' (1952) (3a).

The depressive position supersedes the paranoid position towards the middle of the first year of life. It is correlated with a series of changes affecting the object and ego on the one hand, and the instincts on the other:

a. The mother as whole person may now be perceived, taken as instinctual object and introjected. The 'good' and 'bad'* qualities of the object arc no longer kept radically distinct and attributed to objects that have undergone splitting*; instead, they now relate to a single object. By the same token the gap between the internal phantasy object and the external object is narrowed.

b. The aggressive and libidinal instincts become fused and focus upon the same object; ambivalence (q.v.) is thus established in the full sense of the word: 'Love and hatred have come much closer together and the "good" and "bad" breast, "good" and "bad" mother, cannot be kept as widely separated as in the earlier stage' (3b).

As a corollary of these modifications anxiety changes its character: from now on it centres upon the loss of the internal or external whole object, while its motive is infantile sadism; although according to Klein this sadism is already less intense than in the previous phase, it still threatens, in the child's phantasy world, to destroy, to harm, to provoke abandonment. The infant may try to respond to this anxiety by means of a manic defence using (in more or less modified form) the mechanisms of the paranoid phase (the denial, idealization, splitting or omnipotent control of the object). Depressive anxiety is only successfully overcome and transcended, however, thanks to the two processes of inhibition of aggressiveness and reparation* of the object.

We may add that while the depressive position still holds sway the relationship to the mother begins to lose its exclusiveness and the child enters upon what Klein calls the early stage of the Oedipus complex: '. . . libido and depressive anxiety are deflected to some extent from the mother, and this

115

process of distribution stimulates object-relations as well as diminishes the intensity of depressive feelings' (3c).

(1) Cf. *Contributions*, 282 *ff.*
(2) K LEIN, M. *The Psycho-Analysis of Children* (1932), 218.
(3) *Developments*: a) Cf. 198–236. b) 212. c) 220.

Derivative of the Unconscious

= *D.*: Abkömmling des Unbewussten.–*Es.*: derivado del inconsciente.–
Fr.: rejeton de l'inconscient.–*I.*: derivato dell'inconscio.–
P.: derivado *or* ramificação do inconsciente.

Term often used by Freud within the framework of his dynamic conception of the unconscious: the unconscious tends to thrust certain products back into consciousness and action even though their connection is a more or less distant one. These derivatives of the repressed become in their turn the object of new defensive measures.

This expression occurs above all in the metapsychological texts of 1915. It is not used to refer especially to any particular product of the unconscious, and it covers, for example, symptoms, associations during the session (1a), and phantasies (2).

The term 'derivative of the repressed idea' (1b) or 'of the repressed' (1c) is connected with the theory of the two stages of repression. What has been repressed at the first stage (primal repression*) tends to break through into consciousness in the form of derivatives and is then subjected to a second repression (deferred* repression).

The idea of a derivative illustrates an essential characteristic of the unconscious: it always remains active, exerting a constant pressure in the direction of consciousness.

(1) F REUD, S. 'Repression' (1915*d*): a) Cf. G.W., X, 251–52; S.E., XIV, 149–50. b) G.W. X, 250; S.E., XIV, 148. c) G.W., X, 251; S.E., XIV, 149.
(2) Cf. F REUD, S. 'The Unconscious' (1915*e*), G.W., X, 289; S.E., XIV, 190–91.

Destructive Instinct

= *D.*: Destruktionstrieb.–*Es.*: instinto destructivo *or* destructor.–
Fr.: pulsion de destruction.–*I.*: istinto *or* pulsione di distruzione.–
P.: impulso destrutivo *or* pulsão destrutiva.

Term used by Freud to designate the death instincts* when he is tending to view them in the light of biological and psychological experience. Sometimes it has the same extension as 'death instinct', but for the most part it refers to the death

instinct in so far as it is directed towards the outside world. For this more specific sense Freud also uses the term 'aggressive instinct'* (*Aggressionstrieb*).

When the notion of the death instinct is introduced in *Beyond the Pleasure Principle* (1920g), the context is a frankly speculative one. Freud is concerned from the start, however, to identify its empirical effects. Consequently he often speaks in subsequent writings of a destructive instinct, since this allows him to indicate the aim of the death instinct more precisely.

Considering that these instincts operate, as Freud puts it, 'essentially in silence', and can therefore hardly be recognised save when their action is directed outwards, it is understandable that the term 'destructive instinct' should apply to their more accessible, more manifest effects. The death instinct turns away from the subject's own self because this has been cathected by narcissistic libido, and is directed, with the musculature serving as mediation, towards the external world; it 'would thus seem to express itself–though probably only in part–as an instinct of destruction directed against the external world and other organisms' (1).

In other texts this restricted sense of the destructive instinct relative to the death instinct does not emerge so clearly, for Freud also attributes self-destruction (*Selbstdestruktion*) to it (2). As for the term 'aggressive instinct', it is definitely reserved for destructive tendencies directed outwards.

(1) FREUD, S. *The Ego and the Id* (1923b), G.W., XIII, 269; S.E., XIX, 41.

(2) Cf. FREUD, S. *New Introductory Lectures on Psycho-Analysis* (1933a [1932]), G.W., XV, 112; S.E., XXII, 106.

Direct Analysis

= *D.*: direkte Analyse.–*Es.*: análisis directo.–*Fr.*: analyse directe.–*I.*: analisi diretta.–*P.*: análise direta.

Method of analytic psychotherapy of the psychoses promoted by J. N. Rosen. It owes its name to its use of 'direct interpretations' which are presented to patients and which may be characterised as follows:

a. They concern unconscious contents that the subject expresses verbally or otherwise (mimicry, posture, gestures, behaviour).

b. They do not require analysis of the resistances*.

c. They do not necessarily depend on the mediation of chains of association.

This method further embodies a set of technical procedures designed to establish a close relationship 'between unconscious and unconscious' in which 'the therapist must become to the patient the ever-giving, ever-protecting maternal figure' (1a).

J. N. Rosen has been expounding and elaborating this method since 1946. The epithet 'direct' refers above all to a type of interpretation based on the theory that in the psychoses–and especially in schizophrenia–the subject's unconscious overwhelms the defences and finds direct expression in his words and behaviour. All direct interpretation is supposed to do is to give a clearer explanation of what the subject knows already. Its efficacy therefore depends not on increased insight but rather on the establishment and consolidation of a positive trans-ference: the patient feels *understood* by a therapist to whom he attributes the all-powerful comprehension of an ideal mother; he is *reassured* by statements concerning the infantile content of his anxieties–statements which show him how baseless these anxieties are. Aside from interpretations of this kind, 'direct' analysis, broadly understood, embraces a certain number of active techniques far removed from the neutrality* demanded by the analysis of neurotics, all of which are designed to penetrate the closed universe of the psychotic. By these means, according to Rosen, the analyst comes to fulfil the function of a loving and protective mother, gradually offsetting the effects of the serious privations the subject has invariably suffered in his childhood because of a mother with a perverse maternal instinct (1*b*).

(See also 'Mothering'.)

(1) ROSEN, J. N. *Direct Analysis. Selected Papers* (New York: Grune & Stratton, 1953): a) 139. b) Cf. Chapter IV: 'The Perverse Mother'.

Disavowal (Denial)

= *D*.: Verleugnung.–*Es*.: renegación.–*Fr*.: déni.–*I*.: diniego.–*P*.: recusa.

Term used by Freud in the specific sense of a mode of defence which consists in the subject's refusing to recognise the reality of a traumatic perception–most especially the perception of the absence of the woman's penis. Freud invokes this mechanism particularly when accounting for fetishism and the psychoses.

Freud began using the term '*Verleugnung*' in a comparatively specific sense in 1924. Between that year and 1938 he makes a good number of references to the process thus designated, his most detailed exposition of it being in *An Outline of Psycho-Analysis* (1940a [1938]). Although it would be untrue to say that he worked out a theory of disavowal–he did not even distinguish it in any rigorous way from other closely allied processes–there is nonetheless a definite consistency in the evolution of this concept in his work.

The mechanism of *Verleugnung* is first described by Freud in the course of his discussion of castration. Confronted by the absence of a penis in the girl, children 'disavow (*leugnen*) the fact and believe that they *do* see a penis, all the same' (1). Only gradually do they come to see the absence of the penis as a result of castration.

In 'Some Psychical Consequences of the Anatomical Distinction Between the Sexes' (1925j), disavowal is described as operating in the little girl just as much as in the boy; it should be noticed that Freud compares the process to a psychotic mechanism: '. . . a process may set in which I should like to call a "disavowal" (*Verleugnung*), a process which in the mental life of children seems neither uncommon nor very dangerous but which in an adult would mean the beginning of a psychosis' (2). Inasmuch as disavowal affects *external reality*, Freud sees it as the first stage of psychosis, and he opposes it to repression: whereas the neurotic starts by repressing the demands of the id, the psychotic's first step is to disavow reality (3).

From 1927 onwards, Freud's elaboration of the notion of disavowal relates essentially to the special case of fetishism. In the study he devotes to this perversion–'Fetishism' (1927e)–he shows how the fetishist perpetuates an infantile attitude by holding two incompatible positions at the same time: he simultaneously disavows and acknowledges the fact of feminine castration. Freud's interpretation remains ambiguous, however: on the one hand, he tries to account for this inconsistency of the fetishist by invoking the processes of repression and of a compromise-formation* between the two conflicting forces; on the other hand, he also shows how the inconsistency actually constitutes a splitting* in two (*Spaltung, Zwiespältigkeit*) of the subject.

In the later texts which deal with this topic–'Splitting of the Ego in the Process of Defence' (1940e [1938]) and *An Outline of Psycho-Analysis*–it is this notion of a splitting of the ego which serves to cast a clearer light on the concept of disavowal. The two attitudes of fetishists–their *disavowal* of the perception of the woman's lack of a penis and their *recognition* of this absence and grasp of its consequences (anxiety)–'persist side by side throughout their lives without influencing each other. Here is what may rightly be called a splitting of the ego' (4).

This kind of splitting is to be distinguished from that division in the personality which is brought into being by all neurotic repression. For this there are two reasons: first, what is involved here is the coexistence of two different forms of ego-defence and not a conflict between the ego and the id; secondly, one of these defences of the ego–the disavowal of a perception–is directed towards *external reality*.

This gradual clarification of the process of disavowal may be seen as one of a number of signs of Freud's enduring concern to describe a primal defence mechanism for dealing with external reality. This preoccupation of his is particularly obvious in his first way of conceiving projection (q.v.), in his notion of the withdrawal of cathexis or loss of reality in psychosis, etc. It is within the framework of this line of enquiry that the idea of disavowal has a part to play. To be precise, it was first adumbrated in certain passages of the case-history of the 'Wolf Man': 'In the end there were to be found in him two contrary currents side by side, of which one abominated the idea of castration, while the other was prepared to accept it and console itself with feminity as a compensation. But beyond any doubt a third current, the oldest and deepest, [which had purely and simply repudiated (*verworfen hatte*) castration, and] which did not as yet even raise the question of the reality of castration, was still capable of coming into activity' (5). The idea of a splitting of the personality into various autonomous 'currents' is already present in these lines, as are the conception of a primary defence consisting of a radical repudiation and the notion that such a mechanism bears specifically upon the reality of castration.

Disavowal (Denial)

This last point is without doubt the one which gives us the best key to the Freudian idea of disavowal, but it also brings us to reopen and extend the questions which that idea raises. If the disavowal of castration is the prototype – and perhaps even the origin – of the other kinds of disavowal of reality, we are forced to ask what Freud understands by the 'reality' of castration or by the perception of this reality. If it is the woman's 'lack of a penis' that is disavowed, then it becomes difficult to talk in terms of perception or of reality, for an absence is not perceived as such, and it only becomes real in so far as it is related to a conceivable presence. If, on the other hand, it is castration itself which is repudiated, then the object of disavowal would not be a perception – castration never being perceived as such – but rather a theory designed to account for the facts – a 'sexual theory of children'. It will be recalled in this connection that Freud constantly related the castration complex, or castration anxiety, not to the simple perception of a certain reality but rather to the coming together of two preconditions, namely, the discovery of the anatomical distinction between the sexes and the castration threat by the father (see 'Castration Complex'). These considerations clear the way for the following question: does not disavowal – whose consequences *in* reality are so obvious – bear upon a factor which *founds* human reality rather than upon a hypothetical 'fact of perception'? (See also 'Foreclosure'.)

* * *

[*Translator's note:* '*Verleugnung*' is still widely translated by 'denial', but in the above I have followed the recommendations of the Editors of the *Standard Edition*: 'The word *Verleugnung* has in the past often been translated "denial" and the associated verb by "to deny". These are, however, ambiguous words and it has been thought better to choose "to disavow" in order to avoid confusion with the German "*verneinen*" . . . This latter German word . . . is translated by "to negate" ' (S.E., XIX, 143*n*). This option, however, is at best an unfortunate necessity, as is borne out by the arguments advanced by the authors of the present work to justify their choice of '*déni*' as the French translation of '*Verleugnung*':]

We propose '*déni*' as the best French equivalent of '*Verleugnung*' because it has a number of resonances which the alternative '*dénégation*' does not have:

a. 'Denial' (*déni*) is often a stronger word. We say 'I deny the validity of your statements.'

b. As well as referring to a statement which is being disputed, 'denial' is also used to evoke the withholding of goods or rights.

c. In this last case, the implication is that the prohibition in question is illegitimate: denial of justice, denial of food, etc. – in other words, a withholding of what is due.

These connotations correspond to those of '*Verleugnung*' as used by Freud. (See 'Negation'.)

(1) FREUD, S. 'The Infantile Genital Organization' (1923*e*), G.W., XIII, 296; S.E., XIX, 143–44.

(2) FREUD, S., G.W., XIV, 24; S.E., XIX, 253.

(3) Cf. FREUD, S. 'The Loss of Reality in Neurosis and Psychosis' (1924*e*), G.W., XIII, 364–65; S.E., XIX, 184–85.

(4) FREUD, S. *An Outline of Psycho-Analysis* (1940a [1938]), G.W., XVII, 134; S.E., XXIII, 203.

(5) FREUD, S. 'From the History of an Infantile Neurosis' (1918b [1914]), G.W., XII, 171; S.E., XVII, 85.

Discharge

= *D.*: Abfuhr.–*Es.*: descarga.–*Fr.*: décharge.–*I.*: scarica *or* deflusso.–*P.*: descarga.

'Economic' term used by Freud in the context of his physicalistic models of the psychical apparatus. Discharge means the evacuation into the external world of the energy brought into this apparatus by excitations of either internal or external origin. Such a discharge may be total or partial.

The reader is referred to the articles on the different principles which govern the economic functioning of the psychical apparatus–'Principle of Constancy', 'Principle of Inertia', 'Pleasure Principle'–and, for the pathogenic role of disturbances in discharge, to those on 'Actual Neurosis' and 'Libidinal Stage'.

Displacement

= *D.*: Verschiebung.–*Es.*: desplazamiento.–*Fr.*: déplacement.–*I.*: spostamento.– *P.*: deslocamento.

The fact that an idea's emphasis, interest or intensity is liable to be detached from it and to pass on to other ideas, which were originally of little intensity but which are related to the first idea by a chain of associations.

This phenomenon, though particularly noticeable in the analysis of dreams, is also to be observed in the formation of psychoneurotic symptoms and, in a general way, in every unconscious formation.

The psycho-analytic theory of displacement depends upon the economic hypothesis of a cathectic energy able to detach itself from ideas and to run along associative pathways.

The 'free' displacement of this energy is one of the cardinal characteristics of the primary process* in its role as governor of the functioning of the unconscious system.

a. The notion of displacement makes its appearance as soon as the Freudian theory of the neuroses is conceived (1): it is connected with the clinical evidence for a relative independence of the affect* from the idea*, and with the economic hypothesis which is framed to account for this–the hypothesis of a cathectic energy 'capable of increase, diminution, displacement and discharge' (2a) (see 'Economic', 'Quota of Affect').

121

Displacement

Such a hypothesis reaches full development with Freud's model of the functioning of the 'neuronal apparatus' in his 'Project for a Scientific Psychology' (1950*a* [1895]): the 'quantity' is displaced along pathways made up of neurones which tend towards a complete discharge only, in accordance with the 'principle of neuronal inertia'*. The 'total or primary' process is defined by a displacement of the whole of the energy from one idea to another. So, in the formation of a symptom—that is, of a 'mnemic symbol'* of the hysteric type—'only the distribution [of the quantity] has changed. Something has been added to [the idea] A which has been subtracted from B. The pathological process is one of *displacement*, such as we have come to know in dreams—a primary process therefore' (3*a*).

Displacement is also to be observed in the secondary process*, but here its range is limited and it only involves small quantities of energy (3*b*).

From the psychological point of view, an apparent vacillation on Freud's part is noticeable as regards the extension that should be given to the term 'displacement'. At times he contrasts displacement and conversion*: the phenomenon of *displacement* occurs between different ideas, and is more especially characteristic of obsessional neurosis (cf. Freud's term '*Verschiebungs-ersatz*'—the formation of a substitute by means of displacement); in *conversion*, on the other hand, the affect is eliminated and the cathectic energy changes key by passing from the realm of ideas to the somatic realm (2*b*). At other times, displacement would appear to be a general characteristic of all symptom-formation: '. . . by means of extreme displacement [satisfaction] can be restricted to one small detail of the entire libidinal complex' (4a); to this extent, therefore, conversion itself implies a displacement as, for example, in the case of the displacement of genital pleasure to some other part of the body (4*b*).

b. It was especially in dreams that Freud demonstrated the function of displacement. The comparison of the manifest content of the dream with the latent dream-thoughts reveals that their focus differs: the most important elements of the latent content are represented by insignificant details, which are either recent (and often indifferent) events or else long-past events which have already been the object of a displacement in childhood. From this descriptive standpoint, Freud is led to make a distinction between dreams which do and dreams which do not involve displacement (5*a*). In the latter, 'the different elements were able to retain during the process of constructing the dream the approximate place which they occupied in the dream-thoughts' (5*b*). Such a distinction may appear surprising to those who wish to follow Freud in maintaining that the characteristic mode of operation of unconscious mental processes is *free* displacement. In point of fact, Freud does not deny that displacements may affect each element of a dream; but in *The Interpretation of Dreams* (1900*a*) he usually employs the term 'transference' to designate, in the most general sense, the transposition of psychical energy from one idea to another; 'displacement' he uses rather to refer to a descriptively striking phenomenon, more noticeable in some dreams than in others, whose upshot is the shift in focus of the whole emphasis of the dream which he calls 'the transvaluation of psychical values' (6).

In the analysis of dreams, displacement is closely connected with the other mechanisms of the dream-work*. First, it facilitates condensation* in so far as displacement along two chains of associations leads eventually to ideas or verbal expressions formed at the intersection of the two paths. Represent-ability* too is made easier when a transition is effected, through displacement, between an abstract idea and an equivalent lending itself to visualisation; in this way psychical interest is transformed into sensory intensity. Lastly, secondary elaboration* pursues the work of displacement by subordinating it to its own ends.

*   *   *

Displacement has a clearly defensive function in the various formations in which the analyst encounters it; in a phobia, for instance, displacement on to the phobic object permits the objectivation, localisation and containment of anxiety. In dreams, the relation between displacement and the censorship* is such that the former may appear to be the result of the latter: '*Is fecit cui profuit*. We may assume, then, that dream-displacement comes about through the influence of the same censorship–that is, the censorship of endopsychic defence' (5c). Essentially, however, displacement–in so far as it may be conceived of as operating freely–remains the surest sign of the primary process: 'The cathectic intensities [in the Ucs.] are much more mobile. By the process of *displacement* one idea may surrender to another its whole quota of cathexis' (7). Moreover, these two theses are not really in contradiction with one another, for the censorship does not *provoke* displacement save inasmuch as it represses certain preconscious ideas which, by being drawn into the unconscious, fall under the domination of the laws of the primary process. The censorship *uses* the mechanism of displacement for promoting ideas which are indifferent, transient, or susceptible of integration into associative contexts very far-removed from the defensive conflict, to a privileged position.

The term 'displacement' does not for Freud imply the singling out of any particular type of associative connection–such as association by contiguity or association by similarity–as characteristic of the chain along which the process of displacement operates. The linguist Roman Jakobson has, however, felt justified in correlating the unconscious mechanisms described by Freud and the rhetorical procedures of metaphor and metonymy, which he holds to be the two fundamental poles of all language; he thus brings displacement together with metonymy, in which association is based upon contiguity, while he sees symbolism as corresponding to the metaphoric dimension which is governed by the law of association by similarity (8). Jacques Lacan has taken up these suggestions and developed them, assimilating displacement to metonymy and condensation to metaphor (9); for Lacan, human desire* is structured funda-mentally by the laws of the unconscious, and its nature is metonymic *par excellence*.

(1) Cf. FREUD, S. Letter to Josef Breuer dated June 29, 1892, G.W., XVII, 3–6; S.E., I, 147–8.

(2) FREUD, S. 'The Neuro-Psychoses of Defence' (1894a): a) G.W., I, 74; S.E., III, 60. b) G.W., I, 59–72; S.E., III, 45–58.

(3) FREUD, S.: a) *Anf.*, 429; S.E., I, 350. b) *Anf.*, 446 *ff.*; S.E., I, 366 *ff.*

(4) FREUD, S. *Introductory Lectures on Psycho-Analysis* (1916–17): a) G.W., XI, 381; S.E., XVI, 366. b) G.W., XI, 336; S.E., XVI, 324–25.

Distortion

(5) FREUD, S. *The Interpretation of Dreams* (1900*a*): a) Cf. G.W., II–III, 187; S.E., IV, 180–81. b) G.W., II–III, 311; S.E., IV, 306. c) G.W., II–III, 314; S.E., IV, 308.

(6) FREUD, S. *On Dreams* (1901*a*), G.W., II–III, 667; S.E., V, 655.

(7) FREUD, S. 'The Unconscious' (1915*c*), G.W., X, 285; S.E., XIV, 186.

(8) Cf., for example, JAKOBSON, R. 'Two Aspects of Language and Two Types of Aphasic Disturbances', in *The Fundamentals of Language* (The Hague: Mouton, 1956), 81.

(9) Cf. LACAN, J. 'L'instance de la lettre dans l'inconscient ou la raison depuis Freud', *La Psychanalyse*, 1957, III, 47–81. Reprinted in LACAN, J. *Écrits* (Paris: Seuil, 1966). English translation: 'The Insistence of the Letter', *Yale French Studies*, 1966, 36–37, 112–47; reprinted in EHRMANN, J. (ed.) *Structuralism* (New York: Doubleday Anchor Books, 1970).

Distortion

= *D*.: Enstellung.–*Es*.: deformación.–*Fr*.: déformation.–*I*.: deformazione.–*P*.: deformação.

Overall effect of the dream-work: the latent thoughts are transformed into a manifest formation in which they are not easily recognisable. They are not only transposed, as it were, into another key, but they are also distorted in such a fashion that only an effort of interpretation* can reconstitute them.

For this concept, the reader is referred to the entries 'Dream-Work', 'Manifest Content' and 'Latent Content'.

Dream Screen

= *D*.: Traumhintergrund.–*Es*.: pantalla del sueño.–*Fr*.: écran du rêve.–
I.: schermo del sogno.–*P*.: tela de sonho.

Concept introduced by B. D. Lewin (1): every dream is said to be projected on to a blank screen, generally unperceived by the dreamer, which symbolises the mother's breast as hallucinated by the infant during the sleep which follows feeding; the screen satisfies the wish for sleep. In certain dreams (blank dreams) the screen appears by itself, thus achieving a regression to primary narcissism.

(1) LEWIN, B. D. 'Sleep, the Mouth and the Dream Screen', *P.Q.*, 1946, XV; 'Inferences from the Dream Screen', *I.J.P.*, 1948, XXIX, 4; 'Sleep, Narcissistic Neurosis and the Analytic Situation', *P.Q.*, 1954, IV.

Dream-Work

= *D*.: Traumarbeit.–*Es*.: trabajo del sueño.–*Fr*.: travail du rêve.–*I*.: lavoro del sogno.–
P.: trabalho *or* labor do sonho.

**The whole of the operations which transform the raw materials of the dream–
bodily stimuli, day's residues*, dream-thoughts*–so as to produce the manifest
dream. Distortion* is the result of dream-work.**

At the end of Chapter VI of *The Interpretation of Dreams* (1900*a*), Freud writes:
'Two separate functions may be distinguished in mental activity during the
construction of a dream: the production of the dream-thoughts, and their
transformation into the [manifest] content of the dream' (1*a*). It is this second
operation, constituting the dream-work proper, whose four mechanisms
Freud analysed: *Verdichtung* (condensation*), *Verschiebung* (displacement*),
Rücksicht auf Darstellbarkeit (considerations of representability*) and *sekundäre
Bearbeitung* (secondary revision*).

Freud maintains two complementary theses regarding the nature of the dream-
work:

a. It is absolutely not creative and is restricted to the transformation of the
material.

b. It is the dream-work, however, and not the latent content*, which constitutes
the *essence of the dream*.

The thesis of the non-creative character of dreaming implies, for instance,
that 'everything that appears in dreams as the ostensible activity of the function
of judgement [calculations, argumentations] is to be regarded not as the intellectual achievement of the dream-work but as belonging to the material of the
dream-thoughts' (1*b*). The dream-thoughts present themselves to the dream-
work as material, while the dream-work 'is under some kind of necessity to
combine all the sources which have acted as stimuli for the dream into a single
unity' (1*c*).

As for the second thesis, which maintains that the dream is, in essence, the
work that it carries out, this is stressed by Freud in his 'Remarks on the Theory
and Practice of Dream-Interpretation' (1923*c*) (2), where he warns analysts
against an excessive respect for a 'mysterious unconscious'. The same idea is
noticeable in various notes added to *The Interpretation of Dreams* which constitute a sort of call to order. For example: 'It has long been the habit to regard
dreams as identical with their manifest content; but we must now beware equally
of the mistake of confusing dreams with latent dream-thoughts' (1*d*).

(1) FREUD, S.: a) G.W., II–III, 510; S.E., V, 506. b) G.W., II–III, 447; S.E., V, 445,
c) G.W., II–III, 185; S.E., IV, 179. d) G.W., II–III, 585, *n*. 1; S.E., V, 579, *n*. 1.

(2) Cf. FREUD, S., G.W., XIII, 304; S.E., XIX, 111–12.

Dynamic

= *D.*: dynamisch.–*Es.*: dinámico.–*Fr.*: dynamique.–*I.*: dinamico.–*P.*: dinâmico.

Qualifies a point of view which looks upon psychical phenomena as the outcome of the conflict and of a combination of forces–ultimately instinctual in origin–which exert a certain pressure.

Attention has often been drawn to the fact that psychoanalysis replaces a conception of the unconscious described as static with one which is dynamic. Freud noted himself that what distinguishes his approach from Janet's is that 'We do not derive the psychical splitting from an innate incapacity for synthesis on the part of the mental apparatus; we explain it dynamically, from the conflict of opposing mental forces, and recognise it as the outcome of an active struggling on the part of the two psychical groupings against each other' (1). The 'splitting' in question is that which separates the conscious-preconscious from the unconscious, but clearly this 'topographical'* distinction, far from providing an explanation of the disturbance, presupposes a psychical conflict. The originality of Freud's position is brought out, for example, by his conception of obsessional neurosis: Janet places such symptoms as inhibitions, doubt and abulia in direct relation with an inadequacy of mental synthesis, with a psychical asthenia or 'psychasthenia', whereas for Freud such symptoms are simply the result of an interplay between forces in opposition. The dynamic point of view does not only imply the taking into consideration of the notion of force (which is already done by Janet) but also the idea that, within the psyche, forces must necessarily enter into conflict with each other, this psychical conflict (q.v.) having its ultimate basis in an instinctual dualism.

* * *

In Freud's writings, 'dynamic' is employed in particular to characterise the unconscious, in so far as a permanent pressure is maintained there which necessitates a contrary force–operating on an equally permanent basis–to stop it from reaching consciousness. On a clinical level, this dynamic character is borne out both by the fact that a resistance* is encountered when attempts are made to reach the unconscious, and by the repeated production of derivatives* of repressed material.

The dynamic aspect is further illustrated by the notion of compromise-formations*, the analysis of which shows that they owe their coherence to the fact that they are 'supported from both sides'.

This is Freud's reason for distinguishing two senses of the concept of the unconscious: in the 'descriptive' sense, it connotes whatever is outside the field of consciousness, and to that extent embraces what Freud calls the preconscious*; in the 'dynamic' sense, on the other hand, 'It designates not only latent ideas in general, but especially ideas with a certain dynamic character, ideas keeping apart from consciousness in spite of their intensity and activity' (2).

(1) FREUD, S. 'Five Lectures on Psycho-Analysis', (1910*a*), G.W., VIII, 25; S.E., XI, 25–26.
(2) FREUD, S. 'A Note on the Unconscious in Psycho-Analysis' (1912*g*), S.E., XII, 262; G.W., VIII, 434.

E

Economic

= *D*.: ökonomisch.–*Es*.: económico.–*Fr*.: économique.–*I*.: economico.–*P*.: econômico.

Qualifies everything having to do with the hypothesis that psychical processes consist in the circulation and distribution of an energy (instinctual energy) that can be quantified, i.e. that is capable of increase, decrease and equivalence.

I. Psycho-analysis often evokes the 'economic point of view'. Thus Freud defines metapsychology* as the synthesis of three standpoints–the topographical*, the dynamic* and the economic. The last 'endeavours to follow out the vicissitudes of amounts of excitation and to arrive at least at some *relative* estimate of their magnitude' (1). The economic point of view consists in taking into consideration the cathexes*–their movement, the variations in their intensity, the antagonisms that arise between them (cf. the notion of anticathexis*), etc. Economic considerations are brought forward by Freud throughout his work; in his view, there can be no complete description of a mental process so long as the economy of cathexes has not been assessed.

This requirement of Freudian thought derives on the one hand from a scientific spirit and a conceptual framework which are shot through with notions of energy, and, on the other hand, from a clinical experience that had immediately provided Freud with a certain number of data which, it seemed to him, could only be accounted for in economic terms. For example: the irrepressible nature of the neurotic symptom (often voiced by the patient in such expressions as 'There was something in me that was stronger than me'); the triggering-off of troubles of a neurotic kind following disturbances of sexual discharge (actual neuroses*)–and, inversely, the alleviation and elimination of such troubles once the subject is able, during treatment, to free himself (catharsis*) from his 'strangulated' affects (abreaction*); the separation–observable in the symptom and during the course of treatment–between an idea* and the affect* which was originally bound to it (conversion*, repression*, etc.); the discovery of chains of associations between one idea which gives rise to little or no affective reaction and another, apparently insignificant, one which does occasion such a reaction: this last fact suggests the hypothesis of an actual affective charge which is displaced from one element to the next along a conductor.

Such data as these are the point of departure for the first models worked out by Breuer in his 'Theoretical' contribution to the *Studies on Hysteria* (1895*d*); and by Freud, in his 'Project for a Scientific Psychology' (1950*a* [1895])–a work which is constructed entirely around the notion of a quantity of excitation moving along chains of neurones–and in Chapter VII of *The Interpretation of Dreams* (1900*a*).

127

Economic

Subsequently, a whole range of additional clinical and therapeutic findings served merely to reinforce the economic hypothesis. For example:

a. The study of states such as mourning and the narcissistic neuroses* imposed the idea of an actual *energy balance* between the subject's various cathexes, a withdrawal of cathexis from the external world corresponding to an increase of cathexis of intrapsychic formations (see 'Narcissism', 'Ego-Libido/Object-Libido', 'Work of Mourning').

b. The interest aroused by war neuroses in particular and traumatic neuroses in general. In these cases, the disturbances appear to have been provoked by *too intense* a shock–by an influx of excitation which exceeds the subject's level of tolerance.

c. Limitations in the efficacy of interpretation, and more generally of therapeutic action, in certain recalcitrant cases which necessitate the taking into consideration of the respective *forces* of the different agencies* present, and particularly the force of the instincts, whether this is intrinsic or temporary.

II. The economic hypothesis is a permanent feature of Freud's theory, and he makes use of a whole set of concepts to articulate it. The essential notion here seems to be that of the existence of an *apparatus*–described to begin with as neuronal and later, definitively, as psychical*–whose function is to keep the energy circulating within itself at as low a level as possible. This apparatus carries out certain *work* which Freud describes in different ways: as transformation of free energy into bound energy*, as postponement of discharge, as the psychical *working out* of excitations, etc. Such working out presupposes the distinction between the idea and the *quantum of affect** or *sum of excitation**, which is capable of flowing along associative chains, of *cathecting* a particular idea or ideational complex, etc. From here stem the immediately economic overtones of the notions of *displacement** and *condensation.**

The psychical apparatus is subject to excitations of both external and internal origin; the latter–the *instincts**–exert a constant pressure which constitutes a 'demand for work'. Generally speaking, the whole functioning of the apparatus may be described, in economic terms, as the interplay between cathexes, withdrawals of cathexis, anticathexes and hypercathexes.

The economic hypothesis is closely bound up with the other two metapsychological perspectives, namely the topographical and the dynamic standpoints. Thus Freud defines each agency of the apparatus by invoking a specific modality of energy flow; in the context of the first theory of the psychical apparatus, for example, we find free energy in the system *Ucs*, bound energy in the system *Pcs.* and, in the conscious domain, a mobile hypercathectic energy.

Similarly, the dynamic conception of psychical conflict implies for Freud that the relations between the forces in play–the forces, respectively, of the instincts, of the ego and of the super-ego–be taken into account. The impact of the 'quantitative factor' on the aetiology, as on the therapeutic outcome, of the illness is underlined particularly clearly in 'Analysis Terminable and Interminable' (1937c).

*   *   *

The economic point of view is often looked upon as the most hypothetical aspect of Freud's metapsychology: what exactly *is* this energy, it is asked, to

128

which psycho-analysts are forever referring. A number of points may be raised in this connection:

a. Natural science itself does not pronounce upon the ultimate nature of the quantities whose variations, transformations and equivalences it studies. It is content to define them by their effects (for example, force is that which effects a certain work) and to make comparisons between them (one force is measured by another, or rather, their effects are compared between themselves). In this respect, Freud's position is not exceptional: he defined the pressure of the instinct as 'the measure of the demand for work which it represents' (2), and he readily acknowledges 'that we know nothing of the nature of the excitatory process that takes place in the elements of the psychical systems, and that we do not feel justified in framing any hypothesis on the subject. We are consequently operating all the time with a large unknown factor, which we are obliged to carry over into every new formula' (3).

b. Freud only invokes an energy, therefore, as an underpinning for trans-formations which numerous factors of an empirical nature seem to indicate. Libido*–the energy of the sexual instincts–interests him in so far as it is able to account for the changes undergone by sexual desire as regards its object, its aim and the sources of the excitation. Thus when a symptom mobilises a certain quantity of energy, other activities show signs of impoverishment; similarly, narcissism or libidinal cathexis of the ego is reinforced only to the detriment of object-cathexis, and so on.

Freud even felt that this quantitative factor could be measured, at least in principle, and that such measurement might become a practical proposition in time.

c. When one attempts to clarify the nature of the facts that the economic point of view is meant to explain, it is tempting to conclude that what Freud interprets in physicalistic terms is the same thing that an approach less removed from direct experience describes as the world of 'values'. Daniel Lagache stresses the idea (derived in particular from phenomenology) that the organism structures its surroundings, and its actual perception of objects, according to its vital interests, valorising special objects, fields or perceptual distinctions (the notion of the *Umwelt*). The axiological dimension may be said to be present for all organisms provided that the concept of value is not restricted to the moral, aesthetic or logical realms, where values are defined by their irreducibility to the empirical level, by their essential universality, by the categorical demand that they be fulfilled, etc. It is in this sense that the object cathected by the oral instinct may be said to be aimed at as the object-to-be-absorbed, as food-*qua*-value. As for the phobic object, it is not simply shunned: it is an object-to-be-avoided around which a specific spatio-temporal structure is organised.

It should be noted, however, that this kind of approach cannot convert the entire content of the economic hypothesis into its own terms unless one is pre-pared to look upon the 'values' in question as capable of being exchanged for one another, as susceptible of displacement and equivalence within a system where the 'quantity of value' at the subject's disposal is finite. We should bear in mind that Freud applies economic notions less in the realm of the self-preservative instincts*–although interests, appetites and 'value-objects' (Max Scheler) are clearly present here–than in the sphere of the sexual instincts*, which are able to

Ego

find satisfaction in objects very far removed from the natural one. What Freud means by libidinal economy is, precisely, the *circulation* of value which occurs within the psychical apparatus – usually cloaked by a misapprehension (*méconnaissance*) as a result of which the subject is unable to perceive sexual satisfaction in the suffering caused by the symptom.

(1) FREUD, S. 'The Unconscious' (1915e), G.W., X, 280; S.E., XIV, 181.

(2) FREUD, S. 'Instincts and their Vicissitudes' (1915c), G.W., X, 214; S.E., XIV, 122.

(3) FREUD, S. *Beyond the Pleasure Principle* (1920g), G.W., XIII, 30–31; S.E., XVIII 30–31.

Ego

= *D.*: Ich. – *Es.*: yo. – *Fr.*: moi. – *I.*: io. – *P.*: ego.

Agency which Freud's second theory of the psychical apparatus distinguishes from the id and the super-ego.

Topographically*, the ego is as much in a dependent relation to the claims of the id as it is to the imperatives of the super-ego and the demands of external reality. Although it is allotted the role of mediator, responsible for the interests of the person as a whole, its autonomy is strictly relative.

Seen *dynamically**, the ego is above all the expression of the defensive pole of the personality in neurotic conflict; it brings a set of defensive mechanisms into play which are motivated by the perception of an unpleasurable affect (signal of anxiety*).

Economically*, the ego appears as the 'binding'* factor in the psychical processes; in defensive operations, however, its attempts to bind instinctual energy are subverted by tendencies characteristic of the primary process, and these efforts take on a compulsive, repetitive and unrealistic aspect.

As for the ego's *genesis*, psycho-analytic theory seeks to account for this on two relatively distinct levels. According to the first account, the ego is an agency of adaptation which differentiates itself from the id on contact with external reality. Alternatively, it is described as the product of identifications culminating in the formation, within the personality, of a love-object cathected by the id.

In the context of the first theory of the psychical apparatus, the ego extends beyond the frontiers of the preconscious-conscious system inasmuch as its defensive operations are largely unconscious.

Viewed in its historical development, the topographical conception of the ego appears as the final version of a notion which had constantly engaged Freud's attention from the very start.

Freud worked out two topographies of the psychical apparatus, the first structured in terms of the systems of the *unconscious* and the *preconscious-conscious*, the second in terms of the three agencies of *id*, *ego* and *super-ego*. Consequently psycho-analysts have often held that the concept of the ego only took on a strict, technical and psycho-analytic sense in Freud's thought after the so-called

130

'turning-point' of 1920. This fundamental modification of the theory is supposed further to have corresponded to a fresh practical orientation concerned more with analysing the ego and its defence mechanisms than with unearthing the content of the unconscious. It is argued that although Freud does refer to the ego in his earliest writings he is using the term (*Ich*) in a rather unspecific way (α)–usually as a designation for the personality as a whole. From this point of view the more elaborate conceptualisations of the early work, in which the ego is assigned very precise functions within the psychical apparatus–as, for instance, in the 'Project for a Scientific Psychology' (1950*a* [1895])–are taken as isolated prefigurements of the notions of the second topography. In point of fact, as we shall see, the history of Freud's thought does not admit of such simple interpretation. For one thing, any study of Freud's work in its entirety shows that it is impossible to assign two senses of 'ego' to two different periods: the word is used in its full sense from the start, even though this sense is gradually refined through a series of developments (narcissism*, the emergence of the concept of identification*, etc.). Moreover, the 'turning-point' of 1920 cannot be confined to the definition of the ego as the central agency of the personality: this revision, as is well known, embraces many other essential modifications in the overall structure of the theory–modifications which can only be fully evaluated once their interconnections have been grasped. Finally, it seems inadvisable to draw an outright distinction between the ego as the *person* and the ego as a psychical *agency*, for the very simple reason that the interplay between these two meanings is the core of the problematic of the ego. Freud is implicitly concerned with this question from early days, and his preoccupation with it does not come to an end in 1920. The attempt to identify and eliminate a supposed 'terminological ambiguity' is thus in this case merely a way of avoiding a fundamental problem.

Quite apart from considerations relating to the history of Freud's thought, some authors have sought, for the sake of clarity, to make a conceptual distinction between the ego as agency, as substructure of the personality, and the ego as love-object for the individual himself (i.e. the ego of La Rochefoucauld's *amour-propre* or, in Freudian terms, the ego cathected by narcissistic libido). Hartmann, for example, has suggested a way of getting rid of the ambiguity which arises in his view from the use of terms such as 'narcissism' and 'ego-cathexis' (*Ich-Besetzung*): '. . . in using the term narcissism, two different sets of opposites often seem to be fused into one. The one refers to the self (one's own person) in contradistinction to the object, the second to the ego (as a psychic system) in contradistinction to other substructures of personality. However, the opposite of object cathexis is not ego cathexis, but cathexis of one's own person, that is, self-cathexis; in speaking of self-cathexis, we do not imply whether this cathexis is situated in the id, in the ego, or in the super-ego. [...] It therefore will be clarifying if we define narcissism as the libidinal cathexis not of the ego but of the self' (1).

In our view this position builds upon a purely conceptual distinction, running ahead of a real solution to some essential problems. The danger of proposing a usage of '*Ich*' which is taken to be exclusively psycho-analytical by contrast with other more traditional senses is that the real contributions of the Freudian usage may be lost. For Freud *exploits* traditional usages: he opposes organism to environment, subject to object, internal to external, and so on, while continuing to employ '*Ich*' at these different levels. What is more, he plays on the ambiguities thus created, so that none of the connotations normally attaching to 'ego' or 'I' ('*Ich*') is forgotten (β). It is this complexity that is shunned by those who want a different word for every shade of meaning.

*   *   *

I. Freud introduces the concept of the ego in his earliest writings, and it is worthwhile tracing a certain number of themes and problems which are due to reappear in the later work as they emerge from the texts of the 1894–1900 period.

It was his direct clinical experience of the neuroses that led Freud to transform the traditional concept of the ego in a radical way. By the 1880's the findings of psychology–and particularly of psychopathology–were destroying the idea of an indivisible and permanent ego. The study of '*altérations de la personnalité*', 'dual personality', 'secondary states' and so forth contributed largely to this trend. Pierre Janet, however, was able to go much further. He suggested that, in hysteria, a *simultaneous* double personality could be observed. He spoke of the 'formation, in the mind, of two groups of phenomena: the first constitutes the ordinary personality, while the second–itself liable to subdivision–forms an abnormal personality, different from the first and completely unknown to it' (2). For Janet such a splitting of the personality is a consequence of the 'narrowing of the field of consciousness', of 'a debility of the mental synthesising capacity' which eventually brings the hysteric to effect an 'autotomy'. 'The personality cannot perceive all the phenomena, so some of them are definitively sacrificed; this is a sort of autotomy, after which the rejected phenomena develop in isolation without the subject having any knowledge of their activity' (3). As we know, Freud's contribution to the understanding of such phenomena was to treat them as the expression of a psychical *conflict**: certain ideas call forth a *defence* in so far as they are *incompatible* (*unverträglich*) with the ego.

In the years 1895–1900 Freud employs the term 'ego' frequently and in a variety of ways. It is convenient to view the operation of the concept according to the different contexts in which it occurs: *the theory of the treatment, the model of the defensive conflict, the metapsychology of the psychical apparatus.*

a. In the chapter of the *Studies on Hysteria* (1895*d*) entitled 'The Psycho-therapy of Hysteria', Freud describes how the unconscious pathogenic material, whose high degree of organisation he emphasises, can only be dominated little by little. He compares consciousness or 'ego-consciousness' to a defile through which only one memory is allowed to pass at a time, and which can be blocked so long as the working-through (*Durcharbeiten*)* has not succeeded in breaking down the resistance*: '. . . the single memory which is in the process of breaking through remains in front of the patient until he has taken it up into the breadth of his ego' (4*a*). The closeness of the link between consciousness and the ego is here quite plain–witness the choice of the term 'ego-consciousness' itself. So is the idea that the ego takes in more than immediate consciousness, embracing the whole sphere that Freud will soon incorporate in the 'preconscious'.

In the *Studies on Hysteria* the *resistances* manifested by the patient are said to come first and foremost from the ego, which 'takes pleasure in defence'. Although its vigilance may be momentarily outwitted by some technical device, 'in all fairly serious cases, the ego recalls its aims once more and proceeds with its resistance' (4b).

At the same time, however, the ego is infiltrated by the unconscious 'pathogenic nucleus' so that the dividing-line between the two appears at times to have become purely conventional. Indeed, 'the resistance must be regarded as what is infiltrating' (4c). Here Freud is already hinting at the problematical idea of a truly *unconscious* resistance. He would later suggest two different ways of coping with this implication: first, resort to the notion of an unconscious ego; secondly, the idea that there is a resistance that is peculiar to the id.

b. The concept of the ego plays a constant role in the earliest accounts of neurotic *conflict* that Freud put forward. He attempts to subdivide defence* into different 'modes', 'mechanisms', 'procedures' and 'devices' which he correlates with the various psychoneuroses: hysteria, obsessional neurosis, paranoia, hallucinatory confusion and so on. At the origin of all these different modalities is to be found the incompatibility of a particular idea with the ego.

In hysteria, for instance, the ego intervenes as a defensive agency, but in a complex way. To say that the ego *defends itself* is somewhat ambiguous. Such a statement can be understood as follows: confronted by a situation of conflict– a conflict of interests, of wishes, or one between wishes and prohibitions–the ego, conceived of as a field of consciousness, defends itself by evading this situation, by systematically ignoring it; in which case, the ego is the *area* which has to be protected from the conflict by means of defensive activity. But the psychical conflict whose action Freud observed has another dimension to it: the ego as the 'dominant mass of ideas' is threatened by *one particular* idea considered to be incompatible with it; thus the ego itself is responsible for the repression. The case-history of Lucy R.–one of the first accounts in which Freud brings out the notion of conflict and the part played in it by the ego–provides an especially good illustration of this ambivalence: Freud does not here confine himself to an explanation in terms of the ego's lacking the necessary 'moral courage' to face up to the 'conflict of affects' which is disturbing it. The treatment only makes progress to the degree that it starts trying to elucidate the series of 'mnemic symbols'* of scenes in which a specific unconscious wish appears. Such an unconscious wish is easily identified in that it is incompatible with the self-image which the patient wants to keep up.

The fact that the ego is seen as an active party to the conflict explains why the actual motive for the defensive action–or its *signal*, as Freud was already occasionally calling it–is the feeling of unpleasure which affects the ego and which Freud considers to be directly associated with this incompatibility (4d).

A final point: although the defensive operation in hysteria is attributed to the ego, this does not imply that it is necessarily conceived of as conscious and voluntary. In the 'Project', where Freud presents a schema of hysterical defence, one of the important problems which he endeavours to solve is the way in which 'in the case of an *ego-process* consequences follow to which we are accustomed only with primary processes' (5a). In the formation of the 'mnemic symbol' constituted by the hysterical symptom the whole quota of affect*, the whole weight of meaning, is displaced from what is being symbolised to the symbol itself; this is not true of normal thought processes. This bringing into play of the primary process by the ego happens only when the ego finds itself unable to mobilise its normal defences (e.g. attention, avoidance). In the case of the memory of a sexual trauma (see 'Deferred Action', 'Scene of Seduction'), the ego is taken by surprise by an onslaught from within and has no option but 'to permit a primary process' (5b). The relation of 'pathological defence' to the ego is thus not defined in any clear-cut way; in a sense, the ego is well and truly the agent of defence, but in so far as it cannot defend itself without splitting itself off from that which threatens it, it relinquishes the incompatible idea to a type of process over which it has no control.

c. In his first *metapsychological** description of the psychical apparatus Freud assigns a prime role to the concept of the ego. In the 'Project' its function is essentially inhibitory. In what Freud refers to as the 'experience of satisfaction' (q.v.), the ego's task is to prevent the cathexis of the mnemic image of the earliest satisfying object from acquiring such force as to evoke an 'indication of reality' just as the perception of a real object would do. If the indication of reality is to attain the value of a *criterion* for the subject – if, in other words, hallucination is to be avoided and discharge confined to times when the real object is present – then the primary process, which consists in an unrestricted propagation of the excitation in the direction of the image, has necessarily to be inhibited. It is plain, however, that if the ego enables the subject to make a clear distinction between his internal processes and outside reality, this is not because the ego has any special means of access to the real world or because it disposes of any gauge with which to assess ideas as they present themselves. Such a direct access to reality is reserved by Freud for an independent system known as the 'perceptual system'; designated by the letter W or ω, this is fundamentally distinct (and operates in a completely different mode) from the ψ system of which the ego is a part.

Freud describes the ego as an 'organisation' of neurones or (in the less 'physiological' language he uses elsewhere) as an organisation of ideas. It is distinguished by a number of characteristics: the facilitation* of the associative pathways within this group of neurones; its permanent cathexis* by an endogenous energy, i.e. instinctual energy; its division into a variable and a constant part. It is by virtue of the permanent presence within itself of an adequate level of cathexis that the ego is able to inhibit primary processes – not only those which give rise to hallucination but also any which might be liable to provoke unpleasure ('primary defence'). 'Wishful cathexis to the point of hallucination and the complete generation of unpleasure which involves the complete expenditure of defence are described by us as *psychical primary processes*; by contrast, those processes which are only made possible by a good cathexis of the ego, and which represent a moderation of the foregoing, are described as *psychical secondary processes*' (5c, γ).

So Freud does not identify the ego with the individual as a whole, nor even with the whole of the mental apparatus: it is but a part. At the same time, however, it should be pointed out that he does locate the ego in a privileged position in regard to the individual – both to the individual considered in biological terms (i.e. *qua* organism) and to the individual under his psychical aspects. This fundamental ambiguity of the ego is reflected in the difficulty we encounter when we attempt to give a precise definition of 'internal' or of 'internal excitation'.

Endogenous excitation is successively described as coming from inside the body, from within the psychical apparatus, and finally as stored in the ego–here seen as a reserve of energy (*Vorratsträger*). In view of this series of shifts in perspective it is tempting to place Freud's mechanistic explanatory schemas in parentheses and treat the notion of the ego as a kind of actualised metaphor for the organism.

II. The metapsychological chapter of *The Interpretation of Dreams* (1900*a*) (an exposition of the so-called 'first theory' of the psychical apparatus; this theory is in our view more accurately described, in the light of Freud's posthumous writings, as a *second* metapsychology) marks a definite departure from the conceptions just outlined. The new theory distinguishes the systems of the unconscious, preconscious and conscious, and these provide the framework for an 'apparatus' in which the ego is allotted no place.

Taken up as he is at this time by the discovery of the dream as the 'royal road to the unconscious', Freud emphasises above all the primary mechanisms of the 'dream-work'*, and their way of imposing their logic upon the preconscious material. The passage from one system to another is seen in terms of a translation, and clarified by means of an optical analogy which likens it to the transposition from a given medium to another one with a different refraction index. Defensive activity is by no means absent from dreaming, but in dealing with it Freud has no recourse whatever to the concept of the ego. Various aspects of the ego, as described in the earlier work, can be discerned at various levels of the new scheme.

a. In the first place, the ego's role as an agency of defence is taken over in some measure by the process of censorship*. It is important to note, however, that censorship has a strictly *proscriptive* function, so that it cannot be compared to a complex organisation capable of bringing such specialised mechanisms into play as those which, according to Freud, are involved in neurotic conflicts.

b. The restraining and inhibitory influence exercised by the ego over the primary process is recognisable in the system *Pcs.*, as it operates during waking hours. But there is a striking difference between the conception as it is outlined in the 'Project' and in *The Interpretation of Dreams*: the system *Pcs.* is the actual locus of the operation of the secondary process, whereas the ego of the 'Project' was what instigated the secondary process in accordance with its own organisation.

c. The ego as a libidinally cathected organisation is explicitly present in its role as the carrier of the wish for sleep, which Freud sees as the motive for dream formation (6, δ).

III. The period 1900–15 could be described as a period of groping so far as the concept of the ego is concerned. Schematically, Freud's researches took him in four directions:

a. In his most theoretical expositions of the working of the psychical apparatus Freud invariably refers to the model developed in 1900 on the basis of dreams, while pushing its implications as far as they will go; he makes no use of the notion of the ego in drawing topographical distinctions, nor does he speak of *ego-instincts** in dealing with psychical energy (7).

b. As for the relationship between the ego and the real world, no really new theoretical solution to the problem is brought forward, although there is a change in emphasis. The basic reference-point remains the experience of satisfaction and the primal hallucination:

135

Ego

(i) The value of 'experience of real life' is stressed: 'It was only the non-occurrence of the expected satisfaction, the disappointment experienced, that led to the abandonment of this attempt at satisfaction by means of hallucination. Instead of it, the psychical apparatus had to decide to form a conception of the real circumstances in the external world and to endeavour to make a real alteration in them' (8*a*).

(ii) The recognition of the two main principles of mental functioning introduces a new element into the distinction between the primary and secondary processes. The reality principle emerges as a law which comes from outside to impose its demands on the psychical apparatus; these demands, however, tend to be gradually appropriated by the apparatus itself.

(iii) Freud attributes a unique kind of underpinning to the exigences of the reality principle, in the form of the instincts of self-preservation*. These are quicker to relinquish a *modus operandi* governed by the pleasure principle; since they are more readily educated by reality, they are able to supply the energy underlying an 'ego-reality' which 'need do nothing but strive for what is *useful* and guard itself against damage' (8*b*). In this perspective the ego's access to reality presents little problem. The way the ego eliminates hallucination as a means of satisfying desire takes on a new character: it *tests* reality through the mediation of the instincts of self-preservation; it then attempts to impose the norms of reality upon the sexual instincts*. (For further discussion of this idea, see 'Reality-Testing' and 'Pleasure-Ego/Reality-Ego'.)

(iv) The ego's relationship with the system *Pcs.-Cs.*–and especially with perception and with motility–becomes a very close one.

c. In Freud's description of the defensive conflict, and more particularly in his clinical observation of obsessional neurosis, the ego emerges as the agency which opposes itself to desire. The unpleasurable affect is the sign of this confrontation, which from the beginning assumes the form of a struggle between two forces both of which can be seen to bear the mark of the instinct. In attempting to demonstrate the existence of a 'complete' infantile neurosis in the case of the 'Rat Man', Freud uncovers 'an erotic instinct and a revolt against it; a wish which has not yet become compulsive and, struggling against it, a distressing affect and an impulsion towards the performance of defensive acts' (9). It is his concern to provide the ego with an instinctual basis to counterbalance the instinctual basis of sexuality that leads Freud to describe the conflict as an antagonism between sexual instincts and ego-instincts.

In the same vein, Freud raises the question of the development of the ego-instincts, which he feels deserves the same attention as the development of the libido; he hypothesises that in the case of obsessional neurosis the former might have outstripped the latter (10).

d. It is during this period that a new notion is brought out: the ego as love-object. At first this is applied especially to homosexuality and to the psychoses. By 1914–15, however, in a number of texts which mark a definite turning-point in Freud's thought, this conception of the ego has become dominant.

IV. Three closely linked ideas were worked out in this transition period of 1914–15: narcissism*; identification as constitutive of the ego; and the differentiation, within the ego, of certain 'ideal' components.

136

a. We may summarise the implications of the introduction of narcissism for the definition of the ego as follows:

(i) The ego is not present from the very beginning; it is not even the end-product of a gradual process of psychical differentiation: for it to be constituted, a 'new psychical action' has to take place (11a).

(ii) The ego appears as a *unity* relative to the anarchic, fragmentary functioning of sexuality which characterises auto-erotism*.

(iii) The ego presents itself to sexuality as a love-object, just as external objects do. In outlining the possible genesis of object-choice* Freud goes so far as to suggest the following sequence: auto-erotism, narcissisism, homosexual object-choice, heterosexual object-choice.

(iv) Such a definition of the ego as object prohibits any identification of it with the subject's internal world as a whole. This is why Freud was so concerned, in his controversy with Jung, to preserve a distinction between the introversion* of the libido on to the subject's phantasies and a 'return (of the libido) to his ego' (11b).

(v) From the economic point of view, 'the ego is to be regarded as a great reservoir of libido, from which libido is sent out *to* objects and which is always ready to absorb libido flowing back *from* objects' (12). The implication of this reservoir image is that the ego is not merely an area through which the energy of cathexis passes but that it is the *location* of this energy in a permanently dammed-up state, and even that the ego's actual form is determined by this charge of energy. Whence Freud's characterisation of the ego as an organism –as 'the body of an amoeba' (11c).

(vi) A final point: a 'narcissistic object-choice'*, in which the love-object is defined by its resemblance to the individual's own ego, is described by Freud as typical. But over and above any particular type of object-choice, such as the one manifested in some cases of male homosexuality, it is the entire concept of object-choice itself that Freud is obliged to rethink (including even the so-called anaclitic type*) in order to accommodate the subject's *ego*.

b. During this same period Freud elaborates considerably upon the concept of identification. He now brings forward more basic types of identification in addition to those which he had always recognised in hysteria–where it appears as a transient phenomenon, a means for an unconscious similarity between the person and the other to find expression in a genuine symptom. Identification is now more than the mere expression of a relationship between myself and another person, while the ego may now undergo radical changes because of it, becoming the intrasubjective residue of an intersubjective relationship. Thus, in male homosexuality, 'the young man does not abandon his mother, but identifies himself with her; he transforms himself into her [...]. A striking thing about this identification is its ample scale; it remoulds the ego in one of its important features–in its sexual character–upon the model of what has hitherto been the object' (13).

c. The analysis of melancholia, and of the processes which it exemplifies, results in a profound transformation of the concept of the ego.

(i) Identification with the lost object, which is manifest in melancholics, is interpreted as a regression to a preliminary stage of object-choice in which 'the ego wants to incorporate this object into itself' (14a). This idea clears the way

137

for an ego conceived of as being not only remoulded by secondary identifications but constituted from the beginning by an identification having oral incorporation* as its prototype.

(ii) The introjected object within the ego is described by Freud in anthropomorphic terms: it is subjected to the harshest of treatment, it is made to suffer, suicide threatens to kill it, etc. (14b).

(iii) The introjection* of the object in fact implies the internalisation* of an entire relationship. In melancholia, the conflict due to ambivalence towards the object is transposed into the relationship with the ego.

(iv) The ego is no longer treated as the only agency of the psychical apparatus that is personified. Certain portions can be separated off through splitting, notably the critical agency or conscience: one part of the ego stands face to face with another part, judges it critically and takes it, so to say, as an object.

This reinforces an idea already present in 'On Narcissism: An Introduction' (1914c): the major distinction between ego-libido and object-libido does not suffice to account for all modalities of narcissistic withdrawal of libido. The 'narcissistic' libido can have as its objects a whole series of agencies which together compose a complex system, and whose participation in the ego-system is attested to by Freud's designations for them: ideal ego*, ego-ideal*, super-ego*.

V. The 'turning-point' of 1920: it should be clear from the foregoing–at any rate so far as the development of the concept of the ego is concerned–that this label cannot be unreservedly accepted. It is impossible nevertheless to ignore Freud's own testimony regarding the essential modification which was made in 1920. It would seem that if the second topographical theory treats the ego as a system or agency, this is primarily because it is intended that it should be based more firmly upon the modalities of psychical conflict than was the first theory, which, schematically speaking, took the different modes of mental functioning (primary and secondary processes) as its principal referents. It is the active parties in the conflict–the ego as a defensive agent, the super-ego as a system of prohibitions, the id as the instinctual pole–which are now elevated to the rank of agencies of the psychical apparatus. The changeover from the first topography to the second does not imply that the new 'provinces' supersede the previous lines of demarcation between the unconscious, the preconscious and the conscious; it does mean that functions and processes which were distributed between several systems in the first scheme of things are now to be found together within the agency of the ego:

a. Consciousness, in the very earliest metapsychological model, had the status of a completely autonomous system (the ω system of the 'Project'). Subsequently Freud attached it to the system Pcs., though never without a certain amount of difficulty (see 'Consciousness'). Now at last its topographical position is made clear: it becomes the 'nucleus of the ego'.

b. The functions hitherto attributed to the system Pcs. are now for the most part taken over by the ego.

c. The point upon which Freud places most emphasis is that the ego now appears as largely unconscious. This is borne out by clinical experience, and in particular by unconscious resistances during treatment: 'We have come upon something in the ego itself which is also unconscious, which behaves exactly like the repressed – that is, which produces powerful effects without itself being conscious and which requires special work before it can be made conscious' (15*a*). With these words, Freud opened up an area much explored by his successors: defensive techniques have been described which are not just unconscious in the sense that the subject is ignorant of their motive and mechanism, but more profoundly so in that they present a compulsive, repetitive and unrealistic aspect which makes them comparable to the very repressed against which they are struggling.

The extending of the concept of the ego means that the most varied functions are allotted it in the second topography. These include not only the control of motility and perception, reality-testing*, anticipation, the temporal ordering of the mental processes, rational thought, and so on, but also refusal to recognise the facts, rationalisation* and compulsive defence against instinctual demands. As can be seen, these diverse functions may be organised in antithetical pairs; opposition to the instincts as against satisfaction of the instincts, insight against rationalisation, objective knowledge against systematic distortion, resistance against the removal of resistance, etc. These contradictions are to all intents and purposes merely a reflection of the position assigned the ego *vis-à-vis* the two other agencies and external reality (*ε*). Depending upon his standpoint, Freud at times stresses the heteronomy of the ego, while at others he points up its chances of relative independence. The ego is treated essentially as a mediator attempting to reconcile contradictory demands; it 'owes service to three masters and is consequently menaced by three dangers: from the external world, from the libido of the id and from the severity of the super-ego [...]. As a frontier-creature, the ego tries to mediate between the world and the id, to make the id pliable to the world and, by means of its muscular activity, to make the world fall in with the wishes of the id' (15*b*).

VI. The interest shown by so many authors in the concept of the ego, as well as the diversity of their approaches, gives some measure of the prominence that the idea has attained in psycho-analytic theory. An entire school has set out to relate the acquisitions of psycho-analysis to those of other disciplines (psycho-physiology, learning theory, child psychology, social psychology) in an attempt to found a true general psychology of the ego (*ζ*). This enterprise has led to the introduction of such notions as that of a desexualised, neutralised energy which the ego can command and which has a so-called 'synthetic' function, and that of a conflict-free portion of the ego. The ego is looked upon above all as an apparatus of regulation and adaptation to reality, while an attempt is made to trace its origin and development through maturational and learning processes, starting from the sensory and motor equipment of the infant at the breast. Even supposing that any of these ideas could be shown to have some initial support in Freud's thought, it would still be hard to see how they could be said to represent the most consistent expression of the final Freudian theory of the psychical apparatus. Not that there is any question of setting out some 'true' Freudian theory of the ego to counter these tendencies of ego psychology: indeed, it is remarkably difficult to integrate all the psycho-analytic contributions to the concept of the ego into a unified line of thought. Instead, we shall attempt to consider Freud's ideas on the subject schematically, in terms of two main perspectives, trying to show how each of them deals with three main problems–namely, the ego's *genesis*, its *topographical location* (chiefly its position *vis-à-vis* the id) and the meaning to be given to its *energy*, as seen from the dynamic and economic points of view.

a. Viewed in a first perspective, then, the ego appears as the product of the gradual differentiation of the id resulting from the influence of external reality. This differentiation starts from the system *Pcpt.-Cs.* (perception-consciousness), which is likened to the cortical layer of a vesicle of living matter: the ego 'has been developed out of the id's cortical layer, which, through being adapted to the reception and exclusion of stimuli, is in direct contact with the external world (*reality*). Starting from conscious perception it has subjected to its influence ever larger regions and deeper strata of the id' (16).

The ego is thus seen here as an actual organ which, whatever real setbacks it suffers, is bound by definition, by virtue of its role as the representative of reality, to guarantee a progressive mastery over the instincts: '. . . the ego seeks to bring the influence of the external world to bear upon the id and its tendencies, and endeavours to substitute the reality-principle for the pleasure-principle which reigns unrestrictedly in the id. For the ego, perception plays the part which in the id falls to instinct' (15c). As Freud himself remarks, the ego-id distinction here falls into line with the traditional antagonism between reason and passion (15d).

In this context, the question of the energy that the ego is supposed to have at its command is not an easy one to settle. For if the ego is directly produced by the action of the external world, how can it derive an energy from this outside reality which is capable of performing within a psychical apparatus that operates by definition on its own energy? Freud is at times brought to extend the role of reality: instead of being simply the external data with which the individual has to cope in order to regulate his functioning, it takes on the full responsibility of an actual *agency*–in the sense that the ego and the super-ego are agencies* of the psychical personality–and becomes an active party in the dynamics of the conflict (17). But since the sole energy available to the psychical apparatus is the endogenous energy supplied by the instincts, that available to the ego can only be second-hand, its original source being the id. This is the solution Freud offers most frequently, but it cannot avoid the implication of a 'desexualisation' of libido, and this hypothesis is open to the criticism that it confines the difficulty to one concept (which in any case becomes highly problematical itself) when it is really germane to the entire theory (η).

Two major problems arise when we take an overall view of the approach just outlined. In the first place, how are we to understand the assumption upon which it is based, namely, the differentiation of the ego within a psychical entity whose actual status is poorly defined? Secondly, is not a whole series of essential (and essentially psycho-analytic) contributions to the ego-concept excluded from this well-nigh ideal model of the genesis of the psychical apparatus?

The idea of a genesis of the ego is laden with ambiguity–an ambiguity sustained throughout Freud's work and only aggravated by the model he puts forward in *Beyond the Pleasure Principle* (1920g). The fact is that the evolution of the 'living vesicle' evoked in this text may be understood on different levels: is it supposed to account for the phylogenesis of the human species, or even for the origins of life in general? For the development of the human organism? Or for the differentiation of the psychical apparatus starting from an undifferentiated state of affairs? In the last case, what credibility can be accorded to the hypothesis of a simplified organism which sets up its own boundaries, its receptor apparatus and its protective shield* in response to the impingement of external excitation? Are we being offered a mere analogy using a more or less applicable *image* borrowed from biology (the protozoon) to illustrate the psychical individual's relationship to the outside world? If so, then the body itself must strictly speaking be treated as part of the 'external' world as opposed to whatever it is that constitutes the mental vesicle. Any such notion, however, is quite alien to Freud, for whom there is never any comparison between external excitation and internal excitation–or instinct–which places the psychical apparatus and even the ego under constant attack from the inside, leaving no avenue of escape. We are therefore obliged to seek a more intimate relationship than that of pure metaphor between this biological imagery and its counterpart in the psychical sphere. Freud draws occasionally upon an analogy based on physical reality; for example, he assimilates the ego's functions to the perceptual and protective equipment of the organism: just as the tegument is the surface of the body, so the system *Pcpt.-Cs.* is seen as the 'surface' of the psyche. Such a conception encourages us to view the psychical apparatus as the outcome of a specialisation of the bodily functions, and to look upon the ego as the end-product of a long evolution of the apparatus of adaptation.

Lastly, from another angle, we may well ask whether Freud's insistent use of this metaphor of a living form (defined by its difference of energy level as compared to the exterior, and possessing a frontier subject to breach from without and in constant need of defence and reconstruction) is not based on an *actual* relationship between the genesis of the ego and the structure of the organism. This is a relationship which Freud formulated specifically only on very rare occasions: 'The ego is first and foremost a bodily ego; it is not merely a surface entity, but is itself the projection of a surface' (15e). 'The ego is ultimately derived from bodily sensations, chiefly from those springing from the surface of the body, besides [...] representing the superficies of the mental apparatus' (θ). Such statements suggest that we search for the basis of the agency of the ego in an actual psychical operation consisting in the 'projection' of the organism into the psyche.

b. The last point alone gives us ample justification for bringing together a large group of ideas which are central to the psycho-analytic doctrine and which, taken as a whole, constitute a *second perspective*. This approach does not evade the problem of the ego's genesis, nor does it seek a solution to it by resorting to the idea of a functional differentiation; instead, it introduces specific psychical operations whereby characteristics, images and forms derived from the other person are precipitated, so to speak, into the psyche (see particularly: 'Identification', 'Introjection', 'Narcissism', 'Mirror Phase', 'Good Object/Bad Object'). Psycho-analysts have persistently sought to define the crucial points and the stages of these identifications, trying to decide which of them correspond to each of the psychical agencies (ego, ideal ego, ego-ideal, super-ego). It is worth noting that in this context the relation of the ego to perception and to the outside world, though not suppressed, does take on a new meaning: instead of the ego being seen as an apparatus whose development starts from the system

Pcpt.-Cs., it becomes an internal formation originating from *certain privileged perceptions* which derive not from the external world in general, but specifically from the interhuman world.

In its topographical aspect, the ego new appears as an object *for* the id rather than an emanation *from* the id. For Freud is far from abandoning the theory of narcissism when he brings in the second topography; on the contrary, this theory, along with its corollary, the notion of a libido oriented towards the ego *or* towards an outside object according to the requirements of a true energy-balance, is reaffirmed right up to the end of his work. The clinical experience of psycho-analysis, especially with regard to psychosis, furnishes additional evidence in support of this view, witness the *melancholic's* deprecation and hate of the ego, the extension of the ego in *mania* to the point where it fuses with the ideal ego, the loss of ego 'boundaries' through the withdrawal of cathexis from them which (as Federn has emphasised) typifies states of *depersonalisation*, and so on.

Finally, the problem posed by the source of the energy needed to support the ego's activities is alleviated if it is viewed in relation with the idea of narcissistic cathexis. In this light we no longer have to discover the meaning of the hypothetical qualitative change referred to as desexualisation or neutralisation; we have rather to understand how the ego, as an object of libido, can operate not only as a 'reservoir' but also as the subject of the libidinal cathexes which emanate from it.

This second approach, a few elements of which we have presented, appears less synthetic than the first one precisely inasmuch as it remains closer to analytic experience and analytic discoveries. But it does leave one essential task outstanding: a whole group of activities and operations has yet to be integrated into any genuinely psycho-analytic theory of the mental apparatus, notwithstanding the fact that one psycho-analytic school, in its attempt to construct a general psychology, has categorised them as ego-functions as though this attribution were a matter of course.

(α) This despite the fact that in the passages of the *Studies on Hysteria* relevant to the question of the ego Freud has perfectly specific terms at hand in '*das Individuum*' and '*die Person*'.

(β) The celebrated formula '*Wo Es war, soll Ich werden*' is itself sufficient confirmation of this. Meaning literally 'Where it (id) was, there I (ego) must come about,' this formula occurs at the end of a lengthy exposition of *the* ego, *the* id and *the* super-ego.

(γ) There are a certain number of the ego's characteristics, as it is described in the 'Project for a Scientific Psychology', which make it comparable to the *Gestalt* (form) of some modern thinkers: these are the relative stability of its boundaries, despite their liability to a degree of fluctuation which, thanks to the permanence of the nucleus (*Ichkern*), does not upset the equilibrium of the form as a whole; the maintenance of a constant level of energy in the ego as compared with the rest of the psyche; the free circulation of energy *within* the ego, which contrasts markedly with the barrier constituted by its periphery; and, lastly, the powers of attraction and control, designated by Freud as side-cathexes (*Nebenbesetzung*), which the ego exercises over processes taking place beyond its own borders. It is in a similar fashion that a *Gestalt* polarises and organises the field from which it has detached itself, structuring its own background. Far from the ego being the seat–or even the subject–of thought and of the secondary processes in general, these processes are to be understood, on the contrary, as the consequence of the ego's regulatory capacities.

(δ) Which would appear to justify the following hypothesis: if the defensive function of the ego and even the agency of the ego itself are obscure in *The Interpretation of Dreams*, is this not because the ego finds itself in a completely different position during sleep to the one which it adopts as one of the poles of the defensive conflict? Its narcissistic cathexis (the wish for sleep) broadens the ego, one might say, to the dimensions of the scene of the dream, while at the same time tending to make it coincide with the bodily ego (18).

(ε) For a critique of the inconsistency and inadequacy of the usual theory of the ego's functions, see Daniel Lagache, 'La psychanalyse et la structure de la personnalité' (19).

(ζ) Cf. particularly the work of Hartmann, Kris and Loewenstein, and that of D. Rapaport.

(η) Some authors, aware of this difficulty, have tried endowing the ego with a specific instinct having its own equipment, patterns of operation and form of gratification. Cf. Ives Hendrick's description of an 'instinct to master' (q.v.).

(θ) As the Editors of the *Standard Edition* point out, this footnote does not appear in the German editions of *The Ego and the Id*; it does appear in the English translation of 1927, where it is stated to have received Freud's approval (20).

(1) HARTMANN, H. 'Comments on the Psychoanalytic Theory of the Ego', *Psycho-analytic Study of the Child*, V, 84–85.

(2) JANET, P. *L'automatisme psychologique* (Paris: Alcan, 1889), 367.

(3) JANET, P. *L'état mental des hystériques* (Paris: Alcan, 1893–94). 2nd edn. (1911), 443.

(4) BREUER, J. and FREUD, S. *Studies on Hysteria* (1895*d*): a) G.W., I, 295–96; S.E., II, 291. b) G.W., I, 280; S.E., II, 278. c) G.W., I, 294–95; S.E., II, 290. d) Cf. G.W., I, 174; S.E., II, 116.

(5) FREUD, S. (1950*a* [1895]): a) *Anf.*, 432; S.E., I, 353. b) *Anf.*, 438; S.E., I, 358. c) *Anf.*, 411; S.E., I, 326–27.

(6) Cf. FREUD, S. *On Dreams* (1901*a*), G.W., II–III, 692–94; S.E., V, 679–80.

(7) Cf. FREUD, S. 'A Note on the Unconscious in Psycho-Analysis' (1912*g*); 'The Unconscious' (1915*e*); 'Repression' (1915*d*).

(8) FREUD, S. 'Formulations on the Two Principles of Mental Functioning' (1911*b*): a) G.W., VIII, 231; S.E., XII, 219. b) G.W., VIII, 235; S.E., XII, 223.

(9) FREUD, S. 'Notes upon a Case of Obsessional Neurosis' (1909*d*), G.W., VII, 389; S.E., X, 163.

(10) FREUD, S. 'The Disposition to Obsessional Neurosis' (1913*i*), G.W., VIII, 451; S.E., XII, 324–25.

(11) FREUD, S. 'On Narcissism: An Introduction' (1914*c*): a) G.W., X, 142; S.E., XIV, 77. b) G.W., X, 146; S.E., XIV, 80–81. c) G.W., X, 141; S.E., XIV, 75.

(12) FREUD, S. 'Two Encyclopaedia Articles' (1923*a* [1922]), G.W., XIII, 231; S.E., XVIII, 257.

(13) FREUD, S. *Group Psychology and the Analysis of the Ego* (1921*c*), G.W., XIII, 111; S.E., XVIII, 108.

(14) 'Mourning and Melancholia' (1917*e*): a) G.W., X, 436; S.E., XIV, 249. b) Cf. G.W., X, 428–39; S.E., XIV, 251.

(15) FREUD, S. *The Ego and the Id* (1923*b*): a) G.W., XIII, 244; S.E., XIX, 17. b) G.W., XIII, 286; S.E., XIX, 56. c) G.W., XIII, 252–53; S.E., XIX, 25. d) G.W., XIII, 253; S.E., XIX, 25. e) G.W., XIII, 253; S.E., XIX, 26.

(16) FREUD, S. *An Outline of Psycho-Analysis* (1940*a* [1938]), C.W., XVII, 129; S.E., XXIII, 198–99.

(17) Cf. in particular FREUD, S. 'Neurosis and Psychosis' (1924*b* [1923]) and 'The Loss of Reality in Neurosis and Psychosis' (1924*e*).

(18) Cf. FREUD, S. 'A Metapsychological Supplement to the Theory of Dreams' (1917*d* [1915]), G.W., X, 413; S.E., XIV, 223.

(19) In *La Psychanalyse*, VI (Paris: P.U.F.), especially Chapter VI.

(20) Cf. S.E., XIX, 26.

Ego-Ideal

= *D*.: Ichideal.–*Es*.: ideal del yo.–*Fr*.: idéal du moi.–*I*.: ideale dell'io.–*P*.: ideal do ego.

Term used by Freud in the context of his second theory of the psychical apparatus: an agency of the personality resulting from the coming together of narcissism (idealisation of the ego) and identification with the parents, with their substitutes or with collective ideals. As a distinct agency, the ego-ideal constitutes a model to which the subject attempts to conform.

It is difficult to discern any hard and fast meaning of the term 'ego-ideal' in Freud's writings. The variations in this concept are due to the fact that it is closely bound up with the progressive working out of the idea of the super-ego and, more generally speaking, with that of the second theory of the psychical apparatus. Thus in *The Ego and the Id* (1923*b*) 'ego-ideal' and 'super-ego' appear as synonymous, whereas in other texts the function of the ideal is assigned to a distinct agency or, at any rate, to a specific substructure within the super-ego (q.v.).

It is in 'On Narcissism: An Introduction' (1914*c*) that the term 'ego-ideal' first appears as a designation for a comparatively autonomous intrapsychic formation which serves as a reference-point for the ego's evaluation of its real achievements. Its origin is largely narcissistic: 'What man projects before him as his ideal is the substitute for the lost narcissism of his childhood in which he was his own ideal' (1*a*). This state of narcissism, which Freud compares to a veritable delusion of grandeur, is abandoned as a result, in particular, of the criticism which is directed at the child by its parents. It is noteworthy that this criticism–as internalised in the form of a specific psychical agency with a censoring and self-observing function–is distinguished from the ego-ideal throughout the paper on narcissism: it 'constantly watches the actual ego and measures it by [the ego] ideal' (1*b*).

In *Group Psychology and the Analysis of the Ego* (1921*c*) the role of the ego-ideal is of central importance. Freud sees it as a formation clearly differentiated from the ego which enables us to account in particular for amorous fascination, for subordination to the hypnotist and for submission to leaders–all cases in which the subject substitutes another person for his ego-ideal.

This type of process is the principle on which the constitution of human groups is based. The collective ideal derives its efficacy from a convergence of individual 'ego-ideals': '. . . a number of individuals [...] have put one and the same object in the place of their ego-ideal and have consequently identified themselves with one another in their ego' (2*a*); on the other hand, these individuals, after identifications with their parents, teachers and so on, already harbour a certain number of collective ideals: 'Each individual is a component part of numerous groups, he is bound by ties of identification in many directions, and he has built up his ego-ideal on the most various models' (2*b*).

In *The Ego and the Id*, where it appears for the first time, the super-ego is considered to be indistinguishable from the ego-ideal: there is a single agency, formed through identification with the parents as a corollary of the decline of the Oedipus complex, which combines the functions of prohibition and

144

ideal. The super-ego's 'relation to the ego is not exhausted by the precept: "You ought to be like this (like your father)." It also comprises the prohibition: "You *may not be* like this (like your father)–that is, you may not do all that he does; some things are his prerogative" '(3).

In the *New Introductory Lectures on Psycho-Analysis* (1933a [1932]) a distinction between the two terms appears once more; the super-ego is now described as a comprehensive structure embodying the three functions 'of self-observation, of conscience and of the ideal' (4). The distinction between the last two of these functions is illustrated in particular by the differences which Freud seeks to establish between the sense of guilt and the sense of inferiority. These two sentiments are the outcome of a tension between ego and super-ego, but the former is related to conscience whereas the latter is connected with the ego-ideal inasmuch as this is loved rather than dreaded.

* * *

Psycho-analytic literature testifies to the fact that the term 'super-ego' has not superseded 'ego-ideal': the majority of authors do not use them interchangeably.

There is comparative agreement as regards the denotation of 'ego-ideal'; on the other hand, approaches differ as far as the question of the ego-ideal's relationship with the super-ego and conscience is concerned. The matter is complicated still further by the fact that some writers use 'super-ego' to refer (like Freud in his *New Introductory Lectures*) to an overall structure embodying various sub-structures, while others take it, in a more specific sense, as meaning the 'voice of conscience' in its prohibitive role.

For Nunberg, for instance, the ego-ideal and the prohibitive agency are quite separate. He makes a distinction between them both as regards the motives which they induce in the ego–'Whereas the ego submits to the super-ego out of fear of punishment, it submits to the ego-ideal out of love' (5)–and as regards their respective origins: the ego-ideal is said to be formed principally on the model of loved objects, while the super-ego is formed on that of dreaded figures.

However soundly based such a distinction may appear from a descriptive standpoint, it is hard to assign it any clear meaning in the metapsychological perspective. Which is why many authors, faithful to the suggestions made by Freud in *The Ego and the Id* (cf. the text quoted above), lay the emphasis on the idea that the two aspects–ideal and prohibition–are bound up with one another. Thus Daniel Lagache speaks of a super-ego/ego-ideal system, positing a structural relationship enclosed within this system: '. . . the super-ego corresponds to authority and the ego-ideal to the way in which the subject must behave in order to respond to the expectations of authority' (6).

(1) FREUD, S.: a) G.W., X, 161; S.E., XIV, 94. b) G.W., X, 162; S.E., XIV, 95.

(2) FREUD, S.: a) G.W., XIII, 128; S.E., XVIII, 116. b) G.W., XIII, 144; S.E., XVIII, 129.

(3) FREUD, S., G.W., XIII, 262; S.E., XIX, 34.

(4) FREUD, S., G.W., XV, 72; S.E., XXII, 66.

(5) NUNBERG, H. *Allgemeine Neurosenlehre auf psychoanalytischer Grundlage* (1932). English trans.: *Principles of Psycho-Analysis* (New York: I.U.P., 1955), 146.

(6) LAGACHE, D. 'La psychanalyse et la structure de la personnalité, *La Psychanalyse* (Paris: P.U.F.), VI, 39.

Ego-Instincts

= *D.*: Ichtriebe.—*Es.*: instintos del yo.—*Fr.*: pulsions du moi.—
I.: istinti *or* pulsioni dell'io.—*P.*: impulsos *or* pulsões do ego.

Within the framework of the first theory of the instincts (as formulated) by Freud in the years 1910-15), 'ego-instincts' is the name given to a specific type of instinct whose energy is placed at the service of the ego in the defensive conflict. The ego-instincts are identified with the self-preservative instincts and opposed to the sexual ones.

In the first Freudian theory of the instincts, which sets up an antithesis between the sexual* and the self-preservative* instincts, the latter are still referred to as ego-instincts.

As we know, psychical conflict* had from the outset been described by Freud as opposing sexuality to a repressing, defensive agency, the ego*. But the ego had until now been assigned no specific instinctual support.

At the same time, beginning with the *Three Essays on the Theory of Sexuality* (1905*d*), Freud had definitely contrasted the sexual instincts with what he called 'needs' (or 'functions of vital importance'); he had shown how the sexual instincts come into existence by first attaching themselves to these functions (anaclisis*) and then taking their own path—notably into auto-erotism*. In setting forth his 'first theory of the instincts', Freud seeks to equate two oppositions—namely, the clinical antithesis, in the defensive conflict, between ego and sexual instincts, and the genetic antithesis, at the beginnings of human sexuality, between the self-preservative functions and the sexual instinct.

Only in 'The Psycho-Analytic View of Psychogenic Disturbances of Vision' (1910*i*) did Freud bring all the non-sexual 'great needs' together for the first time under the heading of 'instincts of self-preservation', while proceeding to designate them—under the name 'ego-instincts'—as an active party to the psychical conflict, whose two poles are both, in the last analysis, said to be definable in terms of forces: 'From the point of view of our attempted explanation, a quite specially important part is played by the undeniable opposition between the instincts which subserve sexuality, the attainment of sexual pleasure, and those other instincts which have as their aim the self-preservation of the individual—the ego-instincts. As the poet has said, all the organic instincts that operate in our mind may be classified as "hunger" or "love"' (1*a*).

* * *

What is the meaning of Freud's proposed conflation of self-preservative and ego-instincts? In what sense may a particular group of instincts be considered inherent to the ego?

a. Biologically speaking, Freud finds confirmation of his thesis in the contrast between those instincts which tend towards the preservation of the individual (*Selbsterhaltung*) and those which end by serving the goals of the species (*Arterhaltung*): 'The individual does actually carry on a twofold existence: one to serve his own purposes and the other as a link in a chain, which he serves against his will, or at least involuntarily. [...] The separation of the sexual instincts from the ego-instincts would simply reflect this twofold function of the

146

individual' (2*a*). Seen in this light 'ego-instincts' means 'instincts of self-preservation' in that the ego is the psychical agency to which the task of preserving the individual falls.

b. In the context of the functioning of the psychical apparatus, Freud shows how the self-preservative instincts, in contradistinction to the sexual ones, are particularly well suited to operation in accord with the reality principle. Going much further, he defines a 'reality-ego' by the actual properties of the ego-instincts: '. . . the reality-ego need do nothing but strive for what is *useful* and guard itself against damage' (3).

c. Finally it should not be forgotten that no sooner had the concept of the ego-instincts been introduced than Freud noted the attachment of these instincts –in diametric contrast to the sexual instincts with which they are in conflict–to a specific group of *ideas*, a group 'for which we use the collective concept of the "ego"–a compound which is made up variously at different times' (1*b*).

If we accept the full implications of this remark, we have to conclude that the ego-instincts cathect the 'ego' *qua* 'group of ideas'–that these instincts are *aimed at the ego*. This plainly makes the term 'ego-instincts' ambiguous: these instincts are considered on the one hand as tendencies *emanating* from the organism (or from the ego in so far as it is the agency responsible for the organism's preservation) and directed towards relatively specific external objects (e.g. food); on the other hand, however, they are viewed as attached to the ego as if to their *object*.

*　　　*　　　*

Whenever he brings up the opposition between sexual and ego-instincts in the years 1910–15, Freud rarely fails to declare that this is a hypothesis to which he had been 'compelled' by 'analysis of the pure transference neuroses (hysteria and obsessional neurosis)' (2*b*). It may be pointed out in this connection, however, that in the interpretations of the conflict offered by Freud the instincts of self-preservation are practically never seen to operate as the motor force of repression:

a. In the clinical studies published before 1910 the ego's place in the conflict is often emphasised, but no mention is made of its relationship with the functions necessary for the preservation of the biological individual (see 'Ego'). Later, after the self-preservative instinct has been explicitly posited in theory as an ego-instinct, it is still rarely invoked as an energy of repression: in 'From the History of an Infantile Neurosis' (1918*b* [1914]), the force responsible for repression is sought in 'narcissistic genital libido' (4).

b. In the metapsychological works of 1914–15–'The Unconscious' (1915*e*), 'Repression' (1915*d*), 'Instincts and their Vicissitudes' (1915*c*)–it is to a purely *libidinal* interaction of cathexes, withdrawals of cathexis and anticathexes that repression is attributed in the three major types of transference neurosis: 'Here we may replace "cathexis" by "libido", because, as we know, it is the vicissitudes of *sexual* impulses with which we shall be dealing' (5).

c. In the text which introduces the notion of ego-instincts–one of the few places where Freud attempts to have these play an active part in the conflict– we get the impression that the function of 'self-preservation' (in this instance, vision) is the stake or terrain of the defensive conflict rather than one of its dynamic components.

147

Ego-Instincts

d. In seeking to justify the introduction of this instinctual antagonism, Freud treats it not as a 'necessary postulate' but merely as a 'working hypothesis' reaching well beyond the findings of psycho-analysis. These findings in fact justify nothing beyond the idea of 'a conflict between the claims of sexuality and those of the ego' (6a). The instinctual dualism is grounded instead, in the final analysis, on 'biological' considerations: 'I should like at this point expressly to admit that the hypothesis of separate ego-instincts and sexual instincts [...] rests scarcely at all upon a psychological basis, but derives its principle support from biology' (2c).

*   *   *

The introduction of the idea of narcissism* does not immediately make the opposition between sexual and ego-instincts obsolete in Freud's eyes (2d, 6b), but it does bring in an additional distinction: the sexual instincts can direct their energy either towards an external object (object-libido) or towards the ego (ego-libido or narcissistic libido). The energy of the ego-instincts, meanwhile, is not libido but 'interest'*. This new scheme clearly attempts to get rid of the ambiguity which, as we have just pointed out, had hitherto beset the term 'ego-instincts'. The ego-instincts emanate from the ego and relate to independent objects (such as food); yet the ego may become the object of the sexual instinct (ego-libido).

All the same, the opposition between sexual and ego-instincts soon loses its attraction for Freud, giving way to that between ego-libido and object-libido*.

It now seemed to Freud, in fact, that self-preservation could be brought down to self-love – in other words, to ego-libido. Writing with the benefit of hindsight on the history of his instinct theory, he interprets the turning-point constituted by his introduction of narcissistic libido as a turn towards a monistic theory of instinctual energy – 'as though the slow process of psycho-analytic research was following in the steps of Jung's speculations about a primal libido, especially because the transformation of object-libido into narcissism necessarily carried along with it a certain degree of desexualisation' (7).

It is striking, however, that Freud only discovers this 'monist' phase in his thought at the very moment when he has just posited a *new basic dualism* – that between the life instincts* and the death instincts*.

*   *   *

With the advent of this fresh dualism the term 'ego-instinct' was fated to disappear from Freud's lexicon; not, however, until an attempt had been made in *Beyond the Pleasure Principle* (1920g) to find a place in the new scheme of things for what had hitherto been given this name. This attempt is made in two incompatible ways:

a. Inasmuch as the life instincts are identified with the sexual instincts, Freud seeks a parallel coincidence of ego-instincts and death instincts. In pursuing to its logical conclusion his speculative thesis that the instinct is fundamentally a tendency to restore the inorganic state, Freud treats the self-preservative instincts as 'component instincts whose function it is to assure that the organism shall follow its own path to death' (8a). These instincts are distinct from the immediate tendency towards a return to the inorganic solely to the extent that

148

'the organism wishes to die only in its own fashion. Thus these guardians of life, too, were originally the myrmidons of death' (8*b*).

b. But Freud is brought–in the course of the very same work–to rectify these views by readopting the thesis that the instincts of self-preservation are libidinal in nature (8*c*).

Finally, within the framework of his second theory of the psychical apparatus, Freud no longer postulates a correspondence between particular qualitative types of instinct and particular psychical agencies (as he had sought to do in identifying instincts of *self-preservation* and *ego*-instincts). Although instincts originate in the id they are all to be found at work within each agency. The problem of ascertaining what instinctual energy the ego makes use of more especially is still a preoccupation of Freud's (see 'Ego'), but he makes no mention of ego-instincts in connection with it.

(1) FREUD, S.: a) G.W., VIII, 97–98; S.E., XI, 214–15. b) G.W., VIII, 97; S.E., XI, 213.

(2) FREUD, S. 'On Narcissism: An Introduction' (1914*c*): a) G.W., X, 143; S.E., XIV, 78. b) G.W., X, 143; S.E., XIV, 77. c) G.W., X, 144; S.E., XIV, 79. d) Cf. *passim*.

(3) FREUD, S. 'Formulations on the Two Principles of Mental Functioning' (1911*b*), G.W., VIII, 235; S.E., XII, 223.

(4) FREUD, S., G.W., XII, 73; S.E., XVII, 46.

(5) FREUD, S. 'The Unconscious' (1915*e*), G.W., X, 281; S.E., XIV, 181–82.

(6) FREUD, S. 'Instincts and their Vicissitudes' (1915*c*): a) G.W., X, 217; S.E., XIV, 124. b) Cf. G.W., X, 216 *ff*.; S.E., XIV, 123 *ff*.

(7) FREUD, S. 'Two Encyclopaedia Articles' (1923*a* [1922]), G.W., XIII, 231–32; S.E., XVIII, 257.

(8) FREUD, S.: a) G.W., XIII, 41; S.E., XVII, 39. b) G.W., XIII, 41; S.E., XVII, 39. c) Cf. G.W., XIII, 56; S.E., XVII, 52.

Egoism

= *D*.: Egoismus. – *Es*.: egoísmo. – *Fr*.: égoïsme. – *I*.: egoismo. – *P*.: egoismo.

Interest that the ego directs on to itself.

To begin with, the term 'egoism' helped Freud characterise dreams, which he described as 'egoistic' in the sense that 'the beloved ego appears in all of them' (1*a*). This is not to say that the most 'disinterested' of feelings may not appear in dreams, but simply that the dreamer's ego is invariably present in person or through identifications (1*b*).

With the introduction of the idea of narcissism*, Freud is obliged to distinguish between this new concept and that of egoism: narcissism is 'the libidinal complement of egoism' (2). The two are often confused–but not of necessity. The distinction between them is founded on that between the sexual instincts* and the ego-instincts*: egoism or 'ego-interest' (*Ichinteresse*–see 'Interest') is defined as cathexis by the ego-instincts, narcissism as the cathexis of the ego by the sexual instincts.

Ego-Libido/Object-Libido

(1) *The Interpretation of Dreams* (1900a); a) G.W., II–III, 274; S.E., IV, 267. b) G.W., II–III, 328; S.E., IV, 267.

(2) FREUD, S. 'A Metapsychological Supplement to the Theory of Dreams' (1917d [1915]), G.W., X, 413; S.E., XIV, 223.

Ego-Libido/Object-Libido

= *D.*: Ichlibido/Objektlibido.–*Es.*: libido del yo/libido objetal.–
Fr.: libido du moi/libido d'objet.–*I.*: libido dell'io/libido oggettuale.–
P.: libido do ego/libido objetal.

Terms introduced by Freud to distinguish between two modes of libidinal cathexis: the libido can take as its object either the subject's own self (ego-libido or narcissistic libido) or else an external object (object-libido). According to Freud an energy balance obtains between these two modes of cathexis: object-libido decreases as ego-libido increases, and vice versa.

It was the study of the psychoses, in particular, which led Freud to the recognition that the subject can take his own self as a love-object (see 'Narcissism'); in terms of energy this means that libido may cathect the ego as easily as it does an external object. This is the origin of the distinction that Freud draws between ego-libido and object-libido. The economic problems to which this distinction gives rise are dealt with in 'On Narcissism: An Introduction' (1914c).

According to Freud libido starts by cathecting the ego (primary narcissism*), and it is only thence that it is directed towards external objects: 'Thus we form the idea of there being an original libidinal cathexis of the ego, from which some is later given off to objects, but which fundamentally persists and is related to the object-cathexes much as the body of an amoeba is related to the pseudopodias which it puts out' (1a).

The withdrawal of object-libido on to the ego constitutes secondary narcissism as it is to be observed particularly in psychotic states (hypochondria, delusions of grandeur).

Two terminological points should be borne in mind here. First, in the expression 'object-libido', 'object' is understood in the limited sense of an external object and does not include the ego, which may also be described, more broadly speaking, as the object of the instinct (see 'Object'). Secondly, 'object' and 'ego' in these compound terms refer to the point to which the libido is directed, not to its point of departure.

Difficulties arise from this second point, however, with more than terminological implications.

To begin with Freud recognises only one instinctual dualism–that between sexual instincts* and ego-instincts* (or instincts of self-preservation*). The energy of the former is known as libido, that of the latter as energy of the ego-instincts or ego-interest*. The distinction that Freud introduces later appears at first glance to be a subdivision of the sexual instincts according to which object they cathect:

150

Ego-instincts (interest) | Sexual instincts (libido)

Ego-libido   Object-libido

But however clear-cut the distinction between ego-instincts and ego-libido may be conceptually, it no longer holds good in the case of narcissistic states (sleep, somatic illness): 'Here libido and ego-interest share the same fate and are once more indistinguishable from each other' (1b). Freud does not accept Jung's instinctual monism (α).

A kindred difficulty arises from Freud's frequent use of such formulations as 'the libido is sent out from the ego on to the objects': this surely implies that the ego is not only the object but also the source of 'ego-libido'—in other words, that the ego-libido and the ego-instincts are one and the same. What makes the problem even more thorny is that Freud brings in the notion of ego-libido at the same time as he is working out the strictly topographical conception of the ego. This ambiguity is pointed up in formulations where Freud describes the ego as a 'great reservoir of libido'. The most consistent interpretation of Freud's thinking on this question that we can suggest runs as follows: libido conceived as instinctual energy has its source in the different erotogenic zones; the ego, as total person, serves as a storehouse for this libidinal energy, of which it is the first object; subsequently, however, this 'reservoir' itself functions as a source so far as external objects are concerned, since all cathexes emanate from it.

(α) This is the upshot of Freud's examination of Jung's theses in 1914 (1c). In a retrospective account of the development of 'The Libido Theory' (1923a [1922]) (2) Freud reinterprets this point in his thought as a conflation of ego-instincts and ego-libido—as though, in other words, he had at that time gone along with Jung's views. Note that by 1922 Freud had already worked out a new theory of the instincts, now classified on the basis of the opposition between the life and the death instincts. It is in our opinion a consequence of this development that he becomes less attentive to the distinctions which he had established in 1914–and which, moreover, he had reasserted in the *Introductory Lectures on Psycho-Analysis* (1916–17) (3).

(1) FREUD, S.: a) G.W., X, 140–41; S.E., XIV, 75. b) G.W., X, 149; S.E., XIV, 82. c) Cf. G.W., X, 142–47; S.E., XIV, 77–81.

(2) Cf. FREUD, S., G.W., XIII, 231–32; S.E., XVIII, 257–59.

(3) Cf. FREUD, S., G.W., XI, 435–36; S.E., XVI, 420.

Ego-Syntonic

= *D.*: Ichgerecht.–*Es.*: concorde con el yo.–*Fr.*: conforme au moi.– *I.*: corrispondente all' io, *or* egosintonico.–*P.*: egossintônico.

Term used to describe instincts or ideas that are acceptable to the ego–i.e., compatible with the ego's integrity and with its demands.

This term is occasionally met with in Freud's writings (1, 2). It connotes the idea that the psychical conflict does not imply an opposition between the

151

ego *in abstracto* and all instincts, but rather one between two kinds of instincts, those which are compatible with the ego (ego-instincts*) and those which are antagonistic to it (*ichwidrig*) or dystonic (*nicht ichgerecht*) and consequently repressed. In the context of the first theory of the instincts, whereas the ego-instincts are ego-syntonic by definition, the sexual instincts, whenever they turn out to be irreconcilable with the ego, are bound to be repressed.

The expression 'ego-syntonic' implies a view of the ego as total, integrated, ideal – as it is defined, for example, in 'On Narcissism: An Introduction' (1914c) (see 'Ego'). This implication is present too in Ernest Jones's use of the term: he contrasts *ego-syntonic* and *ego-dystonic* tendencies according to whether or not they are 'consonant, compatible and consistent with the standards of the self' (3).

(1) Cf. FREUD, S. 'Two Encyclopaedia Articles' (1923a), G.W., XIII, 222; S.E., XVIII, 246.

(2) Cf. FREUD, S. 'On Narcissism: An Introduction' (1914c), G.W., X, 167; S.E., XIV, 99.

(3) JONES, E. *Papers on Psycho-Analysis*, 5th edn. (London: Baillière, Tindall & Cox, 1950; Baltimore: Williams & Wilkins, 1949), 497.

Electra Complex

= *D.*: Elektrakomplex. – *Es.*: complejo de Electra. – *Fr.*: complexe d'Électre. – *I.*: complesso di Elettra. – *P.*: complexo de Electra.

Term used by Jung as a synonym for the feminine Oedipus complex in order to bring out the existence of a parallel, *mutatis mutandis*, in the attitudes of the two sexes towards the parents.

Jung introduced the expression 'Electra complex' in *The Theory of Psycho-Analysis* (1913) (1). Freud immediately declared that he was unable to see the usefulness of such a term (2); in his article on 'Female Sexuality' (1931b) he is more categorical: the feminine Oedipus complex, he asserts, is not analogous to the male one. 'It is only in the male child that we find the fateful combination of love for the one parent and simultaneous hatred of the other as a rival' (3).

Freud's rejection of this term, which assumes an analogy between the girl's and the boy's positions *vis-à-vis* their parents, is justified by his findings on the differing effects of the castration complex in the two sexes, on the importance for the girl of the preoedipal attachment to the mother, and on the predominance of the phallus in both sexes.

(1) JUNG, C. G. 'Versuch einer Darstellung der psychoanalytischen Theorie', *Jahrbuch für psychoanalytische und psychopathologische Forschungen*, 1913, V, 370. Trans.: *The Theory of Psycho-Analysis* (New York, 1915).

(2) FREUD, S. 'The Psychogenesis of a Case of Female Homosexuality' (1920a), G.W., XII, 281n; S.E., XVIII, 155n.

(3) FREUD, S., G.W., XIV, 521; S.E., XXI, 229.

Eros

The same Greek word is used in the various languages.

Term used by the Greeks to designate love and the god of Love. Freud employs it in his final instinct theory to connote the whole of the life instincts as opposed to the death instincts.

The reader is referred to the entry 'Life Instincts'; our remarks here will be confined to the use of 'Eros' to designate these instincts.

Freud's concern to relate his conceptions about instincts to general philosophical notions is well known – witness the 'popular' contrast between love and hunger in the first theory, and the Empedoclean one in the final version between φιλία and νεῖκος (love and discord).

Freud refers several times to the Platonic Eros, an idea which he sees as very close to what he understands by *sexuality**; he had in fact emphasised from the start that sexuality was not identical in his eyes with the genital function (1). Those criticisms which claim that Freud brings everything down to sexuality (as commonly understood) do not stand up once this confusion has been dispelled: 'sexual' should be used according to Freud 'in the sense in which it is now commonly employed in psycho-analysis – in the sense of "Eros" ' (2).

Conversely, Freud did not omit to point up the possible disadvantage to the term 'Eros' if it were used to camouflage sexuality. Consider the following passage, for example: 'Anyone who considers sex as something mortifying and humiliating to human nature is at liberty to make use of the more genteel expressions "Eros" and "erotic". I might have done so myself from the first and thus have spared myself much opposition. But I did not want to, for I like to avoid concessions to faintheartedness. One can never tell where that road may lead one; one gives way first in words, and then little by little in substance too' (3). The fact is that using the term 'Eros' risks reducing the import of sexuality in favour of its sublimated manifestations.

If, from *Beyond the Pleasure Principle* (1920g) onwards, Freud readily uses 'Eros' as a synonym for 'life instinct', he does so in order to insert his new theory of the instincts into a philosophical and mythical tradition of universal scope (e.g. Aristophanes's myth in Plato's *Symposium*). Thus Eros is conceived of as what, 'by bringing about a more and more far-reaching combination of the particles into which living substance is dispersed, aims at complicating life and at the same time, of course, at preserving it' (4).

'Eros' is generally used to connote the life instincts when these are being considered in a deliberately speculative way – in a statement such as the following, for instance: 'Our speculations have transformed this opposition [between libidinal instincts and destructive instincts] into one between the life instincts (Eros) and the death instincts' (5*a*).

What is the relationship between *Eros* and *Libido**? When Freud introduces Eros in *Beyond the Pleasure Principle*, he appears to identify the two terms: '. . . the libido of our sexual instincts would coincide with the Eros of the poets and philosophers which holds all living things together' (5*b*). It is worth noting that both these words are borrowed from dead languages and signal a theoretical concern reaching beyond the field of analytic experience (α). This said, however, the fact remains that Freud had always used the term 'libido' in an economic context, and that he continued to do so after his introduction of Eros. 'Libido' designates the energy of the sexual instincts: in *An Outline of Psycho-Analysis* (1940*a* [1938]), for instance, Freud evokes 'the total available energy of Eros, which henceforward we shall speak of as "libido" ' (6).

(α) In this connection it is worth quoting a sentence from the *Studies on Hysteria* (1895*d*) where Breuer uses 'Eros' to denote a daemonic force: 'The girl senses in Eros the terrible power which governs and decides her destiny and she is frightened by it' (7).

(1) Cf. for example FREUD, S. *Three Essays on the Theory of Sexuality*, preface of 1920, G.W., V, 31–32; S.E., VII, 133–34.

(2) FREUD, S. *The Interpretation of Dreams* (1900*a*), note added 1925, G.W., II–III, 167; S.E., IV, 161.

(3) FREUD, S. *Group Psychology and the Analysis of the Ego* (1921*c*), G.W., XIII, 99; S.E. XVIII, 91.

(4) FREUD, S. *The Ego and the Id* (1923*b*), G.W., XIII, 269; S.E., XIX, 40.

(5) FREUD, S.: a) G.W., XIII, 66*n*.; S.E., XVIII, 61*n*. b) G.W., XIII, 54; S.E., XVIII, 50,

(6) FREUD, S., G.W., XVII, 72; S.E., XXIII, 149.

(7) BREUER, J., 1st German edn., 216; S.E., II, 256.

Erotogenic

= *D.*: erogen.–*Es.*: erógeno.–*Fr.*: érogène.–*I.*: erogeno.–*P.*: erógeno.

Related to the production of a sexual stimulus.

This epithet is most frequently used in the expression 'erotogenic zone'*, but it is also found in such terms as 'erotogenic masochism', 'erotogenic activity', etc.

Erotogenic (or Erogenous) Zone

= *D.*: erogene Zone.–*Es.*: zona erogena.–*Fr.*: zone erogene.–*I.*: zona erogena.– *P.*: zona erogena.

Any region of the skin or mucous membrane capable of being the seat of an excitation of a sexual nature.
More specifically, one of those areas which are by function the seat of such excitation: the oral, anal, genital and mamillary zones.

The theory of the erotogenic zones, first outlined by Freud in letters to Fliess dated December 6, 1896 and November 14, 1897, has scarcely undergone any change since its presentation in *Three Essays on the Theory of Sexuality* (1905*d*) (1*a*). Any region of the skin or mucous membrane may operate as an erotogenic zone, and later on Freud even extended the property known as erotogenicity* to all internal organs (2); '. . . in fact the whole body is an erotogenic zone' (3). There are certain zones, however, that seem 'predestined' for this function. Thus in the case of the activity of sucking, the erotogenic role of the oral zone is physiologically determined; in thumbsucking, the thumb plays a part in the sexual excitation as 'a second erotogenic zone, though of an inferior kind' (1*b*). The erotogenic zones are sources* of different component instincts (auto-erotism*). It is they which determine, with varying degrees of specificity, certain types of sexual aim*.

Although the existence and predominance of definite bodily zones in human sexuality remains a fundamental datum of psycho-analytic experience, any account of this fact in merely anatomical and physiological terms is inadequate. What has to be given consideration too is that these zones, at the beginnings of psychosexual development, constitute the favoured paths of exchange with the surroundings, while at the same time soliciting the most attention, care–and consequently stimulation–from the mother (4).

(1) FREUD, S.: a) Cf. G.W., V, 83–85; S.E., VII, 183–84. b) G.W., V, 83; S.E., VII, 182.

(2) Cf. FREUD, S. 'On Narcissism: An Introduction' (1914*c*), G.W., X, 150; S.E., XIV, 84.

(3) FREUD, S. *An Outline of Psycho-Analysis* (1940*a* [1938]), G.W., XVII, 73; S.E., XXIII, 151.

(4) Cf. LAPLANCHE, J. and PONTALIS, J.-B. 'Fantasme originaire, fantasmes des origines, origine du fantasme', *Les temps modernes*, 1964, no. 215, 1833–68. Trans.: 'Fantasy and the Origins of Sexuality', *I.J.P.*, 1968, 49, 1 *ff*.

Erotogenicity (or Erogenicity)

= *D*.: Erogeneität.–*Es*.: erogeneidad.–*Fr*.: érogénéité.–*I*.: erogeneità.–*P*.: erogeneidade.

The capacity of all bodily regions to be the source of a sexual excitation, that is, to behave like an erotogenic zone*.

This term, which is little used, was coined by Freud in 'On Narcissism: An Introduction' (1914*a*) (1). This text defines erotogenicity as that sexual activity of which a particular part of the body is capable (2).

Freud's purpose in using a specific term to denote this 'excitability' (*Erregbarkeit*) is to point out that it is not the special privilege of the particular erotogenic zone where it is most in evidence, but rather a general property of the entire surface of the skin and mucous membrane–and even of the internal organs.

Erotogenicity is conceived of by Freud as a quantitative factor capable of increase and decrease, or of being affected by displacements in its distribution within the organism. In his view such modifications account, for example, for the symptoms of hypochondria.

155

(1) Cf. FREUD, S., G.W., X, 150; S.E., XIV, 84.

(2) Cf. also FREUD, S. *Three Essays on the Theory of Sexuality* (1905d), note added in 1915, G.W., V, 85; S.E., VII, 184.

Experience of Satisfaction

= *D.*: Befriedigungserlebnis.–*Es.*: vivencia de satisfacción.–
  Fr.: expérience de satisfaction.–*I.*: esperienza di soddisfacimento.–
  P.: vivência de satisfação.

Type of primal experience postulated by Freud, consisting in the resolution, thanks to an external intervention, of an internal tension occasioned in the suckling by need. The image of the satisfying object subsequently takes on a special value in the construction of the subject's desire. This image may be recathected in the absence of the real object (hallucinatory satisfaction of the wish). And it will always guide the later search for the satisfying object.

The concept of the experience of satisfaction has no wide currency in psychoanalysis, but it seemed to us that defining it would cast light on some Freudian views which are, for their part, classical and essential. Freud describes and analyses the experience of satisfaction in the 'Project for a Scientific Psychology' (1950a [1895]), and he also refers to it several times in Chapter VII of *The Interpretation of Dreams* (1900a).

The experience of satisfaction is connected with 'the initial helplessness* (*Hilflosigkeit*) of human beings' (1a). The organism is incapable of bringing about the specific action* needed to get rid of the tension that has arisen as a result of the release of endogenous stimuli; this action has therefore to be carried out with the help of an outside person (who, for example, brings food), and only then can the tension be removed.

Over and above this immediate result, the experience has several consequences:

a. Satisfaction is henceforward associated with the image of the object which has procured it, and also with the motor image of the reflex movement which has permitted the discharge. When the state of tension recurs, the image of the object is recathected: '. . . in the first instance this wishful activation will produce the same thing as a perception–namely a *hallucination*. If reflex action is thereupon introduced, disappointment cannot fail to occur' (1b).

At such an early stage, of course, the subject is not equipped to determine that the object is not really there. A cathexis of the image which is too intense produces the same 'indication of reality' as a perception.

b. This experience as a whole–the real satisfaction and the hallucinatory one–constitutes the basis of desire. In fact the wish, though it originates with a search for actual satisfaction, is constituted on the model of the primitive hallucination.

c. The formation of the ego offsets the subject's initial failure to distinguish between hallucination and perception. Thanks to the ego's inhibitory function, the recathexis of the image of the satisfying object is prevented from being too intense.

It is in analogous terms that Freud describes the experience of satisfaction and its consequences in *The Interpretation of Dreams*, but he introduces two new conceptions here: *perceptual identity** and *thought-identity*. He argues that what the subject seeks, whether by direct paths (hallucination) or by indirect ones (action guided by thought), is invariably an identity with 'the perception which was linked with the satisfaction of the need' (2).

In the later writings no explicit mention is made of the experience of satisfaction. It is clear, however, that Freud always continued to make the assumptions on which that notion is founded. The reader is referred, more especially, to the beginning of the article 'Formulations on the Two Principles of Mental Functioning' (1911*b*) and to the paper on 'Negation' (1925*h*). In the latter text, Freud emphasises yet again the irreducible character of primal satisfaction and its decisive role in the subsequent search for objects: '. . . a precondition for the setting up of reality-testing* is that objects shall have been lost which once brought real satisfaction' (3).

The experience of satisfaction–both real and hallucinatory–is the fundamental notion in the Freudian problematic of satisfaction, for it embodies the conjunction of the gratification of needs and the *fulfilment of wishes** (see 'Wish' and 'Phantasy').

(1) FREUD, S. 'Project for a Scientific Psychology' (1950*a* [1895]): a) *Anf.*, 402; S.E., I, 318. b) *Anf.*, 404; S.E., I, 319.

(2) FREUD, S., G.W., II–III, 571; S.E., V, 565.

(3) FREUD, S. 'Negation' (1925*h*), G.W., XIV, 14; S.E., XIX, 238.

F

Facilitation

= *D.*: Bahnung.–*Es.*: facilitación.–*Fr.*: frayage.–*I.*: facilitazione.–*P.*: facilitação.

Term used by Freud at a time when he was putting forward a neurological model of the functioning of the psychical apparatus (1895): the excitation, in passing from one neurone to another, runs into a certain resistance; where its passage results in a permanent reduction in this resistance, there is said to be facilitation; excitation will opt for a facilitated pathway in preference to one where no facilitation has occurred.

Failure Neurosis (or Syndrome)

The notion of facilitation is central to the description of the 'neuronal apparatus' proposed by Freud in his 'Project for a Scientific Psychology' (1950a [1895]). Jones points out that the idea played an important part in Exner's book published a year previously, *Project for a Physiological Explanation for Psychical Phenomena* (*Entwurf au einer physiologischen Erklärung der psychischen Erscheinungen*, 1894) (1). Though he had not abandoned it, Freud makes scant use of the concept in his metapsychological writings. It does recur, however, when he is brought once again–in *Beyond the Pleasure Principle* (1920g)–to use a physiological model (2).

(1) Cf. JONES, E. *Sigmund Freud*, I, 417.
(2) Cf. FREUD, S., G.W., XIII, 26; S.E., XVIII, 26.

Failure Neurosis (or Syndrome)

= *D.*: Misserfolgsneurose.–*Es.*: neurosis de fracaso.–*Fr.*: névrose d'échec.–
I.: nevrosi di scacco.–*P.*: neurose de fracasso.

Term introduced by René Laforgue which has a very wide application: it denotes the psychological structure of a whole variety of subjects, ranging from those patients who, in a general way, seem to be the artisans of their own misfortunes, to those who cannot bear to obtain the very thing that they had appeared to desire the most ardently.

When psycho-analysts speak of failure neurosis, it is failure as a *consequence* of neurotic maladjustment that they have in mind rather than failure as a precipitating *cause* of neurosis (where the disturbance is a reaction to actual failure).

The notion of failure neurosis is associated with the name of René Laforgue, who devoted numerous works to the function of the super-ego, to the mechanism of self-punishment and to the psychopathology of failure (1). Laforgue enumerated many kinds of failure syndrome observable in the emotional and social life of either individuals or social groups–family, class, ethnic group–and sought a common basis for them in the action of the super-ego.

In psycho-analysis, the term 'failure neurosis' is used descriptively rather than nosographically.

Generally speaking, failure is the price paid for every neurosis, in so far as the symptom implies a restriction of the subject's potentialities–a partial block to his energies. But failure neurosis is only evoked in those cases where failure is not just the corollary of the symptom (as in the phobic subject who sees his capacity for movement limited by his precautionary measures), but where it constitutes the symptom itself and so calls for a special explanation.

In 'Some Character-Types Met with in Psycho-Analytic Work' (1916d), Freud had drawn attention to the particular type of subject who is 'wrecked by success', but his treatment of the problem of failure is more restricted than Laforgue's:

158

a. Freud is concerned with subjects whose inability to tolerate satisfaction relates to one particular matter, which is obviously bound up with their unconscious wishes.

b. The case of such individuals presents the following paradox: whereas the external frustration* was not pathogenic, the actual possibility of fulfilling the wish turns out to be intolerable and precipitates 'internal frustration'–the subject denies himself satisfaction.

c. This mechanism does not in Freud's view constitute a neurosis, nor even a syndrome; it is rather one type of precipitating cause of neurosis, and a first symptom of the illness.

In *Beyond the Pleasure Principle* (1920g) Freud relates certain kinds of neurotic failure to the compulsion to repeat*–particularly what he calls the fate compulsions (see 'Fate Neurosis').

(1) Cf. LAFORGUE, R. *Psychopathologie de l'échec* (Paris: Payot, 1939).

(2) Cf. FREUD, S., G.W., X, 372; S.E., XIV, 317–18.

Family Neurosis

= *D*.: Familienneurose.–*Es*.: neurosis familiar.–*Fr*.: névrose familiale.–
I.: nevrosi familiare.–*P*.: neurose familial.

Term used to indicate the fact that individual neuroses, in a given family, complement and condition one another; its use is further intended to point up the pathogenic influence which the family structure may exert over the children (principally the influence of the parental couple).

The term 'family neurosis' has been used for the most part by French-speaking psycho-analysts, in the wake of René Laforgue (1). As these authors say themselves, this neurosis does not constitute a nosological entity.

The term brings together, in a somewhat figurative way, a number of fundamental psycho-analytic conclusions: the central role of identification with the parents in the constitution of the subject, the Oedipus complex as the nuclear complex of neurosis, the important part played by the relationship between the parents in the genesis of the Oedipus complex, and so on. René Laforgue places particular emphasis on the pathogenic influence of a parental couple whose own relationship is based on a certain neurotic compatibility (as in the case of a sado-masochistic couple).

Family neurosis is not invoked in the main, however, as a means of stressing the importance of the environment, but rather in order to underline the role played by each member of the family in a network of unconscious inter-relations (often referred to as the family 'constellation'). The term's chief utility is in the orientation of the psychotherapeutic approach to children, the child's place in the 'constellation' being ascertained from the outset. From a practical point of view, this may lead the psychotherapist not only to attempt to intervene directly in the child's environment, but also to attribute the parent's request for the child to undergo treatment to the family neurosis (in which case the child is seen as in some sense a 'symptom' of the parents).

According to Laforgue the notion of family neurosis derives from the Freudian conception of the super-ego, as expressed in the following passage: '. . . a child's super-ego is in fact constructed on the model not of its parents but of its parents' super-ego; the contents which fill it are the same and it becomes the vehicle of tradition and of all the time-resisting judgements of value which have propagated themselves in this manner from generation to generation' (2).

Present-day psycho-analysts scarcely ever speak of family neurosis. Although the term has the merit of drawing attention to the complementarity of the functions of the various subjects within an unconscious field, its use can encourage an underemphasis on the role of each subject's specific phantasies in favour of a manipulation of the concrete family situation, as though this were an essential determinant of the neurosis.

(1) LAFORGUE, R. 'À propos de la frigidité de la femme', *R.F.P.*, 1935, VIII, 2, 217–26; 'La névrose familiale', *R.F.P.*, 1936, IX, 3, 327–55.

(2) FREUD, S. *New Introductory Lectures on Psycho-Analysis* (1933a), G.W., XV, 73; S.E., XXII, 67.

Family Romance

= *D.*: Familienroman.–*Es.*: novela familiar.–*Fr.*: roman familial.–*I.*: romanzo familiare.– *P.*: romance familial.

Term coined by Freud as a name for phantasies whereby the subject imagines that his relationship to his parents has been modified (as when he imagines, for example, that he is really a foundling). Such phantasies are grounded in the Oedipus complex.

Before devoting an article to them (1909c) (α), Freud had already drawn attention on several occasions to phantasies of a particular type, by means of which the subject invents a new family for himself and in so doing works out a sort of romance (1). Such phantasies are found in a manifest form in paranoiac delusions. Freud was not long in finding them in neurotics in a variety of forms: the child imagines that he was not born of his real parents, but rather of noble ones; or that his father was noble and–to explain this–that his mother has had secret love affairs; or again, that while he is legitimate his brothers and sisters are bastards.

Such phantasies are related to the Oedipal situation–they originate from the pressure exerted by the Oedipus complex*. The precise motives for them are many and mixed; the desire to denigrate the parents from one angle while exalting them from another, notions of grandeur, attempts to circumvent the incest barrier, an expression of fraternal rivalry, etc.

160

(α) Originally incorporated into Otto Rank's *Der Mythus von der Geburt des Helden* (Leipzig and Vienna, 1909). Translation: *The Myth of the Birth of the Hero* (New York, 1914).

(1) Cf. FREUD, S. *Anf.*, Draft M and letter dated June 20, 1898, 219 and 273; S.E., I, 250 and *Origins*, 256.

Fate Neurosis

= *D.*: Schicksalsneurose. – *Es.*: neurosis de destino. – *Fr.*: névrose de destinée. – *I.*: nevrosi di destino. – *P.*: neurose de destino.

This term designates a type of life-pattern characterised by the periodic recurrence of identical chains of – generally unfortunate – events. The subject appears to be the victim of these chains of events, as though they were willed by some external fate, but psycho-analysis teaches that their origin is to be found in the unconscious and, more specifically, in the compulsion to repeat*.

It is at the end of Chapter III of *Beyond the Pleasure Principle* (1920g) (1) that Freud refers, as an example of repetition, to the case of those people who give the impression 'of being pursued by a malignant fate or possessed by some "daemonic" power' (benefactors repeatedly repaid by ingratitude, men invariably betrayed by their friends, and so on). It is worth noting that in speaking of these cases Freud uses the term 'fate compulsion' (*Schicksalszwang*) rather than 'fate neurosis'. The latter, however, has prevailed, no doubt as a result of the extension of psycho-analysis to the so-called 'asymptomatic' neuroses – character neurosis*, failure neurosis*, etc. At all events, the term's value is descriptive not nosographical.

The idea of fate neurosis could easily be taken in a very broad sense: the course of every life-history might be treated as having been 'arranged by the subject in advance'; but if the concept is generalised in this way it is liable to lose even its descriptive value: it would come to connote everything in the behaviour of an individual which is recurrent – or even constant.

It would seem possible to give a more precise meaning to the term 'fate neurosis', and so to differentiate it, in particular, from 'character neurosis', while remaining faithful to Freud's indications in the above-cited passage. The fact is that the examples given by Freud show that his only aim in evoking the 'fate compulsion' is to account for experiences which are relatively specific:

a. They are repeated despite their unpleasant character.

b. They unfold according to an unchanging scenario, and constitute a sequence of events which may imply a lengthy temporal evolution.

c. They appear to be governed by an external fate, whose victim the subject feels himself – with seeming justification – to be. (Freud gives the example of a woman who married three times, only to see each successive husband fall ill soon afterwards and to have to nurse them all on their deathbeds.)

In such cases the repetition can be recognised in a discernible pattern of events. We may say, as a pointer, that in the case of fate neurosis the subject has no access to an unconscious wish, which he thus first encounters coming back at him as it were, from the outside world (whence the 'daemonic' aspect stressed by Freud). In character neurosis, by contrast, it is the compulsive repetition of defence mechanisms and behaviour patterns which is responsible for, and reveals itself in, the rigid maintenance of a particular form (character-trait).

(1) FREUD, S., G.W., XIII, 20–21; S.E., XVIII, 21–22.

Father Complex

= *D*.: Vaterkomplex.–*Es*.: complejo paterno.–*Fr*.: complexe paternel.– *I*.: complesso paterno.–*P*.: complexo paterno.

Term used by Freud to designate one of the chief dimensions of the Oedipus complex*: the ambivalent relation to the father.

Fixation

= *D*.: Fixierung.–*Es*.: fijación.–*Fr*.: fixation.–*I*.: fissazione.–*P*.: fixação.

The fact that libido attaches itself firmly to persons or imagos, that it reproduces a particular mode of satisfaction, that it retains an organisation that is in accordance with the characteristic structure of one of its stages of development. A fixation may be manifest and immediate or else it may be latent – a potentiality constituting the likeliest avenue to a regression that is open to the subject.

The notion of fixation is usually understood within the framework of a general approach presupposing an ordered development of the libido (fixation at a stage*). It may also be viewed, aside from any genetic reference, in the context of the Freudian theory of the unconscious, as a name for the mode of inscription of certain ideational contents (experiences, imagos, phantasies) which persist in the unconscious in unchanging fashion and to which the instinct remains bound.

The idea of fixation is repeatedly encountered in the psycho-analytic doctrine as a way of accounting for a clear empirical fact, namely that the neurotic – or generally speaking any human subject – is marked by childhood experiences and retains an attachment, disguised to a greater or lesser degree, to archaic modes of satisfaction, types of object and of relationship. Psycho-analytic treatment provides evidence of the strength and the repetition of past experiences as it does of the subject's resistance to releasing himself from their grip.

The concept of fixation itself contains no principle of explanation, but its descriptive value is incontestable. For this reason Freud was able to call upon it at all the various stages in the development of his thinking on the subject of what it is in the subject's history that lies at the source of neurosis. Thus he was able to characterise his first aetiological views as essentially bringing into play the idea of a 'fixation to the trauma'* (1a, 2). With the *Three Essays on the Theory of Sexuality* (1905d), fixation is tied in with the theory of the libido and defined as the persistence – especially evident in the perversions – of anachronistic sexual traits: the subject seeks particular kinds of activity or else remains attached to certain properties of 'the object' whose origin can be traced to some specific occasion in the sexual life of his childhood. Although the importance of the trauma is not denied, its role is seen here against the background of a series of sexual experiences which tend to facilitate fixation at a determinate point.

With the development of the theory of the libidinal stages* – particularly the pregenital* stages – the idea of fixation gains in extension: it need not now apply merely to a partial libidinal aim* or object* but instead to the entire structure of the activity characterising one particular stage (see 'Object-Relationship'). Thus fixation at the anal stage* is said to be at the root of obsessional neurosis and of a certain character-type.

In *Beyond the Pleasure Principle* (1920g) (3) Freud has further occasion to refer to the notion of fixation to the trauma: here it is one of the facts which, since they are not fully explained by the persistence of a libidinal mode of satisfaction, oblige him to postulate the existence of a compulsion to repeat*.

Libidinal fixation plays a predominant part in the aetiology of the various forms of mental disturbance, and it has been necessary to clarify its function in neurotic mechanisms:

Fixation is the basis of *repression** and may even be treated as the first stage of repression in a broad sense: 'The libidinal current [which has undergone fixation] behaves in relation to later psychological structures like one belonging to the system of the unconscious, like one that is repressed' (4a). This 'primal repression'* determines repression in the strict sense of the term, which is only made possible by the concerted action, upon the elements destined to be repressed, of a force of repulsion exerted by a higher agency and an attraction exerted by what has already been fixated (5a).

At the same time fixation prepares the points to which that *regression** is going to occur which is met with, under its various aspects, in the neuroses, the perversions and the psychoses.

The *preconditions* for fixation, for Freud, are of two kinds: in the first place, it is brought about by different historical factors (influence of the family configuration, trauma, etc.). Secondly, it is facilitated by constitutional factors: one partial instinctual component may be more powerful than another one; furthermore, there may exist in certain individuals a general 'adhesiveness'* of the libido (1b) which predisposes them to defend 'any position of the libido [...] once taken up [...] from fear of what [they] would lose by giving it up and from mistrust of the probability of a complete substitute being afforded by the new position that [is] in view' (6).

*   *   *

Fixation is often invoked by psycho-analysis but its nature and meaning are ill-defined. Freud at times uses the concept in a descriptive way – as he does the concept of regression. In his most explicit texts fixation is compared to specific biological phenomena in which relics of ontophylogenetic evolution survive

163

in the adult organism. From this genetic standpoint, therefore, what we are dealing with here is an 'inhibition in development', a genetic abnormality, a 'passive lagging behind' (4*b*).

This conception originates and is most at home in the study of the perversions. A first inspection does seem to confirm that certain patterns of behaviour may subsist unchanged within the subject so that he is able to call upon them again. And certain perversions which develop in continuous fashion from childhood onwards even appear to exemplify a fixation evolving into a symptom without our needing to assume the existence of any intermediary regression.

All the same, as advances are made in the theory of the perversions, it becomes doubtful whether these can be said to furnish a model of fixation as nothing more than the survival of an archaic element of development. The fact that conflicts and mechanisms akin to those of neurosis are to be found at the root of the perversions suffices to cast doubt upon the apparent simplicity of the notion of fixation (see 'Perversion').

          *   *   *

The specifically psycho-analytic use of the notion of fixation, as distinct from notions such as that of the survival of anachronistic behaviour patterns, may be brought out by considering the ways in which Freud makes use of the term. Schematically, we may say that he speaks at times of fixation *of* (e.g. fixation of a memory, of a symptom), and at other times of fixation (of the libido) *to* or *at* (a stage, a type of object, etc.). The first of these senses suggests a use of the term compatible with the one accepted by a psychological theory of memory distinguishing between different stages: fixation, conservation, evocation and recognition of the particular memory. It will be noted, however, that for Freud fixation in this sense is understood in a very realistic way: he envisages an actual inscription or registration (*Niederschrift*) of traces in series of mnemic systems–traces which may be 'transposed' from one system to another. As early as a letter to Fliess dated December 6, 1896, a whole theory of fixation had been worked out: 'If a later transcript is lacking the excitation is dealt with in accordance with the psychological laws in force in the earlier psychical period and along the paths open at that time. Thus an anachronism persists: in a certain province *fueros* [ancient laws continuing to apply in particular towns or regions of Spain] are still in force, we are in the presence of "survivals" ' (7). Further, this concept of a fixation *of* ideas* correlates with the concept of a fixation of excitation *to* these ideas. This view of the matter is a fundamental part of the Freudian perspective and it is best formulated in the most complete presentation of the theory of repression that Freud ever gave: 'We have reason to assume that there is a *primal repression*, a first phase of repression, which consists in the physical (ideational) representative of the instinct being denied entrance into the conscious. With this a *fixation* is established; the representative in question persists unaltered from then onwards and the instinct remains attached to it' (5*b*).

The genetic meaning of fixation is certainly not lost in a formulation such as this, but its basis is sought in primal moments at which certain privileged ideas are indelibly inscribed in the unconscious, and at which the instinct itself becomes fixated to its psychical representative*–perhaps by this very process constituting itself *qua* instinct*.

(1) FREUD, S. *Introductory Lectures on Psycho-Analysis* (1916–17): a) G.W., XI, 282 *ff.*; S.E., XVI, 273 *ff.* b) Cf. G.W., XI, 360–61; S.E., XVI, 348.

(2) FREUD, S. 'Five Lectures on Psycho-Analysis' (1910*a*), G.W., VIII, 12; S.E., XI, 17.

(3) Cf. FREUD, S., G.W., XIII, 10; S.E., XVIII, 13.

(4) FREUD, S. 'Psycho-Analytic Notes on an Autobiographical Account of a Case of Paranoia (Dementia Paranoides)' (1911*c*): a) G.W., VIII, 304; S.E., XII, 67. b) G.W., VIII, 304; S.E., XII, 67.

(5) FREUD, S. 'Repression' (1915*d*): a) Cf. G.W., X, 250–51; S.E., XIV, 148. b) G.W., X, 250; S.E., XIV, 148.

(6) FREUD, S. 'From the History of an Infantile Neurosis' (1918*b* [1914]), G.W., XII, 151; S.E., XVII, 115.

(7) FREUD, S., S.E., I, 235.

Flight into Illness

= *D.*: Flucht in die Krankheit.–*Es.*: huída en la enfermedad.–*Fr.*: fuite dans la maladie.–*I.*: fuga nella malattia.–*P.*: fuga para a doença *or* refúgio na doença.

Figurative expression evoking the fact that the subject looks to neurosis as a means of escaping from his psychical conflicts.

The spread of psycho-analysis has given this expression wide currency; today it has come to be applied not only to the field of the neuroses but also to that of organic illnesses where a psychological factor can be shown to be present.

Freud used such expressions as 'flight into psychosis' (1) and 'flight into neurotic illness' (2) before finally settling on 'flight into illness' (3, 4).

The dynamic notion of flight into illness expresses the same idea as the economic notion of gain from illness. Whether the two terms have exactly the same extension it is difficult to decide–the more so since the subdivision of the gain from illness into a primary and a secondary gain is itself hard to define (see 'Gain from Illness'). Freud apparently looks upon flight into illness as an aspect of the primary gain, but at times the expression is used in a broader sense. At all events what this concept is intended to illustrate is that the subject seeks to evade a situation of conflict which is generating tension, and to achieve a reduction of this tension through the formation of symptoms.

(1) FREUD, S. 'The Neuro-Psychoses of Defence' (1894*a*), G.W., I, 75; S.E., III, 59.

(2) FREUD, S. ' "Civilized" Sexual Morality and Modern Nervous Illness' (1908*d*), G.W., VII, 155; S.E., IX, 192.

(3) FREUD, S. 'Some General Remarks on Hysterical Attacks' (1909*a*), G.W., VII, 237; S.E., IX, 231.

(4) FREUD, S. 'Fragment of an Analysis of a Case of Hysteria' (1905*e* [1901]), G.W., V, 202, note 1 added in 1923; S.E., VII, 43*n*.

Foreclosure (Repudiation)

= *D.*: Verwerfung.–*Es.*: repudio.–*Fr.*: forclusion.–*I.*: reiezione.–*P.*: rejeição *or* repúdio.

Term introduced by Jacques Lacan denoting a specific mechanism held to lie at the origin of the psychotic phenomenon and to consist in a primordial expulsion of a fundamental 'signifier' (e.g. the phallus as signifier of the castration complex) from the subject's symbolic* universe. Foreclosure is deemed to be distinct from repression in two senses:

a. Foreclosed signifiers are not integrated into the subject's unconscious.

b. They do not return 'from the inside'–they re-emerge, rather, in 'the Real', particularly through the phenomenon of hallucination.

Lacan, invoking the way in which Freud sometimes uses the term '*Verwerfung*' (repudiation) when referring to psychosis, has proposed '*forclusion*' as the French equivalent.

Lacan's claim of Freudian lineage for this concept calls for comments of two kinds; these concern Freud's terminology and his conception of psychotic defence.

I. A survey of terminology covering the whole of Freud's writings permits the following conclusions to be drawn:

a. Freud uses the term '*Verwerfung*'–and the verbal form '*verwerfen*'–in somewhat disparate senses. Schematically, these meanings may be reduced to three:

(i) The fairly loose sense of a refusal which may operate, for instance, in the mode of repression (1).

(ii) The sense of a repudiation in the form of a conscious judgement of condemnation. In this case, it is most often the compound word '*Urteils-verwerfung*' that Freud employs; he indicates himself that this is synonymous with '*Verurteilung*' (judgement of condemnation*).

(iii) The sense brought to the fore by Lacan, best exemplified in other texts of Freud's. In 'The Neuro-Psychoses of Defence' (1894*a*), for instance, Freud writes apropos of psychosis: 'There is, however, a much more energetic and successful kind of defence. Here, the ego rejects (*verwirft*) the incompatible idea together with its affect and behaves as if the idea had never occurred to the ego at all' (2*a*).

The work from which Lacan has most readily derived support for his promotion of the idea of foreclosure is the case-history of the 'Wolf Man', in which the words '*verwerfen*' and '*Verwerfung*' are to be met with several times. The most telling passage from this point of view is no doubt the one where Freud evokes the coexistence of a number of different attitudes in the subject towards castration: '. . . a third current, the oldest and deepest, [which had purely and simply repudiated (*verworfen*) castration, and] which did not as yet even raise the question of the reality of castration, was still capable of coming into activity. I have elsewhere reported a hallucination which this same patient had at the age of five . . .' (3*a*).

166

b. Apart from '*Verwerfung*', other *terms* are encountered in Freud's work which are used in a sense that would seem, from their context, to authorise their being linked with the *concept* of foreclosure:

> *Ablehnen*, to fend off, to decline (3*b*);
> *Aufheben*, to suppress, to abolish (4*a*);
> *Verleugnen*, to disavow.

To sum up: it may be observed, from a purely terminological standpoint, that in the Freudian usage the term '*Verwerfung*' does not always have the same denotation as 'foreclosure' for Lacan; inversely, other Freudian terms do designate the concept which Lacan wishes to establish.

II. Over and above this strictly terminological approach, it is possible to show that Lacan's introduction of the term 'foreclosure' does constitute the furtherance of a constant injunction of Freud's–the injunction, namely, to define a defence mechanism specific to psychosis. Here, Freud's choice of terms may sometimes lead us astray, particularly when he speaks of 'repression' in connection with psychosis. He pointed to this ambiguity himself: ' . . . a doubt must occur to us whether the process here termed repression has anything at all in common with the repression which takes place in the transference neuroses' (5).

a. Such a train of thought as this regarding psychosis can be traced right the way through Freud's work. In the early writings, it comes out markedly in the discussion on the mechanism of projection, this being understood in the case of the psychotic as a literal and immediate expulsion into the external world and not as a secondary return of the unconscious repressed material. Subsequently, when Freud comes to interpret projection as a mere secondary stage of neurotic repression, he is obliged to admit that–*in this sense*–projection can no longer be looked upon as the essential factor in psychosis: 'It was incorrect to say that the perception which was suppressed (*unterdrückt*) internally is projected outwards; the truth is rather, as we now see, that what was abolished (*das Aufgehobene*) internally returns from without' (4*b*) (see 'Projection').

The expressions 'withdrawal of cathexis from the external word' (4*c*) and 'loss of reality' (6) should also be taken as referring to this *primary* mechanism of separation from and expulsion of the intolerable 'perception' into the outside world.

Finally, in his last works, Freud's thinking centres upon the notion of *Verleugnung*, 'disavowal of reality' (q.v.). Although he studies this mainly in the case of fetishism, he points out explicitly that the presence of such a mechanism here means that this perversion is comparable to psychosis (7, 8*a*). The disavowal which is the common response of the child, the fetishist and the psychotic to the supposed 'reality' of the absence of the penis in the woman is understood as a refusal to admit the 'perception' itself and–*a fortiori*–to draw the inevitable conclusion from it and accept the 'infantile sexual theory' of castration. In 1938, Freud postulates two opposed modes of defence: 'rejection of an instinctual demand from the internal world' and 'disavowal of a portion of the real external world' (8*b*). In 1894, he had already described psychotic defence in almost identical terms: 'The ego breaks away from the incompatible idea; but the latter is inseparably connected with a piece of

167

reality, so that, in so far as the ego achieves this result, it, too, has detached itself wholly or in part from reality' (2*b*).

b. How, in the last reckoning, are we to understand this sort of 'repression' into the external world which is held to be diametrically opposed to neurotic repression? Freud generally describes it in economic terms, speaking of a decathexis of what is perceived, a narcissistic withdrawal of libido possibly accompanied by a withdrawal of the non-libidinal 'interest'*. On other occasions, he seems to be led rather to posit what might be called a withdrawal of significance–a refusal to lend meaning to what is perceived. These two explanations, moreover, were not mutually exclusive for Freud: the withdrawal of cathexis (*Besetzung*) is also a withdrawal of significance (*Bedeutung*) (9).

III. The notion of foreclosure comes as an extension of this line of thought of Freud's within the framework of Lacan's theory of the 'symbolic'*. Lacan bases himself in particular on the passages in the case-history of the 'Wolf Man' where Freud shows how the perceptions made at the moment of the primal scene are only given meaning and interpreted as the result of a 'deferred action'*. In this case, the subject was unable, on the occasion of his first traumatic experience at the age of one and a half, to work out the supposedly brute fact of his mother's lack of a penis in the form of a theory of castration: 'He rejected (*verwarf*) castration, and held to his theory of intercourse by the anus. [...] This really involved no judgement upon the question of its existence, but it was the same as if it did not exist' (3*c*).

An ambiguity certainly exists, in the different Freudian texts, as to what it is that is repudiated (*verworfen*) or disavowed (*verleugnet*) when the child rejects castration. Is it castration itself (3*d*)? If so, then it is an actual theoretical interpretation of the facts–and not a perception–that is repudiated. Or is it a matter of the woman's 'lack of a penis'? In that case, we are still left with a problem, for how can we speak of a 'perception' being disavowed when an *absence* is only a fact of perception in so far as it is related to a possible *presence*?

Lacan's interpretation can be said to clear the way for a solution to these problems. Taking Freud's paper on 'Negation' (1925*h*) as a basis, he defines foreclosure in terms of its relation to a 'primary process' (10) embodying two complementary operations: 'the *Einbeziehung ins Ich*, introduction into the subject, and the *Ausstossung aus dem Ich*, expulsion from the subject'. The first of these operations is what Lacan also calls 'symbolisation' or 'primary' *Bejahung* (postulation, affirmation); the second 'constitutes the Real inasmuch as this is the domain which subsists outside symbolisation'. So foreclosure consists in not symbolising what ought to be symbolised (castration): it is a 'symbolic abolition'. Whence Lacan's formula for the hallucination, which is a translation into his own language of the passage of Freud which we quoted above ('It was incorrect to say . . .'): '. . . what has been foreclosed from the Symbolic reappears in the Real'.

Lacan has since developed the notion of foreclosure in relation to linguistic concepts in his article 'D'une question préliminaire à tout traitement possible de la psychose' (11).

(1) Cf. for example FREUD, S. *Three Essays on the Theory of Sexuality* (1905*d*), G.W., V, 128; S.E., VII, 227.

(2) FREUD, S.: a) G.W., I, 72; S.E., III, 58. b) G.W., I, 73; S.E., III, 59.

(3) FREUD, S. 'From the History of an Infantile Neurosis' (1918*b* [1914]): a) G.W., XII, 117; S.E., XVII, 85. b) Cf. G.W., XII, 49; S.E., XVII, 25. c) G.W., XII, 117; S.E., XVII, 84. d) Cf. G.W., XII, 117; S.E., XVII, 85.

(4) FREUD, S. 'Psycho-Analytic Notes on an Autobiographical Account of a Case of Paranoia' (1911*c*): a) Cf. G.W., VIII, 308; S.E., XII, 71. b) G.W., VIII, 308; S.E., XII, 71. c) G.W., VIII, 307; S.E., XII, 70.

(5) FREUD, S. 'The Unconscious' (1915*e*), G.W., X, 31; S.E., XIV, 203.

(6) Cf. FREUD, S. 'The Loss of Reality in Neurosis and Psychosis' (1924*e*), G.W., XIII, 363–68; S.E., XIX, 183–87.

(7) Cf. for example FREUD, S. 'Fetishism' (1927*e*), G.W., XIV, 310–17; S.E., XXI, 152–57.

(8) FREUD, S. *An Outline of Psycho-Analysis* (1940*a* [1938]): a) Cf. G.W., XVII, 132 *ff.*; S.E., XXIII, 201 *ff.* b) G.W., XVII, 135; S.E., XXIII, 204.

(9) FREUD, S. 'Neurosis and Psychosis' (1924*b* [1923]), G.W., XIII, 389; S.E., XIX, 150–51.

(10) LACAN, J. 'Réponse au commentaire de Jean Hyppolite sur la "Verneinung" de Freud', *La Psychanalyse*, 1956, I, 46. In *Écrits* (Paris: Seuil, 1966), 387–88.

(11) *La Psychanalyse*, 1959, IV, 1–50. In *Écrits* (Paris: Seuil, 1966), 531–83.

Free Association (Method or Rule of)

= *D.*: freie Assoziation.–*Es.*: asociación libre.–*Fr.*: libre association.–*I.*: libera associazione.–*P.*: associação livre.

Method according to which voice must be given to all thoughts without exception which enter the mind, whether such thoughts are based upon a specific element (word, number, dream-image or any kind of idea at all) or produced spontaneously.

The procedure of free association is fundamental to psycho-analytic technique. No precise date can be given as that of its discovery, for it was developed gradually, between 1892 and 1898, from a number of different angles.

a. As the *Studies on Hysteria* (1895*d*) show, free association emerged from preanalytical methods of investigation of the unconscious which relied on suggestion and on the patient's concentrating his mind on a given idea; this persistent search for the pathogenic factor gave way to an emphasis on the patient's spontaneous self-expression. The *Studies on Hysteria* bring out the part played by the patients themselves in this development (α).

b. Meanwhile, Freud was making use of the technique of free association in his self-analysis–especially in the analysis of his dreams. In this context it is an element of the dream which serves as starting-point for the discovery of the chains of association leading to the dream-thoughts.

c. The experiments of the Zurich school (1) followed up the earlier ones of the Wundt school from a psycho-analytic point of view. The Wundt research consisted in a study of reactions–and of the time taken to react, as a function of subjective states–to stimuli-words. What Jung brought out was that associations produced in this way are determined by 'the totality of the ideas related to a specific event that is laden with emotional overtones' (2): to this totality he gives the name 'complex'*.

169

Free Association (Method or Rule of)

In 'On the History of the Psycho-Analytic Movement' (1914*d*), Freud acknowledges the usefulness of these experiments which had made it 'possible to arrive at rapid experimental confirmation of psycho-analytic observations and to demonstrate directly to students certain connections which an analyst would only have been able to tell them about' (3).

d. Perhaps a further source should also be borne in mind—one to which Freud himself drew attention in 'A Note on the Prehistory of the Technique of Analysis' (1920*b*): the writer Ludwig Börne, whom Freud read in his youth, recommended writing down everything which came to mind as a way of 'becoming an original writer in three days' and criticised the effects of self-censorship upon intellectual production (4).

*   *   *

The 'free' in 'free association' calls for the following remarks:

a. Even where a starting-point is provided by a word serving as a stimulus (Zurich experiments) or by a dream element (Freud's method in *The Interpretation of Dreams* [1900*a*]), it is still possible to look upon the unfolding of associations as 'free' so long as it is not steered and controlled by any considerations of selection.

b. This 'freedom' is greater, nevertheless, when no point of departure is stipulated. In that event, the rule of free association is identical with the fundamental rule*.

c. Freedom is not to be understood here, in fact, as implying any absence of determination: the first goal of the rule of free association is the elimination of the voluntary selection of thoughts—or, in the terminology of Freud's first topography, the incapacitation of the *second censorship* (between the conscious and the preconscious). In this way the unconscious defences are revealed—that is, the operation of the *first censorship* (between the preconscious and the unconscious).

Lastly, the free-association method is meant to bring out a determinate order of the unconscious: '. . . when conscious purposive ideas* (*Zielvorstellungen*) are abandoned, concealed purposive ideas assume control of the current of ideas' (5).

(α) Cf. particularly what Freud tells us of his patient Frau Emmy von N.: in answer to Freud's insistent inquiry about the origin of a symptom, she replied that he 'was not to keep on asking her where this and that came from, but to let her tell [him] what she had to say' (6*a*). Of this same patient Freud remarks that 'it is as though she had adopted my procedure'. 'Nor is her conversation [...] so aimless as would appear. On the contrary, it contains a fairly complete reproduction of the memories and new impressions which have affected her since our last talk, and it often leads on, in a quite unexpected way, to pathogenic reminiscences of which she unburdens herself without being asked to' (6*b*).

(1) Cf. JUNG, C. G. *Diagnostische Assoziationsstudien* (1906).

(2) JUNG, C. G. and RICKLIN, F. *Diagnostische Assoziationsstudien, I Beitrag: Experimentelle Untersuchungen über Assoziationen Gesunder* (1904), 57*n*.

(3) FREUD, S., G.W., X, 67; S.E., XIV, 28.

(4) FREUD, S., G.W., XII, 311; S.E., XVIII, 265.

(5) FREUD, S., G.W., II–III, 536; S.E., V, 531.

(6) FREUD, S. *Studies on Hysteria* (1895*d*): a) G.W., I, 116; S.E., II, 63. b) G.W., I, 108; S.E., II, 56.

Free Energy/Bound Energy

= *D.*: freie Energie/gebundene Energie.–*Es.*: energía libre/energía ligada.–
Fr.: énergie libre/énergie liée.–*I.*: energia libera/energia legata.–
P.: energia livre/energia ligada.

Terms connoting the Freudian distinction between the primary and secondary processes when viewed from the economic standpoint. In the primary process, the energy is said to be free or mobile inasmuch as it flows towards discharge in the speediest and most direct fashion possible; in the secondary process, on the other hand, it is bound in that its movement towards discharge is checked and controlled. Genetically speaking, the free state of energy is seen by Freud as prior to the bound one, and the latter is said to be characteristic of a more advanced stage in the structuring of the psychical apparatus.

Freud explicitly attributes the distinction between free and bound energy to Breuer (1, 2). In fact, however, it should be noted that the terms used are not Breuer's, and furthermore that the distinction which Breuer introduced does not have the same meaning as Freud's.

Breuer's antithesis is grounded on the distinction established by physics between two kinds of mechanical energy, whose sum, in an isolated system, remains constant. Helmholtz, for example, whose influence on Breuer's and Freud's thinking is well known, sets up an opposition between 'living forces' (*'lebendige Kräfte'*–a term borrowed from Leibniz) and 'tensile forces' (*'Spannkräfte'*), that is, 'forces which tend to set a point M in motion for as long as they have as yet failed to cause any movement' (3). This opposition parallels the one introduced by other authors during the nineteenth century between actual and potential energy (Rankine), or between kinetic and static energy (Thomson): Breuer refers explicitly to this distinction, and to the terms used by these physicists.

Breuer is mainly concerned to define a kind of potential energy, present in the nervous system, which he calls 'intracerebral tonic excitation', 'nervous tension' or 'quiescent' energy. Just as a reservoir contains a certain quantity of potential energy by virtue of the fact that it holds back the water, so 'the whole immense network [of nerve-fibres] forms a single reservoir of "nervous tension" ' (4a). This tonic excitation is derived from a variety of sources: the nerve-cells themselves, external excitation, excitations originating within the body (physiological needs), and 'psychical affects'. It is put to use or discharged through the various sorts of activity (motor, intellectual, etc.).

Breuer holds that there exists an optimum level of this quiescent energy which permits a good reception of external excitations, the association of ideas and a free circulation of the energy within the whole network of pathways in the nervous system. This is the level that the organism endeavours to keep constant or to re-establish (see 'Principle of Constancy'). There are in fact two sets of circumstances in which it fails to achieve this end: either the nervous energy is exhausted, in which case the organism enters the state of sleep, which permits a recharge of energy, or else the level is too high. Such a rise *above* the

171

optimum level may itself be either generalised and uniform (states of intense expectation) or, alternatively, unevenly spread, as when affects emerge whose energy can be neither discharged nor distributed over the system as a whole by means of associative working over* (it is in this context that Breuer speaks of 'strangulated affects').

It may be seen from the above that:

a. Although Breuer distinguishes between 'quiescent' and 'kinetic' energy, he sees either of these two types as being susceptible of transformation into the other.

b. Kinetic energy enjoys no priority, either from a genetic or from a logical point of view; the Freudian distinction between the primary and secondary processes is apparently alien to Breuer's approach.

c. For Breuer, it is the quiescent state of nervous energy that is fundamental, since it is only after a certain level has been reached that energy can circulate freely. The rift between Breuer and Freud is here strikingly apparent: Breuer, for example, believes that in sleep, when quiescent energy is at a very low level, the free circulation of excitation is *blocked* (4b).

d. Breuer's conception of the principle of constancy differs from Freud's (see 'Principle of Constancy', 'Principle of Neuronal Inertia').

*   *   *

We are thus obliged to conclude that it was indeed Freud who introduced the two antithetical epithets 'free' and 'bound' as applied to psychical energy. It is worth bearing in mind that these were also borrowed from Helmholtz, although the original context in this case was the *second* principle of thermodynamics (gradual loss of energy); 'free energy' Helmholtz defined as that energy which 'is capable of being transformed into other sorts of work', while 'bound energy' was seen by him as the kind 'which can only manifest itself in the form of heat' (5).

This distinction does not correspond exactly to the one between static (or tonic) energy and kinetic energy, for the latter opposition takes only mechanical energy into consideration, whereas that between free and bound energy is taken to apply to different sorts of energy–calorific, chemical, etc.–and to the conditions that make the transition from one kind to another possible or not. Helmholtz's static energy could nevertheless be said to be free in that it is transformable into other kinds of energy, while kinetic energy (or, at least, the kinetic energy of disordered molecular movements) is bound. It thus becomes apparent that by giving the name of bound energy to Breuer's quiescent or tonic energy, and that of free energy to what Breuer called kinetic energy, Freud in effect reversed the meanings that these terms have in physics: by 'free' Freud means not freely *transformable* but rather freely *mobile* (*frei beweglich*).

To recapitulate:

a. The pair of opposites evoked by Breuer (tonic and kinetic energy) is taken from a theory which does not take the second principle of thermodynamics into account. Freud, on the contrary, employs terms ('free' and 'bound' energy) which had appeared in the context of this second principle.

b. Freud, despite the fact that he had a close acquaintance with the conceptions of the Physicalist School (Helmholtz, Brücke), inverts the meanings of these terms borrowed from physics so that they correspond roughly to Breuer's distinction.

c. Despite this apparent correlation, however, Freud's view is in fact completely different from Breuer's, since Freud holds that free energy, being characteristic of the unconscious processes, has *priority* over bound energy. This profound difference of perspective is reflected particularly in the ambiguous formulation of the principle of constancy.

*   *   *

The contrast between two kinds of energy-flow is to be met with in the 'Project for a Scientific Psychology' (1950a [1895]). In the case of the primary functioning of the neuronal apparatus, Freud argues, energy tends towards immediate and total discharge (principle of neuronal inertia); in the secondary process, on the other hand, the energy is bound, that is, it is contained within particular neurones or a particular neuronal system and accumulates there. The conditions making for this binding of energy are, first, the existence of 'contact-barriers' between neurones, which block or restrict the passage of energy from one to the other, and, secondly, the action of a group of neurones which are cathected at a constant level (the ego) upon the other processes which occur within the apparatus: this is what Freud calls side-cathexis (*Nebenbesetzung*), which is the basis of the ego's inhibitory function (6a).

The special case of a 'bound' functioning of energy is illustrated, according to Freud, by the process of thought, which combines the strong cathexis presupposed by attention with the displacement of only small quantities of energy which is essential if thought is to occur at all (6b). This current may be weak in quantitative terms but it circulates easily precisely for that reason: '. . . when the level is high, small quantities can be displaced more easily than when it is low' (6c).

Freud takes up the distinction between free and bound energy once more in *The Interpretation of Dreams* (1900a), although no further reference is made to supposedly distinct states of the neurones; and he always maintains subsequently that this is the economic expression of the basic antithesis between the primary and the secondary process* (see 'Binding').

(1) Cf. for example, FREUD, S. 'The Unconscious' (1915e), end of chapter IV, G.W., X; S.E., XIV.

(2) Cf. for example, FREUD, S. *Beyond the Pleasure Princple* (1920g), G.W., XIII, 26; S.E., XVII, 26–27.

(3) HELMHOLTZ, H. *Über die Erhaltung der Kraft* (Leipzig: Engelmann, 1847), 12.

(4) BREUER, J. and FREUD, S. *Studies on Hysteria* (1895d): a) 1st German edn., 169n.; S.E., II, 194n. b) Cf. German, 168; S.E., II, 192–93.

(5) HELMHOLTZ, H. 'Über die Thermodynamik chemischer Vorgänge' (1882), in *Abhandlungen zur Thermodynamik chemischer Vorgänge* (Leipzig: Engelmann, 1902), 18.

(6) FREUD, S.: a) Cf. Part I, chapter IV. b) Cf. 1st German edn., 447; S.E., I, 368. c) German, 451; S.E., I, 372.

Fright

= *D.*: Schreck.–*Es.*: susto.–*Fr.*: effroi.–*I.*: spavento.–*P.*: susto *or* pavor.

Reaction to a situation of danger, or to very intense external stimulus, which takes the subject by surprise when he is in such a state of unreadiness that he is at a loss either to protect himself against it or to master it.

In *Beyond the Pleasure Principle* (1920g) Freud proposes the following definition: ' "Fright" (*Schreck*), "fear" (*Furcht*) and "anxiety" (*Angst*) are improperly used as synonymous expressions; they are in fact capable of clear distinction in their relation to danger. "Anxiety" describes a particular state of expecting the danger or preparing for it, even though it may be an unknown one. "Fear" requires a definite object of which to be afraid. "Fright", however, is the name we give to the state a person gets into when he has run into danger without being prepared for it; it emphasizes the factor of surprise' (1a).

The difference between fright and anxiety lies in the fact that the first is characterised by unreadiness for danger, whereas 'there is something about anxiety that protects its subject against fright' (1b). It is in this sense that Freud recognises fright as a determining factor of traumatic neurosis, which he even refers to on occasion as '*Schreckneurose*' or 'fright neurosis' (see 'Trauma', 'Traumatic Neurosis').

It should not surprise us therefore that the notion of fright has an important part to play starting from the formative period of the traumatic conception of neurosis. In Breuer's and Freud's earliest theoretical expositions the affect of fright is described as a condition that paralyses mental life, prevents abreaction and fosters the formation of a 'separate psychical group' (2a, 2b). When Freud attempts–in 1895–97–to work out an initial theory of the trauma and sexual repression, the idea of the subject's unpreparedness is essential–as much in dealing with the 'scene of seduction' that occurs before puberty as with the evocation of this scene on a later occasion (see 'Deferred Action', 'Scene of Seduction'). 'Sexual fright' (*Sexualschreck*) connotes an irruption of sexuality into the subject's life.

Generally speaking we may say that the meaning of 'fright' does not vary in Freud's work. It will be noted, however, that the expression tends to be used less frequently after *Beyond the Pleasure Principle*. The opposition that Freud has tried to establish between anxiety on the one hand and fright on the other will be encountered once more, though in the form now of distinctions *within* the concept of anxiety, especially in the contrast between an anxiety that arises 'automatically'* in a traumatic situation and anxiety as signal*, implying an attitude of active expectation (*Erwartung*) which serves as a protection against the development of anxiety proper: 'Anxiety is the original reaction to helplessness in the trauma and is reproduced later on in the danger-situation as a signal for help' (3).

(1) FREUD, S.: a) G.W., XIII, 10; S.E., XVIII, 12–13. b) G.W., XIII, 10; S.E., XVIII, 12–13.

(2) Cf. BREUER, J. and FREUD, S. *Studies on Hysteria* (1895d): a) G.W., I, 89–90; S.E., II, 11. b) 1st German edn., 192; S.E., II, 219–20.

(3) FREUD, S. *Inhibitions, Symptoms and Anxiety* (1926d), G.W., XIV, 199–200; S.E., XX, 166–67.

Frustration

= *D*.: Versagung.–*Es*.: frustración.–*Fr*.: frustration.–*I*.: frustrazione.–*P*.: frustração.

Condition of the subject who is denied, or who denies himself, the satisfaction of an instinctual demand.

Common usage, reinforced by the vogue enjoyed by the term 'frustration' in the English-language literature, has brought about a situation where the German '*Versagung*' is nearly always translated in this way. It is a rendering that deserves some comment:

a. Contemporary psychology, especially research on learning, tends to pair off frustration and gratification, defining them respectively as the condition of an organism subjected either to the absence or to the presence of a pleasurable stimulus. This approach may be said to coincide with certain of Freud's views –particularly with those where he appears to identify frustration with the absence of an external object capable of satisfying the instinct. It is in this sense that, in 'Formulations on the Two Principles of Mental Functioning' (1911b), he contrasts the instincts of self-preservation, which require an external object, with the sexual instincts, which can be satisfied for a long time auto-erotically and in the mode of phantasy: only the self-preservative instincts could, on this view, ever be said to be frustrated (1).

b. For the most part, however, the Freudian '*Versagung*' has other implications: it designates not only an empirical datum but also a relation implying a refusal (as is suggested by the root *sagen* which means 'to say') on the part of the agent and a requirement more or less formulated as a demand on the part of the subject.

c. 'Frustration' would seem to mean that the subject is passively frustrated, but '*Versagung*' in no way lays down *who* does the refusing. In some instances, in fact, the reflexive sense of to deny oneself, to forfeit, seems to predominate.

In our opinion these reservations (α) are lent sanction by various texts which Freud devoted to the concept of *Versagung*. In 'Types of Onset of Neurosis' (1912c) he uses the word to connote all obstacles, whether external or internal, which stand in the way of libidinal satisfaction. He makes a distinction between cases where neurosis is triggered off by a lack in the real world (loss of a love-object, for example) and cases where the subject, as a consequence of internal conflicts or of a fixation, denies himself the satisfactions that reality offers. For Freud *Versagung* is the concept that is best able to cover both these situations. If we bring together the various modes of neurosis-formation, therefore, we reach the conclusion that it is a *relation* that undergoes modification–a certain balance determined at once by external circumstances and by the particular characteristics of the individual.

175

Functional Phenomenon

In the *Introductory Lectures on Psycho-Analysis* (1916–17) Freud stresses the fact that an external deprivation is not pathogenic *per se* and does not become pathogenic except in so far as it affects 'the mode of satisfaction which alone the subject desires' (2).

The paradox presented by those subjects who fall ill at the very moment of achieving success (3) brings out the predominant role of 'internal frustration' –and here Freud goes a step farther: it is the actual satisfaction of his wish that the subject denies himself.

The upshot of these texts of Freud's is that it is not so much the lack of a real object which is at stake in frustration as the response to a demand that requires a given mode of satisfaction or that cannot be satisfied by any means.

From a technical point of view the idea that *Versagung* is the precondition of neurosis forms the basis of the rule of abstinence*; the point here is that the patient should be refused those substitute satisfactions which would appease his libidinal demands: the analyst, in other words, must maintain the frustration.

(α) Given the generality of its use and the difficulty of finding an equivalent which would apply in all cases irrespective of the context, we feel that 'frustration' remains the best rendering of '*Versagung*'.

(1) Cf. FREUD, S., G.W., VIII, 234–35; S.E., XII, 222–23.

(2) FREUD, S., G.W., XI, 357; S.E., XVI, 345.

(3) FREUD, S. 'Some Character-Types Met with in Psycho-Analytic Work' (1916*d*), G.W., X, 364–91; S.E., XIV, 316–31.

(4) Cf. FREUD, S. 'Lines of Advance in Psycho-Analytic Therapy' (1919*a* [1918]), G.W., XII, 183–94; S.E., XVII, 159–68.

Functional Phenomenon

= *D*.: funktionales Phänomen.–*Es*.: fenómeno funcional.–*Fr*.: phénomène fonctionnel.– *I*.: fenomeno funzionale.–*P*.: fenômeno funcional.

Phenomenon discovered by Herbert Silberer (1909) in hypnagogic states and later found by him to be operative in dreams. The functional phenomenon is the transposition into images not of the *content* of the subject's thought but of its present *mode* of operation.

There is an evolution in Silberer's thinking on the subject of the functional phenomenon.

His point of departure was the study of hypnagogic states, which in his view afforded a unique opportunity to observe the birth-process of symbols (the 'auto-symbolic' phenomenon). Silberer distinguishes three kinds of phenomena here: *material* ones, where what is symbolised is the thing on which thought is focussed–i.e. its object; *functional* ones, where what is represented is the functioning of thought at the time–its rapidity or slowness, success or failure, etc.; and *somatic* ones, where it is bodily impressions that are symbolised (1).

For Silberer this categorisation holds for every manifestation in which symbols are involved—especially dreams. Leaving only the symbolisation of the objects of thought and representation under the head of the 'material phenomenon', he eventually categorises as functional phenomena everything which symbolises 'the state, activity or structure of the psyche' (2*a*). Affects, tendencies, intentions, complexes, 'parts of the mind' (especially the censorship*) —all are translated into symbols, and often personified. Clearly Silberer is here generalising to the extreme the idea of a symbolic representation of the *hic-et-nunc* state of consciousness as it creates images.

Lastly, Silberer believes that in symbolism, and above all in dreams, there is a tendency to progress from the material to the functional—a trend towards generalisation, 'away from any particular given theme towards the whole of all those themes that are comparable in affect, or, to put it another way, towards the mental type of the lived event in question' (2*b*). Hence a long thin object that to start with symbolises a phallus may end up (after a series of increasingly abstract intermediate stages) standing for the feeling of potency or power in general. On this view, therefore, the *spontaneous* orientation of the symbolic phenomenon points in the same direction as *anagogic interpretation**—which thus serves merely to strengthen this orientation.

Freud acknowledged the functional phenomenon to be 'one of the few indisputably valuable additions to the theory of dreams. [...] Silberer has [...] demonstrated the part played by observation—in the sense of the paranoic's delusions of being watched—in the formation of dreams' (3). Freud was convinced by the experimental nature of Silberer's discovery, but he restricted the scope of the functional phenomenon to states between sleeping and waking or—in dreams—to 'the dreamer's own perception of his sleeping and waking', which occurs occasionally and which Freud attributes to the *dream censor*, or super-ego.

Freud is critical of the extension taken on by this notion: some people, he writes, 'speak of the functional phenomenon whenever intellectual activities or emotional processes occur in the dream-thoughts, although such material has neither more nor less right than any other kind to find its way into a dream as residues of the previous day' (4). Aside from exceptional cases, therefore, Freud relegates the functional to the same status as bodily stimuli—to the status, that is, of *material*: Freud proceeds in just the opposite direction to Silberer.

For criticism of Silberer's widened conception of the functional phenomenon, the reader may profitably consult Jones's study on 'The Theory of Symbolism' (1916) (5).

(1) Cf. SILBERER, H. 'Bericht über eine Methode, gewisse symbolische Halluzinationserscheinungen hervorzurufen und zu beobachten', *Jahrbuch der Psychoanalyse*, 1909.

(2) SILBERER, H. 'Zur Symbolbildung', *Jahrbuch der Psychoanalyse*, 1909: a) IV, 610. b) IV, 615.

(3) FREUD, S. 'On Narcissism: An Introduction' (1914*c*), G.W., X, 164–65; S.E., XIV, 97.

(4) FREUD, S. *The Interpretation of Dreams* (1900*a*), G.W., II–III, 509; S.E., V, 505.

(5) In JONES, E. *Papers on Psycho-Analysis*. 5th edn. (London: Baillière, Tindall & Cox 1950), 116–37.

Fundamental Rule

= *D.*: Grundregel.–*Es.*: regla fundamental.–*Fr.*: règle fondamentale.–
I.: regola fondamentale.–*P.*: regra fundamental.

Rule which structures the analytic situation: the analysand is asked to say what he thinks and feels, selecting nothing and omitting nothing from what comes into his mind, even where this seems to him unpleasant to have to communicate, ridiculous, devoid of interest or irrelevant.

The fundamental rule makes the free-association* method the basic principle of psycho-analytic treatment. Freud often recalled the path which had led him from hypnosis to suggestion and thence to the institution of this rule. According to his own account, he 'endeavoured to insist on his *unhypnotised* patients giving him their associations, so that from the material thus provided he might find the path leading to what had been forgotten or fended off. He noticed later that the insistence was unnecessary and that copious ideas (*Einfälle*) almost always arose in the patient's mind, but that they were held back from being communicated and even from becoming conscious by certain objections put by the patient in his own way. It was to be expected [...] that everything that occurred to a patient (*alles, was dem Patienten einfiele*) setting out from a particular starting-point must also stand in an internal connection with that starting-point; hence arose the technique of educating the patient to give up the whole of his critical attitude and of making use of the material (*Einfälle*) which was thus brought to light for the purpose of uncovering the connections that were being sought' (1).

A characteristic of this passage deserving of note is Freud's use of the term '*Einfall*' (literally, what falls into the mind, what comes to mind, translated here by 'idea' in the absence of a better equivalent). This term is to be distinguished from '*Assoziation*', which refers to elements composing a chain–either the chain of logical argument or a chain of those associations which, though described as free, are none the less determined. '*Einfall*' designates all the ideas that come to the subject in the course of the analytic session, even where the associative links underlying them are not apparent, and even where they appear subjectively as unconnected with the context.

The effect of the fundamental rule is not that free rein is given to the primary process* to express itself in its pure form, so making possible immediate access to the unconscious chains of associations; all the application of the rule can do is facilitate the emergence of a type of communication in which the unconscious determinism is more accessible as a result of the exposure of fresh connections or of significant *lacunae* in the subject's discourse.

It was only gradually that the rule of free association came to appear *fundamental* to Freud. Thus in 'Five Lectures on Psycho-Analysis' (1910*a*), he enumerates three possible ways of reaching the unconscious and seems to look upon them as of equal status. These ways are the working out of the ideas of the subject who conforms to the main rule (*Hauptregel*), the interpretation of dreams, and the interpretation of parapraxes (2). The rule seems to be conceived of here as intended to assist the emergence of products of the unconscious by eliciting one type of meaningful material among others.

* * *

The fundamental rule has a number of consequences:

a. As the subject who has been asked to apply this rule gradually submits to it, he becomes committed to saying everything and *only* to saying it: his emotions, bodily impressions, ideas, memories–all are channelled into language. An unstated corollary of the rule, therefore, is that a particular portion of the subject's activity comes to be viewed as acting out*.

b. The observance of the rule reveals how the associations originate and the 'nodal points' where they intersect.

c. As has often been noted, the rule is also revealing in the very difficulties the subject runs into in applying it: these may be conscious reticences, or else unconscious resistances to the rule and *by means of* the rule–that is to say, resistances in the actual way in which the rule is used, as, for instance, when certain subjects resort systematically to jibberish, or exploit the rule mainly to show that to apply it strictly is impossible or absurd (α).

These remarks could be extended by emphasising the idea that the rule is more than a technique of investigation–it structures the whole analytic relationship; this is the sense in which it can be described as fundamental, despite the fact that it is not the only component of a situation where other factors–especially the neutrality* of the analyst–play decisive parts. All we shall say here–following Jacques Lacan–is that the fundamental rule contributes to the establishment of the intersubjective relationship between analyst and analysand as a *linguistic relation*. The rule of saying everything must not be taken simply as one method among others of gaining entry into the unconscious–a method that might conceivably be dispensed with at some future date (as was the case with hypnosis, narco-analysis, etc.). It is intended to precipitate the emergence, in the subject's discourse, of the dimension of demand addressed to another. Combined with the analyst's non-action, it brings the subject to formulate his demands in various modes which, at certain stages, have acquired the force of language for him (see 'Regression').

(α) Obviously, the rule of psycho-analysis does not urge the subject to speak in systematically incoherent terms, but simply to avoid making consistency a criterion of selection.

(1) FREUD, S. 'Two Encyclopaedia Articles' (1923a [1922]), G.W., XIII, 214; S.E., XVIII, 238.

(2) Cf. FREUD, S., G.W., VIII, 31; S.E., XI, 33.

(3) Cf. especially LACAN, J. 'La direction de la cure et les principes de son pouvõir', communication to the Colloque International, Royaumont, 1958, in *La Psychanalyse*, VI (Paris: P.U.F., 1961), 149–206. Also in *Écrits* (Paris: Seuil, 1966).

Fusion/Defusion (of Instincts)

= *D*.: Triebmischung/Triebentmischung.–*Es*.: fusión/defusión (de los instintos *or* instintiva).–
Fr.: union/désunion (*or* intrication/désintrication) des pulsions.–
I.: fusione/defusione (delle pulsioni).–*P*.: fusão/desfusão (dos impulsos *or* das pulsões).

Terms used by Freud within the framework of his final instinct theory to describe the relations between the life instincts* and the death instincts* viewed in their concrete manifestations.

The *fusion* of instincts is a true mixing in which each of the two components may be present in variable proportion; *defusion* signifies a process tending to produce a situation in which the two sorts of instincts would operate separately, each pursuing its own aim independent of the other.

It is Freud's final instinct theory, with its radical antithesis between life and death instincts, which raises the question: in a given piece of behaviour, in a given symptom, what are the respective contributions, and the form of association, of the two great classes of instincts? How do they interact, what dialectic operates between them, through the various stages of the subject's development?

It is understandable that it should have been the institution of this new instinctual dualism that induced Freud to envisage the balance of forces between the antagonistic instincts (α).

From this point on, the destructive tendencies are accorded the same force as sexuality; the two face each other on the same ground, and they are met with in forms of behaviour (sado-masochism*), in psychical agencies (super-ego*) and in types of object-relationship* that are accessible to psycho-analytic investigation.

All the same, it should be noted that Freud's approach to the problem of the fusion of the two great instincts does not put the two antagonists on an equal footing. When Freud speaks of defusion he refers–implicitly or explicitly –to the fact that *aggressiveness** has succeeded in breaking all ties with sexuality.

*　　*　　*

How should the fusion of two instincts be visualised? Freud showed no great concern to make this clear. Among the various ideas that play a part in the definition of the instincts, those of *object** and *aim** are above all relevant here. The convergence of two instincts that are distinct from each other in their dynamics upon one and the same *object* does not in itself seem adequate to define fusion; indeed the ambivalence implied by such a definition is in Freud's eyes the most striking illustration of a *defusion* or of a 'fusion that has not been completed' (1*a*). There has in addition to be a harmony of *aim*, a sort of synthesis whose specific tone is attributable to sexuality: 'It is our opinion [...] that in sadism and in masochism we have before us two excellent examples of a mixture of the two classes of instinct, of Eros* and aggressiveness; and we proceed to the hypothesis that this relation is a model one–that every instinctual impulse that we can examine consists of similar fusions or alloys of the two classes of instinct. These fusions, of course, would be in the most varied ratios.

Thus the erotic instincts would introduce the multiplicity of their sexual aims into the fusion, while the others would only admit of mitigations or gradations in their monotonous trend' (2). A similar train of thought brings Freud, in plotting the evolution of sexuality, to show how aggressiveness enters the service of the sexual instinct (3a).

Since the fusion of instincts is a mixture, Freud several times insists on the fact that Eros and aggressiveness may conceivably be present in any proportions, and one might say that there is a kind of complemental series* here: 'Modifications in the proportions of the fusion between the instincts have the most tangible results. A surplus of sexual aggressiveness will turn a lover into a sex-murderer, while a sharp diminution in the aggressive factor will make him bashful or impotent' (4a).

Conversely, defusion could be defined as the outcome of a process which restores independence of aim to each of the instincts concerned. This autonomy of the two great classes of instincts, which existed, according to Freud, at the mythical origins of the living being, can only be conceptualised as an extreme situation of which clinical experience can furnish merely approximations—these being pictured, generally speaking, as regressions vis-à-vis an ideal trend towards the more and more complete integration of aggressiveness into the sexual function. The ambivalence of obsessional neurosis is for Freud one of the best examples of the defusion of instincts (1b).

In the abstract, therefore, we might posit the existence of two complemental series: the first one, *quantitative* in nature, would be a function of the proportions of libido and aggressiveness fused together in each case; the second would register the variable *state* of fusion or defusion of the two instincts relative to each other. In reality, however, Freud considers these as two scarcely compatible ways of formulating the same idea. Libido and aggressiveness are not in fact to be looked upon as two diametrically opposed component elements. Libido, as we know, is in Freud's view a factor tending to bind* (*Bindung*)—and hence also to *fuse*; aggressiveness, on the other hand, tends by its very nature 'to undo connections' (4b). In other words, the more aggressiveness predominates, the more the instinctual fusion tends to disintegrate, while, conversely, the more the libido prevails, the more effective the fusion: '. . . the essence of a regression of libido (e.g. from the genital to the sadistic-anal phase) lies in a defusion of instincts, just as, conversely, the advance from the earlier phase to the definitive genital one would be conditioned by an accession of erotic components' (1c).

*   *   *

Freud used different terms in expounding the idea that death instincts and life instincts combine with each other: '*Verschmalzung*' (conjugation) (3b), '*Legierung*' (mixture) (5), '*sich kombinieren*' (to combine) (4c). But it was the pair '*Mischung*' (or '*Vermischung*') and '*Entmischung*' that he eventually decided upon, and that has passed into accepted psycho-analytic usage. '*Mischung*' means mixture (as of two liquids in given proportions); '*Entmischung*' means the separation of the elements of the mixture.

(α) We may note that from the moment when the hypothesis of an independent aggressive instinct was proposed in psycho-analysis, the need was felt for a concept connoting the alliance

181

of this instinct with the sexual one: Adler speaks of instinctual confluence (*Triebverschränkung*) to bring out the fact that 'the same object serves for the satisfaction of several instincts simultaneously' (6).

(1) FREUD, S. *The Ego and the Id* (1923*b*): a) G.W., XIII, 270; S.E., XIX, 42. b) Cf. G.W., XIII, 270; S.E., XIX, 42. c) G.W., XIII, 270; S.E., XIX, 42.

(2) FREUD, S. *New Introductory Lectures on Psycho-Analysis* (1933*a*), G.W., XV, 111–12; S.E., XXII, 104–5.

(3) FREUD, S. *Beyond the Pleasure Principle* (1920*g*): a) Cf. G.W., XIII, 57–58; S.E., XVIII, 53–54. b) Cf. G.W., XIII, 59; S.E., XVIII, 55.

(4) FREUD, S. *An Outline of Psycho-Analysis* (1940*a* [1938]): a) G.W., XVII, 71; S.E., XXIII, 149. b) G.W., XVII, 71; S.E., XXIII, 148. c) Cf. G.W., XVII, 71; S.E., XXIII, 149.

(5) Cf. FREUD, S. 'Two Encyclopaedia Articles' (1923*a*), G.W., XIII, 233; S.E., XVIII, 258–59.

(6) FREUD, S. 'Instincts and their Vicissitudes' (1915*c*), G.W., X, 215; S.E., XIV, 123.

G

Gain from Illness, Primary and Secondary

= *D*.: primärer und sekundärer Krankheitsgewinn.–
  Es.: beneficio primario y secundario de la enfermedad.–
  Fr.: bénéfice primaire et secondaire de la maladie.–
  I.: utile primario e secondario della malattia.–*P*.: lucro primário e secundário da doença.

In a general sense, 'gain from illness' covers all direct or indirect satisfaction that a patient draws from his condition.

The *primary* gain has a hand in the actual motivation of a neurosis: satisfaction obtained from the symptom, flight into illness*, beneficial change in the subject's relationship with the environment.

Secondary gain may be distinguished from the primary kind by:

a. Its appearance after the fact, in the shape of an extra advantage derived from an already established illness, or a new use to which such an illness is put.

b. Its extraneous character relative to the illness's original determinants and to the meaning of the symptoms.

c. The fact that the satisfactions involved are narcissistic or associated with self-preservation rather than directly libidinal.

From its beginnings the Freudian theory of neurosis is inseparable from the notion that the illness is brought on and maintained by virtue of the satisfaction it affords the subject. The neurotic process complies with the pleasure principle*: it seeks to reap an economic* benefit, to achieve a reduction in tension. The

182

existence of this gain is shown up by the subject's resistance to cure, which counters the conscious will to get better.

The distinction between primary and secondary gain, however, was not drawn by Freud till a late date—and then only in a rough and ready fashion. Thus to begin with, in his study of the 'Dora' case (1905e [1901]), Freud seems to take the view that the motives for the illness are always secondary to the formation of symptoms. The symptoms are said to have no economic function at first, and might enjoy but a transient existence if they did not become fixed as the result of a new development: 'Some psychical current or other finds it convenient to make use of it, and in that way the symptom manages to find a *secondary function* and remains, as it were, anchored fast in the patient's mental life' (1*a*).

Freud subsequently returned to the matter in his *Introductory Lectures on Psycho-Analysis* (1916–17) (2*a*), and in a rectification added to the 'Dora' case-history (1*b*):

The 'primary gain' is bound up with the actual determination of the symptoms. Freud distinguishes between two aspects of it: first, there is an 'internal element in the primary gain' which consists in the reduction of tension achieved by the symptom. However painful the symptom may be, its aim is to free the subject from sometimes even more painful conflicts: here we have the mechanism known as 'flight into illness'. Secondly, the 'external element in the primary gain' is thought of as linked to the changes wrought by the symptom in the subject's interpersonal relationships. Thus a woman 'subjugated by her husband' is able, thanks to her neurosis, to procure more affection and attention while simultaneously getting her own back for the bad treatment she has received.

But Freud's recourse to such epithets as 'accidental' and 'external' to describe this second aspect of the primary gain betrays his discomfiture when he seeks to mark it off clearly from the *secondary* gain.

To describe this secondary gain, Freud refers to the case of traumatic neurosis, and even evokes an instance of physical infirmity resulting from an accident. The secondary gain has here taken the form of an income assured by the disablement—a powerful motive working against recovery: 'If you could put an end to his injury you would make him, to begin with, without means of subsistence; the question would arise of whether he was still capable of taking up his earlier work again' (2*b*).

It is easy, from this simple example, to identify the three defining characteristics of the secondary gain (see our definition above). Yet it must be said that even in a case such as this questions should be raised (as present-day research urges us to do) about the unconscious motives for the accident. And surely the distinctions are even harder to preserve when it comes to neurosis—especially non-traumatic neurosis. A gain obtained at a second juncture in time, and seemingly extraneous, may in reality have been foreseen and aimed for when the symptom was being triggered. As for the objective aspect of the secondary gain, this often merely masks its deeply libidinal nature: the allowance granted the invalid, for example—to come back to Freud's illustration—may be symbolically related to a dependency of the child-mother type.

The topographical* standpoint is perhaps the one which best enables us to understand what is covered by the term 'secondary gain', for it allows us to view the agency of the ego in its tendency–or 'compulsion' even–towards synthesis (see 'Ego'). Freud tackles the problem in the third chapter of *Inhibitions, Symptoms and Anxiety* (1926*d*), where the idea of secondary gain is illuminated by means of a comparison with the 'secondary defensive struggle' which the ego undertakes, not against the wish directly but against an already constituted symptom. Secondary defence and secondary gain emerge as two modalities of the ego's response to that 'foreign body' which the symptom is initially: 'The ego now proceeds to behave as though it recognized that the symptom had come to stay and that the only thing to do was to accept the situation in good part and draw as much advantage from it as possible' (3). Within this secondary gain from illness, which amounts to a veritable incorporation of the symptom into the ego, Freud distinguishes between advantages derived from the symptom which serve the interests of self-preservation and satisfactions that are truly narcissistic in character.

It may be noted in conclusion that invocation of the secondary gain ought not to stand in the way of a search for motives tied more directly to the dynamics of the neurosis. The same applies in the case of those psycho-analytic treatments where the concept of secondary gain is called upon to explain why the patient seems to get more satisfaction from the maintenance of a transference situation than he does from being cured.

(1) FREUD, S. 'Fragment of an Analysis of a Case of Hysteria': a) G.W., V, 203; S.E., VII, 43. b) Cf. G.W., V, 202-3, *n*. 1; S.E., VII, 43, *n*. 1.

(2) FREUD, S.: a) Cf. G.W., XI, 395 *ff*.; S.E., XVI, 381 *ff*. b) G.W., XI, 399; S.E., XVI, 384.

(3) FREUD, S., G.W., XIV, 126; S.E., XX, 99.

Generation of Anxiety

= *D.*: Angstentwicklung.–*Es.*: desarollo de angustia.–*Fr.*: développement d'angoisse.– *I.*: sviluppo d'angoscia.–*P.*: desenvolvimento de angústia.

Expression coined by Freud which denotes anxiety viewed in its temporal development as it increases in the individual.

This term is to be met with on several occasions in Freud's writings, particularly in the *Introductory Lectures on Psycho-Analysis* (1916–17) and in *Inhibitions, Symptoms and Anxiety* (1926*d*). It is a descriptive term which takes on its full meaning within the framework of a theory of anxiety which distinguishes between a traumatic situation where the anxiety cannot be controlled (automatic anxiety*), and anxiety as a signal* intended to ward off automatic anxiety. The 'generation of anxiety' means the process which, in cases where the signal-anxiety has not been effective, leads from the first to the second of these two moments.

Genital Love

= *D.*: genitale Liebe.–*Es.*: amor genital.–*Fr.*: amour génital.–*I.*: amore genitale.–
P.: amor genital.

Term much used in contemporary psycho-analytical parlance to designate that form of love achieved by the subject at the term of his psychosexual development, an achievement implying not only the accession to the genital stage but also the overcoming of the Oedipus complex.

The term 'genital love' is never used by Freud himself. All the same, he certainly does express the idea of a final form of sexuality–and even that of a 'completely normal attitude in love' (1*a*) which combines the trends of sensuality and 'affection' (*Zärtlichkeit*). The separation between these two currents is epitomised for Freud in that common psycho-analytic subject, the man who can not desire the woman he loves–or rather, idealises–nor love the woman he desires (the prostitute).

The evolution of the sensual current, described in *Three Essays on the Theory of Sexuality* (1905*d*), comes to an end with the genital organisation*: with puberty, 'a new sexual aim appears, and all the component instincts combine to attain it, while the erotogenic zones become subordinated to the primacy of the genital zone. [...] The sexual instinct is now subordinated to the reproductive function' (2).

As for affectionate feelings, Freud traces their origin back to the most primitive relationship between mother and child, to that primary object-choice in which sexual satisfaction and the satisfaction of vital needs operate indistinguishably in anaclisis* (see 'Affection').

*   *   *

In an article devoted to the question of genital love, Michael Balint (3*a*) notes that this is most often referred to negatively, just as Abraham's *post-ambivalent stage** is defined essentially by the absence of the characteristics of earlier stages.

Attempts to define genital love positively have difficulty avoiding a normative approach, and even fall into an openly moralistic language of comprehension of and respect for the other person, of devotion, of the ideal of marriage, etc.

As far as psycho-analytic theory is concerned, the notion of genital love justifies a number of questions and comments:

a. Genital satisfaction–whether it is attained by the subject, by his partner or by both–in no way implies the existence of love. On the other hand, love surely implies a bond going beyond genital satisfaction (3*b*).

b. A psycho-analytic conception of love, setting aside as it must any appeal to norms, cannot overlook the discoveries of psycho-analysis itself as regards love's genesis:

(i) as regards object-relationships*: incorporation*, mastery, fusion* with hate (4).

(ii) as regards the modalities of pregenital* satisfaction, to which genital satisfaction is inseparably linked;

185

Genital Stage or Organisation

(iii) as regards the object: the 'full object-love' of which Freud speaks is surely always marked by primary narcissism*, irrespective of whether the object-choice* in question is anaclitic or narcissistic proper. It was, after all, the 'erotic life of human beings' that furnished Freud with the basis for the introduction of the idea of narcissism* (5).

c. The current application of the notion of genital love often evokes the idea of a complete satisfaction of the instincts, and even of the resolution of all conflict. 'In a word,' one author has felt able to write, 'the genital relationship has no history' (6). There can be no doubt that such a view is in contradiction with the Freudian theory of sexuality as expressed, for example, in the following lines: '. . . we must reckon with the possibility that something in the nature of the sexual instinct itself is unfavourable to the realization of complete satisfaction' (1b).

d. It seems, broadly speaking, that the current use of the term 'genital love' confuses several levels which are not necessarily concordant: that of libidinal development, which is supposed to lead to the synthesis of the component instincts under the primacy of the genital organs; that of object-relationships, which presupposes the overcoming of the Oedipus complex; and, lastly, that of the individual encounter. It is a striking fact, moreover, that those authors who invoke genital love never fail to fall into the following contradiction: the love-object is conceived of as both *interchangeable* (since the 'genital' must of necessity find an object) and *unique* (since the 'genital' takes the singularity of the other person into account).

(1) FREUD, S. 'On the Universal Tendency to Debasement in the Sphere of Love' (1912d): a) G.W., VIII, 79; S.E., XI, 180. b) G.W., VIII, 89; S.E., XI, 188–89.

(2) FREUD, S., G.W., V, 108–9; S.E., VII, 207.

(3) Cf. BALINT, M. 'On Genital Love' (1947) in *Primary Love and Psychoanalytic Technique* (London: Hogarth, 1952): a) *passim*. b) *passim*.

(4) Cf. FREUD, S. 'Instincts and their Vicissitudes' (1915c), G.W., X, 230 *ff*.; S.E., XIV, 138 *ff*.

(5) Cf. FREUD, S. 'On Narcissism: An Introduction' (1914c), G.W., X, 153 *ff*.; S.E., XIV, 87 *ff*.

(6) BOUVET, M. in *La psychanalyse d'aujourd'hui* (Paris: P.U.F., 1956), I, 61.

Genital Stage or Organisation

= *D*.: genitale Stufe (*or* Genitalorganisation).–*Es*.: fase *or* organización genital.– *Fr*.: stade (*or* organisation) génital(e).–*I*.: fase (*or* organizzazione) genitale.– *P*.: fase (*or* organização) genital.

Stage of psychosexual development characterised by the organisation of the component instincts under the primacy of the genital zones. This organisation holds sway twice, its dominance being interrupted by the latency period*: first during the phallic phase* (infantile genital organisation) and subsequently at puberty, when genital organisation proper takes over.

Some authors restrict the term 'genital organisation' to this second period, classing the phallic phase among the pregenital* organisations.

186

As the first edition of the *Three Essays on the Theory of Sexuality* (1905*d*) shows, there was initially only one organisation of sexuality for Freud–the genital organisation which is instituted at puberty and which stands in opposition to the 'polymorphous perversity' and auto-erotism* of infantile sexuality. Subsequently, this first conception of Freud's undergoes gradual modification:

a. Pregenital organisations are described (1913, 1915–see 'Organisation of the Libido').

b. In an addition to the *Three Essays*–the section on 'The Phases of Development of the Sexual Organisation'–Freud evolves the idea that a sexual object-choice* is already made in childhood: '. . . the whole of the sexual currents have become directed towards a single person in relation to whom they seek to achieve their aims. This then is the closest approximation possible in childhood to the final form taken by sexual life after puberty. The only difference lies in the fact that in childhood the combination of the component instincts and their subordination under the primacy of the genitals have been effected only very incompletely or not at all. Thus the establishment of that primacy in the service of reproduction is the last phase through which the organisation of sexuality passes' (1).

c. The theory proposed in this last sentence is itself thrown into question with Freud's recognition of the existence, before the latency period, of a 'genital organisation' described as phallic, the sole difference between this phase and the postpubertal genital organisation being that in the first case a single genital organ is what counts for either sex–namely, the phallus* (1923–see 'Phallic Stage').

It will be seen that the evolution of Freud's ideas regarding psychosexual development pushed him constantly in the direction of an equation of infantile and adult sexuality. All the same, his original conception does not disappear: it is still with the genital organisation of puberty that the component instincts are definitively fused and ordered according to a hierarchy, that the pleasure attached to the non-genital erotogenic zones becomes 'preliminary' to orgasm, etc.

This is why Freud laid strong emphasis on the fact that infantile genital organisation is characterised by a disjunction between Oedipal demands and the degree of biological development reached.

(1) FREUD, S., G.W., V, 100; S.E., VII, 199.

(2) Cf. FREUD, S. 'The Dissolution of the Oedipus Complex' (1924*d*), G.W., XIII, 395–402; S.E., XIX, 173–79.

'Good' Object/'Bad' Object

= *D*.: 'gutes' Objekt/'böses' Objekt.–*Es*.: object 'bueno'/objeto 'malo'.–
Fr.: 'bon' objet/'mauvais' objet.–*I*.: oggetto 'buono'/oggetto 'cattivo'.–
P.: objeto 'bom'/objeto 'mau'.

Terms introduced by Melanie Klein to designate the earliest partial or whole instinctual objects in the form in which they appear in the infant's phantasy life.

'Good' Object/'Bad' Object

The qualities 'good' and 'bad' are attributed to these objects not only in consequence of their gratifying or frustrating nature but also because of the subject's projection of his libidinal or destructive instincts on to them. According to Klein, the part-object* (breast, penis) is split into a 'good' and a 'bad' object, this split constituting a primary mode of defence against anxiety. The whole object is said to be split in a similar fashion (the 'bad' mother and the 'good' mother, etc.).

'Good' and 'bad' objects are subject to the processes of introjection* and projection*.

The dialectic between 'good' and 'bad' objects lies at the centre of the psychoanalytic theory that Melanie Klein derived from the analysis of the most primitive phantasies.

We cannot describe this whole complex dialectic here, so we shall simply point out some of the main characteristics of the notions of 'good' and 'bad' objects and try to dispel certain ambiguities.

a. The inverted commas which Melanie Klein often uses serve to underscore the phantasy nature of these properties of the object.

We are indeed concerned here with 'imagos, which are a phantastically distorted picture of the real objects upon which they are based' (1). This distortion is the product of two factors: in the first place, the gratification that the breast affords makes it into a 'good' breast; conversely, the withdrawal or denial of the breast leads to the image of a 'bad' breast being formed. Secondly, the child projects its love on to the breast that gratifies and (above all) its aggressiveness on to the bad breast. Although these two factors together constitute a vicious circle ('The breasts hate me and deprive me, because I hate them' (2)), Melanie Klein places most of the emphasis on the element of projection.

b. The principle governing the interplay between good and bad objects is the duality of the life* and the death instincts*, which Klein sees as an irreducible datum at work from the beginning of the individual's existence. She even holds that sadism is at its 'zenith' at the start of life, with the balance between libido and destructiveness tending to tip at this point in favour of destructiveness.

c. Inasmuch as the two types of instinct are present from the outset, both directed towards a sole object (the breast), one may justifiably speak here of *ambivalence**. Such ambivalence, however, being anxiogenic for the child, is immediately checked by the mechanism of *splitting of the object** and of the affects related to this object.

d. The phantasy nature of these objects must not allow us to lose sight of the fact that they are dealt with as though they were substantial and *real* (in the sense in which Freud speaks of psychical *reality**). Klein describes them as contents 'inside' the mother; she defines their introjection and projection as operations which affect, not good or bad *qualities*, but rather the objects in which such qualities inhere. Moreover, the object–whether good or bad–is phantastically endowed with powers analogous to those of a person ('bad persecuting breast', 'good reassuring breast', attack on the mother's body by bad objects, struggle between good and bad objects within the body, etc.).

The breast is the first object to be split in this way. All part-objects suffer

188

a comparable division (penis, faeces, child, etc.). And the same goes for whole objects, once the child is able to apprehend them. 'The good breast–external and internal–becomes the prototype of all helpful and gratifying objects, the bad breast the prototype of all external and internal persecutory objects' (3).

We may note as a final point that the Kleinian conception of the splitting of the object into 'good' and 'bad' should be seen in connection with certain suggestions made by Freud, notably in 'Instincts and their Vicissitudes' (1915c) and in 'Negation' (1925h) (see 'Pleasure-Ego/Reality-Ego').

(1) KLEIN, M. 'A Contribution to the Psychogenesis of Manic-Depressive States' (1934), in *Contributions*, 282.

(2) RIVIERE, J. 'On the Genesis of Psychical Conflict in Earliest Infancy' (1936), in *Developments*, 47.

(3) KLEIN, M. 'Some Theoretical Conclusions regarding the Emotional Life of the Infant' (1952), in *Developments*, 200.

H

Helplessness

= *D*.: Hilflosigkeit.–*Es*.: desamparo.–*Fr*.: incapacité à s'aider.–*I*.: l'essere senza aiuto.–
P.: desamparo *or* desarvoramento.

This common word has a specific meaning in Freudian theory, where it is used to denote the state of the human suckling which, being entirely dependent on other people for the satisfaction of its needs (hunger, thirst), proves incapable of carrying out the specific action necessary to put an end to internal tension.

For the adult, the state of helplessness is the prototype of the traumatic situation which is responsible for the generation of anxiety.

The word '*Hilflosigkeit*' constitutes a permanent reference-point for Freud, and it deserves to be signalled out and translated consistently. This state of helplessness is an essentially objective *datum*–the situation of impotence in which the newborn human infant finds itself. The baby is incapable of undertaking co-ordinated and effective action (see 'Specific Action'); Freud calls this state of affairs motor helplessness (*motorische Hilflosigkeit*) (1a). And, from the economic* point of view, this situation results in an increase of the tension brought about by need–an increase which the psychical apparatus is as yet unable to control: this is what is meant by psychical helplessness (*psychische Hilflosigkeit*).

189

Hospitalism

The idea of an initial state of helplessness is at the root of several lines of psycho-analytic inquiry:

a. Genetically speaking (2), it is on the basis of this idea that we are able to understand the primordial role played by the *experience of satisfaction**, its hallucinatory reproduction and the distinction between the primary and secondary processes*.

b. As a corollary of the total dependence of the human infant on its mother, the state of helplessness implies the mother's *omnipotence*. It thus has a decisive influence on the structuring of the psyche–a process which is destined to come about entirely on the basis of the relationship with the other person.

c. Within the framework of the theory of anxiety, helplessness becomes the prototype of the traumatic situation. Thus Freud, in *Inhibitions, Symptoms and Anxiety* (1926d), recognises that what the 'internal dangers' have in common is a loss or separation occasioning a progressive increase in tension, until eventually the subject finds himself to be incapable of mastering the excitations and is overwhelmed by them: this is what defines the state which generates the feeling of helplessness.

d. Lastly, it may be noted that Freud explicitly relates the state of helplessness to the fact of the *prematurity* of the human infant: its 'intra-uterine existence seems to be short in comparison with that of most animals, and it is sent into the world in a less finished state. As a result, the influence of the real external world upon it is intensified and an early differentiation between the ego and the id is promoted. Moreover, the dangers of the external world have a greater importance for it, so that the value of the object which can alone protect it against them and take the place of its former intra-uterine life is enormously enhanced. The biological factor, then, establishes the earliest situations of danger and creates the need to be loved which will accompany the child through the rest of its life' (1b).

(1) Cf. FREUD, S. *Inhibitions, Symptoms and Anxiety* (1926d): a) G.W., XIV, 200; S.E., XX, 167. b) G.W., XIV, 186–87; S.E., XX, 154–55.

(2) Cf. in particular FREUD, S. 'Project for a Scientific Psychology' (1950a [1895]), Part I.

Hospitalism

= *D.*: Hospitalismus.–*Es.*: hospitalismo.–*Fr.*: hospitalisme.–*I.*: ospedalismo.– *P.*: hospitalismo.

Term used since René Spitz's work on the subject to denote whatever somatic and psychical disturbances result in infants (up to eighteen months old) who undergo a prolonged stay in a hospital-type institution completely separated from their mother.

The reader is referred to the specialised work which has been done on this topic (1), and particularly to the contributions of Spitz, who has become the recognised authority on the matter (2). Spitz's conclusions are based on extensive

and in-depth study, and on comparisons between different categories of infants
–those raised in orphanages, those in a nursery with some presence of the
mother, those brought up by their mother, and so on.

It is when the baby is raised in the total absence of its mother, in an institution
where it is looked after in an anonymous fashion, so that no emotional link
can be established, that the disorders which Spitz has grouped together under
the name of hospitalism set in. These disorders are: retardation of corporal
development, of body mastery, of adaptation to the environment, of linguistic
capacity; reduced resistance to disease; and, in the most serious cases, wasting
and death.

The effects of hospitalism are long-term, if not irreparable. Spitz, after
describing hospitalism, has attempted to situate it in relation to the whole
group of troubles brought about by a disturbed relationship between mother
and child: by defining it as a *total* emotional deprivation, he distinguishes it
from *anaclitic depression**, which is the consequence of a *partial* affective deprivation in a child which has previously enjoyed a normal relationship with its
mother–a deprivation which may come to an end once the mother has been
found again (3).

(1) Cf. the bibliography of Spitz's article (2).

(2) SPITZ, R. A. 'Hospitalism–An Enquiry into the Genesis of Psychiatric Conditions in
Early Childhood' (1945), *Psychoanal. Study Child*, I, 53–74.

(3) Cf. SPITZ, R. A. *La Première année de la vie de l'enfant* (Paris, 1953).

Hypercathexis

= *D.*: Überbesetzung.–*Es.*: sobrecarga.–*Fr.*: surinvestissement.–*I.*: superinvestimento.–
P.: sobrecarga *or* superinvestimento.

**Charge of supplementary cathexis received by already cathected ideas, perceptions,
etc. This term applies above all to the process of attention, within the framework
of the Freudian theory of consciousness.**

The 'economic' term 'hypercathexis' carries with it no overtones as regards
either the object or the source of the additional cathexis in question. We may
say, for example, that an unconscious idea is hypercathected when a supplementary charge of instinctual energy is directed on to it; Freud also speaks of
hypercathexis in the case of narcissistic withdrawal of libido on to the ego in
schizophrenia.

All the same the term is introduced and most often used in order to provide
an economic basis for what Freud describes as a 'particular psychical function'
(1), namely attention, of which he proposes a highly elaborate theory–mainly
in the 'Project for a Scientific Psychology' (1950*a* [1895]). In this text he pro-
pounds the 'biological rule' which the ego obeys in the process of attention:
'If an indication of reality appears, then the perceptual cathexis which is
simultaneously present is to be hypercathected' (2) (see 'Consciousness').

191

Hypnoid Hysteria

From a rather similar perspective, Freud later gives the name of hypercathexis to the preparation for danger which permits the subject to avoid or to check the trauma: 'In the case of quite a number of traumas, the difference between systems that are unprepared and systems that are well prepared through being hypercathected may be a decisive factor in determining the outcome' (3).

(1) FREUD, S. *The Interpretation of Dreams* (1900*a*), G.W., II–III, 599; S.E., V, 593.

(2) FREUD, S. *Anf.*, 451; S.E., I, 371.

(3) FREUD, S. *Beyond the Pleasure Principle* (1920*g*), G.W., XIII, 32; S.E., XVIII, 31-32.

Hypnoid Hysteria

= *D.*: Hypnoidhysterie.–*Es.*: histeria hipnoide.–*Fr.*: hystérie hypnoïde.– *I.*: isteria ipnoida.–*P.*: histeria hipnóide.

Term used by Breuer and Freud in 1894–95 to refer to a form of hysteria supposed to originate in hypnoid states: the subject is unable to integrate the ideas which emerge in these states into his self and his history. The ideas are then formed into a separate, unconscious psychical group which is liable to have pathogenic effects.

The reader is referred to our article on the 'Hypnoid State' for the theory which underpins this notion. It may be remarked here that the term 'hypnoid hysteria' is not to be met with in the texts signed by Breuer alone, from which it would seem logical to infer that this denomination is to be attributed to Freud. For Breuer, indeed, all hysterias are 'hypnoid' in that he considers the hypnoid state to be their ultimate basis. In Freud's view, on the contrary, hypnoid hysteria is just one form of that disorder, alongside retention hysteria* and defence hysteria* (which really overshadows it); starting from this distinction, moreover, Freud was enabled first to restrict and eventually to reject the role of the hypnoid state as compared with that of defence*.

Hypnoid State

= *D.*: hypnoider Zustand.–*Es.*: estado hipnoide.–*Fr.*: état hypnoïde.–*I.*: stato ipnoide.– *P.*: estado hipnóide.

Term introduced by Breuer to designate a state analogous to the one produced by hypnosis. The contents of consciousness which arise in such states are supposed to have little or no associative connection with the remainder of mental life, the result being the formation of groups of split-off associations.

Breuer sees the hypnoid state, which introduces a split (*Spaltung*) into mental life, as the constitutive phenomenon of hysteria.

192

The term 'hypnoid state' continues to be associated with the name of Breuer, although Breuer himself evoked Moebius as his forerunner as regards its use.

Breuer was led to put forward the notion of hypnoid states by the relation between hypnosis and hysteria, and in particular by the resemblance between phenomena provoked by hypnosis and certain hysterical symptoms. The effects of events which take place while the subject is under hypnosis–such as the hypnotist's instructions–remain independent and are liable to re-emerge, in isolated fashion, either during a second hypnosis or else in the waking state, in apparently aberrant actions unconnected with the rest of the subject's behaviour at the time. Hypnosis and its effects thus provide a sort of experimental model of what, in hysteria, appears as behaviour which is radically at odds with the patient's motivations.

Hypnoid states are thus seen as natural equivalents, at the root of hysteria, to those states which hypnosis induces by artificial means. 'It [the hypnoid state] must correspond to some kind of vacancy of consciousness in which an emerging idea meets with no resistance from any other–in which, so to speak the field is clear for the first comer' (α).

According to Breuer, a hypnoid state comes about when two conditions are fulfilled: an *affect** must emerge during a state of *reverie* (day-dreaming or twilight-state); spontaneous auto-hypnosis is triggered by 'affect being introduced into a habitual reverie' (1*a*). Certain situations, such as that of the languishing lover or of someone watching at the sick-bed of a person dear to him, are conducive to the conjunction of these two factors: '. . . in sick-nursing the quiet by which the subject is surrounded, his concentration on an object, his attention fixed on the patient's breathing–all this sets up precisely the conditions demanded by many hypnotic procedures and fills the twilight-state produced in this way with the affect of anxiety' (1*b*). Moreover, Breuer asserts that in extreme cases hypnoid states may be provoked by just one of the two above-mentioned conditions acting alone: a reverie may be transformed into an auto-hypnosis without the intervention of an affect, or an intense emotion may on occasion paralyse the flow of associations (see 'Fright').

In their 'Preliminary Communication' (1893*a*), Breuer and Freud had tackled the problem in a slightly different way. The question here is not so much to ascertain the respective roles of the state of reverie and of affects in the production of hypnoid states as to determine the relative responsibility of the hypnoid state and of the traumatising affect in the origin of hysteria: if the trauma can cause the hypnoid state, or if it can appear during such a state, then it can also be a pathogenic factor in its own right.

The pathogenic capacity of the hypnoid state is seen as resulting from the exclusion of the ideas* which arise during such a state from 'associative communication', and hence from any 'associative working-over*'. These ideas come in this way to form a 'separate psychical group' whose charge of affect is liable, if it does not enter into communication with the whole of the contents of consciousness, to be connected up with other such groups which have arisen in similar states. A splitting of mental life has thus occurred such as is particularly noticeable in cases of dual personality, which exemplify the mental dissociation of conscious and unconscious.

Breuer saw the hypnoid state as the basic condition of hysteria. Freud at first emphasised what in his view constituted the positive side of such a theory (especially in comparison to Janet's) as an attempt to explain the existence in hysterics of 'a splitting of consciousness, accompanied by the formation of separate psychical groups' (2a). Whereas Janet, according to Freud, invokes 'an innate weakness of the capacity for psychical synthesis and the narrowness of the "field of consciousness (*champ de conscience*)" ' (2b, β), Breuer has the merit of showing that the splitting of consciousness, as the fundamental characteristic of hysteria, itself admits of a genetic explanation based on the exceptional moments which hypnoid states constitute.

But it was not long before Freud qualified the importance of Breuer's views by developing the notion of defence hysteria*.

He was finally, in retrospect, to reject those views completely: '. . . the hypothesis of "hypnoid states" [...] sprang entirely from the initiative of Breuer. I regard the use of such a term as superfluous and misleading, because it interrupts the continuity of the problem as to the nature of the psychical process accompanying the formation of hysterical symptoms' (3).

(α) Moebius's definition in *Über Astasie-Abasie* (1894), quoted by Breuer in his 'Theoretical' chapter of the *Studies on Hysteria* (1c).

(β) In point of fact, Janet's thesis appears to be subtler than Freud suggests. For one thing, he does recognise the importance of the trauma, and, secondly, he does not hold that 'mental weakness' is necessarily innate (4).

(1) BREUER, J. and FREUD, S. *Studies on Hysteria* (1895d): a) 1st German edn., 191; S.E., II, 218–19. b) German, 191; S.E., II, 219. c) German, 188; S.E., II, 215.

(2) FREUD, S. 'The Neuro-Psychoses of Defence' (1894a): G.W., I, 60; S.E., III, 46. b) G.W., I, 60; S.E., III, 46.

(3) FREUD, S. 'Fragment of an Analysis of a Case of Hysteria' (1905e [1901]), G.W., V, 185n.; S.E., VII, 27n.

(4) Cf. partic. JANET, P. *L'état mental des hystériques* (Paris: Alcan, 1892), 635–37.

Hysteria

= D.: Hysterie.–Es.: histeria *or* histerismo.–Fr.: hystérie.–I.: isteria *or* isterismo.– P.: histeria.

Class of neuroses presenting a great diversity of clinical pictures. The two best-isolated forms, from the point of view of symptoms, are *conversion hysteria**, in which the psychical conflict is expressed symbolically in somatic symptoms of the most varied kinds: they may be paroxystic (e.g. emotional crises accompanied by theatricality) or more long-lasting (anaesthesias, hysterical paralyses, 'lumps in the throat', etc.); and *anxiety hysteria**, where the anxiety is attached in more or less stable fashion to a specific external object (phobias).

Freud discovered major aetio-pathogenic characteristics in conversion hysteria. It is this development which has enabled psycho-analysis to reduce a variety of clinical types affecting the organisation of the personality and the mode of existence of the subject to a single common hysterical structure—and this even where there are no phobic symptoms and no obvious conversions.

The specificity of hysteria is to be found in the prevalence of a certain kind of identification and of certain mechanisms (particularly repression, which is often explicit) in an emergence of the Oedipal conflict occurring mainly in the phallic and oral libidinal spheres.

The idea of an hysterical disease is very ancient, for it dates back to Hippo-crates. Its demarcation has followed the meanderings of the history of medicine, and the reader is referred to the abundant literature on its evolution (1, 2a).

At the end of the nineteenth century, particularly as a result of Charcot's teaching, the problem which hysteria presented to medical thought and to the accepted methods of clinical anatomy began to receive attention. Very roughly speaking, we may say that a solution was sought in two directions. One sugges-tion was that, considering the absence of any organic lesion, hysterical symptoms should be treated as the result of suggestion or auto-suggestion–or even as simulation (a line of thought destined, later, to be taken up and systematised by Babinski). The alternative proposal was that hysteria should be raised to the status of a disease like any other, as well-defined and precise in its symptoms as, say, a neurological condition (cf. the work of Charcot). The approach adopted by Breuer and Freud–and, from another angle, by Janet–allowed them to transcend this particular choice of paths. Freud–like Charcot, the influence of whose lessons upon him needs no reiteration–looked upon hysteria as a well-defined psychical disorder requiring explanation in terms of a specific aetiology. On the other hand, in trying to ascertain its 'psychical mechanism', Freud aligned himself with a whole current of opinion which saw hysteria as a 'malady through representation' (2b). It was of course in the process of bringing the psychical aetiology of hysteria to light that psycho-analysis made its principal discoveries: the unconscious, phantasy, defensive conflict and repression, identification, transference, etc.

Following Freud, psycho-analysts have consistently looked upon hysterical neurosis and obsessional neurosis as the two major divisions of the field of the neuroses (α); this does not imply any obstacle to their possible combination, as structures, in particular clinical pictures.

There is a further type of neurosis, whose most apparent symptoms are of a phobic character, which Freud considers to be an expression of the basic hysterical structure; to this he gives the name 'anxiety hysteria' (q.v.).

(α) Must we admit the existence of an hysterical *psychosis* as a nosographical entity in its own right? The question arises when we are confronted with states presenting, in particular, hallucinations often of a visual kind in which there is a dramatic participation of the subject. Freud–at least to begin with–did posit such an independent category (3), and several of the cases dealt with in the *Studies on Hysteria* (1895d) certainly raise this problem in the mind of the reader.

(1) Cf. Rosolato, G. 'Introduction à l'étude de l'hystérie', in Ey, H. *Encyclopédie médico-chirurgicale (Psychiatrie)* (1955), 37355 A 10; Zilboorg, G. *A History of Medical Psychology* (New York: Norton, 1941).

(2) Cf. Janet, P. *L'état mental des hystériques* (Paris: Alcan, 1894): a) *passim*. b) Première Partie, chap. VI, 40–47. English translation: *The Mental State of Hystericals* (New York and London: Putnam's, 1901), cf. 486–88.

(3) Cf. Freud, S. 'Draft H' of the Fliess papers, *Anf.*, 118–24; S.E., I, 206–12.

Hysterogenic Zone

= *D.*: hysterogene Zone.–*Es.*: zona histerógena.–*Fr.*: zone hystérogène.–
I.: zona isterogena.–*P.*: zona histerógena.

**Particular bodily areas which Charcot, and later Freud, showed to be the seat of
specific sensory phenomena in certain cases of conversion hysteria. Such areas,
described by the patient as painful, turn out under examination to be libidinally
cathected. As a result their stimulation causes reactions similar to those accompanying sexual pleasure which may even lead up to an hysterical attack.**

Charcot described hysterogenic zones as 'more or less circumscribed regions of
the body where pressure or simple rubbing brings about the more or less rapid
occurrence of the phenomenon of the *aura*; this may be followed on occasion,
if one persists, by an hysterical attack. These points–or rather, these areas–
have the further property of being the seat of a permanent sensitivity [...]. Once
developed, the attack may often be halted by means of a vigorous pressure
exerted at these same points' (1).

In the *Studies on Hysteria* (1895*d*), Freud adopted Charcot's term 'hysterogenic zone' and expanded its meaning: he reported that if the physician pressed
or pinched the areas described by hysterical patients as painful he could provoke
reactions suggesting that the subject was experiencing a 'voluptuous tickling
sensation' (2*a*). Freud likens these reactions to an hysterical attack–itself
deemed 'an equivalent of coition' (3).

An hysterogenic zone is thus a part of the body that has become erotogenic.
Freud stresses in the *Three Essays on the Theory of Sexuality* (1905*d*) that
'erotogenic and hysterogenic zones show the same characteristics' (4). In fact
he demonstrated (see 'Erotogenic Zone') that any area of the body could become
erotogenic by virtue of a displacement from those zones that are predisposed by
their function to procure sexual pleasure. This process of erogenisation is
particularly active in hysterics.

The preconditions for this type of displacement are to be found in the subject's
history. The case of Elisabeth von R., for example, reveals how an hysterogenic
zone is constituted: 'The patient surprised me [...] by announcing that she knew
why it was that the pains always radiated from that particular area of the right
thigh and were at their most painful there: it was on this place that her father
used to rest his leg every morning, while she renewed the bandage around it,
for it was badly swollen. This must have happened a good hundred times, yet
she had not noticed the connection till now. In this way she gave me the explanation that I needed of the emergence of what was an atypical hysterogenic zone'
(2*b*).

It can thus be seen that the notion of the hysterogenic zone is modified in two
respects as it passes from Charcot to Freud: in the first place, Freud considers
such zones to be the seat of sexual excitations; secondly, he does not hold to the
set topography that Charcot wished to lay down, since on his view any bodily
region can become hysterogenic.

(1) CHARCOT, J.-M. *Leçons sur les maladies du système nerveux* (Paris: Lecrosnier & Babé, 1890), III, 88.

(2) FREUD, S.: a) G.W., I, 198; S.E., II, 137. b) G.W., I, 211–12; S.E., II, 148.

(3) FREUD, S. 'Some General Remarks on Hysterical Attacks' (1919*a*), G.W., VII, 239; S.E., IX, 234.

(4) FREUD, S., G.W., V, 83; S.E., VII, 184.

I

Id

= *D.*: Es.–*Es.*: ello.–*Fr.*: ça.–*I.*: es.–*P.*: id.

One of the three agencies* distinguished by Freud in his second theory of the psychical apparatus. The id constitutes the instinctual pole of the personality; its contents, as an expression of the instincts, are unconscious, a portion of them being hereditary and innate, a portion repressed and acquired.

From the economic* point of view, the id for Freud is the prime reservoir of psychical energy; from the dynamic* point of view, it conflicts with the ego and the super-ego–which, genetically speaking, are diversifications of the id.

The term '*das Es*' is first used in *The Ego and the Id* (1923*b*). Freud borrows it from Georg Groddeck (*a*), citing the precedent set by Nietzsche, who apparently used the expression 'for whatever in our nature is impersonal and, so to speak, subject to natural law' (1*a*).

The word attracted Freud's attention because it evokes the idea, developed by Groddeck, that 'what we call our ego behaves essentially passively in life, and that [...] we are "lived" by unknown and uncontrollable forces' (1*b*, *β*); this notion is consistent, moreover, with the language used spontaneously by patients: ' "It shot through me," people say; "there was something in me at that moment that was stronger than me." "C'était plus fort que moi" ' (2).

The term 'id' first appears during Freud's revision of his topography* between 1920 and 1923. The position occupied by the id in the second topography may be looked upon as roughly equivalent to that held by the unconscious* system (*Ucs.*) in the first one–provided always that a number of differences are borne in mind. These differences may be described as follows:

a. Aside from certain phylogenetically acquired patterns or contents, the unconscious of the first topography is indistinguishable from the *repressed*.

In *The Ego and the Id* (Chapter I), by contrast, Freud stresses the fact that the *repressing* agency–the ego–and its defensive operations are also for the most part unconscious. Consequently, the id, though it includes the same contents as the system *Ucs.* has done hitherto, no longer covers the whole area of the unconscious psyche.

b. The revision of the instinct theory and the development of the notion of the ego* bring about a further change. The neurotic conflict had at first been defined by the antagonism between the sexual instincts* and the ego-instincts*, he latter having a fundamental part to play in the motivation of defence (see 'Psychical Conflict'). From 1920–23 onwards, the group of ego instincts loses its autonomy by being dissolved into the great opposition between the life instincts* and the death instincts*. Thus the ego is no longer characterised by a specific form of instinctual energy, since the new agency of the id includes the two types of instincts from the outset.

In short, the agency against which defence operates is no longer defined as the unconscious pole but rather as the instinctual pole of the personality.

It is in this sense that the id is depicted as the 'great reservoir' of libido (γ) and, more generally, of instinctual energy (1*c*, 1*d*). The energy utilised by the ego is drawn from this common fund, especially in the form of 'desexualieds and sublimated' energy.

c. The limits of the new agency relative to the other agencies and to the biological domain are drawn differently and, broadly speaking, less distinctly than they were in the first topography:

i. The boundary with the ego is less rigorous than the former frontier, constituted by the censorhip*, between *Ucs.* and *Pcs.-Cs.*: 'The ego is not sharply separated from the id; its lower portion merges into it. But the repressed merges into the id as well, and is merely a part of it. The repressed is only cut off sharply from the ego by the resistances of repression; it can communicate with the ego through the id' (1*e*).

This blending of the id with the repressing agency is a consequence above all of the genetic definition of this agency that Freud proposes, and according to which the ego is 'that part of the id which has been modified by the direct influence of the external world through the medium of the *Pcpt.-Cs.* [perception-consciousness] system' (1*f*).

ii. By the same token, the super-ego* is not a completely autonomous agency: it 'merges into the id' (3*a*).

iii. Lastly, the distinction between the id and a biological substratum of the instinct is not so hard and fast as that between the unconscious and the source* of the instinct: the id is 'open at its end to somatic influences' (3*b*). The idea of an 'inscription' of the instinct, previously lent support by the notion of 'representatives'*, though not rejected outright here, is not reasserted.

d. Does the id have a *mode of organisation*–a specific internal structure? Freud himself asserted that the id was 'a chaos': 'It is filled with energy reaching it from the instincts, but it has no organisation, produces no collective will' (3*c*). The characteristics of the id are supposedly only definable in negative terms–through contrast with the ego's organisational mode.

The fact is, however–and it should be emphasised–that Freud transfers to the id most of the properties which in the first topography had defined the system *Ucs.*, and which constitute a positive and unique form of organisation: operation according to the primary process*, structure based on complexes*, genetic layering of the instincts, etc. Similarly, the freshly introduced dualism of life and death instincts implies that these properties are organised into a dialectical opposition. Thus the id's lack of organisation is only relative, implying merely the absence of the type of relations that characterise the ego's organisation. This absence is epitomised by the fact that 'contrary [instinctual] impulses exist side by side, without cancelling each other out or diminishing each other' (3*d*). As Daniel Lagache has stressed, it is the absence of a coherent subject that best typifies the organisation of the id–an absence which accounts for Freud's choice of a neuter pronoun to designate this organisation (4).

e. In the last analysis, we are best able to grasp the transition from the unconscious in the first topography to the id in the second by considering the difference in the *genetic perspectives* to which they belong.

The unconscious owed its formation to that repression which in its dual historical and mythical role introduced into the psyche the radical split between the systems *Ucs.* and *Pcs.-Cs.*

With the advent of the second topography this instant of schism between the agencies of the psyche loses its fundamental character. The genesis of the different agencies is now viewed rather as a gradual process of differentiation as the various systems emerge. Hence Freud's concern to lay stress on continuity in the evolution from biological need to the id, and from the id to the ego as well as to the super-ego. It is for this reason that Freud's new conception of the psychical apparatus lends itself more readily than did the first one to a 'biologistic' or 'naturalistic' reading.

(α) Groddeck was a German psychiatrist close to psycho-analytical circles; he was the author of several works inspired by Freud's ideas, notably *Das Buch vom Es: psychoanalytische Briefe an eine Freundin* (1923); translation: *The Book of the It* (London: Vision Press, 1949; New York: Vintage Books, n.d.).

(β) Groddeck describes what he means by '*das Es*' as follows: 'I hold the view that man is animated by the Unknown, that there is within him an "Es", an "It", some wondrous force which directs both what he himself does, and what happens to him. The affirmation "I live" is only conditionally correct, it expresses only a small and superficial part of the fundamental principle, "Man is lived by the It" ' (5).

(γ) On this point, the reader may profitably consult the comments of the Editors of the *Standard Edition* (XIX, 63–66).

(1) FREUD, S.: a) G.W., XIII, 251, *n*. 2; S.E., XIX, 23, *n*. 3. b) G.W., XIII, 251; S.E., XIX, 23. c) Cf. G.W., XIII, 258*n*.; S.E., XIX, 30, *n*. 1. d) Cf. G.W., XIII, 275; S.E., XIX, 46. e) G.W., XIII, 251–52; S.E., XIX, 24. f) G.W., XIII, 252; S.E., XIX, 25.

(2) FREUD, S. *The Question of Lay Analysis* (1926*e*), G.W., XIV, 222; S.E., XX, 195.

(3) FREUD, S. *New Introductory Lectures on Psycho-Analysis* (1933*a* [1932]): a) G.W., XV, 85; S.E., XXII, 79. b) G.W., XV, 80; S.E., XXII, 73. c) G.W., XV, 80; S.E., XXII, 73. d) G.W., XV, 80; S.E., XXII, 73–74.

(4) Cf. LAGACHE, D. 'La psychanalyse et la structure de la personnalité', in *La psychanalyse*, VI (Paris: P.U.F., 1961), 21.

(5) GRODDECK, G. *Das Buch vom Es*, 10–11; Vintage edn., 11.

Idea (or Presentation or Representation)

= *D*.: Vorstellung. – *Es*.: representación. – *Fr*.: représentation. – *I*.: rappresentazione. – *P*.: representação.

Classical term in philosophy and psychology for 'that which one represents to oneself, that which forms the concrete content of an act of thought', and 'in particular the reproduction of an earlier perception' (1). Freud contrasts the idea with the affect*: these two elements suffer distinct fates in psychical processes.

The word '*Vorstellung*' is part of the traditional vocabulary of German philosophy. Freud does not set out immediately to change its meaning, but he does use it in an original way (α). The following brief remarks are intended to show in what respect this is so.

a. Freud's earliest theoretical models designed to account for the psychoneuroses* are centred on the distinction between the 'quota of affect'* and the idea. In *obsessional neurosis*, the quota of affect is displaced from the pathogenic idea – which is bound to the traumatic event – on to another idea regarded by the subject as insignificant. In *hysteria*, the quota of affect is converted into somatic energy, while the repressed idea is symbolised by a bodily zone or activity. This thesis, according to which the separation of affect and idea is a defining principle of repression, leads to the description of distinct fates for each of these elements and the postulation of different processes for dealing with them: the idea is 'repressed'*, the affect 'suppressed'*, etc.

b. Freud excuses himself for speaking of 'unconscious ideas': he was of course fully aware of the paradoxical effect of juxtaposing the two words. The fact that he persisted nevertheless in doing so is a sure sign that in his use of '*Vorstellung*' one aspect of its meaning predominant in classical philosophy has faded into the background – namely, the connotation of the act of subjective presentation of an object to consciousness. For Freud, an idea or presentation is to be understood rather as what comes from the object and is registered in the 'mnemic systems'.

c. Now we know that Freud does not picture memory as a pure and simple receptacle of images, after the fashion of a strict empiricist model; instead he speaks of mnemic systems and breaks the memory up into different series of associations, while what he calls a memory-trace* is less a 'weak impression', preserving its relation to the object through its resemblance to it, than a sign invariably co-ordinated with other signs and not bound to any particular sensory quality. From this point of view, some authors have felt justified in comparing Freud's '*Vorstellung*' to the linguistic notion of the signifier (*le signifiant*).

d. We ought, however, to remember the distinction Freud draws here between two levels of operation of 'ideas': the distinction between 'thing-presentations'* and 'word-presentations'. The purpose of this distinction is to point up a difference which is in Freud's view of fundamental topographical* import; thing-presentations, which are characteristic of the unconscious sytem, have a more immediate relationship with things: in the case of the 'primal hallucination', the

200

child is held to take the thing-presentation as equivalent to the perceived object and to cathect it in the absence of that object (see 'Experience of Satisfaction').

Similarly, when Freud seeks the 'unconscious pathogenic idea' at the end of associative pathways (as he does, notably, in his first descriptions of psycho-analytic treatment in 1894–96 (2)), the aim of his investigation is the ultimate point where the object cannot be dissociated from its traces–where, in other words, what is signified is indistinguishable from its signifier.

e. Although the distinction between the memory-trace and the idea as a cathexis of the memory-trace is always implicit in Freud's approach (3), it is not always clearly drawn (4). The reason for this, no doubt, is that Freud found it hard to conceive of a *pure memory-trace*–i.e. an idea from which all cathexis has been withdrawn, not only by the conscious system but also by the un-conscious one.

(α) The possible influence on Freud of the idea of an actual 'mechanics of ideas' (*Vorstel-lungsmechanik*), as developed by Herbart, has often been remarked upon. As Ola Andersson points out, 'Herbartianism was the dominant psychology in the scientific world in which Freud lived during the formative years of his scientific development' (5).

(1) LALANDE, A. *Vocabulaire technique et critique de la philosophie* (Paris: P.U.F., 1951).

(2) Cf. FREUD, S. *Studies on Hysteria* (1895d), *passim*.

(3) Cf. FREUD, S. 'The Unconscious' (1915e), G.W., X, 300; S.E., XIV, 201–2.

(4) Cf. FREUD, S. *The Ego and the Id* (1923b), G.W., XIII, 247; S.E., XIX, 20.

(5) ANDERSSON, O. *Studies in the Prehistory of Psycho-Analysis* (Norstedts: Svenska Bokförlaget, 1962), 224. (Also New York: Humanities Press, 1962.)

Ideal Ego

= *D*.: Idealich.–*Es*.: yo ideal.–*Fr*.: moi idéal.–*I*.: io ideale.–*P*.: ego ideal.

Intrapsychic formation which some authors distinguish from the ego-ideal and define as an ideal of narcissistic omnipotence constructed on the model of infantile narcissism.

Freud coined the term '*Idealich*' which is to be found in 'On Narcissism: An Introduction' (1914c) and in *The Ego and the Id* (1923b). On the other hand, he makes no distinction, conceptually speaking, between '*Idealich*' (ideal ego) and '*Ichideal*' (ego-ideal*).

A number of post-Freudian authors have used the pair constituted by these two terms to designate two distinct intrapsychic formations.

Nunberg, in particular, looks upon the ideal ego as a formation with genetic priority over the super-ego: 'The as-yet unorganised ego which feels at one with the id corresponds to an ideal condition . . .' (1). In the course of his develop-ment, the subject is said to leave this narcissistic ideal behind but to aspire to return to it–a return which occurs mainly, though not exclusively, in the psychoses.

Idealisation

Daniel Lagache has stressed the advantage that is to be obtained by contrasting the pole of identifications represented by the ideal ego with that constituted by the 'ego-ideal/super-ego system'. Lagache also sees the ideal ego as an unconscious narcissistic formation, but his approach differs from Nunberg's: 'The Ideal Ego, understood as a narcissistic ideal of omnipotence, does not amount merely to the union of the Ego with the Id, but also involves a primary identification with another being invested with omnipotence–namely, the mother' (2a). The ideal ego serves as the basis of what Lagache has called *heroic identification*, i.e. identification with outstanding and admirable personalities: 'The Ideal Ego is further revealed by cases of passionate admiration for great historical or contemporary figures who are remarkable for their independence, nobility or superiority. As the treatment progresses, we see the Ideal Ego taking shape and emerging as a formation which cannot be confused with the Ego-Ideal' (2b). Lagache holds that the formation of the ideal ego has sado-masochistic implications, particularly the negation of the other as a corollary of self-affirmation (see 'Identification with the Aggressor').

For Jacques Lacan too the ideal ego is an essentially narcissistic formation, originating in the mirror phase* and belonging to the order of the Imaginary* (3).

Despite their divergent standpoints, these authors are agreed, first, in asserting that it is worth while in psycho-analytic theory to specify the ideal ego as an unconscious formation in its own right and, secondly, in bringing the narcissistic nature of this formation to the fore. Moreover, note that in the same text which contains Freud's first reference to the ideal ego, the process of idealisation whereby the subject sets out to recover the supposedly omnipotent state of infantile narcissism is placed at the start of the development of the personality's ideal agencies.

(1) NUNBERG, H. *Allgemeine Neurosenlehre auf psychoanalytischer Grundlage* (1932). English trans.: *Principles of Psycho-Analysis* (New York: I.U.P., 1955), 126.

(2) LAGACHE, D. 'La psychanalyse et la structure de la personnalité', *La Psychanalyse*, 1958, VI: a) 43. b) 41–42.

(3) LACAN, J. 'Remarques sur le rapport de Daniel Lagache', *La Psychanalyse*, 1958, VI, 133–46. Reprinted in *Écrits* (Paris: Seuil, 1966), 647*ff*.

Idealisation

= *D*.: Idealisierung.–*Es*.: idealización.–*Fr*.: idéalisation.–*I*.: idealizzazione.–*P*.: idealização.

Mental process by means of which the object's qualities and value are elevated to the point of perfection. Identification with the idealised object contributes to the formation and elaboration of the individual subject's so-called ideal agencies (ideal ego, ego-ideal).

Freud observed the operation of this process before having occasion to define it–notably in the sphere of love (sexual overvaluation). When he does define it, it is in the context of his introduction of the concept of narcissism*. He draws a distinction between idealisation and sublimation*: 'Sublimation is a process that concerns object-libido and consists in the instinct's directing itself towards an aim other than, and remote from, sexual satisfaction [...]. Idealisation is a process that concerns the *object*; by it that object, without any alteration in its nature, is aggrandised and exalted in the subject's mind. Idealisation is possible in the sphere of ego-libido as well as in that of object-libido' (1).

Idealisation–especially idealisation of the parents–has a vital part in the setting up of the ideal agencies within the subject (see 'Ideal Ego', 'Ego-Ideal'). Yet it is not synonymous with the *formation* of a person's *ideals*. Indeed, it may apply to an independent object–e.g. idealisation of a loved object. Even in this event, however, the process is always heavily marked by narcissism: 'We see that the object is being treated in the same way as our own ego, so that when we are in love a considerable amount of narcissistic libido overflows on to the object' (2).

*   *   *

Many authors have underscored the defensive function fulfilled by idealisation– notably Melanie Klein. For Klein, idealisation of the object is essentially a defence against the destructive instincts; in this sense it is looked upon as a corollary of an extreme split between, on the one hand, an idealised 'good' object*, endowed with all possible virtues (e.g. an ever-ready, inexhaustible maternal breast), and, on the other hand, a bad object whose persecutory traits are by the same token of the most extreme kind (3).

(1) FREUD. S. 'On Narcissism: An Introduction' (1914c), G.W., X, 161; S.E., XIV, 94.

(2) FREUD, S. *Group Psychology and the Analysis of the Ego* (1921c), G.W., XIII, 124; S.E., XVIII, 112.

(3) Cf. for example KLEIN, M. 'Some Theoretical Conclusions regarding the Emotional Life of the Infant' (1952), in *Developments*, 202.

Ideational Representative (α)

= *D.*: Vorstellungsrepräsentanz (*or* Vorstellungsrepräsentant).–
  Es.: representante ideativo.–*Fr.*: représentant–représentation.–
  I.: rappresentanza data da una rappresentazione.–*P.*: representante ideativo.

Idea or group of ideas to which the instinct becomes fixated in the course of the subject's history; it is through the mediation of the ideational representative that the instinct leaves its mark in the psyche.

'Representative' renders '*Repräsentanz*' (β), a German term of Latin origin which should be understood as implying *delegation* (γ). '*Vorstellung*' is a philo-sophical term whose traditional English equivalent is 'idea'*. '*Vorstellungsre-präsentanz*' means a delegate (in this instance, a delegate of the instinct) in the

203

sphere of ideas; it should be stressed that according to Freud's conception it is the idea that represents the instinct, not the idea itself that is represented by something else–Freud is quite explicit about this (1*a*, 2).

*   *   *

The notion of ideational representatives is met with in those texts where Freud defines the relationship between soma and psyche as that of the instinct to its representatives. It is defined and used above all in the metapsychological works of 1915–'Repression' (1915*d*), 'The Unconscious' (1915*e*)–while it appears in its clearest form in Freud's most thorough presentation of the theory of repression.

It will be recalled that the instinct, in so far as it is somatic, is not directly involved in the psychical operation of repression into the unconscious. This operation can only affect the instinct's psychical representatives–or, more properly, the ideational representatives.

In fact Freud makes a clear distinction between two components of the instinct's psychical representative–namely, the idea and the affect–and he points out that each of them meets a different fate: only the first–the ideational representative–passes unchanged into the unconscious system. (For this distinction, see 'Psychical Representative', 'Affect', 'Repression'.)

What picture are we to form of the ideational representative? Freud never really clarified this concept. As regards 'representative' and the relationship of delegation that it implies between the instinct and itself, see our article on the 'Psychical Representative'. And for 'ideational' (as opposed to affective), the following entries should be consulted: 'Idea' (*Vorstellung*) and 'Thing-Presentation/Word-Presentation' (*Sachvorstellung* or *Dingsvorstellung*, and *Wortvorstellung*).

In the theory of the unconscious system presented in his 1915 article on repression, Freud looks upon ideational representatives not only as '*contents*' of the *Ucs.* but also as what actually constitutes it. In fact it is through a single and unitary process–primal repression*–that the instinct becomes fixated to a representative and that the unconscious is constituted: 'We have reason to assume that there is a *primal repression*, a first phase of repression, which consists in the psychical (ideational) representative of the instinct being denied entrance into the conscious. With this a *fixation* is established; the representative in question persists unaltered from then onwards and the instinct remains attached to it' (1*b*).

In a passage such as this, the term 'fixation'* brings together two different ideas: first, the idea, which is central to the genetic conception, of a fixation of the instinct at a stage or to an object; and secondly, the notion of an inscription of the instinct in the unconscious. This second idea–or, perhaps better, this image–is undoubtedly a very old one in Freud's work: it is advanced as early as the correspondence with Fliess in one of the very first models of the psychical apparatus, here said to comprise several layers of registrations of signs (*Niederschriften*) (3); and it is taken up again in *The Interpretation of Dreams* (1900*a*), notably in a passage dealing with the hypothesis of the transcription of ideas as they pass out of one system into another (4).

This analogy between the instinct's relationship to its representative and the inscription of a sign (or, to borrow a term from linguistics, of a 'signifier') might perhaps serve to shed light on the nature of the ideational representative.

(α) See note (α) to the article 'Instinctual Representative'.

(β) The usual term in German is '*der Repräsentant*', but this is rarely employed by Freud, who prefers the form '*die Repräsentanz*', closer to the Latin and no doubt more abstract.

(γ) 'X is my representative'.

(1) FREUD, S. 'Repression' (1915*d*): a) Cf. G.W., X, 255; S.E., XIV, 152–53. b) G.W., X, 250; S.E., XIV, 148.

(2) Cf. FREUD, S. 'The Unconscious' (1915*e*), G.W., X, 275–76; S.E., XIV, 177.

(3) Cf. FREUD, S., letter dated December 6, 1896, *Anf.*, 185–86; S.E., I, 233.

(4) Cf. FREUD, S., G.W., II–III, 615; S.E., V, 610.

Identification

= *D*.: Identifizierung.–*Es*.: identificación.–*Fr*.: identification.–*I*.: identificazione.–*P*.: identificação.

Psychological process whereby the subject assimilates an aspect, property or attribute of the other and is transformed, wholly or partially, after the model the other provides. It is by means of a series of identifications that the personality is constituted and specified.

a. Since the term 'identification' also has a place in both common and philosophical usage, it may be helpful from the semantic point of view if we begin by delimiting its application in psycho-analytic language.

The substantive 'identification' can be understood in two ways: transitively, in a sense corresponding to the verbal 'to identify', and reflexively, in a sense corresponding to 'to identify (oneself) with'. This is true for both the meanings of the term distinguished by Lalande as follows:

(i) 'Action of identifying, that is, of recognising as identical; either numerically, e.g. "identification of a criminal", or by kind, as for example when an object is recognised as belonging to a certain class [...] or again, when one class of facts is seen to be assimilable to another.'

(ii) 'Act whereby an individual becomes identical with another or two beings become identical with each other (whether in thought or in fact, completely or *secundum quid*)' (1).

Freud uses the word in both these senses. Identification in the sense of the procedure whereby the relationship of similitude–the 'just-as-if' relationship–is expressed through a substitution of one image for another, is described by him as characteristic of the dream-work* (2*a*). This is undoubtedly an instance of Lalande's meaning (i), although identification does not here entail cognition: it is an active procedure which replaces a partial identity or a latent resemblance by a total identity.

Psycho-analysis uses the term above all, however, in the sense of *identification of oneself with*.

Identification

b. In everyday usage, identification in this last sense overlaps a whole group of psychological concepts–e.g. imitation, *Einfühlung* (empathy), sympathy, mental contagion, projection*, etc.

It has been suggested for the sake of clarity that a distinction be drawn within this field, according to the direction in which the identification operates, between an identification that is *heteropathic* (Scheler) and *centripetal* (Wallon), where the subject identifies his own self with the other, and an *idiopathic* and *centrifugal* variety in which the subject identifies the other with himself. Finally, in cases where both these tendencies are present at once, we are said to be dealing with a more complex form of identification, one which is sometimes invoked to account for the constitution of a 'we'.

*   *   *

In Freud's work the concept of identification comes little by little to have the central importance which makes it, not simply one psychical mechanism among others, but the operation itself whereby the human subject is constituted. This evolution is correlated chiefly, in the first place, with the coming to the fore of the Oedipus complex viewed in the light of its structural consequences, and secondly, with the revision effected by the second theory of the psychical apparatus, according to which those agencies that become differentiated from the id are given their specific characters by the identifications of which they are the outcome.

Identification was nevertheless evoked by Freud in very early days, principally apropos of hysterical symptoms. The phenomenon known as imitation or mental contagion had, of course, long been recognised, but Freud went further when he explained such phenomena by positing the existence of an unconscious factor common to the individuals involved: '. . . identification is not simple imitation but *assimilation* on the basis of a similar aetiological pretension; it expresses a resemblance and is derived from a common element which remains in the unconscious' (2*b*). This common element is a phantasy*: the agoraphobic identifies unconsciously with a 'streetwalker', and her symptom is a defence against this identification and against the sexual wish that it presupposes (3*a*). Lastly, Freud notes at a very early date that several different identifications can exist side by side: 'Multiplicity of Psychical Personalities. The fact of identification perhaps allows us to take the phrase *literally*' (3*b*).

The notion of identification is subsequently refined thanks to a number of theoretical innovations:

a. The idea of oral incorporation emerges in the years 1912–15 (*Totem and Taboo* [1912–13]; 'Mourning and Melancholia' [1917*e*]). In particular, Freud brings out the role of incorporation in melancholia, where the subject identifies in the oral mode with the lost object by regressing to the type of object-relationship characteristic of the oral stage* (see 'Incorporation', 'Cannibalistic').

b. The idea of narcissism* is evolved. In 'On Narcissism: An Introduction' (1914*c*), Freud introduces the dialectic which links the narcissistic object-choice* (where the object is chosen on the model of the subject's own self) with identification (where the subject, or one or other of his psychical agencies, is constituted on the model of earlier objects, such as his parents or people around him).

206

c. The effects of the Oedipus complex* on the structuring of the subject are described in terms of identification: cathexes* of the parents are abandoned and identifications take their place (4).

Once the Oedipus complex has been expressed as a general formula, Freud shows that these identifications form a complicated structure inasmuch as father and mother are each both love-object and object of rivalry. It is probable, moreover, that an ambivalence of this kind with respect to the object is a precondition of the institution of any identification.

d. The development of the second theory of the psychical apparatus testifies to the new depth and growing significance of the idea of identification. The individual's mental agencies are no longer described in terms of systems in which images, memories and psychical 'contents' are inscribed, but rather as the relics (in different modes) of object-relationships.

This elaboration of the notion is not carried so far, either in Freud or in psycho-analytic theory as a whole, as a systematisation of the various modes of identification. In fact Freud admits to dissatisfaction with his own formulations on the subject (5a). The most thorough exposition of the matter that he did attempt will be found in Chapter VII of *Group Psychology and the Analysis of the Ego* (1921c). In this text Freud eventually distinguishes between three modes of identification:

(i) The primal form of the emotional tie with the object.

(ii) The regressive replacement for an abandoned object-choice.

(iii) In the absence of any sexual cathexis of the other person the subject may still identify with him to the extent that they have some trait in common (e.g. the wish to be loved): owing to displacement, identification in such a case will occur in regard to some other trait (hysterical identification).

Freud also indicates here that in certain cases identification does not affect the object as a whole but merely a 'single trait' from it (6).

Finally, the study of hypnosis, of being in love and of the psychology of groups leads Freud to contrast that identification which constitutes or enriches an agency of the personality with the opposite trend, where it is the object which is 'put in the place' of a psychical agency—as for example in the case of the leader who replaces the ego-ideal* of the members of his group. It is noteworthy that in such instances there is also a mutual identification between the individuals in the group, but this requires as a precondition that a 'replacement' of the kind just described has occurred. The distinctions we took note of above (centripetal, centrifugal and reciprocal identifications) can thus be recognised in this context, which views them from a structural standpoint.

*   *   *

The term 'identification' should be distinguished from other, kindred terms like 'incorporation', 'introjection' and 'internalisation'*.

Incorporation and introjection are prototypes of identification—or at any rate of certain modes of identification where the mental process is experienced and symbolised as a bodily one (ingesting, devouring, keeping something inside oneself, etc.).

The distinction between identification and internalisation is a more complex one, since it brings into play theoretical assumptions concerning the nature of

207

what it is that the subject assimilates himself to. From a purely conceptual point of view we may say that he identifies with *objects*–i.e. with a person ('the assimilation of one ego to another one' (5*b*)), with a characteristic of a person, or with a part-object*–whereas he internalises intersubjective *relations*. The question which of these two processes is the primary one, however, remains unanswered. We may note that the identification of a subject A with a subject B is not generally total but *secundum quid*–a fact which sends us back to some particular aspect of A's *relationship* to B: I do not identify with my boss but with some trait of his which has to do with my sado-masochistic relationship to him. But at the same time the identification always preserves the stamp of its earliest prototypes: incorporation affects *things*, with the relationship in question being indistinguishable from the object which embodies it; the object with which the child entertains an aggressive relationship becomes in effect the 'bad object' which is then introjected. A further point–and an essential one–is that a subject's identifications viewed as a whole are in no way a coherent relational system. Demands coexist within an agency like the super-ego*, for instance, which are diverse, conflicting and disorderly. Similarly, the ego-ideal* is composed of identifications with cultural ideals that are not necessarily harmonious.

(1) LALANDE, A. *Vocabulaire technique et critique de la philosophie* (Paris: P.U.F., 1951).

(2) FREUD, S. *The Interpretation of Dreams* (1900a): a) Cf. G.W., II–III, 324–25; S.E., IV, 319–20. b) G.W., II–III, 155–56; S.E., IV, 150.

(3) FREUD, S.: a) *Anf.*, 193–94; *Origins*, 181–82. b) *Anf.*, 211; S.E., I, 249.

(4) Cf. notably FREUD, S. 'The Dissolution of the Oedipus Complex' (1924d), G.W., XIII, 395–402; S.E., XIX, 171–79.

(5) FREUD, S. *New Introductory Lectures on Psycho-Analysis* (1933a [1932]): a) Cf. G.W., XV, 70; S.E., XXII, 63. b) Cf. G.W., XV, 69; S.E., XXII, 63.

(6) Cf. FREUD, S., G.W., XIII, 117; S.E., XVIII, 107.

Identification with the Aggressor

= *D*.: Identifizierung mit dem Angreifer.–*Es*.: identificación con el agresor.–
Fr.: identification à l'agresseur.–*I*.: identificazione con l'aggressore.–
P.: identificação ao agressor.

Defence mechanism identified and described by Anna Freud (1936): faced with an external threat (typically represented by a criticism emanating from an authority), the subject identifies himself with his aggressor. He may do so either by appropriating the aggression itself, or else by physical or moral emulation of the aggressor, or again by adopting particular symbols of power by which the aggressor is designated. According to Anna Freud, this mechanism predominates in the constitution of the preliminary stage of the super-ego: aggression at this time is still directed outwards and has not as yet been turned round against the subject in the shape of self-criticism.

This expression does not occur in Freud's writings, but it has been pointed out that he does describe the mechanism to which it refers–notably in Chapter III of *Beyond the Pleasure Principle* (1920g), in connection with certain children's games.

Ferenczi speaks of identification with the aggressor in a very specific sense: the aggression he has in mind is the sexual attack made by an adult who lives in a world of passion and guilt upon a supposedly innocent child (see 'Scene of Seduction'). The behaviour concerned, described as the consequence of fear, is a total submission to the will of the aggressor; the change brought about in the personality is 'the introjection of the guilt feelings of the adult' (1).

Anna Freud sees identification with the aggressor at work in a variety of contexts–in physical aggression, criticism, etc.; the phenomenon may occur either after or before the feared aggression. The behaviour we observe is the outcome of a reversal of roles: the aggressed turns aggressor.

Those authors who assign to this mechanism an important part in the individual's development differ in their assessment of its scope, especially with regard to the setting up of the super-ego. In Anna Freud's opinion, the subject passes through a first stage in which the whole aggressive relationship is reversed: the aggressor is introjected while the person attacked, criticised or guilty is projected outwards. Only at a second stage is the aggressiveness turned inwards, and the entire relationship internalised*.

Daniel Lagache, for his part, holds that identification with the aggressor occurs rather at the beginning of the formation of the ideal ego*: within the framework of the conflict of demands between child and adult, the subject identifies with the adult, whom he endows with omnipotence; this implies that the other person is misperceived, subjugated, even abolished altogether (2).

René Spitz makes great use of this idea in his *No and Yes* (1957). In his view the turning round of aggressiveness against the aggressor is the predominant mechanism in the acquisition of the capacity to say no, whether in word or gesture–an attainment which Spitz places at about the fifteenth month of life.

*   *   *

Where should identification with the aggressor be placed within psycho-analytic theory as a whole? Is it a highly specific mechanism or, alternatively, simply an important part of what is usually called *identification**? And in particular, what are its links with what is classically referred to as identification with the rival in the Oedipal situation? Those authors who have given a prominent role to this mechanism do not appear to have formulated the problem in such terms. Nonetheless, it is striking that the observations reported have as a rule situated identification with the aggressor in the context not of a triangular but of a dual relationship–a relationship whose basis, as Lagache has so often stressed, is sado-masochistic in character.

(1) FERENCZI, S. 'Sprachverwirrung zwischen den Erwachsenen und dem Kind' (1932–33). English trans.: 'Confusion of Tongues between Adults and the Child', in *Final Contributions*, 162.

(2) LAGACHE, D. 'Pouvoir et personne', *L'évolution psychiatrique*, 1962, I, 111–19.

Imaginary (sb. & adj.)

= *D.*: das Imaginäre. – *Es.*: imaginario. – *Fr.*: imaginaire. – *I.*: immaginario. – *P.*: imaginário.

In the sense given to this term by Jacques Lacan (and generally used substantively): one of the three essential orders of the psycho-analytic field, namely the Real, the Symbolic* and the Imaginary (α). The imaginary order is characterised by the prevalence of the relation to the image of the counterpart (*le semblable*).

The concept of the 'Imaginary' can be grasped initially by reference to one of Lacan's earliest theoretical developments of the theme of the *mirror stage**. In his work on this topic, Lacan brought forward the idea that the ego of the human infant–as a result, in particular, of its biological prematurity–is constituted on the basis of the image of the counterpart (specular ego).

Bearing in mind this primordial experience: we may categorise the following as falling into the Imaginary:

a. from the intrasubjective point of view, the basically narcissistic relation of the subject to his ego (1);

b. from the intersubjective point of view, a so-called *dual* relationship based on–and captured by–the image of a counterpart (erotic attraction, aggressive tension). For Lacan, a counterpart (i.e. another who is me) can only exist by virtue of the fact that the ego is originally another (2);

c. As regards the environment (*Umwelt*) a relation of a type that animal ethologists (Lorenz, Tinbergen) have described and which bears out the importance that a particular *Gestalt* may have in the triggering-off of behaviour;

d. lastly, as regards meaning, the Imaginary implies a type of apprehension in which factors such as resemblance and homoeomorphism play a decisive role, as is borne out by a sort of coalescence of the signifier with the signified.

Lacan's use of the term 'Imaginary' is highly idiosyncratic, yet it is not entirely unrelated to the usual meaning, for he holds that all imaginary behaviour and relationships are irremediably deceptive.

Lacan insists on the difference, and the opposition, between the Imaginary and the Symbolic, showing that intersubjectivity cannot be reduced to the group of relations that he classes as imaginary; it is particularly important, in his view, that the two 'orders' should not be confused in the course of analytic treatment.

(α) *Translator's note:* in capitalising these terms, I have followed the proposal of Lacan's translator, Anthony Wilden; cf. *The Language of the Self* (Baltimore: Johns Hopkins Press, 1968), xv.

(β) Cf. the use of the simulacrum in ethology as a means of proving this empirically (employment of artificial stimuli/signals to trigger off instinctual patterns of response).

(1) Cf. LACAN, J. 'Le stade du miroir comme formateur de la fonction du Je', *R.F.P.* 1949, XIII, 449–53. Also in *Écrits* (Paris: Seuil, 1966), 93–100.

(2) Cf., for example, LACAN, J. 'L'agressivité en psychanalyse', *R.F.P.*, 1948, XII, 367–88. Also in *Écrits* (Paris: Seuil, 1966), 101–24.

(3) Cf. LACAN, J. 'La direction de la cure et les principes de son pouvoir', *La Psychanalyse*, 1958, VI; and in *Écrits* (Paris: Seuil, 1966), 585–645.

Imago

(The Latin word has been adopted in the different languages.)

Unconscious prototypical figure which orientates the subject's way of apprehending others; it is built up on the basis of the first real and phantasied relationships within the family environment.

The concept of the imago is attributable to Jung who, in his 'Wandlungen und Symbole der Libido' of 1911 (translation: *Psychology of the Unconscious* [New York: 1916; London: 1919]), describes maternal, paternal and fraternal imagos.

Imago and complex* are related concepts: they both deal with the same area –namely, the relations between the child and its social and family environment. The notion of the complex refers, however, to the effect upon the subject of the interpersonal situation as a whole, whereas that of the imago evokes an imaginary residue of one or other of the participants in that situation.

The imago is often defined as an 'unconscious representation'. It should be looked upon, however, as an acquired imaginary set rather than as an image: as a stereotype through which, as it were, the subject views the other person. Feelings and behaviour, for example, are just as likely to be the concrete expressions of the imago as are mental images. Nor, it may be added, should the imago be understood as a reflection of the real world, even in a more or less distorted form: the imago of a terrifying father, for instance, may perfectly well be met with in a subject whose real father is unassertive.

Incorporation

= *D*.: Einverleibung.–*Es*.: incorporación.–*Fr*.: incorporation.–*I*.: incorporazione.– *P*. incorporação.

Process whereby the subject, more or less on the level of phantasy, has an object penetrate his body and keeps it 'inside' his body. Incorporation constitutes an instinctual aim* and a mode of object-relationship* which are characteristic of the oral stage*; although it has a special relationship with the mouth and with the ingestion of food, it may also be lived out in relation with other erotogenic zones and other functions. Incorporation provides the corporal model for introjection* and identification*.

Freud introduces the term 'incorporation' while developing the notion of the oral stage (1915); its use puts the emphasis on the relationship to the object, where formerly–notably in the first edition of the *Three Essays on the Theory of Sexuality* (1905d)–Freud had described oral activity from the relatively limited viewpoint of pleasure derived from sucking.

Several instinctual aims are involved in the process of incorporation. In

211

Infantile Amnesia

1915, in the context of what was then his theory of the instincts (the opposition between sexual instincts on the one hand and the ego-instincts or instincts of self-preservation on the other), Freud stresses that the two functions of sexuality and nourishment are closely bound up with one another.

Within the framework of his final instinct theory (opposing life to death instincts), it is above all the fusion of libido and aggressiveness that Freud brings to the fore: 'During the oral stage of organisation of the libido, the act of obtaining erotic mastery over an object coincides with that object's destruction' (2). This approach was to be developed by Abraham and, later, by Melanie Klein (see 'Oral-Sadistic Stage').

Actually incorporation contains three meanings: it means to obtain pleasure by making an object penetrate oneself; it means to destroy this object; and it means, by keeping it within oneself, to appropriate the object's qualities. It is this last aspect that makes incorporation into the matrix of introjection and identification.

Incorporation is confined neither to oral activity proper nor to the oral stage, though orality does furnish the prototype of incorporation. Other erotogenic zones and other functions may in fact serve as its basis (incorporation via the skin, respiration, sight, hearing). Similarly, there is an anal incorporation in so far as the rectal cavity is identified with a mouth, and a genital incorporation that is most strikingly manifested in the phantasy of the retention of the penis within the body.

Abraham and subsequently Klein have pointed out that the incorporation process and cannibalism* can also be partial–that is to say, they can operate on part-objects*.

(1) Cf. FREUD, S.: section 6, inserted in 1915, G.W., V, 98; S.E., VII, 197.
(2) FREUD, S. *Beyond the Pleasure Principle* (1920g), G.W., XIII, 58; S.E., XVIII, 54.

Infantile Amnesia

= *D.*: infantile Amnesie. – *Es.*: amnesia infantil. – *Fr.*: amnésie infantile. – *I.*: amnesia infantile. – *P.*: amnésia infantil.

That amnesia which generally affects the facts of the first years of life. Freud does not consider this amnesia to be the result of any functional inability of the young child to record his impressions; instead, he attributes it the repression which falls upon infantile sexuality and extends to nearly all the events of early childhood. The temporal limit of the field covered by infantile amnesia is constituted by the decline of the Oedipus complex* and the entry into the latency period*.

Infantile amnesia is not one of the discoveries of psycho-analysis. Faced with the clear evidence of this phenomenon, however, Freud was not satisfied by an explanation of it founded on functional immaturity, and he proposed a specific interpretation of his own. Just like hysterical amnesia, infantile amnesia

212

can in principle be dispelled; it does not imply any destruction or absence of registrations of memories, but is the outcome of a repression (1). Freud further sees such amnesia as the prerequisite of subsequent repressions*–and especially of hysterical amnesia. (On this question, see especially the passage of the *Three Essays* just referred to.)

(1) Cf. FREUD, S. *Three Essays on the Theory of Sexuality* (1905d), G. W., V, 175–77; S.E., VII, 174–76.

Inferiority Complex

= *D.*: Minderwertigkeitskomplex.–*Es.*: complejo de inferioridad.–
Fr.: complexe d'infériorité.–*I.*: complesso d'inferiorità–*P.*: complexo de inferioridade.

Term deriving from Adler's psychology: a very general designation for the whole of the attitudes, ideas and types of behaviour that are more or less masked expressions or reactions of a feeling of inferiority.

See 'Sense of Inferiority'.

Innervation

= *D.*: Innervation.–*Es.*: inervación.–*Fr.*: innervation.–*I.*: innervazione.–*P.*: inervação.

Term used by Freud in his earliest works to denote the fact that a certain energy is transported to a particular part of the body where it brings about motor or sensory phenomena.
    Innervation, which is a physiological phenomenon, is possibly produced by the conversion* of psychical into nervous energy.

The term 'innervation' may pose a problem for the reader of Freud. The fact is that it is generally used nowadays to mean a detail of anatomy: the route of a nerve on its way to a given organ. For Freud, however, innervation was a physiological process: the transmission, generally in an efferent direction, of energy along a nerve-pathway. Witness this statement apropos of hysteria: '. . . the affect that is torn from [the idea is] used for a somatic innervation. (That is, the excitation is "converted".)' (1)

(1) FREUD, S. and BREUER, J. *Studies on Hysteria* (1895d), G.W., I, 228; S.E., II, 285.

Instinct (or Drive)

= I. *D.*: Instinkt.–*Es.*: instinto.–*Fr.*: instinct.–*I.*: istinto.–*P.*: instinto.
II. *D.*: Trieb.–*Es.*: instinto.–*Fr.*: pulsion (*or* instinct).–*I.*: istinto *or* pulsione.–
P.: impulso or pulsão.

I. Traditionally, a hereditary behaviour pattern peculiar to an animal species, varying little from one member of this species to another and unfolding in accordance with a temporal scheme which is generally resistant to change and apparently geared to a purpose.

II. Term generally accepted by English-speaking psycho-analytic authors as a rendering of the German '*Trieb*': dynamic process consisting in a *pressure* (charge of energy, motricity factor) which directs the organism towards an aim. According to Freud, an instinct has its *source* in a bodily stimulus; its *aim* is to eliminate the state of tension obtaining at the instinctual source; and it is in the *object*, or thanks to it, that the instinct may achieve its aim.

I. The word 'instinct' is used to translate two different German words, '*Instinkt*' and '*Trieb*'. The latter is of Germanic origin, has long been in use and retains overtones suggestive of pressure (*Treiben* = to push); the use of '*Trieb*' accentuates not so much a precise goal as general orientation, and draws attention to the irresistible nature of the pressure rather than to the stability of its aim and object.

Some writers seem to use '*Instinkt*' and '*Trieb*' interchangeably (α); others apparently draw an implicit distinction by keeping '*Instinkt*' as a designation (in zoology, for example) for behaviour predetermined by heredity and appearing in virtually identical form in all individual members of a single species (1).

In Freud's work the two terms are used in quite distinct senses. The Freudian conception of *Trieb*–a pressure that is relatively indeterminate both as regards the behaviour it induces and as regards the satisfying object–differs quite clearly from theories of instinct, whether in their traditional form or in the revised version proposed by modern researchers (the concepts of behaviour patterns, innate trigger-mechanisms, specific stimuli-signals, etc.). When Freud does use the word '*Instinkt*' it is in the classical sense: he speaks of *Instinkt* in animals confronted by danger and of the 'instinctive recognition of dangers' (2), etc. Moreover, when Freud asks whether 'inherited mental formations exist in the human being–something analogous to instinct (*Instinkt*) in animals' (3), he does not look for such a counterpart in what he calls *Triebe*, but instead in that 'hereditary, genetically acquired factor in mental life' (4) constituted by *primal phantasies** (primal scene*, castration*).

Thus Freud makes use of two terms that it is quite possible to contrast with each other, though no such contrast has an explicit place in his theory. The distinction has hardly ever been drawn in the psycho-analytic literature, however, especially since 'instinct' is used to translate both words (β). There is consequently a risk that the Freudian theory of the instincts may be confused with psychological conceptions of animal instinct, and the unique aspects of Freud's approach may be blurred, particularly the thesis of the relatively undetermined

214

nature of the motive force in question, and the notions of contingence of object*
and variability of aim*.

II. Although the term '*Trieb*' makes its first appearance in Freud's writings
only in 1905, the idea originates as an energetic notion in a distinction that
Freud made in very early days between two types of excitation (*Reiz*) to which
the organism is subjected, and which it must discharge in accordance with the
principle of constancy*. Alongside external excitations, from which the subject
may take flight, there exist internal sources of a constant inflow of excitation
which the organism cannot evade and which is the basis of the functioning of
the psychical apparatus*.

Three Essays on the Theory of Sexuality (1905*d*) was the work which introduced the term '*Trieb*', and along with it the distinction (which Freud never
ceased using thenceforward) between *source*, *object* and *aim*. The Freudian
conception of instinct emerges in the course of the description of human sexuality. Basing himself notably upon the study of the perversions* and of the
modes of infantile sexuality, Freud contests the so-called popular view that
assigns to the sexual instinct a specific aim and object and localises it in the
excitation and operation of the genital apparatus. He shows how, on the contrary,
the object is variable, contingent and only chosen in its definitive form in consequence of the vicissitudes of the subject's history. He shows too how aims are
many and fragmented (see 'Component Instinct'), and closely dependent on
somatic sources which are themselves manifold, and capable of acquiring and
retaining a predominant role for the subject (erotogenic zones*): the component
instincts only become subordinate to the genital zone and integrated into the
achievement of coitus at the end of a complex evolution which biological
maturation alone does not guarantee.

The final element that Freud introduced in connection with the idea of the
instinct was that of *pressure*, conceived as a quantitative economic factor—a
'demand made upon the mind for work' (5*a*). It is in 'Instincts and their Vicissitudes' (1915*c*) that Freud brings together these four aspects—pressure, source,
object, aim—and proposes an overall definition of the instinct (5*b*).

III. What is the *location* of this force that attacks the organism from within,
exerting pressure on it to carry out particular actions liable to precipitate a
discharge of excitation? Are we concerned here with a somatic force or with a
psychical energy? This question, which Freud raises himself, receives a variety
of answers—precisely because the instinct is defined as 'lying on the frontier
between the mental and the physical' (6). The matter is bound up for Freud
with the concept of 'representative', by which he means a sort of delegate sent
into the psyche by the soma. For a more thorough discussion of this question
the reader is referred to our commentary at 'Psychical Representative'.

IV. The idea of the instinct, then, is analysed on the model of sexuality, yet
from the start the Freudian theory opposes other instincts to the sexual one. It
is well known that Freud's instinct theory was always dualistic; the first dualism
he evokes is that between sexual instincts* and ego-instincts* or instincts of
self-preservation*; by these last Freud means the great needs or functions that
are indispensable for the preservation of the individual, the prototype here
being hunger and the function of nutrition.

This polarity obtains, according to Freud, right from the beginnings of

Instinct (or Drive)

sexuality, when the sexual instinct detaches itself from its anaclitic dependence on the self-preservative functions (see 'Anaclisis'). It is postulated in order to account for the psychical conflict*, with the ego deriving the essential part of the energy it needs for defence against sexuality from the instinct of self-preservation.

The new instinctual dualism introduced in *Beyond the Pleasure Principle* (1920g) contrasts life instincts* and death instincts*, modifying the function and location of the instincts in the conflict.

a. The topographical conflict (between the defensive agency and the repressed agency) no longer coincides with the instinctual conflict: the id* is pictured as an instinctual reservoir containing both types of instinct. The energy used by the ego* is drawn from this common fund, particularly in the form of 'desexualised and sublimated' energy.

b. The two great classes of instincts are postulated in this last theory less as the concrete motive forces of the actual functioning of the organism than as fundamental principles which *ultimately* regulate its activity: 'The forces which we assume to exist behind the tensions caused by the needs of the id are called *instincts*' (7). This shift of emphasis is especially clear in a familiar statement of Freud's: 'The theory of the instincts is so to say our mythology. Instincts are mythical entities, magnificent in their indefiniteness' (8).

*   *   *

The Freudian approach, as even this brief survey shows, tends to overturn the traditional conception of instinct. It does so in two contrasting ways. In the first place, the concept of 'component instinct' underscores the idea that the sexual instinct exists to begin with in a 'polymorphous' state and aims chiefly at the elimination of tension at the level of the somatic source, and that it attaches itself in the course of the subject's history to representatives which determine the object and the mode of satisfaction: initially indeterminate, the internal pressure faces vicissitudes that will stamp it with highly individualised traits. But at the same time, far from postulating–as the instinct theorists so readily do–that behind each type of activity there lies a corresponding biological force, Freud places all instinctual manifestations under the head of a single great basic antagonism. What is more, this antagonism is derived from the mythical tradition: first, between Hunger and Love, and later, between Love and Discord.

(α) Cf., for example, *Der Begriff des Instinktes einst und jetzt* (The notion of instinct formerly and today), third edition (Jena, 1920), where Ziegler speaks now of *Geschlechtstrieb*, now of *Geschlechtsinstinkt*.

(β) *Translator's note:* The authors of the present work argue for the use of the term '*pulsion*' as the French equivalent of '*Trieb*' rather than the common rendering '*instinct*'. *Mutatis mutandis*, their arguments would support the replacement of the English 'instinct', wherever it stands for '*Trieb*', by one or other of the much less popular alternatives 'drive' (9) or 'urge'. Given the almost general adoption of 'instinct', however, it has been retained throughout this book. The question is discussed in the General Introduction to the *Standard Edition*, where the editors give their reasons for choosing 'instinct'.

(1) Cf. HEMPELMANN, F. *Tierpsychologie* (Leipzig: Akademische Verlagsgesellschaft, 1926), *passim*.

(2) FREUD, S. *Inhibitions, Symptoms and Anxiety* (1926d), G.W., XIV, 201; S.E., XX, 168.

(3) FREUD, S. 'The Unconscious' (1915e), G.W., X, 294; S.E., XIV, 195.

(4) FREUD, S. 'From the History of an Infantile Neurosis' (1918b [1914]), G.W., XII, 156; S.E., XVII, 120–21.

(5) FREUD, S. 'Instincts and their Vicissitudes' (1915c): a) G.W., X, 214; S.E., XIV, 122. b) Cf. G.W., X, 214–15; S.E., XIV, 122.

(6) FREUD, S. *Three Essays on the Theory of Sexuality* (1905d), G.W., V, 67; S.E., VII, 168.

(7) FREUD, S. *An Outline of Psycho-Analysis* (1940a [1938]), G.W., XVII, 70; S.E., XXIII, 148.

(8) FREUD, S. *New Introductory Lectures on Psycho-Analysis* (1933a [1932]), G.W., XV, 101; S.E., XXII, 95.

(9) Cf. for example KRIS, E., HARTMANN, H. and LOEWENSTEIN, R. 'Notes on the Theory of Aggression', *Psychoanalytic Study of the Child*, 1946, III–IV, 12–13.

Instinct to Master (or for Mastery)

= *D.*: Bemächtigungstrieb.–*Es.*: instinto de dominio.–*Fr.*: pulsion d'emprise.–
I.: istinto *or* pulsione d'impossessamento.–*P.*: impulso *or* pulsão de apossar-se.

Although Freud uses this term on a number of occasions, its sense cannot be tied down with any degree of accuracy. What Freud understands by it is a non-sexual instinct which only fuses with sexuality secondarily and the aim of which is to dominate the object by force.

The term '*Bemächtigungstrieb*' is not easy to translate. The usual rendering 'instinct to master' is not thoroughly satisfactory: mastery suggests a controlled domination whereas *sich bemächtigen* means to seize or dominate by force.

What is Freud's conception of this instinct? An examination of the texts reveals that, schematically speaking, he viewed it in two ways:

a. In writings antedating *Beyond the Pleasure Principle* (1920g), the *Bemächtigungstrieb* is described as a non-sexual instinct which only fuses with sexuality secondarily; it is directed from the outset towards outside objects and constitutes the sole factor present in the primal cruelty of the child.

Freud speaks of such an instinct for the first time in the *Three Essays on the Theory of Sexuality* (1905d): the origin of infantile cruelty is sought in an instinct to master whose original aim is not to make the other person suffer–rather, it simply fails to take the other person into account (this phase precedes pity as well as sadism*) (1a). The instinct to master is said to be independent of sexuality, even though it 'may become united with it at an early stage owing to an anastomosis near their points of origin' (1b).

In 'The Disposition to Obsessional Neurosis' (1913i), the instinct to master is brought up in connection with the relationship between the pair of opposites activity/passivity*, which is predominant at the anal-sadistic stage*: while passivity is based on anal erotism, 'Activity is supplied by the common instinct of mastery, which we call sadism when we find it in the service of the sexual function' (2).

217

Instinct to Master (or for Mastery)

Returning to the question of activity and passivity during the anal-sadistic stage in the 1915 edition of the *Three Essays*, Freud posits the muscular apparatus as the basis of the instinct to master.

Finally, in 'Instincts and their Vicissitudes' (1915c), where the first of Freud's theses regarding sado-masochism* is clearly worked out, the primary aim of 'sadism' is defined as the degradation of the object and its subjugation by violence (*Überwältigung*). Causing suffering is not part of the original aim; the aim of producing pain and the fusion with sexuality occur only with the turning round* into masochism: sadism in the erotogenic sense is the upshot of a second turning round–the turning round of masochism on to the object.

b. With *Beyond the Pleasure Principle* and the introduction of the death instinct*, the question of a specific instinct to master is posed in a different way.

The genesis of sadism is now described as a diversion of the death instinct, which is originally aimed at the destruction of the subject himself, on to the object: 'Is it not plausible to suppose that this sadism is in fact a death instinct which, under the influence of the narcissistic libido, has been forced away from the ego and has consequently only emerged in relation to the object? It now enters the service of the sexual function' (3a).

As to the aim of masochism and sadism–treated henceforward as incarnations of the death instinct–the accent falls no longer on mastery but on destruction.

What becomes then of the mastery that has to be attained over the object? It is no longer assigned to a special instinct, and appears instead as a *form* that the death instinct is able to take on when it 'enters the service' of the sexual instinct: 'During the oral stage of organization of the libido, the act of obtaining erotic mastery (*Liebesbemächtigung*) over an object coincides with that object's destruction; later, the sadistic instinct separates off, and finally, at the stage of genital primacy, it takes on, for the purposes of reproduction, the function of overpowering the sexual object to the extent necessary for carrying out the sexual act' (3b).

*   *   *

It should be noted further that apart from '*Bemächtigung*' Freud also fairly often uses the term '*Bewältigung*', which has a rather similar meaning. As a rule he employs the latter term to denote mastery achieved over an excitation–be it instinctual or external in origin–and the 'binding' (q.v.) of this excitation (α). No strict distinction is drawn between the two terms, however–particularly since there is more than one point of overlap, so far as analytic theory is concerned, between mastery attained over the object and mastery of excitations. Thus in *Beyond the Pleasure Principle*, explaining the role of repetition in children's play as in traumatic neurosis, Freud can postulate–among other hypotheses–that this 'might be put down to an instinct for mastery' (3c). Here the mastery of the object (which, in symbolic shape, is at the subject's entire command) goes hand in hand with the binding together of the traumatic memory and the energy which cathects it.

*   *   *

One of the only authors to have attempted an elaboration of Freud's sparse hints concerning the *Bemächtigungstrieb* is Ives Hendrick, who devoted a series

218

of articles to reopening the question in the context of a developmental ego-psychology inspired by research on learning. His theses may be schematically summarised as follows:

a. There exists an instinct to master, a need to control the environment, which has been neglected by psycho-analysts in favour of the mechanisms of the search for pleasure. This is 'an inborn drive to do and to learn how to do' (4).

b. This instinct is originally asexual; it may be libidinalised secondarily by virtue of a fusion with sadism.

c. It involves a specific kind of pleasure – the pleasure derived from the successful carrying out of a function: '. . . primary pleasure is sought by efficient use of the central nervous system for the performance of well-integrated ego functions which enable the individual to control or alter his environment' (5a).

d. Why should we speak of an *instinct* to master in preference to treating the ego as an organisation which procures types of pleasure that are not instinctual gratifications? In the first place, Hendrick states his aim as the establishment of 'a concept explaining what forces make the ego function' (6) – a 'definition of the ego in terms of instinct'. Secondly, what we are confronted with here, in Hendrick's view, is definitely an instinct 'psychoanalytically defined as the biological source of tensions impelling to specific patterns of action' (5b).

Such a conception has something in common with the view of the instinct to master that we have tried to extract from Freud's writings; what Hendrick is concerned with, however, is a second-level mastery – a progressively adapted control of action itself.

As a matter of fact Freud did not entirely overlook this idea of a mastery established over one's own body, and he saw its basis as lying in 'the child's efforts to gain control (*Herr werden*) over his own limbs' (7).

(α) For such uses of '*Bewältigung*', see, for example, a number of Freud's texts (8). Elsewhere he also uses such terms as '*bändigen*' (to tame) and '*Triebbeherrschung*' (domination of the instinct) (9).

(1) FREUD, S.: a) Cf. G.W., V, 93–94; S.E., VII, 192–93. b) G.W., V, 94; S.E., VII, 193, *n.* 1.

(2) FREUD, S., G.W., VIII, 448; S.E., XII, 322.

(3) FREUD, S.: a) G.W., XIII, 58, S.E., XVIII, 54. b) G.W., XIII, 58; S.E., XVIII, 54. c) G.W., XIII, 14; S.E., XVIII, 16.

(4) HENDRICK, I. 'Instinct and the Ego during Infancy', *P.Q.*, 1942, XI, 40.

(5) HENDRICK, I. 'Work and the Pleasure Principle', *P.Q.*, 1943, XII: a) 311. b) 314.

(6) HENDRICK, I. 'The Discussion of the "Instinct to Master" ', *P.Q.*, 1943, XII, 563.

(7) FREUD, S. 'Instincts and their Vicissitudes' (1915c), G.W., X, 223; S.E., XIV, 130.

(8) FREUD, S. 'On the Grounds for Detaching a Particular Syndrome from Neurasthenia under the Description "Anxiety Neurosis" ' (1895b), G.W., I, 336 and 338; S.E., III, 110 and 112. 'On Narcissism: An Introduction' (1914c), G.W., X, 152; S.E., XIV, 85–86. 'From the History of an Infantile Neurosis' (1918b [1914]), G.W., XII, 83–84; S.E. XVII, 54–55.

(9) Cf. FREUD, S. 'Analysis Terminable and Interminable' (1937c), G.W., XVI, 69 and 74; S.E., XXIII, 225 and 229–30.

Instincts of Self-Preservation

= *D*.: Selbsterhaltungstriebe. – *Es*.: instintos de autoconservación. –
  Fr.: pulsions d'auto-conservation. – *I*.: instinti *or* pulsioni d'autoconservazione. –
  P.: impulsos *or* pulsões de autoconservação.

Term by which Freud designates all needs associated with bodily functions necessary for the preservation of the individual; hunger provides the model of such instincts.
   Within the framework of his first theory of the instincts Freud opposes the instincts of self-preservation to the sexual instincts.

Although this term makes its first appearance in Freud's work only in 1910, the notion of opposing another type of instinct to the sexual one dates back further. It is in fact implicit in what Freud has to say, beginning with *Three Essays on the Theory of Sexuality* (1905*d*), about the anaclitic relationship of sexuality to other somatic functions (see 'Anaclisis'). At the oral level, for instance, sexual pleasure rests upon the activity of taking nourishment: 'The satisfaction of the erotogenic zone is associated, in the first instance, with the satisfaction of the need for nourishment' (1*a*). In the same context Freud also speaks of a 'nutritional instinct' (1*b*).
   In 1910 Freud proposed the distinction that was to remain central to his first instinct theory: '. . . a quite specially important part is played by the undeniable opposition between the instincts which subserve sexuality, the attainment of sexual pleasure, and those other instincts, which have as their aim the self-preservation of the individual–the ego-instincts. As the poet has said, all the organic instincts that operate in our mind may be classified as "hunger" or "love" ' (2). This antithesis has two aspects, which Freud brings out together in the writings of this period: the anaclitic relationship of the sexual instincts to the self-preservative ones, and the decisive role of the antagonism between them in the psychical conflict*. This double aspect is evident, for example, in hysterical disturbances of vision: a sole organ, the eye, is the basis of two distinct types of instinctual activity; should conflict develop between them, it also becomes the locus of the symptom.
   As regards the question of *anaclisis*, the reader is referred to our commentary on this term. As to the way in which the two great classes of instincts come to confront one another in the defensive conflict, one of Freud's most explicit passages appears in 'Formulations on the Two Principles of Mental Functioning' (1911*b*). The ego-instincts, since they can only be satisfied by a real object, very quickly make the transition from the pleasure principle to the reality principle, until a point is reached where they become the agents of reality and so stand opposed to the sexual instincts which, being able to achieve satisfaction in a phantasy mode, have remained longer under the exclusive sway of the pleasure principle: 'An essential part of the psychical predisposition to neurosis [...] lies in the delay in educating the sexual instincts to pay regard to reality' (3).
   This view of the matter is summed up in the idea, occasionally voiced by Freud, that the conflict between sexual and self-preservative instincts can

provide a key to the understanding of the transference neuroses* (on this point see our commentary on 'Ego-Instincts').

*   *   *

Freud never made any great effort to present an overall exposition of the different varieties of self-preservative instincts; he generally speaks of them generically or else extrapolates from the special case of hunger. He nonetheless appears to admit the existence of numerous such instincts–as many, in fact, as there are great organic functions (nutrition, defecation, micturition, muscular activity, vision, etc.).

The Freudian antithesis between sexual and self-preservative instincts may raise doubts about the legitimacy of using the one term '*Trieb*' for both categories. It should be noted first of all that when Freud deals with instinct in general he is actually referring, more or less explicitly, to the sexual instinct alone: for instance, he attributes to instinct in general such characteristics as variability of aim and contingency of object. For the self-preservative instincts, however, the paths of access to reality are ready-formed, while the satisfying object is determined from the start; to use a phrase of Max Scheler's, the hunger of the infant at the breast implies an 'intuition of the value food' (4). As is shown by Freud's conception of the anaclitic type of object-choice*, it is the self-preservative instincts which lead sexuality to the object. No doubt it was this distinction that prompted Freud on several occasions to use the term 'need' (*Bedürfnis*) as a designation for self-preservative instincts (5a). In this connection one cannot but stress the artificiality of attempts to establish a strict parallelism, genetically speaking, between the self-preservative functions and the sexual instincts, on the grounds that both are equally subject to begin with to the pleasure principle, before gradually coming under the dominion of the reality principle. In fact the self-preservative functions ought instead to be assigned to the side of the reality principle from the start, and the sexual instincts to the side of the pleasure principle.

Freud's successive revisions of the theory of the instincts caused him to shift the location of the self-preservative functions. In the first place, it is noteworthy that in these attempts at reclassification the hitherto interchangeable concepts of ego-instincts and self-preservative instincts undergo transformations that are not altogether identical. As regards the question of the ego-instincts–the question, in other words, of the nature of the instinctual energy that is placed at the service of the agency of the ego–the reader is referred to our commentaries on 'Ego-Instincts', 'Ego-Libido/Object-Libido' and 'Ego'. Confining ourselves to the self-preservative instincts, we may say–schematically–that:

a. With the introduction of narcissism* (1915), these instincts remain opposed to the sexual ones, despite the fact that the latter are now subdivided according to whether they are directed towards outside objects (object-libido) or on to the ego (ego-libido).

b. Between 1915 and 1920, when Freud makes an 'apparent approach to Jung's views' (5b) and is tempted to adopt an instinctual monism, the self-preservative instincts tend to be looked upon as a particular case of self-love or ego-libido.

c. After 1920 a new dualism is brought forward–that between death instincts* and life instincts*. At first Freud hesitates (6a) as to the position of the self-preservative instincts in this scheme: he begins by classing them among the death instincts, asserting that they merely institute detours which express the fact that 'the organism wishes to die only in its own fashion' (6b); but he reverses this position immediately and treats the preservation of the individual as a particular instance of the work of the life instincts.

The subsequent writings uphold this second view of the matter: 'The contrast between the instincts of self-preservation and the preservation of the species, as well as the contrast between ego-love and object-love, fall within Eros' (7).

(1) FREUD, S.: G.W., V, 82; S.E., VII, 181–82. b) G.W., V, 83; S.E., VII, 182.

(2) FREUD, S. 'The Psycho-Analytic View of Psychogenic Disturbances of Vision' (1910i), G.W., VIII, 97–98; S.E., XI, 214.

(3) FREUD, S., G.W., VIII, 235; S.E., XII, 223.

(4) SCHELER, M. Wesen und Formen der Sympathie (1913).

(5) Cf. FREUD, S. 'Two Encyclopaedia Articles' (1923a [1922]): a) G.W., XIII, 221; S.E. XVIII, 245. b) G.W., XIII, 231–32; S.E., XVIII, 257.

(6) FREUD, S. Beyond the Pleasure Principle (1920g): a) passim. b) G.W., XIII, 41; S.E., XVIII, 39.

(7) FREUD, S. An Outline of Psycho-Analysis (1940a [1938]), G.W., XVII, 71; S.E., XXIII, 148.

Instinctual Component

= D.: Triebkomponente.–Es.: componente instinctivo.–Fr.: composante pulsionnelle.– I.: componente di pulsione.–P.: componente impulsor(a) or pulsional.

See 'Component Instinct'.

Instinctual Impulse

= D.: Triebregung.–Es.: impulso instintual.–Fr.: motion pulsionelle.– I.: moto pulsionale or istintivo.–P.: moção impulsora or pulsional.

Term used by Freud to designate the instinct seen under its dynamic aspect, i.e. in so far as it takes on concrete and specific form in a determinate internal stimulus.

This term appears for the first time in 'Instincts and their Vicissitudes' (1915c), but the idea connoted is a very old one in Freud's work. Thus he means exactly the same thing when he speaks in the 'Project for a Scientific Psychology' (1950a [1895]) of endogenous stimuli (endogene Reize).

There is very little difference between 'Triebregung' and 'Trieb' (instinct*)–in fact Freud often uses the two interchangeably. A reading of all the relevant texts, however, does make a real distinction feasible here: the instinctual impulse is the instinct in action, the instinct considered at the moment when it is set in motion by an organic change.

Thus Freud places the instinctual impulse on the same level as the instinct. When the instinct is conceived of as a biological modification–and consequently as deeper, strictly speaking, than the distinction between conscious and unconscious–then the same goes for the instinctual impulse: 'When we [...] speak of an unconscious instinctual impulse or of a repressed instinctual impulse, the looseness of phraseology is a harmless one. We can only mean an instinctual impulse the ideational representative of which is unconscious, for nothing else comes into consideration' (1).

It is worth noting that Freud uses '*Regung*' in compound terms other than '*Triebregung*', always with the same connotation of internal movement: for example, '*Wunschregung*' (wishful impulse), '*Affektregung*' (affective impulse).

(1) FREUD, S. 'The Unconscious' (1915e), G.W., X, 276; S.E., XIV, 177.

Instinctual Representative (α)

= *D*.: Triebrepräsentanz (*or* Triebrepräsentant).–
   Es.: representación *or* representante del instinto.–*Fr*.: représentant de la pulsion.–
   I.: rappresentanza *or* rappresentante della pulsione.–
   P.: representante do impulso *or* pulsional (da pulsão).

Term used by Freud to designate the elements or the process by means of which the instinct finds psychical expression. At times it is synonymous with 'ideational representative'*, while at others its meaning is broadened so as to embrace the affect as well.

As a general rule Freud makes no distinction between the instinctual representative and the ideational one. In his description of the phases of repression*, the fate of the ideational representative is envisaged alone until another 'element of the psychical representative' has to be taken into account–namely, the quota of affect* (*Affektbetrag*), which 'corresponds to the instinct in so far as the latter has become detached from the idea and finds expression, proportionate to its quantity, in processes which are sensed as affects' (1a).

Alongside the ideational element in the instinctual representative, therefore, we also find a quantitative or affective factor. Freud does not, however, use a term 'affective representative', although one might well do so by analogy with 'ideational representative'.

The fate of the affective factor is nevertheless of cardinal importance for repression, whose 'motive and purpose', in fact, is 'nothing else than the avoidance of unpleasure. It follows that the vicissitude of the quota of affect belonging to the representative is far more important than the vicissitude of the idea' (1b).

It will be recalled that this 'vicissitude' may take a variety of forms: if the affect is preserved, it may be displaced on to another idea; alternatively, it may be transformed into another affect–especially anxiety; or again, it may be

223

Intellectualisation

suppressed (1c, 2a). But a suppression* of this kind, be it noted, is not a repression into the unconscious in the same sense as the one which affects the idea; in fact it is impossible, properly, to speak of an unconscious affect. What is loosely referred to in this way consists solely, in the system *Ucs.*, of a 'potential beginning which is prevented from developing' (2b).

Strictly speaking, then, the instinct may be said to be represented by the affect only at the level of the system *Pcs.-Cs.*–or, in other words, at the level of the ego.

(α) In the interests of clarity we are devoting separate articles to three terms whose meaning is so nearly identical that in most Freudian texts they are used interchangeably: 'Instinctual Representative', 'Psychical Representative' and 'Ideational Representative'. The three articles are all concerned with a single concept, but we have chosen to give over each of our commentaries to the discussion of a particular point.

The present article recalls the respective functions assigned by Freud to the idea and the affect in so far as they represent the instinct. At the entry 'Psychical Representative' we have concentrated on defining what Freud means when he speaks of a 'representative' (of the somatic domain in the psychical one). Lastly, the article 'Ideational Representative' shows that the job of representing the instinct falls principally to the lot of the *idea* (*Vorstellung*).

Further, the articles 'Idea' and 'Thing-Presentation/Word-Presentation' deal with aspects of the same conceptual framework.

(1) FREUD, S. 'Repression' (1915d): a) G.W., X, 255; S.E., XIV, 152. b) G.W., X, 256; S.E., XIV, 153. c) Cf. G.W., X, 255–56; S.E., XIV, 153.

(2) FREUD, S. 'The Unconscious' (1915e): a) Cf. G.W., X, 276–77; S.E., XIV, 178. b) G.W. X, 277; S.E., XIV, 178.

Intellectualisation

= *D.*: Intellektualisierung.–*Es.*: intelectualización.–*Fr.*: intellectualisation.– *I.*: intellettualizzazione.–*P.*: intelectualização.

Process whereby the subject, in order to master his conflicts and emotions, attempts to couch them in a discursive form.

The term usually has a pejorative ring to it: it denotes the preponderance, particularly during treatment, of abstract thought over the emergence and acknowledgement of affects and phantasies.

The term 'intellectualisation' is not met with in Freud's writings, and psychoanalytic literature as a whole contains few theoretical accounts of the process. Among the most explicit texts is Anna Freud's, which describes intellectualisation in the adolescent as a defence mechanism but looks upon it as the exacerbation of a normal process whereby the 'ego' attempts 'to lay hold on the instinctual processes by connecting them with ideas which can be dealt with in consciousness'; intellectualisation, according to this writer, constitutes 'one of the most general, earliest and most necessary acquirements of the human ego' (1).

The term is used above all as a designation for a mode of resistance met with

224

in treatment. This is more or less patent but invariably constitutes a means of evading the implications of the fundamental rule*.

Thus a given patient will only present his problems in rational and general terms: faced with a choice in his love life, for example, he will hold forth on the relative merits of marriage and free love. Another subject, though describing his own history, character and conflicts accurately, will couch this description in a language of coherent reconstruction (a language he may even borrow from psycho-analysis): instead of talking of his relations with his father, he will mention his 'opposition to authority'. A subtler form of intellectualisation may be compared to what Karl Abraham described as early as 1919 in 'A Particular Form of Neurotic Resistance Against the Psycho-Analytic Method': certain patients seem, so far as the analysis is concerned, to be doing 'good work' and applying the rule; they offer memories, dreams, and even emotional experiences, yet everything suggests that what they say is preplanned and that they are attempting to behave like model subjects; by imposing their own interpretation they avoid possible intrusions of the unconscious or interventions by the analyst, both of which they look upon as dangerous threats.

A number of reservations should be made regarding the use of this term:

a. As our last example shows, it is not always easy to distinguish this mode of resistance from that necessary and fruitful time during which the subject formulates and assimilates discoveries that have been made and interpretations that have been put forward (see 'Working-Through').

b. The idea of intellectualisation harks back to a distinction inherited from the psychology of 'faculties'–namely the distinction between *intellectual* and *affective*. There is a danger of the criticism of intellectualisation leading to an overestimation of 'lived emotional experience' in the psycho-analytic cure, with the result that this cure may become indistinguishable from the cathartic method*. Fenichel puts these two diametrically opposed modes of resistance on a par with each other: in the first type of case, the resistance 'consists in the patient's always being reasonable and refusing to have any understanding for the logic of emotions', while in the second 'the patient floats continuously in unclear emotional experiences without getting the necessary distance and freedom' (2).

*   *   *

Intellectualisation is comparable to other mechanisms described by psycho-analysis, and particularly to rationalisation*. One of the main aims of intel-lectualisation is to keep the affects at arm's length and to neutralise them. In this respect, rationalisation has a different role: instead of implying a systematic avoidance of affects, it merely assigns them motives that are more plausible than true, justifying them in terms of what is rational or ideal (sadistic behaviour, for example, may be justified in wartime by an appeal to the necessity of fighting, to love for one's country, etc.).

(1) FREUD, A. *The Ego and the Mechanisms of Defence* (London: Hogarth Press, 1937; New York: I.U.P. 1946), 178.

(2) FENICHEL, C. *The Psychoanalytic Theory of Neurosis* (New York: Norton, 1945), 28.

Interest, Ego-Interest

= *D.*: Interesse, Ichinteresse.–*Es.*: interés (del yo).–*Fr.*: intérêt, intérêt du moi.–
I.: interesse (dell' io).–*P.*: interesse (do ego).

**Term used by Freud in the context of his first instinctual dualism: the energy of
the instincts of self-preservation as opposed to that of the sexual instincts (libido).**

The specific meaning of 'interest' as indicated in the above definition was
developed in Freud's writings between 1911 and 1914. As we know, libido* is
the name for the cathectic energy of the sexual instincts*; parallel with this,
according to Freud, there is also a cathectic energy that belongs to the instincts
of self-preservation*.

In certain contexts 'interest' is taken in a broader sense to denote both these
types of cathexis, as is the case, for example, in the following passage, where
Freud is using the term for the first time: the paranoic withdraws perhaps 'not
only his libidinal cathexis, but also his interest in general–that is, the cathexes
that proceed from his ego as well' (1). As a reaction to Jung's thesis (α) which
rejects any distinction between libido and 'psychical energy in general', Freud
is led to emphasise the opposition by keeping the term 'interest' exclusively for
those cathexes which emanate from the instincts of self-preservation or ego-
instincts* (see 'Egoism').

For an example of this more specific sense, the reader is referred to the
Introductory Lectures on Psycho-Analysis (1916–17) (3).

(α) Jung maintains that Claparède suggested the term 'interest', and that it was in fact as a
synonym for 'libido' that he did so (4).

(1) FREUD, S. 'Psycho-Analytic Notes on an Autobiographical Account of a Case of
Paranoia (Dementia Paranoides)' (1911c), G.W., XVIII, 307, *n.* 3; S.E., XII, 70, *n.* 2.

(2) Cf. FREUD, S. 'On Narcissism: An Introduction' (1914c), G.W., X, 145–47; S.E., XIV,
79–81.

(3) Cf. FREUD, S., G. W., XI, 430; S.E., XVI, 414.

(4) Cf. JUNG, C. G., 'Versuch einer Darstellung der psychoanalytischen Theorie', *Jahrbuch
psa. Forsch.*, 1913, V, 337 *ff.*

Internalisation

= *D.*: Verinnerlichung.–*Es.*: interiorización–*Fr.*: intériorisation.–*I.*: interiorizzazione.–
P.: interiorização.

a. Term often used as a synonym for 'introjection'*.
**b. More specifically, process whereby intersubjective relations are transformed
into intrasubjective ones (internalisation of a conflict, of a prohibition, etc.).**

This term is in common use in psycho-analysis. It is often taken, particularly
by the Kleinians, to mean the same thing as introjection, namely the trans-

position in phantasy of an external 'good' or 'bad' object, or of a whole or part-object, to the 'inside' of the subject.

In a narrower sense, we only speak of internalisation when it is a *relationship* that is transposed in this way–for example, the relation of authority between father and child is said to be internalised in the relation between super-ego and ego. This process presupposes a structural differentiation within the psyche such that relations and conflicts may be lived out on the intrapsychic level. Such internalisation is correlated with Freud's topographical* notions and particularly with his second theory of the psychical apparatus.

Although, for reasons of terminological accuracy, we have distinguished two meanings of 'internalisation' (a and b above), the two senses are in fact closely linked together: we may say, for instance, that with the decline of the Oedipus complex the subject *introjects* the paternal imago while *internalising* the conflict of authority with the father.

Interpretation

= *D.*: Deutung.–*Es.*: interpretación.–*Fr.*: interprétation.–*I.*: interpretazione.–*P.*: interpretação.

a. Procedure which, by means of analytic investigation, brings out the latent meaning in what the subject says and does. Interpretation reveals the modes of the defensive conflict and its ultimate aim is to identify the wish that is expressed by every product of the unconscious.

b. In the context of the treatment, the interpretation is what is conveyed to the subject in order to make him reach this latent meaning, according to rules dictated by the way the treatment is being run and the way it is evolving.

Interpretation is at the heart of the Freudian doctrine and technique. Psycho-analysis itself might be defined in terms of it, as the bringing out of the latent meaning of given material.

The first example and paradigm of interpretation was furnished by Freud's approach to dreams. 'Scientific' theories of dreams had attempted to account for them as a phenomenon of mental life by invoking a drop in psychical activity, a loosening of associations; certain such theories did define the dream as a specific activity, but all of them failed to take into consideration its *content* and, *a fortiori*, the relation existing between this content and the dreamer's personal history. On the other hand, 'dream-book' types of interpretation (Classical and Oriental) do not overlook the dream's content and acknowledge that it has a meaning. To this extent, therefore, Freud claims allegiance to this tradition; but he places all the stress on the sole application of the dream's symbolism to the individual in question, and in this respect his approach parts company with the 'decoding' method of dream-books (1*a*).

Starting from the account given by the dreamer (the *manifest content**), the interpretation, according to Freud, uncovers the meaning of the dream as it is

227

Interpretation

formulated in the *latent content** to which the free associations lead us. The ultimate goal of the interpretation is the unconscious wish, and the phantasy in which this wish is embodied.

Naturally the term 'interpretation' is not reserved for the dream–that major product of the unconscious: it is also applied to its other products (parapraxes, symptoms, etc.) and, more generally, to whatever part of the speech and behaviour of the subject bears the stamp of the defensive conflict.

*   *   *

Since conveying his interpretation is the analyst's form of action *par excellence*, an absolute use of the term 'interpretation' has the additional, technical sense of an *interpretation made known to the patient*.

Interpretation understood in this technical sense has a role dating back to the beginnings of psycho-analysis. It may be noted, however, that at the stage represented by the *Studies on Hysteria* (1895d), in so far as the main objective was the recovering of the unconscious pathogenic *memories*, interpretation had not as yet emerged as the chief mode of therapeutic action (the term itself is not in fact to be found in this work).

It was to be assigned this central role as soon as psycho-analytic technique began to take on definite shape; interpretation now became an integral part of the dynamics of the treatment, as is shown by the article on 'The Handling of Dream-Interpretation in Psycho-Analysis' (1911e): 'I submit, therefore, that dream-interpretation should not be pursued in analytic treatment as an art for its own sake, but that its handling should be subject to those technical rules that govern the conduct of the treatment as a whole' (2). It is respect for these 'technical rules' which must dictate the *level* (relative 'depth'), *type*, (interpretation of the resistances, of the transference, etc.) and ultimate *order* of the interpretations.

But we do not intend to deal here with the problems surrounding interpretation–problems which have been the subject of many technical debates: criteria, form and formulation, timing, 'depth', order, etc. (α). We would merely point out that interpretation does not cover the entirety of the analyst's *contributions* to the treatment: for example, it does not cover encouraging the patient to speak, reassuring him, explaining mechanisms or symbols, injunctions, constructions*, etc.–though all these *can* take on an interpretative sense within the analytic situation.

*   *   *

A terminological point: 'interpretation' does not correspond exactly to the German word '*Deutung*'. The English term tends to bring to mind the subjective –perhaps even the forced or arbitrary–aspects of the attribution of a meaning to an event of statement. '*Deutung*' would seem to be closer to 'explanation' or 'clarification' and, in common usage, has fewer of the pejorative overtones that are at times carried by the English word (β). Freud writes that the *Deutung* of a dream consists in ascertaining its *Bedeutung* or meaning (1b).

Nonetheless, Freud does not omit to point out the kinship which exists between interpretation in the analytic sense of the word and other mental processes where an interpretative activity is evident.

228

Thus the secondary revision* constitutes a 'first interpretation' aiming to lend a certain degree of consistency to the elements which are the outcome of the dream-work*: certain dreams 'have been subjected to a far-reaching revision by this psychical function that is akin to waking thought; they appear to have a meaning, but that meaning is as far removed as possible from their true significance [*Bedeutung*]. [...] They are dreams which might be said to have been already interpreted once, before being submitted to waking interpretation' (1*c*). In secondary revision the subject deals with the dream-content exactly as he deals with any unfamiliar perceptual content: he tends to reduce it to what is familiar by means of certain 'anticipatory ideas' (*Erwartungsvorstellungen*) (3). Freud further draws attention to the connections which exist between paranoic interpretation (and also the interpretation of signs in superstitions) and the analytic kind (4*a*). For paranoics, indeed, everything is interpretable: ' . . . they attach the greatest significance to the minor details of other people's behaviour which we ordinarily neglect, interpret (*ausdeuten*) them and make them the basis of far-reaching conclusions' (4*b*). In their interpretations of the behaviour of others, paranoics often display a greater perspicacity than the normal subject. But the reverse side of the paranoic's lucidity towards other people is a fundamental inability to understand his own unconscious.

(α) The reader wishing guidance on these problems is referred to Edward Glover's *The Technique of Psycho-Analysis* (New York: I.U.P., 1955).

(β) In German psychiatry, it may be noted, paranoid delusions are scarcely ever described as delusions of interpretation.

(1) FREUD, S. *The Interpretation of Dreams* (1900*a*): a) Cf. Chapter I and beginning of Chapter II. b) Cf. G.W., II–III, 100–1; S.E., IV, 96. c) G.W., II–III, 494; S.E., V, 490.

(2) FREUD, S., G.W., VIII, 354; S.E., XII, 94.

(3) Cf. FREUD, S. 'On Dreams' (1901*a*), G.W., II–III, 679–80; S.E., V, 666.

(4) Cf. particularly FREUD, S. *The Psychopathology of Everyday Life* (1901*b*): a) G.W. IV., 283–89; S.E., VI, 254–60. b) G.W., IV, 284; S.E., VI, 255.

Introjection

= *D*.: Introjektion.–*Es*.: introyección.–*Fr*.: introjection.–*I*.: introiezione.–*P*.: introjeção.

Process revealed by analytic investigation: in phantasy, the subject transposes objects and their inherent qualities from the 'outside' to the 'inside' of himself.

Introjection is close in meaning to incorporation*, which indeed provides it with its bodily model, but it does not necessarily imply any reference to the body's real boundaries (introjection into the ego, into the ego-ideal, etc.).

It is closely akin to identification*.

It was Sandor Ferenczi who introduced the term 'introjection', which he coined as the opposite of 'projection'. In 'Introjection and Transference' (1909) he writes: 'Whereas the paranoiac expels from his ego the impulses that have

Introjection

become unpleasant, the neurotic helps himself by taking into the ego as large as possible a part of the outside world, making it the object of unconscious phantasies. [...] One might give to this process, in contrast to projection, the name of *Introjection*' (1*a*). In this article as a whole, however, it is hard to discern a precise meaning of the concept of introjection, for Ferenczi seems to use the word in a broad sense to indicate a 'passion for the transference' which leads the neurotic 'to mollify the free-floating affects by extension of his circle of interest' (1*b*). He ends up by using the word to designate a type of behaviour (chiefly in hysterics) that might equally well be described as projection.

In adopting the term, Freud distinguishes it clearly from projection. His most explicit text on this point is 'Instincts and their Vicissitudes' (1915*c*), which envisages the genesis of the opposition between subject (ego) and object (outside world) in so far as it can be correlated with that between pleasure and un-pleasure: the 'purified pleasure-ego' is constituted by an introjection of every-thing that is a source of pleasure and by the projection outwards of whatever brings about unpleasure (see 'Pleasure-Ego/Reality-Ego'). We find the same contrast in 'Negation' (1925*h*): '. . . the original pleasure-ego wants to introject into itself everything that is good and to eject from itself everything that is bad' (2*a*).

Introjection is further characterised by its link with oral incorporation; indeed the two expressions are often used synonymously by Freud and many other authors. Freud shows how the antagonism between introjection and projection, before it becomes general, is first expressed concretely in an oral mode: 'Expressed in the language of the oldest – the oral – instinctual impulses, the judgement is: "I should like to eat this", or "I should like to spit it out"; and, put more generally: "I should like to take this into myself and to keep that out" ' (2*b*).

We thus have grounds – as this last-quoted passage in fact suggests – for preserving a distinction between incorporation and projection. In psycho-analysis the bounds of the body provide the model of all separations between an inside and an outside. Incorporation involves this bodily frontier literally. Introjection has a broader meaning in that it is no longer a matter only of the interior of the body but also that of the psychical apparatus, of a psychical agency, etc. Thus we speak of introjection into the ego, into the ego-ideal, etc.

Introjection was initially brought out by Freud in his analysis of melancholia (3), but then it was acknowledged to be a more general process (4). This realisa-tion constituted a renewal of the Freudian theory of identification*.

Inasmuch as introjection continues to bear the stamp of its bodily prototype it finds expression in phantasies applying to objects – whether part-objects or whole ones. Consequently the notion plays an important part for such writers as Abraham and – particularly – Melanie Klein, who sought to describe the phanta-sied comings and goings of 'good' and 'bad' objects* (introjection, projection, reintrojection). These authors speak essentially of introjected *objects*, and there are indeed good reasons for restricting the use of the term to cases where objects, or their intrinsic qualities, are under examination. This would make it strictly incorrect to speak – as Freud was capable of doing – of an 'introjection of aggressiveness' (5); it would be preferable here to say 'turning round upon the subject's own self'*.

230

(1) Cf. FERENCZI, S. *First Contr.*: a) 40. b) 43.

(2) FREUD, S.: a) G.W., XIV, 13; S.E., XIX, 237. b) G.W., XIV, 13; S.E., XIX, 237.

(3) Cf. FREUD, S. 'Mourning and Melancholia' (1917e), G.W., X, 42–46, S.E., XIV, 243–58

(4) Cf. ABRAHAM, K. 'Versuch einer Entwicklungsgeschichte der Libido auf Grund der Psychoanalyse seelischer Störungen' (1924). English trans.: 'A Short Study of the Development of the Libido, Viewed in the Light of Mental Disorders', in *Selected Papers* (London, Hogarth Press, 1927; New York: Basic Books, 1953), 438 *ff.*

(5) Cf. FREUD, S. *Civilization and its Discontents* (1930a), G.W., XIV, 482; S.E., XXI, 123.

Introversion

= *D.*: Introversion.–*Es.*: introversión.–*Fr.*: introversion.–*I.*: introversione.– *P.*: introversão.

Term introduced by Jung as a general designation for the detachment of libido from external objects and its withdrawal on to the subject's internal world.

Freud adopted the word but confined its application to a withdrawal of libido which results in the cathexis of imaginary intrapsychic formations, as distinct from a withdrawal of libido on to the ego (secondary narcissism).

The term 'introversion' makes its first appearance in Jung's work in 'Über Konflikte der kindlichen Seele' (1910) (1). It recurs in many subsequent writings, notably in *Psychology of the Unconscious* (1913) (2). The notion has since enjoyed a wide vogue in post-Jungian typologies (cf. the contrast between introverted and extraverted types).

Although he accepted the term Freud expressed immediate reservations concerning its extension.

For Freud introversion means the withdrawal of libido on to imaginary objects or phantasies. In this sense it constitutes a stage in the formation of neurotic symptoms, a period which follows upon frustration and which may lead up to regression. The libido 'turns away from reality, which, owing to the obstinate frustration, has lost its value for the subject, and turns towards the life of phantasy, in which it creates new wishful structures and revives the traces of earlier, forgotten ones' (3).

In 'On Narcissism: An Introduction' (1914c), Freud criticises Jung's use of 'introversion' as too broad. This use had led Jung to categorise psychosis as introversion neurosis. Freud, on the other hand, contrasts the concept of (secondary) narcissism with introversion understood as withdrawal of libido on to phantasies, while he places psychosis under the head of narcissistic neurosis*.

(1) *Jb. psychoan. psychopath. Forsch.*, II.

(2) *Wandlungen und Symbole der Libido* (Leipzig and Vienna, 1912). Translation: *Psychology of the Unconscious* (New York, 1916; London, 1919).

(3) FREUD, S. 'Types of Onset of Neurosis' (1912c), G.W., VIII, 323–24; S.E., XII, 232.

Isolation

= *D*.: Isolieren *or* Isolierung. – *Es*.: aislamiento. – *Fr*.: isolation. – *I*.: isolamento. – *P*.: isolamento.

Mechanism of defence, particularly characteristic of obsessional neurosis, which consists in isolating thoughts or behaviour so that their links with other thoughts or with the remainder of the subject's life are broken. Among the procedures used for isolation are: pauses in the train of thought, formulas, rituals and, in a general way, all those measures which facilitate the insertion of a hiatus into the temporal sequence of thoughts or actions.

The most explicit passage concerning isolation in Freud's work is to be found in *Inhibitions, Symptoms and Anxiety* (1926*d*) (1*a*), where it is described as a technique peculiar to obsessional neurosis*.

Some patients defend themselves against an idea, an impression or an action by isolating it from its context by means of a pause 'during which nothing further must happen – during which [they] must perceive nothing and do nothing' (1*b*). This active, 'motor' technique is qualified by Freud as magical; he likens it to the normal operation of concentration in the subject who is trying not to let his attention be diverted from the object upon which it is presently focused.

Isolation is displayed in various obsessional symptoms; it is particularly evident in psycho-analytic treatment, where the rule of free association*, by working against it, serves to make it clearly visible (subjects who make a radical separation between their analysis and their life, between a specific train of thought and the session as a whole, or between a particular idea and the ideas and emotions surrounding it).

In the last analysis Freud brings the tendency to isolate down to an archaic mode of defence against the instinct – namely, the prohibition of touching, since 'touching and physical contact are the immediate aim of the aggressive as well as the loving object-cathexes' (1*c*).

Seen in this light, isolation appears as the removal of 'the possibility of contact; it is a method of withdrawing a thing from being touched in any way. And when a neurotic isolates an impression or an activity by interpolating an interval, he is letting it be understood symbolically that he will not allow his thoughts about that impression or activity to come into associative contact with other thoughts' (1*d*).

It should be pointed out that this passage of *Inhibitions, Symptoms and Anxiety* does not reduce isolation to a specific type of symptom but gives it a broader extension. A parallel is evoked between isolation and hysterical repression*: if the traumatic experience is not repressed into the unconscious, 'it is deprived of its affect, and its associative connections are suppressed (*unterdrückt*) or interrupted so that it remains as though isolated and is not reproduced in the ordinary processes of thought' (1*e*). The isolating techniques observable in the symptoms of obsessional neurosis are merely a reversion to and a reinforcement of this earlier form of splitting.

In this broader sense the idea of isolation is one that is evident in Freud's

232

thinking from his earliest reflections on defensive activity in general. Thus in 'The Neuro-Psychoses of Defence' (1894*a*) defence is conceived of as isolation as much in hysteria as in the group of phobias and obsessions: '. . . defence against the incompatible idea [is] effected by separating it from its affect; the idea itself [remains] in consciousness, even though weakened and isolated' (2).

*　　*　　*

The term 'isolation' is occasionally used in psycho-analytical parlance in a rather loose way which calls for reservations.

Isolation is thus often confused with processes which can be combined with it or from which it may result, such as displacement*, neutralisation of the affect or even psychotic dissociation.

Sometimes too people speak of isolation of the symptom in the case of subjects who experience and represent their symptoms as unconnected with anything else and alien to them. What is actually involved here is a mode of being where the underlying process need not necessarily be the obsessional mechanism of isolation. Notice also that the localisation of the conflict is a very general property of symptoms, so any symptom may appear isolated relative to the subject's existence as a whole.

In our view, in fact, there is a good case for using the term 'isolation' solely to denote a specific defensive process which ranges from compulsion to a systematic and concerted attitude, and which consists in the severing of the associative connections of a thought or act–especially its connections with what precedes and succeeds it in time.

(1) FREUD, S.: a) Cf. G.W., XIV, 150–52; S.E., XX, 120–22. b) G.W., XIV, 150; S.E., XX, 120. c) G.W., XIV, 152; S.E., XX, 122. d) G.W., XIV, 152; S.E., XX, 122. e) G.W., XIV, 150; S.E., XX, 120.

(2) FREUD, S., G.W., I, 72; S.E., III, 58.

L

Latency Period

= *D.*: Latenzperiode *or* Latenzzeit, *or occasionally* Aufschubsperiode.–
Es.: período de latencia.–*Fr.*: période de latence.–*I.*: periodo di latenza.–
P.: período de latência.

Period which extends from the dissolution of infantile sexuality (at the age of five or six) to the onset of puberty, constituting a pause in the evolution of sexuality. This stage sees a decrease in sexual activity, the desexualisation of object-relationships and of the emotions (particularly the predominance of tenderness* over sexual desire), and the emergence of such feelings as shame and disgust along with moral and aesthetic aspirations.

According to psycho-analytic theory the latency period has its origin in the dissolution of the Oedipus complex; it represents an intensification of repression which brings about an amnesia affecting the earliest years, a transformation of object-cathexes into identifications with the parents, and a development of sublimations.

The idea of a latency period (α) may be understood in the first instance, in purely biological terms, as a predetermined hiatus between two surges of libidinal 'pressure' (*Drang*) (β). From this point of view no psychological explanation is called for as far as the genesis of the period is concerned: it may be adequately described largely in terms of its effects–and this is what Freud does in the *Three Essays on the Theory of Sexuality* (1905d) (1a).

Such is Freud's view too when he relates the latency period to the dissolution of the Oedipus complex: '. . . the Oedipus complex must collapse because the time has come for its disintegration, just as the milk-teeth fall out when the permanent ones begin to grow' (2a). But while the 'pressure' of puberty which signals the end of the latency period is an indisputable fact, the biological factor determining the onset of the period is less evident. And Freud notes that there is 'no need to expect that anatomical growth and psychical development must be exactly simultaneous'.

Thus it is that Freud is led, in order to account for the dissolution of the Oedipus complex, to invoke this complex's 'internal impossibility' (2b)–a kind of disjunction between the Oedipal structure and biological immaturity: '. . . the absence of the satisfaction hoped for, the continued denial of the desired baby, must in the end lead the small lover to turn away from his hopeless longing' (2c).

It is strictly impossible, then, to understand the entry into the latency period other than by reference to the evolution of the Oedipus complex and to the modes of its resolution in the two sexes (see 'Oedipus Complex', 'Castration Complex').

Secondarily, social formations, combining their action with that of the

234

super-ego, serve to reinforce sexual latency, which can 'only give rise to a complete interruption of sexual life in cultural organisations which have made the suppression of infantile sexuality a part of their system. This is not the case with the majority of primitive peoples' (3).

It will be noticed that Freud speaks of a *period* of latency, not of a stage*. The significance of this is that during the period in question, although manifestations of a sexual nature are to be observed, there is strictly speaking no new *organisation** of sexuality.

(α) Freud claims to have borrowed this term from Wilhelm Fliess.

(β) A first reference by Freud to periods of life (*Lebensalter*), and to 'transitional periods (*Übergangszeiten*) during which repression for the most part occurs', is to be found in his letter to Fliess dated May 30, 1896 (4).

(1) FREUD, S.: a) G.W., V, 77–80; S.E., VII, 176–79. b) G.W., V, 77, note 2 added in 1920; S.E., VII, 177*n*.

(2) FREUD, S. 'The Dissolution of the Oedipus Complex' (1924*d*): a) G.W., XIII, 395; S.E., XIX, 173. b) G.W., XIII, 395; S.E., XIX, 173. c) G.W., XIII, 395; S.E., XIX, 173.

(3) FREUD, S. *An Autobiographical Study* (1925*d* [1924]), G.W., XIX, 64, *n.* 2 added in 1935; S.E., XX, 37, *n.* 1.

(4) FREUD, S., S.E., I, 229.

Latent Content

= *D*.: latenter Inhalt.–*Es*.: contenido latente.–*Fr*.: contenu latent.–
I.: contenuto latente.–*P*.: conteúdo latente.

Group of meanings revealed upon the completion of an analysis of a product of the unconscious—particularly a dream. Once decoded, the dream no longer appears as a narrative in images but rather as an organisation of thoughts, or a discourse, expressing one or more wishes.

This term may be understood in a broad sense as a designation for everything that analysis gradually uncovers (the associations* of the subject, the interpretations* of the analyst). The latent content of a dream would thus be said to consist of day's residues*, childhood memories, bodily impressions, allusions to the transference situation, etc.

In a more restricted sense, the latent content means the complete and genuine translation of the dreamer's discourse, the adequate formulation of his desire*; as such it stands in opposition to the manifest content*, which is both incomplete and mendacious. The manifest content (often referred to by Freud simply as the 'content') is as it were the abridged version, while the latent content (also called the 'dream-thoughts' or 'latent dream-thoughts') which is revealed by analysis is the correct version: the two 'are presented to us like two versions of the same subject-matter in two different languages, or, more properly, the dream-content seems like a transcript of the dream-thoughts into another mode of expression, whose characters and syntactic laws it is our business to discover by comparing the original and the translation. The dream-thoughts are immediately comprehensible, as soon as we have learnt them' (1a).

According to Freud the latent precedes the manifest content, the dream-work* transforming the former into the latter so that, in this sense, it is 'not creative' (2). This does not mean that the analyst can rediscover everything: 'There is often a passage in even the most thoroughly interpreted dream which has to be left obscure [...]. This is the dream's navel' (1b). Nor does it mean, consequently, that a definitive interpretation of a dream can ever be made (see 'Over-interpretation').

(1) FREUD, S. *The Interpretation of Dreams* (1900a): a) G.W., II–III, 283; S.E., IV, 277. b) G.W., II–III, 530; S.E., V, 525.

(2) FREUD, S. *On Dreams* (1901a), G.W., II–III, 680; S.E., V, 667.

Libidinal Stage (or Phase)

= D.: Libidostufe (*or* -phase).–*Es*.: fase libidinosa.–*Fr*.: stade (*or* phase) libidinal(e).– *I*.: fase libidica.–*P*.: fase libidinal.

Period of childhood development characterised by a specific (more or less marked) organisation* of the libido under the primacy of one erotogenic zone*, and by the dominance of one mode of object-relationship*. The idea of the stage has acquired a broader extension in psycho-analysis as a consequence of the attempt to identify stages in the evolution of the ego.

When stages are mentioned in psycho-analysis this usually means the stages of libidinal development. But it is of note that a Freudian concern with distinguishing between the different 'ages of life', 'phases' or 'periods' of development is evident even before the earliest formulations of the concept of *organisation* of the libido: this concern parallels the discovery that the various psychoneurotic affections have their roots in childhood. Thus, around 1896–97, Freud's correspondence with Wilhelm Fliess–who, as we know, had himself worked out a whole theory of periods (1)–contains an attempt to establish a series of periods in childhood and adolescence which can be tied down chronologically with varying degrees of precision; this attempt is closely bound up with the notion of deferred action*, and with the theory of seduction* which Freud worked out at this time. In fact certain of the periods in question ('periods of the event', *Ereigniszeiten*) are those during which the 'sexual scenes' occur, while others are 'periods of repression' (*Verdrängungszeiten*). To this succession of periods Freud relates the 'choice of neurosis'*: 'The different neuroses have their particular chronological requirements for their sexual scenes. [...] Thus the periods at which *repression* occurs are of no significance for the choice of neurosis, the periods at which the *event* occurs are decisive' (2a). Further, the transition from one of these periods to the next is correlated with the stratification of the psychical apparatus into systems of 'registrations': transitions from one period to

236

another and from one system to another are compared to a 'translation' that may be more or less successful (2*b*).

It was not long before the idea emerged of tieing these successive periods to the dominance and the relinquishment of specific 'sexual' or 'erotogenic zones' (the anal region, the region of mouth and pharynx and–in the case of the girl –the clitoral region). Freud pursues this line of advance rather a long way– witness his letter to Fliess dated November 14, 1897: the process of so-called normal repression is seen here as closely related to the relinquishing of one zone in favour of another, to the 'decline' of a particular zone.

Such conceptions are in many respects adumbrations of what is to become, in its more finished form, the theory of libidinal stages. But it is a striking fact that these ideas fade into the background with the first account that Freud gives of the evolution of sexuality, and they are taken up and clarified only at a later point. In the first edition of the *Three Essays on the Theory of Sexuality* (1905*d*), the chief distinction is that between the sexuality of puberty and adulthood on the one hand, organised under genital primacy, and infantile sexuality on the other, where the sexual aims are multiple, as are the erotogenic zones that support them, without any one of these zones–or any type of object-choice–being at all capable of establishing a primacy. No doubt this opposition is lent particular emphasis by Freud in this context because of the didactic and expository nature of this work, and because of the novelty of the thesis that it seeks to impose: the thesis of the originally perverse and polymorphous character of sexuality (see 'Sexuality', 'Auto-Erotism').

Between 1913 and 1923 this thesis undergoes a gradual elaboration as a result of the introduction of the notion of pregenital* stages preceding the institution of the genital stage–namely, the oral*, anal*, and phallic* stages.

What characterises these stages is a specific mode of organisation* of sexual life. The notion of the primacy of an erotogenic *zone* does not suffice to account for the structural and normative overtones of the concept of stage. This concept is based exclusively upon a type of activity which is linked, it is true, to an erotogenic zone, but it is also an activity that can be observed at different levels of the object-relationship*. Thus incorporation*, which characterises the oral stage, is seen as a pattern that can be found in numerous phantasies underlying activities other than nutritional ones (e.g. 'devouring with the eyes').

* * *

For psycho-analysis, then, the model for the notion of the stage is sought on the plane of the evolution of libidinal activity; but we should note that other developmental schemas have also been outlined:

a. Freud points to a temporal scale of periods based on access to the libidinal object, a scale according to which the subject passes in succession through auto-erotism*, narcissism*, the homosexual choice and the heterosexual one.

b. Another avenue leads to the identification of different stages in that evolution which culminates in the establishment of the hegemony of the reality principle over the pleasure principle. An attempt to systematise this approach was made by Ferenczi (4).

c. Some authors consider that only the formation of the ego can account for the changeover from the pleasure to the reality principle. The ego 'enters

Libidinal Stage (or Phase)

the process as an independent variable' (5). The development of the ego is what permits the differentiation of the self from the outside world, the postponement of satisfaction, the relative control over instinctual stimulation, etc. Freud himself, although he remarked on the utility of ascertaining the precise nature of the ego's evolution and stages, made no attempt to follow this up. It is interesting that when he does raise the problem—as, for example, in 'The Disposition to Obsessional Neurosis' (1913*i*)–the notion of the ego is not as yet restricted to the precise topographical sense that it is to have in *The Ego and the Id* (1923*b*). He suggests that 'a chronological outstripping of libidinal development by ego development should be included in the disposition to obsessional neurosis', but he points out that 'the stages of development of the ego-instincts are at present very little known to us' (6).

Anna Freud too, in *The Ego and the Mechanisms of Defence*, declines to set up a temporal scheme for the appearance of the various mechanisms of ego-defence (7).

What overall view may be formed of these different approaches? The most thoroughgoing attempt to establish correlations between the different types of stages is still Abraham's 'Short Study of the Development of the Libido, Viewed in the Light of Mental Disorders' (1924) (8). Robert Fliess has completed the picture proposed by Abraham (9).

We must stress that Freud for his part never undertook the formulation of a holistic theory of stages which would be able to embrace not only the evolution of the libido but also that of the defences, of the ego, etc.; such a theory eventually comes to include the development of the whole of the personality in a single genetic sequence under the general heading of the notion of object-relations. In our view, Freud's failure to reach such a position does not simply mean that he did not round out his thinking in this area; in fact the gap –and the possibility of a dialectic–between these different developmental sequences are in Freud's eyes an essential factor in the determination of neurosis.

In this sense, even though the Freudian theory may have been one of the chief contributors in the history of psychology to the spread of the idea of stages, it would seem that in its fundamental inspiration it is at odds with the way this idea is used by genetic psychology, which postulates the existence, at each point in development, of an overall structure with an integrative function (10).

(1) Cf. KRIS, E., Preface to FREUD, S. *Anf.*, 9–12; *Origins*, 4–8.

(2) FREUD, S.: a) *Anf.*, 175–76; S.E., I, 229–31. b) *Anf.*, 185–92; S.E., I, 233–39.

(3) Cf. FREUD, S. 'Psycho-Analytic Notes on an Autobiographical Account of a Case of Paranoia (Dementia Paranoides)' (1911c), G.W., VIII, 296–97; S.E., XII, 60–61.

(4) Cf. FERENCZI, S. 'Stages in the Development of the Sense of Reality', 1913, in *First Contributions*.

(5) HARTMANN, H, KRIS, E. and LOEWENSTEIN, M. 'Comments on the Formation of Psychic Structure', *Psa. Study of the Child*, 1946, II, 23.

(6) FREUD, S., G.W., VIII, 451; S.E., XII, 325.

(7) Cf. FREUD, A. (London: Hogarth Press, 1937; New York: I.U.P., 1946), 57.

(8) Cf. ABRAHAM, K. *Selected Papers* (London: Hogarth Press, 1927), 418–501.

(9) Cf. FLIESS, R. 'An Ontogenetic Table', 1942, in *The Psychoanalytic Reader* (London: Hogarth Press, 1950), 254–55.

(10) Cf. 'Symposium de l'Association de Psychologie scientifique de langue française', various authors, Geneva, 1955, in *Le problème des stades en psychologie de l'enfant* (Paris: P.U.F., 1956).

Libido

Energy postulated by Freud as underlying the transformations of the sexual instinct with respect to its object (displacement of cathexes), with respect to its aim (e.g. sublimation), and with respect to the source of sexual excitation (diversity of the erotogenic zones).

For Jung, the notion of libido extends to embrace 'psychical energy' in general, present in every 'tendency towards' or *appetitus.*

The Latin word *libido* means wish or desire. Freud claims to have borrowed it from Moll (*Untersuchungen über die Libido sexualis*, Vol. I, 1898), but in point of fact it appears several times in the letters and manuscripts sent to Fliess, and for the first time in Draft E, the probable date of which is June, 1894.

A satisfactory definition of libido is difficult to give. This is not only because the theory of libido evolved hand in hand with the different stages of the instinct theory, but also because the concept of libido itself has never been clearly defined (α). Two specific characteristics, however, were invariably posited by Freud:

a. *Qualitatively* speaking, libido cannot be reduced—as Jung would have us do—to an indeterminate mental energy. If it can be 'desexualised'—particularly in the case of narcissistic cathexes—this is invariably a secondary process involving a renunciation of the specifically sexual aim.

At the same time, Freud's libido never extends to the whole domain of the instincts. As first conceived, libido stands opposed to the instincts of self-preservation*. When these instincts are seen, in Freud's final account, as libidinal in nature, the antagonism is merely displaced: libido is now opposed to the death instincts. Thus Freud never accepts Jung's monism and persists in upholding the sexual character of libido.

b. The role of libido as a *quantitative* concept is increasingly emphasised by Freud: it serves 'as a measure of processes and transformations occurring in the field of sexual excitation'. Its 'production, increase or diminution, distribution and displacement should afford us possibilities for explaining the psychosexual phenomena observed' (1).

Both these aspects are stressed in the following definition: 'Libido is an expression taken from the theory of the emotions. We call by that name the energy, regarded as a quantitative magnitude (though not at present actually measurable), of those instincts which have to do with all that may be comprised under the word "love" ' (2).

In so far as the sexual instinct lies on the borderline between the somatic and the psychical, libido represents the mental side; it is 'the dynamic manifestation of [the sexual instinct] in mental life' (3). When the concept of libido is

239

Libido

introduced by Freud in his first writings on anxiety neurosis* (1896), it is presented as an energy quite distinct from somatic sexual excitation: an insufficiency of 'psychical libido' causes the tension to be maintained on the somatic level, where it is transformed, without psychical working over*, into symptoms. When 'there is something lacking in the psychical determinants' (4), the endogenous sexual excitation is not mastered, the tension cannot be utilised by the psyche, there is a split between somatic and psychical, and anxiety arises.

In the first edition of the *Three Essays on the Theory of Sexuality* (1905d), libido–which stands in the same relation to love as hunger does to the nutritional instinct–is not much different from sexual desire in search of satisfaction, and serves to identify the forms taken by this desire. For at this point only object-libido is involved; we observe it as it focusses on objects–either becoming fixated there or abandoning them–and as it leaves one object for another.

Inasmuch as the sexual instinct represents a force exerting a 'pressure'* libido is defined by Freud as the energy of this instinct. It is this quantitative aspect which predominates in what, on the basis of the concepts of narcissism and of an ego-libido, is to become the 'libido theory'.

The notion of 'ego-libido' does in fact entail a generalisation of the libidinal economy so as to embrace the whole of the interplay between cathexes and anticathexes, while whatever overtones of subjectivity the term 'libido' may have had hitherto are attenuated; as Freud acknowledges, the libido theory becomes frankly speculative. Perhaps Freud was trying to restore the subjective and qualitative dimension originally intrinsic to the idea of libido–but on the level, now, of a biological myth–when, in *Beyond the Pleasure Principle* (1920g), he brought in the notion of Eros* as the basic principle of the life instincts, as a tendency for organisms to maintain the cohesion of living matter and to create new unities.

(α) The most explicit texts on the development of the libido theory are the article 'Libido-theorie' (1923a) and Chapter XXVI of the *Introductory Lectures on Psycho-Analysis* (1916–17).

(1) FREUD, S. *Three Essays on the Theory of Sexuality* (1905d), passage added in 1915, G.W., V, 118; S.E., VII, 217.

(2) FREUD, S. *Group Psychology and the Analysis of the Ego* (1921c), G.W., XIII, 98; S.E., XVIII, 90.

(3) FREUD, S. 'Two Encyclopaedia Articles' (1923a [1922]). G.W., XIII, 220; S.E., XVIII, 244.

(4) FREUD, S., *Anf.*, 101; S.E., I, 193.

Life Instincts

= *D.*: Lebenstriebe.–*Es.*: instintos de vida.–*Fr.*: pulsions de vie.–
I.: instinti *or* pulsioni di vita.–*P.*: impulsos *or* pulsões de vida.

Great class of instincts which Freud contrasts in his final theory with the death instincts*. The tendency of the life instincts is to create and maintain ever greater unities. Known also as 'Eros'*, they embrace not only the sexual instincts* proper but also the instincts of self-preservation*.

It was in *Beyond the Pleasure Principle* (1920g) that Freud introduced the great antithesis between the death instincts and the life instincts which he was to uphold until the end of his work. The death instincts tend towards the destruction of vital unities, the absolute equalisation of tensions and a return to the hypothesised inorganic state of complete repose. The life instincts tend not only to preserve existing vital unities but also to constitute, on the basis of these, new and more inclusive ones. Thus, even on the cellular level, a tendency is said to exist 'which seeks to force together and hold together the portions of living substance' (1*a*). This tendency is found in the individual organism in so far as this seeks to sustain its unity and its existence (self-preservative instincts, narcissistic libido*). Sexuality in its manifest forms is itself defined as a principle of *union* (union of individuals in coitus, union of gametes in fertilisation).

The best way to grasp what Freud means by the life instincts is to view them in their opposition to the death instincts: the two types of instinct stand opposed to one another as two great principles said to be already observable in the inanimate world (attraction/repulsion) and, above all, to be the basis of the phenomena of life (anabolism/catabolism).

The new instinctual dualism gives rise to a number of problems:

a. Freud's introduction of the death instinct is an upshot of his reflection upon what is the most basic aspect of all instincts–namely, the return to an earlier state. In the evolutionist perspective explicitly chosen by Freud, this regressive tendency can only be aimed at the restoration of less differentiated, less organised forms–forms devoid, ultimately, even of differences in energy level. This tendency is expressed *par excellence* in the death instinct, while the life instinct, for its part, is defined by the opposite trend: the establishment and maintenance of more differentiated, more organised forms, *constancy* of the energy level and even the *widening of differences* in it as between the organism and its surroundings. In the case of the life instincts Freud had to admit his inability to show how these could be said to obey what he had described as the basic trait of any instinct–its conservative (or, better, regressive) character. 'In the case of Eros (or the love instinct) we cannot apply this formula. To do so would presuppose that living substance was once a unity which had later been torn apart and was now striving towards re-union' (2*a*). Freud is consequently driven to refer to a myth–the one recounted by Aristophanes in Plato's *Symposium*–according to which sexual union is an attempt to restore the lost wholeness of an originally androgynous being said to have existed before the separation of the sexes (1*b*).

241

Life Instincts

b. The same opposition–and the same problem–recur on the level of the two principles of mental functioning which correspond to the two great classes of instincts: the Nirvana principle*, which corresponds to the death instincts, is clearly defined, but the pleasure principle (and its modified form, the reality principle*), which is supposed to represent the demands of the life instincts, is hard to understand in any economic sense, and Freud reformulates it in 'qualitative' terms (see 'Pleasure Principle', 'Principle of Constancy').

Freud's last formulations on the question–in *An Outline of Psycho-Analysis* (1940a [1938])–indicate that the principle underlying the life instincts is a principle of *binding**: 'The aim of [Eros] is to establish ever greater unities and to preserve them thus–in short, to bind together; the aim of [the destructive instinct] is, on the contrary, to undo connections and so to destroy things' (2b).

It is clear therefore that from the economic standpoint too the life instincts fit badly into the energy-based model of the instinct as a tendency towards the reduction of tensions. In certain passages (3) Freud goes so far as to oppose Eros to the general conservative nature of the instincts.

c. A final point is that when Freud claims to see the life instincts as identical with what he had formerly called the sexual instinct*, we are justified in asking whether this conflation does not reflect a shift in sexuality's location in the framework of Freud's dualistic conception. Up until this point, sexuality had played the part of an essentially subversive force, represented by the first components of the major antitheses recognised by Freud: free energy* as opposed to bound, primary* as opposed to secondary processes, the pleasure principle as opposed to the reality principle and–in the 'Project for a Scientific Psychology' (1950a [1895])–the principle of inertia* as opposed to the principle of constancy. With the advent of the final instinctual dualism, the death instinct takes over as the 'primal', 'demoniac' force which is of the essence of instinct, while sexuality–paradoxically–goes over to the side of the binding process.

(1) FREUD, S.: a) G.W., XIII, 66n.; S.E., XVIII, 60n. b) Cf. G.W., XIII, 62–63; S.E., XVIII, 57–58.

(2) FREUD, S. *An Outline of Psycho-Analysis* (1940a [1938]): a) G.W., XVII, 71; S.E., XXIII, 149. b) G.W., XVII, 71; S.E., XXIII, 148.

(3) Cf. FREUD, S. *Civilization and its Discontents* (1930a), G.W., XIV, 477n.; S.E., XXII, 118, *n*. 2.

M

Manifest Content

= *D*.: manifester Inhalt.–*Es*.: contenido manifiesto.–*Fr*.: contenu manifeste.–
I.: contenuto manifesto.–*P*.: conteúdo manifesto *or* patente.

Designates the dream before it receives any analytic investigation, as it appears to the dreamer who recounts it. By extension, we speak of the manifest content of any verbal product—from phantasies to literary works—which we intend to interpret according to the analytic method.

The expression 'manifest content' was introduced by Freud in *The Interpretation of Dreams* (1900*a*) as a correlate to 'latent content'*. The unqualified 'content' is often used to refer to the same thing and contrasted with the 'dream-thoughts' or 'latent dream-thoughts'. For Freud the manifest content is the product of the dream-work*, while the latent content is the product of the opposite type of work–interpretation*.

This account has been criticised from a phenomenological point of view: Politzer holds that the dream, strictly speaking, can only have one content. On his view, what Freud understands by the manifest content constitutes the descriptive narrative that the subject puts forward at a time when he does not have the full meaning of his dream at his disposal (1).

(1) Cf. POLITZER, G. *Critique des fondements de la psychologie* (Paris: Rieder, 1928).

Masculinity/Femininity

= *D*.: Männlichkeit/Weiblichkeit.–*Es*.: masculinidad/feminidad.–*Fr*.: masculinité/féminité.–
I.: mascolinità/femminilità.–*P*.: masculinidade/feminidade.

Antithesis taken up by psycho-analysis, which shows that it is much more complex than generally thought: the way the subject situates himself *vis-à-vis* his biological sex is the variable outcome of a process of conflict.

Freud pointed out the variety of meanings covered by the terms 'masculine' and 'feminine'. First, they have a *biological* significance, which relates the subject to his primary and secondary sexual characteristics; here the concepts have an exact sense, but psycho-analysis has shown that such biological data do not suffice in accounting for psychosexual behaviour. Secondly, they have a *sociological* significance, which varies according to the real and symbolic functions assigned to the man and the woman in the culture under consideration. And lastly, they have a *psychosexual* significance, which necessarily interlocks with the other two meanings, though particularly with the social one. In other words, these notions are highly problematic and should be approached with circumspection. For example, a woman with a professional activity demanding qualities of independence, character, initiative, etc., should not necessarily be looked upon as more 'masculine' than other women. Generally speaking, the decisive factor in the assessment of behaviour from the point of view of the masculinity–femininity dichotomy is the underlying phantasies which psychoanalysis alone is able to uncover.

The notion of bisexuality*, whether it is assigned a biological foundation or whether it is understood in terms of identifications or Oedipal positions, always implies that in every human being a synthesis takes place between masculine and feminine traits – a synthesis which may be more or less harmonious, more or less well integrated.

In terms of individual development, psycho-analysis shows that the masculine–feminine distinction is not present in the child from the outset, but that this differentiation is preceded by stages in which other oppositions predominate – first the active-passive antithesis (see 'Activity/Passivity'), then the phallic-castrated one; this holds good for both sexes (see 'Phallic Stage').

From this position, Freud does not speak for example of femininity until the little girl has succeeded – at least partially – in the accomplishment of her double task: the switch of major erotogenic zone (from the clitoris to the vagina) and the change of love-object (from the mother to the father) (1).

(1) Cf. particularly FREUD, S. *New Introductory Lectures on Psycho-Analysis* (1933*a* [1932]), Chapter XXXIII on 'Femininity', G.W., XV; S.E., XXII.

Masochism

= *D.*: Masochismus. – *Es.*: masoquismo. – *Fr.*: masochisme. – *I.*: masochismo. – *P.*: masoquismo.

Sexual perversion in which satisfaction is tied to the suffering or humiliation undergone by the subject.

Freud extends the notion of masochism beyond the perversion as described by sexologists. In the first place, he identifies masochistic elements in numerous types of sexual behaviour and sees rudiments of masochism in infantile sexuality. Secondly, he describes derivative forms, notably 'moral masochism', where the subject, as a result of an unconscious sense of guilt*, seeks out the position of victim without any sexual pleasure being directly involved.

Krafft-Ebing was the first to offer a thorough description of a sexual perversion which he named after Sacher Masoch. 'All the clinical manifestations are mentioned: physical pain induced by pricking, bastinado, flagellation; moral humiliation through an attitude of servility towards women, accompanied by the corporal chastisement that is considered indispensable. The part played by maso-chistic phantasies did not escape Krafft-Ebing. He further indicated the relation-ship between masochism and its opposite, sadism, and had no hesitation in looking upon the whole of masochism as a pathological outgrowth of feminine psychical elements–a morbid reinforcement of certain characteristics of woman's soul' (1*a*).

For the intimate links between masochism and sadism, and the function Freud assigns to this pair of opposites in mental life, the reader is referred to the entry 'Sado-Masochism'. Here we shall confine ourselves to remarks on some conceptual distinctions proposed by Freud and often used in psycho-analysis.

In 'The Economic Problem of Masochism' (1924*c*), Freud distinguishes three forms of masochism: erotogenic, feminine and moral. If the idea of 'moral masochism' can easily be tied down (see our definition above and the following articles: 'Need for Punishment', 'Sense of Guilt', 'Super-Ego', 'Failure Neurosis', 'Negative Therapeutic Reaction'), the other two forms, by contrast, can give rise to misunderstandings.

a. There is a tendency to use the term 'erotogenic masochism' to mean masochistic sexual perversion (1*b*). Although such a denomination might seem legitimate–since it is *erotic* excitation that the masochistic pervert seeks in pain–it does not correspond to what Freud apparently means. He is not con-cerned with a clinically identifiable form of masochism, but rather with a state of affairs that lies at the root of the masochistic perversion and that is also to be found in moral masochism: the fact of sexual pleasure being bound to pain.

b. By 'feminine masochism' one is naturally tempted to understand a 'masochism of women'. Freud certainly used such terms to mean the 'expression of the feminine essence', but in the context of the theory of bisexuality* feminine masochism is an immanent possibility for any human being regardless of sex. What is more, it is under this heading that Freud describes what constitutes the essence of the masochistic perversion in *men*: '. . . if one has an opportunity of studying cases in which the masochistic phantasies have been especially richly elaborated, one quickly discovers that they place the subject in a character-istically female situation' (2).

*　　　*　　　*

Two other classical notions are those of *primary* and *secondary* masochism.

By primary masochism Freud understands a state in which the death instinct is still directed towards the subject himself, although it is bound by the libido and fused with it. Such a masochism is termed 'primary' because it is not subsequent to a period in which aggressiveness is turned upon an external object, and also in so far as it is opposed to a secondary masochism which, for its part, is defined as a turning round of sadism against the subject's own self, and which supplements the primary type.

The idea of a masochism that cannot be adequately explained as a turning round of sadism against the self was only accepted by Freud once he had put forward the hypothesis of the death instinct*.

(1) NACHT, S. 'Le masochisme', *R.F.P.*, 1938, X, 2: a) 177. b) Cf. 193.

(2) FREUD, S., G.W., XIII, 374; S.E., XIX, 162.

Material

= *D*.: Material.–*Es*.: material.–*Fr*.: matériel.–*I*.: materiale.–*P*.: material.

Term commonly used in psycho-analysis to designate the patient's words and behaviour as a whole, in so far as they offer a sort of raw material for interpretations and constructions.

This term complements 'interpretation'* and 'construction'*, which refer to the elaboration of the brute data furnished by the patient.

Freud often compared the work of analysis to that of the archaeologist reconstructing a long-lost building on the basis of fragments brought to light during the digging. The analogy of successive layers is still used in speaking of the material as being 'deeper' or 'not so deep' as measured by genetic and structural yardsticks.

Freud is sometimes led–for example, in 'Constructions in Analysis' (1937*d*) –to draw a clear distinction within the work of analysis between the production of material and its elaboration. Such a distinction is obviously only a schematic one:

a. It is impossible to make a division between two successive stages in the history of the treatment, one set aside for the production, the other for the elaboration of material. In practice what we see is a constant interplay between the two. We see, for instance, that the outcome of an interpretation is that it has made new material emerge (memories, phantasies).

b. Nor is it possible to define the production of material and the elaboration of it as two functions of which the former is to be attributed to the subject and the latter to the analyst. For in point of fact the analysand may take an active part in the interpretation of the material, he is supposed to assimilate the interpretations (see 'Working-Through'), etc.

With these reservations, however, the term 'material' does stress an essential aspect of the products originating in the unconscious–namely, their alien quality as far as the conscious subject is concerned. This is true whether the subject looks upon them from the start as relatively foreign to his personality and so deems them to constitute *material*, or whether, as one of the first results of the analytic work and of the application of the fundamental rule*, he becomes aware of the symptomatic and uncontrollable character of certain behaviour. Only at this point does he come to consider this behaviour as incommensurate with his conscious motives–and thus a *material* to be analysed.

Beyond its relatively loose sense in common psycho-analytical parlance, this term takes on its full meaning in the context of the Freudian realism of the unconscious: in Freud's view there exist unconscious 'contents'–i.e. an unconscious pathogenic material.

(1) Cf. FREUD, S. 'Analysis of a Phobia in a Five-Year-Old Boy' (1909*b*), G.W., VII, 356; S.E., X, 181.

Memory-Trace (or Mnemic Trace)

= *D.*: Erinnerungsspur *or* Erinnerungsrest.–*Es.*: huella mnémica.–*Fr.*: trace mnésique.–
I.: traccia mnemonica.–*P.*: traço *or* vestígio mnêmico.

Term used by Freud throughout his work to denote the way in which events are inscribed upon the memory. Memory-traces, according to Freud, are deposited in different systems; they subsist permanently, but are only reactivated once they have been cathected.

The psycho-physiological notion of the memory-trace, which Freud evokes constantly in his metapsychological works, implies a conception of memory that he never fully expounded. This lack of explicitness has given rise to mistaken interpretations, according to which a term such as 'memory-trace' is said to be nothing more than a vestige of outdated neurophysiological thinking. While making no claim here to present a Freudian theory of memory, we may recall the fundamental requirements which were the underlying reason for Freud's adoption of the term 'memory-trace': the task with which he was confronted was to assign memory a place within a topographical* schema and to provide an explanation of its functioning in economic terms.

a. The necessity of defining each psychical system in terms of a specific function, and of making Perception-Consciousness the function of one system in particular (see 'Consciousness'), leads to the postulation of an incompatibility between consciousness and memory: 'We find it hard to believe, however, that permanent traces of excitation such as these are also left in the system *Pcpt.-Cs.* If they remained constantly conscious, they would very soon set limits to the system's aptitude for receiving fresh excitations. If, on the other hand, they were unconscious, we should be faced with the problem of explaining the existence of unconscious processes in a system whose functioning was otherwise accompanied by the phenomenon of consciousness. We should, so to say, have altered nothing and gained nothing by our hypothesis relegating the process of becoming conscious to a special system' (1). This is an idea which dates from the origins of psycho-analysis. Breuer put it forward for the first time in the *Studies on Hysteria* (1895d): 'It is impossible for one and the same organ to fulfil these two contradictory conditions. The mirror of a reflecting telescope cannot at the same time be a photographic plate' (2). Freud later sought to illustrate this topographical conception by means of an analogy with the way in which the 'mystic writing-pad' works (3).

b. Freud introduces topographical distinctions inside memory itself. Thus a given event may be registered in different 'mnemic systems'. He proposes several more or less figurative models of this stratification of the memory in systems. In the *Studies on Hysteria*, he compares the organisation of memory to complicated archives in which the individual memories are arranged according to different methods of classification: according to chronological order, according to the links in chains of associations, and according to their degree of accessibility to consciousness (4). In his letter to Fliess dated December 6, 1896, and in *The Interpretation of Dreams* (1900a), this notion of an ordered

247

succession of registrations in the mnemic systems is taken up once more and given a more definitive exposition: the distinction between preconscious and conscious is now assimilated to that between two mnemic systems. In the 'descriptive' sense, all mnemic systems are held to be unconscious, but the traces in the system *Ucs.* are unable to emerge into consciousness as they are, whereas preconscious memories (i.e. 'memory' in the everyday sense of the word) can be actualised in specific sorts of behaviour.

c. The Freudian conception of infantile amnesia* throws light on the meta-psychological theory of memory-traces. We know that, for Freud, the fact that we do not remember the events of our earliest years is not due to any failure of recollection but rather the outcome of repression*. Generally speaking, all memories are recorded as a matter of course, but their evocation depends on the way in which they are cathected*, decathected and counter-cathected. This view of the matter is grounded on that distinction which clinical experience brings to light between the idea* and the quota of affect*: '. . . in mental functions something is to be distinguished–a quota of affect or sum of excitation–which [...] is capable of increase, diminution, displacement and discharge, and which is spread over the memory-traces of ideas somewhat as an electric charge is spread over the surface of a body' (5).

*   *   *

It is thus plain that the Freudian concept of the memory-trace is quite distinct from the empiricist notion of the engram, defined as an impression bearing a resemblance to the corresponding reality. In fact:

a. The memory-trace is invariably recorded in systems, and stands there in relation to other traces. Freud goes so far as to attempt to distinguish the *different* systems in which the traces of a *single* object are recorded, this according to the type of association involved (simultaneity, causality, etc.) (6, 7a). As far as evocation is concerned, a memory may be reactualised in one associative context while, in another, it will remain inaccessible to consciousness (see 'Complex').

b. Freud even tends to deny any sensory quality to memory-traces: '. . . if memories become conscious once more, they exhibit no sensory quality or a very slight one in comparison with perceptions' (7b).

It might be supposed that the 'Project for a Scientific Psychology' (1950a [1895]), with its neurophysiological orientation, would furnish the best support for any assimilation of the memory-trace to the 'simulacrum'-type image. In point of fact, however, this work provides instead the best point of access to what is most original in the Freudian theory of memory. In the 'Project', Freud attempts to account for the registration of the memory in the neuronal apparatus without making any appeal to a resemblance between trace and object. The memory-trace is simply a particular arrangement of facilitations*, so organised that one route is followed in preference to another. The functioning of memory in this way might be compared to what is known as 'memory' in the theory of cybernetic machines, which are built on the principle of binary oppositions, just as Freud's neuronal apparatus is defined by its successive bifurcations.

It should be noted, nevertheless, that Freud's way of referring to memory-traces in his later works–where he often also uses the term 'mnemic image'

synonymously–does indicate that when he is not considering the process whereby they are constituted he is led to speak of them as reproductions of things
in the sense in which this is understood by an empiricist psychology.

(1) FREUD, S. *Beyond the Pleasure Principle* (1920*g*), G.W., XIII, 24; S.E., XVIII, 25.

(2) BREUER, J. 'Theoretical' chapter of *Studies on Hysteria* (1895*d*), 1st German edn., 164*n.*;
S.E., II, 188–89*n*.

(3) Cf. FREUD, S. 'A Note upon the "Mystic Writing-Pad"' (1925*a* [1924]), G.W., XIV,
3–8; S.E., XIX, 227–32.

(4) Cf. FREUD, S., G.W., I, 295*ff.*; S.E., II, 291*ff*.

(5) FREUD, S. 'The Neuro-Psychoses of Defence' (1894*a*), G.W., I, 74; S.E., III, 60.

(6) Cf. FREUD, S. *Anf.*, 186; S.E., I, 233–4.

(7) FREUD, S. *The Interpretation of Dreams* (1900*a*): a) Cf. G.W., II–III, 544; S.E., V,
538–9. b) G.W., II–III, 545; S.E., V, 540.

Metapsychology

= *D.*: Metapsychologie.–*Es.*: metapsicología.–*Fr.*: métapsychologie.–*I.*: metapsicologia.–
P.: metapsicologia.

**Term invented by Freud to refer to the psychology of which he was the founder
when it is viewed in its most theoretical dimension. Metapsychology constructs an
ensemble of conceptual models which are more or less far-removed from empirical
reality. Examples are the fiction of a psychical apparatus* divided up into agencies*,
the theory of the instincts*, the hypothetical process of repression*, and so on.**

**Metapsychology embraces three approaches, known as the dynamic*, the
topographical* and the economic* points of view.**

The term 'metapsychology' is to be met with from time to time in Freud's
letters to Fliess. He makes use of it to define the originality of his own attempt
to construct a psychology 'that leads behind consciousness' (1*a*), as compared
to the classical psychologies of consciousness. It is impossible to overlook the
similarity of the terms 'metapsychology' and 'metaphysics', and indeed Freud
very likely intended to draw this analogy, for we know from his own admission
how strong his philosophical vocation was: 'I hope you will lend me your ear
for a few metapsychological questions. [...] When I was young, the only thing
I longed for was philosophical knowledge and now that I am going over from
medicine to psychology I am in the process of attaining it' (1*b*).

But Freud's reflection upon the relations between metaphysics and metapsychology does not come to an end with this simple parallel: in a significant
passage, he defines metapsychology as a scientific endeavour to redress the
constructions of 'metaphysics'. He sees these–like superstitious beliefs or
certain paranoiac delusions–as projecting what in reality are the properties of
the unconscious on to forces in the outside world: '. . . a large part of the
mythological view of the world, which extends a long way into the most modern
religions, *is nothing but psychology projected into the external world*. The obscure

249

recognition (the endopsychic perception, as it were) of psychical factors and relations in the unconscious is mirrored [...] in the construction of a *super-natural reality*, which is destined to be changed back once more by science into the *psychology of the unconscious*. One could venture [...] to transform *metaphysics* into *metapsychology*' (2).

Much later, Freud took the term up once more and gave it precise definition: 'I propose that when we have succeeded in describing a psychical process in its dynamic, topographical and economic aspects, we should speak of it as a *metapsychological* presentation (*Darstellung*)' (3, α). Rather than treating as metapsychological works all the theoretical studies involving concepts and hypotheses intrinsic to these three points of view, it might be preferable to reserve this description for texts which are more basic in that they develop or expound the hypotheses which underpin psycho-analytic psychology–its 'principles' (*Prinzipien*), 'fundamental concepts' (*Grundbegriffe*) and theoretical 'models' (*Darstellungen, Fiktionen, Vorbilder*). If so, then we shall find a certain number of *strictly* metapsychological texts punctuating Freud's work–in particular, the 'Project for a Scientific Psychology' (1950a [1895]); Chapter VII of *The Interpretation of Dreams* (1900a); 'Formulations on the Two Principles of Mental Functioning' (1911b); *Beyond the Pleasure Principle* (1920g); *The Ego and the Id* (1923b); *An Outline of Psycho-Analysis* (1940a [1938]). A final point worth noting is that in 1915 Freud conceived and partially carried through the project of writing a book on the *Preliminaries to a Metapsychology* (*Zur Vorbereitung einer Metapsychologie*), his intention being 'to clarify and carry deeper the theoretical assumptions on which a psycho-analytic system could be founded' (4, β).

(α) Hartmann, Kris and Loewenstein have suggested adding the *genetic* point of view to Freud's triple perspective of the topographical, the dynamic and the economic (see 'Stage'). David Rapaport adds the point of view of *adaptation*.

(β) Five of the planned articles were published, while seven others were apparently written but destroyed.

(1) FREUD, S.: a) letter to Fliess dated March 10, 1898, *Anf.*, 262; S.E., I, 274. b) letter to Fliess dated 2 April, 1896, *Anf.*, 176; *Origins*, 161–62.

(2) FREUD, S. *The Psychopathology of Everyday Life* (1901b), G.W., IV, 287–88; S.E., VI, 258–59.

(3) FREUD, S. 'The Unconscious' (1915e), G.W., X, 281; S.E., XIV, 181.

(4) FREUD, S. 'A Metapsychological Supplement to the Theory of Dreams (1917d [1915]), G.W., X, 412, *n*. 1; S.E., XIV, 222, *n*. 1.

Mirror Phase (or Stage)

= *D.*: Spiegelstufe.–*Es.*: fase del espejo.–*Fr.*: stade du miroir.–*I.*: stadio dello specchio.– *P.*: fase do espelho.

According to Jacques Lacan, a phase in the constitution of the human individual located between the ages of six and eighteen months (α). Though still in a state of powerlessness and motor incoordination, the infant anticipates on an imaginary

plane the apprehension and mastery of its bodily unity. This imaginary unification comes about by means of identification with the image of the counterpart as total *Gestalt*; it is exemplified concretely by the experience in which the child perceives its own reflection in a mirror.

The mirror phase is said to constitute the matrix and first outline of what is to become the ego.

The idea of the mirror phase was one of Lacan's earliest contributions, first proposed at the 1936 Marienbad International Congress of Psycho-Analysts (1*a*).

The concept is grounded upon a number of empirical data:

a. Data taken from child psychology and comparative psychology concerning the infant's behaviour when confronted with its reflection in a mirror (2). Lacan draws attention to 'the triumphant assumption of the image, with the accompanying jubilant mimicry and the playful complacency with which the specular identification is controlled' (3*a*).

b. Data derived from animal ethology, which demonstrates how certain results of maturation and biological organisation are attained solely by the visual perception of the counterpart (3*b*).

According to Lacan, the import of the mirror phase in human development is attributable to the prematurity of birth (β), as evidenced by the anatomically incomplete pyramidal system and the motor incoordination of the first months of life (γ).

*   *   *

I. As far as the structure of the subject is concerned, the mirror phase is said to represent a genetic moment: the setting up of the first roughcast of the ego. What happens is that the infant perceives in the image of its counterpart–or in its own mirror image–a form (*Gestalt*) in which it anticipates a bodily unity which it still objectively lacks (whence its 'jubilation'): in other words, it identifies with this image. This primordial experience is basic to the imaginary nature of the ego, which is constituted right from the start as an 'ideal ego' and as the 'root of the secondary identifications' (1*b*). It is obvious that from this point of view the subject cannot be equated with the ego, since the latter is an imaginary agency in which the subject tends to become alienated.

II. For Lacan, in so far as the intersubjective relationship bears the mark of the mirror phase, it is an imaginary, dual relationship inevitably characterised by an aggressive tension in which the ego is constituted as another and the other as an *alter ego* (see 'Imaginary').

III. This approach might be compared to Freud's own views on the transition from auto-erotism*–which precedes the formation of an ego–to narcissism* proper: what Lacan calls the phantasy of the 'body-in-pieces' (*le corps morcelé*) would thus correspond to the former stage, while the mirror stage would correspond to the onset of primary narcissism. There is one important difference, however: Lacan sees the mirror phase as responsible, retroactively, for the emergence of the phantasy of the body-in-pieces. This type of dialectical relation may be observed in the course of psycho-analytic treatment, where anxiety about fragmentation can at times be seen to arise as a consequence of loss of narcissistic identification, and vice versa.

(α) As Lacan has indicated himself, the word 'phase' (*phase*) is no doubt better adapted here than 'stage' (*stade*), in that it suggests a turning-point rather than a period in the process of psycho-biological maturation.

(β) Freud had already laid emphasis on this basic notion of the incompleteness of the human offspring at birth. Cf. our commentary on 'Helplessness', particularly the passage quoted there from *Inhibitions, Symptoms and Anxiety* (1926*d*).

(γ) The reader is referred to the writings of the embryologists, and in particular to those of Louis Bolk (1866–1930) concerning foetalisation (4).

(1) LACAN, J. 'Le stade du miroir comme formateur de la fonction du Je, telle qu'elle nous est révélée dans l'expérience psychanalytique', *R.F.P.*, 1949, XIII, 4; and in *Écrits* (Paris: Seuil, 1966): a) 449–55; *Écrits*, 93–100. b) 450; *Écrits*, 94.

(2) Cf. especially WALLON, H. 'Comment se développe chez l'enfant la notion du corps propre', *Journal de Psychologie*, 1931, 705–48.

(3) LACAN, J. 'Propos sur la causalité psychique', *L'évolution psychiatrique*, 1947; and in *Écrits* (Paris: Seuil, 1966): a) 34; *Écrits*, 185. b) Cf. 38–41; *Écrits*, 189–92.

(4) Cf. BOLK, L. 'Das Problem der Menschwerdung' (1926). French translation: *Arguments*, 1960, No. 18, 3–13.

Mixed Neurosis

= *D*.: gemischte Neurose.–*Es*.: neurosis mixta.–*Fr*.: névrose mixte.–*I*.: nevrosi mista.– *P*.: neurose mista.

Form of neurosis characterised by the coexistence of symptoms belonging to neuroses which Freud considers to be aetiologically distinct.

In Freud's work, the term 'mixed neurosis' is met with chiefly in the earliest writings (1), where he calls upon it to account for the fact that psychoneurotic symptoms are often combined with actual ones, and that the symptoms of one psychoneurosis may be accompanied by those of another.

The implication of the term is not merely that there is a complex clinical picture. In cases of mixed neurosis, according to Freud, each type of symptom exhibited can be related, ideally at any rate, to a corresponding mechanism: 'Wherever a mixed neurosis is present, it will be possible to discover an admixture of several specific aetiologies' (2).

That neuroses are rarely to be encountered in a pure state is very widely acknowledged in psycho-analytic clinical practice. For example, psycho-analysis lays emphasis on the existence of hysterical characteristics at the root of every obsessional neurosis (3), as it does on the actual nucleus of all psycho-neuroses (see 'Actual Neurosis'). What, since Freud, have been known as *borderline cases**–illnesses displaying both neurotic and psychotic components –also testify to the way in which psychopathological structures overlap.

But the concept of mixed neurosis must not lead to the rejection of all noso-graphical classification (4). On the contrary, the notion implies that it is always

possible in a given complex clinical case to ascertain what part is to be ascribed
to a particular structure or a particular mechanism.

(1) Cf., for example, FREUD, S. 'On the Grounds for Detaching a Particular Syndrome
from Neurasthenia under the Description "Anxiety Neurosis"' (1895b). And 'The Psychotherapy of Hysteria', in *Studies on Hysteria* (1895d), especially G.W., I, 256; S.E., II, 259.

(2) 'On the Grounds for Detaching a Particular Syndrome from Neurasthenia under the
Description "Anxiety Neurosis"' (1895b), G.W., I, 339; S.E., III, 113.

(3) Cf., for example, FREUD, S. 'From the History of an Infantile Neurosis' (1918b [1914]),
G.W., XII, 107; S.E., XVII, 75. And *Inhibitions, Symptoms and Anxiety* (1926d), G.W., XIV,
143; S.E., XX, 113.

(4) Cf., for example, FREUD, S. *Introductory Lectures on Psycho-Analysis* (1916–17), G.W.,
XI, 405; S.E., XVI, 390.

Mnemic Symbol

= *D.*: Erinnerungssymbol.–*Es.*: símbolo mnémico.–*Fr.*: symbole mnésique.–
I.: simbolo mnestico.–*P.*: símbolo mnêmico.

**Term often employed by Freud in his earliest writings to qualify the hysterical
symptom.**

In several texts dating from around 1895–'The Neuro-Psychoses of Defence'
(1894a), 'Further Remarks on the Neuro-Psychoses of Defence' (1896b),
Studies on Hysteria (1895d), etc.–Freud defines the hysterical symptom as a
mnemic symbol of the pathogenic trauma or of the conflict. He writes, for
example: 'By this means the ego succeeds in freeing itself from the contradiction; but instead, it has burdened itself with a mnemic symbol which finds a
lodgement in consciousness, like a sort of parasite, either in the form of an
unresolvable motor innervation or as a constantly recurring hallucinatory
sensation' (1). Elsewhere, Freud compares hysterical symptoms to monuments
erected to commemorate events; thus Anna O.'s symptoms are seen as the
'mnemic symbols' of the illness and death of her father (2).

(1) FREUD, S. 'The Neuro-Psychoses of Defence' (1894a), G.W., I, 63; S.E., III, 49.

(2) FREUD, S. 'Five Lectures on Psycho-Analysis' (1910a) G.W., VIII, 11–12; S.E., XI,
16–17.

Mothering

= *D.*: Bemuttern *or* mütterliches Betreuen.–*Es.*: maternalización.–*Fr.*: maternage.–
I.: maternage.–*P.*: maternagem.

**Technique used in the psychotherapy of the psychoses, particularly schizophrenia,
the aim of which is to establish a relationship between therapist and patient that**

Mothering

operates in a mode at once symbolic and real – a relationship analogous to the one thought to obtain between a 'good mother' and her child.

The technique of mothering is based on an aetiological view of psychosis which ascribes it to primitive, essentially oral frustrations experienced by the subject in earliest infancy because of his mother.

The term 'mothering' has been used in a broad sense to connote 'all care lavished on the infant in that atmosphere of active, devoted, watchful and constant tenderness which typifies maternal feeling' (1a). As a rule, however, the word covers only the psychotherapeutic technique.

The function of this procedure is primarily reparation. However, although it does aim to supply the patient with those real satisfactions in regard to which he has been frustrated in his relationship to his mother, its prime goal is the comprehension of fundamental needs. As Racamier points out (1b), we have to identify the needs which underlie the psychotic defences, pick out those among them which are deserving of preferential treatment ('basic needs') and – most importantly – answer them by means other than classical analytic interpretation*.

As to the nature of these means, each of the authors who have pursued this line of inquiry over the past thirty years (Schwing, Rosen, Sechehaye, among others) has his own view. We cannot describe here the various techniques – and the various insights – which, broadly speaking, come under the head of mothering. It may be pointed out, however, that:

a. Mothering is not a matter of reconstructing the relationship between suckling and mother in its full reality.

b. As all the authors stress, mothering requires more of the therapist than a maternal attitude – it requires a true emotional commitment on his part: 'The mothering relationship springs from the encounter between a patient deeply, vitally, avidly in need of passive gratification and a therapist at once capable of understanding him and desirous of reaching out to him like a mother reaching out to an abandoned infant' (1c).

Lastly, a consistent theory of mothering would have to determine what portion of the therapeutic action in question may be properly ascribed to real satisfaction, what portion to the symbolic gift and what portion to interpretation.

(1) RACAMIER, P.-C. 'Psychothérapie psychanalytique des psychoses', in *La psychanalyse d'aujourd'hui* (Paris: P.U.F., 1956): a) II, 599. b) II, 601–2. c) II, 601.

N

Narcissism

= *D.*: Narzissmus.–*Es.*: narcisismo.–*Fr.*: narcissisme.–*I.*: narcisismo.–*P.*: narcisismo.

By reference to the myth of Narcissus, love directed towards the image of oneself.

I. The term 'narcissism' (α) appears in Freud's work for the first time in 1910, when it is called upon to account for object-choice in homosexuals, who 'take *themselves* as their sexual object. That is to say, they proceed from a narcissistic basis and look for a young man who resembles themselves and whom *they* may love as their mother loved *them*' (1*a*).

The discovery of narcissism leads Freud–in the Schreber case (1911*c*)–to posit the existence of a *stage* in sexual development between auto-erotism* and object-love. The subject 'begins by taking himself, his own body, as his love-object' (2), which allows a first unification of the sexual instincts. This view of the matter is again put forward in *Totem and Taboo* (1912–13).

II. Thus Freud was already making use of the concept of narcissism before he 'introduced' it in a paper devoted to the topic: 'On Narcissism: An Introduction' (1914*c*). It is this text, nevertheless, which integrates the notion into the psycho-analytic theory as a whole, particularly by relating it to libidinal cathexes. It now becomes clear that the possibility of the libido's recathecting the ego while withdrawing cathexis from the object is illustrated by psychosis ('narcissistic neurosis'*); the implication of this is that 'an original libidinal cathexis of the ego [...] fundamentally persists and is related to the object-cathexes much as the body of an amoeba is related to the pseudopodia which it puts out' (3*a*). Basing himself on a sort of principle of conservation of libidinal energy, Freud postulates a seesaw balance between *ego-libido** (i.e. libido which cathects the ego) and *object-libido*: 'The more of the one is employed, the more the other becomes depleted' (3*b*). 'The ego is to be regarded as a great reservoir of libido from which libido is sent out *to* objects and which is always ready to absorb libido flowing back *from* objects' (4).

In this way we are brought–in the context of an approach based on energy and asserting the permanence of a libidinal cathexis of the ego–to define narcissism *structurally*: instead of appearing as a developmental stage, narcissism now emerges as a damming up of the libido* which no object-cathexis can completely overcome.

III. Such a process of withdrawal of cathexis from the object and its turning back on to the subject had already been identified in 1908 by Karl Abraham, who drew on the example of dementia praecox: 'The psychosexual characteristic of dementia praecox is the return of the patient to auto-erotism [...]. The mental patient transfers on to himself alone as his only sexual object the whole of the libido which the healthy person turns upon all living and inanimate objects in his environment' (5). Freud adopted these ideas of Abraham's, which 'have been accepted in psycho-analysis and have become the basis of our attitude to the psychoses' (6). But he added the idea–which facilitates a clear distinction between narcissism and auto-erotism–that the ego does not exist from the very first as a unity, and that 'a new psychical action' has to take place in order to bring about narcissism (3c).

If we are to preserve a distinction between a state on the one hand in which the sexual instincts attain satisfaction anarchically, independently of one another, and narcissism on the other hand, where it is the ego in its entirety which is taken as love-object, then we must inevitably make the period of infantile narcissism's dominance coincide with the formative moments of the ego.

On this point psycho-analytic theory is somewhat ambivalent. From the genetic point of view, the establishment of the ego can be conceived of as the formation of a psychical unit paralleling the constitution of the bodily schema. One may further suppose that this unification is precipitated by the subject's acquisition of an image of himself founded on the model furnished by the other person–this image being the ego itself. Narcissism then appears as the amorous captivation of the subject by this image. Jacques Lacan has related this first moment in the ego's formation to that fundamentally narcissistic experience which he calls the *mirror stage** (7). In this light, with the ego taking form by virtue of an identification with the other, narcissism–and even 'primary narcissism'–is no longer seen as a state independent of any inter-subjective relationship, but rather as the internalisation of a relationship. There is no doubt that this approach is consistent with the conception of narcissism proposed in such a text as 'Mourning and Melancholia' (1917e [1915]), where Freud certainly appears to see nothing more in it than a 'narcissistic identification' with the object (8).

This attitude fades into the background, however, with the advent of the second theory of the psychical apparatus, by which time Freud has come to maintain an absolute opposition between a first (objectless) narcissistic state and object-relations. This primitive state, now called primary narcissism*, is supposed to be characterised by the total absence of any relationship to the outside world, and by a lack of differentiation between ego and id; intra-uterine existence is taken to be its prototypical form, while sleep is deemed a more or less successful imitation of that ideal model (9).

The idea of a narcissism contemporaneous with the formation of the ego through identification with the other person does survive nevertheless. It is now known as 'secondary' rather than 'primary' narcissism: 'The libido which flows into the ego owing to the identifications [...] brings about its "secondary narcissism" ' (10a). 'The narcissism of the ego is thus a secondary one which has been withdrawn from objects' (10b).

This profound modification of Freud's views is correlated, in the first place, with the introduction of the notion of the id* as a separate agency from which the other agencies derive through a process of differentiation; secondly, with an evolution of the concept of the ego which places the emphasis as much on its adaptive role *qua* differentiated agency as on the identifications of which it is a product; and lastly, with the fading of the distinction between auto-erotism and narcissism. If we pursue this line of thought to the letter we incur two risks.

First, there is a danger of running counter to experience by asserting that the newborn baby is without any perceptual outlet on to the external world. Secondly, we may find ourselves re-opening the door–and in the naïvest way– to a version of the idealist fallacy made all the more flagrant by being expressed in 'biological' language: just how are we supposed to picture the transition from a monad shut in upon itself to a progressive discovery of the object?

(α) Freud opens 'On Narcissism: An Introduction' (1914c) by stating that he has borrowed the term from Paul Näcke, who used it (in 1899) to describe a perversion. This statement was corrected, however, in a note added in 1920 to the *Three Essays on the Theory of Sexuality* (1905d). Freud now asserted that it was to Havelock Ellis that the introduction of the term should rightly be attributed (1b). In point of fact Näcke had indeed invented the actual word '*Narzissmus*', but in the course of commenting on Ellis's views; it was Ellis who, in his *Auto-erotism, a Psychological Study* (1898), first invoked the myth of Narcissus to help describe a case of perverted behaviour.

(1) FREUD, S. *Three Essays on the Theory of Sexuality* (1905d): a) G.W., V, 44, *n.* 1; S.E., VII, 145, *n.* 1. b) Cf. G.W., V, 119, *n.* 3; S.E., VII, 218, *n.* 3.

(2) FREUD, S. 'Psycho-Analytic Notes on an Autobiographical Account of a Case of Paranoia (Dementia Paranoides)' (1911c), G.W., VIII, 296–97; S.E., XII, 60–61.

(3) FREUD, S. 'On Narcissism: An Introduction' (1914c): a) G.W., X, 141; S.E., XIV, 75–76. b) G.W., X, 141; S.E., XIV, 75–76. c) G.W., X, 142; S.E., XIV, 77.

(4) FREUD, S. 'Two Encyclopaedia Articles' (1923a [1922]), G.W., XIII, 231; S.E., XVIII, 257.

(5) ABRAHAM, K. 'The Psycho-Sexual Differences between Hysteria and Dementia Praecox' (1908), in *Selected Papers* (London: Hogarth, 1927), 73–75.

(6) FREUD, S. *Introductory Lectures on Psycho-Analysis* (1916–17), G.W., XI, 430; S.E., XVI, 415.

(7) Cf. LACAN, J. 'Le stade du miroir comme formateur de la fonction du Je', *R.F.P.*, 1949, XIII, 4, 449–55. Reprinted in his *Écrits* (Paris: Seuil, 1966), 93–100. Trans.: 'The Mirror-Phase', *New Left Review*, 1968, 51, 71–77.

(8) Cf. FREUD, S., G.W., X, 435–37; S.E., XIV, 249–51.

(9) Cf. FREUD, S. *Group Psychology and the Analysis of the Ego* (1921c), G.W., XIII, 146; S.E., XVIII, 130–31.

(10) FREUD, S. *The Ego and the Id* (1923b): a) G.W., XIII, 258n.; S.E., XIX, 30. b) G.W., XIII, 275; S.E., XIX, 46.

Narcissistic Libido

= *D.*: narzisstische Libido.–*Es.*: libido narcisista.–*Fr.*: libido narcissique.– *I.*: libido narcisistica.–*P.*: libido narcísica.

See 'Ego-Libido/Object-Libido'.

Narcissistic Neurosis

= *D.*: narzisstische Neurose.–*Es.*: neurosis narcisista.–*Fr.*: névrose narcissique.–
I.: nevrosi narcisistica.–*P.*: neurose narcísica.

Term tending to disappear from present-day psycho-analytic usage but found in Freud's writings as a designation for a mental illness characterised by the withdrawal of libido from the outside world and its direction on to the ego. Narcissistic neurosis thus stands in opposition to the transference neuroses*.

Nosographically, the group of narcissistic neuroses comprises all functional psychoses (i.e. psychoses whose symptoms are not caused by somatic lesions).

The term 'narcissistic neurosis' has its origin in the exposition of narcissism to which Freud was led in particular by the application of psycho-analytic conceptions to the psychoses (1). Freud used the term mostly as the antithesis of 'transference neurosis'.

This opposition is of both a technical order (difficulty or impossibility of libidinal transference) and a theoretical one (withdrawal of libido on to the ego). In other words, the narcissistic relation is predominant in the structures under consideration. In this sense Freud holds the narcissistic neuroses to be identical to the psychoses (which he is still referring to as paraphrenias*).

Later–especially in his article on 'Neurosis and Psychosis' (1924*b* [1923])– Freud limits the application of the name 'narcissistic neurosis' to conditions of the melancholic type, which are thus treated as distinct from both the transference neuroses and the psychoses* (2).

Today, the term is tending to fall out of use.

(1) Cf. FREUD, S. 'On Narcissism: An Introduction' (1914*c*), G.W., X, 138–70; S.E., XIV, 73–102.

(2) Cf. FREUD, S., G.W., XIII, 390; S.E., XIX, 151–52.

Narcissistic Object-Choice

= *D.*: narzisstische Objektwahl.–*Es.*: elección objetal narcisista.–
Fr.: choix d'objet narcissique.–*I.*: scelta d' oggetto narcisistica.–
P.: escolha narcísica de objeto.

Type of object-choice* operating on the model of the subject's relationship to his own self, with the object representing some aspect or other of himself.

The discovery that specific subjects, particularly homosexuals, 'have taken as a model [...] their own selves' in the choice of a love-object was for Freud 'the strongest of the reasons which have led us to adopt the hypothesis of narcissism' (1*a*). The narcissistic object-choice is opposed to the anaclitic one* in that it does not reproduce a pre-existing object-relationship, but is instead the formation of an object-relationship on the model of the subject's relationship to himself. In his first attempts to work out the idea of narcissism, Freud makes the homosexual narcissistic choice into an interim stage between narcissism and heterosexuality: the child is said to choose an object initially whose genital organs resemble its own (2).

But the idea of the narcissistic choice is not a straightforward one even in the case of homosexuality: the object is chosen on the model of the little child or adolescent that the subject once was, while the subject identifies with the mother who used to take care of him (3).

The paper 'On Narcissism: An Introduction' (1914c) expands the notion of the narcissistic choice, and Freud sets forth the following schema:

'A person may love [...] according to the narcissistic type:

'a. what he himself is (i.e., himself),

'b. what he himself was,

'c. what he himself would like to be,

'd. someone who was once part of himself' (1b).

These headings cover very varied phenomena. The first three instances concern the choice of an object resembling the subject's own self, but it must be stressed, first, that what serves as model for the choice is an image or ideal, and, secondly, that the similarity between the object chosen and the model may be quite partial, amounting to nothing more than a few common traits. Under d., what Freud has in mind is the mother's narcissistic love for her child, who was 'once part of herself'. Here the situation is very different, for the object chosen does not resemble the subject as a unified individual but is, rather, the thing that allows the subject to rediscover and restore his lost unity.

'On Narcissism' contrasts the male object-choice, said to operate more usually in the anaclitic mode, with that of the woman, which is as a rule narcissistic. Freud points out, however, that this distinction is only a schematic one, and that 'both kinds of object-choice are open to each individual' (1c).

The two types of object-choice are thus looked upon as purely ideal, and as liable to alternate or to be combined in any actual individual case.

Yet it is doubtful whether an antithesis between the narcissistic and the anaclitic object-choices, even as ideal types, is tenable. It is in 'complete object-love of the attachment type' that Freud observes 'the marked sexual over-valuation which is doubtless derived from the child's original narcissism and thus corresponds to a transference of that narcissism to the sexual object' (1d). Conversely, he describes the case of 'narcissistic women' in the following terms: 'Strictly speaking, it is only themselves that such women love with an intensity comparable to that of the man's love for them. Nor does their need lie in the direction of loving, but of being loved; and the man who fulfils this condition is the one who finds favour with them' (1e). It may be asked whether a case such as this, described here as *narcissistic*, does not display a subject seeking to reproduce the child's relationship to the mother who feeds it – an aim which according to Freud is a defining characteristic of the *anaclitic* object-choice.

(1) FREUD, S. 'On Narcissism: An Introduction' (1914c): a) G.W., X, 154; S.E., XIV, 88. b) G.W., X, 156; S.E., XIV, 90. c) G.W., X, 154; S.E., XIV, 88. d) G.W., X, 154; S.E., XIV, 88. e) G.W., X, 155; S.E., XIV, 89.

(2) Cf. FREUD, S. 'Psycho-Analytic Notes on an Autobiographical Account of a Case of Paranoia (Dementia Paranoides)' (1911c), G.W., VII, 297; S.E., XII, 60–61.

(3) Cf. FREUD, S. *Leonardo da Vinci and a Memory of his Childhood* (1910c), G.W., VIII, 170; S.E., XI, 99–100.

Need for Punishment

= *D.*: Strafbedürfnis.–*Es.*: necesidad de castigo.–*Fr.*: besoin de punition.– *I.*: bisogno di punizione.–*P.*: necessidade de castigo *or* de punição.

Requirement of internal origin postulated by Freud as lying at the root of the behaviour of certain subjects who are shown by psycho-analytic investigation to be seeking out unpleasant or humiliating situations, from which they derive enjoyment (moral masochism). Whatever is irreducible in such behaviour must, in the last reckoning, be ascribed to the death instinct.

The existence of phenomena implying self-punishment aroused Freud's interest very early on: among such phenomena were *dreams* of punishment, which resemble a tribute paid to the censorship for a wish-fulfilment (1), and–above all–the symptoms of *obsessional neurosis*. As early as his first studies of this condition, Freud describes self-reproaches; then, in 'Notes upon a Case of Obsessional Neurosis' (1909*d*), he deals with self-punishing forms of behaviour; more generally speaking, it is the overall symptomatology of this neurosis, with the suffering it entails, that makes the obsessional patient into his own tormentor.

The clinical picture presented by *melancholia* reveals the violence of a compulsion to self-punishment that can go as far as suicide. But it is also one of the contributions of Freud and of psycho-analysis to have shown that self-punishment is the true motive for types of behaviour where punishment is only *apparently* the unwished-for consequence of certain *aggressive and criminal acts* (2). In this sense we may speak of 'criminals out of self-punishment' without necessarily implying that this process is the only motive for what is inevitably a complex phenomenon.

Lastly, in the context of the *treatment*, Freud was led to pay more and more attention to what he terms a negative therapeutic reaction*: the analyst has the impression, he writes, that he is confronted by 'a force which is defending itself by every possible means against recovery and which is absolutely resolved to hold on to illness and suffering' (3*a*).

The deeper investigation, in the context of the second theory of the psychical apparatus, of the metapsychological problems raised by these phenomena, the advances made in his thinking about sado-masochism*, the introduction of the death instinct*–all these enabled Freud to better circumscribe and differentiate self-punishing behaviour.

a. Freud himself expressed reservations concerning the expression 'unconscious sense of guilt*', the term 'need for punishment' seeming to him more appropriate (4*a*).

b. From a topographical standpoint, self-punishing behaviour is explained by Freud in terms of the tension between an especially demanding super-ego and the ego.

c. But the use of the term 'need for punishment' does bring out the irreducible factor in the force which impels certain subjects to suffer, along with the paradoxical nature of the satisfaction they get from their suffering. Freud is led to distinguish between two types of cases: certain individuals 'give an impression of being morally inhibited to an excessive degree, of being under the domination of an especially sensitive conscience, although they are not conscious of any of this ultra-morality. On closer inspection, we can see the difference there is between an unconscious extension of morality of this kind and moral masochism. In the former, the accent falls on the heightened sadism of the super-ego to which the ego submits; in the latter, it falls on the ego's own masochism which seeks punishment, whether from the super-ego or from the parental powers outside' (4b). To this extent, then, the sadism of the super-ego and the ego's masochism cannot be treated purely and simply as the two diametrically opposed forces constituting a single tension.

d. Pursuing this line of thought, Freud goes so far—in 'Analysis Terminable and Interminable' (1937c)—as to put forward the hypothesis that it is impossible to account adequately for the need for punishment, as an expression of the death instinct, by invoking the conflictual relationship of the super-ego and the ego. If it is true that one portion of the death instinct is 'psychically bound by the super-ego', other portions, 'whether bound or free, may be at work in other, unspecified places' (3b).

(1) Cf. FREUD, S. *The Interpretation of Dreams* (1900a), G.W., II–III, 476–80, 563–66; S.E., V, 473–76, 557–60.

(2) Cf. FREUD, S. *The Ego and the Id* (1923b), G.W., XIII, 282; S.E., XIX, 52.

(3) FREUD, S. 'Analysis Terminable and Interminable' (1937c): a) G.W., XVI, 88; S.E., XXIII, 242. b) G.W., XVI, 88; S.E., XXIII, 242–43.

(4) FREUD, S. 'The Economic Problem of Masochism' (1924c): a) Cf. G.W., XIII, 378–79; S.E., XIX, 166. b) G.W., XIII, 381; S.E., XIX, 168–69.

Negation

= *D.*: Verneinung.–*Es.*: negación.–*Fr.*: (dé)négation.–*I.*: negazione.–*P.*: negação.

Procedure whereby the subject, while formulating one of his wishes, thoughts or feelings which has been repressed hitherto, contrives, by disowning it, to continue to defend himself against it.

This word calls first of all for a few remarks of a terminological order:

a. The common linguistic consciousness of each language does not always distinguish clearly between terms which denote the act of negating, while it is even rarer to find one-to-one correspondences between the various terms in the different languages.

Negation

In German, '*Verneinung*' denotes *negation* in the logical and grammatical sense (there is no verb '*neinen*' or '*beneinen*'), but it also means *denial* in the psychological sense of rejection of a statement which I have made or which has been imputed to me, e.g. 'No, I did not say that, I did not think that'. In this second sense, '*verneinen*' comes close to '*verleugnen*' (or '*leugnen*'), to disown, deny, disavow, refute.

b. When we turn to the specifically Freudian usage, there seems to be a justification for distinguishing between '*verneinen*' and '*verleugnen*'. Towards the end of his work, Freud tends to reserve the latter verb for the refusal to perceive a fact which is imposed by the external world. The Editors of the *Standard Edition*, who recognised the special sense taken on by '*Verleugnung*' in Freud's later work, elected to translate it 'disavowal' (q.v.) (1).

As for Freud's use of '*Verneinung*', the English reader inevitably loses the ambiguity which derives from the term's meaning both negation and denial–an ambiguity which may even be one of the sources of the richness of the article that Freud devoted to 'Negation' (1925*h*).

It is worth noting that the German term of Latin origin '*Negation*' is also met with on occasion in Freud's writings (2).

*　　*　　*

Freud brought the procedure of negation to light in the course of his experience of treatment. In the hysterics with whom he was dealing, he very soon encountered a particular kind of resistance: 'The deeper we go the more difficult it becomes for the emerging memories to be recognised, till near the nucleus we come upon memories which the patient disavows even in reproducing them' (3). A good example of negation is furnished by the 'Rat Man', who had thought as a child that he would win the love of a little girl on condition that some misfortune should befall him, '. . . and as an instance of such a misfortune his father's death had forced itself upon his mind. He had at once rejected the idea with energy. And even now he could not admit the possibility that what had arisen in this way could have been a "wish"; it had clearly been no more than a "train of thought".–By way of objection I asked him why, if it had not been a wish, he had repudiated it.–Merely, he replied, on account of the content of the idea, the notion that his father might die' (4*a*). The continuation of the analysis brings proof positive that there was indeed a hostile wish directed towards the father: '. . . the "No" with which the fact is first denied is immediately followed by a confirmation of it, though, to begin with, only an indirect one' (4*b*).

The notion that, during treatment, negation often marks the bringing to consciousness of repressed material is the starting-point of Freud's paper on the subject of 1925. 'There is no stronger evidence that we have been successful in our effort to uncover the unconscious than when the patient reacts to it with the words "I didn't think that", or "I didn't (ever) think of that" ' (5*a*).

Negation is held to have this same significance when it is opposed to the interpretation* of the analyst. This tenet gives rise to an objection concerning first principles which Freud did not overlook: in 'Constructions in Analysis' (1937*d*), he poses the question whether such a hypothesis does not run the risk of claiming infallibility for the analyst on the grounds that 'if the patient agrees with us, then the interpretation is right; but if he contradicts us, that is only a sign of his resistance, which again shows that we are right' (6*a*). Freud's answer to such a criticism is a measured one: he urges the analyst to seek confirmation in the context and development of the treatment (6*b*). It is certainly true, all the same, that negation has an indicative value for Freud, signalling as it does the moment when an unconscious idea or wish begins to re-emerge, whether during the course of treatment or outside it.

Freud offers a very exact metapsychological explanation of the phenomenon, notably in the paper on 'Negation'. His exposition develops three closely linked assertions:

a. 'Negation is a way of taking cognizance of what is repressed. [...]

b. '. . . only one consequence of the process of negation is undone–the fact, namely, of the ideational content of what is repressed not reaching consciousness. The outcome of this is a kind of intellectual acceptance of the repressed, while at the same time what is essential to the repression persists. [...]

c. 'With the help of the symbol of negation, thinking frees itself from the restrictions of repression' (5*b*).

This last proposition shows that in Freud's view the negation dealt with in psycho-analysis and negation in the logical and linguistic sense–the 'symbol of negation'–share the same origin; this is in fact the central thesis of his paper.

(1) Cf. S.E., XIX, 143*n*.

(2) Cf. FREUD, S. 'The Unconscious' (1915*e*), G.W., X, 285; S.E., XIV, 186.

(3) FREUD, S. *Studies on Hysteria* (1895*d*), G.W., I, 293; S.E., II, 289.

(4) FREUD, S. 'Notes upon a Case of Obsessional Neurosis' (1909*d*): a) G.W., VII, 402; S.E., X, 178–79. b) G.W., VII, 406*n*.; S.E., X, 183, *n*. 2.

(5) FREUD, S. 'Negation' (1925*h*): a) G.W., XIV, 15; S.E., XIX, 239. b) G.W., XIV, 12–13; S.E., XIX, 235–36.

(6) FREUD, S.: a) G.W., XVI, 43; S.E., XXIII, 257. b) Cf. G.W., XVI, 49–52; S.E.,XXIII, 262–65.

Negative Therapeutic Reaction

= *D*.: negative therapeutische Reaktion.–*Es*.: reacción terapeútica negativa.–
Fr.: réaction thérapeutique négative.–*I*.: reazione terapeutica negativa.–
P.: reação terapêutica negativa.

Phenomenon met with in some courses of psycho-analytic treatment as a type of resistance to cure that is particularly hard to overcome: at every point where an advance might be expected in the progress of the treatment, the patient gets worse instead, as though certain subjects preferred suffering to being cured. Freud connects this phenomenon with an unconscious sense of guilt inherent in certain masochistic structures.

Freud's most complete description and analysis of the negative therapeutic reaction is given in *The Ego and the Id* (1923*b*). In the case of certain subjects, 'Every partial solution that ought to result, and in other people does result, in an improvement or a temporary suspension of symptoms produces in them for the time being an exacerbation of their illness; they get worse during the treatment instead of getting better' (1*a*).

Earlier–for example in 'Remembering, Repeating and Working-Through' (1914*g*)–Freud had already drawn attention to the problem of 'deterioration during treatment' (2). The proliferation of the symptoms can be explained by that return of the repressed* which is facilitated by a more tolerant attitude towards the neurosis, or else by the patient's desire to prove to the analyst how dangerous the treatment is.

Freud also speaks of 'negative reactions' in 'From the History of an Infantile Neurosis' (1918*b*): '. . . every time something had been conclusively cleared up [the Wolf Man] attempted to contradict the effect for a short while by an aggravation of the symptom' (3); but it is only with *The Ego and the Id* that a more specific theory is put forward. The negative therapeutic reaction is to be distinguished from other types of resistance* that would in the normal way be invoked as an explanation: adhesiveness* of the libido–in other words, an unusual difficulty encountered by the subject in getting rid of his fixations; negative transference; the subject's wish to prove his own superiority over the analyst; the 'narcissistic inaccessibility' of certain serious cases; and even the gain from illness*. In Freud's view we are confronted here by an *inverse* reaction in which the patient, at each stage of the analysis, prefers to go on suffering rather than be cured. Freud treats this as the expression of an unconscious sense of guilt* of which it is very hard to form a clear picture: '. . . as far as the patient is concerned this sense of guilt is dumb; it does not tell him he is guilty; he does not feel guilty, he feels ill' (1*b*).

Freud returns to the question in 'The Economic Problem of Masochism' (1924*c*): if we are justified in speaking of a gain from illness in connection with the negative therapeutic reaction, it is in so far as the masochist gets his satisfaction through suffering and seeks to maintain 'a certain amount of suffering' (4) at all costs.

Can the negative therapeutic reaction be viewed as a super-ego resistance? This appears to be Freud's opinion, at any rate in those cases where the sense of guilt may be seen as 'a *borrowed* one–when it is the product of an identification with some other person who was once the object of an erotic cathexis' (1*c*). When Freud evokes super-ego resistance in *Inhibitions, Symptoms and Anxiety* (1926*d*), it is to the negative therapeutic reaction that he is alluding (5).

Nonetheless Freud left leeway from the start for something that cannot always be adequately accounted for by the role of the super-ego and secondary masochism. The clearest expression of this idea may be found in 'Analysis Terminable and Interminable' (1937*c*), where the negative therapeutic reaction is directly linked with the death instinct (q.v.). The effects of this instinct cannot be located entirely in the conflict between ego and super-ego (sense of guilt, need for punishment*); this only represents 'the portion of it which is, as it were, psychically bound by the super-ego and thus becomes recognisable; other quotas of the same force, whether bound or free, may be at work in other, unspecified places' (6). If it is impossible on occasion to overcome the negative therapeutic reaction, or even to interpret it satisfactorily, this is because its ultimate *raison d'être* is to be found in the irreducible nature of the death instinct.

264

It is clear that the expression 'negative therapeutic reaction' is meant–at any rate as far as Freud is concerned–to designate a very specific clinical phenomenon where the resistance to cure can apparently not be explained by means of the notions that are usually called upon. The paradoxical character of this reaction, which cannot be accounted for by the operation of the pleasure principle no matter how complex this is taken to be, was one of a number of motives Freud had for forming the hypothesis of primary masochism (see 'Masochism').

All the same, psycho-analysts often employ the expression in a more descriptive way, without restricting its meaning so narrowly, as a designation for any particularly obstinate form of resistance to change met with during the treatment.

(1) FREUD, S.: a) G.W., XIII, 278; S.E., XIX, 49. b) G.W., XIII, 279; S.E., XIX, 50. c) G.W., XIII, 279n.; S.E., XIX, 50n.

(2) FREUD, S., G.W., X, 131–32; S.E., XII, 152.

(3) FREUD, S., G.W., XII, 100; S.E., XVII, 69.

(4) FREUD S., G.W., XIII, 379; S.E., XIX, 166.

(5) Cf. FREUD, S., G.W., XIV, 193; S.E., XX, 160.

(6) FREUD, S., G.W., XVI, 88; S.E., XXIII, 242–43.

Neurasthenia

= *D*.: Neurasthenie.–*Es*.: neurastenia.–*Fr*.: neurasthénie.–*I*.: nevrastenia.–
P.: neurastenia.

Condition described by the American physician George Beard (1839–83). According to Beard neurasthenia presents a clinical picture centred around a physical fatigue of 'nervous' origin but embracing symptoms of the most varied kinds.

Freud was among the first to draw attention to the fact that this syndrome was being invoked too widely. He felt that the category of neurasthenia should be broken down and part of its extension be taken over by other nosographical denominations. He nonetheless held neurasthenia to be a neurosis in its own right, characterised by feelings of physical tiredness, intracranial pressure, dyspepsia, constipation, spinal paraesthesias and the impoverishment of sexual activity. He placed it under the head of the actual neuroses, alongside anxiety neurosis*, and sought its aetiology in a type of sexual functioning incapable of adequately discharging libidinal tension (masturbation).

It was George Beard who coined the term 'neurasthenia', the etymological meaning of which is nervous weakness; the reader is referred to this author's work for the clinical picture which he described as typical of this condition (1).

Freud concerned himself with neurasthenia chiefly in his earliest work, where he was led to limit and subdivide the field of the actual neuroses (q.v.) (2, 3). He did subsequently persist, however, in asserting the specificity of this neurosis (4).

Neuro-Psychosis (or Psychoneurosis) of Defence

(1) Cf. BEARD, G. *American Nervousness, its Causes and Consequences* (New York, 1881), and *Sexual Neurasthenia (Nervous Exhaustion), its Hygiene, Causes, Symptoms and Treatment* (New York, 1884).

(2) Cf. FREUD, S. 'On the Grounds for Detaching a Particular Syndrome from Neurasthenia under the Description "Anxiety Neurosis" ' (1895*b*).

(3) Cf. FREUD, S. 'Sexuality in the Aetiology of the Neuroses' (1898*a*).

(4) Cf. notably FREUD, S. *Introductory Lectures on Psycho-Analysis* (1916–17), Chapter XXIV.

Neuro-Psychosis (or Psychoneurosis) of Defence

= *D.*: Abwehr-Neuropsychose.–*Es.*: psiconeurosis de defensa.–
Fr.: psychonévrose de défense.–*I.*: psiconevrosi da difesa.–*P.*: psiconeurose de defesa.

Term employed by Freud in the years 1894–96 to denote a certain number of psychoneurotic conditions–hysteria, phobia, obsessions, some psychoses–while bringing out the role of defensive conflict, first discovered in hysteria.

Once the idea that defence has an essential function in every psychoneurosis had gained acceptance, the term, whose value had been heuristic, gave way to 'psychoneurosis'*.

The term was introduced in 'The Neuro-psychoses of Defence' (1894*a*), an article in which Freud attempts to bring out the role of defence in the field of hysteria before going on to show that this mechanism–though in other guises– has a part to play in phobias, obsessions and certain hallucinatory psychoses. At this stage in his thought, Freud made no claim to extend the notion of defence to either hysteria as a whole (see 'Defence Hysteria') or to all the psychoneuroses, although he did do so a little later. By the time of his 'Further Remarks on the Neuro-Psychoses of Defence' (1896*a*), Freud feels that it is now established that defence is 'the nuclear point in the psychical mechanism of the neuroses in question' (1).

(1) FREUD, S., G.W., I, 379–80; S.E., III, 162.

Neurosis

= *D.*: Neurose.–*Es.*: neurosis.–*Fr.*: névrose.–*I.*: nevrosi.–*P.*: neurose.

A psychogenic affection in which the symptoms are the symbolic expression of a psychical conflict whose origins lie in the subject's childhood history; these symptoms constitute compromises* between wish* and defence*.

The extension of the term 'neurosis' has varied; it is now usually reserved, when unqualified, for those clinical pictures which can be ascribed to obsessional neurosis, hysteria or phobic neurosis. Present-day nosography thus distinguishes

clearly between neuroses, psychoses, perversions, psychosomatic disturbances; on the other hand, the nosographical status of what are known as 'actual neuroses', 'traumatic neuroses' and 'character neuroses' is still the object of controversy.

The term 'neurosis' appears to have been first used by the Scottish doctor William Cullen, in a medical treatise published in 1777, *First Lines of the Practice of Physic*. The second part of this work is entitled 'Neurosis or Nervous Diseases' and deals not only with mental illnesses or 'vesaniae' but also with dyspepsia, cardiac palpitations, colic, hypochondria and hysteria.

Nineteenth-century authors consistently brought a whole range of disorders under the rubric of neurosis, according to the following criteria:

a. Neuroses were deemed to have a precisely localised origin in the organism, whence the terms 'digestive neurosis', 'cardiac neurosis', 'neurosis of the stomach', etc.; and in the cases of hysteria and hypochondria such an origin was hypothesised (uterus, alimentary canal).

b. They were defined as functional disorders, that is to say that there were no signs of 'inflammation or structural lesion' (1) in the relevant organ.

c. They were held to be illnesses of the nervous system.

The nineteenth-century concept of neurosis appears, in its comprehension, to have been comparable to the modern notions of psychosomatic disorder and organ-neurosis. In nosographical extension, however, the term covered troubles which would now come under one of three headings: *neurosis* (hysteria for example), *psychosomatic conditions* (neurasthenia, digestive troubles) and *neurological affections* (epilepsy, Parkinson's disease).

An account of the change undergone by the idea of neurosis at the end of the last century would demand an extensive historical inquiry, the more so since its evolution varies from country to country. This cannot be undertaken here, but it will make things clearer if we bear in mind that the majority of the authors of the time seem to have been aware of the heterogeneous nature of the disorders classed as 'neurosis' (α).

Troubles for which there seemed good reason to postulate a lesion in the nervous system, such as epilepsy, Parkinson's disease and chorea, were progressively set apart from this original amalgam.

At the same time, the group of the neuroses tended to annex clinical syndromes lying on the other side of its ill-defined frontier with mental illness, with the result that obsessions and phobias came under its aegis, though some authors continued to classify them as 'psychoses', '*folies*' or 'delusional states'.

In France, Pierre Janet's position no doubt bears the mark of this evolution of the end of the century: we find him making a general distinction between two major categories of neurosis: hysteria and psychasthenia (the latter covering in large part what Freud meant by obsessional neurosis*).

*   *   *

Where does Freud stand at this period (1895–1900)? It would seem that German-language psychiatric culture was able to provide him with a comparatively well-grounded distinction, clinically speaking, between psychosis* and neurosis. Apart from a very few fluctuations in his terminology, he can be said to use these two terms to refer to conditions which even today would still be categorised in the same way.

Freud's principal concern at this time, however, is not to demarcate the respective domains of psychosis and neurosis, but rather to point up the psychogenic mechanism in a whole series of disorders. Consequently, the main axis of his classification separates the *actual neuroses**, whose aetiology is sought in shortcomings of the somatic functioning of sexuality, from the *psychoneuroses**, where psychical conflict is the determining factor. This latter group – the 'neuropsychoses of defence'* – embraces neuroses such as hysteria* and certain psychoses, sometimes called defence psychoses, like paranoia* (2, 3).

Following the same line of reasoning, Freud subsequently attempted to get the term 'narcissistic (psycho)neurosis'* accepted for what contemporary psychiatry called psychoses. But he eventually returned to the usual psychiatric system of classification and reserved the term 'narcissistic neurosis' for manic-depression (4). A final point worth remembering is that Freud made a clear distinction very early in his work between the field of the neuroses and that of the perversions*.

The following table attempts to recapitulate the above by presenting a schematic picture of the evolution in the extension of the concept of neurosis in psycho-analytic nosography:

		Psychoneuroses		
1915	Actual neuroses	transference	narcissistic	
1924	Actual neuroses	Neuroses	Narcissistic neuroses	Psychoses
Present-day class-ification	Psycho-somatic con-ditions	Neuroses	Psychoses manic-depressive	paranoia schizo-phrenia

Although the subdivisions of the group of the neuroses are liable to vary according to the writer – phobia, for example, may be considered as an epiphenomenon in hysteria or as a disorder in its own right – there is visibly a very large measure of agreement today over the clinical demarcation of all the syndromes which are looked upon as neurotic. The recognition of 'borderline cases'* by modern clinicians can be seen in one sense as an acknowledgement that neurosis is – at least in principle – a clearly defined category. Moreover, psycho-analytic thought is very largely at one with the clinical boundary-lines which have been adopted by the overwhelming majority of psychiatric schools.

How is the notion of neurosis to be defined from the point of view of its 'comprehension'? Such a definition might–in theory–be approached from two different angles: it could be attempted in terms of symptomatology, which would involve the listing of a certain number of characteristics so as to make a distinction possible between the symptoms of neurosis and those of psychosis or perversion; alternatively, a structural approach could be adopted.

In practice, the majority of attempts at definition by psychiatric writers–if ever they get beyond a simple distinction of degree between 'more serious' and 'less serious' disorders–vacillate between these two lines of attack. To give an example, it is worth quoting an attempt at definition in a recent manual: 'The clinical picture of neurosis is characterised:

'a. By *neurotic symptoms*. These are disturbances of behaviour, of the emotions or of thought which *make manifest* a defence against anxiety and constitute a compromise in respect of this internal conflict from which the subject, in his neurotic position, derives a certain advantage (secondary gain from neurosis).

'b. By the *neurotic character of the Ego*. The Ego, being unable to identify its own personality, is thus prevented from establishing either viable relationships with others or a satisfactory internal equilibrium' (5).

*   *   *

The task of trying to define neurosis, as revealed by clinical experience, in terms of the comprehension of the *concept* of neurosis, tends to become indistinguishable from the psycho-analytic theory itself, in that this theory was basically constituted as a theory of neurotic conflict and its modes.

It is scarcely possible to claim that an effective distinction has yet been established between the structures of neurosis, psychosis and perversion. As a consequence, our own definition of neurosis is inevitably open to the criticism that it is too broad, in so far as it applies at least in part to the perversions and the psychoses as well.

(α) Cf., for example, A. Axenfeld: 'The whole class of the neuroses has been founded on a negative conception; it was born the moment pathological anatomy, which had been enjoined to explain illnesses by the deterioration of organs, found itself face to face with a certain number of morbid states whose *raison d'être* escaped it' (6).

(1) B ARRAS *Traité sur les gastralgies et les entéralgies, ou maladies nerveuses de l'estomac et de l'intestin* (Paris and Brussels, 1829).

(2) Cf. FREUD, S. 'The Neuro-Psychoses of Defence' (1894a), G.W., I, 74; S.E., III, 60.

(3) Cf. FREUD, S. 'Further Remarks on the Neuro-Psychoses of Defence' (1896b), G.W., I, 392; S.E., III, 174.

(4) Cf. FREUD, S. 'Neurosis and Psychosis' (1924b [1923]), G.W., XIII, 390; S.E., XIX, 152.

(5) EY, H., BERNARD, P. and BRISSET, C. *Manuel de psychiatrie* (Paris: Masson, 1963).

(6) AXENFELD, A. *Traité des névroses* (2nd edn.: Germer Baillière, 1883), 14.

Neurosis of Abandonment

= *D.*: Verlassenheitsneurose.–*Es.*: neurosis de abandono.–*Fr.*: névrose d'abandon.–
I.: nevrosi d'abbandono.–*P.*: neurose de abandono.

**Term introduced by Swiss psycho-analysts (Germaine Guex, Charles Odier) as a
name for a clinical picture in which anxiety about abandonment and insecurity
predominate. It is suggested that this is a neurosis with a preoedipal aetiology. The
subject may not necessarily have been the victim of abandonment during his
childhood. Patients suffering from this neurosis have been termed 'abandonic'
('*abandonniques*').**

In her work *La névrose d'abandon* (1), Germaine Guex considers it necessary to
isolate this type of neurosis as not falling into any of the traditional nosographical categories (α).

At first sight, the symptomatology of the condition in question–anxiety,
aggressiveness, masochism, feelings of worthlessness–does not present anything
of strict specificity; the thesis is, however, that these symptoms cannot be explained in terms of the conflicts that psycho-analysis usually brings out (especially
Oedipal conflicts), but that they are only intelligible if one supposes a basic
emotional insecurity.

The unlimited need for love, manifested in a polymorphous way which often
makes it unrecognisable, is held to indicate a search for a lost security epitomised
by a primitive fusion of the child with its mother. This is not necessarily a
consequence of a real desertion by the mother, of the kind whose effects have
been studied by René Spitz (see 'Hospitalism', 'Anaclitic Depression'); rather,
it is essentially the result of an affective attitude on the mother's part which is
experienced by the child as a refusal of love (as, for example, in the case of the
'false presence' of the mother). Germaine Guex feels that, in addition, a psycho-
organic constitutional factor should be taken into account (affective 'gluttony',
intolerance of frustrations, neuro-vegetative imbalance).

Guex maintains that the 'abandonic' patient has never entered the Oedipal
phase, which constituted too large a threat to his security; the neurosis of
abandonment should be attributed to a 'disturbance of the ego' which frequently
only appears in the course of psycho-analytic treatment.

It may be noted that the term 'abandonic' is used descriptively, even by authors
who have not adopted Guex's views (presented here in very condensed form),
either from a nosographical or from an aetiological point of view.

(α) In a private communication, Germaine Guex has indicated to us that it would be preferable to speak of a *syndrome* rather than a *neurosis* of abandonment.

(1) Paris: P.U.F., 1950.

270

Neutrality

= *D.*: Neutralität.-*Es.*: neutralidad.-*Fr.*: neutralité.-*I.*: neutralità.-*P.*: neutralidade.

One of the defining characteristics of the attitude of the analyst during the treatment. The analyst must be *neutral* in respect of religious, ethical and social values – that is to say, he must not direct the treatment according to some ideal, and should abstain from counselling the patient; he must be *neutral* too as regards manifestations of transference (this rule usually being expressed by the maxim, 'Do not play the patient's game'); finally, he must be *neutral* towards the discourse of the patient: in other words, he must not, *a priori*, lend a special ear to particular parts of this discourse, or read particular meanings into it, according to his theoretical preconceptions.

Psycho-analysis was led towards the idea of neutrality as it gradually marked itself off from the methods of suggestion, which presuppose a deliberate influence exercised over the patient by the therapist. Traces of part of this development are to be found in the *Studies on Hysteria* (1895*d*). At the end of that work, Freud writes apropos of the therapist's conduct of the treatment: 'One works, to the best of one's power, as an elucidator [*Aufklärer*] (where ignorance has given rise to fear), as a teacher, as a father confessor who gives absolution, as it were, by a continuance of his sympathy and respect after the confession has been made' (1).

Freud gives the clearest indication of how neutrality should be understood in his 'Recommendations to Physicians Practising Psycho-Analysis' (1912*e*). In this paper, he castigates 'therapeutic ambition' and 'educative ambition' and deems it wrong to set a patient tasks, such as collecting his memories or thinking over some particular period of his life' (2*a*). The analyst should model himself on the surgeon, who has one aim and one aim only: '. . . performing the operation as skilfully as possible' (2*b*).

In 'On Beginning the Treatment' (1913*c*), Freud sees the establishment of a successful transference as being dependent on analytic neutrality: 'It is certainly possible to forefeit the first success if from the start one takes up any other standpoint than one of sympathetic understanding, such as a moralizing one, or if one behaves like the representative or advocate of some contending party' (3). The idea of neutrality is expressed once again – and with a good deal of force – in this passage from 'Lines of Advance in Psycho-analytic Therapy' (1919*a*), which is aimed at the followers of Jung: 'We refused most emphatically to turn a patient who puts himself in our hands in search of help into our private property, to decide his fate for him, to force our own ideals upon him, and with the pride of a Creator to form him in our own image and to see that it is good' (4).

It may be noted that the expression 'benevolent neutrality', borrowed no doubt from diplomatic language, which has become a classical definition of the analyst's proper attitude, is nowhere to be found in Freud's work. We ought to add that the demand for neutrality is strictly relative to the treatment: it is a technical requirement, and in no way does it imply or guarantee a sovereign

271

'objectivity' in the person who exercises the profession of psycho-analyst (5). Neutrality is a qualification not of the actual analyst himself but of his function: the person who interprets and who sustains the transference should be neutral in that he does not make himself felt in his own psycho-social specificity; neutrality is, obviously, an ideal to be aimed at rather than an absolute injunction.

Although not always adhered to, the whole series of recommendations relating to neutrality does not as a rule meet with opposition from psycho-analysts. Even the most orthodox, however, may be led in particular cases–especially cases involving anxiety in children, the psychoses and certain perversions–to waive the rule of complete neutrality on the grounds of its being neither desirable nor practicable.

(1) FREUD, S. 'The Psychotherapy of Hysteria', in *Studies on Hysteria* (1895*d*), G.W., I, 285; S.E., II, 282.

(2) FREUD, S.: a) G.W., VIII, 386; S.E., XII, 119. b) G.W., VIII, 381; S.E., XII, 115.

(3) FREUD, S., G.W., VIII, 474; S.E., XII, 140.

(4) FREUD, S., G.W., XII, 190; S.E., XVII, 164.

(5) Some pertinent comment on this point will be found in GLOVER, E. *The Technique of Psycho-Analysis* (London: Baillière, Tindall & Cox, 1955; New York: I.U.P., 1955) 167 *ff.*

Nirvana Principle

= *D.*: Nirwanaprinzip.–*Es.*: principio de nirvana.–*Fr.*: principe de Nirvana.– *I.*: principio del Nirvana.–*P.*: princípio de nirvana.

Term proposed by Barbara Low and adopted by Freud to denote the tendency of the psychical apparatus to reduce the quantity of excitation in itself, whether of internal or of external origin, to zero–or, failing that, to as low a level as possible.

The term 'Nirvana', which was given currency in the West by Schopenhauer, is drawn from Buddhism, where it connotes the 'extinction' of human desire, the abolition of individuality when it is fused into the collective soul, a state of quietude and bliss.

In *Beyond the Pleasure Principle* (1920*g*), Freud adopts the expression suggested by the English psycho-analyst Barbara Low and formulates the Nirvana principle as a tendency expressing 'the effort to reduce, to keep constant or to remove internal tension due to stimuli' (1).

This formulation is identical with the one Freud puts forward, in the same work, as a definition of the principle of constancy; he thus takes up an ambiguous position, for he equates the tendency to maintain a certain constant level with the tendency to reduce all tension to zero-point (for a discussion of this see 'Principle of Constancy').

It is well worth noting, however, that Freud's introduction of the term 'Nirvana', with its philosophical resonance, comes in a text in which he ventures a very long way along the path of speculation; indeed, what he sees in the

Nirvana of the Hindus or of Schopenhauer is an echo of the idea of the death instinct*. This is a parallel which he stresses once again in 'The Economic Problem of Masochism' (1924c): 'The *Nirvana* principle expresses the trend of the death instinct' (2). To this extent, the Nirvana principle must be understood as something more than a law of constancy or of homeostasis: it is, rather, the radical tendency to reduce excitation to zero-point, as postulated much earlier by Freud under the name of the 'principle of inertia'*.

At the same time, the word 'Nirvana' evokes a profound link between pleasure and annihilation: this is a link that always remained problematic for Freud.

(1) FREUD, S., G.W., XIII, 60; S.E., XVIII, 55–56.
(2) FREUD, S., G.W., XIII, 373; S.E., XIX, 160.

O

Object

= *D*.: Objekt.–*Es*.: objeto.–*Fr*.: objet.–*I*.: oggetto.–*P*.: objeto.

Psycho-analysis considers the notion of object from three main points of view:

I. In correlation with the instinct: the object is the thing in respect of which and through which the instinct seeks to attain its aim* (i.e. a certain type of satisfaction). It may be a person or a part-object*, a real object or a phantasied one.

II. In correlation with love (or hate): the relation in question here is that between the whole person, or the agency of the ego, and an object which is itself focussed upon in its totality (person, entity, ideal, etc.).

III. In the sense traditional to the philosophy and psychology of knowledge, in correlation with the perceiving and knowing subject: an object is whatever presents itself with fixed and permanent qualities which are in principle recognisable by all subjects irrespective of individual wishes and opinions (the adjective corresponding to this sense of 'object' is 'objective').

In psycho-analytic literature the word 'object' occurs both alone and in many compound forms such as 'object-choice'*, 'object love', 'object-loss', 'object-relationship'*, etc.–terms which may confuse the non-specialist reader. 'Object' is understood here in a sense comparable to the one it has in the literary or archaic 'the object of my passion, of my hatred, etc.'. It does not imply, as it does ordinarily, the idea of a 'thing', of an inanimate and manipulable object as opposed to an animate being or person.

Object

I. These various uses of the term stem from the Freudian conception of the instinct. As soon as he turned his attention to the analysis of the instinct, Freud drew a distinction between the instinctual object and the instinctual aim*: 'I shall now introduce two technical terms. Let us call the person from whom sexual attraction proceeds the *sexual object* and the act towards which the instinct tends the *sexual aim*' (1). This distinction was to be preserved throughout Freud's work; he reaffirmed it notably in the most complete definition of the instinct that he ever offered: 'The object of an instinct is the thing in regard to which or through which the instinct is able to achieve its aim' (2*a*); at the same time the object is defined as a means contingent upon satisfaction: 'It is what is most variable about an instinct and is not originally connected with it, but becomes assigned to it only in consequence of being peculiarly fitted to make satisfaction possible' (2*b*). This major and constant tenet of Freud's, the contingency of the object, does not mean that *any* object can satisfy the instinct, but that the instinctual object, which is often distinguished by highly specific traits, is determined by the history of each individual subject–particularly by his childhood history. The object is the aspect of the instinct least conditioned by constitutional factors.

This view of the matter has not passed unchallenged. The question that arises here might be summed up by reference to a distinction of Fairbairn's: is the libido *pleasure-seeking* or *object-seeking* (3)? There is no doubt in Freud's mind that the libido, even if it is marked very early on by some particular object (see 'Experience of Satisfaction'), is to begin with entirely oriented towards satisfaction and the resolution of tension via the shortest available path that is consistent with the specific modalities of activity of each erotogenic zone*. Nevertheless, the idea (which is pointed up by the concept of object-relationship) that a close tie exists between the nature and 'vicissitudes' of the aim and those of the object is not foreign to Freud's thinking (for discussion of this point, see 'Object-Relationship').

Furthermore, the Freudian conception of the instinctual object was constructed–in the *Three Essays on the Theory of Sexuality* (1905*d*)–on the basis of the analysis of the *sexual* instincts. What of the object of the other instincts– and particularly, in the context of Freud's first dualism, the object of the instincts of self-preservation*? In the case of these instincts the object (e.g. food) is manifestly more determined by the demands of vital functions.

This difference between the sexual and the self-preservative instincts, however, does not warrant an overly strict distinction regarding the character of their respective objects: the one is not completely contingent, the other is not absolutely predetermined and conditioned by biology. As Freud shows, the sexual instincts operate to begin with thanks to an anaclitic dependence on the self-preservative ones; this means, notably, that the self-preservative instincts show the sexual instincts the path to the object.

The appeal to the notion of anaclisis* provides the key to the tangled problem of the instinctual object. Let us consider the oral stage by way of illustration: in the language of the self-preservative instinct, the object here is that which provides nourishment; in the language of the oral instinct, it is that which is incorporated–and embraces the whole phantasy dimension that incorporation* implies. The analysis of oral phantasies reveals that the activity of incorporation

274

can involve objects quite other than nutritional ones, and this is what defines the 'oral object-relationship'.

II. The psycho-analytic conception of the object is not to be understood only in its relation to the instinct (if indeed the instinct's operation *can* be apprehended in a pure form). The notion also refers to whatever is an object of attraction or love for the subject–usually, a person. Only analytic investigation, by going beyond this general relation of the ego to its love-objects, lets us discover the specific role of the instincts, with all their polymorphousness, variations and phantasy-level correlates. During the period in which Freud was first analysing the notions of sexuality and instinct, the problem of the connection between the object of the instinct and the love-object did not arise explicitly. Nor could it have done so, since the first version of the *Three Essays* (1905) is based on the assumed major distinction between the functioning of sexuality in childhood and the functioning of sexuality after puberty. The former is defined as essentially auto-erotic*, and at this stage in Freud's thinking little attention is paid to the problem of its relation to objects other than the subject's own body–not even phantasied ones. In the child, the instinct is described as *partial*–more by reason of its mode of satisfaction (localised pleasure or *organ-pleasure**) than by reason of the type of object towards which it is directed. Although 'prefigurements' and 'adumbrations' of it can no doubt be found in childhood, it is really only with puberty that a true *object-choice* comes into play, so allowing sexual life not only to become unified but also to orient itself definitively around the other person.

As we know, the period 1905–24 sees the gradual attenuation of the contrast between infantile auto-erotism and the object-choice of puberty. A series of pregenital* libidinal stages are described, each with its unique mode of 'object-relationship'. The ambiguity to which the notion of auto-erotism had been prone–in that it could be taken as implying that initially the subject has no knowledge of any real or even phantasied external objects–is dispelled. The partial or component instincts*, whose interplay had defined auto-erotism, are now deemed partial inasmuch as their satisfaction is tied, not only to a determinate erotogenic zone, but also to what psycho-analytic theory is to name *part-objects**. Between these objects symbolic equivalents are established, which Freud brought to light in 'On the Transformations of Instinct, as Exemplified in Anal Erotism' (1917c); as a result of such substitutions the life of the instincts passes through a sequence of metamorphoses. The emergence of the set of problems surrounding part-objects has the effect of breaking down whatever generality the relatively undifferentiated notion of the sexual object had been able to claim in the earliest stages of Freudian thought. Indeed, it now becomes necessary to distinguish the instinctual object proper from the love-object. The first is defined essentially by its ability to procure satisfaction for the instinct concerned. Such an object may be a person, but not necessarily: satisfaction may also be assured, notably, by a part of the body. The accent here falls on the object's contingence–its subordination to satisfaction. As for the relationship to the love-object, this–along with hate–involves a different pair of factors: the terms of 'love and hate cannot be made use of for the relations of *instincts* to their objects, but are reserved for the relations of the *total* ego to objects' (2c). A terminological point should be made here: despite the fact that he has now brought out relations with part-objects, Freud keeps the expression 'object-choice' for a person's relationship to his love-objects, which are themselves essentially whole persons.

Taking a genetic view of psychosexual development, one might be tempted to infer from this dichotomy between the *part-object* (the object of the instinct and, essentially, the pregenital* object) and the *total object* (the love-object and, essentially, the genital object) that the subject passes from the former to the latter thanks to a gradual integration of his component instincts within the genital* organisation. On this view, the genital stage entails increased consideration being given to the diversity and richness of the object's qualities, and to its autonomy. The love-object is thus no longer looked upon as a mere correlate of the instincts, with the instinct's satisfaction as its sole *raison d'être*.

Despite the undeniable import of the distinction between the instinctual part-object and the love-object, however, it does not necessarily justify a reading of this kind. For one thing, the part-object may be held to be an irreducible or insuperable pole of the sexual instinct. Moreover, analytic investigation shows that the whole object, far from representing a definitive form, is never free of narcissistic undertones; it owes its existence less to a happy synthesis of the part-objects than to a sort of precipitation of them into a form modelled on the ego (α).

A text such as 'On Narcissism: An Introduction' (1914c) does not make it easy to assign a precise status to the love-object: on the one hand, we have the object of the anaclitic type of choice*, where sexuality makes way for the functions of self-preservation, and on the other hand, the object of the narcissistic choice*, which is a replica of the ego: in other words, 'the mother who feeds, the father who protects' as against 'what one is, was or would like to be'.

III. Lastly, psycho-analytic theory also evokes the object in its traditional philosophical sense, the sense in which it is coupled with the notion of a perceiving and knowing subject. The problem naturally arises of the relation between the object so understood and the sexual object. If we think of an evolution of the sexual object and, *a fortiori*, if we see this as leading up to the constitution of a genital love-object defined by its complexity, its autonomy and its total character, then we are unavoidably bringing this object into relation with the gradual construction of the object of perception. There have been a number of attempts to correlate psycho-analytic ideas on the evolution of object-relationships with the findings of a developmental psychology of knowledge, and even to outline a 'psycho-analytic theory of knowledge'. (For the pointers offered by Freud himself, see 'Pleasure-Ego/Reality-Ego', 'Reality-Testing'.)

(α) In narcissism the ego is itself defined as the love-*object*; it may even be deemed the prototype of love-objects, as illustrated especially by the narcissistic type of object-choice. The text in which Freud sets forth this theory, however, is the very one where he introduces the now classic distinction between ego-libido* and object-libido; 'object' is understood here in the restricted sense of external object.

(1) FREUD, S. *Three Essays on the Theory of Sexuality* (1905d), G.W., V, 34; S.E., VII, 135–36.

(2) FREUD, S. 'Instincts and their Vicissitudes' (1915c): a) G.W., X, 215; S.E., XIV, 122. b) G.W., X, 215; S.E., XIV, 122. c) G.W., X, 229; S.E., XIV, 137.

(3) Cf. FAIRBAIRN, W. R. D. 'A Revised Psychopathology of the Psychoses and Psychoneuroses', *I.J.P.*, 1941, XXII, 250–79.

Object-Choice

= *D.*: Objektwahl.–*Es.*: elección de objeto *or* objetal.–*Fr.*: choix d'objet *or* objectal.–
I.: scelta d'oggetto.–*P.*: escolha de objeto *or* objetal.

The act of selecting a person or a type of person as love-object.

A distinction is drawn between an infantile object-choice and a pubertal one, with the former pointing the way for the latter.

Freud considers that object-choice operates in two modes: the anaclitic and the narcissistic types of object-choice.

Freud introduced the term 'object-choice' in his *Three Essays on the Theory of Sexuality* (1905*d*); it is still part of common psycho-analytical usage.

'Object' in this context is to be understood in the sense of love-object (see 'Object').

As for 'choice', it is not to be taken here–any more than in the expression 'choice of neurosis'*–to mean an intellectual choice between various equally accessible alternatives. Rather, it evokes the irrevocable and determining character of the subject's selection of his type of love-object at a decisive moment in his history. In the *Three Essays* Freud also speaks of '*Objecktfindung*' – the finding of an object.

It should be noted that the term 'object-choice' is used to designate either the choice of a particular person (e.g. 'his object-choice is directed on to his father'), or else the choice of a certain type of object (e.g. 'homosexual object-choice').

As we know, the development of Freud's view of the relation between infantile and post-pubertal sexuality led him to identify the two more and more closely, until he reached the point of acknowledging the existence of a 'full object-choice' in infancy itself (α).

In 'On Narcissism: An Introduction' (1914*c*), Freud assigns the various object-choices to two major categories, namely, *anaclitic* and *narcissistic* (see separate articles).

(α) Cf. Freud's recapitulation of this development of his thought at the beginning of 'The Infantile Genital Organisation' (1923*e*) (1); also articles in the present work on 'Genital Stage', 'Organisation of the Libido', 'Phallic Stage'.

(1) Cf. FREUD, S., G.W., XIII, 293–94; S.E., XIX, 141–42.

Object-Relation(ship)

= *D.*: Objektbeziehung.–*Es.*: relación de objeto *or* objetal.–*Fr.*: relation d'objet.–
I.: relazione oggetuale.–*P.*: relação de objeto *or* objetal.

Term enjoying a very wide currency in present-day psycho-analysis as a designation for the subject's mode of relation to his world; this relation is the entire complex outcome of a particular organisation of the personality, of an apprehension of objects that is to some extent or other phantasied, and of certain special types of defence.

277

Object-Relation(ship)

We may speak of the object-relationships of a specific subject, but also of *types* of object-relationship by reference either to points in development (e.g. an oral object-relationship) or else to psychopathology (e.g., a melancholic object-relationship).

The term 'object-relationship' does occur occasionally in Freud's writings (1), so the claim that he was unfamiliar with it, which has sometimes been made, is mistaken. It is certainly true, however, that this idea plays no part in Freud's conceptual scheme.

But since the 'thirties the notion of object-relationship has gradually attained so much importance in the psycho-analytical literature that today it constitutes the major theoretical parameter for many authors. As Daniel Lagache has often stressed, this development is part of a movement of ideas not confined to psycho-analysis: the tendency to stop considering the organism in isolation, but rather in its interaction with its surroundings (2). Michael Balint has maintained that there is a split in psycho-analysis between a technique based on communication, on person-to-person relationships, and a theory which is still–to use an expression of Rickman's–a 'one-body psychology'. For Balint, who urged that more attention be paid to the development of object-relationships as early as 1935, all psycho-analytic terms and concepts except for 'object' and 'object-relationship' refer to the individual alone (3). In the same vein, René Spitz has noted that, apart from a passage in the *Three Essays on the Theory of Sexuality* (1905*d*) dealing with the mutual relations between mother and child, Freud views the libidinal object solely from the point of view of the subject (cathexes, object-choice) (4).

The upgrading of the notion of the object-relationship has resulted in a change of perspective in the clinical, technical and genetic fields. Even a brief summary of this development is impossible here. We shall confine ourselves to commenting on terminology and attempting to give some pointers towards a broad definition of the present-day use of the notion seen in the light of Freud's work.

I. The reader unfamiliar with the psycho-analytical literature may easily be misled by the term 'object-relationship'. 'Object' is to be taken here in the special sense which it has for psycho-analysis in such expressions as 'object-choice'* and 'object love'. As we know, a person is described as an object in so far as the instincts are directed towards him; there is nothing pejorative in this–no particular implication that the person concerned is in any sense not a *subject*.

'Relationship' should be understood in the strong sense of the term–as an *inter*relationship, in fact, involving not only the way the subject constitutes his objects but also the way these objects shape his actions. An approach such as Melanie Klein's lends even more weight to this idea: objects (projected, introjected) actually *act* upon the subject–they persecute him, reassure him, etc. (see ' "Good" Object/"Bad" Object').

That we speak of the 'object-relationship' rather than of the relationship to the object serves to point up this connotation of interaction: to use the second formulation would imply that the object or objects predate the subject's relations with them and, by the same token, that the subject has already been constituted.

278

II. How does the original Freudian theory stand relative to the current notion of object-relationship?

We know that in seeking to analyse the concept of instinct Freud distinguished between the instinctual source*, object* and aim*. The *source* of the instinct is that zone or somatic apparatus which is the seat of the sexual excitation; its importance in Freud's eyes is attested to by the fact that he names each stage of libidinal development after the corresponding predominant erotogenic zone. As to the *aim* and *object*, Freud preserved the distinction between them throughout his work. Thus separate sections in the *Three Essays* deal in turn with 'deviations in respect of the aim' (e.g. sadism) and 'deviations in respect of the object' (e.g. homosexuality). Similarly, in 'Instincts and their Vicissitudes' (1915c), there is a difference between those transformations of the instinct tied to changes of aim and those where the process essentially concerns the object.

A distinction of this nature is based in particular on the idea that the instinctual aim is determined by the component instinct concerned, and, in the last reckoning, by the bodily source. For example, incorporation* is the mode of activity proper to the oral instinct; it is capable of being displaced on to apparatuses other than the mouth, of reverting into its opposite (devouring/being devoured), of being sublimated, etc., yet its plasticity* is only relative. As regards the object, Freud often underscores what is described as its contingence – a term connoting two strictly complementary ideas:

a. The object has no conditions imposed upon it other than the requirement that it procure satisfaction. In this sense it is relatively interchangeable. At the oral stage, for instance, every object is treated according to the possibility of its being incorporated.

b. The object may become so specific during the subject's history that only a precise object – or a substitute endowed with the essential traits of the original – is capable of procuring satisfaction. In this sense, the object's characteristics are highly particularised.

We may thus understand how it is possible for Freud to assert not only that the object is 'what is most variable about an instinct' (5a), but also that 'the finding of an object is in fact a refinding of it' (6).

The distinction between source, object and aim, which Freud uses as a frame of reference, loses its seeming rigidity when he brings his attention to bear on instinctual life.

To say that at a given stage the functioning of a particular somatic apparatus (the mouth) determines a mode of relationship with the object (incorporation) is tantamount to treating this functioning as a prototype: all the subject's other activities, somatic or not, may on this view be invested with oral meanings. Similarly, numerous connections exist between object and aim. Modifications of the instinctual aim appear as governed by a dialectic in which the object has its part to play; particularly in the cases of sadism/masochism and voyeurism/exhibitionism, 'the turning round upon the subject's self [change of *object*] and the transformation from activity to passivity [change of *aim*] converge or coincide' (5b). Sublimation* is said to supply a further illustration of this correlation between object and aim.

Lastly, Freud envisaged character-types and types of relationship to the object in conjunction with each other (7), and in his clinical works he was able to show how the same set of problems may be identified in what are apparently quite distinct activities of a given subject.

III. It may therefore be asked what is new in the post-Freudian conception of the object-relationship. This question is difficult to answer, for those authors who make use of the notion have widely varying approaches, and it would be artificial to try and find common denominators. The following remarks will have to suffice:

a. The present-day concept of object-relationship, while it does not strictly speaking imply a revision of Freud's instinct theory, does involve a shift in emphasis.

The source of the instinct, as organic substrate, is definitively assigned a secondary role; its status as mere prototype, already recognised by Freud, is stressed. Consequently the aim is considered less as the sexual satisfaction of a particular erotogenic zone: the very concept of aim tends to fade and give way to that of relationship. In the case of the 'oral object-relationship', for example, what now become the centre of interest are the various guises of incorporation and the way this is to be found as the meaning and the dominant phantasy at the kernel of all the subject's relations with the world. As for the status of the object, it would seem that very many contemporary analysts accept neither its highly variable character as far as the satisfaction sought is concerned, nor its uniqueness in so far as it is a part of the individual's particular history: they tend rather to adhere to the idea that each relational mode has a *typical* object (speaking of an oral object, an anal object, etc.).

b. The search for typical forms is taken further: for a given mode of the object-relationship, in fact, it is not only the instinctual life that is evoked, but also, in so far as they are also specific to the relationship in question, the corresponding defence mechanisms, the degree of development and the structure of the ego, etc. (α). Thus the concept of object-relationship emerges as both comprehensive (or 'holistic') and typological when applied to the development of the personality.

We may note in this connection that the term 'stage'* is tending to be replaced by 'object-relationship'. The advantage of such a change of emphasis is that it helps clarify the fact that several types of object-relationship may be combined, or may alternate, in the same subject. To talk of the coexistence of different stages, by contrast, amounts to a contradiction in terms.

c. Inasmuch as the notion of object-relationship places the accent, by definition, on the relational aspect of the subject's life, there is a danger of its leading some authors to look upon real relations with others as the chief determining factor. This is a deviation that must be rejected by every analyst for whom the object-relationship has to be studied essentially in terms of phantasy* (though of course phantasies can modify the apprehension of reality and actions directed towards reality).

(α) Freud did of course recognise other lines of development than that constituted by the libidinal stages, yet he did not really go into the problem of their mutual correspondence – or rather, he left open the possibility that they might not correspond (see 'Stage').

(1) Cf. for example FREUD, S. 'Mourning and Melancholia' (1917e), G.W., X, 435; S.E., XIV, 249.

(2) Cf. LAGACHE, D. 'La psychanalyse. Évolution, tendances et problèmes actuels', *Cahiers d'actualité et de synthèse de l'Encyclopédie française permanente*, VIII, suppl., 23–34.

(3) Cf. BALINT, M. 'Critical Notes on the Theory of the Pregenital Organisations of the Libido' (1935), *passim*. And 'Changing Therapeutic Aims and Techniques in Psycho-Analysis' (1949). Both in *Primary Love and Psychoanalytic Technique* (London: Hogarth Press, 1952).

(4) Cf. SPITZ, R. *La première année de la vie de l'enfant: Genèse des premières relations objectales* (Paris: P.U.F., 1958).

(5) FREUD, S.: a) G.W., X, 215; S.E., XIV, 122. b) G.W., X, 220; S.E., XIV, 127.

(6) FREUD, S. *Three Essays on the Theory of Sexuality* (1905d), G.W., V, 123; S.E., VII, 222.

(7) Cf. for example FREUD, S. 'Character and Anal Erotism' (1908b), G.W., VII, 203–9; S.E., IX, 169–75.

Obsessional Neurosis

= *D.*: Zwangsneurose.–*Es.*: neurosis obsesiva.–*Fr.*: névrose obsessionnelle.– *I.*: nevrosi ossessiva.–*P.*: neurose obsessiva.

Class of neurosis identified by Freud and constituting one of the major frames of reference of psycho-analytic clinical practice.

In the most typical form of obsessional neurosis, the psychical conflict is expressed through *symptoms* which are described as compulsive–obsessive ideas, compulsions towards undesirable acts, struggles against these thoughts and tendencies, exorcistic rituals, etc.–and through a *mode of thinking* which is characterised in particular by rumination, doubt and scruples, and which leads to inhibitions of thought and action.

Freud brought out the aetio-pathogenic specificity of obsessional neurosis from a succession of standpoints: first, from the point of view of the *mechanisms* involved (displacement* of the affect* on to ideas* removed to a varying degree from the original conflict; isolation*; undoing* what has been done); next, from the point of view of *instinctual life* (ambivalence*, fixation at the anal stage*, and regression*); and finally from the *topographical* standpoint (internalisation of a sado-masochistic relation in the shape of tension between the ego and a particularly cruel super-ego). This exposition of the underlying dynamics of obsessional neurosis, together with the description of the anal character and of the reaction-formations* which constitute it, enable us to assign to this neurosis clinical pictures in which the symptoms proper are not at first sight apparent.

It should first of all be emphasised that obsessional neurosis, which is today a universally accepted nosographical category, was first isolated by Freud, in 1894–95: 'I was obliged to begin my work with a nosographic innovation. I found reason to set alongside of hysteria the obsessional neurosis (*Zwangsneurose*) as a self-sufficient and independent disorder, although the majority of the authorities place obsessions among the syndromes constituting mental degeneracy or confuse them with neurasthenia' (1a). Freud began by analysing the psychological mechanism of obsessions (*Zwangsvorstellungen*) (2), and then proceeded to bring together (3, 1b) under the head of a single psychoneurotic condition a series of symptoms (compulsive emotions, ideas, behaviour, etc.)

281

which had been described long before but assigned to very varied nosographical categories (Magnan's '*dégénérescence*', Dupré's '*constitution émotive*', Beard's 'neurasthenia', etc.). A short while after Freud, Janet used the term 'psychasthenia' to describe a neurosis close to Freud's 'obsessional neurosis', but his conception was centred on a different aetiology: it was a state of deficiency, a weakness of mental synthesis, a psychical asthenia which Janet held to be fundamental and to determine the obsessional struggle itself, whereas for Freud doubts and inhibitions were the consequence of a conflict which both mobilises and blocks the subject's energies (4).

Since that time the specificity of obsessional neurosis has become a more and more certain tenet of psycho-analytic theory.

The evolution of psycho-analysis has led to an increasing emphasis being placed on the obsessional *structure* to the detriment of the *symptoms*. From the terminological point of view, this must raise doubts as to the descriptive value of the term '*obsessional* neurosis'.

A first point to note here is that 'obsessional neurosis' is not an exact equivalent of the German term '*Zwangsneurose*': '*Zwang*' can refer not only to compulsive thoughts or obsessions (*Zwangsvorstellungen*) but also to compulsive acts (*Zwangshandlungen*) and emotions (*Zwangsaffekte*) (see 'Compulsion') (α). A further consideration is that the term 'obsessional neurosis' directs attention to a symptom–albeit an essential one–rather than to the structure; yet it frequently happens that mention is made of an obsessional structure, an obsessional character or an obsessional patient in the absence of explicit signs of obsession. It is significant, moreover, that there is a tendency in contemporary usage to keep the term 'obsessed' for the patient who exhibits clearly characterised obsessions.

(α) Freud himself renders *Zwangsneurose* by *névrose des obsessions* (1c) or *névrose d'obsessions* (1d). [In the English-language literature, this difficulty has led to inconsistency: thus 'obsessive-compulsive neurosis' is frequently used in preference to 'obsessional neurosis', while 'compulsion neurosis' is also to be met with occasionally.–*tr.*]

(1) FREUD, S. 'Heredity and the Aetiology of the Neuroses' (1896a): a) G.W., I, 411; S.E., III, 146. b) G.W., I, 407–22; S.E., III, 143–56. c) G.W., I, 411; S.E., III, 146. d) G.W., I, 420; S.E., III, 155.

(2) Cf. FREUD, S. 'The Neuro-Psychoses of Defence' (1894a), G.W., I, 59–74; S.E., III, 45–68.

(3) Cf. FREUD, S. 'Further Remarks on the Neuro-Psychoses of Defence' (1896b), G.W., I, 377–403; S.E., III, 162–85.

(4) Cf. JANET, P. *Les obsessions et la psychasthénie* (1903).

Oedipus Complex

= *D.*: Ödipuskomplex.–*Es.*: complejo de Edipo.–*Fr.*: complexe d'Oedipe.–
I.: complesso di Edipo.–*P.*: complexo de Édipo.

Organised body of loving and hostile wishes which the child experiences towards its parents. In its so-called *positive* form, the complex appears as in the story of

Oedipus Rex: a desire for the death of the rival–the parent of the same sex–and a sexual desire for the parent of the opposite sex. In its *negative* form, we find the reverse picture: love for the parent of the same sex, and jealous hatred for the parent of the opposite sex. In fact, the two versions are to be found in varying degrees in what is known as the *complete* form of the complex.

According to Freud, the peak period for the experience of the Oedipus complex lies between the ages of three and five years, that is, during the phallic stage*; its decline signals entry into the latency period*. At puberty the complex is revived and is then surmounted with a varying degree of success by means of a particular sort of object-choice.

The Oedipus complex plays a fundamental part in the structuring of the personality, and in the orientation of human desire*.

Psycho-analysis makes it the major axis of reference for psychopathology, and attempts to identify the particular modes of its presentation and resolution which characterise each pathological type.

Psycho-analytical anthropology seeks to uncover the triangular structure of the Oedipus complex, which it holds to be universal, in the most varied cultures, including those where the conjugal family is not predominant.

Although the actual term 'Oedipus complex' does not make its first appearance in Freud's writings until 1910 (1), it is clear from the context that the concept was by that time already accepted in psycho-analytical usage (α). Freud's actual discovery of the Oedipus complex was made during his self-analysis–though the ground had long been prepared by the analysis of his patients (see 'Seduction')–when he was brought to recognise the love for his mother which was in himself, alongside a jealousy of his father which conflicted with the affection in which he held him; on October 15, 1897, he wrote to Fliess that 'we can understand the riveting power of *Oedipus Rex* [...]. The Greek legend seizes on a compulsion which everyone recognises because he feels its existence within himself' (2a).

Observe that even in this first formulation Freud spontaneously refers to a myth transcending the history and the variations of the individual life-experience. He asserts the universal validity of the Oedipus complex from the very first, and will adhere to this thesis ever more firmly as time goes on: 'Every new arrival on this planet is faced with the task of mastering the Oedipus complex' (3).

We do not intend to trace all the twists and turns in the gradual elaboration which the discovery of the Oedipus complex underwent: the history of these researches is in reality coextensive with that of psycho-analysis itself. It is significant, moreover, that Freud himself nowhere gives any systematic account of the Oedipus complex. So we shall do no more here than consider certain questions relating to this complex's functions, to its effects and to its role in the evolution of the individual.

I. The Oedipus complex was first discovered only in its 'simple' or 'positive' version, and it is also in this form that it appears in the myth. But as Freud notes, this is but 'a simplification or schematisation' when it is set against the complexity of actual experience: '. . . a boy has not merely an ambivalent attitude towards his father and an affectionate object-choice towards his mother, but at the same time he also behaves like a girl and displays an affectionate feminine attitude to his father and a corresponding jealousy and hostility towards his mother' (4). In practice, a whole range of hybrid cases stretches between the two poles constituted by the positive and the negative forms of the Oedipus complex. In each case the two coexist in dialectical relation to each other, and the task of the analyst is to ascertain what the different postures are which the patient takes up as he assumes and resolves his Oedipus complex.

In this context–as Ruth Mack Brunswick has emphasised–*the Oedipus complex* connotes the child's situation in the triangle (5). The description of the complex in its complete form allows Freud to elucidate ambivalence towards the father (in the case of the little boy) in terms of the play of heterosexual and homosexual components, instead of making it simply the result of a situation of rivalry.

a. The earliest versions of the theory of the Oedipus complex were developed on the model of the little boy. For a long time Freud accepted that such a description of the complex was applicable, *mutatis mutandis*, to the girl. Eventually, however, several factors brought this assumption into question.

(i) First, Freud's article on the infantile genital organisation of the libido (1923) develops the hypothesis that for both sexes in the phallic stage–i.e. at the high-point of the Oedipus complex's dominance–there is only one organ which comes into account: the phallus* (6).

(ii) Secondly, the increased emphasis on preoedipal attachment to the mother. In the female, this preoedipal phase is particularly well defined, in so far as the Oedipus complex must necessarily represent for her a change of love-object from the mother to the father (7*a*).

These have been the two starting-points of subsequent psycho-analytic work which has tried to bring out the specificity of the Oedipus complex in women.

b. To begin with, Freud did not postulate any very definite age for the experience of the Oedipus complex. For example, in the *Three Essays on the Theory of Sexuality* (1905d), the object-choice* is not fully effected until puberty, and infantile sexuality remains basically auto-erotic in character. According to this approach, the Oedipus complex, though outlined in infancy, only comes to the fore at puberty and is then rapidly overcome. Freud's vagueness on this matter was still present in the *Introductory Lectures on Psycho-Analysis* (1916–17), even though he was by this time able to recognise the existence of an infantile object-choice very similar to the adult one (8).

In Freud's final perspective, once the existence of an infantile genital organisation or phallic stage has been postulated, the Oedipus complex is integrated into it, so becoming attached, schematically speaking, to the period in the child's development between the ages of three and five.

c. As is evident from the above, Freud always accepted the existence of a period in the child's life prior to the dominance of the Oedipus complex. Those who distinguish between the *preoedipal* and the oedipal phase and even go so far as to postulate an opposition between them, claim that it is necessary to go beyond any such mere acknowledgement: they stress the existence and the effects of a complex relationship with two elements–the mother and the child–

rather than three as in the Oedipal situation. They seek to identify fixations to this relationship in the most varied psychopathological structures. This approach would seem to challenge the absolute validity of the celebrated formula according to which the Oedipus complex is the 'nucleus of the neuroses'.

A considerable number of authors maintain that such a purely dualistic structure precedes the triangular relation of the Oedipus complex, and that the conflicts originating in this first period can be analysed without taking rivalry with a third person into account.

The Kleinian school, whose essential emphasis on the earliest stages of infancy is well known, does not strictly treat any phase as preoedipal; for the Kleinians, the Oedipus complex comes into play with the 'depressive position'*, that is, as soon as the child relates to whole persons (9).

As for the possibility of a preoedipal *structure*, Freud's own position was always reserved. He did acknowledge that he had been late in recognising the full implications of the primal link to the mother, admitting that the findings brought forward on the preoedipal phase in girls–particularly by women analysts–had taken him by surprise (7*b*). But these facts, Freud felt, could still be explained without necessarily having recourse to a frame of reference other than the Oedipal one (see 'Preoedipal').

II. This refusal to put Oedipal and preoedipal relations on the same footing, either structurally or aetiologically, is consistent with Freud's constant adherence to the thesis of the predominance of the Oedipus complex. The strength of this assumption of Freud's is borne out by the basic functions which he assigns to the complex:

a. The choice of love-object, which after puberty bears the stamp both of the object-cathexes and identifications which are inherent in the Oedipus complex, and of the prohibition against incest.

b. The accession to genitality, which biological maturation in itself in no way guarantees. The genital organisation presupposes the establishment of the primacy of the phallus, and this can hardly be held to have been achieved without the resolution of the Oedipal crisis by means of identification*.

c. The complex's effects on the structuring of the personality–on the constitution of the different agencies, particularly the super-ego* and the ego-ideal*.

Freud relates this structuring role in the genesis of the intrapersonal topography to the decline of the Oedipus complex and the entry into the latency period*. He sees this process as more than a repression: 'It is equivalent, if ideally carried out, to a destruction and an abolition of the complex [...]. If the ego has in fact not achieved much more than a *repression* of the complex, the latter persists in an unconscious state in the id and will later manifest its pathogenic effect' (10*a*). In the article from which this quotation is taken, Freud discusses the different factors which bring about the decline of the Oedipus complex. In the young boy, it is the 'threat of castration' by the father which is the determining factor in the renunciation of the incestuous object, and the dominance of the Oedipus complex comes to an end in a fairly abrupt fashion. In little girls, however, the relation between the Oedipus complex and the castration complex* is very different: 'Whereas in boys the Oedipus complex is destroyed by the castration complex, in girls it is made possible and led up to by the castration complex' (11). Here 'renunciation of the penis is not tolerated by the girl without some attempt at compensation. She slips–along the line of a symbolic equation, one might say–from the penis to a baby. Her Oedipus complex culminates in a desire, which is long retained, to receive a baby from her father as a gift–to bear him a child' (10*b*). Consequently, it is more difficult in this case to identify the precise moment when the complex loses its force.

III. The above description does not do justice to the *founding* character which the Oedipus complex had for Freud. This idea is brought out particularly in the hypothesis proposed in *Totem and Taboo* (1912–13) of the killing of the primal father–an act seen as the first moment in the genesis of mankind. Questionable as it is from an historical point of view, this hypothesis should be understood primarily as the mythical transposition of the inevitability, for every human, of being an 'Oedipus in germ' (2*b*). The Oedipus complex is not reducible to an actual situation–to the actual influence exerted by the parental couple over the child. Its efficacity derives from the fact that it brings into play a proscriptive agency (the prohibition against incest) which bars the way to naturally sought satisfaction and forms an indissoluble link between *wish** and *law* (a point which Jacques Lacan has emphasised). Seen in this light, the criticisms first voiced by Malinowski and later taken up by the 'culturalist' school lose their edge. The objection raised was that no Oedipus complex was to be found in certain civilisations where there is no onus on the father to exercise a repressive function. In its stead, these critics postulated a nuclear complex typifying one or another given social structure. In practice, when confronted with the cultures in question, psycho-analysts have merely tried to ascertain which social roles–or even which institution–incarnate the proscriptive agency, and which social modes specifically express the triangular structure constituted by the child, the child's natural object and the bearer of the law.

Such a structural conception of the Oedipus complex conforms to the thesis put forward by Claude Lévi-Strauss who, in his *Structures élémentaires de la parenté*, makes the prohibition against incest the universal law and the minimal condition of the differentiation of a 'culture' from 'nature' (12).

The interpretation of the Oedipus complex which sees it as transcending the individual lived experience in which it is manifested can find support in another Freudian conception: the notion of the 'primal phantasies'*. Said to be 'transmitted phylogenetically', these are patterns structuring the imaginative life of the subject and, in reality, just so many variants of the triangular situation (seduction*, primal scene*, castration*, etc.).

It should be pointed out that in concentrating on the triangular relationship itself, we are led to assign an essential role in the constitution of a given Oedipus complex to the other poles of this relationship–the unconscious desires of both parents, seduction, and the relations between the parents–as well as to the subject and his instincts.

It is the different types of relation between the three points of the triangle which–at least as much as any particular parental image–are destined to be internalised and to survive in the structure of the personality.

(α) Freud also uses the term '*Kernkomplex*' (nuclear complex). Usually employed as an equivalent to 'Oedipus complex', it first appears in 'On the Sexual Theories of Children' (1908*c*). As Daniel Lagache has noted, what is envisaged in this text is the conflict between children's sexual explorations and demands for information on the one hand, and the deceitful replies of adults on the other (13).

(1) Cf. FREUD, S. 'A Special Type of Choice of Object Made by Men' (1910h), G.W., VIII, 73; S.E., XI, 171.

(2) FREUD, S.: a) Anf., 238; S.E., I, 265. b) Anf., 238; S.E., I, 265.

(3) FREUD, S. Three Essays on the Theory of Sexuality (1905d), G.W., V, 127, n. 2 (added 1920); S.E., VII, 226, n. 1.

(4) FREUD, S. The Ego and the Id (1923b), G.W., XIII, 261; S.E., XIX, 33.

(5) Cf. BRUNSWICK, R. M. 'The Preoedipal Phase of the Libido Development' (1940), in Psa. Read., 232.

(6) Cf. FREUD, S. 'The Infantile Genital Organisation' (1923e), G.W., XIII, 294–95; S.E., XIX, 142.

(7) Cf. FREUD, S. 'Female Sexuality' (1931b): a) G.W., XIV, 517–37; S.E., XXI, 223–43. b) G.W., XIV, 519; S.E., XXI, 226–27.

(8) Cf. FREUD, S., G.W., XI, 338; S.E., XVI, 326.

(9) Cf. KLEIN, M. 'Some Theoretical Conclusions regarding the Emotional Life of the Infant' (1952). In Developments.

(10) FREUD, S. 'The Dissolution of the Oedipus Complex' (1924d): a) G.W., XIII, 399; S.E., XIX, 177. b) G.W., XIII, 401; S.E., XIX, 178–79.

(11) FREUD, S. 'Some Psychical Consequences of the Anatomical Distinction between the Sexes' (1925j), G.W., XIV, 28; S.E., XIX, 256.

(12) Cf. LÉVI-STRAUSS, C. (Paris, P.U.F., 1949), Introduction and whole of Chapter II. Trans.: The Elementary Structures of Kinship (London: Eyre and Spottiswoode, 1969; Boston: Beacon Press, 1969).

(13) Cf. FREUD, S., G.W., VII, 176; S.E., IX, 213–14.

Oral Stage (or Phase)

= D.: orale Stufe (or Phase).–Es.: fase oral.–Fr.: stade oral.–I.: fase orale.–P.: fase oral.

The first stage of libidinal development: sexual pleasure at this period is bound predominantly to that excitation of the oral cavity and lips which accompanies feeding. The activity of nutrition is the source of the particular meanings through which the object-relationship is expressed and organised; the love-relationship to the mother, for example, is marked by the meanings of *eating* and *being eaten*.

Abraham suggested that this stage be subdivided according to two different activities: sucking (early oral stage) and biting (oral-sadistic stage).

In the first edition of the *Three Essays on the Theory of Sexuality* (1905d), Freud describes an oral *sexuality*, whose existence he demonstrates in adults (perverted or preliminary activity) and which he also identifies in children on the basis of the observations of the paediatrician Lindner (masturbatory significance of thumb-sucking) (1a). Yet he no more speaks here of an oral *stage* or organisation than he does of an anal one.

Nonetheless, the activity of sucking takes on an exemplary value for Freud from this point on, allowing him to show how the sexual instinct, which is at

287

first satisfied by means of an anaclitic* relationship to a vital function, later becomes autonomous and attains pleasure auto-erotically. Furthermore, the *experience of satisfaction**, which furnishes the prototype for the fixation of the wish to a specific object, is an oral experience; one may therefore advance the hypothesis that desire* and satisfaction are forever marked by this first experience.

In 1915, after recognising the existence of the anal organisation, Freud describes the oral or cannibalistic* stage as the first stage of sexual life. The source* is the oral zone; the object* is closely associated with that of the ingestion of food; the aim* is incorporation* (1*b*). Thus the accent no longer falls only upon an erotogenic zone–i.e. upon a specific excitation and pleasure–but also upon a relational mode: incorporation; psycho-analysis reveals that in childhood phantasies this mode is not attached solely to oral activity but that it may be transposed on to other functions (e.g. respiration, sight).

According to Freud the distinction between activity* and passivity which characterises the anal stage does not exist at the oral stage. Karl Abraham seeks to identify the types of relationship in play in the oral period, and is led in the process to distinguish between an early stage of preambivalent* sucking–seemingly closer to what Freud had initially described as the oral stage–and an oral-sadistic* stage concurrent with teething in which the activity of biting and devouring implies a destruction of the object; as a corollary of this we find the presence of the phantasy of being eaten or destroyed by the mother (2).

The increased attention paid to object-relationships has led certain psycho-analysts (notably Melanie Klein and Bertram D. Lewin) to describe the meanings connoted by the concept of the oral stage in more complex fashion.

(1) Cf. FREUD, S.: a) G.W., V, 80; S.E., VII, 179. b) G.W., V, 98; S.E., VII, 198.
(2) Cf. ABRAHAM, K. 'A Short Study of the Development of the Libido, Viewed in the Light of Mental Disorders', in *Selected Papers* (London: Hogarth Press, 1927), 442–53.

Oral-Sadistic Stage (or Phase)

= *D.*: oral-sadistische Stufe (*or* Phase).–*Es.*: fase oral-sádica.–*Fr.*: stade sadique-oral.–*I.*: fase sadico-orale.–*P.*: fase oral-sádica.

According to a subdivision introduced by Karl Abraham, the second phase of the oral stage*. It is distinguished by the appearance of teeth and the activity of biting. At this point incorporation* has the meaning of a destruction of the object, implying that ambivalence* has come into play in the object-relationship.

In 'A Short Study of the Development of the Libido, Viewed in the Light of Mental Disorders' (1924), Karl Abraham differentiates two subsidiary stages within the oral stage: an early sucking stage, which is 'preambivalent', and an oral-sadistic stage which corresponds to the teething period; biting and devouring here implies a destruction of the object and instinctual ambivalence makes its appearance (libido and aggressiveness directed towards a single object).

With Melanie Klein oral sadism takes on added importance. Indeed the oral stage for Klein is the culminating point of infantile sadism. In contrast to Abraham, however, she sees sadistic tendencies as playing a part from the outset: '. . . aggression forms part of the infant's earliest relation to the breast, though it is not usually expressed in biting at this stage' (1). 'The libidinal desire to suck is accompanied by the destructive aim of sucking out, scooping out, emptying, exhausting' (2). Although Klein rejects Abraham's distinction between sucking and biting oral stages she considers the oral stage as a whole to be of an oral-sadistic nature.

(1) KLEIN, M. 'Some Theoretical Conclusions regarding the Emotional Life of the Infant' (1952), in *Developments*, 206, *n.* 2.

(2) HEIMANN, P. and ISAACS, S. 'Regression' (1952), in *Developments*, 185–86.

Organisation of the Libido

= *D.*: Organisation der Libido.–*Es.*: organización de la libido.–*Fr.*: organisation de la libido.– *I.*: organizzazione della libido.–*P.*: organização da libido.

Relative coordination of the component instincts, which are characterised by the primacy of one erotogenic zone and by a specific mode of object-relationship. Viewed in temporal succession, the organisations of the libido serve to define the stages of the psychosexual development of childhood.

The evolution of Freud's views regarding the organisation of the libido may be schematically pictured as follows: in the first edition of the *Three Essays on the Theory of Sexuality* (1905*d*), oral or anal activities are certainly treated as precocious sexual activities, but no mention is made of an organisation in this connection; the child only emerges from the anarchy of the component instincts once the primacy of the genital zone has been established. Even though the central theme of the *Three Essays* is the demonstration of the existence of a sexual function extending beyond the genital one, the fact remains that the genital function is alone capable of *organising* the sexual function as a whole. Schematising the modifications brought about by puberty, Freud writes in 1905: 'The sexual instinct has hitherto been predominantly auto-erotic; it now finds a sexual object. Its activity has hitherto been derived from a number of separate instincts and erotogenic zones, which, independently of one another, have pursued a certain sort of pleasure as their sole sexual aim. Now, however, a new sexual aim appears, and all the component instincts combine to attain it, while the erotogenic zones become subordinated to the primacy of the genital zone' (1*a*). It will be noted that Freud makes no mention at this date of a pregenital organisation, and that it is strictly the discovery of the object which permits the coordination of the instincts.

Matters are again viewed from the point of view of the object when Freud later discovers a mode of organisation of sexual life which he interpolates between the unorganised state of the instincts and full object-choice: narcissism*. Here the object is the ego as a unity.

Only in his article on 'The Disposition to Obsessional Neurosis' (1913*i*) does Freud introduce the concept of a pregenital* organisation: the unification of the instincts at such a stage is explained by the predominance of a sexual activity connected with a specific erotogenic zone. First Freud describes an anal organisation (1913*i*), then an oral (in the 1915 edition of the *Three Essays* (1*b*)), and finally a phallic one (in 'The Infantile Genital Organisation' [1923*e*]). Note, however, that after describing these three organisations Freud reasserts that 'the complete organisation is only achieved at puberty, in a fourth, genital phase' (2)

In his attempt to define the modes of the pregenital organisation of sexuality, Freud pursued two trains of thought which are not strictly compatible with one another. According to the first approach, it is the *object* which fulfils the function of organiser: the different modes of organisation are spaced out in a series leading from auto-erotism to the heterosexual object via narcissism and the homosexual object-choice. In the other perspective each organisation is centred upon a *specific mode of sexual activity* which depends on a determinate erotogenic zone.

How, from this second point of view, are we to understand the primacy of an erotogenic zone, and the activity corresponding to this primacy?

As far as the oral organisation is concerned, (oral) primacy may be taken to mean a virtually exclusive relationship to the environment. But what of the later organisations, which do not imply the elimination of non-predominant types of activity? What does it mean, for example, to talk about the primacy of anality? This cannot be taken as indicating a suspension of all oral sexuality, nor even its relegation to the background; in fact oral sexuality is integrated into the anal organisation, and oral exchange becomes imbued with meanings associated with anal activity.

(1) FREUD, S. *Three Essays on the Theory of Sexuality* (1905*d*): a) G.W., V, 108; S.E., VII, 207. b) Cf. G.W., V, 98; S.E., VII, 198.

(2) Cf. FREUD, S. *An Outline of Psycho-Analysis* (1940*a* [1938]), G.W., XVII, 77; S.E., XXIII, 155.

Organ-Pleasure

= *D*.: Organlust.–*Es*.: placer de órgano.–*Fr*.: plaisir d'organe.–*I*.: piacere d'organo.– *P*.: prazer de órgão.

Mode of pleasure characteristic of the auto-erotic satisfaction of the component instincts*: the excitation of an erotogenic zone* is appeased at the same place where it is produced, independently of the satisfaction of the other zones and in the absence of any direct link with the carrying out of a function.

The term 'organ-pleasure' is used by Freud on a number of occasions. This does not appear to constitute any terminological innovation on his part. The expression suggests a contrast with the commoner one 'functional pleasure', which refers to satisfaction tied to the carrying out of a vital function (e.g. the pleasure of feeding).

Freud evokes organ-pleasure above all in attempting to give greater depth to his hypotheses concerning the origin and nature of sexuality* in the sense given it by psycho-analysis, which extends its meaning well beyond the genital function. The point of emergence of sexuality is sought in the so-called auto-erotic* phase, which is typified by the independent functioning of each component instinct.

In the suckling, sexual pleasure proper detaches itself from the function upon which it has at first depended anaclitically (see 'Anaclisis') and of which it is the 'marginal product' (*Nebenprodukt*). Henceforward this sort of pleasure is pursued for its own sake. Sucking, for instance, is an attempt to alleviate a tension in the erotogenic zone of mouth and lips, and it is quite independent of any nutritional need.

The concept of organ-pleasure crystallises those traits which in Freud's view are the essential defining attributes of infantile sexuality, which 'at its origin [...] attaches itself [anaclisis] to one of the vital somatic functions; it has as yet no sexual object, and is thus auto-erotic; and its sexual aim is dominated by an erotogenic zone' (1).

In the *Introductory Lectures on Psycho-Analysis* (1916–17), Freud deals at length with the question whether it is possible to define the very essence of sexuality by reference to those manifestations whose kinship and continuity with genital pleasure psycho-analysis has shown up. The categorisation of these manifestations as 'organ-pleasure' is presented by Freud in this context as an attempt on the part of his scientific opponents to furnish a physiological explanation of infantile pleasures which he deems to be sexual. In this passage Freud criticises such a categorisation in so far as it results in a negation or limitation of the discovery of infantile sexuality. While challenging this polemical use of the term, however, he is quite ready to adopt it himself inasmuch as it accentuates the specificity of infantile sexual pleasure as distinct from pleasure associated with the functions of self-preservation. Thus he writes in 'Instincts and their Vicissitudes' (1915c): 'This much can be said by way of a general characterization of the sexual instincts. They are numerous, emanate from a great variety of organic sources, act in the first instance independently of one another and only achieve a more or less complete synthesis at a later stage. The aim which each of them strives for is the attainment of "organ-pleasure" ' (2).

(1) FREUD, S. *Three Essays on the Theory of Sexuality* (1905d), G.W., V, 83; S.E., VII, 182–83.

(2) FREUD, S., G.W., X, 218; S.E., XIV, 125–26.

Over-Determination, Multiple Determination

= *D.*: Überdeterminierung *or* mehrfache Determinierung.–*Es.*: superdeterminación.–
Fr.: surdétermination *or* détermination multiple.–*I.*: sovradeterminazione.–
P.: superdeterminação *or* determinação múltipla.

The fact that formations of the unconscious (symptoms, dreams, etc.) can be attributed to a plurality of determining factors. This can be understood in two different ways:

a. The formation in question is the result of several causes, since one alone is not sufficient to account for it.

b. The formation is related to a multiplicity of unconscious elements which may be organised in different meaningful sequences, each having its own specific coherence at a particular level of interpretation. This second reading is the most generally accepted one.

However distinct these two senses of over-determination may be, it is not impossible to find bridges between them.

In the *Studies on Hysteria* (1895*d*) they are to be found in juxtaposition. Sometimes (1*a*) the hysterical symptom is said to be over-determined in that it is the outcome both of a constitutional predisposition and of a number of traumatic events: one of these factors on its own is not enough to produce or to sustain the symptom, and this is why the cathartic method* of treatment, although it does not attack the constitutional causes of the hysteria, is nonetheless able to get rid of the symptom through the recollection and abreaction of the trauma. Another passage of Freud's in the same work comes much closer to using the second sense of over-determination: the chain of associations which links the symptom to the 'pathogenic nucleus' is here said to constitute 'a ramifying system of lines and more particularly [...] a converging one' (1*b*).

The study of dreams throws the clearest light on the phenomenon of over-determination. In fact analysis reveals that 'each of the elements of the dream's content turns out to have been "over-determined"–to have been represented in the dream-thoughts many times over' (2*a*). Over-determination is a consequence of the work of condensation*. It is not expressed only on the level of isolated elements of the dream–the dream as a whole may be over-determined: 'The achievements of condensation can be quite extraordinary. It is sometimes possible by its help to combine two quite different latent trains of thought into one manifest dream, so that one can arrive at what appears to be a sufficient interpretation of a dream and yet in doing so can fail to notice a possible "over-interpretation" ' (3*a*) (see 'Over-Interpretation').

It should be emphasised that over-determination does not mean that the dream or symptom may be interpreted in an infinite number of ways. Freud compares dreams to certain languages of antiquity in which words and sentences appear to have various possible interpretations (3*b*): in such languages ambiguity is dispelled by the context, by intonation or by extra signs. In dreams, the lack of determination is more fundamental, yet the different interpretations may still be verified scientifically.

Nor does over-determination imply the independence or the parallelism of the different meanings of a single phenomenon. The various chains of meanings intersect at more than one 'nodal point', as is borne out by the associations; the symptom bears the traces of the interaction of the diverse meanings out of which it produces a *compromise*. Taking the hysterical symptom as his model, Freud shows that this 'develops only where the fulfilments of two opposing wishes, arising each from a different psychical system, are able to converge in a single expression' (2*b*).

What remains then of our first definition (a) of over-determination? The phenomenon with which we are concerned is a *result*; over-determination is a positive characteristic, not merely the absence of a unique, exhaustive meaning. Jacques Lacan has stressed that over-determination is a trait common to all unconscious formations: '. . . for a symptom to be admitted as such in psycho-analytical psychotherapy–whether a neurotic symptom or not–Freud insists on the minimum of over-determination as constituted by a double meaning: it must symbolise a conflict long dead over and above its function in a *no less symbolic* present conflict' (4). The reason for this is that the symptom (in the broad sense) is 'structured like a language', and thus naturally constituted by elision and layering of meaning; just as a word cannot be reduced to a signal, a symptom cannot be the unambiguous sign of a single unconscious content.

(1) FREUD, S.: a) Cf. G.W., I, 261; S.E., II, 262–63. b) G.W., I, 293–94; S.E., II, 289.

(2) FREUD, S. *The Interpretation of Dreams* (1900*a*): a) G.W., II–III, 289; S.E., IV, 283. b) G.W., II–III, 575; S.E., V, 569.

(3) FREUD, S. *Introductory Lectures on Psycho-analysis* (1916–17): a) G.W., XI, 176; S.E., XV, 173. b) Cf. G.W., XI, 234–39; S.E., XV, 228–33.

(4) LACAN, J. 'Fonction et champ de la parole et du langage en psychanalyse', *La Psych-analyse*, 1956, I, 114. Reprinted in *Écrits* (Paris: Seuil, 1967). Translation: 'The Function of Language in Psychoanalysis', in WILDEN, A. *The Language of the Self* (Baltimore: Johns Hopkins, 1968), 32.

Over-Interpretation

= *D.*: Überdeutung.–*Es.*: superinterpretación.–*Fr.*: surinterprétation.–
I.: sovrinterpretazione.–*P.*: superinterpretação

Term used a number of times by Freud, apropos of dreams, to designate an interpretation* which emerges after it has already been possible to develop a first one that is consistent and apparently complete. The essential precondition of over-interpretation is to be found in over-determination*.

In several passages of *The Interpretation of Dreams* (1900*a*) Freud raises the question whether an interpretation can ever be said to be complete. For example, he writes: 'I have already had occasion to point out that it is in fact never possible to be sure that a dream has been completely interpreted. Even if the solution seems satisfactory and without gaps the possibility always remains that the dream may have yet another meaning' (1*a*).

Over-Interpretation

Freud speaks of over-interpretation whenever a fresh interpretation is added to one that has already shown its own consistency and worth; it is in rather varied contexts, however, that he calls upon this notion.

Over-interpretation can be explained as the superimposition of layers of meaning. Different ways of picturing a stratification of this kind are to be found in Freud's writings.

Thus it is possible to speak of over-interpretation in one sense–albeit a rather loose and superficial one–as soon as new associations of the subject come to light, enlarging the material and so justifying the analyst's making new connections. Over-interpretation in this case is simply a function of the growth of the material*.

In another sense–already more rigourous–over-interpretation is related to meaning, and becomes synonymous with 'deeper' interpretation. And it is true that interpretation is brought to bear at various levels, ranging from the level where it merely brings out or clarifies the subject's behaviour and statements, to the level where it comes to grips with unconscious phantasy*.

But what make the over-interpretation of a dream possible, and even essential, are the mechanisms at work in the formation of that dream–especially the mechanism of condensation*: a single image may refer back to a whole series of 'trains of unconscious thought'. We must no doubt go further and acknowledge that a single dream may be the expression of several wishes. 'Dreams frequently seem to have more than one meaning. Not only [...] may they include several wish-fulfilments one alongside the other; but a succession of meanings or wish-fulfilments may be superimposed on one another, the bottom one being the fulfilment of a wish dating from earliest childhood' (1*b*).

It may be asked whether this last-mentioned wish does not constitute the ultimate point beyond which it is impossible to go–the *nec plus ultra* of over-interpretation. Perhaps this is what Freud means when, in a famous passage of *The Interpretation of Dreams*, he uses the image of the *dream's navel*: 'There is often a passage in even the most thoroughly interpreted dream which has to be left obscure; this is because we become aware during the work of interpretation that at that point there is a tangle of dream-thoughts which cannot be unravelled and which moreover adds nothing to our knowledge of the content of the dream. This is the dream's navel, the spot where it reaches down into the unknown. The dream-thoughts to which we are led by interpretation cannot, from the nature of things, have any definite ending; they are bound to branch out in every direction into the intricate network of our world of thought. It is at some point where this meshwork is particularly close that the dream-wish grows up, like a mushroom out of its mycelium' (1*c*).

(1) FREUD, S.: a) G.W., II–III, 285; S.E., IV, 279. b) G.W., II–III, 224; S.E., IV, 214. c) G.W., II–III, 530; S.E., V, 525.

294

P

Pair of Opposites

= *D*.: Gegensatzpaar.–*Es*.: par antitético.–*Fr*.: couple d'opposés.–*I*.: coppia d'opposti.–
P.: par antitético.

**Term often used by Freud to designate great basic antitheses, either on the plane
of psychological or psychopathological phenomena (e.g. sadism/masochism*,
voyeurism/exhibitionism) or else in the realm of metapsychology (e.g. life
instincts*/death instincts*).**

In the *Three Essays on the Theory of Sexuality* (1905*d*), Freud uses this term
to point up a basic characteristic of certain perversions: 'We find, then, that
certain among the impulses to perversion occur regularly as pairs of opposites;
and this [...] has a high theoretical significance' (1*a*). The study of sadism, for
instance, shows up the presence, alongside the dominant sadistic tendencies,
of a masochistic pleasure; similarly, voyeurism and exhibitionism are closely
coupled together as the active and passive forms of the same component
instinct*. Though especially visible in the perversions, such pairs of opposites
are also regularly met with in the psycho-analysis of neuroses (1*b*).

Over and above its application to these clinical data, the idea of the pair of
opposites is part of a permanent and essential element in Freud's thinking–
namely, the basic dualism which provides the ultimate explanation of psychical
conflict.

Whatever the form taken by this dualistic conception at the various stages
in Freud's doctrine, one is constantly coming across such terms as 'pair of
opposites', 'opposition' (*Gegensätzlichkeit*), 'polarity' (*Polarität*) (2), etc. The
idea is not only used descriptively–it also appears at various levels of conceptualisation: in the three antitheses which define the successive libidinal
positions of the subject, namely active/passive, phallic/castrated and masculine/
feminine; in the pleasure-unpleasure opposition; and, at a more radical level,
in the instinctual dualism (love/hunger, life instincts/death instincts).

Note that the terms paired off in this way invariably belong on the same plane
but that neither can be reduced to the other; the one cannot engender the other
in dialectical fashion–rather, the pair is the root of all conflict, the motor of
any dialectic.

(1) FREUD, S.: a) G.W., V, 59; S.E., VII, 160. b) Cf. G.W., V, 66–67; S.E., VII, 166–67.
(2) Cf. FREUD, S. 'Instincts and their Vicissitudes' (1915*c*), G.W., X, 226; S.E., XIV, 133.

Paranoia

= *D*.: Paranoia.–*Es*.: paranoia.–*Fr*.: paranoïa.–*I*.: paranoia.–*P*.: paranóia.

Chronic psychosis characterised by more or less systematised delusion, with a predominance of ideas of reference but with no weakening of the intellect and, generally speaking, no tendency towards deterioration.

As well as delusions of persecution, Freud places erotomania, delusional jealousy and delusions of grandeur under the heading of paranoia.

The word 'paranoia' is Greek in origin, and means madness or disorder of the mind. Psychiatry has long made use of it, and the term's complicated history has often been summarised in the textbooks, to which the reader is referred (1). It is well known that 'paranoia'–which in nineteenth-century German psychiatry tended to take in delusional states of all kinds–came in the present century, principally as a result of Kraepelin's influence, to have a preciser meaning and a more restricted application. Even today, however, divergences persist among the different schools over the exact extension of this nosological category.

Psycho-analysis does not appear to have had any direct influence upon this evolution of the concept, though it did have an indirect effect through its contribution, via Bleuler, to the definition of the neighbouring field of schizophrenia*.

It may help the student of Freud to see how the use of the term in Freud's work corresponds to this historical development of the concept. In his correspondence with Fliess, as in his earliest published works, Freud seems still to accept the pre-Kraepelinian conception of paranoia, looking upon it as a very broad clinical type covering most forms of chronic delusional conditions. In the writings published from 1911 onwards, he accepts Kraepelin's major distinction between paranoia and dementia praecox: 'I am of opinion that Kraepelin was entirely justified in taking the step of separating off a large part of what had hitherto been called paranoia and merging it, together with catatonia and certain other forms of disease, into a new clinical unit' (*2a*). Kraepelin, of course, acknowledged the existence, alongside the hebephrenic and catatonic forms of dementia praecox, of a paranoid form marked by delusions, though little-systematised ones, which are accompanied by lack of affectivity and which lead towards terminal dementia. It was the adoption of the Kraepelinian terminology which led Freud to emend a diagnosis in one of his early publications: 'chronic paranoia' became 'dementia paranoides' (3).

In agreement with Kraepelin, Freud always kept all conditions involving systematised delusions apart from the dementia praecox group by giving them the name of 'paranoia', under which he includes not only delusions of persecution but also erotomania, delusional jealousy and delusions of grandeur. His position differs markedly from that of his pupil Bleuler, who places paranoia in the group of schizophrenias, whose common denominator is considered by him to be a primary, fundamental disturbance, namely, 'dissociation' (4) (see

'Schizophrenia'). This approach prevails nowadays in the American school of psycho-analytically orientated psychiatry.

Freud's attitude, however, is far from inflexible: although he seeks on several occasions to distinguish paranoia from schizophrenia in regard to their respective fixation points and the mechanisms in play in either case, he nevertheless acknowledges that 'paranoid and schizophrenic phenomena may be combined in any proportion' (2b); and he explains such complex structures in genetic terms. If we take the distinction introduced by Kraepelin as a point of reference, then Freud's position appears as directly opposite to Bleuler's. Kraepelin differentiates clearly between paranoia on the one hand and the paranoid form of dementia praecox on the other; Bleuler treats paranoia as a sub-category of dementia praecox, or the group of schizophrenias; as for Freud, he is quite prepared to see certain so-called paranoid forms of dementia praecox brought under the head of paranoia, mainly because he does not consider the 'systematisation' of delusions to be a good criterion for defining paranoia. As is plain from his account of the case of Schreber (1911c) (and as the form of the title of this account itself indicates), this case of 'paranoid dementia' is essentially a paranoia proper in Freud's eyes.

It is not our intention here to give an exposition of a Freudian theory of paranoia. It should be noted, however, that paranoia is defined in psychoanalysis, whatever the variations in its delusional modes, as a defence against homosexuality (2c, 5, 6). When this mechanism is found to be prevalent in a so-called paranoid delusional state, Freud considers this to be a major reason for evoking paranoia, even where there is no 'systematisation'.

Though worked out on a somewhat different basis, the position of Melanie Klein follows this tendency of Freud's to seek a common foundation for paranoid schizophrenia and paranoia. This is one of the explanations for the apparent ambiguity of her term 'paranoid position'*. The paranoid position is centred on the phantasy of persecution by 'bad' part-objects, and Klein finds this phantasy in both paranoid and paranoiac delusional states.

(1) For example: EY, H. 'Groupe des psychoses schizophréniques et des psychoses délirantes chroniques' (1955), in EY, H. *Encyclopédie médico-chirurgicale* (*Psychiatrie*), 37281 A 10; EY, H. and PUJOL, R. 'Groupe des délires chroniques: III. Les deux grands types de personnalités délirantes' (1955), *ibid.*, 37299 C 10; POROT, A. *Manuel alphabétique de psychiatrie* (Paris, 1960), see article on 'Paranoia'.

(2) FREUD, S. 'Psycho-Analytic Notes on an Autobiographical Account of a Case of Paranoia (Dementia Paranoides)' (1911c): a) G.W., VIII, 312; S.E., XII, 75. b) G.W., VIII, 314; S.E., XII, 77. c) Cf. G.W., VIII, 295–302; S.E., XII, 59–65.

(3) FREUD, S. 'Further Remarks on the Neuro-Psychoses of Defence' (1896b), G.W., I, 392n.: S.E., III, 174n.

(4) BLEULER, E. *Dementia Praecox oder Gruppe der Schizophrenien* (Leipzig & Vienna, 1911), *passim*. English translation: *Dementia Praecox or the Group of Schizophrenias* (New York, 1950).

(5) FREUD, S. 'A Case of Paranoia Running Counter to the Psycho-Analytic Theory of the Disease' (1915f), G.W., X, 234–46; S.E., XIV, 263–72.

(6) FREUD, S. 'Some Neurotic Symptoms in Jealousy, Paranoia and Homosexuality' (1922b), G.W., XIII, 198–204; S.E., XVIII, 225–30.

Paranoid Position

= *D.*: paranoide Einstellung.–*Es.*: posición paranoide.–*Fr.*: position paranoïde.–
I.: posizione paranoide.–*P.*: posição paranóide.

**According to Melanie Klein, a mode of object-relations which is specific to
the first four months of life but which may also be met with subsequently, in the
course of childhood and particularly in paranoic and schizophrenic states in the
adult.**

**The paranoid position is characterised as follows: the aggressive instincts
exist from the start side by side with the libidinal ones and are especially strong;
the object* is partial (chiefly the mother's breast) and split into two: the 'good'
and the 'bad' object*; the predominant mental processes are introjection* and
projection*; anxiety, which is intense, is of a persecutory type (destruction by
the 'bad' object).**

First some comment on usage is called for. In the (German) psychiatric
terminology inherited from Kraepelin, the adjective 'paranoid' is reserved for
a form of schizophrenia resembling paranoia in that delusions occur, but
different from it chiefly on account of dissociation (1). English usage, however,
has failed to preserve the distinction implied: 'paranoid' and 'paranoi(a)c' are
applied indiscriminately whether it is paranoia itself or paranoid schizophrenia
that is at issue (2).

Nor is it Melanie Klein's intention to challenge the nosological distinction
between these two conditions when she uses the term 'paranoid' to designate the
persecutory aspect of both of them; in fact she had begun by speaking of a
'persecutory phase'. In her latest writings she adopted the expression 'paranoid-
schizoid position'–the first term accentuating the persecutory character of the
anxiety and the second the schizoid nature of the mechanisms at work.

As to the word 'position', Klein gives the following reason for preferring it
to 'phase': '. . . these groupings of anxieties and defences, although arising first
during the earliest stages, are not restricted to them but occur and recur during
the first years of childhood and under certain circumstances in later life' (3*a*).

From the beginning of her work Klein brings to light phantasied fears of
persecution met with in the analysis of children, especially psychotic children.
Only at a later point does she speak of a 'rudimentary paranoid state' which
she looks upon as an early developmental phase (4). At first she locates this
phase within Abraham's first anal stage*, but later on she makes it the first
type of object-relation in the oral stage* and gives it the name 'paranoid
position'. Her most systematic description of it is to be found in 'Some
Theoretical Conclusions regarding the Emotional Life of the Infant' (1952) (3*b*).

The paranoid-schizoid position may be schematically characterised as follows:

a. As regards the instincts, libido and aggressiveness (oral-sadistic instincts:
devouring, tearing) are present and fused from the outset: in this sense
ambivalence* exists in Klein's view as early as the first oral (sucking) stage (3*c*).
The emotions associated with instinctual life are intense (greed, anxiety, etc.).

b. The object is partial, its prototype being the maternal breast.

c. This part-object* is split from the start into a 'good' and a 'bad' object, not only inasmuch as the mother's breast gratifies or frustrates, but also because the child projects its love or hate on to it.

d. The good and bad objects which are the outcome of this splitting attain a relative independence of one another, and each of them becomes subject to the processes of introjection and projection.

e. The good object is 'idealized'*: it is capable of providing 'unlimited, immediate and everlasting gratification' (3d). Its introjection defends the infant against persecutory anxiety (reassurance). The bad object, on the other hand, is a terrifying persecutor; its introjection exposes the child to endogenous threats of destruction.

f. The ego, because of its 'lack of integration', has only a limited tolerance of anxiety. As means of defence, aside from splitting and idealization, it uses *denial* (disavowal*), which seeks to divest the persecuting object of all reality, and omnipotent *control* of the object.

g. 'These first introjected objects form the core of the super-ego' (3e) (see 'Super-Ego').

* * *

It should be stressed that in the Kleinian view every individual passes in the normal course of events through phases in which psychotic anxieties or mechanisms predominate: first the paranoid position, then the depressive position*. The overcoming of the paranoid position depends in particular on the relative strength of the libidinal instincts as compared with the aggressive ones.

(1) Cf. for example POROT, A. *Manuel alphabétique de psychiatrie* (Paris: P.U.F., 1960).

(2) Cf. ENGLISH, H. B. and ENGLISH, H. C. *A Comprehensive Dictionary of Psychological and Psychoanalytical Terms* (1958).

(3) Cf. KLEIN, M. 'Some Theoretical Conclusions regarding the Emotional Life of the Infant', in *Developments:* a) 236. b) 198. c) 206n. d) 202. e) 200n.

(4) Cf. KLEIN, M. *The Psycho-Analysis of Children* (1932), 232–33.

Paraphrenia

= *D.*: Paraphrenie.–*Es.*: parafrenia.–*Fr.*: paraphrénie.–*I.*: parafrenia.–*P.*: parafrenia.

I. Term proposed by Kraepelin to denote chronic delusional psychoses, such as paranoia, which are not accompanied by intellectual deterioration and which do not evolve in the direction of dementia; these psychoses are comparable to schizophrenia by virtue of the presence of complex, badly systematised constructions based on hallucinations and confabulations.

II. Term proposed by Freud for denoting either schizophrenia ('paraphrenia proper') or the paranoia-schizophrenia group as a whole.

Today, Kraepelin's definition has completely prevailed over Freud's proposal.

Parapraxis

Kraepelin proposed the term 'paraphrenia' before Freud–between 1900 and 1907. For his nosological conception of paraphrenia, which has now achieved classical status, the reader is referred to the psychiatric textbooks.

It was in a quite different sense that Freud wished to use the term. He considered the designation of 'dementia praecox' to be inappropriate, as he did that of 'schizophrenia'*. He preferred the name 'paraphrenia' on the grounds that it did not imply the same assumptions as regards the fundamental mechanism of the illness; furthermore, '*para*phrenia' resembled '*para*noia', thus drawing attention to the affinity between these two affections (1).

Subsequently, in 'On Narcissism: An Introduction' (1914c), Freud uses the term once more in a broader sense to denote the paranoia-schizophrenia group, but he nevertheless continues to refer to schizophrenia as 'paraphrenia proper' (*eigentliche Paraphrenie*) (2).

Freud soon abandoned this terminological suggestion–doubtless as a result of the success encountered by Bleuler's 'schizophrenia'.

(1) Cf. FREUD, S. 'Psycho-Analytic Notes on an Autobiographical Account of a Case of Paranoia (Dementia Paranoides)' (1911c), G.W., VIII, 312–13; S.E., XII, 75.

(2) Cf. FREUD, S., G.W., X, 138–70; S.E., XIV, 73–102.

Parapraxis

= *D.*: Fehlleistung.–*Es.*: acto fallido.–*Fr.*: acte manqué.–*I.*: atto mancato.–
P.: ato falho *or* perturbado.

Act whose explicit goal is not attained; instead, this goal turns out to have been replaced by another one. When speaking of parapraxes we do not include all failures of memory, speech or action, but just those acts which the subject is normally able to perform successfully, so that he is inclined to attribute his failure to mere lack of concentration or to happenstance.

Freud showed that parapraxes, like symptoms, are compromise-formations* resulting from the antagonism between the subject's conscious intentions and what he has repressed*.

For the theory of parapraxes the reader is referred to Freud's *Psychopathology of Everyday Life* (1901b), in which it transpires that what appear to be bungled actions turn out in fact–on another level–to be quite successful ones, and that unconscious wishes are fulfilled by such behaviour in a manner that is often very plain to see.

The German term '*Fehlleistung*'–literally, 'faulty function'–is understood by Freud as connoting not only acts proper but also all kinds of errors and slips in speech and in mental operations.

The German language brings out the common denominator of all these mistakes by giving the prefix '*ver-*' to many of the words which describe them: *das Vergessen* (forgetting), *das Versprechen* (slip of the tongue), *das Verlesen* (misreading), *das Verschreiben* (slip of the pen), *das Vergreifen* (bungled action), *das Verlieren* (mislaying).

It is worth noting that before Freud these marginal phenomena of everyday life had never been seen as connected or brought together under one heading— witness the lack of a generic concept for them. It was Freud's theory which gave birth to the concept of the parapraxis and, as the editors of the *Standard Edition* point out, the English term had to be coined especially to render Freud's '*Fehlleistung*'.

Part-Object

= *D.*: Partialobjekt.–*Es.*: objeto parcial.–*Fr.*: objet partiel.–*I.*: oggetto parziale.–
P.: objeto parcial.

Type of object towards which the component instincts* are directed without this implying that a person as a whole is taken as love-object. In the main part-objects are parts of the body, real or phantasied (breast, faeces, penis), and their symbolic equivalents. Even a person can identify himself or be identified with a part-object.

It was the Kleinian school of psycho-analysis that introduced the term 'part-object' and assigned it a leading role in the psycho-analytic theory of object-relationships*.

However, the idea that the instinct's object* is not necessarily a whole person is already explicit in Freud's work. No doubt when he speaks of object-choice* or of object love Freud generally refers to a whole person, but when he deals with the object towards which the component instincts are directed it is clearly a part-object that he has in mind (breast, food, faeces, etc.) (1). What is more, Freud brought out the equations and relationships which come to hold between various part-objects (child = penis = faeces = money = gift). Of particular relevance in this connection is the article 'On the Transformations of Instinct, as Exemplified in Anal Erotism' (1917*c*). Freud also points out how the woman progresses from a wish for the penis to a wish for the man, leaving open the possibility of a 'temporary regression from man to penis as the object of her wish' (2). Lastly, on the plane of symptomatology, fetishism attests in Freud's view to the possibility of the sexual instinct's fixation to a part-object: as we know, Freud defines the fetish as a substitute for the mother's penis (3).

As for the now classic notion of the identification of a whole person with a part-object, especially with the phallus (4, 5), sporadic references to this too may be found in Freud (see 'Phallus').

With Karl Abraham, the antinomy between part and whole in the development of object-relationships takes on prime importance. In this author's essentially genetic approach there is a correlation between the evolution of the object and that of the libidinal aims* which characterise the different psycho-sexual stages* (6). Partial object-love constitutes one of the phases of the 'development of object love'.

Penis Envy

Melanie Klein's work follows the direction first pointed out by Abraham. The notion of the part-object is central to the reconstructed picture which she proposes of the child's world of phantasy. While this theory cannot be summarised here, we can at any rate name the pairs of opposites upon which Klein's dialectic of phantasy is based: good object/bad object*, introjection*/ projection*, part/whole (see these terms and also 'Paranoid Position' and 'Depressive Position').

It should be pointed out nevertheless that Abraham does not look upon the evolution of the object-relationship simply as a progression from the part-object to the whole one: his conception of it is much more complex. Thus the stage of partial object-love, for example, is itself preceded by a type of relationship implying a total incorporation* of the object.

Specifically, the *part-object* is in fact what is involved in the process of incorporation–although Abraham seems never to have used the actual term itself.

In Klein's use of 'part-object', 'object' is meant in its fullest psycho-analytic sense: though partial, the object (breast or other part of the body) is endowed in phantasy with traits comparable to a person's (e.g. it can be persecutory, reassuring, benevolent, etc.).

A final point: for the Kleinians, the relationship to part-objects does more than typify a stage of psychosexual development (the paranoid position): it continues to play a big part even after the relation to whole objects has become established. Jacques Lacan also stresses this. With Lacan, however, the specifically genetic aspect of the part-object is relegated to the background: he has sought to assign to the part-object a special place in a *topography* of desire* (7).

(1) Cf. FREUD, S. *Three Essays on the Theory of Sexuality* (1905d), G.W., V, 98–101; S.E., VII, 197–206.

(2) FREUD, S., G.W., X, 406; S.E., XVII, 130.

(3) Cf. FREUD, S. 'Fetishism' (1927e), G.W., XIV, 310–17; S.E., XXI, 152–57.

(4) Cf. FENICHEL, O. 'Die symbolische Gleichung: Mädchen = Phallus', *Internationale Zeitschrift für Psychoanalyse*, 1936, XXII, 299–314; in *Collected Papers* (London: Routledge & Kegan Paul, 1955), 3–18.

(5) Cf. LEWIN, B. 'The Body as Phallus', *P.Q.*, 1933, II, 24–47.

(6) Cf. ABRAHAM, K. 'A Short Study of the Development of the Libido, Viewed in the Light of Mental Disorders. Part II: Origins and Growth of Object-Love' (1924), in *Selected Papers* (London: Hogarth Press, 1927; New York: Basic Books, 1953), 480–501.

(7) Cf. especially LACAN, J. 'Le désir et son interprétation', *compte-rendu* of seminar by J.-B. Pontalis, *Bulletin de Psychologie*, 1960, XIII, No. 5.

Penis Envy

= *D.*: Penisneid.–*Es.*: envidia del pene.–*Fr.*: envie du pénis.–*I.*: invidia del pene.– *P.*: inveja do pênis.

Fundamental element in female sexuality and root of its dialectic.

Penis envy originates in the discovery of the anatomical distinction between

302

the sexes: the little girl feels deprived in relation to the boy and wishes to possess a penis as he does (castration complex). Subsequently, in the course of the Oedipal phase, this penis envy takes on two secondary forms: first, the wish to acquire a penis within oneself (principally in the shape of the desire to have a child) and, secondly, the wish to enjoy the penis in coitus.

Penis envy may follow many pathological or sublimated paths.

The notion of penis envy took on more and more importance in Freud's theory as he was gradually brought to specify female sexuality, which he had at first assumed to correspond exactly to that of the boy.

No reference is made to penis envy in the first edition of *Three Essays on the Theory of Sexuality*, which is centred on the development of sexuality in the male. The first mention of it in Freud's work comes only in the article 'On the Sexual Theories of Children' (1908c), where he draws attention to the little girl's interest in the boy's penis–an interest which 'falls under the sway of envy (*Neid*). [...] When a girl declares that "she would rather be a boy", we know what deficiency her wish is intended to put right' (1).

By the time Freud used it–in 1914 (2)–to denote the expression of the castration complex in the girl, the term 'penis envy' had, apparently, already gained acceptance in psycho-analytical parlance.

In 'On the Transformations of Instinct, as Exemplified in Anal Erotism' (1917c), however, the term's denotation is no longer restricted to the female's desire to have a penis like the boy's: it now also covers the main derivative versions of penis envy–namely, the wish for a child, in accordance with the symbolic equivalence of penis and child, and the desire for the male as an 'appendage to the penis' (3).

The Freudian conception of female sexuality (4) gives penis envy an essential place in the psychosexual development towards femininity–a development which entails a switch in erotogenic zone (from the clitoris to the vagina) and a change of object (the preoedipal attachment to the mother giving way to the Oedipal love for the father). It is the castration complex* and penis envy which –at different levels–serve as the crux of this double reorientation:

a. Resentment towards the mother who has failed to provide the daughter with a penis.

b. Depreciation of the mother, who now appears as castrated.

c. Renunciation of phallic activity (clitoral masturbation) as passivity takes over.

d. Symbolic equivalence between penis and child.

'The wish (*Wunsch*) with which the girl turns to her father is no doubt originally the wish for the penis which her mother has refused her and which she now expects from her father. The feminine situation is only established, however, if the wish for a penis is replaced by one for a baby, if, that is, a baby takes the place of a penis in accordance with an ancient symbolic equivalence' (5a).

Freud draws attention on several occasions to the way in which penis envy can persist in a woman's character (e.g. the 'masculinity complex') and in her neurotic symptoms. It is in fact these adult relics which are commonly meant

303

Penis Envy

when mention is made of penis envy; psycho-analysis recognises them beneath the greatest variety of disguises.

In one of his last writings, Freud—who had always stressed the way in which penis envy persists in the unconscious in spite of apparent renunciations of it—even asserts that it may, in some degree, prove impervious to analysis (6).

*　　*　　*

The term 'penis envy' obviously embodies a certain measure of ambiguity; Jones emphasises this, and attempts to remedy it by differentiating three meanings: '(i) The wish to acquire a penis, usually by swallowing, and to retain it within the body, often converting it there into a baby; (ii) the wish to possess a penis in the clitoritic region [...]; (iii) the adult wish to enjoy a penis in coitus' (7).

However useful this distinction may be, it must not lead to the assumption that these three modalities of penis envy are in any way exclusive of one another; on the contrary, the role of the psycho-analytic approach is precisely to describe the links and equivalences between them (α).

*　　*　　*

Several writers (Karen Horney, Helene Deutsch, Ernest Jones, Melanie Klein) have debated the Freudian thesis which treats penis envy as a primary *datum* and not as a formation which is constructed or used in a secondary manner in order to fend off earlier wishes. Though we cannot summarise this important discussion here, it may be remarked that the justification for Freud's maintenance of his argument lies in the central function which he assigns to the phallus in both sexes (see 'Phallic Stage', 'Phallus').

(α) Two variants of the term are in fact to be met with in certain passages of Freud's writings: 'envy' (*Neid*) and 'desire' (*Wunsch*) for the penis; there are no grounds for inferring, however, that any distinction is intended. (Cf., for example, the *New Introductory Lectures on Psycho-Analysis* (5b).)

(1) FREUD, S., G.W., VII, 180; S.E., IX, 218.

(2) Cf. FREUD, S. 'On Narcissism: An Introduction' (1914c), G.W., X, 159; S.E., XIV, 92.

(3) FREUD, S., G. W., X, 405; S.E., XVII, 129.

(4) Cf. especially: FREUD, S. 'Some Psychical Consequences of the Anatomical Distinction between the Sexes' (1925j); 'Female Sexuality' (1931b); *New Introductory Lectures on Psycho-Analysis* (1933a). And BRUNSWICK, R. M. 'The Preoedipal Phase of the Libido Development' (1940), in *Psa. Read.*

(5) FREUD, S. *New Introductory Lectures on Psycho-Analysis* (1933a [1932]): a) G.W., XV, 137; S.E., XXII, 128. b) G.W., XV, 137–39; S.E., XXII, 128–30.

(6) Cf. FREUD, S. 'Analysis Terminable and Interminable' (1937c), G.W., XVI, 97–98; S.E., XXIII, 250–51.

(7) JONES, E. 'The Phallic Phase' (1932) in *Papers on Psycho-Analysis*, fifth edition (London: Baillière, 1950; Baltimore: Williams and Wilkins, 1949), 469.

Perceptual Identity/Thought Identity

= *D.*: Wahrnehmungsidentität/Denkidentität.–
Es.: identitad de percepción/identitad de pensamiento.–
Fr.: identité de perception/identité de pensée.–
I.: identità di percezione/identità di pensiero.–
P.: identidade de percepção (*or* perceptual)/identidade de pensamento.

These terms are used by Freud to denote the goals of the primary process and the secondary process respectively. The primary process endeavours to find a perception identical with the image of the object which results from the experience of satisfaction. In the secondary process, the identity sought is that between one thought and another.

These terms make their one and only appearance in Chapter VII of *The Interpretation of Dreams* (1900*a*). They are related to the Freudian conception of the experience of satisfaction*. The primary and secondary processes* can be defined in purely economic terms–the primary process as immediate discharge, the secondary process as inhibition, postponement of satisfaction and diversion. With the notion of perceptual identity, we leave the economic realm and direct our attention to the equivalences which are set up between ideas*.

The search for perceptual identity has its origin in the experience of satisfaction, which binds* the idea of a special object to an eminently satisfying discharge. From then on, the subject is destined to seek 'a repetition of the perception which was linked with the satisfaction of the need' (1*a*). The primal hallucination is the shortest route available for obtaining such a perceptual identity. More generally speaking, we may say that the primary process functions in accordance with this model; in another chapter of *The Interpretation of Dreams*, Freud shows that the relation of identity between two images–'identification'–is the type of logical relation which best corresponds to the sort of mental functioning which characterises dreaming (1*b*).

Thought-identity stands in a dual relationship to perceptual identity.

In the first place, it constitutes a modification of perceptual identity in that its aim is to free mental processes from the exclusive control of the pleasure principle: 'Thinking must concern itself with the connecting paths between ideas, without being led astray by the *intensities* of those ideas' (1*c*). In this sense, such a modification could be said to constitute the emergence of what logicians call the principle of identity.

In a second sense, however, thought-identity remains in the service of perceptual identity: '. . . all the complicated thought-activity which is spun out from the mnemic image to the moment at which the perceptual identity is established by the external world–all this activity of thought merely constitutes a *roundabout path to wish-fulfilment* which has been made necessary by experience' (1*d*).

These terms may not appear again in Freud's writings, yet the idea of an opposition, from the point of view of thought and judgement, between the primary and the secondary processes retains its central place in his theory. It

Perversion

may be recognised – to give just one example of its persistence – in the distinction between thing-presentations* and word-presentations.

*　　*　　*

In France, Daniel Lagache has on many occasions stressed the great utility of Freud's antithesis between perceptual identity and thought-identity; in particular, he sees this contrast as a means of distinguishing between defensive compulsions, on the one hand, where the ego remains in the grip of perceptual identity, and the working-off mechanisms* on the other, which bring an attentive, discriminating consciousness to bear – a consciousness that is capable of resisting the intrusions of unpleasurable ideas and affects: '. . . the task of objectifying identification, which preserves the individual identity of each object of thought, is to oppose syncretic identification' (2).

It should further be noted that the distinction between these two modes of 'identity' cannot be brought down to the traditional opposition between affectivity and reason, or even between 'emotional logic' (*logique affective*) and the logic of reason. For does not the whole of *The Interpretation of Dreams* aim to establish, in the face of 'scientific' prejudices, that the dream obeys laws which constitute a primary mode of functioning of the *logos*?

(1) FREUD, S.: a) G.W., II–III, 571; S.E., V, 566. b) Cf. G.W., II–III, 324 *ff*.; S.E., IV, 319 *ff*. c) G.W., II–III, 607–8; S.E., V, 602. d) G.W., II–III, 572; S.E., V, 566–67.

(2) LAGACHE, D. 'La Psychanalyse et la structure de la personnalité', *La Psychanalyse*, 1958, VI, 51.

Perversion

= *D*.: Perversion. – *Es*.: perversión. – *Fr*.: perversion. – *I*.: perversione. – *P*.: perversão.

Deviation from the 'normal' sexual act when this is defined as coitus with a person of the opposite sex directed towards the achievement of orgasm by means of genital penetration.

Perversion is said to be present: where the orgasm is reached with other sexual objects (homosexuality, paedophilia, bestiality, etc.) or through other regions of the body (anal coitus, etc.); where the orgasm is subordinated absolutely to certain extrinsic conditions, which may even be sufficient in themselves to bring about sexual pleasure (fetishism, transvestitism, voyeurism and exhibitionism, sado-masochism).

In a more comprehensive sense, 'perversion' connotes the whole of the psycho-sexual behaviour that accompanies such atypical means of obtaining sexual pleasure.

I. It is difficult to comprehend the idea of perversion otherwise than by reference to a norm. Before Freud's time the term was used, as indeed it still is, to denote 'deviations' of instinct* (in the traditional sense of predetermined behaviour characteristic of a particular species and comparatively invariable as regards its performance and its object).

Those authors who accept a plurality of instincts are thus brought to make a very broad category out of perversion and to posit a multitude of forms for it to take: perversions of the 'moral sense' (delinquency), of the 'social instincts' (prostitution), of the instinct of nutrition (bulimia, dipsomania) (1). In a similar vein, it is common to speak of perversion in order to qualify the character and behaviour of certain subjects who manifest particular cruelty or malevolence.

In psycho-analysis, the word 'perversion' is used exclusively in relation to sexuality. Where Freud recognises the existence of instincts other than sexual ones, he does not evoke perversion in connection with them. In the domain of what he calls the instincts of self-preservation*–in the case, say, of hunger –he makes no mention of perversion when he is describing troubles affecting nutrition which many authors would refer to as perversions of the instinct of nutrition. Such troubles, according to Freud, should be ascribed to the impact of sexuality on the alimentary function (libidinisation); one might say, in fact, that this function is 'perverted' by sexuality.

II. The systematic study of the sexual perversions was topical when Freud was beginning to work out his theory of sexuality: Krafft-Ebing's *Psychopathia Sexualis* dates from 1893, Havelock Ellis's *Studies in the Psychology of Sex* from 1897. These works already described the whole of the adult sexual perversions, and Freud's originality lies in the fact that he used the existence of perversion as a weapon with which to throw the traditional definition of sexuality into question. This traditional definition he summed up as follows: the sexual instinct is 'understood to be absent in childhood, to set in at the time of puberty in connection with the process of coming to maturity and to be revealed in the manifestation of an irresistible attraction exercised by one sex upon the other; while its aim is presumed to be sexual union, or at all events action leading in that direction' (2a). The frequency of typically perverse types of behaviour, and especially the persistence of perverse tendencies, whether these underpin neurotic symptoms or are integrated into the normal sexual act in the guise of 'forepleasure', led Freud to the idea that 'the disposition to perversions is itself of no great rarity but must form a part of what passes as the normal constitution' (2b). This conclusion serves as both confirmation and explanation of the existence of an infantile sexuality. This sexuality, in so far as it is subject to the interplay of the component instincts* and closely bound up with the diversity of the erotogenic zones*, and in so far as it develops prior to the establishment of the genital functions proper, may be described as a 'polymorphously perverse disposition'. Adult perversion appears in this light as the persistence or re-emergence of a component part of sexuality. Freud's subsequent recognition of stages* of libidinal organisation* within infantile sexuality, and of an evolution in the choice of object, permits this definition to be made more precise (fixation* at a particular stage or type of object-choice*): perversion can now be seen as a regression* to an earlier fixation of libido.

III. It is obvious what repercussions the Freudian conception of sexuality can have upon the actual definition of the term 'perversion'. So-called normal sexuality cannot be seen as an *a priori* aspect of human nature: '... the exclusive sexual interest felt by men for women is also a problem that needs elucidating and is not a self-evident fact' (2c). A perversion such as homosexuality, for instance, appears as a *variant* of sexual life: 'Psycho-analytic research is most decidedly opposed to any attempt at separating off homosexuals from the rest of mankind as a group of a special character. [...] it has found that all human beings are capable of making a homosexual object-choice and have in fact made one in their unconscious' (2d). One could pursue this line of reasoning further still and define human sexuality itself as essentially 'perverse' inasmuch as it never fully detaches itself from its origins, where satisfaction was sought not in a specific activity but in the 'pleasure gain' associated with functions or activities depending on other instincts (see 'Anaclisis'). Even in the performance of the genital act itself, it suffices that the subject should develop an excessive attachment to forepleasure for him to slip towards perversion (2e).

IV. Which said, the fact remains that Freud and all psychoanalysts do talk of 'normal' sexuality. Even if we admit that the polymorphously perverse disposition typifies all infantile sexuality, that the majority of perversions are to be found in the psychosexual development of every individual, and that the outcome of this development–the genital* organisation–'is not a self-evident fact' and has to be set up and governed not by nature but by the process of personal evolution–even if we admit all this, it is still true that the notion of development itself implies a norm.

Are we to conclude that Freud returns to the normative conception of sexuality that he emphatically challenged at the outset of his *Three Essays on the Theory of Sexuality*–basing it now on genetic criteria? Does he end up by categorising as perversions exactly what has always been so categorised?

In answering these questions, it must be said first of all that inasmuch as Freud does accept a norm he does not seek it in a social consensus any more than he reduces perversion to a deviant path in contrast to the dominant tendency of the social group: homosexuality is not considered abnormal because it is condemned, nor does it cease to be a perversion in those societies where it is very widespread and accepted.

Is it then the establishment of the genital organisation that institutes the norm in that it unifies sexuality and subordinates partial sexual activities to the genital act, so that the former are relegated to a preparatory role *vis-à-vis* the latter? This is the explicit thesis of the *Three Essays*, and Freud never completely abandoned this view, even after the discovery of the successive pregenital* 'organisations' had had the effect of narrowing the rift between infantile and adult sexuality; indeed, Freud writes that 'the complete organisation is only achieved [in the] genital phase' (3a).

It is nonetheless reasonable to ask whether it is merely its unifying character –its force as a 'totality' as opposed to the 'component' instincts–that confers a normative role upon genitality. Numerous perversions, such as fetishism, most forms of homosexuality and even incest when it is actually practised, presuppose an organisation dominated by the genital zone. This surely suggests that the norm should be sought elsewhere than in genital functioning itself. It is worth recalling that the transition to the complete genital organisation implies for Freud that the Oedipus complex has been transcended, the castration complex assumed and the prohibition on incest accepted. Moreover, Freud's last researches on perversion show how fetishism is bound up with the 'disavowal' of castration.

V. In a famous formulation, Freud connects and contrasts neurosis and perversion: 'Neuroses are the negative of perversions' (2*f*). This dictum is too often given in an inverted form: perversion is described as the negative of neurosis; this amounts to treating perversion as the brute, non-repressed manifestation of infantile sexuality. In point of fact, the researches of Freud and the psycho-analysts on the perversions reveal that they are highly differentiated conditions. Of course, Freud does often contrast them with the neuroses in so far as, in the case of perversions, the mechanism of repression is absent; but at the same time he is at pains to show that *other* forms of defence come into operation here. His last works, especially those on fetishism (3*b*, 4), emphasise the complexity of these defences: disavowal* of reality, splitting* (*Spaltung*) of the ego, etc.; these are mechanisms, moreover, bearing significant resemblance to those found in psychosis.

(1) Cf. BARDENAT, C., article on 'Perversions' in POROT, A. *Manuel alphabétique de psychiatrie* (Paris: P.U.F., 1960).

(2) FREUD, S. *Three Essays on the Theory of Sexuality* (1905*d*): a) G.W., V, 33; S.E., VII, 135. b) G.W., V, 71; S.E., VII, 171. c) G.W., V, 44, *n.* 1; S.E., VII, 144, *n.* 1. d) G.W., V, 44, *n.* 1; S.E., VII, 144, *n.* 1. e) Cf. G.W., V, 113–14; S.E., VII, 211–12. f) G.W., V, 65 and 132; S.E., VII, 165 and 231.

(3) FREUD, S. *An Outline of Psycho-Analysis* (1940*a* [1938]): a) G.W., XVII, 77; S.E., XXIII, 155. b) Cf. G.W., XVII, 133–35; S.E., XXIII, 202–4.

(4) Cf. FREUD, S. 'Splitting of the Ego in the Process of Defence' (1940*e* [1938]), G.W., XVII, 59–62; S.E., XXIII, 275–78.

Phallic Stage (or Phase)

= *D.*: phallische Stufe (*or* Phase).–*Es.*: fase fálica.–*Fr.*: stade phallique.–*I.*: fase fallica.–*P.*: fase fálica.

Stage of childhood libidinal organisation succeeding the oral* and anal* stages and characterised by a unification of the component instincts under the primacy of the genital organs. By contrast with the situation obtaining in the genital organisation of puberty, however, the child at this stage, whether boy or girl, knows but one genital organ–the male one–and the opposition of the sexes is equivalent to that of *phallic* and *castrated*. The phallic stage corresponds to the culmination and dissolution of the Oedipus complex*; the castration complex* is predominant.

The notion of the phallic stage (α) emerges late on in Freud's work, making its first appearance only in 'The Infantile Genital Organisation' (1923*e*). The groundwork for it can be seen in the development of Freud's ideas concerning the successive modes of organisation of the libido and in his views on the primacy of the phallus*–two lines of approach worth distinguishing in the interests of clarity:

a. As for the first approach, we may recall that to begin with (1905) Freud

Phallic Stage (or Phase)

saw the absence of organisation* as the distinguishing mark of infantile sexuality as opposed to sexuality after puberty: the child can only emerge from the anarchy of the component instincts* once puberty has guaranteed the primacy of the genital zone. The introduction of the anal and oral pregenital* organisations (1913, 1915) implicitly challenges the genital zone's hitherto uncontested right to organise the libido; for the time being, however, it is only a matter of 'abortive beginnings and preliminary stages' (1*a*) of an organisation* in the full sense of the term. 'The combination of the component instincts and their subordination under the primacy of the genitals have been effected only very incompletely or not at all' (1*b*). By introducing the idea of a phallic phase, Freud recognises the existence, from infancy onwards, of a true organisation of sexuality very close to that found in the adult: 'This phase, which already deserves to be described as genital, presents a sexual object and some degree of convergence of the sexual impulses upon that object; but it is differentiated from the final organisation of sexual maturity in one essential respect. For it knows only one kind of genital: the male one' (1*c*).

b. This idea of a primacy of the phallus is already adumbrated in texts dating from well before 1923. As early as the *Three Essays on the Theory of Sexuality* (1905*d*), we find these two theses:

(i) Libido is 'of a masculine nature, whether it occurs in men or in women' (1*d*).

(ii) 'The leading erotogenic zone in female children is located at the clitoris, and is thus homologous to the masculine genital zone of the glans penis' (1*e*, 2).

The analysis of 'Little Hans' (1909*b*), where the notion of the castration complex is developed, brings to the fore the option facing boys: either to possess a penis or to be castrated. And lastly, the article 'On the Sexual Theories of Children' (1908*c*)–though, just like the *Three Essays*, it envisages sexuality from the boy's point of view–accentuates the special attention paid to the penis by the little girl, her envy of it and her feeling of being deprived as compared with the little boy.

*   *   *

The gist of the Freudian conception of the phallic phase is to be found in three articles: 'The Infantile Genital Organisation' (1923*e*), 'The Dissolution of the Oedipus Complex' (1924*d*), and 'Some Psychical Consequences of the Anatomical Distinction between the Sexes' (1925*j*). Freud's account of the phase may be schematically summarised as follows:

a. From the genetic point of view, the 'pair of opposites'* constituted by activity* and passivity, which is dominant during the anal stage, is transformed into the polarity of phallic and castrated; only at puberty is the opposition between masculinity* and femininity established.

b. So far as the Oedipus complex is concerned, the existence of a phallic stage has an essential role: the dissolution of the complex (in the case of the boy) is determined by the threat of castration, the effectiveness of which depends first on the narcissistic interest directed by the little boy towards his own penis and secondly on his discovery of the lack of a penis in the little girl (see 'Castration Complex').

c. A phallic organisation exists in girls. The discovery of the difference between the sexes gives rise to an *envy of the penis**; the effect of this envy on the relationship with the parents is that a resentment develops towards the mother who has not given the daughter a penis, while the father is now chosen as love-object inasmuch as he can offer the penis or its symbolic equivalent–the child. Thus the girl's development does not parallel the boy's (Freud does not recognise any knowledge of the vagina on the part of the girl); but both evolutions are orientated around the phallic organ.

The meaning of the phallic phase, especially in girls, has occasioned important debates in the history of psycho-analysis. Those authors (Horney, Klein, Jones) who accept the existence in the little girl of sexual feelings that are specific from the outset–particularly a primary intuitive knowledge of the vaginal cavity–are obliged to look upon the phallic phase as nothing more than a secondary formation serving a defensive function.

(α) It is also permissible to speak, of a phallic *phase* or *position*; these terms emphasise the fact that we are here concerned with an intersubjective moment embedded in the Oedipal dialectic rather than a stage of libidinal development properly speaking.

(1) FREUD, S. *Three Essays on the Theory of Sexuality* (1905d): a) G.W., V, 98; S.E., VII, 197–98 (added 1915). b) G.W., V, 100; S.E., VII, 199 (added 1915). c) G.W., V, 100; S.E., VII, 199 (note added 1924). d) G.W., V, 120; S.E., VII, 219. e) G.W., V, 121; S.E., VII, 220.

(2) Cf. FREUD, S., letter to Fliess dated November 14, 1897, *Anf.*, 244–49; S.E., I, 268–71.

Phallic Woman, Phallic Mother

= *D.*: phallische (Frau *or* Mutter).–*Es.*: fálica (mujer *or* madre).–
   Fr.: phallique (femme *or* mère).–*I.*: fallica (donna *or* madre).–*P.*: fálica (mulher *or* mãe).

Woman endowed, in phantasy, with a phallus. This image has two main forms: the woman is represented either as having an external phallus or phallic attribute, or else as having preserved the male's phallus inside herself.

The image of women equipped with male sexual organs is often met with by psycho-analysis in dreams and phantasies.

Theoretically speaking, the basis for the image of the phallic mother was provided by the gradual bringing to light of a 'sexual theory of children'–and of a libidinal phase proper–in which both sexes were viewed as having only one sexual organ–the phallus (see 'Phallic Stage').

According to Ruth Mack Brunswick, an imago of this kind appears 'to insure the mother's possession of the penis, and as such probably arises at the moment when the child becomes uncertain that the mother does indeed possess it. Previously [...] it seems more than probable that the executive organ of the active mother is the breast; the idea of the penis is then projected back upon the active mother after the importance of the phallus has been recognised' (1).

On the clinical plane, Freud showed for example how the fetishist uses his fetish as a substitute for the maternal phallus whose absence he disavows* (2).

311

Phallus

Following another avenue, one opened up by Boehm (3), some psycho-analysts have uncovered, especially in the analysis of male homosexuals, an anxiety-generating phantasy in which the mother has kept the phallus received in coitus inside her body. Melanie Klein's idea of the 'combined parent'* extends the field of operation of this phantasy.

In the main, the term 'phallic woman' denotes the woman *who has* a phallus – not the image of the woman or little girl *identified with* the phallus (4). Lastly, it should be pointed out that this expression is often employed in a loose way as a description of a woman with allegedly masculine character-traits – e.g. authoritarianism – even when it is not known what the underlying phantasies are.

(1) BRUNSWICK, R. M. 'The Preoedipal Phase of the Libido Development', *P.Q.*, 1940, IX, 304; *Psa. Read.*, 240.

(2) Cf. FREUD, S., 'Fetishism' (1927e), G.W., XIV, 312; S.E., XXI, 152–53.

(3) Cf. BOEHM, F. 'Homosexualität und Ödipuskomplex', *Internationale Zeitschrift für Psychoanalyse*, 1926, XII, 66–99.

(4) Cf. FENICHEL, O. 'Die symbolische Gleichung: Mädchen = Phallus', *Internationale Zeitschrift für Psychoanalyse*, 1936, XXII, 299–314; in *Collected Papers* (London: Routledge & Kegan Paul, 1955), 3–18.

Phallus

= *D.*: Phallus. – *Es.*: falo. – *Fr.*: phallus. – *I.*: fallo. – *P.*: falo.

In classical antiquity, the figurative representation of the male organ.

In psycho-analysis, the use of this term underlines the symbolic function taken on by the penis in the intra- and inter-subjective dialectic, the term 'penis' itself tending to be reserved for the organ thought of in its anatomical reality.

Only on a few occasions does the term 'phallus' occur in Freud's writings. In its adjectival form, however, it is used in a variety of expressions, the most important being 'phallic stage'*. In contemporary psycho-analytical literature there has been a gradual tendency to use 'penis' and 'phallus' in distinct senses: the former denotes the male organ in its bodily reality, while the latter lays the stress on the symbolic value of the penis.

The phallic organisation, which Freud gradually came to recognise as a stage* of libidinal development in both sexes, occupies a central position in that it is correlated with the castration complex at its acme and governs the setting-up and the resolution of the Oedipus complex. The choice offered the subject at this stage is simply that between having the phallus and being castrated. Clearly the opposition here is not between two terms denoting two anatomical realities – as is the case when we contrast penis and vagina – but rather between the presence and the absence of a single factor. In Freud's view, this primacy of the phallus for both sexes is a corollary of the fact that the little girl is ignorant of the existence of the vagina. Even though the mode of the castration complex varies from the boy to the girl, it is nevertheless centred solely, in both cases,

312

on the phallus, which is thought of as detachable from the body. In this light, an article such as 'On Transformations of Instinct, as Exemplified in Anal Erotism' (1917*c*) serves to show how the male organ has a part to play in a series of interchangeable elements constituting 'symbolic equations' (penis = faeces = child = gift, etc.); a common trait of these elements is that they are detachable from the subject and capable of circulating from one person to another.

For Freud, the male organ is not only a reality that can be identified as the ultimate point of reference in a whole series of references. The theory of the castration complex* also assigns a dominant role to it, as a symbol this time, in so far as its absence or presence transforms an anatomical distinction into a major yardstick for the categorisation of human beings, and in so far as, for each individual subject, this absence or presence is not taken for granted and remains irreducible to a mere *datum*: instead, it is the problematic outcome of an intra- and inter-subjective process (the assumption by the subject of his own sex). It is doubtless with this symbolic value in mind that Freud, and, more systematically, contemporary psycho-analysis, speaks of the phallus: reference is made, with varying degrees of explicitness, to the use of this term in antiquity to refer to the figurative representation (painted, sculpted, etc.) of the male member as an object of veneration with a pivotal role in initiation ceremonies (Mysteries). 'In this distant period, the erect phallus symbolised sovereign power, magically or supernaturally transcendent virility as opposed to the purely priapic variety of male power, the hope of resurrection and the force that can bring it about, the luminous principle that brooks neither shadows nor multiplicity and maintains the eternal springs of being. The ithyphallic gods Hermes and Osiris are the incarnation of this essential inspiration' (1).

How are we to understand 'symbolic value' here? First, it would be mistaken to assign a specific allegorical meaning to the phallus-symbol, however broad it might be (fecundity, potency, authority, etc.). Secondly, what is symbolised here cannot be reduced to the male organ or penis itself, in its anatomical reality. Lastly, the phallus turns out to be the meaning–i.e. what is *symbolised*– behind the most diverse ideas just as often as (and perhaps more often than) it appears as a symbol in its own right (in the sense of a schematic, figurative representation of the male member). Freud pointed out in his theory of symbolism that the phallus was one of the universal objects of symbolisation; and he thought that the property of being something little (*das Kleine*) could provide a *tertium comparationis* between the male organ and what is used to represent it (2*a*). Yet to pursue the logic of this remark, we might conclude that what really characterises the phallus and reappears in all its figurative embodiments is its status as a detachable and transformable object–and in this sense as a part-object*. Nor is this conclusion contradicted by the fact that the subject as whole person may be identified with the phallus–a fact perceived by Freud as early as *The Interpretation of Dreams* (1900*a*) (2*b*, 2*c*) and largely borne out by analytic investigation. For what happens at such moments is that the person himself is assimilated to an object that can be seen and exhibited, or that can circulate, be given and received. In particular, Freud showed how, in the case of female sexuality, the wish to receive the father's phallus is transformed into the wish to have a child by him. This instance, furthermore, casts doubt on the

Phantasy (or Fantasy)

wisdom of setting up a radical distinction between penis and phallus in psycho-analytic terminology. The term *'Penisneid'* (see 'Penis Envy') crystallises an ambiguity which may be a fruitful one, and which cannot be disposed of by making a schematic distinction between, say, the wish to derive pleasure from the real man's penis in coitus and the desire to possess the phallus *qua* virility symbol.

In France, Jacques Lacan has attempted a reorientation of psycho-analytic theory around the idea of the phallus as the 'signifier of desire'. The Oedipus complex, in Lacan's reformulation of it, consists in a dialectic whose major alternatives are to be or not to be the phallus, and to have it or not to have it; the three moments of this dialectic are centred on the respective positions occupied by the phallus in the desires of the three protagonists (3).

(1) LAURIN, C. 'Phallus et sexualité féminine', *La Psychanalyse*, 1964, VII, 15.

(2) FREUD, S. *The Interpretation of Dreams* (1900a): a) G.W., II–III, 366; S.E., V, 362–63. b) G.W., II–III, 370–71; S.E., V, 366. c) G.W., II–III, 399; S.E., V. 394.

(3) Cf. LACAN, J. 'Les formations de l'inconscient', *comptes-rendus* of seminars, 1957–58, by PONTALIS, J.-B., in *Bulletin de Psychologie*, 1958, XI, 4/5; XII, 2/3; XII, 4.

Phantasy (or Fantasy)

= *D.*: Phantasie.–*Es.*: fantasia.–*Fr.*: fantasme.–*I.*: fantasia *or* fantasma.–*P.*: fantasia.

Imaginary scene in which the subject is a protagonist, representing the fulfilment of a wish (in the last analysis, an unconscious wish) in a manner that is distorted to a greater or lesser extent by defensive processes.

Phantasy has a number of different modes: conscious phantasies or day-dreams*, unconscious phantasies like those uncovered by analysis as the structures underlying a manifest content*, and primal phantasies*.

I. The German word *'Phantasie'* means imagination, though less in the philosophical sense of the faculty of imagining (*Einbildungskraft*) than in the sense of the world of the imagination, its contents and the creative activity which animates it. Freud exploited these different connotations of the common German usage.

In French, the term *'fantasme'* was revived by psycho-analysis, with the result that it has more philosophical overtones than its German equivalent; nor does it correspond exactly to the German, in that it has a more restricted extension: *'fantasme'* refers to a specific imaginary production, not to the world of phantasy and imaginative activity in general.

Daniel Lagache has suggested that *'fantaisie'* should be revived in its old sense, the advantage of this being that it denotes both a creative activity and the products of this activity; the drawback, however, is that French usage makes it difficult to erase connotations of whimsy, eccentricity, triviality, etc. [It is

314

because 'fantasy' has similar overtones that most English psycho-analytic writers have preferred to write 'phantasy' but, as Charles Rycroft remarks in his *Critical Dictionary of Psychoanalysis*, 'few, if any, American writers have followed them in doing so'–*tr.*]

II. The use of the term 'phantasy' cannot fail to evoke the distinction between imagination and reality (perception). If this distinction is made into a major psycho-analytic axis of reference, we are brought to define phantasy as a purely illusory production which cannot be sustained when it is confronted with a correct apprehension of reality. It is true, what is more, that certain of Freud's writings seem to back up this type of approach. Thus in 'Formulations on the Two Principles of Mental Functioning' (1911*b*), Freud sets the internal world, tending towards satisfaction by means of illusion, against an outside world which gradually imposes the reality principle* upon the subject through the mediation of the perceptual system.

Another instance often invoked to lend support to this orientation is the way in which Freud discovered the importance of phantasies in the aetiology of the neuroses: Freud, so the argument runs, had at first believed that the pathogenic infantile scenes rediscovered during the course of analysis were real; he subsequently abandoned this conviction, however, and admitted his 'error', affirming that the apparently material reality of these scenes was in fact no more than 'psychical reality'* (α).

It is right to emphasise at this point, however, that the expression 'psychical reality' itself is not simply synonymous with 'internal world', 'psychological domain', etc. If taken in the most basic sense that it has for Freud, this expression denotes a nucleus within that domain which is heterogeneous and resistant and which is alone in being truly 'real' as compared with the majority of psychical phenomena. 'Whether we are to attribute *reality* to unconscious wishes, I cannot say. It must be denied, of course, to any transitional or intermediate thoughts. If we look at unconscious wishes reduced to their most fundamental and truest shape, we shall have to conclude, no doubt, that *psychical* reality is a particular form of existence not to be confused with *material* reality' (1*a*).

An explanation of the stability, efficacity and relatively coherent nature of the subject's phantasy life is precisely the goal to which Freud's efforts, and the efforts of psycho-analytic thought as a whole, are directed. It was in this perspective that Freud, as soon as his attention had been focussed on phantasies, identified typical modes of phantasy scenes–the 'family romance'*, for example. He refuses to be restricted to a choice between one approach, which treats phantasy as a distorted derivative of the memory of actual fortuitous events, and another one which deprives phantasy of any specific reality and looks upon it merely as an imaginary expression designed to conceal the reality of the instinctual dynamic. The typical phantasies uncovered by psycho-analysis led Freud to postulate the existence of unconscious schemata transcending individual lived experience and supposedly transmitted by heredity; these he called 'primal phantasies'*.

III. The term 'phantasy' is very widely used in psycho-analysis. According to some authors, the drawback of this is that the *topographical* position of these products is not specified–it is not made clear, in other words, whether they are conscious, preconscious or unconscious.

315

Phantasy (or Fantasy)

If the Freudian notion of *Phantasie* is to be properly understood, a distinction should be made between a number of different levels:

a. What Freud means in the first place by '*Phantasien*' are day-dreams*, scenes, episodes, romances or fictions which the subject creates and recounts to himself in the waking state. In the *Studies on Hysteria* (1895d), Breuer and Freud demonstrated the frequency and importance of such phantasy activity in hysterics, describing it as often 'unconscious'–that is, as occurring during states of absence of mind or hypnoid states*.

In *The Interpretation of Dreams* (1900a), Freud continues to base his description of phantasies on the model of day-dreaming. According to his analysis, they are compromise-formations*: he shows that their structure is comparable to that of dreams. These phantasies or day-dreams are used by the secondary revision*, which is the part of the dream-work* closest to waking activity.

b. Freud often speaks of 'unconscious phantasy' without always implying a clearly demarcated metapsychological position. He seems at times to be referring to a subliminal, preconscious revery into which the subject falls and of which he may or may not become reflexively aware (2). In the article on 'Hysterical Phantasies and their Relation to Bisexuality' (1908a), 'unconscious' phantasies are held to be precursors of hysterical symptoms and are described as being closely connected with day-dreams.

c. When Freud follows up an alternative line of thought, phantasy emerges as having a much more intimate relation to the unconscious. In Chapter VII of *The Interpretation of Dreams*, he quite clearly considers that certain phantasies operate, topographically speaking, at an unconscious level. The phantasies in question are those which are bound to unconscious wishes and which are the starting-point of the metapsychological process of dream formation: the first portion of the 'journey' which ends with the dream 'was a progressive one, leading from the unconscious scenes or phantasies to the preconsciuos' (1b).

d. It is thus possible to distinguish–although Freud himself never did so explicitly–between several levels at which phantasy is dealt with in Freud's work: conscious, subliminal and unconscious (β). Freud's principal concern, however, seems to have been less with establishing such a differentiation than with emphasising the links between these different aspects:

(i) In dreams, the day-dreams utilised by the secondary revision may be directly connected with the unconscious phantasy which constitutes the 'nucleus of the dream': 'The wishful phantasies revealed by analysis in night-dreams often turn out to be repetitions or modified versions of scenes from infancy; thus in some cases the façade of the dream directly reveals the dream's actual nucleus, distorted by an admixture of other material' (3). So, in the dream-work, phantasy is to be found at both poles of the process: on the one hand, it is bound to the deepest unconscious wishes, to the 'capitalist' aspect of the dream, while at the other extreme it has a part to play in the secondary revision. The two extremities of the dream process and the two corresponding modes of phantasy seem therefore to join up, or at least to be linked internally with each other –they appear, as it were, to symbolise each other.

(ii) Freud presents phantasy as a unique *focal point* where it is possible to observe the process of *transition* between the different psychical systems *in vitro* –to observe the mechanism of repression* or of the return of the repressed* in action. Phantasies 'draw near to consciousness and remain undisturbed so long as they do not have an intense cathexis, but as soon as they exceed a certain height of cathexis they are thrust back' (4a).

(iii) In the most complete metapsychological definition of phantasy that he proposed, Freud establishes a link between those aspects of it which appear to be the furthest away from one another: 'On the one hand, they [phantasies] are highly organised, free from self-contradiction, have made use of every acquisition of the system *Cs.* and would hardly be distinguished in our judgement from the formations of that system. On the other hand they are unconscious and are incapable of becoming conscious. Thus *qualitatively* they belong to the system *Pcs.*, but *factually* to the *Ucs.* Their origin is what decides their fate. We may compare them with individuals of mixed race who, taken all round, resemble white men, but who betray their coloured descent by some striking feature or other, and on that account are excluded from society and enjoy none of the privileges of white people' (4b).

It would seem, therefore, that the Freudian problematic of phantasy, far from justifying a distinction in kind between unconscious and conscious phantasies, is much more concerned with bringing forward the analogies between them, the close relationship which they share and the transitions which take place between one and the other: 'The contents of the clearly conscious phantasies of perverts (which in favourable circumstances can be transformed into manifest behaviour), of the delusional fears of paranoics (which are projected in a hostile sense on to other people) and of the unconscious phantasies of hysterics (which psycho-analysis reveals behind their symptoms)—all of these coincide with one another even down to their details' (5). In imaginary formations and psycho-pathological structures as diverse as those enumerated here by Freud, it is possible to meet with an identical content and an identical organisation irrespective of whether these are conscious or unconscious, acted out or imagined, assumed by the subject or projected on to other people.

Consequently, the psycho-analyst must endeavour in the course of the treatment to unearth the phantasies which lie behind such products of the unconscious as dreams, symptoms, acting out*, repetitive behaviour, etc. As the investigation progresses, even aspects of behaviour that are far removed from imaginative activity, and which appear at first glance to be governed solely by the demands of reality, emerge as emanations, as 'derivatives' of unconscious phantasy. In the light of this evidence, it is the subject's life as a whole which is seen to be shaped and ordered by what might be called, in order to stress this structuring action, 'a phantasmatic' (*une fantasmatique*). This should not be conceived of merely as a thematic—not even as one characterised by distinctly specific traits for each subject—for it has its own dynamic, in that the phantasy structures seek to express themselves, to find a way out into consciousness and action, and they are constantly drawing in new material.

IV. Phantasy has the closest of links with desire*, a fact to which an expression of Freud's bears witness: '*Wunschphantasie*', or wishful phantasy (6). How should we conceive of this relationship? We know that desire has its origin and its prototype in the *experience of satisfaction**: 'The first wishing (*Wünschen*) seems to have been a hallucinatory cathecting of the memory of satisfaction' (1c). Does this mean that the most primitive phantasies are the ones which tend

317

Phantasy (or Fantasy)

to recover the hallucinatory objects that are bound to the very earliest experiences of the rise and resolution of internal tension? May we say that the first phantasies are object-phantasies–or phantasy-objects–which desire is directed towards in the same way as need is directed towards its natural object?

The relationship between phantasy and desire seems to us to be more complicated than that. Even in their least elaborate forms, phantasies do not appear to be reducible to an intentional aim on the part of the desiring subject:

a. Even where they can be summed up in a single sentence, phantasies are still scripts (*scénarios*) of organised scenes which are capable of dramatisation–usually in a visual form.

b. The subject is invariably present in these scenes; even in the case of the 'primal scene'*, from which it might appear that he was excluded, he does in fact have a part to play not only as an observer but also as a participant, when he interrupts the parents' coitus.

c. It is not an *object* that the subject imagines and aims at, so to speak, but rather a *sequence* in which the subject has his own part to play and in which permutations of roles and attributions are possible. (The reader's attention is drawn, in particular, to Freud's analysis of the phantasy ' "A Child is Being Beaten" ' (1919*e*), and to the syntactical changes which this sentence undergoes; cf. also the transformations of the homosexual phantasy in the account of the Schreber case (1911*c*).)

d. In so far as desire is articulated in this way through phantasy, phantasy is also the locus of defensive operations: it facilitates the most primitive of defence processes, such as turning round upon the subject's own self*, reversal into the opposite*, negation* and projection*.

e. Such defences are themselves inseparably bound up with the primary function of phantasy, namely the *mise-en-scène* of desire–a *mise-en-scène* in which what is *prohibited* (*l'interdit*) is always present in the actual formation of the wish.

(*α*) On several occasion, Freud described this turning-point in his thought (7) in terms which lend weight to this interpretation. But a careful study of Freud's concepts and their evolution between 1895 and 1900 reveals that his own–extremely schematic–account does not take into consideration the complexity and depth of his views on phantasy. (For an interpretation of this period, cf. Laplanche and Pontalis, 'Fantasme originaire, fantasmes des origines, origine du fantasme' (1964) (8).)

(*β*) In her article of 1948, 'The Nature and Function of Phantasy' (9), Susan Isaacs proposes that the two alternative spellings *fantasy* and *phantasy* should be used to denote 'conscious daydreams, fictions and so on' and 'the primary content of unconscious mental processes' respectively. Isaacs feels that such an innovation in psycho-analytic terminology would be consistent with Freud's thought. In our view, however, the suggested distinction does not do justice to the complexity of Freud's views. In any case, it would lead to problems of translation: if, for every occurrence of '*Phantasie*' in Freud's writings, a choice had to be made between '*ph*antasy' and '*f*antasy', the door would be open to the most arbitrary of interpretations.

(1) FREUD, S. *The Interpretation of Dreams* (1900*a*): a) G. W., II–III, 625; S. E., V, 620. b) G. W., II–III, 579; S.E., V, 574. c) G.W., II–III, 604; S.E., V, 598.

(2) Cf. FREUD, S. 'Hysterical Phantasies and their Relation to Bisexuality' (1908*a*), G.W., VII, 192–93; S.E., IX, 160.

(3) FREUD, S. *On Dreams* (1901*a*), G.W., II–III, 680; S.E., V, 667.

(4) FREUD, S. 'The Unconscious' (1915*e*): a) G.W., X, 290; S.E., XIV, 191. b) G.W., X, 289; S.E., XIV, 190–91.

(5) F R E U D, S. *Three Essays on the Theory of Sexuality* (1905*d*), G.W., V, 65, *n.* 1; S.E., VII, 165, *n.* 2.

(6) Cf. F R E U D, S. 'A Metapsychological Supplement to the Theory of Dreams' (1917*d* [1915]), *passim.*

(7) Cf., for example, F R E U D, S. *Introductory Lectures on Psycho-Analysis* (1916–17).

(8) *Les Temps Modernes*, No. 215, 1833–68. English trans.: 'Fantasy and the Origins of Sexuality'. *I.J.P.*, 1968. 49, 1 *ff.*

(9) I S A A C S, S., *I.J.P.*, 1948, XXIX, 73–97. Also in *Developments*, 67–121.

Phobic Neurosis

= *D.*: phobische Neurose.–*Es.*: neurosis fóbica.–*Fr.*: névrose phobique.– *I.*: nevrosi fobica.–*P.*: neurose fóbica.

See 'Anxiety Hysteria'.

Plasticity of the Libido

= *D.*: Plastizität der Libido.–*Es.*: plasticidad de la libido.–*Fr.*: plasticité de la libido.– *I.*: plasticità della libido.–*P.*: plasticidade da libido.

The degree of facility with which the libido is able to change its object and mode of satisfaction.

Plasticity (or free mobility: *freie Beweglichkeit*) may be looked upon as the opposite property to *adhesiveness*. The reader is referred to our commentary on this last term, which Freud uses much more readily than 'plasticity'.

This expression evokes an idea that is vital to psycho-analysis: the libido is at first relatively undetermined in regard to its object*, and it is always capable of changing it.

There is also a plasticity of aim*: the non-satisfaction of a particular component instinct is compensated for by the satisfaction of another one, or by a sublimation*. One of the sexual instincts, Freud writes, 'can take the place of another, one of them can take over another's intensity; if the satisfaction of one of them is frustrated by reality, the satisfaction of another can afford complete compensation. They are related to one another like a network of intercommunicating channels filled with a liquid' (1).

Plasticity varies according to the individual, his age and his history. It is an important factor in the indication and prognosis of psycho-analytic treatment, for according to Freud the capacity for change rests on the capacity to modify libidinal cathexes*.

(1) F R E U D, S. *Introductory Lectures on Psycho-Analysis* (1916–17), G.W., XI, 358; S.E., XVI, 345.

319

Pleasure-Ego/Reality-Ego

= *D.*: Lust-Ich/Real-Ich.–*Es.*: yo placer/yo realidad.–*Fr.*: moi-plaisir/moi-réalité.–
I.: io-piacere/io-realtà.–*P.*: ego-prazer/ego-realidade.

Terms used by Freud with reference to the genesis of the subject's relationship to the outside world and of his mode of access to reality. The two expressions are invariably opposed to one another, but their sense varies too much to allow of a clearcut definition; nor can we offer several alternative definitions, for the different usages overlap to a large degree.

The antithesis between the pleasure-ego and the reality-ego is expounded by Freud chiefly in the following works: 'Formulations on the Two Principles of Mental Functioning' (1911*b*), 'Instincts and their Vicissitudes' (1915*c*) and 'Negation' (1925*h*). The first point to note is that these three texts, though they date from different stages in Freud's work, are nevertheless consistent with each other and show no trace of the revisions made in the definition of the ego* with the transition from the first to the second topography*.

a. In 'Formulations on the Two Principles of Mental Functioning' the opposition between pleasure-ego and reality-ego is bound up with that between the pleasure* and the reality principles*. Freud calls upon the terms '*Lust-Ich*' and '*Real-Ich*' in describing the evolution of the ego-instincts*. The instincts, which function initially in accordance with the pleasure principle, gradually come under the sway of the reality principle, but this development is not so rapid nor so complete in the case of the sexual instincts since they are more difficult to 'educate' than the ego-instincts. 'Just as the pleasure-ego can do nothing but *wish*, work for a yield of pleasure, and avoid unpleasure, so the reality-ego need do nothing but strive for what is *useful* and guard itself against damage' (1). Note that the ego is here viewed essentially from the standpoint of the instincts which are supposed to supply its energy; the pleasure-ego and the reality-ego are not two radically distinct forms of the ego but, rather, descriptions of two modes of operation of the ego-instincts, one based on the pleasure principle, the other on the reality principle.

b. The standpoint taken in 'Instincts and their Vicissitudes' is again a genetic one, but what is envisaged here is neither the mutual articulation of the two principles nor the evolution of the ego-instincts: instead, it is the genesis of the opposition between subject (ego) and object (outside world) in so far as it is correlated with the pleasure-unpleasure antagonism.

In this perspective Freud distinguishes two stages: in the first, the subject 'coincides with what is pleasurable and the external world with what is indifferent' (2*a*); in the second, subject is opposed to outside world as pleasurable versus unpleasurable. The subject in the first stage is described as a pleasure-ego and, in the second, as a reality-ego. It will be noticed that the order of the terms here is the reverse of what it was in the article on 'The Two Principles of Mental Functioning'. But the expressions–especially 'reality-ego'–are not being used in the same way: the opposition between reality-ego and pleasure-ego now comes about prior to the emergence of the reality principle, and the transition from reality-ego to pleasure-ego is accomplished 'under the dominance of the pleasure principle' (2*b*).

This 'original reality-ego' is so named because it 'distinguishes internal and external by means of a sound objective criterion' (2*c*)–an assertion that may be understood as follows: it is indeed an *objective* position which allows the subject, from the beginning, to receive sensations of pleasure and unpleasure without making these into properties of the external world, which is, *per se*, neutral.

How is the pleasure-ego constituted? The subject, just like the external world, is split into pleasurable and unpleasurable parts. Starting from this situation, a new arrangement is made wherein the subject coincides with all that is pleasurable and the world with all that is unpleasurable. This new distribution is achieved by means of an introjection* of the portion of the objects in the external world which are sources of pleasure and a projection* outwards of whatever is a cause of unpleasure within. The subject's new position allows him to be defined as a 'purified pleasure-ego', all unpleasure now being located outside him.

Clearly then, the term 'pleasure-ego' as used in 'Instincts and their Vicissitudes' no longer means simply an ego regulated by the pleasure-unpleasure principle, but instead an ego identified with the pleasurable as opposed to the unpleasurable. In this new sense, it is still two stages of the ego that stand opposed to each other, but now they are defined by a modification in the ego's boundary and contents.

c. In 'Negation' Freud calls once more upon the distinction between pleasure-ego and reality-ego, and here the perspective is once more that of 'Instincts and their Vicissitudes': how is the antithesis between subject and external world constituted? The expression 'original reality-ego' does not recur explicitly, but Freud does not seem to have rejected this idea, for he maintains that the subject has an objective grasp of reality at his command from the start: '. . . originally the mere existence of a presentation was a guarantee of the reality of what was presented' (3*a*).

The second stage–that of the 'pleasure-ego'–is described in the same way as in 'Instincts': '. . . the original pleasure-ego wants to introject into itself everything that is good and to eject from itself everything that is bad. What is bad, what is alien to the ego and what [s external are, to begin with, identical' (3*b*).

The expression 'definitive reality-ego' is here used to refer to a third phase in which the subject seeks to rediscover a real object in the outside world that is equivalent to his image of the lost satisfying object of a primitive period (see 'Experience of Satisfaction'): here we have the basic principle of the process of *reality-testing*.*

The transition from the pleasure-ego to the reality-ego depends here–as it did in 'Two Principles of Mental Functioning'–on the establishment of the reality principle.

*   *   *

This antithesis was never integrated by Freud into his metapsychological approach as a whole, nor, more especially, into his theory of the ego as an agency of the psychical apparatus. The advantages to be gained by so doing are, however, plain: such an integration would help solve a number of problems raised by the psycho-analytic theory of the ego*:

a. Freud's views on the development of the pleasure-ego and the reality-ego constitute an attempt to establish a mediation, a genetic line (albeit a mythical one) from the biopsychological individual (identical in our opinion with Freud's 'original reality-ego') to the ego *qua* psychical agency.

b. These views further ground such a genesis upon primitive mental operations of introjection and projection whereby the boundaries of an ego comprising an inside and an outside are laid down.

c. Freud's approach has the additional merit of dispelling the confusion, always endemic to psycho-analytic theory, which surrounds such terms as 'primary narcissism'* inasmuch as they are often taken to mean a hypothetical original state in which the individual does not have even the most rudimentary kind of access to the world outside.

(1) FREUD, S., G.W., VIII, 235; S.E., XII, 223.

(2) FREUD, S.: a) G.W., X, 227: S.E., XIV, 135. b) G.W., X, 228; S.E., XIV, 135–36. c) G.W., X, 228; S.E., XIV, 135–36.

3) FREUD, S.: a) G.W., XIV, 14; S.E., XIX, 237. b) G.W., XIV, 13; S.E., XIX, 237.

Pleasure Principle

= D.: Lustprinzip. – Es.: principio de placer. – Fr.: principe de plaisir. – I.: principio di piacere. – P.: princípio de prazer.

One of the two principles which, according to Freud, govern mental functioning: the whole of psychical activity is aimed at avoiding unpleasure and procuring pleasure. Inasmuch as unpleasure is related to the increase of quantities of excitation, and pleasure to their reduction, the principle in question may be said to be an economic one.

The idea of grounding a regulatory principle of mental functioning on pleasure is by no means Freud's own. Fechner, whose ideas, as is well known, left a profound mark on Freud, had himself put forward a 'principle of the pleasure of action' (1a). What Fechner understood by this, in contradistinction to traditional hedonist doctrines, was not that the final purpose of human action is pleasure, but rather that our acts are determined by the pleasure or unpleasure procured *in the immediate* by the idea of the action to be accomplished or of its consequences. He further noted that these motives are not necessarily perceived consciously: '... it is quite natural that, since the motives are lost in the unconscious, the same should hold good in respect of pleasure and unpleasure' (1b, α).

This immediate aspect of motivation is also at the core of Freud's approach: the psychical apparatus* is regulated by the avoidance or discharge of unpleasurable tension. It is worth noting that Freud at first calls this principle the 'unpleasure principle' (2a): the motive is present unpleasure as opposed to pleasure in prospect. Regulation by this mechanism is said to be 'automatic' (2b).

* * *

The idea of the pleasure principle undergoes little modification throughout Freud's work. What is problematic for him, on the other hand, is the position of this principle in its relation to other theoretical points of reference, and he offers various ways out of this difficulty.

A first obstacle, already apparent in the actual formulation of the principle, arises over the definition of pleasure and unpleasure. Consider one of Freud's permanent theses regarding his model of the psychical apparatus: an operating principle of the perception-consciousness system is that, while it is sensitive to a great diversity of qualities originating in the external world, it can only apprehend internal reality in terms of the increase and decrease of tension, as expressed on a single qualitative axis – namely, the pleasure-unpleasure scale (2c, β). Must we therefore be content with a purely economic definition and accept that pleasure and unpleasure are nothing more than the translation of quantitative changes into qualitative terms? And what then is the precise correlation between these two aspects, the qualitative and the quantitative? Little by little, Freud came to lay considerable emphasis on the great difficulty encountered in the attempt to provide a simple answer to this question. If, to begin with, he is satisfied by the mere postulation of an equivalence between pleasure and the reduction of tension, and between unpleasure and a corresponding increase in it, he soon abandons the idea that this relationship is an evident and simple one: 'We will, however, carefully preserve this assumption in its present highly indefinite form, until we succeed, if that is possible, in discovering what sort of relation exists between pleasure and unpleasure, on the one hand, and fluctuations in the amounts of stimulus affecting mental life, on the other. It is certain that many very various relations of this kind, and not very simple ones, are possible' (3).

As regards the nature of the mechanism in question, it is hard to find more than a few brief pointers in Freud's work. In *Beyond the Pleasure Principle* (1920g), he remarks that unpleasure and the feeling of tension should not be treated as identical: pleasurable tensions, in other words, do exist. 'Is the feeling of tension to be related to the absolute magnitude, or perhaps to the level, of the cathexis, while the pleasure and unpleasure series indicates a change in the magnitude of the cathexis *within a given unit of time*?' (4a). It is again a temporal factor – rhythm – that is taken into account in a later text, at the same moment when the essentially qualitative aspect of pleasure is reinstated (5a).

Whatever the obstacles may be which hinder the laying down of exact quantitative equivalents to pleasure and unpleasure as qualitative states, the advantages of an economic interpretation of these states for psycho-analytic theory are obvious: such an explanation clears the way for the formulation of a principle which holds good as much for the unconscious agencies of the personality as for its conscious aspects. To speak, for example, of unconscious pleasure as being associated with a manifestly distressing symptom is to court criticisms from the point of view of psychological description. Freud takes as his standpoint a psychical apparatus and the modifications which occur within it. He thus has at his disposal a model which enables him to consider each substructure as regulated by the same principle as the apparatus as a whole. He can also put in parenthesis the difficult problem of determining, for each of these substructures, the mode and the occasion of an increase in tension becoming an effective motive-force in the form of perceived unpleasure. The problem, however, is not neglected in Freud's work: it is dealt with specifically, apropos of the ego, in *Inhibitions, Symptoms and Anxiety* (1926*d*) (the concept of anxiety as a signal* or motive for defence).

*   *   *

A further problem – not unrelated, in fact, to the last one – arises as regards the relationship between *pleasure* and *constancy*. For, even if we accept the validity of an economic, quantitative account of pleasure, we have still not answered the question whether what Freud calls the pleasure principle implies the maintenance of energy at a constant level or a radical reduction of tensions to the minimum level. Many of Freud's formulations, assimilating the pleasure principle as they do to the principle of constancy, appear to indicate an option for the first of these two alternatives. But, on the other hand, if we take an overall view of Freud's basic theoretical references (as they emerge, in particular, from works such as the 'Project for a Scientific Psychology' (1950*a* [1895]) and *Beyond the Pleasure Principle*), we find that his tendency is rather to oppose the pleasure principle to the maintenance of constancy. Either this principle is seen to stand for the free flow of energy whereas constancy implies that it is bound*, or, alternatively, Freud goes so far as to ask whether the pleasure principle is not 'in the service of the death instincts' (4*b*, 5*b*). We discuss this issue at greater length in dealing with the 'Principle of Constancy'.

The question, often debated in psycho-analysis, of what lies 'beyond the pleasure principle' is one which cannot be validly posed until the problems raised by the concepts of pleasure, constancy, binding and the reduction of tension to zero have been fully resolved. The fact is that Freud only postulates the existence of principles or instinctual forces which transcend the pleasure principle on those occasions when he is opting for an interpretation of this principle tending to identify it with the principle of constancy. Whenever he is tempted, on the contrary, to conflate the pleasure principle with a principle of reduction of tension to zero (Nirvana principle), then there is no doubt in his mind that it has the fundamental character of a first principle (see especially 'Death Instincts').

*   *   *

The notion of the pleasure principle assumes its main function in psycho-analytic theory when coupled with the reality principle. Thus when Freud comes to expound the two principles of mental functioning in explicit fashion it is this major axis of reference that he brings to the fore. The instincts, he argues, at first have discharge alone as their aim – they seek satisfaction via the shortest route. The nature of reality is only learnt gradually, but this learning process is the only way for the instincts, after the necessary detours and postponements, to reach the sought-for satisfaction. In this simplified thesis, it can be seen how the pleasure-reality relation poses a problem which is itself dependent on the meaning psycho-analysis assigns to the term 'pleasure'. If we understand

324

pleasure essentially as the fulfilment of a need, after the fashion of the satisfaction of the self-preservation instincts, then the opposition between the pleasure principle and the reality principle has no radical implications, especially as it will be readily granted that the living organism is naturally endowed with predispositions which treat pleasure as a guiding principle, but that these are subordinated to adaptive behaviour and functions. It is in quite another context, however, that psycho-analysis emphasises the notion of pleasure–a context in which it appears to be connected with processes (experience of satisfaction) and with phenomena (the dream) whose unrealistic character is patent. And from this standpoint the two principles emerge as fundamentally antagonistic, in that the fulfilment of unconscious wishes (*Wunscherfüllung*) is a response to very different requirements, and functions according to very different laws, from the satisfaction (*Befriedigung*) of the vital needs (see 'Self-Preservation Instincts').

(α) It is interesting to note that Fechner never made any explicit connection between his 'pleasure principle' and his 'stability principle'. Freud refers to the latter only.

(β) This is only a simplified model. Freud is in fact forced to attempt some account of a whole series of 'qualitative' phenomena which do *not* derive from an immediate external perception: the association of thought-processes with verbal memories ('*langage intérieur*'), memory-images, dreams and hallucinations. He maintains, notwithstanding, that in the last analysis qualities always have their origin in a simultaneous stimulus in the perceptual system. The difficulties encountered as a result of this claim–which leaves so little room, between *langage intérieur* and hallucination, for that domain which, since Sartre, we know as the 'imaginary'–are particularly apparent in 'A Metapsychological Supplement to the Theory of Dreams' (1917*d*) (see also 'Memory-Trace').

(1) FECHNER, G. T. 'Über das Lustprinzip des Handelns', in *Zeitschrift für Philosophie und Philosophische Kritik* (Halle, 1848): a) 1–30 and 163–94. b) 11.

(2) FREUD, S. *The Interpretation of Dreams* (1900*a*): a) G.W., II–III, 605; S.E., V, 574. b) G.W., II–III, 580; S.E., V, 574. c) Cf. G.W., II–III, 621; S.E., V, 616.

(3) FREUD, S. 'Instincts and their Vicissitudes' (1915*c*), G.W., X, 214; S.E., XIV, 120–21.

(4) FREUD, S.: a) G.W., XIII, 69; S.E., XVIII, 63. b) G.W., XIII, 69; S.E., XVIII, 63.

(5) FREUD, S. 'The Economic Problem of Masochism' (1924*c*): a) G.W., XIII, 372–73; S.E., XIX, 160–61. b) G.W., XIII, 372; S.E., XIX, 160.

Preconscious (sb. and adj.)

= D.: das Vorbewusste, vorbewusst.–*Es*.: preconsciente.–*Fr*.: préconscient.– *I*.: preconscio.–*P*.: preconsciente.

I. Term used by Freud in the context of his first topography: as a substantive, it denotes a system of the psychical apparatus that is quite distinct from the unconscious system (*Ucs*.); as an adjective, it qualifies the operations and contents of this preconscious system (*Pcs*.). As these are not currently present in the field of consciousness, they are unconscious in the 'descriptive' sense of the term (α) (see 'Unconscious', definition II), but they differ from the contents of the unconscious system in that they are still in principle accessible to consciousness (e.g. knowledge and memories that are not presently conscious).

Preconscious (sb. and adj.)

From the metapsychological point of view, the preconscious system is governed by the secondary process. It is separated from the unconscious system by the censorship*, which does not permit unconscious contents and processes to pass into the preconscious without their undergoing transformations.

II. In the context of the second topography the term 'preconscious' is used above all adjectivally, to describe what escapes immediate consciousness without being unconscious in the strict sense of the word. As far as *systems* are concerned, the term qualifies contents and processes associated, mainly, with the ego–but also, to some extent, with the super-ego.

The distinction between preconscious and unconscious is a fundamental one for Freud. It is true, however, that apologetic considerations–the need to support the hypothesis of an unconscious psyche in general–led him on occasion to invoke the incontestable existence of a mental life extending beyond the boundaries of the immediate field of consciousness (1*a*). And, if we understand 'unconscious' in what Freud calls the 'descriptive' sense–i.e. as meaning that which lies outside consciousness–the distinction between preconscious and unconscious fades away. This distinction has therefore to be taken essentially as a topographical* (or systematic) and dynamic* one.

In developing his metapsychological views, Freud had established this division very early on (2*a*). In *The Interpretation of Dreams* (1900*a*), the preconscious system lies between the unconscious* system and consciousness*; it is cut off from the former by the censorship, which seeks to prohibit unconscious contents from taking the path towards the preconscious and consciousness; and at its other extremity it commands access to consciousness and motility. In this sense, therefore, consciousness may be looked upon as connected with the preconscious–Freud speaks of the system *Pcs.-Cs.* But in other passages of *The Interpretation* the preconscious and what Freud calls the perception-consciousness system are sharply demarcated off from each other. This ambiguity apparently derives from the fact (later noted by Freud) that consciousness does not lend itself easily to a structural approach (1*b*) (see 'Consciousness'). Freud considers that passage from the preconscious to the conscious is controlled by a 'second censorship', but that this differs from the censorship proper (that between *Ucs.* and *Pcs.*) in that it *distorts* less than it *selects*–its function consists essentially in preventing disturbing thoughts from reaching consciousness. In this way the focussing of attention is facilitated.

The preconscious system is distinguished from the unconscious one by the form of its energy (which is 'bound'*) and by the type of process occurring there (secondary process*). This distinction is not an absolute one, however: just as certain contents of the unconscious (e.g. phantasies) are modified by the secondary process, a point stressed by Freud, so preconscious elements may be governed by the primary process (e.g. the day's residues* in dreams). In a more general way, examination of preconscious operations in their defensive aspect reveals the control exercised by the pleasure principle* and the influence of the primary process.

Freud always put the difference between *Ucs.* and *Pcs.* down to the fact that preconscious ideas are bound to verbal language–to 'word-presentations'*.

It may be added that the relation between the preconscious and the ego* is clearly a very close one. Significantly, when Freud first introduces the preconscious he identifies it with 'our official ego' (2b). Later, when the ego is redefined in the second topography, the preconscious system falls automatically within its confines, although the two are not seen as coextensive, part of the ego being unconscious. Lastly, the newly identified agency of the super-ego* may be shown to have preconscious dimensions.

* * *

What does the notion of the preconscious correspond to in the subject's lived experience, especially in the experience of the treatment? The most frequently given illustration is that of memories which are not immediately conscious but which the subject can recall at will. More generally, the preconscious is understood to designate whatever is *implicitly* present in mental activity without constituting an object of consciousness; this is what Freud means when he defines the preconscious as 'descriptively' unconscious yet accessible to consciousness, whereas the unconscious remains cut off from the conscious realm.

In 'The Unconscious' (1915e) Freud describes the preconscious system as 'conscious knowledge' (*bewusste Kenntnis*) (1c). The choice of terms here is significant in that it stresses distinctiveness from the unconscious: 'knowledge' implies a certain cognisance regarding the subject and his personal world, while 'conscious' points up the fact that the contents and processes in question, though non-conscious, are attached to the conscious from a topographical point of view.

A dynamic validation of the topographical distinction is furnished by the treatment–particularly by a fact that has been underlined by Daniel Lagache: while the subject's acknowledgement of preconscious contents may occasion *reticence*–the reticence which the rule of free association* aims to eliminate– the recognition of unconscious elements runs up against *resistances*, themselves unconscious, which the analysis must gradually interpret and overcome (though, naturally, reticences are for the most part *based* on resistances).

(α) This word of Freud's does not seem to be a very happy choice. It is possible, in fact, while limiting oneself to the level of description alone, and without calling upon any topographical distinctions, to establish differences between what is preconscious and what is unconscious. The formulation 'unconscious in the descriptive sense' is an indiscriminate designation for all psychical contents and processes having in common the sole–negative– characteristic of not being conscious.

(1) Cf. FREUD, S. 'The Unconscious' (1915e): a) G.W., X, 264–65; S.E., XIV, 166–67. b) G.W., X, 291; S.E., XIV, 192. c) G.W., X, 265; S.E., XIV, 167.
(2) Cf. FREUD, S., letter to Fliess dated December 6, 1896: a) *Anf.*, 185; S.E., I, 234. b) *Anf.*, 186; S.E., I, 234–35.

Pregenital

= *D.*: prägenital.–*Es.*: pregenital.–*Fr.*: prégénital.–*I.*: pregenitale.–*P.*: pregenital.

Adjective used to qualify instincts, organisations, fixations, etc., which are related to the period of development preceding the establishment of the primacy of the genital zone (see 'Organisation of the Libido').

The introduction of this term by Freud in 'The Disposition to Obsessional Neurosis' (1913*i*) coincides with that of the idea of a libidinal *organisation* earlier than the one which takes form under the dominance of the genital organs. As we know, Freud had very much earlier recognised the existence of an infantile sexual life prior to the institution of this dominance. As early as his letter to Fliess dated November 14, 1897 (1), he speaks of later-to-be-abandoned sexual zones; and in the *Three Essays on the Theory of Sexuality* (1905*d*), he describes the originally anarchic functioning of the non-genital component instincts.

The adjective 'pregenital' has been applied very widely. In present-day psycho-analytical language it qualifies not only instincts or libidinal organisations but also fixations and regressions to these early modes of psychosexual functioning. We speak of pregenital neuroses when such fixations predominate. The word has even been used substantivally as a denomination for a particular personality-type.

(1) Cf. FREUD, S. *Anf.*, 244–49; S.E., I, 268–71.

Preoedipal

= *D.*: präoedipal.–*Es.*: preedípico.–*Fr.*: préœdipien.–*I.*: preedipico.–*P.*: pré-edipiano.

Qualifies the period of psychosexual development preceding the formation of the Oedipus complex; during this period attachment to the mother predominates in both sexes.

This term makes a very late appearance in Freud's work, at the point at which he found himself obliged to make clear the specificity of feminine sexuality and, in particular, to emphasise the importance, complexity and duration of the primary relationship between the little girl and her mother (1*a*). A phase of this kind occurs also in the case of the little boy, but it is neither as prolonged nor as rich in consequences and it is harder to distinguish from Oedipal love, since the object remains the same.

From the terminological point of view, a clear-cut distinction ought to be made between the terms 'preoedipal' and 'pregenital'*, which are often confused. 'Preoedipal' refers to the interpersonal situation (absence of the Oedipal triangle) while 'pregenital' concerns the type of sexual activity in question.

True, the evolution of the Oedipus complex comes to a close in principle with the institution of the genital organisation, but it is a normative approach to claim a coincidence between genitality and the full object-choice which is a corollary of the Oedipus complex. Experience teaches, in fact, that a satisfactory genital activity is possible short of the culmination of the Oedipus complex, and also that the Oedipal conflict may be worked out in pregenital sexual modes.

Is it strictly permissible to speak of a preoedipal *phase*–i.e. a period characterised exclusively by the two-way relationship of mother and child? Freud did not pass over this question. He remarks that even when the relation with the mother is dominant the father is still present as a 'troublesome rival'; in his view the facts may be equally well summarised by saying 'that the female only reaches the normal positive Oedipus situation after she has surmounted a period before it that is governed by the negative complex' (1b)–a formulation that for Freud has the merit of preserving the idea that the Oedipus complex is the nuclear complex of the neuroses.

Schematically, it may be said that two possible lines of approach are opened up by Freud's rather complex thesis: one may either accentuate the exclusiveness of the dual relationship or else identify signs of the Oedipus complex so early on that it becomes impossible to isolate a strictly preoedipal phase.

An example of the first approach is to be found in the work of Ruth Mack Brunswick (2), which is the outcome of a long collaboration with Freud and which in her opinion represents a faithful expression of his thinking:

a. She holds that the father, though certainly present in the psychological field, is not perceived as a rival.

b. She accords a certain specificity to the preoedipal phase, which she attempts to describe, and attaches particular significance to the predominance of the opposition between activity and passivity*.

By contrast, Melanie Klein's school, on the basis of the analysis of the most primitive phantasies, holds that the father intervenes very early on in the relationship with the mother, as is shown notably by the phantasy of the father's penis being kept within the mother's body (see 'Combined Parents'). It may be asked, however, whether the presence of a third term (phallus) in the primitive mother–child relationship is enough to warrant the description of this period as an 'early Oedipal stage'. The father is not in fact present at this point as an agent of prohibition (see 'Oedipus Complex'). In this context, in examining the Kleinian conception, Jacques Lacan has spoken of a 'preoedipal triangle' in order to designate the mother–child–phallus relation, the third term of which comes into play as the phantasy object of the desire of the mother (3).

(1) FREUD, S. 'Female Sexuality' (1931b): a) Cf. G.W., XIV, 515–37; S.E., XXI, 223–43. b) G.W., XIV, 518; S.E., XXI, 226.

(2) Cf. BRUNSWICK, R. M. 'The Preoedipal Phase of the Libido Development', 1940, in *The Psychoanalytic Reader* (London: Hogarth Press, 1950), 231–53.

(3) Cf. LACAN, J. 'La relation d'objet et les structures freudiennes', *compte-rendu* by J.-B. Pontalis in *Bul. Psycho.*, 1956–57.

Pressure (of the Instinct)

= *D.*: Drang.–*Es.*: presión.–*Fr.*: poussée.–*I.*: spinta.–*P.*: pressão.

Variable quantitative factor which affects each instinct and which accounts, in the last analysis, for the action triggered off in order to achieve satisfaction; even when this satisfaction is passive (being seen, being beaten), the instinct is active in so far as it exerts a 'pressure'.

In the analysis of the concept of instinct to be found at the beginning of 'Instincts and their Vicissitudes' (1915c), Freud considers the instinct's 'pressure' along with its source*, its object* and its aim*. This pressure he defines as follows: 'By the pressure of an instinct we understand its motor factor, the amount of force or the measure of the demand for work which it represents. The characteristic of exercising pressure is common to all instincts; it is in fact their very essence. Every instinct is a piece of activity; if we speak loosely of passive instincts, we can only mean instincts whose *aim* is passive' (1).

This text lays emphasis on two characteristics of instincts:

a. The quantitative factor, which Freud always stresses, and which he sees as a determining element in pathological conflict (see 'Economic').

b. The active character of all instincts. Here Freud's remarks are addressed to Adler, who makes activity the prerogative of one instinct only, the aggressive instinct: 'It appears to me that Adler has mistakenly promoted into a special and self-subsisting instinct what is in reality a universal and indispensable attribute of all instincts–their instinctual and "pressing" character (*das Drängende*), what might be described as their capacity for initiating movement' (2).

The idea that the instincts are to be defined essentially by the pressure that they exert dates from the beginnings of Freud's theoretical thought, which were influenced by Helmholtzian conceptions. The 'Project for a Scientific Psychology' (1950a [1895]) opens by making a basic distinction between external excitations which the organism may evade by resorting to flight, and endogenous ones deriving from somatic factors: 'From these the organism cannot withdraw [...]. It must put up with [maintaining] a store of Q [quantity]' (3). It is the exigencies of life (*die Not des Lebens*) which exert pressure on the organism to accomplish the specific action* which is alone capable of resolving the tension.

(1) FREUD, S., G.W., X, 214–15; S.E., XIV, 122.

(2) FREUD, S. 'Analysis of a Phobia in a Five-Year-Old Boy' (1909b), G.W., VII, 371; S.E., X, 140–41.

(3) FREUD, S. *Anf.*, 381; S.E., I, 357–58.

Primal Phantasies

= *D.*: Urphantasien. – *Es.*: protofantasías. – *Fr.*: fantasmes originaires.
I.: fantasmi (*or* fantasie) originari(e), primari(e). –
P.: protofantasias, *or* fantasias primitivas, *or* originárias.

Typical phantasy structures (intra-uterine existence, primal scene, castration, seduction) which psycho-analysis reveals to be responsible for the organisation of phantasy life, regardless of the personal experiences of different subjects; according to Freud, the universality of these phantasies is explained by the fact that they constitute a phylogenetically transmitted inheritance.

The term '*Urphantasien*' made its first appearance in Freud's work in 1915: 'I call such phantasies – of the observation of sexual intercourse between the parents, of seduction, of castration, and others – "primal phantasies" ' (1). Such so-called primal phantasies are met with very generally in human beings, although it is not possible in every case to point to scenes really experienced by the individual in question. They therefore call, Freud argues, for an explanation in phylogenetic terms – an explanation in which reality is enabled to reassert itself: castration, for example, was actually carried out by the father in the archaic past of humanity: 'It seems to me quite possible that all the things that are told to us today in analysis as phantasy [...] were once real occurrences in the primaeval times of the human family, and that children in their phantasies are simply filling in the gaps in individual truth with prehistoric truth' (2). In other words, what was factual reality in prehistory is said to have become psychical reality*.

Considered in isolation, what Freud means by primal phantasy is difficult to understand; the fact is that the notion is introduced at the end of an extended discussion of the ultimate factors that psycho-analysis can uncover at the origins of neurosis and, more generally speaking, beneath the phantasy life of every individual.

At a very early stage in his work, Freud sought to discover real, primitive events capable of providing the ultimate basis of neurotic symptoms. He gave the name of 'primal scenes' (*Urszenen*) to those actual traumatic events whose memory is sometimes elaborated and concealed by phantasies. One among these was destined to keep the denomination of '*Urszene*' in psycho-analytic terminology, namely the scene of parental coitus which the child is supposed to have witnessed (see 'Primal Scene'). It is significant that these inaugural events are referred to as *scenes*, and that Freud attempted from the outset to identify a limited number of them as archetypal scenarios (3).

This is not the place to plot the development in Freud's thought which runs from this realist conception of 'primal scenes' to the notion of 'primal phantasy': this development, in all its complexity, parallels the working-out of the psycho-analytic concept of phantasy*. It would be over-schematic to assume that Freud simply abandoned his initial approach, which sought the aetiology of the neuroses in circumstantial infantile traumas, in favour of a theory which, since it looked upon phantasy as the forerunner of the symptom, could only accord

331

reality to phantasy in so far as it gave expression–in an imaginary mode–to an instinctual life whose main trends are biologically determined. In point of fact, psycho-analysis endows the phantasy world from the very start with the coherence, organisation and efficacity which are clearly implied, for example, by the term 'psychical reality'.

Between 1907 and 1909 phantasy occasioned a great deal of research on Freud's part, and he now came to accord full recognition to its unconscious effect. He realised, for instance, that phantasy underlies hysterical attacks, which are symbolic expressions of it. He sought to bring to light typical sequences, imaginary scenarios (family romance*) or theoretical constructions (sexual theories of children) whereby the neurotic–and perhaps 'all human beings'–seek an answer to the central enigmas of their existence.

It is remarkable, nevertheless, that the full recognition of phantasy as an autonomous sphere, capable of being explored and having its own specific coherence, does not imply for Freud that the question of the *origin* of phantasy can be shelved. The most striking confirmation of this is to be met with in the analysis of the 'Wolf Man'. Freud here seeks to establish the reality of the scene of observation of parental intercourse by reconstituting it in its minutest detail. When his argument appears to have been shattered by Jung's thesis that such scenes are merely phantasies constructed retrospectively by the adult subject, he still persists in maintaining that perception has furnished the child with the clues and–even more important–he introduces the notion of primal phantasy. This notion responds to two demands: first, the need to find what might be called the bedrock of the event (and, should the contours of this be ill-defined in the history of the individual, through being refracted and, as it were, demultiplied, then we must look further back still–back, if necessary, into the history of the species); secondly, the need to found the structure of the phantasy itself on something other than the event. At times, this latter requirement even led Freud to assert that presubjective structures may predominate over individual experience: 'Wherever experiences fail to fit in with the hereditary schema, they become remodelled in the imagination [...]. It is precisely such cases that are calculated to convince us of the independent existence of the schema. We are often able to see the schema triumphing over the experience of the individual; as when in our present case [the 'Wolf Man'] the boy's father became the castrator and the menace of his infantile sexuality in spite of what was in other respects an inverted Oedipus complex. [...] The contradictions between experience and the schema seem to supply the conflicts of childhood with an abundance of material' (4).

If we consider the themes which can be recognised in primal phantasies (primal scene*, castration*, seduction*), the striking thing is that they have one trait in common: they are all related to the origins. Like collective myths, they claim to provide a representation of and a 'solution' to whatever constitutes a major enigma for the child. Whatever appears to the subject as a reality of such a type as to require an explanation or 'theory', these phantasies dramatise into the primal moment or original point of departure of a history. In the 'primal scene', it is the origin of the subject that is represented; in seduction phantasies, it is the origin or emergence of sexuality; in castration phantasies, the origin of the distinction between the sexes.

In conclusion, it should be noted that the notion of primal phantasy is of central importance for analytic practice and theory. Whatever reservations may be justified as regards the theory of an hereditary, genetic transmission, there is no reason, in our view (α), to reject as equally invalid the idea that structures exist in the phantasy dimension (*la fantasmatique*) which are irreducible to the contingencies of the individual's lived experience.

(α) We have proposed an interpretation of Freud's notion of primal phantasy in our article 'Fantasme originaire, fantasmes des origines, origine du fantasme' (5). The universality of these structures should be related to the universality that Freud accords to the Oedipus complex (q.v.) as a nuclear complex whose structuring *a priori* role he often stressed: 'The content of the sexual life of infancy consists in auto-erotic activity on the part of the dominant sexual components, in traces of object-love, and in the formation of that complex which deserves to be called *the nuclear complex of the neuroses*. [...] The uniformity of the content of the sexual life of children, together with the unvarying character of the modifying tendencies which are later brought to bear upon it, will easily account for the constant sameness which as a rule characterizes the phantasies that are constructed around the period of childhood, irrespective of how greatly or how little real experiences have contributed towards them. It is entirely characteristic of the nuclear complex of infancy that the child's father should be assigned the part of a sexual opponent and of an interferer with auto-erotic sexual activities; and real events are usually to a large extent responsible for bringing this about' (6).

(1) FREUD, S. 'A Case of Paranoia Running Counter to the Psycho-Analytic Theory of the Disease' (1915*f*), G.W., X, 242; S.E., XIV, 269.

(2) FREUD, S. *Introductory Lectures on Psycho-Analysis* (1916–17), G.W., XI, 386; S.E., XVI, 371.

(3) Cf. FREUD, S. Draft M of the Fliess Papers, *Anf.*, 215–19; S.E., I, 250–53.

(4) FREUD, S. 'From the History of an Infantile Neurosis' (1918*b* [1914]), G.W., XII, 155; S.E., XVII, 119–20.

(5) Cf. LAPLANCHE, J. and PONTALIS, J.-B., *Les Temps modernes*, 1964, No. 215, 1833–68. English trans.: 'Fantasy and the Origins of Sexuality'. *I.J.P.*, 1968, 49, 1 *ff*.

(6) FREUD, S. 'Notes upon a Case of Obsessional Neurosis' (1909*d*), G.W., VII, 428*n*.; S.E., X, 208*n*.

Primal Repression

= *D*.: Urverdrängung.–*Es*.: represión primitiva *or* originaria.–*Fr*.: refoulement originaire.– *I*.: rimozione originaria *or* primaria.–*P*.: recalque (*or* recalcamento) primitivo *or* originário.

Hypothetical process described by Freud as the first phase of the operation of repression*. Its effect is the formation of a certain number of unconscious ideas– the 'primal repressed'. The unconscious nuclei constituted in this way then parti- cipate in repression proper: the attraction which they exert upon those contents of consciousness which are due to be repressed joins forces with repulsion operating from the direction of the superior agencies.

It would seem preferable to translate '*Urverdrängung*' by 'primal repression' rather than by the frequently used alternative of 'primary repression'; the prefix *Ur-* is invariably rendered by 'primal' in the cases of *Urphantasie* (primal phantasy*) and *Urszene* (primal scene*).

333

Primal Repression

However obscure the notion of primal repression may be, it is nonetheless a cardinal element in the Freudian theory of repression, and it is to be met with constantly in Freud's work from *The Case of Schreber* (1911c) onwards. Primal repression is postulated above all on the basis of its effects. According to Freud, an idea cannot be repressed without undergoing two simultaneous influences, namely, an action directed towards it from a superior psychical agency and an attraction exerted upon it by contents which are already unconscious. But this of course fails to account for the initial presence of some formations in the unconscious which cannot have been drawn there by other ones; hence the part attributed to a 'primal repression' as distinct from repression proper or after-pressure (*Nachdrängen*). As late as 1926 Freud remarks on the very limited state of knowledge about the nature of primal repression (1a). A number of points may be put forward, however, on the basis of the Freudian hypotheses (α):

a. There is a close connection between primary repression and fixation*. In Freud's study of the Schreber case, the first phase of repression is already described as fixation (2). In this text, however, fixation is conceived of as an 'inhibition in development', whereas elsewhere the term has a less narrowly genetic meaning and denotes not only fixation at a libidinal stage but also the fixation of the instinct to an idea and the 'registration' (*Niederschrift*) of this idea in the unconscious: 'We have reason to assume that there is a *primal repression*, a first phase of repression, which consists in the psychical (ideational) representative* of the instinct being denied entrance into the conscious. With this a *fixation* is established; the representative in question persists unaltered from then onwards and the instinct remains attached to it' (3).

b. Although primal repression is at the origin of the first unconscious formations, its mechanism is not to be explained by a cathexis* on the part of the unconscious; nor does it arise from a withdrawal of cathexis* by the pre-conscious-conscious system, but solely from an anticathexis*: 'It is this [the anticathexis] which represents the permanent expenditure of a primal repression, and which also guarantees the permanence of that repression. Anticathexis is the sole mechanism of primal repression; in the case of repression proper ('after-pressure') there is in addition withdrawal of the *Pcs.* cathexis' (4).

c. As regards the nature of this anticathexis, it remains obscure. Freud considers that it is unlikely to derive from the super-ego, whose formation is subsequent to primal repression. Its origin should probably be sought in very intense archaic experiences: 'It is highly probable that the immediate precipitating causes of primal repressions are quantitative factors such as an excessive degree of excitation and the breaking through of the protective shield against stimuli (*Reizschutz*)' (1b).

(α) An attempt at an interpretation of the notion of primal repression will be found in LAPLANCHE, J. and LECLAIRE, S. 'L'inconscient', *Les Temps Modernes*, 1961, XVII, No. 183.

(1) FREUD, S. *Inhibitions, Symptoms and Anxiety* (1926d): a) Cf. G.W., XIV, 121; S.E., XX, 94. b) G.W., XIV, 121; S.E., XX, 94.

(2) Cf. FREUD, S. 'Psycho-Analytic Notes on an Autobiographical Account of a Case of Paranoia' (1911c), G.W., VIII, 303-4; S.E. XII, 67.

(3) FREUD, S. 'Repression' (1915d), G.W., X, 250; S.E., XIV, 148.

(4) FREUD, S. 'The Unconscious' (1915e), G.W., X, 280; S.E., XIV, 181.

Primal Scene

= *D*.: Urszene.–*Es*: escena primitiva *or* originaria, *or* protoescena.–*Fr*.: scène originaire.–
I.: scena originaria *or* primaria.–*P*.: cena primitiva *or* originária, *or* protocena.

Scene of sexual intercourse between the parents which the child observes, or infers on the basis of certain indications, and phantasises. It is generally interpreted by the child as an act of violence on the part of the father.

The term '*Urszenen*' makes its first appearance in a manuscript of Freud's dating from 1897 (1), where it is used to connote certain traumatic infantile experiences which are organised into scenarios or scenes (see 'Phantasy'); at this point Freud gives no special consideration to the type of scene involving parental intercourse.

In *The Interpretation of Dreams* (1900*a*), there is no mention of primal scenes as such, but Freud does underline the importance of the observation of coitus between the parents in so far as it generates anxiety: 'I have explained this anxiety by arguing that what we are dealing with is a sexual excitation with which their [children's] understanding is unable to cope and which they also, no doubt, repudiate because their parents are involved in it' (2).

Analytic experience was to cause Freud to attribute an increasing importance to the scene where the child happens to witness sexual relations between its parents: 'Among the store of phantasies of all neurotics, and probably of all human beings, this scene is seldom absent' (3). It falls into the category of what Freud calls the primal phantasies* (*Urphantasien*). It is in his account of the case of the 'Wolf Man'–'From the History of an Infantile Neurosis' (1918*b* [1914])– that the observation of parental intercourse is called 'the primal scene'. Basing himself upon this case, Freud brings out different aspects: first, the act of coitus is understood by the child as an aggression by the father in a sado-masochistic relationship; secondly, the scene gives rise to sexual excitation in the child while at the same time providing a basis for castration anxiety; thirdly, the child interprets what is going on, within the framework of an infantile sexual theory, as anal coitus.

In addition, according to Ruth Mack Brunswick, 'the understanding and interest which the child brings to the parental coitus are based on the child's own preoedipal physical experiences with the mother and its resultant desires' (4).

Should we look upon the primal scene as the memory of an actually experienced event or as a pure phantasy? Freud debated this problem with Jung, he debated it in his own mind, and it is raised at several points in the case-history of the Wolf Man. However varied Freud's proposed solutions may seem, they invariably fall within certain bounds. In the first version of *The Wolf Man*, where he is concerned to establish the reality of the primal scene, he is already laying stress on the fact that it is only through a deferred action* (*nachträglich*) that it is grasped and interpreted by the child. At the other end of the scale, when he comes to emphasise the role of retrospective phantasies (*Zurück-phantasien*), he still maintains that reality has at least provided certain clues (noises, animal coitus, etc.) (5).

Primary Identification

Over and above the discussion of the respective dosages of phantasy and reality in the primal scene, what Freud seems to be getting at and what he wants to uphold, particularly against Jung, is the idea that this scene belongs to the (ontogenetic or phylogenetic) past of the individual and that it constitutes a happening which may be of the order of myth but which is *already given* prior to any meaning which is attributed to it after the fact.

(1) Cf. FREUD, S. *Anf.*, 210; S.E., I, 248.

(2) FREUD, S., G.W., II–III, 591; S.E., V, 585.

(3) FREUD, S. 'A Case of Paranoia Running Counter to the Psycho-Analytic Theory of the Disease' (1915*f*), G.W., X, 242; S.E., XIV, 269.

(4) BRUNSWICK, R. M. 'The Preoedipal Phase of the Libido Development' (1940) in *The Psycho-Analytic Reader* (1950), 243.

(5) Cf. FREUD, S., G.W., XII, 137*n*.; S.E., XVII, 103*n*.

Primary Identification

= *D.*: primäre Identifizierung.–*Es.*: identificación primaria.–*Fr.*: identification primaire.–*I.*: identificazione primaria.–*P.*: identificação primária.

Primitive mode of the constitution of the subject on the model of the other person – a mode not dependent upon any prior establishment of a relationship in which the object can at first lay claim to an autonomous existence. Primary identification is closely bound up with the relation known as oral incorporation*.

The notion of primary identification, though now assured of a permanent place in analytic terminology, is used in rather different senses depending on the various authors' reconstructions of the very earliest phases of the individual's existence.

Primary identification is opposed to the secondary identifications that are superimposed on it, not only because of its chronological priority but also because its establishment does not wait upon an object-relationship proper – because it is the 'original form of emotional tie with an object' (1*a*). 'At the very beginning, in the individual's primitive oral stage, object-cathexis and identification are no doubt indistinguishable from each other' (2*a*). This modality of the infant's tie to another person has been described in the main as the first relationship to the *mother*, before the differentiation of ego and *alter ego* has been firmly established. Such a relation would clearly bear the stamp of the process of incorporation. But it should be pointed out that, strictly speaking, it is difficult to ascribe primary identification to an absolutely undifferentiated and objectless state.

It is interesting to note that Freud, on the rare occasions when he in fact uses the expression 'primary identification', does so in order to designate an identification with the *father* in the individual's 'own personal prehistory': the little boy takes the father as an ideal or model (*Vorbild*). This is 'a direct and immediate identification and takes place earlier than any object-cathexis' (2*b*, 1*b*).

336

(1) FREUD, S. *Group Psychology and the Analysis of the Ego* (1921c): a) G.W., XIII, 118; S.E., XVIII, 107. b) G.W., XIII, 115 *ff.*; S.E., XVIII, 105 *ff.*

(2) FREUD, S. *The Ego and the Id* (1923b): a) G.W., XIII, 257; S.E., XIX, 29. b) G.W., XIII, 259; S.E., XIX, 31.

Primary Narcissism, Secondary Narcissism

= *D.*: primärer Narzissmus, sekundärer Narzissmus.–
Es.: narcisismo primario, narcisismo secundario.–
Fr.: narcissisme primaire, narcissisme secondaire.–
I.: narcisismo primario, narcisismo secondario.–
P.: narcisismo primário, narcisismo secundário.

'Primary narcissism' denotes an early state in which the child cathects its own self with the whole of its libido. 'Secondary narcissism' denotes a turning round upon the ego of libido withdrawn from the objects which it has cathected hitherto.

These terms are put to such varied uses in psycho-analytic literature–and even within Freud's own work–that it is impossible to give a more precise yet consistent definition than the one offered above.

I. The expression 'secondary narcissism' is less problematic than 'primary narcissism'. Freud uses it as early as his paper 'On Narcissism: An Introduction' (1914c) to designate such states as schizophrenic narcissism: 'This leads us to look upon the narcissism which arises through the drawing in of object-cathexes as a secondary one, superimposed upon a primary narcissism that is obscured by a number of different influences' (1). For Freud secondary narcissism does not only connote certain extreme forms of regression–it is also a permanent structural feature of the subject: a) economically* speaking, object-cathexes do not supplant ego-cathexes: rather, a veritable balance of energy is struck between these two kinds of cathexis*; b) from the topographical* point of view, the ego-ideal* constitutes a narcissistic formation which is never abandoned.

II. The notion of primary narcissism undergoes extreme variations in sense from one author to the next. The problem here is the definition of a hypothetical stage in the development of the infantile libido, and there are complex debates over the way such a state should be described as well as over its chronological position, while for some theorists its very existence is debatable.

In Freud's work primary narcissism refers in a general way to the first narcissism–that of the child who takes itself as its love-object before choosing external objects. This kind of state is said to correspond to the child's belief in the omnipotence of its thoughts (2).

In attempting to ascertain the exact moment of the establishment of this state we are faced–even in Freud's own case–with a variety of views. Freud's works of the period 1910–15 (3) place the phase in question between the phases of primitive auto-erotism and of object-love; it thus seems to be contemporaneous with the first emergence of a unified subject–in other words, of an ego. Subsequently, with the elaboration of the second topography, Freud uses the term

337

Primary Narcissism, Secondary Narcissism

'primary narcissism' to mean rather a first state of life, prior even to the formation of an ego, which is epitomised by life in the womb (4). The upshot of this development is that the distinction between auto-erotism* and narcissism is eradicated. From a topographical standpoint, it is difficult to see just *what* is supposed to be cathected in primary narcissism thus conceived.

This latter conception of primary narcissism generally prevails today in psychoanalytic thought, with the result that the importance and the implications of the debate are reduced: whether the notion is accepted or rejected, the term is invariably taken to mean a strictly 'objectless'–or at any rate 'undifferentiated' –state, implying no split between subject and external world.

There are two sorts of objections that may be made to this way of understanding narcissism:

a. As regards terminology, this approach loses sight of the reference to an image of the self or to a mirror-type relation which is implicit in the etymology of 'narcissism'. If we are talking about an objectless state, then in our opinion it is inappropriate to describe it as primary narcissism.

b. Empirically, the existence of such a state is highly problematic, and there are some authors who hold that object-relations*–in the shape of a 'primary object-love' (5)–are evident from the very first in the suckling: they thus reject as mythical the notion of a primary narcissism understood as the first, objectless state of extra-uterine existence. For Melanie Klein, there is no justification for speaking of a narcissistic stage because object-relations are contracted from the very beginning; it is only legitimate to evoke narcissistic 'states' characterised by a turning round of libido on to internalised objects.

It seems to us that it is possible, by taking such criticisms as a starting-point, to retrieve the ultimate sense of Freud's intentions when he took the notion of narcissism, which had been brought into psychopathology by Havelock Ellis, and broadened its meaning so that it became an indispensable stage in the development from the anarchic, auto-erotic functioning of the component instincts* to the object-choice*. There seems to be no reason why 'primary narcissism' should not designate an early phase, or formative moments, marked by the emergence of a first adumbration of the ego* and its immediate libidinal cathexis. This is not to say that this first narcissism represents the earliest state of the human being, nor, economically speaking, that such a predominance of self-love rules out any object-cathexis (see 'Narcissism').

(1) Freud, S., G.W., X, 140; S.E., XIV, 75.

(2) Cf. Freud, S. *Totem and Taboo* (1912–13), *passim.*

(3) Cf. Freud, S. 'Psycho-Analytic Notes on an Autobiographical Account of a Case of Paranoia (Dementia Paranoides)' (1911c); *Totem and Taboo* (1912–13); and 'On Narcissism: An Introduction' (1914c).

(4) Cf. Freud, S. *Introductory Lectures on Psycho-Analysis* (1916–17), G. W., XI, 431–32; S.E., XVI, 415–16.

(5) Cf. Balint, M. 'Early Developmental States of the Ego. Primary Object-Love' (1937), in *Primary Love and Psychoanalytic Technique* (London: Hogarth Press, 1952), 103–8.

Primary Process /Secondary Process

= *D*.: Primärvorgang/Sekundärvorgang.–*Es*.: proceso primario/proceso secundario.–
Fr.: processus primaire/ processus secondaire.–*I*.: processo primario/processo secondario.–
P.: processo primário/processo secundário.

The two modes of functioning of the psychical apparatus as specified by Freud. They are to be distinguished radically:

a. from the *topographical* point of view, in that the primary process is characteristic of the unconscious system, while the secondary process typifies the preconscious-conscious system;

b. from the *economico-dynamic* point of view: in the case of the primary process, psychical energy flows freely, passing unhindered, by means of the mechanisms of condensation and displacement, from one idea to another and tending to completely recathect the ideas attached to those satisfying experiences which are at the root of unconscious wishes (primitive hallucination); in the case of the secondary process, the energy is bound at first and then it flows in a controlled manner: ideas are cathected in a more stable fashion while satisfaction is postponed, so allowing for mental experiments which test out the various possible paths leading to satisfaction.

The opposition between the primary process and the secondary process corresponds to that between the pleasure principle and the reality principle.

Freud's distinction between the primary and secondary processes is contemporaneous with his discovery of the unconscious processes, and it is in fact the first theoretical expression of this discovery. It is to be met with as from the 'Project for a Scientific Psychology' (1950*a* [1895]); Freud developed it in Chapter VII of *The Interpretation of Dreams* and it always remained an unchanging co-ordinate of his thought.

The study of symptom-formation and the analysis of dreams led Freud to recognise a type of mental functioning that was very different from the thought-processes which had been the object of traditional psychological observation. This method of functioning, which had its own mechanisms and which was regulated by specific laws, was particularly well illustrated by dreaming: where classical psychology had asserted that dreams were characterised by their absence of meaning, Freud now maintained rather that they exhibited a constant sliding of meaning. The mechanisms which are in operation here, according to Freud, are displacement*, on the one hand, whereby an often apparently insignificant idea comes to be invested with all the psychical value, depth of meaning and intensity originally attributed to another one; and, on the other hand, condensation*, a process which enables all the meanings in several chains of association to converge on a single idea standing at their point of intersection. A further instance of this specifically unconscious type of functioning is afforded by the overdetermination* of the symptom.

It was also the model of the dream which caused Freud to postulate that the aim of the unconscious process was to establish a perceptual identity* by the shortest available route–i.e. by means of the hallucinatory reproduction of those

339

ideas upon which the original experience of satisfaction* has conferred a special value.

It is by way of contrast with this mode of mental functioning that the operations traditionally described by psychology–waking thought, attention, judgement, reasoning, controlled action–may be referred to as *secondary* processes. In the secondary process, it is thought-identity* that is sought: 'Thinking must concern itself with the connecting paths between ideas, without being led astray by the *intensities* of those ideas' (1). From this standpoint, the secondary process constitutes a modification of the primary one. It exercises a regulatory function made possible by the establishment of the ego, whose prime role is to inhibit the primary process (see 'Ego'). This does not mean, however, that all the processes in which the ego plays a part should be looked upon as secondary ones: Freud drew attention from the outset to the way in which the ego can come under the sway of the primary process, particularly in the case of the pathological mode of defence. The primary character of this type of defence is indicated clinically by its compulsive nature or, in economic terms, by the fact that the energy in play seeks discharge in a total and immediate fashion, via the most direct path (α): 'Wishful cathexis to the point of hallucination [and] complete generation of unpleasure which involves a complete expenditure of defence are described by us as *psychical primary processes*; by contrast, those processes which are only made possible by a good cathexis of the ego, and which represent a moderation of the foregoing, are described as *psychical secondary processes*' (2a).

The opposition between primary and secondary processes corresponds to that between the two ways in which psychical energy circulates, according to whether it is 'free' or 'bound'*. It should also be seen as parallel with the contrast between the pleasure principle and the reality principle.

*　　*　　*

The terms 'primary' and 'secondary' have temporal and even genetic implications which increase in force with the advent of Freud's second theory of the psychical apparatus, where the ego is defined as the outcome of a gradual process of differentiation from the id*.

These overtones are nonetheless present even in Freud's first theoretical model. In the 'Project', for instance, the two sorts of process appear to correspond not only to modes of functioning on the level of ideas, but also to two *stages* in the diversification of the neuronal apparatus–and even in the development of the organism. Freud distinguishes between a 'primary function'–in which the organism and the specialised part of it known as the neuronal system work on the model of the 'reflex arc', with a total and immediate discharge of the quantity of excitation–and a 'secondary function' involving flight from external stimuli but presupposing a certain storing of energy to meet the need for the specific action which is alone capable of putting an end to endogenous tension: 'All the functions of the nervous system can be comprised either under the aspect of the primary function or of the secondary one imposed by the exigencies of life [*Not des Lebens*]' (2b). It was inevitable that Freud should endeavour to fulfil what he considered to be a fundamental scientific requirement–that he should try to insert his discovery of primary and secondary processes of the mind into a biological framework involving types of response of

340

the organism to an influx of stimuli. The outcome of this attempt, however, was that Freud made a number of claims that it would be hard to validate from a biological point of view. A case in point is his conception of the reflex arc, deemed to transmit the same quantity of excitation at its motor extremity as it has taken in at its sensory one. Another example is afforded, at a profounder level, by the notion that an organism could go through a stage in which it functioned solely according to the principle of discharging all the energy that it receives completely: the paradoxical implication of this hypothesis is that it is only the 'exigencies of life' which make it possible for the living being to come into existence at all (see 'Principle of Constancy').

It will be noticed, however, that even at this point, where Freud has his closest commitment to his biological frame of reference, he does not equate the organism's primary and secondary 'functions' with the primary and secondary 'processes', which he sees as two modalities of the functioning of the psyche or ψ system (2c).

(α) In the 'Project' Freud also refers to the primary process as a 'full' or total (*voll*) process.

(1) FREUD, S., G.W., II–III, 607–8; S.E., V, 602.
(2) FREUD, S. 'Project for a Scientific Psychology' (1950a [1895]): a) *Anf.*, 411; S.E., I, 326–27. b) *Anf.*, 381; S.E., I, 297. c) *Anf.*, cf. 409–11; S.E., I, cf. 324–27.

Principle of Constancy

= *D.*: Konstanzprinzip.–*Es.*: principio de constancia.–*Fs.*: principe de constance.–
I.: principio di costanza.–*P.*: princípio de constância.

Principle according to which the psychical apparatus tends to keep the quantity of excitation in itself at as low a level – or, at any rate, as constant a level – as possible. Constancy is achieved on the one hand through the *discharge* of the energy already present, and, on the other hand, by *avoidance* of whatever might increase the quantity of excitation and *defence* against any such increase that does occur.

The principle of constancy is a cornerstone of Freudian economic* theory. It plays a part from Freud's earliest works, and he constantly makes the implicit assumption that it controls the functioning of the psychical apparatus. The thesis is that this apparatus endeavours to keep all excitations in itself at a constant level. This it succeeds in doing, as far as external stimuli are concerned, by setting avoidance mechanisms in motion. As regards increases in tension of internal origin, the same result is achieved by means of the mechanisms of defence and discharge (abreaction). The most diverse manifestations of mental life, when reduced to their ultimate economic form, are to be understood as more or less successful attempts to maintain or restore this constancy.

The principle of constancy is closely allied with the pleasure principle, in that unpleasure can be seen in an economic perspective as the subjective perception of an increase of tension, and pleasure as corresponding to a decrease in it.

341

Principle of Constancy

But the relationship between subjective sensations of pleasure-unpleasure and the economic processes that are said to underlie them appeared to Freud, on reflection, to be a highly complicated one: it may happen, for instance, that the sensation of pleasure accompanies an *increase* in tension. The upshot is that the relation between the principle of constancy and the pleasure principle must be defined in terms other than those of a pure and simple equivalence between the two (see 'Pleasure Principle').

*   *   *

When Freud–as well as Breuer–postulates a law of constancy as part of the groundwork of psychology, he is only confronting in his turn a requirement which was very widely acknowledged in the scientific circles of the latter part of the nineteenth century–namely, the call to extend the most general principles of physics, in so far as these stand at the very basis of all science, to psychology and psychophysiology. One could find a large number of attempts to demonstrate the action of a law of constancy in psychophysiology–attempts both prior to Freud's (most importantly, Fechner's claim of universality for his 'principle of stability' (1)) and contemporaneous with it.

But–as Freud himself was aware–the apparent simplicity of the concept of constancy is deceptive, for 'the most various things might be understood by it' (2*a*).

Psychology, borrowing the idea from physics, has invoked a principle of constancy in a number of senses. These may be schematically outlined as follows:

a. Some authors restrict themselves to the application to psychology of the principle of conservation of energy. According to this principle, the sum of energy in any closed system remains constant. To submit the data of mental functioning to such a rule is equivalent to postulating the existence of a psychical or nervous energy whose quantity remains invariable irrespective of the different transformations and displacements that it undergoes. The enunciation of this law clears the way for the translation of psychological facts into the language of energy. It should be borne in mind that this principle, which is basic to the economic theory in psycho-analysis, does not operate on the same plane as that regulatory principle which Freud calls the principle of constancy.

b. The principle of constancy is sometimes understood in a sense that makes it analogous to the second principle of thermodynamics, which states that in a closed system the differences between levels of energy tend to even out, the ideal final state of affairs being one of equilibrium. Fechner's 'principle of stability' has comparable implications. In the case of this kind of parallel, however, it has to be made clear exactly what system is involved: we have to decide whether the law applies to the psychical apparatus and the energy circulating within it, or whether, on the other hand, it applies to the system constituted by the psychical apparatus and the organism together–or even to the organism-environment system. Depending on which of these options is taken, in fact, the notion of the tendency towards equalisation takes on quite contrary meanings. Thus, if we accept the third possibility, then the outcome of this tendency is the reduction of internal energy in the organism to a level which implies the latter's return to a non-organic state (see 'Nirvana Principle').

c. Lastly, the principle of constancy may be understood as a principle of self-regulation–in other words, the system in question is said to operate in such a

342

way that it seeks to keep the difference between its level of energy and that obtaining in the environment constant. From this point of view, the principle of constancy amounts to an assertion that there exist comparatively closed systems (either the psychical apparatus or the organism as a whole) which tend to maintain and to restore their specific configuration and energy level despite all exchanges with the surrounding world. The idea of constancy taken in this sense has been fruitfully compared to the notion of homoeostasis, as developed by the physiologist Cannon (α).

* * *

It is difficult to fix on one or another of these multiple possible meanings of the principle of constancy as being the sense in which Freud understood it. The formulations of the principle which he proposes–and with which, as he notes himself, he is dissatisfied (3a)–are often ambiguous and sometimes even self-contradictory: '. . . the mental apparatus endeavours to keep the quantity of excitation present in it as low as possible or at least to keep it constant' (3b). Freud evidently looks upon 'the effort to reduce, to keep constant or to remove internal tension due to stimuli' (3c) as manifestations of a single principle. Yet the trend of the internal energy in a system to fall to zero-point is scarcely comparable with the peculiar tendency of living organisms to maintain an equilibrium with their surroundings at a constant (and possibly very high) level. This second tendency, in fact, may, depending upon the circumstances, just as easily take the form of a search for excitation as a discharge of it.

The only way to clear up the contradictions, inconsistencies and conflations of meaning which beset Freud's pronouncements on this question is to try and bring out–more clearly than Freud did himself–the nature of the empirical factors and the theoretical requirements which occasioned his more or less successful endeavours to put forward a psycho-analytic law of constancy.

* * *

The principle of constancy is part of the theoretical apparatus which Breuer and Freud constructed in common around the period between 1892 and 1895 in order to account, in particular, for the phenomena which they had encountered in hysteria: they related the symptoms to defective abreaction and sought the basis of the cure in a sufficient discharge of affect. Nevertheless, if we compare two theoretical texts which were not co-authored–each bearing the respective signature of one of the two men–it becomes evident that a distinct difference of perspective lies beneath their seeming concord.

Breuer, in his 'Theoretical' contribution to the *Studies on Hysteria* (1895d), considers the conditions of the functioning of a relatively autonomous system– namely, the central nervous system. He distinguishes between two sorts of energy active in this system: a quiescent energy or 'intracerebral tonic excitation', and a kinetic energy which circulates in the apparatus. The principle of constancy regulates the sphere of tonic excitation only: '. . . there exists in the organism a "tendency to keep intracerebral excitation constant" ' (4). Three essential points must be emphasised here:

First, the law of constancy is understood by Breuer as implying an optimum– a favourable level of energy which has to be restored by discharges when a

343

tendency to increase occurs, but also by recharging (particularly in the form of sleep) in the event of too great a fall.

Secondly, constancy may be threatened either by generalised and uniform states of excitation or else by an unequal distribution of excitation inside the system (affects).

Lastly, the existence and restoration of an optimum level are the preconditions of the free circulation of kinetic energy. Provided that thought activity functions without hindrance, and that associations of ideas come about in normal fashion, then the undisturbed self-regulation of the system is assured.

Freud, too, studies the conditions of the functioning of the neuronal apparatus – in his 'Project for a Scientific Psychology' (1950a [1895]). But it is not a principle of constancy in the sense of the maintenance of a certain energy-level that he posits to begin with: instead, he lays down a principle of neuronal inertia* according to which neurones tend to divest themselves of the quantity of excitations, to offload it completely. Further on in the 'Project', it is true, Freud assumes that a tendency to constancy does exist, but he sees this as a 'secondary function imposed by the exigencies of life', that is, as a mere modification of the principle of inertia: '. . . the nervous system is obliged to abandon its original trend to inertia (that is, to bringing the level [of $Q\dot{\eta}$] to zero. It must put up with [maintaining] a store of $Q\dot{\eta}$ sufficient to meet the demand for a specific action. Nevertheless, the manner in which it does this shows that the same trend persists, modified into an endeavour at least to keep the $Q\dot{\eta}$ as low as possible and to guard against any increase of it – that is, to keep it constant' (2b). Freud maintains that the principle of inertia regulates the primary type of functioning of the apparatus, the circulation of free energy*. As for the law of constancy – even though it is not formulated explicitly as an autonomous principle – it corresponds to the secondary process in which the energy is bound, or, in other words, kept at a determinate level.

It should be plain by now that, although Breuer and Freud may appear at first sight to share a conceptual apparatus, their respective theoretical models are in point of fact radically at odds. Breuer's is evolved in a biological perspective which foreshadows modern conceptions of homoeostasis and self-regulating systems (β). Freud's constructions, on the other hand, might well seem absurd from the standpoint of the biological sciences, in that they claim to *deduce* an organism – with its vital capacities, its adaptive functions and its energy constants – from a principle which is the very negation of any sustained difference in level.

This disparity between Breuer's views and Freud's – which was, moreover, never acknowledged explicitly (γ) – is nevertheless rich in lessons. The fact is that what Freud sees as regulated by the principle of inertia is a type of process whose existence he had been led to postulate as a result of his very recent discovery of the unconscious. This is the primary process*, described in the 'Project' on the basis of special instances such as dreams and the formation of symptoms, particularly as met with in hysteria. The primary process is characterised essentially by an unhindered flow – by the 'ease with which $Q\dot{\eta}$ is displaced' (2c). What is observed at the level of psychological analysis is that one idea can end up by substituting itself for another one completely, taking over all its properties and efficacity: 'The *hysteric*, who weeps at A, is quite unaware that he is doing so on account of the association A-B, and B itself plays no part at all in his psychical life. The symbol has in this case taken the place of the *thing* entirely' (2*d*). The phenomenon of a total displacement of meaning from one idea to another, and the clinical observation of the intensity and efficacity exhibited by the substitute idea – these are the data which seem to Freud to be explained in a perfectly natural way by the economic terms of the principle of inertia. The free circulation of meaning and the discharge of energy to the point of complete evacuation are seen by Freud as one and the same. Obviously, such a process is quite opposed to the maintenance of constancy.

The trend to constancy is invoked in the 'Project', certainly, but it is looked upon as a force which simply moderates and inhibits the basic tendency towards absolute discharge. It is to the ego that the task falls of binding psychical energy and keeping it at a higher level; that this should be the function of the ego is attributable to the fact that the ego itself constitutes an ensemble of neurones or ideas in which a constant level of cathexis is maintained (see 'Ego').

The relationship between the primary and the secondary processes should not therefore be looked upon as an actual succession in the order of life, as though the role of the principle of constancy, in the history of organisms, took over from the principle of inertia; this relationship only obtains in the context of a psychical apparatus in which Freud, from the start, points to the presence of two kinds of process, two principles of mental functioning (δ).

It will be recalled that Chapter VII of *The Interpretation of Dreams* (1900*a*) is based upon this distinction. Freud there pursues the hypothesis of 'a primitive psychical apparatus whose activities are regulated by an effort to avoid an accumulation of excitation and to maintain itself so far as possible without excitation' (5*a*). This trend, which is characterised by the 'free discharge of the quantities of excitation', Freud calls the 'principle of unpleasure'. It regulates the functioning of the unconscious system, whereas the preconscious-conscious system operates in accordance with a second mode, in that 'by means of the cathexes emanating from it, [it] succeeds in *inhibiting* this [free] discharge and in transforming the cathexis into a quiescent one, no doubt with a simultaneous raising of its potential' (5*b*). In Freud's later work, the antithesis between the modes of operation of the two systems is as a rule assimilated with the opposition between the pleasure principle* and the reality principle*. Considerations of conceptual clarity, however, urge that a distinction be preserved between a tendency to reduce the quantity of excitation to zero on the one hand, and a tendency to keep this quantity at a constant level on the other; to meet this demand, the pleasure principle must be seen as correlative with the former trend, and the maintenance of constancy treated as a corollary of the action of the reality principle.

*   *   *

Only with *Beyond the Pleasure Principle* (1920*g*) does Freud put forward an explicit formulation of the principle of constancy. There are several points to be noted here:

a. The principle of constancy is posited as the economic foundation of the pleasure principle (3*d*).

Principle of Constancy

b. The definitions which Freud proposes are all ambiguous in that the tendency towards an absolute reduction and the trend to constancy are treated as identical.

c. At the same time, the tendency to zero-point–now referred to as the Nirvana principle*–is considered to be fundamental and the other principles to be mere modifications of it.

d. Although Freud appears to consider that a sole tendency, whatever the modifications it undergoes, is at work in 'mental life, and perhaps [in] nervous life in general' (3e), he simultaneously introduces a basic and irreducible dualism on the plane of the instincts–namely, that between the death instincts, which tend towards the absolute reduction of tension, and the life instincts* which seek on the contrary to maintain and create vital unities presupposing a high level of tension. This dualism–best understood, as not a few authors have pointed out, as a dualism of *principles*–becomes clearer in the light of its comparison with certain fundamental oppositions which are permanent features of Freudian thought: bound energy and free energy*; release and binding* (*Entbindung/Bindung*); primary process and secondary process* (see also 'Death Instincts').

On the other hand, Freud never clearly elucidated the antithesis which ought logically to parallel the above distinctions on the plane of the economic principles of mental functioning. Although he did hint at such an antithesis in the 'Project', in the form of his contrast between a principle of inertia and a trend to constancy, this never came in the later work to constitute the explicit point of reference which might perhaps have served to dispel the confusion still surrounding the notion of the principle of constancy.

(α) In his book *The Wisdom of the Body* (1932), W. B. Cannon gave the name of homoeostasis to the physiological processes by which means the body tends to keep the composition of the bloodstream constant. He describes this process as it operates in the cases of the different components of the blood–water, salt, sugar, proteins, fat, calcium, oxygen, hydrogen ions (acid-base balance)–and in the case of the blood temperature. This list could naturally be extended to cover other elements (minerals, vitamins, hormones, etc.).

Thus the idea of homoeostasis clearly implies a dynamic equilibrium characteristic of the human body, and in no way a reduction of tension to a minimum level.

(β) It will be remembered that Breuer collaborated with the neurophysiologist Hering in his work on one of the most important self-regulating systems in the organism–respiration.

(γ) There are clear indications that the two collaborators had difficulty in reaching agreement over a definition of the principle of constancy. These are to be found in the extant succession of versions of the 'Preliminary Communication' to the *Studies on Hysteria*.

In 'On the Theory of Hysterical Attacks' (1940d [1892]), a manuscript sent to Breuer for his approval, and in a letter to Breuer dated June 29, 1892 (6), Freud speaks of a tendency to 'keep constant' what may be called the 'sum of excitation' in the nervous system.

In the lecture given by Freud ten days after the publication of the 'Preliminary Communication', and published under the same title in the *Wiener medizinische Presse* (1893h), Freud only mentions a tendency 'to diminish the sum of excitation' (7).

And finally, in the definitive version of the 'Preliminary Communication' as it appears in the *Studies*, the principle of constancy is not put forward.

(δ) The problems with which Breuer and Freud are struggling to come to grips at this point may be made somewhat clearer if we separate out a number of different spheres:

a. The *organism*, regulated by homoeostatic mechanisms and therefore functioning solely in accordance with the principle of constancy. Such a principle holds good not only for the organism as a whole but also for the specialised apparatus of the nervous system, which cannot

346

operate without the maintenance or restoration of constant conditions. This is what Breuer has in mind when he speaks of a constant level of intracerebral tonic excitation.

b. The human *psyche*, which is the object of Freud's researches. This second sphere may be further broken down into:

(i) The unconscious processes which, in the last reckoning, imply an unlimited mobility of meanings, or, to put this into terms of energy, a completely unfettered discharge of the quantity of excitation.

(ii) The secondary process, as identified in the preconscious-conscious system, presupposing a binding of the energy undertaken by a particular 'form' which tends to maintain and to restore its boundaries and its level of energy: the ego.

Broadly speaking, therefore, it might be said that Breuer and Freud simply do not have the same reality in view: while Breuer poses the problem of the neurophysiological conditions of normal psychical functioning, Freud is concerned with how the primary mental process in man comes to be limited and regulated.

Nevertheless, an ambiguity persists in Freud's approach – and this is true of the 'Project' as much as of later works such as *Beyond the Pleasure Principle*. For there is a persistent incompatibility between the derivation of the secondary psychical process from the primary one and the postulation of a quasi-mythical genesis of the organism as a permanent form, as a being tending to affirm its existence from a starting-point in a purely inorganic state.

It is our view that this fundamental ambiguity in Freudian thought cannot be interpreted unless the ego itself is thought of as a 'form' or *Gestalt* constructed on the model of the organism, or, to put it another way, as an actualised metaphor of the organism.

(1) Cf. FECHNER, G. T. *Einige Ideen zur Schöpfungs- und Entwicklungsgeschichte der Organismen* (Leipzig: Breitkopf und Härtel, 1873).

(2) FREUD, S.: a) *Anf.*, 148; *Origins*, 137. b) *Anf.*, 381; S.E., I, 297. c) *Anf.*, 425; S.E., I, 342. d) *Anf.*, 425; S.E., I, 349.

(3) FREUD, S. *Beyond the Pleasure Principle* (1920*g*): a) Cf. G.W., XIII, 68; S.E., XVIII, 62. b) G.W., XIII, 5; S.E., XVIII, 9. c) G.W., XIII, 60; S.E., XVIII, 55–56. d) Cf.G.W.,XIII, 5; S.E., XVIII, 9. e) G.W., XIII, 60; S.E., XVIII, 55–56.

(4) BREUER, J., 1st German edition, 171; S.E., II, 197.

(5) FREUD, S.: a) G.W., II–III, 604; S.E., V, 598. b) G.W., II–III, 605; S.E., V, 489.

(6) Cf. FREUD, S., G.W., XVII, 12; S.E., I, 147.

(7) FREUD, S., S.E., III, 36.

Principle of (Neuronal) Inertia

= *D.*: Prinzip der Neuronenträgheit *or* Trägheitsprinzip. –
Es.: principio de inercia neurónica. – *Fr.*: principe d'inertie neuronique. –
I.: principio dell'inerzia neuronica. – *P.*: princípio de inércia neurônica.

Principle of the functioning of the neuronal system postulated by Freud in his 'Project for a Scientific Psychology' (1950*a* [1895]): neurones tend to divest themselves completely of the quantities of energy which they receive.

In his 'Project for a Scientific Psychology' Freud enunciates a principle of inertia as the law governing the functioning of what at this time he calls the neuronal system. In his subsequent metapsychological writings he does not readopt this expression. The notion belongs therefore to the period in which the Freudian conception of the psychical apparatus is being worked out. It will be

Principle of (Neuronal) Inertia

recalled that in the 'Project' Freud describes a neuronal system on the basis of two fundamental notions–the notion of the neurone and the notion of quantity. The quantity is supposed to circulate in the system, and to take some particular path through the successive bifurcations of the neurones, in accordance with the resistance ('contact-barrier') or the facilitation* which it encounters in passing from one neuronal element to another. There is an obvious analogy to be drawn between this account in the language of neurophysiology and Freud's subsequent descriptions of the psychical apparatus which also bring two factors into play–ideas organised in chains or systems, and psychical energy.

The interest presented by this old idea of the principle of inertia lies in the fact that it helps to clarify the meaning of the basic economic principles which regulate the working of the psychical apparatus.

* * *

In physics, inertia consists in the fact that 'a point which is unaffected by any mechanical force, and which is the object of no action, permanently conserves a motion constant in both velocity and direction (including the case where the motion is zero, i.e. where the body in question is at rest)' (1).

a. The principle laid down by Freud concerning the neuronal system is certainly comparable with the law of inertia in physics; Freud formulates his principle in the following terms: 'Neurones tend to divest themselves of Q [quantity]' (2).

The model for this type of functioning is provided by a particular conception of reflex movement: in the reflex arc, the quantity of excitation received by the sensory neurone is deemed to be completely discharged at the motor extremity. More generally, Freud's neuronal apparatus behaves as though it tended not only to discharge excitations but also to draw itself away, subsequently, from the sources of the stimuli. As far as internal excitations are concerned, the principle of inertia, short of radical modification, does not operate; in fact a specific action* is needed to assure an adequate discharge, and such an action, if it is to be carried through, demands a certain stocking of energy.

b. The relationship between Freud's use of the idea of the principle of inertia and its use in physics remains a fairly loose one:

(i) In physics, inertia is a property of bodies in motion; for Freud, on the other hand, it is not a property of the *mobile* element under consideration– namely, excitation–but rather an active tendency of the *system* in which the quantities circulate.

(ii) In physics, the principle of inertia is a universal law which *defines* the phenomena in question: it can be shown to hold good even in cases which seem to the superficial observer to constitute exceptions to the rule. The motion of a projectile, for instance, tends apparently to come to a stop of its own accord, but physics teaches us that it really stops only as a result of air-resistance; once we recognise the effect of this contingent factor, we see that the validity of the law of inertia is in no way put in doubt. In Freud's transposition of this notion into psychophysiological terms, however, the principle of inertia is no longer constitutive of the natural order in view, and it is liable to be countered by another mode of functioning which limits the range of its applicability. The fact is that the formation of groups of neurones with a constant charge implies the action of a law–the law of constancy*–whose dominance runs counter to the free flow of energy. It is only by using a form of deduction which appeals to a *purpose* that Freud is able to claim that the principle of inertia employs a certain amount of accumulated energy for its own ends.

(iii) This shift from mechanism to purpose may also be seen in the fact that Freud infers, on the basis of the principle of discharge of excitation, that there exists a tendency to avoid all sources of excitation.

c. It is easy to see why Freud, in so far as he was committed to maintaining some level of biological credibility, found himself obliged to modify the principle of inertia quite considerably. For how could an organism functioning according to this principle survive? How could it even *exist*, for that matter, for the very concept of an organism implies the permanent maintenance of an energy-level different from that obtaining in the environment.

*   *   *

In our opinion, however, the contradictions which can be shown to exist in Freud's notion of the principle of neuronal inertia should not be used to discredit the basic intuition which lies behind his evocation of it. This intuition is bound up with the actual discovery of the unconscious; what Freud expresses in terms of the free circulation of energy in the neurones is simply a transposition of his clinical experience of that free circulation of meaning which is characteristic of the primary process*.

To this extent the Nirvana principle*, as it appeared very much later in Freud's work at a decisive moment in his thought (the 'turning-point' of the 'twenties), may legitimately be seen as a reaffirmation of the fundamental insight which already lay behind the enunciation of the principle of inertia.

(1) LALANDE, A. *Vocabulaire technique et critique de la philosophie* (Paris: P.U.F., 1951).
(2) FREUD, S., *Anf.*, 380; S.E., I, 296.

Projection

= *D*.: Projektion.–*Es*.: proyección.–*Fr*.: projection.–*I*.: proiezione.–*P*.: projeção.

I. Term used in a very general sense in neurophysiology and psychology to designate the operation whereby a neurological or psychological element is displaced and relocated in an external position, thus passing either from centre to periphery or from subject to object. Used in this way, 'projection' has a number of rather varied connotations (see commentary below).

II. In the properly psycho-analytic sense: operation whereby qualities, feelings, wishes or even 'objects'*, which the subject refuses to recognise or rejects in himself, are expelled from the self and located in another person or thing. Projection so understood is a defence of very primitive origin which may be seen at work especially in paranoia, but also in 'normal' modes of thought such as superstition.

Projection

I. The term 'projection' is in very wide use today, as much in psychology as in psycho-analysis. It is understood in a variety of ways which–as has often been noted–are badly demarcated. It may be helpful if–confining ourselves at first to the semantic plane–we enumerate the term's different connotations:

a. In *neurology*, 'projection' is used in a sense derived from the one it has in geometry, where it designates a point-by-point correspondence between, say, a figure in space and a figure in a plane. Hence a neurologist may say that a particular cerebral area constitutes the projection of a particular (receptor or effector) somatic apparatus: the correlation in question may be established, in accordance with specific laws, either point by point or from structure to structure, and it may operate in a centripetal direction as easily as in a centrifugal one.

b. A second use of the word derives from the above but specifically implies a movement from centre to periphery. In the language of psychophysiology, it has been said, for instance, that olfactory sensations are located in the receiving apparatus by virtue of projection. Freud has the same sense in mind when he speaks of 'a sensation of itching or stimulation which is centrally conditioned and projected on to the peripheral erotogenic zone' (1). And from a similar standpoint we may follow English and English in defining 'eccentric' projection as the 'localisation of a sense datum at the position in space of the stimulating object, rather than at the point of stimulation on the body' (2a).

In *psychology*, 'projection' may denote the following processes:

c. The subject perceives his surroundings and responds according to his own interests, aptitudes, habits, long-standing or transient emotional states, expectations, wishes, etc. This type of correlation between *Innenwelt* and *Umwelt* is one of the contributions of modern biology and psychology, under the influence, notably, of Gestalt psychology. It is corroborated at all levels of behaviour: the animal selects special stimuli from its field of perception which govern its entire behaviour; a particular businessman sees all objects in terms of what can be bought and sold ('occupational distortion'); a good-humoured person is inclined to view things through 'rose-tinted spectacles'; and so on. Less superficially, essential structures or characteristics of the personality are liable to emerge in manifest behaviour. This fact furnishes the basic principle of so-called projective techniques: a child's drawings reveal its personality; in standardised tests–that is, in projective tests proper (e.g. Rorschach, T.A.T.)–the subject is confronted by relatively unstructured situations and ambiguous stimuli, which allows us 'to read off, according to the rules of decoding suited to the proposed type of material and of creative activity, certain traits of his character and certain patterns of organisation of his behaviour and emotions' (3).

d. The subject shows by his attitude that he has identified one person with another: it may be said in such a case that he is 'projecting' the image of his father, for example, on to his employer. 'Projection' is being employed here as a rather inappropriate designation for the psycho-analytic discovery correctly referred to as 'transference'*.

e. The subject identifies himself with other people or, conversely, he identifies people, animate or inanimate beings with himself. It is thus commonly asserted that the novel-reader projects himself on to a particular hero or–in the obverse sense–that La Fontaine, for example, projected anthropomorphic feelings or reasoning into the animals of his *Fables*. Processes of this type would be more aptly placed under the head of what psycho-analysis calls 'identification'*.

f. The subject attributes tendencies, desires, etc., to others that he refuses to recognise in himself: the racist, for instance, projects his own faults and unacknowledged inclinations on to the group he reviles. This type of projection, which English and English call 'disowning projection' (2*b*), seems to come closest to the Freudian sense of the term.

II. Freud called upon projection to account for a variety of manifestations of normal and pathological psychology:

a. Projection was first discovered in *paranoia**. As early as 1895–96 Freud devoted two brief texts (4*a*) to this affection, as well as Chapter III of 'Further Remarks on the Neuro-Psychoses of Defence' (1896*b*). Projection is described here as a primary defence which misuses a normal mechanism, namely, the search for an external source for an unpleasurable experience. The paranoic projects his intolerable ideas outwards, whence they return in the shape of reproaches: '. . . *the subject-matter remains unaffected*; what is altered is something in the *placing* of the whole thing' (4*b*).

On every subsequent occasion when Freud deals with paranoia he invokes projection–especially in the Schreber case-history (1911*c*). But it should be noticed how he restricts its role: projection is now seen as but one portion of the mechanism of paranoic defence, and it is not present to the same degree in all forms of the disturbance (5*a*).

b. In 1915 Freud describes the entire *phobic* construction as a veritable 'projection' of the instinctual threat into outside reality: 'The ego behaves as if the danger of a development of anxiety threatened it not from the direction of an instinctual impulse but from the direction of perception, and it is thus enabled to react against this external danger with the attempts at flight represented by phobic avoidances' (6).

c. Freud sees projection at work in what he names 'projected jealousy' (7), which he distinguishes on the one hand from 'normal' jealousy and on the other from the delusional jealousy of the paranoic. In projected jealousy the subject fends off his desire to be unfaithful by imputing jealousy to his spouse; in this way he turns his attention away from his own unconscious and redirects it on to the unconscious of the other person, so gaining a great insight regarding the other person while falling into just as great a misapprehension regarding himself. It is thus at times impossible, and always vain, to denounce projection as misperception.

d. Freud insisted several times on the *normal* character of the mechanism of projection. Thus he considers that it operates in superstition, in mythology, in 'animism'. 'The obscure recognition (the endopsychic perception, as it were) of psychical factors and relations in the unconscious is mirrored [...] in the construction of a *supernatural reality*, which is destined to be changed back once more by science into the *psychology of the unconscious*' (8).

e. Lastly, it was only on rare occasions that Freud invoked projection in connection with the analytic situation. He never describes transference in general as a projection; he only uses the term to denote a specific phenomenon associated with the transference, namely, the subject's attribution to the analyst of words or thoughts which are really his own (e.g. 'Now you'll think I mean [...] but really I've no such intention' (9a)).

It will be evident from the foregoing that although Freud recognises projection in rather diverse areas he assigns it a fairly strict meaning. It always appears as a defence, as the attribution to another (person or thing) of qualities, feelings or wishes that the subject repudiates or refuses to recognise in himself. The example of animism is the one which best illustrates the fact that Freud does not understand projection in the sense of a simple identification of the other person with oneself. Animistic beliefs have indeed been accounted for very often by the supposed inability of primitive people to conceive of nature otherwise than after the model of the human being; similarly, it is often said of mythology that the ancients 'projected' human qualities and passions on to the forces of nature. For his part–and this is his major contribution here–Freud holds that such assimilations have a *refusal to recognise something* as their basic principle and *raison d'être*: 'demons' and 'ghosts' are embodiments of bad unconscious desires.

III. For the most part, when Freud mentions projection he avoids dealing with the matter as a whole. In the Schreber case-history he justifies this attitude in the following terms: since 'more general psychological problems are involved in the question of the nature of projection, let us make up our minds to postpone the investigation of it (and with it that of the mechanism of paranoic symptom-formation in general) until some other occasion' (5b). It is possible that such a study was indeed made, but if so it was never published. All the same, Freud did on several occasions throw out hints regarding the metapsychology of projection, so we can attempt to bring together the elements of his theory and the problems that it raises:

a. The most general principle underlying projection is to be found in the Freudian conception of the instinct. As we know, Freud holds that the organism is subject to two kinds of tension-generating excitations: those which it can flee and against which it can protect itself, and those which it cannot evade and against which there exists at first no protective apparatus or shield*; here we have the first criterion of what is external and what internal. Projection emerges at this point as the primal means of defence against those endogenous excitations whose intensity makes them too unpleasurable: the subject projects these outside so as to be able to flee from them (e.g. phobic avoidance) and protect himself from them. 'There is a tendency to treat them as though they were acting, not from the inside, but from the outside, so that it may be possible to bring the shield against stimuli into operation as a means of defence against them. This is the origin of *projection*' (10). There is a drawback to this solution, however: as Freud noted, the subject now finds himself obliged to believe completely in something that is henceforth subject to the laws of external reality (4c).

b. Freud makes projection (along with introjection*) play an essential part in the genesis of the opposition between subject (ego) and object (outside world). 'In so far as the objects which are presented to it are sources of pleasure, [the ego] takes them into itself, "introjects" them (to use Ferenczi's term); and, on the other hand, it expels whatever within itself becomes a cause of unpleasure (the mechanism of projection)' (11). This process of introjection and projection is expressed in the 'language of the oral instinct' (9b) through the contrast between ingesting and expelling. This is the stage of what Freud calls the 'purified pleasure-ego' (see 'Pleasure-Ego/Reality-Ego'). Those authors who seek to place this conception of Freud's in a chronological perspective raise the question whether the operation of projection and introjection *presupposes* the differentiation between internal and external or whether it *constitutes* it. Thus Anna Freud takes the first view: '. . . we might suppose that projection and introjection were methods which depended on the differentiation of the ego from the outside world' (12). In this she stands opposed to the Kleinian school, which has brought to the fore the dialectic of the introjection/projection of 'good' and 'bad' objects*, and which treats this dialectic as the actual basis of discrimination between inside and outside.

IV. Freud did therefore point out what he considered to be the mainspring of projection; but his approach leaves a number of fundamental questions in the air–questions to which it is impossible to find unequivocal answers in his work.

a. An initial difficulty arises over *what it is* that is projected. Freud often describes projection as the distortion of a normal process by means of which we seek the *cause* of our effects in the outside world: such would appear to be his conception of projection as observable in phobia. By contrast, in the analysis of the mechanism of paranoia offered by Freud in *Schreber*, the appeal to causality appears as an *a posteriori* rationalisation of projection: '. . . the proposition "I hate him" becomes transformed by *projection* into another one: "*He hates* (persecutes) *me*, which will justify me in hating him" ' (5c). Here it is the *affect* of hate–the *instinct* itself, so to speak–which is projected. Finally, in such metapsychological writings as 'Instincts and their Vicissitudes' (1915c) and 'Negation' (1925h), what is projected is what is 'hated' or 'bad'. By now we are very close to the 'realistic' view of projection which was to come to full flower in the work of Melanie Klein: for Klein, the thing projected is the phantasied 'bad' object, as though it were necessary, if the instinct or the affect is to be truly expelled, for it to become embodied in an *object*.

b. A second major difficulty is illustrated by the Freudian view of paranoia. The fact is that Freud does not always locate projection in the same place within the overall defensive process of this affection. In the first writings dealing with paranoic projection he conceives of it as a primary defence-mechanism whose nature is revealed by comparison with the repression at work in obsessional neurosis. In obsessional neurosis, primary defence consists in a repression into the unconscious of the whole of the pathogenic memory and its replacement by a 'primary defensive symptom'–namely, self-distrust. In paranoia, the primary defence has the same co-ordinates: there is a repression here too, but it is a repression into the outside world, while the primary defensive symptom is distrust of *other people*. As for delusions, these are looked upon as a failure of this defence and as a 'return of the repressed'* from without (4d).

In the Schreber case-history projection has a very different role: it is described as occurring during the period of 'symptom-formation'*. This approach tends to bring the mechanism of paranoia closer to that of the neuroses: in a first phase, the intolerable feeling (homosexual love) is said to be repressed inwards, into the unconscious, and transformed into its opposite; a subsequent phase

353

sees its projection into the outside world. Projection here is the way in which what has been repressed into the unconscious makes its return.

This variation in the conceptualisation of the mechanism of paranoia results in our having two distinct senses of projection:

(i) A sense comparable to the cinematographic one: the subject sends out into the external world an image of something that exists in him in an unconscious way. Projection is defined here as a mode of *refusal to recognise* (*méconnaissance*) which has as its counterpart the subject's ability to recognise in others precisely what he refuses to acknowledge in himself.

(ii) A sense in which it means a quasi-real process of expulsion: the subject ejects something he does not want and later rediscovers it in outside reality. One might say schematically that projection is defined in this sense not as 'not wishing to know' but as 'not wishing to be'.

The first meaning confines projection to the status of an illusion, while the second roots it in a primal division between subject and outside world (see 'Foreclosure').

Nor is this second view of the matter absent from *Schreber*, witness the following: 'It was incorrect to say that the perception which was suppressed internally is projected outwards; the truth is rather, as we now see, that what was abolished (*aufgehobene*) internally returns from without' (5*d*). It will be noticed that what Freud continues to call 'projection' in this passage–i.e. what we have just described as a mode of plain refusal to recognise something–is in his opinion now inadequate, when so defined, to account for the psychosis.

c. We run into a further difficulty when we come to the Freudian theory of hallucinations and dreams as projections. If, as Freud maintains, it is the unpleasurable that is projected, how are we to account for the projection of a wish-fulfilment? Freud did not overlook the problem, and his proposed solution to it might be stated thus: if the dream fulfils a pleasant wish in its *content*, it is still defensive in its primary function–its prime aim is to keep at arm's length whatever threatens to disturb sleep: '. . . the internal demand which was striving to occupy [the sleeper] has been replaced by an external experience, whose demand has been disposed of. A dream is, therefore, among other things, a *projection*: an externalization of an internal process' (13).

V. a. Despite these basic difficulties the Freudian usage of the term 'projection' is–as will by now be plain–a clearly circumscribed one. It is always a matter of throwing out what one refuses either to *recognise* in oneself or to *be* oneself. But this overtone of rejection or expulsion does not seem to have attached in any great degree to the pre-Freudian use of 'projection'–consider, for instance, Renan's 'L'enfant projette sur toutes choses le merveilleux qu'il porte en lui'. Naturally the earlier sense has survived Freud's novel idea of projection and this fact explains a number of the term's current ambiguities in psychology and even at times among psycho-analysts (α).

b. Our concern to preserve the clarity of Freud's conception of projection does not imply any wish to deny the existence of all the processes we have sought to distinguish and classify above (cf. I). At the same time the psycho-analyst will inevitably wish to point out that a part is played in these processes by projection *qua* expulsion, *qua* refusal to recognise:

Even the simple projection of a state of tension or a diffused suffering on to one bodily organ allows it to be localised and its true source misapprehended (cf. I, b above).

Similarly, it would be easy to show, with regard to projective tests (cf. I, c above), that these do not only involve the structuring of stimuli in accordance with the personality structure: the subject–particularly when he is confronted with T.A.T. pictures–undoubtedly projects what he *is*, but he also projects what he *refuses to be*. It is even legitimate to ask whether the projective technique does not tend above all to stimulate the mechanism of the projection outwards of whatever is 'bad'.

It should also be pointed out that psycho-analysts do not equate the transference as a whole with a projection (cf. I, d above); on the other hand, they do acknowledge the way in which projection may have a hand in the transference. They will say, for example, that the subject is projecting his super-ego on to the analyst, and that this expulsion helps him achieve a more advantageous situation and a relief from his internal strife.

Lastly, the relationship between identification and projection is highly confused, owing in part to sloppy linguistic usage. The hysteric, for instance, is sometimes described interchangeably as *projecting himself on to* or *identifying himself with* such and such a character. (So great is the confusion, in fact, that Ferenczi even used 'introjection' to denote this same process.) Without in any way going into the question of the interconnections between the two mechanisms, we may say that such a use of 'projection' is incorrect, since the precondition always assumed in the psycho-analytic definition of the term is not met by a case of this kind: there is no division within the person, no expulsion into the other of the part of the self which is rejected.

(α) An anecdote may help clear up this confusion. During a debate between philosophers of two different persuasions, one participant asks: 'Surely we have the same position?' 'I hope not,' replies a member of the opposing group. In the ordinary psychological sense it is the first man who is 'projecting' here; in the Freudian sense, we may take it that it is the second, in so far as his posture attests a radical rejection of his opponent's ideas–ideas which he is afraid to discover in himself.

(1) FREUD, S. *Three Essays on the Theory of Sexuality* (1905*d*), G.W., V, 85; S.E., VII, 184.

(2) ENGLISH, H. B. and ENGLISH, A. C. *A Comprehensive Dictionary of Psychological and Psychoanalytical Terms* (1958): a) See 'Projection, eccentric'. b) See 'Projection', 3.

(3) ANZIEU, D. *Les méthodes projectives* (Paris: P.U.F., 1960), 2–3.

(4) FREUD, S.: a) *Anf.*, 118–24 and 163–64; S.E., I, 207–12 and 226–28. b) *Anf.*, 120; S.E., I, 208. c) Cf. *Anf.*, 118–24 and 163–64; S.E., I, 207–12 and 226–28. d) Cf. *ibid.*

(5) FREUD, S. 'Psycho-Analytic Notes on an Autobiographical Account of a Case of Paranoia (Dementia Paranoides)' (1911*c*): a) Cf. G.W., VIII, 302–3; S.E., XII, 66. b) G.W., VIII, 303; S.E., XII, 66. c) G.W., VIII, 299; S.E., XII, 63. d) G.W., VIII, 508; S.E., XII, 71.

(6) FREUD, S. 'The Unconscious' (1915*e*), G.W., X, 283; S.E., XIV, 184.

(7) Cf. FREUD, S. 'Some Neurotic Symptoms in Jealousy, Paranoia and Homosexuality' (1922*b*), G.W., XIII, 195–98; S.E., XIII, 223–25.

(8) FREUD, S. *The Psychopathology of Everyday Life* (1901*b*), G.W., IV, 287–88; S.E., VI, 258–59.

(9) Cf. for example FREUD, S. 'Negation' (1925*h*): a) G.W., XIV, 11; S.E., XIX, 235. b) G.W., XIV, 13; S.E., XIX, 237.

(10) FREUD, S. *Beyond the Pleasure Principle* (1920*g*), G.W., XIII, 29; S.E., XVIII, 29.

(11) FREUD, S. 'Instincts and their Vicissitudes' (1915*c*), G.W., X, 228; S.E., XIV, 136.

(12) FREUD, A. *The Ego and the Mechanisms of Defence* (London: Hogarth, 1937; New York: I.U.P., 1946), 55.

(13) FREUD, S. 'A Metapsychological Supplement to the Theory of Dreams' (1917*d* [1915]), G.W., X, 214; S.E., XIV, 223.

Projective Identification

= *D.*: Projektionsidentifizierung.–*Es.*: identificación proyectiva.–
Fr.: identification projective.–*I.*: identificazione proiettiva.–*P.*: identificação projetiva.

Term introduced by Melanie Klein: a mechanism revealed in phantasies in which the subject inserts his self– in whole or in part– into the object in order to harm, possess or control it.

The expression 'projective identification' has been used by Melanie Klein in an idiosyncratic sense which is not the one that the conjunction of these two words might suggest at first glance–namely, an attribution to the other person of certain traits of the self, or even of an overall resemblance to one's self.

In *The Psycho-Analysis of Children* (1932), Klein describes phantasies of attacking the inside of the mother's body and of invading it sadistically (1). Only later, however, does she introduce the term 'projective identification' as a designation for 'a particular form of identification which establishes the prototype of an aggressive object-relation' (2*a*).

This mechanism, which is closely associated with the paranoid-schizoid position*, consists in the phantasied projection of split-off parts of the subject's own self–or even his whole self (not just partial bad objects)–into the interior of the mother's body, so as to injure and control the mother from within. This phantasy lies at the root of such anxieties as the fear of being imprisoned and persecuted within the mother's body; and by a reverse process, projective identification may result in introjection* being experienced 'as a forceful entry from the outside into the inside, in retribution for violent projection' (2*b*). A further danger is that the ego may become weak and impoverished in so far as projective identification deprives it of 'good' parts of itself; this is the way in which an agency such as the ego-ideal* may become external to the subject (2*c*).

Melanie Klein and Joan Riviere see phantasies of projective identification at work in a variety of pathological conditions such as depersonalisation and claustrophobia.

Projective identification may thus be considered as a mode of *projection**. If Klein speaks of *identification* here it is because it is the subject's self that is projected. The Kleinian usage is consistent with the narrow sense to which psycho-analysis tends to confine the term 'projection': the ejection into the outside world of something which the subject refuses in himself–the projection of what is bad.

*   *   *

This approach fails to tackle the problem of whether there is a valid distinction to be made, within the category of identification, between those modes of the process where the subject makes himself one with the other person and those where he makes the other person one with himself. To bring the latter together under the heading of projective identification results in an erosion of the psycho-analytic concept of projection; there is therefore a case for preferring to formulate this distinction in terms of *centrifugal* and *centripetal* identification, for example.

(1) K LEIN, M., third edn. (London: Hogarth Press, 1949), 187–89.

(2) K LEIN, M. 'Notes on some Schizoid Mechanisms', in *Developments* (1952): a) 300. b) 304. c) Cf. 301.

Protective Shield (Against Stimuli)

= *D*: Reizschutz.–*Es.*: protector *or* protección contra las excitaciones.–*Fr.*: pare-excitations.– *I.*: apparato protettivo contro lo stimolo.–*P.*: paraexcitações.

Term used by Freud within the framework of a psychophysiological model to denote a particular function and the apparatus which carries it out. The function consists in protecting (*schützen*) the organism against excitations deriving from the outside world which threaten to destroy it by their intensity. The apparatus responsible for this protective action is conceived of as a superficial layer enveloping the organism and passively filtering the excitations.

The literal meaning of the term '*Reizschutz*' is protection against excitation. Freud introduces it in *Beyond the Pleasure Principle* (1920*g*) and makes notable use of it in 'A Note upon the "Mystic Writing-Pad" ' (1925*a* [1924]) and *Inhibitions, Symptoms and Anxiety* (1926*d*). He calls upon it to account for a protective *function*, it is true, but also–and above all–a specialised *apparatus*. Freud's English and French translators have not always used the same rendering for these different senses of the German term.

Beginning with his 'Project for a Scientific Psychology' (1950*a* [1895]), Freud posits the existence of protective apparatuses (*Quantitätschirme*) located at the point of exogenous excitation. The quantities of energy at work in the outside world are not commensurate with those which the psychical apparatus is equipped to discharge, whence the necessity on the frontier between external and internal for ' "nerve-ending apparatuses" [...] through which only *quotients* of exogenous Qs [quantities] will pass' (1). At the point of emergence of excitations coming from within the body there is said to be no need for any such apparatus, since the quantities involved are from the outset of the same order as those circulating between neurones.

Notice that Freud connects the existence of protective devices with the primal tendency of the neuronal system to keep quantity at zero-level (*Trägheitsprinzip*: principle of inertia*).

357

Psychical (or Psychic or Mental) Apparatus

In framing a theory of the trauma* in *Beyond the Pleasure Principle*, Freud bases himself upon a simplified picture of the living vesicle. In order to subsist, such a vesicle must surround itself with a protective layer that loses its properties of living matter and becomes a barrier with the function of protecting the vesicle from outside stimuli incomparably stronger than the internal energies of the system, though at the same time letting these stimuli through in quantities proportional to their intensity so that the organism may receive information from the outside world. Seen in the light of this analogy, the trauma can be defined in its first stage as a widescale breach of the protective shield.

The hypothesis of the protective shield can be incorporated into a topographical* perspective: below this protective layer lies another stratum, the receptor layer, defined in *Beyond the Pleasure Principle* as the perception-consciousness system (*Pcpt.-Cs.*). Freud later compared this layered structure to a 'mystic writing-pad'.

It will be noted that if, in the texts we are dealing with here, Freud denies the existence of a shield against *internal* stimuli, this is because he is describing the psychical apparatus in a period logically prior to the institution of defences*.

The resolution of the problem of the nature of the protective shield presupposes a treatment of the whole question of the validity of physiological models. We shall merely remark here that Freud often attributes physical actuality to this device: in the 'Project' he refers to the receptive sensory organs; in *Beyond the Pleasure Principle* he locates the sense organs underneath the body's 'general shield against stimuli' (*allgemeiner Reizschutz*), which thus appears in this context as a tegument (2). But Freud also gives the protective shield a broader, psychological sense implying no determinate bodily underpinning. He goes so far as to assign it a purely functional role, with protection against excitation being guaranteed by periodic cathexis and decathexis of the perception-consciousness system. Hence this system simply takes 'samples' of the external world. The breaking-down of the mass of stimuli may therefore be treated as the work not of a purely spatial apparatus but of a temporal mode of functioning which assures a 'periodic non-excitability' (3).

(1) FREUD, S., *Anf.*, 390; S.E., I, 306.

(2) Cf. FREUD, S., G.W., XIII, 27; S.E., XVIII, 28.

(3) FREUD, S. 'A Note upon the "Mystic Writing-Pad"' (1925a [1924]), G.W., XIV, 8; S.E., XIX, 231.

Psychical (or Psychic or Mental) Apparatus

= D.: psychischer *or* seelischer Apparat.–*Es.*: aparato psíquico.–*Fr.*: appareil psychique.– *I.*: apparato psichico *or* mentale.–*P.*: aparêlho psíquico *or* mental.

Term which underscores certain characteristics attributed to the psyche by the Freudian theory: its capacity to transmit and transform a specific energy and its subdivision into systems or agencies.

In *The Interpretation of Dreams* (1900*a*) Freud defines the psychical apparatus in terms of a comparison with optical apparatuses. His purpose in making this analogy is, as he puts it, 'to assist us in our attempt to make the complications of mental functioning intelligible by dissecting the function and assigning its different constituents to different component parts of the apparatus' (1*a*).

This kind of statement calls for a number of comments:

a. When he speaks of a psychical apparatus, Freud is suggesting the idea of a certain arrangement, of an internal disposition, but he is not merely allotting different functions to particular 'mental spaces', for he assigns to these a given *order* implying a specific temporal succession. The coexistence of the different systems which make up the psychical apparatus is not to be taken in an anatomical sense, as would be the case in a theory of cerebral localisation. This coexistence means simply that excitations must follow a progression determined by the position of the various systems (2).

b. The word 'apparatus' evokes the idea of a task, or even that of *work*. The dominant schema here was taken over by Freud from a particular conception of the reflex arc which sees this as transmitting the energy it receives in its entirety: '... the psychical apparatus must be constructed like a reflex apparatus. Reflex processes remain the model (*Vorbild*) of every psychical function' (1*b*).

In the last analysis, the function of the psychical apparatus is to keep the internal energy of an organism at the lowest possible level (see 'Principle of Constancy'). Its diversification into substructures makes it easier to conceptualise the *transformations of energy* (from the free* to the bound state – see 'Working Out') and the interplay of cathexes, anticathexes and hypercathexes.

c. These brief remarks show that the psychical apparatus serves for Freud's purposes as a *model* – or, as he said himself, as a 'fiction' (1*c*). This model may at times be a physical one, as is the case in the first quotation above or again in the first chapter of the *Outline of Psycho-Analysis* (1940*a* [1938]); on other occasions, it is derived instead from biology (the 'protoplasmic vesicle' of *Beyond the Pleasure Principle* [1920*g*]). And thus discussion of the notion of the psychical apparatus has led us towards an overall evaluation of Freudian metapsychology and of the metaphors that it brings into play.

(1) FREUD, S.: a) G.W., II–III, 541; S.E., V, 536. b) G.W., II–III, 543; S.E., V, 538. c) G.W., II–III, 604; S.E., V, 598.

(2) Cf. for example FREUD, S., letter to Fliess dated December 6, 1896, *Anf.* and S.E., I, 233 *ff.*

Psychical Conflict

= *D*.: psychischer Konflikt. – *Es*.: conflicto psíquico. – *Fr*.: conflit psychique. – *I*.: conflitto psichico. – *P*.: conflito psíquico.

Psycho-analysis speaks of conflict when contradictory internal requirements are opposed to each other in the subject. The conflict may be manifest – between

a wish and a moral imperative, for example, or between two contradictory emotions – or it may be latent, in which event it is liable to be expressed in a distorted fashion in the manifest conflict, emerging especially in the formation of symptoms, behavioural troubles, character disturbances, etc. Psycho-analysis considers that conflict is a constitutive part of the human being, and this remains true when it is viewed in various perspectives: conflict between desire and defence, between the different systems or agencies, between instincts, and, lastly, the Oedipal conflict, in which there is not only a confrontation between contrary wishes but also one between these wishes and the prohibition imposed upon them.

From its beginnings, psycho-analysis was confronted with psychical conflict, and this rapidly became the pivotal concept of the theory of the neuroses. The *Studies on Hysteria* show how, during the treatment, as he gets closer and closer to the pathogenic memories, Freud encounters a growing resistance (q.v.); this resistance is itself merely the temporary or 'actual' expression of an intra-subjective defence against ideas which Freud describes as 'incompatible' (*unverträglich*). As from 1895–96, this defensive activity is recognised to be the principal mechanism in the aetiology of hysteria (see 'Defence Hysteria') and, by extension, in that of the other 'psychoneuroses', known at this point as the 'neuro-psychoses of defence'. The neurotic symptom comes to be defined as the product of a compromise* between two groups of ideas acting as two opposed forces, each as immediate and exigent as the other: 'The process which we here see at work – conflict, repression, substitution involving a compromise – returns in all psychoneurotic symptoms' (1). In an even more general sense, this process is met with once again in such phenomena as dreams, parapraxes, screen memories, etc.

Although conflict is without doubt a major datum of psycho-analytic experience, relatively simple to describe in its clinical modes, it is more difficult to work out a metapsychological theory to deal with it. Throughout Freud's work, the solutions proposed for the problem of the ultimate basis of conflict are various. It should be noted to begin with that conflict may be accounted for on two comparatively distinct planes: first, in topographical* terms, as conflict between systems or agencies*, and secondly, from an economico-dynamic point of view, as conflict between instincts. It is this second type of explanation which Freud looks upon as the more radical, but the articulation between the two levels is often difficult to clarify, since a particular agency, though an active pole of the conflict, may not necessarily correspond to a specific type of instinct.

In the framework of the first metapsychological theory, the conflict can be brought down schematically, from the topographical point of view, to the opposition between the *Ucs.* system on the one hand and the *Pcs.-Cs.* system on the other, the two being separated by the censorship*. This antagonism corresponds, furthermore, to the dualism of the pleasure and reality principles, with the latter seeking to establish its superiority over the former. We may say that at this point the two conflicting forces for Freud are sexuality* and an agency of repression comprising in particular the ethical and aesthetic aspirations of the personality. The motive for the repression lies in specific traits of the sexual ideas which supposedly make them incompatible with the 'ego'* and generate unpleasure for this agency.

Only at a rather late stage did Freud seek an instinctual basis for the repressing agency. The dualism of the sexual* and self-preservative* instincts (the latter being defined as 'ego-instincts'*) is then taken to underpin the psychical conflict: 'we must, on the psycho-analytic view, assume that [certain] ideas have come into opposition to other, more powerful ones, for which we use the collective concept of the "ego"–a compound which is made up variously at different times–and have for that reason come under repression. But what can be the origin of this opposition, which makes for repression, between the ego and various groups of ideas? [...] Our attention has been drawn to the importance of the instincts in ideational life. We have discovered that every instinct tries to make itself effective by activating ideas that are in keeping with its aims. These instincts are not always compatible with one another; their interests often come into conflict. Opposition between ideas is only an expression of struggle between the various instincts' (2). All the same, it is clear that even at that stage in Freud's thinking where there is a correlation between the defensive agency of the ego and a specific type of instinct, the ultimate 'hunger-love' opposition is expressed in the concrete modes of the conflict only via a series of mediations that are very hard to characterise.

Subsequently, the introduction of the second topography provides us with a model of the personality which is more differentiated and closer to these concrete modes. This model deals with conflicts between agencies, and conflicts within a particular agency, such as the one between the poles of paternal and maternal identification which is to be found in the super-ego.

The new instinctual dualism that Freud invokes between the life* and the death* instincts might be expected, given the radical opposition that it brings into play, to furnish a foundation for the theory of conflict. In point of fact, however, it is very far indeed from providing any such superimposition of the level of first principles (Eros and the death instincts) upon that of the concrete dynamics of the conflict (on this point, see 'Death Instinct'). Nevertheless, the new dualism does revise the notion of conflict:

a. Instinctual forces are more and more clearly seen to animate the different agencies (for example, Freud describes the super-ego as sadistic), even though none of these is affected exclusively by one type of instinct.

b. The life instincts appear to cover the greater part of the conflictual oppositions previously identified by Freud on the basis of clinical experience: 'The contrast between the instincts of self-preservation and the preservation of the species, as well as the contrast between ego-love and object-love, fall within Eros' (3a).

c. The death instinct is interpreted by Freud on occasion not as a pole of the conflict but rather as the very principle of strife, like the νεῖκος (hate) which for Empedocles already stood opposed to love (φιλία).

Thus it is that Freud comes to specify a 'tendency towards conflict' as a variable whose intervention results in certain cases in the transformation of the bisexuality proper to the human being into a conflict between strictly irreconcilable requirements; should this variable not come into play, by contrast, then nothing ought to stand in the way of a balanced resolution of homosexual and heterosexual trends.

We may interpret the role Freud assigns to the concept of instinctual fusion along similar lines. This concept does not only mean a distribution of sexuality and aggression in variable proportions: the death instinct is itself responsible for defusion (see 'Fusion/Defusion of Instincts').

*　　*　　*

If we take an overview of the development of Freud's way of picturing conflict we are struck, first, by the fact that he invariably attempts to bring it down to an irreducible dualism which can only be based, in the last reckoning, on a quasi-mythical opposition between two great contradictory forces; and secondly, by the fact that one of the poles of the conflict is always sexuality*, although the other is sought in a reality which varies ('ego', 'ego-instincts', 'death instincts'). From the very beginning of his work (see 'Seduction')–but also in the *Outline of Psycho-Analysis* (1940a [1938])–Freud insists upon the necessity of maintaining an intrinsic link between sexuality and conflict. It is true that an abstract theoretical model of this connection might be proposed which would apply to 'any sort of instinctual demand', but 'our observation shows us invariably, so far as we can judge, that the excitations which play this pathogenic part arise from the component instincts of sexual life' (3b). What is the final theoretical justification of this privileged role accorded to sexuality in the conflict? The question is left in the air by Freud, who at several points in his work pointed out the peculiar temporal characteristics of human sexuality, which result in the fact that 'the weak point in the ego's organisation seems to lie in its attitude to the sexual function' (3c).

Any psycho-analytic attempt to elucidate the question of conflict in depth must inevitably open on to what is the nuclear conflict for the human subject– the Oedipus complex*. The conflict here, before it becomes defensive conflict, is already inscribed, presubjectively, as a dialectical and primal conjunction of desire and prohibition.

In so far as it constitutes the major, ineluctable datum which orientates the child's intersubjective field, the Oedipus complex may be recognised behind the most varied modes of the defensive conflict (as, for example, in the ego's relationship to the super-ego). More fundamentally, if one takes the Oedipus complex as a structure in which the subject has to find his place, the conflict appears as already present in it prior to the interplay of instincts and defences which is to constitute the psychical conflict specific to each individual.

(1) FREUD, S. 'Screen Memories' (1899a), G.W., I, 537; S.E., III, 308.

(2) FREUD, S. 'The Psycho-Analytic View of Psychogenic Disturbances of Vision' (1910i), G.W., VIII, 97; S.E., XI, 213.

(3) FREUD, S. *An Outline of Psycho-Analysis* (1940a [1938]): a) G.W., XVII, 71; S.E., XXIII, 148. b) G.W., XVII, 112; S.E., XXIII, 186. c) G.W., XVII, 113; S.E., XXIII, 186.

Psychical Reality

= *D.*: psychische Realität.–*Es.*: realidad psíquica.–*Fr.*: réalité psychique.–
I.: realtà psichica.–*P.*: realidade psíchica.

**Term often used by Freud to designate whatever in the subject's psyche presents
a consistency and resistance comparable to those displayed by material reality;
fundamentally, what is involved here is unconscious desire and its associated
phantasies.**

When Freud speaks of psychical reality he is not simply referring to the proper
field of psychology, conceived as having its own order of reality and as being
open to scientific investigation: he means everything in the psyche that takes
on the force of reality for the subject.

The idea of psychical reality emerges in the history of psycho-analysis
according as the theory of seduction*, and of the pathogenic role of real infantile
traumas, is abandoned–or at least restricted. Phantasies, even if they are not
based on real events, now come to have the same pathogenic effect for the
subject as that which Freud had at first attributed to 'reminiscences': '. . . phantasies possess *psychical* as contrasted with material reality [for] *in the world of
the neuroses it is psychical reality which is the decisive kind*' (1*a*).

A theoretical problem is undoubtedly raised by the relationship between the
phantasy and the events that have served as a basis for it (see 'Phantasy');
Freud remarks, however, that 'up to the present we have not succeeded in pointing to any difference in the consequences, whether phantasy or reality has had
the greater share in these events of childhood' (1*b*). Thus the psycho-analytic
treatment starts out on the assumption that the neurotic symptoms are grounded
at least upon a *psychical* reality, and that in this sense the patient 'must surely
be right in some way' (2). On several occasions, Freud stresses the idea that
even those affects which appear the most unmotivated, such as the sense of
guilt* in obsessional neurosis, are actually fully justified in that they rest upon
psychical realities.

Generally speaking, neurosis, and *a fortiori* psychosis, are characterised by
the predominance of psychical reality in the life of the subject.

This notion is bound up with the Freudian hypothesis about unconscious
processes: not only do these processes take no account of external reality, they
also replace it with a psychical one (3). In its strictest sense, 'psychical reality'
denotes the unconscious wish and the phantasy associated with it. Apropos
of the analysis of dreams, Freud asks whether we must attribute reality to
unconscious wishes: 'It must be denied, of course, to any transitional or
intermediate thoughts. If we look at unconscious wishes reduced to their most
fundamental and truest shape, we shall have to conclude, no doubt, that
psychical reality is a particular form of existence not to be confused with
material reality' (4, α).

(α) For the history of the concept of 'psychical reality' and the set of problems surrounding
it, we venture to refer the reader to our article 'Fantasme originaire, fantasme des origines,
origine du fantasme', *Les temps modernes*, No. 215, April, 1964. Translated as 'Fantasy and
the Origins of Sexuality', *I.J.P.*, 1968, 49, 1 *ff*.

Psychical Representative (α)

(1) FREUD, S. *Introductory Lectures on Psycho-Analysis* (1916–17): a) G.W., XI, 383; S.E., XVI, 368. b) G.W., XI, 385; S.E., XVI, 370.

(2) FREUD, S. 'Mourning and Melancholia' (1917e), G.W., X, 432; S.E., XIV, 246.

(3) Cf. FREUD, S. 'The Unconscious' (1915e), G.W., X, 286; S.E., XIV, 187.

(4) FREUD, S. *The Interpretation of Dreams* (1900a), G.W., II–III, 625; S.E., V, 620.

Psychical Representative (α)

= *D*.: psychische Repräsentanz *or* psychischer Repräsentant. – *Es*.: representante psíquico. – *Fr*.: représentant psychique. – *I*.: rappresentanza psichica *or* rappresentante psichico. – *P*.: representante psíquico.

Term used by Freud within the framework of his instinct theory to designate the expression of endosomatic excitations on the psychical level.

This term cannot be understood save by reference to the concept of *instinct**–a concept which in Freud's view bridges the gap between the somatic and the mental. On the somatic side, the instinct has its source* in organic phenomena generating tension from which the subject is unable to escape; but at the same time, by virtue of its aim* and of the objects* to which it becomes attached, the instinct undergoes a 'vicissitude' (*Triebschicksal*) that is essentially psychical in nature.

This borderline position of the instinct no doubt accounts for Freud's calling upon the notion of a representative–by which he means a kind of *delegation*– of the soma within the psyche. This notion of delegation, however, is formulated in two different ways.

Sometimes the instinct itself is presented as 'the psychical representative of the stimuli originating from within the organism and reaching the mind' (1, 2). At other times the instinct becomes part of the process of somatic excitation, in which case it is represented in the psyche by 'instinctual representatives'* which comprise two elements–the ideational representative* and the quota of affect* (3).

We cannot accept the suggestion made in the *Standard Edition* that it is possible to discern a development in Freud's thinking on this point: the two formulations we have just mentioned were both put forward by him in the same year–1915. As to the claim that Freud opted for the second view of the matter in his last works, it is even less convincing: in fact it is the *first* one that is propounded in the *Outline of Psycho-Analysis* (1940a [1938]). Are we then obliged–as the *Standard Edition* further proposes–to dismiss this contradiction by putting it down to the ambiguity of the concept of instinct with its frontier status between body and mind (4)? Perhaps; but it seems to us that Freud's thinking on this point can be clarified.

a. Although the two formulations are at first sight contradictory they both contain the same idea: the *relation* between soma and psyche is conceived of as neither parallelistic nor causal; rather, it is to be understood by analogy with the relationship between a delegate and his mandator (β).

364

Since this relation is constant in Freud's propositions we may reasonably assume that the difference between them is merely semantic. Thus the somatic modification in question may be said to be designated in the first formulation by the term 'instinct' (*Trieb*), and in the second by 'excitation' (*Reiz*). As for the psychical representative, it is referred to in the first case as the ideational representative and in the second as the instinct.

b. This said, however, there is still in our opinion a difference between the two accounts. The solution which has the instinct, considered as somatic, delegate its psychical representatives seems to us more accurate: first, because it does not just invoke an overall relation of *expression* between the somatic and the psychical, and further, because it is more in tune with the notion of the *registration of ideas* which is inseparable from the Freudian conception of the unconscious*.

(α) See note (α) to the article 'Instinctual Representative'.

(β) It is a commonplace that, though in principle he is nothing more than the proxy of his mandator, the delegate in such cases enters in practice into a new system of relationships which is liable to change his perspective and cause him to depart from the directives he has been given.

(1) FREUD, S. 'Instincts and their Vicissitudes' (1915c), G.W., X, 214; S.E., XIV, 122.

(2) Same formulation found in: FREUD, S. 'Psycho-Analytic Notes on an Autobiographical Account of a Case of Paranoia (Dementia Paranoides)' (1911c), G.W., VIII, 311; S.E., XII, 73–74; FREUD, S. *Three Essays on the Theory of Sexuality* (1905d), passage added in 1915, G.W., V, 67; S.E., VII, 168; FREUD, S. *An Outline of Psycho-Analysis* (1940a [1938]), G.W., XVII, 70; S.E., XXIII, 148.

(3) Cf. FREUD, S. 'Repression' (1915d), G.W., X, 254–55; S.E., XIV, 152.

(4) S.E., XIV, 113.

Psychical Working Out (or Over)

= D.: psychische Verarbeitung (*or* Bearbeitung, *or* Ausarbeitung, *or* Aufarbeitung).–
Es.: elaboración psíquica.–*Fr.*: élaboration psychique.–*I*: elaborazione psichica.–
P.: elaboração psíquica.

Term used by Freud in different contexts to designate the work the psychical apparatus carries out in order to control the excitations which reach it and whose accumulation threatens to become pathogenic. This work consists in integrating the excitations into the psyche and establishing associative links between them.

'*Arbeit*' (work) is a component of numerous Freudian expressions: *Traumarbeit* (dream-work*), *Trauerarbeit* (work of mourning*), *Durcharbeiten* (working-through*), and various terms which are translated into English as 'working out' or 'working over' (*Verarbeitung, Bearbeitung, Ausarbeitung, Aufarbeitung*). By applying it in this way to intrapsychical operations, Freud is using the concept of work in a novel manner. This use may be understood by referring to the Freudian conception of a psychical apparatus* which transforms and

365

transports the energy entering it, the instinct being defined in this perspective as 'a measure of the demand made upon the mind for work' (1).

Understood very broadly, psychical working out might be said to cover all the operations of the psychical apparatus. Freud's sense of it, however, would seem to be a more specific one: psychical working out is the transformation of the quantity of energy so that it may be mastered by means of diversion or binding*.

Freud and Breuer found the term in Charcot, who spoke, apropos of hysterics, of a period of psychical working out between the trauma and the appearance of symptoms (2). When they adopted it in their theory of hysteria, the context, so far as aetiology and treatment were concerned, was a different one. In the normal way, the traumatic effect of an event is eliminated either through abreaction* or else through its integration into 'the great complex of associations' (3) (which thus exercises a corrective function). In the hysteric, various factors (see 'Hypnoid Hysteria', 'Defence Hysteria') obstruct such an elimination of the trauma's effects; there is no associative working out (*Verarbeitung*): the memory of the trauma remains in the state of a 'separate psychical group'. The cure is effected through the establishment of those associative links that facilitate the gradual elimination of the trauma (see 'Cathartic Method').

The term 'working out' is also used in the theory of the actual neuroses*: the lack of any psychical working out of the somatic sexual tension leads to the direct rechannelling of this tension into symptoms. The mechanism resembles the one found in hysteria (4), but the lack of working out is more fundamental here: 'Where there is an abundant development of physical sexual tension but this cannot be turned into affect by psychical working-over [...] the sexual tension is transformed into *anxiety*' (5).

In 'On Narcissism: An Introduction' (1914c), Freud picks up and elaborates upon the idea that, since they bring about the damming up* of libido, the absence or defectiveness of psychical working out are fundamental, in one mode or another, to neurosis and psychosis.

*   *   *

Taking an overview of Freud's different uses of the notion of psychical working out in the theory of hysteria and in that of the actual neuroses, one might distinguish between two aspects of the process in question: first, the transformation of physical quantity into psychical quality; and secondly, the setting up of associative pathways (for which a transformation of this kind is a prerequisite).

Such a distinction is also suggested in 'On Narcissism', where Freud asserts that an actual neurosis lies at the root of every psychoneurosis, thus implying that the damming up of libido and psychical working out are two successive stages.

Working out might therefore be seen as a frontier-concept between the economic* and symbolic* dimensions of Freudianism. For discussion of this question, the reader is referred to our commentary at 'Binding'.

We may note finally that working out and working through* cannot be divorced from one another: there is an analogy to be drawn between the way the work of the treatment proceeds and the way the psychical apparatus works of its own accord.

(1) FREUD, S. *Three Essays on the Theory of Sexuality* (1905*d*), G.W., V, 67; S.E., VII, 168.

(2) Cf. CHARCOT, J. M. *Leçons du mardi à la Salpêtrière* (Paris, 1888), I, 99.

(3) FREUD, S. *Studies on Hysteria* (1895*d*), G.W., I, 87; S.E., II, 9.

(4) Cf. FREUD, S. 'On the Grounds for Detaching a Particular Syndrome from Neurasthenia under the Description "Anxiety Neurosis" ' (1895*b*), G.W., I, 336, 342; S.E., III, 109, 115.

(5) FREUD, S. *Anf.*, 103; S.E., I, 194.

Psycho-Analysis

= *D.*: Psychoanalyse.–*Es.*: psicoanálisis.–*Fr.*: psychanalyse.–
I.: psicoanalisi *or* psicanalisi.–*P.*: psicanálise.

Discipline founded by Freud, whose example we follow in considering it under three aspects:

a. As a method of investigation which consists essentially in bringing out the unconscious meaning of the words, the actions and the products of the imagination (dreams, phantasies, delusions) of a particular subject. The method is founded mainly on the subject's free associations*, which serve as the measuring-rod of the validity of the interpretation*. Psycho-analytical interpretation can, however, be extended to human productions where no free associations are available.

b. As a psychotherapeutic method based on this type of investigation and characterised by the controlled interpretation of resistance*, transference* and desire*. It is in a related sense that the term 'psycho-analysis' is used to mean a course of psycho-analytic treatment, as when one speaks of undergoing psychoanalysis (or analysis).

c. As a group of psychological and psychopathological theories which are the systematic expression of the data provided by the psycho-analytic method of investigation and treatment.

Freud first used the terms 'analysis', 'psychical analysis', 'psychological analysis' and 'hypnotic analysis' in his early article on 'The Neuro-Psychoses of Defence' (1894*a*) (1). It was only later, in an article on the aetiology of neuroses published in French, that he introduced the name *'psycho-analyse'* (2). The German *'Psychoanalyse'* made its first appearance in 1896, in 'Further Remarks on the Neuro-Psychoses of Defence' (1896*b*) (3). The adoption of this term served as formal confirmation that catharsis* under hypnosis and suggestion had been dropped and that the obtaining of material* would henceforward depend exclusively on the rule of free association. Freud gave several definitions of psycho-analysis. One of the most explicit is to be found at the beginning of an encyclopaedia article written in 1922: 'Psycho-analysis is the name (i) of a procedure for the investigation of mental processes which are almost inaccessible in any other way, (ii) of a method (based upon that investigation) for the treatment of neurotic disorders and (iii) of a collection of psychological information obtained along those lines, which is gradually being accumulated into a new scientific discipline' (4).

Psycho-Analysis

The definition which we have proposed above is a more detailed version of the one given by Freud in this article.

As regards the choice of the term 'psycho-analysis', we can do no better than quote Freud himself, who invented the name while in the process of following up his discovery: 'The work by which we bring the repressed mental material into the patient's consciousness has been called by us psycho-analysis. Why "analysis" – which means breaking up or separating out, and suggests an analogy with the work carried out by chemists on substances which they find in nature and bring into their laboratories? Because in an important respect there really is an analogy between the two. The patient's symptoms and pathological manifestations, like all his mental activities, are of a highly composite kind; the elements of this compound are at bottom motives, instinctual impulses. But the patient knows nothing of these elementary motives or not nearly enough. We teach him to understand the way in which these highly complicated mental formations are compounded; we trace the symptoms back to the instinctual impulses which motivate them; we point out to the patient these instinctual motives, which are present in his symptoms and of which he has hitherto been unaware – just as a chemist isolates the fundamental substance, the chemical 'element', out of the salt in which it had been combined with other elements and in which it was unrecognisable. In the same way, as regards those of the patient's mental manifestations that were not considered pathological, we show him that he was only to a certain extent conscious of their motivation – that other instinctual impulses of which he had remained in ignorance had co-operated in producing them.

'Again, we have thrown light on the sexual impulses in man by separating them into their component elements; and when we interpret a dream we proceed by ignoring the dream as a whole and starting associations from its single elements.

'This well-founded comparison of medical psycho-analytic activity with a chemical procedure might suggest a new direction for our therapy. [...] We have been told that after an analysis of a sick mind a synthesis of it must follow. And, close upon this, concern has been expressed that the patient might be given too much analysis and too little synthesis; and there has then followed a move to put all the weight on this synthesis as the main factor in the psychotherapeutic effect, to see in it a kind of restoration of something that had been destroyed – destroyed, as it were, by vivisection.

'[...] The comparison with chemical analysis has its limitation: for in mental life we have to deal with trends that are under a compulsion towards unification and combination. Whenever we succeed in analysing a symptom into its elements, in freeing an instinctual impulse from one nexus, it does not remain in isolation, but immediately enters into a new one.

'[...] The psycho-synthesis is thus achieved during analytic treatment without our intervention, automatically and inevitably' (5).

A list of the principal general expositions of psycho-analysis published by Freud is to be found in the *Standard Edition* (6).

The fashionableness of psycho-analysis has led many authors to place a large number of works under this rubric even though their content, method and results have only the loosest of connections with psycho-analysis proper.

(1) Cf. FREUD, S., G.W., I, 59–74; S.E., III, 45–68.

(2) Cf. FREUD, S. 'Heredity and the Aetiology of the Neuroses' (1896a), G.W., I, 407–22; S.E., III, 143–56.

(3) Cf. FREUD, S., G.W., I, 379, 383; S.E., III, 162, 165–66.

(4) FREUD, S. 'Two Encyclopaedia Articles' (1923a), G.W., XIII, 211; S.E., XVIII, 235.

(5) FREUD, S. 'Lines of Advance in Psycho-Analytic Therapy' (1919a [1918]), G.W., XII 184–86; S.E., XVII, 159–61.

(6) S.E., XI, 56.

Psychoneurosis or Neuro-Psychosis

= D.: Neuropsychose.–Es.: psico-neurosis.–Fr.: psychonévrose.–I.: psiconevrosi.– P.: psiconeurose.

Term used by Freud to characterise certain psychical affections, namely, the transference neuroses* and the narcissistic neuroses*, as opposed to the actual neuroses*; the symptoms of the psychoneuroses are the symbolic expression of infantile conflicts.

The concept of psychoneurosis appears very early in Freud's work, for example in his article on 'The Neuro-Psychoses of Defence' (1894a), which, as the subtitle indicates, attempts 'a psychological theory of acquired hysteria, of many phobias and obsessions and of certain hallucinatory psychoses'.

When speaking of psychoneurosis, Freud stresses the psychogenic nature of the conditions in question. He uses the term essentially as the opposite of 'actual neurosis', as can be seen in 'Heredity and the Aetiology of the Neuroses' (1896a) and in 'Sexuality in the Aetiology of the Neuroses' (1898a). The same opposition recurs in the *Introductory Lectures on Psycho-Analysis* (1916–17).

Thus the term is not synonymous with 'neurosis'*: for one thing, it does not cover the actual neuroses, while it does embrace the narcissistic neuroses (which Freud also called psychoses–thereby adopting a psychiatric usage which has attained even greater acceptance since his time).

It is also worth noting that there is a certain ambiguity in common psychiatric parlance as regards the meaning of 'psychoneurosis': it appears that for some people the root *psycho* evokes psychosis, with the result that 'psychoneurosis' is mistakenly employed in order to lend an extra suggestion of seriousness, or even to imply the existence of an organic factor.

Psychosis

= D.: Psychose.–Es.: psicosis.–Fr.: psychose.–I.: psicosi.–P.: psicose.

a. In clinical psychiatry, the concept of psychosis is usually given a very broad extension covering a whole range of mental illnesses, whether they are clearly

of organic origin (general paralysis, for example) or whether their ultimate aetiology is obscure (as in the case of schizophrenia).

b. In psycho-analysis, there was no immediate attempt to develop a system of classification to deal with all the mental disorders a psychiatrist must know; instead, interest was at first directed towards the conditions which were most immediately accessible to analytic investigation, and within this field – narrower than that of psychiatry – the major distinctions were those between the perversions*, the neuroses* and the psychoses.

Within this last group, psycho-analysis has tried to define different structures: on the one hand, paranoia (including, in a rather general way, delusional conditions) and schizophrenia; on the other, melancholia and mania. Fundamentally, psycho-analysis sees the common denominator of the psychoses as lying in a primary disturbance of the libidinal relation to reality; the majority of manifest symptoms, and particularly delusional construction, are accordingly treated as secondary attempts to restore the link with objects.

The appearance of the word 'psychosis' in the nineteenth century came at the end of an evolution which had led to the establishment of mental illness as a separate domain, distinct not only from illnesses of the brain or nerves but also from what an age-old philosophical tradition looked upon as 'maladies of the spirit' – i.e. error and sin (α).

During the course of the last century, the term gained an increasingly wide currency, particularly in German psychiatric literature, as a designation for mental illness in general, for madness or lunacy – although this did not imply a psychogenic theory of madness. It was only at the close of the century, however, that the opposition between 'neurosis' and 'psychosis' as mutually exclusive categories (at least in principle) came into use. In fact the two terms evolved in differing contexts. The group of the neuroses, for its part, was demarcated gradually, starting from a certain number of disturbances which were looked upon as nervous disorders: these might be affections where a given organ was suspected but where, in the absence of any lesion, the blame was put on faulty functioning of the nervous system (cardiac neurosis, digestive neurosis, etc.); or there might be neurological indications but no discoverable lesion and no temperature (chorea, epilepsy, neurological manifestations of hysteria). One might say, schematically, that those patients whose condition was diagnosed as neurosis would consult their doctor but would not be committed to an asylum; furthermore, the term 'neurosis' implied a categorisation based on aetiology (functional illness of the nerves).

Inversely, the term 'psychosis' was at that time used to denote those conditions which, since they found their expression in an essentially psychical symptomatology, called for the competence of an alienist, although this is no way implied that the psychoses were considered by the authors who used the term to have causes outside the nervous system.

*   *   *

A well-established distinction between psychosis and neurosis is to be found in Freud's earliest works, as in the correspondence with Fliess. Thus in 'Draft

370

H', dated January 24, 1894, Freud considers the following states to be psychoses: hallucinatory confusion, paranoia and hysterical psychosis (this last as distinct from hysterical neurosis). Similarly, in the two texts which he devotes to the psychoneuroses of defence, he appears to take the distinction between psychosis and neurosis for granted and speaks for example of 'defence psychoses' (1).

At this period, however, Freud's essential concern is to define the notion of defence and to show its different modes in operation in a variety of conditions. From a nosographical standpoint, his major distinction is that between psychoneuroses (of defence)* and actual neuroses*. Later, though preserving this distinction, Freud places an increasing emphasis on the need for differentiation within the group of the psychoneuroses, with the result that the dividing-line between neurosis and psychosis does come to occupy the centre of the Freudian system of classification. (For the evolution of this system, see particularly 'Neurosis' and 'Narcissistic Neurosis'.)

*   *   *

There is today a very large measure of agreement in psychiatric clinical practice, in spite of the diversity of schools, over the delimitation of the respective fields of psychosis and neurosis; for confirmation of this, the reader may consult, for example, the *Encyclopédie médico-chirurgicale (Psychiatrie)*, edited by Henri Ey. It is obviously very difficult to assess the possible role played by psycho-analysis in the stabilisation of these nosological categories, as its history, since Bleuler and the Zurich School, has been closely interwoven with the development of psychiatric thinking as a whole.

As regards the *comprehension* of the concept, psychiatry's definition of psychosis is still more intuitive than systematic, invoking as it does characteristics which are so often not of the same order at all. Thus current definitions can often be seen to juxtapose such disparate criteria as social inadaptability (the problem of hospitalisation); the degree of 'seriousness' of the symptoms; disturbance of the capacity to communicate; the lack of awareness of the morbid state; loss of contact with reality; the 'incomprehensibility' (Jaspers' term) of the trouble; its determination by organogenic or psychogenic factors; the more or less profound, or more or less irreversible, deterioration of the ego.

In so far as it can be argued that psycho-analysis is largely responsible for the neurosis-psychosis opposition, the task of working out a coherent and structural definition of psychosis cannot be left to other psychiatric schools. Such a concern, though not central to Freud's preoccupations, is nonetheless present in his work. This is shown by the approaches he made to the problem on several occasions. All we can do here is sketch the general direction of these attempts.

a. In his first writings, there can be no doubt that Freud seeks to show the defensive conflict against sexuality at work in the case of certain psychoses—having just discovered the function of this conflict in the neurotic symptom. Nonetheless, he does at this same time attempt to identify specific mechanisms which come into operation *straight away in the subject's relation with the outside world*: one such mechanism is the outright 'rejection' (*verwerfen*) of an idea from consciousness in the case of hallucinatory confusion (2) (see 'Foreclosure'); another is a kind of primal projection of a 'self-reproach' on to the outside world (3) (see 'Projection').

Psychosis

b. Between 1911 and 1914, Freud takes the question up once again, this time in the context of his first theory of the psychical apparatus and the instincts (cf. the analysis of the case of Schreber [1911c] and the paper 'On Narcissism' [1914d]). He approaches the matter from the standpoint of the relations between libidinal cathexes and cathexes of objects by the ego-instincts (ego-interest*). This orientation allows of a subtle and flexible account of those clinical observations which belie any constant and indiscriminate enlistment of the idea of 'loss of reality' in explaining the psychoses.

c. In the second theory of the psychical apparatus, the opposition between neurosis and psychosis puts the ego's role as intermediary between the id and reality into question. Whereas in neurosis the ego bows to the demands of reality (and of the super-ego) and represses instinctual claims, in the case of psychosis a rupture between ego and reality occurs straight away, leaving the ego under the sway of the id; then, at a second stage–that of the onset of delusions–the ego is supposed to reconstruct a new reality in accordance with the desires of the id. It is clear that, as all the instincts are thus gathered together at the same pole of the defensive conflict–the id–Freud is obliged to make reality play the part of an actual autonomous force, almost as though it was itself an agency* of the psychical apparatus. The distinction fades between libidinal cathexis and ego-interest (whose task had formerly been to act as a mediational link within the psychical apparatus ensuring an adaptative relation to reality).

d. Freud himself did not in fact look upon this simplified schema–which has too often been treated as the last word of Freudian theory on the psychoses–as completely satisfactory (4). In the final stage of his work he started looking once again for a completely original mechanism of rejection of reality–or rather, of a highly specific 'reality', namely, castration*; his insistence on the notion of disavowal (q.v.) was the result.

(α) According to R. A. Hunter and I. Macalpine (5), the term 'psychosis' was introduced in 1845 by Feuchtersleben in his *Medical Psychology* (*Lehrbuch der ärztlichen Seelenkunde*). For this author it denotes mental illness (*Seelenkrankheit*), whereas 'neurosis' denotes affections of the nervous system–only some of which may be expressed through the symptoms of a 'psychosis'. 'Every psychosis,' he writes, 'is at the same time a neurosis, because without an intervention of nervous life no modification of the psychical is manifested; but every neurosis is not necessarily a psychosis.'

(1) FREUD, S., G.W., I, 74 and 392–93; S.E., III, 60 and 174–75.

(2) FREUD, S. 'The Neuro-Psychoses of Defence' (1894a), G.W., I, 72–74; S.E., III, 58–61.

(3) FREUD, S. 'Further Remarks on the Neuro-Psychoses of Defence' (1896b), G.W., I, 392–403; S.E., III, 174–85.

(4) FREUD, S. 'Fetishism' (1927e), cf. especially G.W., XIV, 315; S.E., XXI, 155–56.

(5) Cf. HUNTER, R. A. and MACALPINE, I. Introduction to SCHREBER, D. P. *Memoirs of my Nervous Illness* (London, Dawson, 1955), 16. English translation of Feuchtersleben: *Medical Psychology* (London, 1847).

Psychotherapy

= *D*.: Psychotherapie.–*Es*.: psicoterapia.–*Fr*.: psychothérapie.–*I*.: psicoterapia.–
P.: psicoterapia.

I. In a broad sense, any method of treating psychic or somatic disorders which utilises psychological means–or, more specifically, the therapist–patient relationship: hypnosis, suggestion, psychological re-education, persuasion, etc. In this sense psycho-analysis is a variety of psychotherapy.

II. In a narrower sense, psychotherapy in its various forms is often contrasted with psycho-analysis. There is a whole set of reasons for this distinction, but the most notable one is the major part played in psycho-analysis by the interpretation of the unconscious conflict, with the analysis of the transference tending to resolve this conflict.

III. The name 'analytic psychotherapy' is given to any form of psychotherapy which is based on the theoretical and technical principles of psycho-analysis without, however, fulfilling the requirements of a psycho-analytic treatment as strictly understood.

Purposive Idea

= *D*.: Zielvorstellung.–*Es*: representación-meta.–*Fr*.: représentation-but.–
I.: rappresentazione finalizzata.–*P*.: representação-meta.

Term coined by Freud to account for what directs the flow of thoughts, as much conscious as preconscious and unconscious ones: on each of these levels there is a purpose at work ordering thoughts in a way that is not merely mechanical, but that is determined by certain special ideas which wield a veritable force of attraction over the others (examples of such special ideas would be the *task to be accomplished* in the case of conscious ideas, and, in the case of the subject's submitting to the rule of free association*, the *unconscious phantasy**).

The term 'purposive idea' is particularly used by Freud in his first metapsychological writings–in the 'Project for a Scientific Psychology' (1950*a* [1895]) and in Chapter VII of *The Interpretation of Dreams* (1900*a*), where it occurs several times. It brings out what is original in Freud's view of psychical determinism: the flow of thoughts is never indeterminate, never independent of any law. Moreover, the laws which do govern this flow are not those purely mechanical ones identified by the doctrine of associationist psychology, according to which the stream of associations can always be accounted for in terms of juxtaposition and similarity alone, there being no need to seek any deeper significance. 'Whenever one psychical element is linked with another by an objectionable or superficial association, there is also a legitimate and deeper link between them which is subjected to the resistance of the censorship' (1).

The term 'purposive idea' underscores the fact that in Freud's view associations are subordinated to a specific aim. This aim is manifest in the case of

373

attentive, discriminating thought, where selection is governed by the goal being pursued. It is latent–though discoverable by psycho-analysis–in cases where the associations are apparently free-flowing (see 'Free Association').

Why Freud speaks of a purposive *idea* instead of speaking simply of a purpose or aim is a question that arises above all when he considers unconscious goals. One possible answer is that the relevant ideas are, quite simply, unconscious phantasies. Such an interpretation can find support in the first models of the operation of thought that Freud worked out: thought–including the exploration which characterises the secondary process*–is only possible by virtue of the fact that the purpose (or purposive idea) remains cathected, exerting an attraction which keeps all the pathways leading in its direction more permeable–or, better, more 'facilitated'*. The aim in question is the 'wishful idea' (*Wunschvorstellung*) derived from the experience of satisfaction* (2).

(1) FREUD, S. *The Interpretation of Dreams* (1900*a*), G.W., II–III, 535; S.E., V, 530.

(2) Cf. FREUD, S. *Anf.*, 411–16; S.E., I, 327–32.

Q

Quota of Affect

= *D*.: Affektbetrag.–*Es*.: cuota *or* suma de afecto.–*Fr*.: quantum d'affect.–
I.: importo *or* somma d'affetto.–*P*.: quota *or* soma de afeto.

A quantitative factor postulated as the substratum of the affect as this is experienced subjectively. The 'quota of affect' is the element that remains invariable despite the various modifications which the affect* undergoes–displacement*, detachment of the idea* and qualitative transformations.

The term 'quota of affect' is one of a number that Freud uses in framing his economic* hypothesis. This same underlying quantitative factor is given various names, such as 'cathectic energy', 'instinctual force', 'pressure' of the instinct or, when the sexual instinct alone is under consideration, 'libido'. This particular term is most often employed by Freud when he is dealing with the fate of the affect and its autonomy *vis-à-vis* the idea: '. . . in mental functions something is to be distinguished–a quota of affect or sum of excitation–which possesses all the characteristics of a quantity (though we have no means of measuring it), which is capable of increase, diminution, displacement and discharge, and which is spread over the memory-traces of ideas somewhat as an electric charge is spread over the surface of a body' (1).

374

As Jones points out, 'the idea of the affect being independent and detachable differentiated it sharply from the old conception of an "affective tone" ' (2, α). The concept of the quota of affect is metapsychological rather than descriptive: 'It corresponds to the instinct in so far as the latter has become detached from the idea and finds expression, proportionate to its quantity, in processes which are sensed as affects' (3). It is possible, however, to find examples of a looser usage of the two terms 'affect' and 'quota of affect' where the contrast between them–which corresponds, schematically, to that between quality and quantity–becomes blurred.

(α) It is worth noting, however, that in his article written in French, 'Some Points for a Comparative Study of Hysterical and Motor Paralyses' (1893c) Freud chose to render '*Affektbetrag*' by '*valeur affective*'.

(1) FREUD, S. 'The Neuro-Psychoses of Defence' (1894a), G.W., I, 74; S.E., III, 60.
(2) JONES, E. *Sigmund Freud*, I, 435.
(3) FREUD, S. 'Repression' (1915d), G.W., X, 255; S.E., XIV, 152.

R

Rationalisation

= *D*.: Rationalisierung.–*Es*.: racionalización.–*Fr*.: rationalisation.–*I*.: razionalizzazione.–*P*.: razionalização.

Procedure whereby the subject attempts to present an explanation that is either logically consistent or ethically acceptable for attitudes, actions, ideas, feelings, etc., whose true motives are not perceived. More specifically, we speak of the rationalisation of a symptom, of a defensive compulsion or of a reaction-formation. Rationalisation also occurs in delusional states and tends towards a more or less thoroughgoing systematisation.

This term was brought into common psycho-analytical usage by Ernest Jones in his article on 'Rationalisation in Everyday Life' (1908).

Rationalisation is a very common process which occurs throughout a broad field stretching from deliria to normal thought. Since any behaviour is susceptible of a rational explanation, it is often difficult to decide when such an explanation is spurious–not in what it says but in what it neglects to say. In psycho-analytic treatment, specifically, all the intermediary stages between two extremes are to be found. At one pole, it is easy to show the patient the artificiality of the motives

375

he claims and so to discourage him from being content with the account he has given. In other cases, on the contrary, the rational motives are especially well founded (the resistances that can be dissimulated by the 'appeal to reality', for example, are particularly well known to analysts); but even here it may be of use to place these motives 'in parentheses' in order to uncover the satisfactions or unconscious defences which are additional motivating factors.

Instances of the first type of case are furnished by rationalisations of neurotic or perverse symptoms (e.g. masculine homosexual behaviour is explained by an appeal to the male's supposed intellectual and aesthetic superiority); and of defensive compulsions (e.g. rituals associated with feeding are justified in terms of hygiene).

In the case of character traits or behaviour well integrated into the ego it is more difficult to make the subject aware of the part played by rationalisation.

Despite its patent defensive function rationalisation is not usually looked upon as one of the mechanisms of defence*. The reason for this is that it is not aimed directly against instinctual satisfaction, but rather operates secondarily, camouflaging the various factors in the defensive conflict. Thus defences, resistances arising during the treatment and reaction-formations are themselves subject to rationalisation. The process finds solid support in established ideologies, received morality, religions, political beliefs, etc.; in such cases the action of the super-ego comes to the aid of the ego-defences.

Rationalisation is comparable to secondary revision*, which subjects the dream-images to the logic of a consistent narrative.

It is definitely in this restricted sense, according to Freud, that rationalisation should be evoked in giving an account of delusional states. Indeed Freud considers rationalisation incapable of inventing delusional themes (1), so contesting the classical view that looks upon megalomania, for example, as a rationalisation of persecutory delusions ('I must be a great person to deserve to be persecuted by such powerful beings').

'Intellectualisation'* is a term close in meaning to 'rationalisation', but they should nonetheless be kept distinct.

(1) Cf. FREUD, S. 'Psycho-Analytic Notes on an Autobiographical Account of a Case of Paranoia (Dementia Paranoides)' (1911c), G.W., VIII, 248; S.E., XII, 48–49.

Reaction-Formation

= D.: Reaktionsbildung.–Es.: formación reactiva.–Fr.: formation réactionnelle.– I.: formazione reattiva.–P.: formação reativa or de reação.

Psychological attitude or habitus diametrically opposed to a repressed wish, and constituted as a reaction against it (e.g. bashfulness countering exhibitionistic tendencies).

In economic* terms, reaction-formation is the countercathexis* of a conscious element; equal in strength to the unconscious cathexis, it works in the contrary direction.

Reaction-formations may be highly localised, manifesting themselves in specific

behaviour, or they may be generalised to the point of forming character-traits more or less integrated into the overall personality.

From the clinical point of view, reaction-formations take on a symptomatic value when they display a rigid, forced or compulsive aspect, when they happen to fail in their purpose or when–occasionally–they lead directly to the result opposite to the one consciously intended (*suumum jus summa injuria*).

Beginning with his first descriptions of obsessional neurosis, Freud brings out a specific psychical mechanism consisting in a direct struggle with the distressing idea* and its replacement by a 'primary symptom of defence' or 'counter-symptom'. The personality traits of conscientiousness, shame and self-distrust are symptoms of this kind: they are the antithesis of the childhood sexual activity in which the subject has formerly taken pleasure during a first period of so-called 'childhood immorality'. These are instances of 'successful defence' inasmuch as the elements involved in the conflict–the sexual idea as well as the 'self-reproach' to which it gives rise–are radically excluded from consciousness to the benefit of extreme moral rectitude (1).

The subsequent development of psycho-analysis has only served to confirm the importance of this form of defence in the clinical picture of obsessional neurosis. The description of its manifestations as *reaction*-formations effectively underlines their direct opposition to the actualisation of desire, both in terms of their meaning and from the economic and dynamic points of view.

In obsessional neurosis reaction-formations take the form of character-traits or 'alterations of the ego'*. These constitute defensive systems which conceal the specificity of the ideas and phantasies involved in the conflict: thus a subject will show pity towards living beings *in general* although his unconscious aggression is directed against *particular* people. A reaction-formation constitutes a permanent countercathexis: 'The person who has built up reaction-formations does not develop certain defence mechanisms for use when an instinctual danger threatens; he has changed his personality structure as if this danger were continually present, so that he may be ready whenever the danger occurs' (2). Reaction-formations are especially marked in 'anal characters' (see 'Character Neurosis').

The mechanism of reaction-formation is not specific to the obsessional structure and it may be observed, more particularly, in hysteria. 'But the difference between reaction-formations in obsessional neurosis and in hysteria is that in the latter they do not have the universality of a character-trait but are confined to particular relationships. A hysterical woman, for instance, may be especially affectionate with her own children who at bottom she hates; but she will not on that account be more loving in general than other women, or even more affectionate to other children' (3*a*).

*   *   *

The term 'reaction-*formation*' itself invites comparisons with other forms of symptom-formation*–with substitutive formation* and compromise-formation*. Theoretically, the distinction is easy to establish: in the case of a compromise-formation, the satisfaction of the repressed wish can invariably be

377

Reaction-Formation

recognised, bound up with the defensive action (for example, in an obsession); in a reaction-formation, on the other hand, only the *opposition* to the instinct is supposed to appear – and this in particularly explicit fashion, as when an attitude of extreme cleanliness serves as a complete mask for an active anal erotism. But these remain *model* mechanisms, and, in practice, when one is confronted with an actual reaction-formation, it *is* possible to recognise the action of the instinct against which the subject is defending himself. For one thing, this instinct tends to manifest itself in abrupt outbursts at certain moments or in certain sectors of the subject's activity – and it is precisely these blatant short-comings, in their sharp contrast to the rigid attitude usually adopted, which allow us to recognise that a given personality trait has the force of a symptom. Furthermore, the subject may come close to satisfying the demands of the opposing instinct while actually engaged in the pursuit of the virtue which he affects, if this pursuit is followed through to its most extreme consequences; as a result, the threatening instinct eventually succeeds in infiltrating the whole defensive system. Does not the housewife who is obsessed with cleanliness end up by concentrating her whole existence on dust and dirt? Similarly, the lawyer who pushes his concern with equity to the extreme point of fastidiousness may in this way show his systematic lack of concern for the real problems presented to him by the defence of those who depend on him: he is thus satisfying his sadistic tendencies under a cloak of virtue. . . .

Going further, we might put even more emphasis on the relation between the instinct and the reaction-formation, treating the latter as the virtually direct expression of the conflict between two opposed instinctual feelings (a conflict which is fundamentally ambivalent): '. . . one of the two conflicting feelings (usually that of affection) becomes enormously intensified and the other vanishes' (3*b*). Were this the case, then the reaction-formation could be defined as a utilisation by the ego of the opposition intrinsic to instinctual ambivalence*.

*   *   *

Can the idea of reaction-formation be used outside the strictly pathological domain? When Freud introduces the term in the *Three Essays on the Theory of Sexuality* (1905*d*), he mentions the part played by reaction-formations in the development of every individual in that they are built up during the latency period: the sexual excitations 'evoke opposing mental forces (reacting impulses) which, in order to suppress this unpleasure [resulting from sexual activity] effectively, build up the mental dams [of] disgust, shame and morality' (4*a*). To this extent, then, Freud draws attention to the importance of reaction-formations, alongside sublimation*, in the construction of human character and human virtues (4*b*). When he introduces the concept of the super-ego* he assigns a considerable place in its genesis to the mechanism of reaction-formation (5).

(1) Cf. FREUD, S. 'Further Remarks on the Neuro-Psychoses of Defence' (1896*b*), G.W., I, 386–87; S.E., III, 169–70. Cf. also *Anf.*, 159–60; S.E., I, 222–25.

(2) FENICHEL, O. *The Psychoanalytic Theory of Neurosis* (New York: Norton, 1945), 151.

(3) FREUD, S. *Inhibitions, Symptoms and Anxiety* (1926*d*): a) G.W., XIV, 190; S.E., XX, 158. b) G.W., XIV, 130; S.E., XX, 102.

(4) FREUD, S.: a) G.W., V, 79; S.E., VIII, 178. b) Cf. G.W., V, 140–41; S.E., VII, 238–39.

(5) Cf. FREUD, S. *The Ego and the Id* (1923*b*), G.W., XIII, 262–63; S.E., XIX, 34–35.

Realistic Anxiety

= *D.*: Realangst.–*Es.*: angustia real.–*Fr.*: angoisse devant un danger réel.–
I.: angoscia (di fronte a una situazione) reale.–*P.*: angústia real.

Term used by Freud in the context of his second theory of anxiety. Realistic anxiety is anxiety occasioned by an external danger which constitutes a real threat to the subject.

The term '*Realangst*' is introduced in *Inhibitions, Symptoms and Anxiety* (1926*d*). '*Real*' is substantival–it does not qualify the anxiety itself but rather the thing motivating that anxiety. Realistic anxiety is contrasted with anxiety *vis-à-vis* the instinct. For some authors, notably Anna Freud, the instinct is anxiogenic only to the extent that it is liable to provoke a danger in the outside world; the majority of psycho-analysts maintain, however, that there is such a thing as an instinctual threat capable of generating anxiety.

Without going into the Freudian theory of anxiety we may note that the term '*Angst*', in German common usage as in its psycho-analytic sense, is not exactly equivalent to 'anxiety'. Everyday expressions such as '*ich habe Angst vor*' have to be rendered 'I am afraid to', etc. The contrast frequently made between *fear*, which is said to have a specific object, and *anxiety*, defined by the absence of any object, does not correspond precisely with the Freudian distinctions.

Reality Principle

= *D.*: Realitätsprinzip.–*Es.*: principio de realidad.–*Fr.*: principe de réalité.–
I.: principio di realtà.–*P.*: princípio de realidade.

One of the two principles which for Freud govern mental functioning. The reality principle is coupled with the pleasure principle, which it modifies: in so far as it succeeds in establishing its dominance as a regulatory principle, the search for satisfaction does not take the most direct routes but instead makes detours and postpones the attainment of its goal according to the conditions imposed by the outside world.

Viewed from the economic standpoint, the reality principle corresponds to a transformation of free energy into bound energy*; from the topographical standpoint, it is essentially characteristic of the preconscious-conscious system; and from the dynamic perspective, psycho-analysis seeks to base the intervention of the reality principle on a particular type of instinctual energy said to be more specifically in the service of the ego (see 'Ego-Instincts').

The reality principle was adumbrated in Freud's earliest metapsychological writings but only stated explicitly in 'Formulations on the Two Principles of Mental Functioning' (1911*b*). Freud relates it, in a genetic perspective, to the pleasure principle, from which it is said to take over. To begin with, the suckling

379

attempts to discover a way of discharging instinctual tension immediately, by means of hallucination (see 'Experience of Satisfaction'): 'It was only the non-occurrence of the expected satisfaction, the disappointment experienced, that led to the abandonment of this attempt at satisfaction by means of hallucination. Instead of it, the psychical apparatus had to decide to form a conception of the real circumstances in the external world and to endeavour to make a real alteration in them. A new principle of mental functioning was thus introduced; what was presented in the mind was no longer what was agreeable but what was real, even if it happened to be disagreeable' (1a). As a regulatory principle of mental functioning, the reality principle emerges secondarily, modifying the pleasure principle which has been dominant up to this point; its establishment goes hand in hand with a whole series of adaptations which the psychical apparatus has to undergo: the development of conscious functions – attention, judgement, memory; the replacement of motor discharge by an action aimed at an appropriate transformation of reality; the beginnings of thought, defined as a 'testing activity' in which small quantities of cathexis are displaced and which implies a transformation of *free* energy*, tending to circulate without hindrance from one idea to another, into *bound* energy (see 'Perceptual Identity/Thought Identity'). The transition from the pleasure to the reality principle does not, however, involve the suppression of the pleasure principle. For one thing, the reality principle assures that satisfactions are attained in the real world, while the pleasure principle continues to reign over a whole range of psychical activities – over a sort of preserve which is given over to phantasy and which functions in accordance with the laws of the primary process*: the unconscious*.

Such is the most general model that Freud worked out within the framework of what he himself called a 'genetic psychology' (1b). He points out that this schema has a different application according to whether it is the evolution of the sexual or of the self-preservative instincts that is under consideration. Whereas the instincts of self-preservation, as they develop, are gradually obliged to bow completely to the authority of the reality principle, the sexual instincts, for their part, can only be 'educated' belatedly – and never totally, even then. A secondary result of this is that the sexual instincts are said to continue as the field of the pleasure principle's action *par excellence*, while the instincts of self-preservation are quickly able to represent the requirements of reality within the psychical apparatus. In this light, the psychical conflict between the ego and the repressed emerges as definitely anchored in an instinctual dualism that in its turn parallels the dualism of the two principles.

Despite its apparent simplicity, this approach raises difficulties which Freud himself perceived and to which he drew attention on numerous occasions:

a. As regards the *instincts*, the idea that the sexual and the self-preservative instincts evolve according to a common pattern hardly seems satisfactory. In the case of the self-preservative instincts, it is hard to form a clear picture of this first period which is supposedly regulated solely by the pleasure principle, for surely these instincts are oriented from the outset towards the real satisfying object, as Freud himself maintained in order to distinguish them from the sexual instincts (2). Inversely, the link between sexuality* and phantasy* is so essential that the notion of a progressive learning of reality becomes highly questionable – the more so considering that this link is confirmed by analytic experience.

It has often been asked why the child should ever have to seek a real object if it can attain satisfaction on demand, as it were, by means of hallucination. We may resolve this difficult problem by looking upon the sexual instinct as emerging from the instinct of self-preservation, to which it stands in a double relationship of both anaclisis* and separation. Schematically, the self-preservative functions bring into play behavioural patterns and perceptual sets whieh are directed–albeit unskilfully–towards a real adequate object (breast, food). The sexual instinct comes into being secondarily in the course of the attainment of this natural function, and it only achieves an authentic independence through the trend which separates it off both from the function in question and from the object, as the pleasure is repeated auto-erotically and as selected ideas, organised into phantasies, become the aim. It is clear that from this point of view the link between the two types of instinct under consideration can by no means be seen as a secondary acquisition: the relationship between self-preservation and reality is closely knit from the start and, inversely, sexuality emerges at the same moment as phantasy and hallucinatory wish-fulfilment.

b. Critics have often attributed to Freud the idea that the human being has to emerge from a hypothetical state in which he creates a sort of closed system given over entirely to 'narcissistic'* pleasure if he is to gain access, by some obscure route, to reality. This allegation is belied by not a few of Freud's formulations: he maintains, in fact, that the real world is accessible, at least in some areas, and particularly in that of perception, from the beginning. It would seem that the contradiction arises rather from the fact that, in the field of investigation proper to psycho-analysis, the problematic of the real world presents itself in quite different terms from those familiar to a psychology oriented towards the analysis of child behaviour. It may be argued that what Freud holds–unjustifiably–to be valid for the whole of the development of the human subject has its true field of application on the plane of unconscious desire*–a plane which is unrealistic from the outset. It is in the evolution of human sexuality, and in the way that it is structured by the Oedipus complex, that Freud seeks the preconditions of access to what he calls 'full object-love'. Without this reference to the Oedipal dialectic and to the identifications which are its corollary it is well-nigh impossible to grasp the significance of a reality principle capable of changing the course of sexual desire (see 'Object').

c. Freud assigns an important part to the notion of *reality-testing**, though without ever developing a consistent theoretical explanation of this process and without giving any clear account of its relationship to the reality principle. The way he uses this notion reveals even more clearly that it covers two very different lines of thought: on the one hand, a genetic theory of the learning of reality– of the way in which the instinct is put to the test of reality by means of a sort of 'trial-and-error' procedure–and, on the other hand, a quasi-transcendental theory dealing with the constitution of the object in terms of a whole range of antitheses: internal-external, pleasurable-unpleasurable, introjection-projection. (For discussion of this problem, see 'Reality-Testing' and 'Pleasure-Ego/Reality-Ego.')

d. Inasmuch as Freud defines the *ego* in his final topography as a differentiation of the id resulting from direct contact with outside reality, he makes it into the agency which must assume the task of assuring the authority of the reality principle. The ego's 'constructive function consists in interpolating, between the demand made by an instinct and the action that satisfies it, the activity of thought which, after taking its bearings in the present and assessing earlier experiences, endeavours by means of experimental actions to calculate the consequences of the course of action proposed. In this way the ego comes to a decision on whether the attempt to obtain satisfaction is to be carried out or postponed or whether it may not be necessary for the demand by the instinct to be suppressed altogether as being dangerous. (Here we have the *reality principle*.)' (3). Such a statement exemplifies Freud's most thoroughgoing affirmation of his attempt to subordinate the individual's adaptative functions to the ego (see 'Ego', commentary, VI). This approach calls for reservations of two kinds: first, it is not certain that education in the exigencies of reality can be consigned entirely to the action of an agency of the psychical personality whose own development and function are affected by identifications and conflicts. Secondly, has not the concept of reality, in the specific field of psychoanalysis, been profoundly modified by such fundamental discoveries as that of the Oedipus complex and of the gradual constitution of the libidinal object? What psycho-analysis understands by 'access to reality' cannot be reduced either to the idea of a capacity to discriminate between the unreal and the real, or to the notion of phantasies and unconscious desires being put to the test on contact with an outside world which would indeed in that case be the sole authority.

(1) FREUD, S.: *a*) G.W., VIII, 231–32; S.E., XII, 219. b) G.W., VIII, 235; S.E., XII, 223.

(2) Cf. FREUD, S. 'Instincts and their Vicissitudes' (1915*c*), G.W., X, 227*n*.; S.E., XIV, 134–35.

(3) FREUD, S. *An Outline of Psycho-Analysis* (1940*a* [1938]), G.W., XVII, 129; S.E., XXIII, 199.

Reality-Testing

= *D*.: Realitätsprüfung.–*Es*.: prueba de realidad.–*Fr*.: épreuve de réalité.–
I.: esame di realtà.–*P*.: prova de realidade.

Process postulated by Freud which allows the subject to distinguish stimul originating in the outside world from internal ones, and to forestall possible confusion between what he perceives and what he only imagines–a confusion supposedly fundamental to hallucination.

The term '*Realitätsprüfung*' does not make its appearance in Freud's work until 'Formulations on the Two Principles of Mental Functioning' (1911*b*). The problem with which it is associated, however, had been raised as early as the first theoretical writings.

One of the basic assumptions of the 'Project' (1950*a* [1895]) is that the psychical apparatus disposes to begin with of no yardstick for telling the difference between a heavily cathected *idea* of the satisfying object and the *per-*

ception of that object. It is true that perception–which Freud attributes to a specialised system of the neuronal apparatus–has a direct relationship to real external objects and provides 'indications of reality'; but such indications may equally well be caused by the cathexis of a memory, which, if it is sufficiently intense, eventually produces hallucination. Before the indication of reality (also referred to as the 'indication of quality') can serve as a trustworthy criterion, an inhibition of the cathexis of memories must necessarily take place, and this presupposes the constitution of an ego.

At this point in Freud's thinking, clearly, it is not a 'test' that determines the reality of ideas*, but rather a mode of internal functioning of the psychical apparatus*. In *The Interpretation of Dreams* (1900a) the problem is still posed in comparable terms: the hallucinatory fulfilment of the wish, in dreams especially, is conceived of as the outcome of a 'regression' whereby the perceptual system is cathected by internal excitations.

Only with 'A Metapsychological Supplement to the Theory of Dreams' (1917d [1915]) does the question receive more systematic treatment:

a. How is belief in an idea's reality ensured in dreams and hallucinations? Regression is an adequate explanation only if we assume a recathexis not only of mnemic images but also of the system *Pcs.-Cs.* itself.

b. Reality-testing is defined as a device (*Einrichtung*) which allows us to discriminate between external stimuli which motor action is able to influence and internal ones which such action cannot eliminate. This device is assigned to the system *Cs.* in that this controls motility; Freud classes it 'among the major *institutions of the ego*' (1a, α).

c. Reality-testing can be put out of action in the case of hallucinatory disturbances and dreams inasmuch as a partial or total turning away from reality is equivalent to a withdrawal of cathexis from the system *Cs.*, which is thus left open to any cathexis reaching it from an internal source: '. . . the excitations which [...] have entered on the path of regression will find that path clear as far as the system *Cs.* where they will count as undisputed reality' (1b).

It would seem that in this text two different conceptions coexist as to what it is that permits discrimination between perceptions and endogenous ideas. On the one hand, we have an economic explanation: the difference between dream and waking state is accounted for by a differing distribution of cathexes among systems. On the other hand, there is a more empiricist view which ascribes the carrying out of this discriminatory function to motor exploration.

In one of his last works, *An Outline of Psycho-Analysis* (1940a [1938]), Freud returned to this question. Reality-testing is there defined as a 'special device' which is only needed once internal processes have become capable of affecting consciousness otherwise than through quantitative variations of pleasure and unpleasure (2a). 'Since memory-traces can become conscious just as perceptions do, especially through their association with residues of speech, the possibility arises of a confusion which would lead to a mistaking of reality. The ego guards itself against this possibility by the institution of *reality-testing*' (2b).

Freud's aim in this work is not to describe the nature of reality-testing but rather to deduce its *raison d'être*.

*   *   *

Reality-Testing

The term 'reality-testing' is often used in the psycho-analytic literature as though its sense were generally agreed upon; in point of fact its meaning is still indeterminate and confused. The different problems in connection with which it occurs may profitably be distinguished from one another.

I. Keeping strictly to Freud's conceptualisation:

a. Reality-testing is evoked as a rule apropos of the distinction between hallucinations and perceptions.

b. It would be a mistake, however, to suppose reality-testing capable of discriminating for the subject between one and the other. Once a hallucinatory state or a dream-state holds sway there is no 'test' that can counter it. So even in cases where reality-testing should theoretically be equipped to play a discriminatory role it is apparently ineffectual in practice from the start (hence the uselessness of recourse to motor action by the hallucinating subject as a way of distinguishing between subjective and objective).

c. Freud is thus obliged to ascertain the conditions that can actually prevent the hallucinatory state itself from occurring. This means, however, that there can no longer be any question of a 'test'—with its implicit connotation of a task carried out over a period of time and based on approximation, on trial and error. Freud's principle of explanation now becomes a set of metapsychological conditions (economic and topographical ones essentially).

II. In order to get out of this impasse one can try to see the Freudian model of the suckling's hallucinatory satisfaction not as an explanation of the phenomenon of hallucination in the form known to clinical experience, but rather as a genetic hypothesis relating to the ego's constitution as it evolves through the different modes of the opposition between ego and non-ego.

If, following Freud, we attempt a schematic picture of this constitutional process (see 'Pleasure-Ego/Reality-Ego'), three stages may be discerned. During a first period, access to the real world is as yet unbeset by problems: '. . . the original "reality-ego" [...] distinguished internal and external by means of a sound objective criterion' (3). At this early stage the 'equation perception = reality (external world)' still holds good (2c). Originally 'the mere existence of a presentation was a guarantee of the reality of what was presented' (4a).

At a second stage, described as that of the 'pleasure-ego', the pair of opposites in force is no longer the subjective and the objective but instead the pleasurable and the unpleasurable, the ego being identical with whatever is a source of pleasure and the non-ego with everything unpleasurable. Freud never explicitly identifies this stage with the period of 'hallucinated' satisfaction, but it seems reasonable to do so since there is no criterion available to the 'pleasure-ego' which would enable it to discern whether or not satisfaction is linked with an outside object.

The third stage—that of the 'definitive reality-ego'—supposedly corresponds to the emergence of a distinction between what is merely 'represented' and what is 'perceived'. Reality-testing is described as the mechanism which permits this discrimination, so paving the way for the constitution of an ego that becomes differentiated from outside reality as part of the same process that institutes it as an *internal* reality. Thus in 'Negation' (1925*h*) Freud terms reality-testing the basis of the judgement of existence (the judgement which affirms or denies that a given idea corresponds to something real). What makes it necessary is 'the fact

384

that thinking possesses the capacity to bring before the mind once more something that has once been perceived, by reproducing it as a presentation without the external object having still to be there' (4*b*).

III. It would still seem, however, that the term 'reality-testing' covers, and so confuses, two rather different functions: on the one hand, the basic function of discrimination between the merely represented and the actually perceived – and hence too between the internal and the external world; and on the other hand, the function which consists in comparing what is perceived objectively with mental representations so as to *rectify* possible distortions in the latter. Freud explicitly brings both these functions under the head of reality-testing (4*c*), which thus subsumes not only that motor action which is alone able to assure the differentiation of external and internal (1*c*), but also – in the case of mourning, for instance – the fact that the subject faced with the loss of a loved object learns to modify his personal world, his projects and his wishes in accordance with this real loss.

Nowhere, however, did Freud make this distinction clear, and the confusion intrinsic to the notion of reality-testing seems to have been preserved if not aggravated by present-day usage. Indeed, the term can be taken as meaning that reality is what serves to test or measure the degree of realism of the subject's wishes and phantasies, acting as the standard against which these may be judged. This line of reasoning ends by treating psycho-analytic therapy as nothing more than a gradual reduction of whatever 'unrealistic' elements may be present in the subject's personal world. This is to lose sight of one of the fundamental principles of psycho-analysis: '. . . one must never allow oneself to be misled into applying the standards of reality to repressed psychical structures, and on that account, perhaps, into undervaluing the importance of phantasies in the formation of symptoms on the ground that they are not actualities, or into tracing a neurotic sense of guilt back to some other source because there is no evidence that any actual crime has been committed' (5). Similarly, the purpose of such expressions as 'thought-reality' (*Denkrealität*) and 'psychical reality'* is to bring out the idea that unconscious structures not only have to be considered as having a specific reality answerable to its own laws, but also that they can achieve the full force of reality for the subject (see 'Phantasy').

(α) A certain hesitation is observable in Freud's work with regard to the topographical position of reality-testing. At one point in his thinking he mooted the interesting idea that it might be dependent on the ego-ideal* (6).

(1) FREUD, S.: a) G.W., X, 424; S.E., XIV, 233. b) G.W., X, 425; S.E., XIV, 234. c) Cf. G.W., X, 423–24; S.E., XIV, 232.

(2) FREUD, S.: a) Cf. G.W., XVII, 84; S.E., XXIII, 162. b) G.W., XVII, 130; S.E., XXIII, 199. c) G.W., XVII, 84; S.E., XXIII, 162.

(3) FREUD, S. 'Instincts and their Vicissitudes' (1915*c*), G.W., X, 228; S.E., XIV, 136.

(4) FREUD, S. 'Negation' (1925*h*): a) G.W., XIV, 14; S.E., XIX, 237. b) G.W., XIV, 14; S.E., XIX, 237. c) Cf. G.W., XIV, 14; S.E., XIX, 237.

(5) FREUD, S. 'Formulations on the Two Principles of Mental Functioning' (1911*b*), G.W., VIII, 238; S.E., XII, 225.

(6) Cf., for example, FREUD, S. *Group Psychology and the Analysis of the Ego*, G.W., XIII, 126; S.E., XVIII, 114.

Regression

= *D*.: Regression.–*Es*.: regresión.–*Fr*.: régression.–*I*.: regressione.–*P*.: regressão.

Applied to a psychical process having a determinate course or evolution, 'regression' means a return from a point already reached to an earlier one.

Topographically speaking, regression occurs, according to Freud, along a series of psychical systems through which excitation normally runs in a set direction.

In *temporal* terms, regression implies the existence of a genetic succession and denotes the subject's reversion to past phases of his development (libidinal stages*, object-relationships*, identifications*, etc.).

In the *formal* sense, regression means the transition to modes of expression that are on a lower level as regards complexity, structure and differentiation.

The idea of regression is evoked very often in psycho-analysis and modern psychology; it is generally conceived of as a reversion to earlier forms in the development of thought, of object-relationships or of the structure of behaviour.

Freud's first description of regression, however, placed it in a purely genetic context. A terminological point should be made in this connection: literally, to regress means to walk back, to retrace one's steps – which can be understood as readily in a logical or spatial sense as in a temporal one.

Freud introduces the idea of regression in *The Interpretaion of Dreams* (1900*a*) in order to account for an essential characteristic of dreams: the dream-thoughts* arise for the most part in the form of sensory images which impose themselves upon the subject in a quasi-hallucinatory fashion. The explanation of this trait calls for a topographical conception of the psychical apparatus which views it as made up of an ordered succession of systems. In the waking state, these systems are traversed by excitations in a *progressive* direction (travelling from perception towards motor activity); during sleep, by contrast, the thoughts, finding their access to motor activity barred, *regress* towards the perceptual system (*Pcpt.*) (1*a*). It is thus above all in a topographical sense that regression is understood by Freud when he introduces the idea (α).

The temporal meaning of the term, latent at the outset, was to gain constantly in importance with each of Freud's successive contributions concerning the individual's psychosexual development.

Although the term 'regression' does not itself appear in the *Three Essays on the Theory of Sexuality* (1905*d*), this work already hints at the possibility of a return of libido to 'collateral channels' to satisfaction (2*a*), and to earlier objects (2*b*). Note that those passages which deal explicitly with regression were added in 1915. In fact Freud himself remarked that it was only belatedly that he had discovered the idea of a regression of libido to a previous mode of organisation (3*a*). The full development of the notion of temporal regression had indeed waited upon the gradual discovery (1910–12) of the stages of infantile psychosexual development which follow each other in a predetermined order. In 'The Disposition to Obsessional Neurosis' (1913*i*), for example, Freud contrasts those cases where, 'once the sexual organisation which contains the disposition to obsessional neurosis is established, it is never afterwards completely surmounted', with other cases where this organisation is 'replaced to begin with by the higher stage of development, and then [...] reactivated by regression from the latter' (4).

At this point Freud was obliged to differentiate within the concept of regression, witness the following passage added to *The Interpretation of Dreams* in 1914: 'Three kinds of regression are thus to be distinguished; a. *topographical* regression, in the sense of the schematic picture [of the psychical apparatus]; b. *temporal* regression, in so far as what is in question is a harking back to older psychical structures; and c. *formal* regression, where primitive methods of expression and representation take the place of the usual ones. All these three kinds of regression are, however, one at bottom and occur together as a rule; for what is older in time is more primitive in form and in psychical topography lies nearer to the perceptual end' (1*b*).

Topographical regression is especially evident in dreams, where it is carried through completely. It is also found in other, pathological, processes, where it is less inclusive (hallucination), and even in some normal processes, where it is less thoroughgoing (memory).

The idea of *formal* regression is less often evoked by Freud, although numerous phenomena involving a reversion from the secondary to the primary process* may be placed under this heading (transition from a psychical functioning based on thought-identity* to one based on perceptual identity). What Freud calls formal regression may be compared to what Gestalt psychology and Jacksonian neurophysiology refer to as a destructuring (of behaviour, of consciousness, etc.). The order assumed here is not one made up of a sequence of stages actually passed through by the individual, but rather one constituted by a hierarchy of functions or structures.

Within the framework of *temporal* regression, Freud distinguishes, according to different lines of development, between a regression as regards the object, a regression as regards the libidinal stage and a regression in the evolution of the ego (3*b*).

All these distinctions do more than answer a need for classification. The fact is that in certain normal and pathological structures the different types of regression do not coincide; for example, as Freud notes, 'it is true that in hysteria there is a regression of the libido to the primary incestuous sexual objects and that this occurs quite regularly; but there is as good as no regression to an earlier stage of the sexual organisation' (3*c*).

*　　　*　　　*

Freud often laid stress on the fact that the infantile past–of the individual or even of humanity as a whole–remains forever within us: '. . . the primitive stages can always be re-established; the primitive mind is, in the fullest meaning of the word, imperishable' (5). He was able to identify this idea of a reversion to an earlier point in the most varied domains: psychopathology, dreams, the history of civilisations, biology, etc. The re-emergence of the past in the present is pointed up once more by the concept of the repetition compulsion*. Moreover, '*Regression*' is not the only word in the Freudian lexicon to express this idea, witness such kindred terms as '*Rückbildung*', '*Rückwendung*', '*Rückgreifen*', etc.

Reparation

The concept of regression is a predominantly descriptive one, as Freud himself indicated. Its evocation alone is clearly not enough to tell us in what *manner* the subject is returning to the past. Certain striking psychopathological states encourage us to understand regression in a literal way: it is sometimes said of the schizophrenic that he turns back into a baby at the breast, or of the catatonic that he returns to the foetal state. On the other hand, it is obviously not in the same sense that we are able to say that an obsessional subject has regressed to the anal stage*. And it is in an even more restricted sense – if we consider the subject's behaviour as a whole – that we speak of regression in the transference*.

Even if these distinctions of Freud's do not manage to provide the notion of regression with a rigourous theoretical basis, at least they prevent us from treating regression as a massive phenomenon. Nor should it be forgotten that the notion of regression is linked to that of fixation, and that this cannot be reduced to the implantation of a behavioural pattern. In so far as fixation is to be understood as an 'inscription' (see 'Fixation', 'Ideational Representative'), regression might be interpreted as the bringing back into play of what has been 'inscribed'. When mention is made of 'oral regression' – particularly during the treatment – we ought, from this point of view, to take this as meaning that the subject's speech and attitudes represent a rediscovery of what Freud called 'the language of the oral instinctual impulses' (6).

(α) The idea of a 'retrogressing' (*rückläufige*) excitation of the perceptual apparatus in hallucinations and dreams – found in Breuer as from the *Studies on Hysteria* (1895*d*) (7) and in Freud as early as the 'Project for a Scientific Psychology' (1950*a* [1895]) (8) – appears to have been fairly widespread among those nineteenth-century authors who dealt with hallucination.

(1) FREUD, S.: a) Cf. G.W., II-III, 538–55; S.E., V, 533–49. b) G.W., II-III, 554; S.E., V, 548.

(2) Cf. FREUD, S.: a) G.W., V, 69–70; S.E., VII, 170–71. b) G.W., V, 129; S.E., VII, 228.

(3) FREUD, S. *Introductory Lectures on Psycho-Analysis* (1916–17): a) Cf. G.W., XI, 355–57; S.E., XVI, 343–44. b) Cf. G.W., XI, 353–57 & 370–71; S.E., XVI, 340–44 & 357. c) G.W., XI, 355; S.E., XVI, 343.

(4) FREUD, S., G.W., VIII, 448; S.E., XII, 322.

(5) FREUD, S. 'Thoughts for the Times on War and Death' (1915*b*), G.W., X, 337; S.E., XIV, 286.

(6) FREUD, S. 'Repression' (1915*d*), G.W., XIV, 13; S.E., XIX, 237.

(7) Cf. BREUER, J. and FREUD, S., 1st German edn., 164–65; S.E., II, 188–89.

(8) Cf. FREUD, S., *Anf.*, 423; S.E., I, 339.

Reparation

= *D*.: Wiedergutmachung. – *Es*.: reparación. – *Fr*.: réparation. – *I*.: riparazione. – *P*.: reparação.

Mechanism described by Melanie Klein whereby the subject seeks to repair the effects his destructive phantasies have had on his love-object. This mechanism is associated with depressive anxiety and guilt: the phantasied reparation of the external and internal maternal object is said to permit the overcoming of the

depressive position by guaranteeing the ego a stable identification with the beneficial object.

It should be pointed out first of all that Melanie Klein's writings contain several terms that are very close to one another in meaning: *'Weiderherstellung'* (or 'restoration'), *'Wiedergutmachung'* ('restitution' or 'reparation' in the English texts, with the latter being preferred in Klein's later work). In their Kleinian usage these terms retain the various overtones they have in common parlance; 'reparation', specifically, has the same sense here as is found in 'to repair something' as well as in 'to make reparation to someone'.

The idea of reparation is part of the Kleinian conception of early infantile sadism, which finds expression in phantasies of destruction (*Zerstörung*), fragmentation (*Ausschneiden; Zerschneiden*), devouring (*Fressen*), etc. Reparation is linked essentially with the depressive position (q.v.), which coincides with the establishment of a relation to the whole object*. It is in response to the anxiety and guilt intrinsic to this position that the child attempts to maintain or restore the wholeness of the mother's body. Various phantasies represent this endeavour to repair 'the disaster created through the ego's sadism' (1*a*): preserving the mother's body from the attacks of 'bad' objects*, putting the dispersed bits of it back together again, bringing what has been killed back to life, etc. By thus restoring its wholeness to the loved object and negating all the evil that has been done it, the child is said to be assured of the possession a thoroughly 'good' and stable object whose introjection will strengthen his ego. Phantasies of reparation therefore play a structuring role in ego-development.

To the extent that their operation is defective, mechanisms of reparation may come to resemble sometimes maniac defences (feeling of omnipotence), and sometimes obsessional ones (compulsive repetition of reparatory acts). Successful reparation, according to Klein, implies a victory of the life instincts over the death instincts (see these terms).

Melanie Klein has emphasised the part played by reparation in the work of mourning* and in sublimation*: '... the effort to undo the state of disintegration to which [the object] has been reduced presupposes the necessity to make it beautiful and "perfect" ' (1*b*, 1*c*).

(1) KLEIN, M. *Contributions to Psycho-Analysis*: a) 289. b) 290. c) Cf. 227–35.

Representability, Considerations of

= D.: Rücksicht auf Darstellbarkeit.–*Es*.: consideración a la reprentabilidad.–
Fr.: prise en considération de la figurabilité.–*I*.: riguardo per la raffigurabilità.–
P.: consideração à representabilidade *or* figurabilidade.

Requirement imposed on the dream-thoughts; they undergo selection and transformation such as to make them capable of being represented by images–particularly visual images.

389

Repression

The expressive system constituted by dreams has its own laws. It demands that all meanings, even the most abstract thoughts, be expressed through images. Speeches and words, according to Freud, enjoy no special privileges in this respect: their role in dreams is limited to that of meaningful elements and has no relation to the sense they might have in spoken language.

This condition has two consequences:

a. It means that 'of the various subsidiary thoughts attached to the essential dream-thoughts, those will be preferred which admit of visual representation' (1*a*). In particular, the logical connections between the dream-thoughts are eliminated or replaced more or less effectively by the forms of expression that Freud describes in *The Interpretation of Dreams* (1900*a*) (Chapter VI, Part C: 'The Means of Representation in Dreams').

b. It directs displacements towards pictorial substitutes. Thus the displacement of expressions (*Ausdrucksverschiebung*) can provide a bridge–a concrete word– between an abstract notion and a sensory image (for example, the replacement of the term of 'aristocrat' by that of 'highly placed'–which can be represented by a *high tower*).

This condition regulating the dream-work undoubtedly originates in 'regression'*–regression at once topographical, formal and temporal. In regard to the temporal aspect Freud stresses the polarising role played by infantile scenes of an essentially visual character in the fabrication of dream images: '. . . the transformation of thoughts into visual images may be in part the result of the attraction which memories couched in visual form and eager for revival bring to bear upon thoughts cut off from consciousness and struggling to find expression. On this view a dream might be described as *a substitute for the infantile scene modified by being transferred on to a recent experience*. The infantile scene is unable to bring about its own revival and has to be content with returning as a dream' (1*b*).

(1) FREUD, S.: a) G.W., II–III, 349; S.E., V, 344. b) G.W., II–III, 551–52; S.E., V, 546.

Repression

= *D*.: Verdrängung.–*Es*.: represión.–*Fr*.: refoulement.–*I*.: rimozione.– *P*.: recalque *or* recalcamento.

I. Strictly speaking, an operation whereby the subject attempts to repel, or to confine to the unconscious, representations (thoughts, images, memories) which are bound to an instinct. Repression occurs when to satisfy an instinct–though likely to be pleasurable in itself–would incur the risk of provoking unpleasure because of other requirements.

Repression is particularly manifest in hysteria, but it also plays a major part in other mental illnesses as well as in normal psychology. It may be looked upon as a universal mental process in so far as it lies at the root of the constitution of the unconscious as a domain separate from the rest of the psyche.

II. In a looser sense, the term 'repression' is sometimes used by Freud in a way

which approximates it to 'defence'*. There are two reasons for this: first, the operation of repression in sense I constitutes one stage–to say the least–in many complex defensive processes (and Freud takes the part for the whole); secondly, the theoretical model of repression is used by Freud as the prototype of other defensive procedures.

A distinction between two senses of the term 'repression' appears to be unavoidable, a conclusion borne out by Freud's own remarks, made in 1926, on the subject of his use of 'repression' and 'defence': 'It will be an undoubted advantage, I think, to revert to the old concept of 'defence', provided we employ it explicitly as a general designation for all the techniques which the ego makes use of in conflicts which may lead to a neurosis, while we retain the word 'repression' for the special method of defence which the line of approach taken by our investigations made us better acquainted with in the first instance' (1).

In point of fact the development of Freud's views on the question of the relation between repression and defence does not correspond exactly to the picture of it put forward in these lines, and a number of comments are called for on the actual evolution of his attitude:

a. In texts prior to *The Interpretation of Dreams* (1900a) the terms 'repression' and 'defence' are used with comparable frequency. It is only on very rare occasions, however, that Freud employs them as if they were quite simply interchangeable. It would be wrong, moreover, to assert on the basis of Freud's subsequent testimony that the only mode of defence known to him during this early period was repression–as the mode of defence specific to hysteria–and that he thus treated the particular as the general. In the first place, he was quite able to specify the various psychoneuroses according to clearly differentiated modes of defence, which did not include repression. Thus in the two papers dealing with the neuro-psychoses of defence* (1894a; 1896b), it is the *conversion** of the affect which is seen as the defence mechanism of hysteria, and the transposition or displacement of the affect as that of obsessional neurosis, while in the case of psychosis Freud looks to such mechanisms as the simultaneous repudiation (*verwerfen*) of idea and affect, or projection. Furthermore, 'repression' is used to denote the fate of those ideas cut off from consciousness which constitute the nucleus of a separate psychical group–a process to be observed in obsessional neurosis as well as in hysteria (2).

Even if the concepts of defence and repression both extend beyond the context of any particular psychopathological condition, they clearly do not do so in the same manner. Defence is a *generic* concept from the start, and it designates a general tendency 'linked to the most fundamental conditions of the psychical mechanism (the law of constancy)' (3a). This trend may take normal forms as well as pathological ones. In the latter, it is expressed specifically in complex 'mechanisms' in which idea and affect are subject to different vicissitudes. It is true that repression too is universally present in the various illnesses, and that it is not merely a particular defence mechanism specific to hysteria, but this is because the different psychoneuroses all imply a separate unconscious (q.v.)–an unconscious of which repression *is the foundation*.

b. After 1900, the term 'defence' tends to be used less often, but it is far from disappearing completely as Freud claimed–' "repression" (as I now began to say instead of "defence")' (4)–and it preserves the same generic meaning. Freud continues to speak of 'mechanisms of defence', 'defensive struggle', etc.

As for 'repression', it never loses its *specificity* so as to become simply a comprehensive concept connoting all the defensive techniques used for dealing with psychical conflict. It is significant, for example, that in his treatment of 'secondary defence'–defence against the symptom itself–Freud never refers to it as secondary 'repression' (5). In the paper which he devoted to the notion of repression in 1915, it retains at bottom the meaning we have outlined above: '. . . *the essence of repression lies simply in turning something away, and keeping it at a distance, from the conscious*' (6a). In this sense, repression is sometimes looked upon as a particular 'defence mechanism'–or rather as an 'instinctual vicissitude'–liable to be employed as a defence. It plays a major part in hysteria, while in obsessional neurosis it is embedded in a more complex defensive process (6b). One should not therefore argue–as the editors of the *Standard Edition* do (7)–that, since repression is described as present in several neuroses, 'repression' and 'defence' may therefore be treated as synonymous. The fact is that repression is to be met with in each condition as one moment of the defensive operation–and this in its precise sense of repression into the unconscious.

It is true, nonetheless, that the mechanism of repression studied by Freud in its different stages does constitute in his eyes a sort of prototype of other defensive operations. Thus in his account of the case of Schreber (1911c), while actually trying to isolate a defence mechanism specific to psychosis, he refers to the three phases of repression and exploits the opportunity to present his theory of this process. It is no doubt in such a text as this that the confusion between the concepts of repression and defence is at its greatest–and it is more than terminological confusion, for it gives rise to basic problems (see 'Projection').

c. Finally, it should not pass unnoticed that Freud, after subsuming repression under the category of the mechanisms of defence, wrote as follows in his commentary on Anna Freud's book: 'There was never any doubt that repression was not the only procedure which the ego could employ for its purposes. Nevertheless, repression is something quite peculiar and is more sharply differentiated from the other mechanisms than they are from each other' (8).

*   *   *

'The theory of repression is the cornerstone on which the whole structure of psycho-analysis rests' (9). The term is already to be met with in Herbart (10) and some authors have suggested that Herbart's work was known to Freud through Maynert (11). Be that as it may, it was as a clinical *datum* that repression imposed itself from Freud's earliest treatment of hysterics onwards. Freud found that his patients did not have certain memories at their disposition, although these were perfectly vivid once they *had* been recalled: '. . . it was a question of things which the patient wished to forget, and therefore intentionally repressed from his conscious thought and inhibited and suppressed' (12).

It is clear from this, the formative moment of the notion of repression, that it appeared from the beginning in correlation to the concept of the unconscious (in fact the word 'repressed' remained a synonym of 'unconscious' right up until the introduction of the idea of unconscious defences of the ego). As for the qualification 'intentionally', Freud does not make it unreservedly even at this period (1895): the splitting of consciousness is only *initiated* by an intentional act. In fact the repressed contents escape the control of the subject and they are governed–as a 'separate psychical group'–by their own laws (the primary process*). A repressed idea itself constitutes a 'nucleus of crystallization' capable of attracting other incompatible ideas without the intervention of any conscious intention (13). To this extent the operation of repression itself bears the mark of the primary process. Indeed, this is what distinguishes it as a pathological form of defence as compared with a normal type of defence such as avoidance (3*b*). Lastly, repression is described from the outset as a dynamic operation implying the maintenance of an anticathexis*, and liable at any moment to be defeated by the strength of the unconscious wish which is striving to return into consciousness and motility (see 'Return of the Repressed', 'Compromise-Formation').

In the years 1911–15, Freud endeavoured to develop a detailed theory of repression by distinguishing different phases of the process. It should be noted in this connection, however, that this was not in fact his first theoretical elaboration of the matter. In our view, his *theory* of seduction* must be looked upon as a first systematic attempt to account for repression–an attempt which is all the more interesting in that this mechanism is not described in isolation from its object *par excellence*–namely, sexuality.

In his article on 'Repression' (1915*d*), Freud makes a distinction between repression in a broad sense, comprising three phases, and in a more restricted sense which refers to the second phase taken alone. The first phase is a 'primal repression'*, not directed against the instinct as such but against its signs or 'representatives', which are denied entrance to the conscious and to which the instinct remains fixated. In this way a first unconscious nucleus is formed which acts as a pole of attraction for the elements due to be repressed.

Repression proper (*eigentliche Verdrängung*) or 'after-pressure' (*Nachdrängen*) is therefore a dual process, in that it adds to this attraction a repulsion (*Abstossung*) operating from the direction of a higher agency.

The third and last phase is the 'return of the repressed' in the guise of symptoms, dreams, parapraxes, etc. What does repression act *upon*? It must be emphasised that it acts neither upon the instinct* (14*a*) which, in so far as it is organic, escapes the split between conscious and unconscious, nor upon the affect*. The affect may undergo various transformations as an indirect result of repression but it cannot become unconscious in any strict sense (14*b*) (see 'Suppression'). It is only the ideational representatives* of the instinct (ideas, images, etc.) that are repressed. These representative elements are bound to the primal repressed material, either because they originate from it or because they become connected with it fortuitously. The fate reserved for each one by repression is quite distinct and 'highly individual', according to its degree of distortion, its remoteness from the unconscious nucleus or its affective value.

$$* \quad * \quad *$$

The repressive operation may be viewed in the triple perspective of metapsychology*:

First, from the *topographical* point of view: although repression is described

393

in the first theory of the psychical apparatus as exclusion from consciousness, Freud does not identify consciousness and the repressing agency*; it is, rather, the *censorship** which provides a model here. In the second topography repression is held to be a defensive operation of the ego (partially unconscious).

Secondly, from the *economic** point of view, repression implies a complex interplay of decathexes*, recathexes and anticathexes affecting the instinctual representatives.

Lastly, from the *dynamic** standpoint, the main question is that of the *motives* for repression: how does it come about that an instinct—whose satisfaction must by definition engender pleasure—occasions instead such unpleasure that the repressive operation is triggered off? (On this point, see 'Defence'.)

(1) FREUD, S. *Inhibitions, Symptoms and Anxiety* (1926*d*), G.W., XIV, 195; S.E., XX, 163.

(2) Cf., for example, FREUD, S. 'The Neuro-Psychoses of Defence' (1894*a*), G.W., I, 68–69; S.E., III, 54–55.

(3) FREUD, S.: a) *Anf.*, 157; S.E., I, 221. b) *Anf.*, 431–32; S.E., I, 409–10.

(4) FREUD, S. 'My Views on the Part Played by Sexuality in the Aetiology of the Neuroses' (1906*a* [1905]), G.W., V, 156; S.E., VII, 276.

(5) Cf. FREUD, S. 'Notes upon a Case of Obsessional Neurosis' (1909*d*), G.W., VII, 441–42; S.E., X, 224–25.

(6) FREUD, S. 'Repression' (1915*d*): a) G.W., X, 250; S.E., XIV, 147. b) G.W., X, 259-61; S.E., XIV, 156–58.

(7) Cf. S.E., XIV, 144.

(8) FREUD, S. 'Analysis Terminable and Interminable' (1937*c*), G.W., XVI, 81; S.E., XXIII, 236.

(9) FREUD, S. 'On the History of the Psycho-Analytic Movement' (1914*d*), G.W., X, 54; S.E., XIV, 16.

(10) Cf. HERBART, J. F. *Psychologie als Wissenschaft* (1824), 341; and *Lehrbuch zur Psychologie* (1806), in *Samtliche Werke*, V, 19.

(11) Cf. JONES, E. *Sigmund Freud*, I, 309; and ANDERSSON, O. *Studies in the Prehistory of Psycho-analysis* (Norstedts: Svenska Bokförlaget, 1962), 116–17. Another edn.: New York: Humanities Press, 1962.

(12) BREUER, J. and FREUD, S. 'On the Psychical Mechanism of Hysterical Phenomena: Preliminary Communication' (1893*a*), in *Studies on Hysteria* (1895*d*), G.W., I, 89; S.E., II, 10.

(13) Cf. FREUD, S. *Studies on Hysteria* (1895*d*), G.W., I, 182; S.E., II, 123.

(14) Cf. FREUD, S. 'The Unconscious' (1915*e*): a) G.W., X, 275–76; S.E., XIV 177 b) G.W., X, 276–77; S.E., XIV, 177–78.

Resistance

= *D.*: Widerstand. – *Es.*: resistencia. – *Fr.*: résistance. – *I.*: resistenza. – *P.*: resistência.

In psycho-analytic treatment the name 'resistance' is given to everything in the words and actions of the analysand that obstructs his gaining access to his unconscious. By extension, Freud spoke of *resistance to psycho-analysis* when referring to a hostile attitude towards his discoveries in so far as they exposed unconscious desires and inflicted a 'psychological blow' upon man (α).

The concept of resistance was introduced by Freud very early on; it may be said to have played a decisive part in the foundation of psycho-analysis. In fact hypnosis and suggestion were rejected essentially because the passive resistance that certain patients set up against them seemed to Freud at once legitimate (β) and impossible to overcome or to interpret (γ) by such methods. Psychoanalysis, by contrast, made it possible to achieve these aims in that it permitted the gradual bringing to light of the resistances, which are expressed particularly by the different ways in which the patient breaks the fundamental rule*. A first inventory of the various forms of resistance–some manifest, some concealed–is to be found in the *Studies on Hysteria* (1895d) (1a).

Resistance was first discovered as an obstacle to the elucidation of the symptoms and to the progress of the treatment; it is the resistance that 'finally brings work to a halt' (2a, δ). To start with, Freud tried to overcome this obstacle by insistence (application of a countervailing force to the resistance) and persuasion, but then he realised that resistance was itself a means of reaching the repressed and unveiling the secret of neurosis; in fact the forces to be seen at work in resistance and in repression were one and the same. In this sense–as Freud stresses in his technical writings–all progress made in analytic technique may be summed up as the increasingly accurate evaluation of the resistance–that is, of the clinical fact that conveying the meaning of his symptoms to the patient does not suffice to eliminate the repression. As we know, Freud held steadfastly to the view that the interpretation of resistance, along with that of the transference*, constituted the specific characteristics of his technique. What is more, he considers that the transference is to be looked upon as in part a resistance itself, in that it substitutes acted-out repetition for verbalised recollection; it must be borne in mind, however, that although resistance may make use of the transference it does not constitute it.

Freud's views regarding the explanation of the resistance phenomenon are harder to ascertain. In the *Studies on Hysteria* he forms the following hypothesis: memories may be considered as grouped, according to their degree of resistance, in concentric layers around a central pathogenic nucleus; in the course of treatment, therefore, each time the frontier is crossed between one circle and the next nearest the nucleus, the resistance increases correspondingly (1b). From this period on, Freud treats resistance as a manifestation, specific to the treatment and to the recollection this requires, of that same force which the ego directs against unpleasurable ideas. He seems, however, to see the ultimate source of resistance in a repelling force derived from the repressed itself–an expression of the difficulty the repressed has in becoming conscious, and particularly in gaining the subject's full acceptance. We are here faced therefore with two kinds of explanation: according to one, the resistance is governed by its distance from the repressed; according to the other, it is equivalent to a defensive function. This ambiguity subsists in Freud's writings on technique.

With the advent of the second topography, however, the emphasis shifts to the defensive aspect of the resistance; such defence, as several texts make clear, is carried out by the ego. 'The unconscious–that is to say, the "repressed"–offers no resistance whatever to the efforts of the treatment. Indeed, it itself has no other endeavour than to break through the pressure weighing down on it and force its way either to consciousness or to a discharge through some real action. Resistance during treatment arises from the same higher strata and systems of the mind which originally carried out repression' (3).

Resistance

This predominant role of ego-defence is asserted by Freud right up until one of his last writings: '. . . the defensive mechanisms directed against former danger recur in the treatment as *resistances* against recovery. It follows from this that the ego treats recovery itself as a new danger' (4*a*). From this standpoint the analysis of resistances is indistinguishable from that of the permanent ego-defences as they emerge in the analytic situation (Anna Freud).

Yet Freud does explicitly state that the manifest defence put up by the ego is not sufficient to account for the difficulties met with as the work of analysis is carried through and concluded; the analyst, in his clinical experience, encounters resistances that he cannot put down to alterations* of the ego (4*b*).

At the end of *Inhibitions, Symptoms and Anxiety* (1926*d*), Freud distinguishes five types of resistances. Three are ascribed to the ego: repression, transference resistance, and that resistance which proceeds from the secondary gain* from illness and which is 'based upon an assimilation of the symptoms into the ego'. This still leaves the resistance of the unconscious or the id and that of the super-ego. The former is what makes working-through* (*Durcharbeiten*) technically indispensable: it is the 'power of the compulsion to repeat–the attraction exerted by the unconscious prototypes upon the repressed instinctual process'. Finally, the resistance of the super-ego derives from unconscious guilt and the need for punishment* (5*a*) (see 'Negative Therapeutic Reaction').

Here we have an attempt at metapsychological classification with which Freud was not satisfied but which at least has the merit of pointing up his steadfast refusal to lump the interpersonal and intrapersonal phenomenon of resistance together with the defence mechanisms intrinsic to the structure of the ego. For Freud the question of *who resists* remains open and vexed (*ε*). There is no getting around the fact that beyond the ego, 'which clings to its anticathexes' (5*b*), there lies a final obstacle to the work of analysis–a fundamental resistance about the nature of which Freud's hypotheses were at variance, but which, in any event, cannot be placed in the category of defensive operations (see 'Repetition Compulsion').

(α) This is an idea that emerges as early as 1896: 'I am met with hostility and live in such isolation that one might suppose I had discovered the greatest truths' (2*b*). As to the 'psychological blow', cf. 'A Difficulty in the Path of Psycho-Analysis' (1917*a*) (6).

(β) 'When a patient who showed himself unamenable was met with the shout: "What are you doing? *Vous vous contre-suggestionnez!*", I said to myself that this was an evident injustice and an act of violence. For the man certainly had a right to counter-suggestion if people were trying to subdue him with suggestions' (7).

(γ) Suggestive technique 'does not permit us, for example, to recognise the *resistance* with which the patient clings to his disease and thus even fights against his own recovery' (8).

(δ) Cf. the definition of resistance given in *The Interpretation of Dreams* (1900*a*): '. . . whatever interrupts the progress of analytic work is a resistance' (9).

(ε) The reader is referred to Edward Glover's *The Technique of Psycho-Analysis*. After methodically enumerating the resistances *qua* manifestations–brought out by analysis–of the permanent defences of the mental apparatus, Glover acknowledges the existence of a residue: '. . . having exhausted the possibilities of resistance arising from the ego or the super-ego, we are faced with the bare fact that a set of presentations is being repeated before us again and again. [...] We expected that by removing the ego and the super-ego resistances we should bring about something like automatic release of pressure, that the charge would either dissipate itself explosively and openly, or that some other manifestation of defence would immediately arise to bind the freed energy, as happens in transitory symptom-formation. Instead, we seem

396

to have given a fillip to the repetition-compulsion, and the id has made use of weakened ego-defences to exercise an increased attraction on preconscious presentations' (10).

(1) Cf. FREUD, S.: a) G.W., I, 280; S.E., II, 278. b) G.W., I, 284; S.E., II, 289.

(2) FREUD, S.: a) letter of October 27, 1897, *Anf.*, 240; S.E., I, 266. b) letter of March 13, 1896, *Anf.*, 172; *Origins*, 161.

(3) FREUD, S. *Beyond the Pleasure Principle* (1920g), G.W., XIII, 17; S.E., XVIII, 19.

(4) FREUD, S. 'Analysis Terminable and Interminable' (1937c): a) G.W., XVI, 84; S.E., XXIII, 238. b) Cf. G.W., XVI, 86; S.E., XXIII, 241.

(5) FREUD, S.: a) Cf. G.W., XIV, 191–93; S.E., XX, 158–60. b) G.W., XIV, 191–93; S.E., XX, 158–60.

(6) Cf. FREUD, S., G.W., XII, 1–26; S.E., XVII, 137–44.

(7) FREUD, S. *Group Psychology and the Analysis of the Ego* (1921c), G.W., XIII, 97; S.E., XVIII, 89.

(8) FREUD, S. 'On Psychotherapy' (1905a [1904]), G.W., V, 18; S.E., VII, 261.

(9) FREUD, S., G.W., II–III, 521; S.E., V, 517.

(10) GLOVER, E. (London: Baillière, 1955; New York: I.U.P., 1955), 81.

Retention Hysteria

= *D.*: Retentionshysterie.–*Es.*: histeria de retención.–*Fr.*: hystérie de rétention.–
I.: isteria da ritenzione.–*P.*: histeria de retenção.

Form of hysteria* distinguished by Breuer and Freud in 1894–95 from two others: hypnoid hysteria* and defence hysteria*.

Pathogenically, this hysteria is characterised by the existence of affects which have not undergone abreaction, particularly as a result of unfavourable outside circumstances.

It was in 'The Neuro-Psychoses of Defence' (1894a) that Freud first identified retention hysteria as a specific form of hysteria.

In the 'Preliminary Communication' (1893a), the notion of retention–though not the actual term–was used to evoke a set of aetiological conditions where, in contradistinction to the hypnoid state, it is the *nature* of the trauma (determined either by the social circumstances surrounding it or by defence on the part of the subject himself) which excludes the possibility of abreaction (1a).

The idea of retention, more descriptive than explanatory, was destined soon to disappear, for in attempting to account for the phenomenon of retention Freud encountered defence*. An example of this was his therapeutic experience in the case of Rosalia H. (1b), to which he is no doubt alluding when he makes the following observation: 'I had a case which I looked upon as a typical retention hysteria and I rejoiced in the prospect of an easy and certain success. But this success did not occur, though the work was in fact easy. I therefore suspect, though subject once again to all the reserve which is proper to ignorance, that at the basis of retention hysteria, too, an element of defence is to be found which has forced the whole process in the direction of hysteria' (1c).

397

(1) FREUD, S. *Studies on Hysteria* (1895*d*): a) Cf. G.W., I, 89; S.E., II, 10. b) Cf. G.W., I, 237–41; S.E. II, 169–73. c) G.W., I, 289–90; S.E. II, 286.

Return of the Repressed

= *D.*: Wiederkehr (*or* Rückkehr) des Verdrängten.–*Es.*: retorno de lo reprimido.–
Fr.: retour du refoulé.–*I.*: ritorno del rimosso.–*P.*: retôrno do recalcado.

Process whereby what has been repressed–though never abolished by repression–tends to reappear, and succeeds in so doing in a distorted fashion in the form of a compromise.

Freud always insisted on the 'indestructibility' of the contents of the unconscious (1). Repressed material not only escapes destruction, it also has a permanent tendency to re-emerge into consciousness. It does so by more or less devious routes, and through the intermediary of secondary formations–'derivatives of the unconscious'*–which are unrecognisable to a greater or lesser degree (α).

The idea that symptoms may be explained in terms of a return of what has been repressed is brought forward from the earliest of Freud's psychoanalytic writings. Another essential idea is also present from the outset–namely, the notion that this return of the repressed comes about by means of 'a *compromise* between the repressed ideas and the repressing ones' (2). As regards the relation between the mechanisms of repression* and the return of the repressed, however, Freud's view varied considerably:

a. For example, in *Delusions and Dreams in Jensen's 'Gradiva'* (1907*a*), Freud is led to place the emphasis on the fact that the repressed, in order to return, makes use of the same chains of association which have served as the vehicle for repression in the first place (3*a*). The two operations are thus seen as being intimately connected, each presenting the mirror-image of the other, as it were. In this context, Freud evokes the excuse of the ascetic monk who, while seeking to banish temptation by gazing at an image of the Crucifixion, is rewarded by the appearance of a naked woman in the place of the crucified Saviour: '. . . in and behind the repressing force, what is repressed proves itself victor in the end' (3*b*).

b. Freud did not stand by this conception, however: he revises it, for instance, in a letter to Ferenczi dated December 6, 1910, in which he asserts that the return of the repressed is a specific mechanism (4). This hypothesis is further developed, especially in 'Repression' (1915*d*), where the return of the repressed is conceived of as a third, independent stage in the operation of repression when the latter is understood in its broadest sense (5). Freud here describes the process in the various neuroses, and the upshot of his analysis is that the return of the repressed comes about by means of displacement*, condensation*, conversion*, etc.

Freud also outlined the general preconditions for the return of the repressed: these are the weakening of the anticathexis*, the reinforcement of the instinctual pressure (under the biological influence of puberty, for instance), and the occurrence, in the present, of events which call forth the repressed material.

(α) As regards the problems to which such an approach gives rise, the reader's attention is drawn to a note in *Inhibitions, Symptoms and Anxiety* (1926d) in which Freud asks whether repressed wishes end up by transferring all their energy to their derivatives or whether they themselves remain present in the unconscious (7).

(1) Cf. FREUD, S. *The Interpretation of Dreams* (1900a), G.W., II–III, 583; S.E., V, 577.

(2) FREUD, S. 'Further Remarks on the Neuro-Psychoses of Defence' (1896b), G.W., I, 387; S.E., III, 170.

(3) FREUD, S.: a) Cf. G.W., VII, 60–61; S.E., IX, 35. b) G.W., VII, 50–61, S.E., IX, 35.

(4) Cf. JONES, E. *Sigmund Freud*, II, 499.

(5) Cf. FREUD, S., G.W., X, 256–58; S.E., XIV, 154–56.

(6) Cf. FREUD, S. *Moses and Monotheism* (1939a), G.W., XVI, 210–12; S.E., XXIII, 95–96.

(7) Cf. FREUD, S., G.W., XIV, 173n.; S.E., XX, 142n.

Reversal into the Opposite

= *D.*: Verkehrung ins Gegenteil.–*Es.*: transformación en lo contrario.–
Fr.: renversement dans le contraire.–*I.*: conversione nell' opposto.–
P.: interversão do impulso *or* da pulsão.

Process whereby the aim of an instinct is transformed into its opposite in the transition from activity to passivity.

In 'Instincts and their Vicissitudes' (1915c) Freud counts reversal into the opposite and turning round upon the subject's own self* among the 'instinctual vicissitudes' alongside repression* and sublimation*. He immediately points out that these two processes, one concerning the aim*, the other the object*, are so closely bound up with each other–as is shown by the two major instances of sadism/masochism* and voyeurism/exhibitionism–that they cannot be described separately.

The turning round of sadism into masochism implies both the transition from activity to passivity* and an inversion of roles between the one who inflicts and the one who undergoes suffering. This process may be arrested at an intermediate point where, though there is a turning round upon the subject's own self (change of *object*), yet the *aim* has not become passive but merely reflexive (making oneself suffer). In its complete form, with the transition to passivity made, masochism implies that 'An extraneous person is once more sought as object; this person, in consequence of the alteration which has taken place in the instinctual aim, has to take over the role of subject' (1a). Such a transformation is inconceivable unless it is assumed that phantasy has an organising part to play: in imagination, another person becomes the subject at whom the instinctual activity is directed.

The two processes may of course function in the reverse direction: the transformation of passivity into activity, or a turning round from the self on to

399

the other person: '. . . there is no difference in principle between an instinct turning from an object to the ego and its turning from the ego to an object' (2).

One might ask whether the return of libido from an outside object to the ego (ego-libido* or narcissistic libido) could not also be described as a 'turning round upon the self'. Freud, it may be noted, preferred in such cases to use such expressions as 'withdrawal of the libido on to' or 'into the ego'.

Alongside the reversal of activity into passivity, which affects the mode or 'form' of activity, Freud envisages a reversal 'of the content', a 'material' reversal: love turns into hate. But to speak of turning round here seems to him valid at a descriptive level only, for love and hate cannot be understood as the vicissitudes of a single instinct. Thus in the first instinct theory (1b), as in the second (3), Freud assigns them distinct origins.

Anna Freud classes reversal into the opposite and turning round upon the self among the mechanisms of defence and asks whether we ought not to view them as the most primitive of defensive processes (4) (see 'Identification with the Aggressor'). Certain passages in Freud tend to support this position (1c).

(1) FREUD, S.: a) G.W., X, 220; S.E., XIV, 127. b) Cf. G.W., X, 225 *ff*.; S.E., XIV, 133 *ff*. c) Cf. G.W., X, 219; S.E., XIV, 126–27.

(2) FREUD, S. *Beyond the Pleasure Principle* (1920*g*), G.W., XIII, 59; S.E., XVIII, 54.

(3) Cf. FREUD, S. *The Ego and the Id* (1923*b*), G.W., XIII, 271 *ff*.; S.E., XIX, 42 *ff*.

(4) Cf. FREUD, A. *The Ego and the Mechanisms of Defence* (1936), German edn., 41; English edn. (London: Hogarth Press, 1937; New York: I.U.P., 1946), 47.

S

Sadism

= *D*.: Sadismus.–*Es*.: sadismo.–*Fr*.: sadisme.–*I*.: sadismo.–*P*.: sadismo.

Sexual perversion in which satisfaction is dependent on suffering or humiliation inflicted upon others.

Psycho-analysis extends the notion of sadism beyond the perversion described by sexologists: in the first place it identifies numerous more embryonic forms– especially infantile ones; secondly, it makes sadism into one of the fundamental components of instinctual life.

For a description of the different forms and degrees of the sadistic perversion, the reader is referred to the works of the sexologists–particularly those of Krafft-Ebing and Havelock Ellis (α).

As regards terminology, it should be noted that Freud tends for the most part to reserve the term 'sadism' (cf. for example *Three Essays on the Theory of Sexuality* [1905d]) or 'sadism proper' (1) for cases where there is an association between sexuality and violence used against others.

Speaking more loosely, however, he does at times use the word to mean such violence whether or not it is accompanied by sexual satisfaction (2) (see 'Instinct to Master', 'Aggressiveness', 'Sadism/Masochism'). This sense of the word has attained wide currency in psycho-analysis despite Freud's emphasis on the fact that it is not absolutely strict. The danger of this usage is that it encourages an unjustified conflation of sadism and aggressiveness. It is especially marked in the writings of Melanie Klein and her followers.

(α) It was Krafft-Ebing who suggested giving this perversion the name of sadism, with reference to the work of the Marquis de Sade.

(1) FREUD, S. 'The Economic Problem of Masochism' (1924c), G.W., XIII, 376; S.E., XIX, 163.

(2) Cf., for example, FREUD, S. 'Instincts and their Vicissitudes' (1915c), G.W., X, 221; S.E., XIV, 128.

Sadism/Masochism, Sado-Masochism

= *D.*: Sadismus/Masochismus, Sadomasochismus.–
  Es.: sadismo/masoquismo, sado-masoquismo.–
  Fr.: sadisme/masochisme, sado-masochisme.–
  I.: sadismo/masochismo, sado-masochismo.–
  P.: sadismo/masoquismo, sado-masoquismo.

The coupling of sadism and masochism is not just a way of stressing whatever isomorphism and complementarity there may be between the two perversions: the compound term denotes a pair of opposites* that is as fundamental to the *evolution* of instinctual life as it is to its *manifestations*.

It is in this sense that the term 'sado-masochism', used in sexology to designate combined forms of these perversions, has been adopted by psycho-analysis (and particularly, in France, by Daniel Lagache) to bring out the interplay between the two postures, not only in the intersubjective conflict (domination-submission) but also in the structure of the individual (self-punishment).

The reader will find remarks of a mainly terminological kind at the entries 'Masochism' and 'Sadism'. The present article is only concerned with the pair of opposites sadism/masochism, with the relationship psycho-analysis establishes between these two poles and with the function it attributes to this relationship.

The idea of a connection between the sadistic and masochistic perversions had already been noted by Krafft-Ebing. Freud stresses it as early as the *Three Essays on the Theory of Sexuality* (1905d), treating sadism and masochism as

401

the two faces of a single perversion whose active and passive forms are to be found in variable proportions in the same individual: 'A sadist is always at the same time a masochist, although the active or the passive aspect of the perversion may be the more strongly developed in him and may represent his predominant sexual activity' (1*a*).

In the subsequent development of Freud's work and of psycho-analytic thought two ideas receive increasing emphasis in this connection:

a. The correlation between the two terms of the pair is so close that they cannot be studied in isolation either in their genesis or in any of their manifestations.

b. The importance of this pair of opposites extends far beyond the realm of the perversions: 'Sadism and masochism occupy a special position among the perversions, since the contrast between activity and passivity which lies behind them is among the universal characteristics of sexual life' (1*b*).

*   *   *

As regards the respective origins of sadism and masochism, Freud's ideas evolved in parallel with his successive revisions of the instinct theory. Where the frame of reference is the first version of the theory in its final form, as propounded in 'Instincts and their Vicissitudes' (1915*c*), it is commonly held that sadism is prior to masochism, and that masochism is sadism turned round upon the subject's own self. In fact sadism in this context has the sense of an aggression against the other person in which the other's suffering is not a relevant factor – an aggression unconnected with any sexual pleasure. 'Psychoanalysis would appear to show that the infliction of pain plays no part among the original, purposive actions of the instinct. A sadistic child takes no account of whether or not he inflicts pain, nor does he intend to do so' (2*a*). What Freud refers to as sadism at this point is the exercise of the instinct to master*.

Masochism corresponds to a turning round* against the subject's own self and at the same time to a reversal* of activity into passivity. Only with the masochistic period does instinctual activity take on a sexual meaning, and only then does the infliction of suffering become intrinsic to this activity: '. . . sensations of pain, like other unpleasurable sensations, trench upon sexual excitation and produce a pleasurable condition, for the sake of which the subject will even willingly experience the unpleasure of pain' (2*b*). Freud points out two stages in this process of turning round upon the self: in the first, the subject inflicts suffering on himself – an attitude particularly evident in obsessional neurosis; in the second, characteristic of masochism proper, the subject has pain inflicted upon himself by another person. Thus before passing into the 'passive' voice the verb 'to inflict suffering' goes into the reflexive, 'middle' voice (2*c*). Finally, sadism, in the sexual sense of the term, is achieved by virtue of another turning round of the masochistic position.

Freud underscores the role of phantasied identification with the other person in these two successive about-turns: in masochism, 'the passive ego [places] itself back in phantasy in its first role, which has now in fact been taken over by the extraneous subject' (2*d*). Similarly, in sadism, 'while these pains are being inflicted on other people, they are enjoyed masochistically by the subject through his identification of himself with the suffering object' (2*e*, α).

It will be noted that sexuality's intervention in the process is correlated with the emergence of the intersubjective dimension and of phantasy.

Although Freud later felt able to say of this stage in his thought, by way of contrast with the succeeding one, that he deduced masochism from sadism and did not as yet accept the thesis of a primary masochism, it is nonetheless quite evident – provided the masochism/sadism dichotomy is taken in its strict (i.e. sexual) sense – that he already looked upon the masochistic period as the primary or fundamental one.

With the introduction of the death instinct Freud makes a basic postulate of the existence of what he calls primary masochism. At a first – mythical – stage, the whole death instinct is turned against the subject himself – but this is not yet what Freud calls primary masochism. It falls to the lot of the libido to divert a large portion of the death instinct on to the external world: 'A portion of the instinct is placed directly in the service of the sexual function, where it has an important part to play. This is sadism proper. Another portion does not share in this transposition outwards; it remains inside the organism and, with the help of the accompanying sexual excitation […], becomes libidinally bound there. It is in this portion that we have to recognise the original, erotogenic masochism' (3a).

Overlooking a certain terminological looseness of which Freud himself was conscious (3b), we may say that that primary state in which the death instinct is directed in its entirety against the individual himself no more corresponds to a masochistic attitude than it does to a sadistic one.

It is as part of a single process that the death instinct, attaching itself to the libido, splits into sadism and erotogenic masochism. We may note, lastly, that this sadism too may be turned round against the subject in a 'secondary masochism […] which is added to the original masochism' (3c).

*　　*　　*

Freud described the part played by sadism and masochism in the various libidinal organisations of childhood development. First and most importantly, he recognised their action in the anal-sadistic* organisation; but they are present in the other stages too (see 'Oral-Sadistic Stage', 'Cannibalistic', 'Fusion/Defusion'). As we know, the pair activity/passivity*, expressed *par excellence* in the opposition between sadism and masochism, is treated by Freud as one of the great polarities which characterise the sexual life of the subject; we know too that it is again recognisable in the later oppositions phallic/castrated and masculine/feminine*.

The intrasubjective function of the sadism/masochism opposition was discovered by Freud, particularly its role in the dialectic between the sadistic super-ego and the masochistic ego (3d, 4).

*　　*　　*

It was not only in manifest perversions that Freud drew attention to the inter-relation between sadism and masochism; he further noted the interchangeability of the two postures in phantasy and ultimately in intrasubjective conflict. Pursuing this line of thought, Daniel Lagache has laid especial stress upon the notion of *sado-masochism*, making it the chief axis of the intersubjective

403

relationship. Psychical conflict – and its essential form, Oedipal conflict – can be understood as a conflict of demands (see 'Psychical Conflict'): '. . . the position of he who demands is potentially a persecuted-persecutor position, because the mediation of the demand necessarily introduces those sado-masochistic relationships based on domination and submission that are implicit in any intervention of authority' (5).

(α) For the interconnections between sadism and masochism in the structure of phantasy, see Freud's ' "A Child is Being Beaten" ' (1919e).

(1) FREUD, S.: a) G.W., V, 59; S.E., VII, 159. b) passage added in 1915: G.W., V, 58; S.E., VII, 159.

(2) FREUD, S.: a) G.W., X, 221; S.E., XIV, 128. b) G.W., X, 221; S.E., XIV, 128. c) Cf. G.W., X, 221; S.E., XIV, 128. d) G.W., X, 220; S.E., XIV, 128. e) G.W., X, 221; G.W., XIV, 129.

(3) FREUD, S. 'The Economic Problem of Masochism' (1924c): a) G.W., XIII, 376; S.E., XIX, 163–64. b) Cf. G.W., XIII, 377; S.E., XIX, 164. c) G.W., XIII, 377; S.E., XIX, 164. d) Cf. passim.

(4) Cf. FREUD, S. The Ego and the Id (1923b), Chapter V: G.W., XIII, 277–89; S.E., XIX, 48–59.

(5) LAGACHE, D. 'Situation de l'agressivité', Bull. Psycho., 1960, XIV, 1, 99–112.

Scene of Seduction; Theory of Seduction

= D. Verführung (Verführungsszene, Verführungstheorie). –
Es.: escena de –, teoría de la seduccíon. – Fr: scène de –, théorie de la séduction. –
I.: scena di – , teoria della seduzione. – P.: cena de – , teoria da sedução.

I. **Real or phantasied scene in which the subject, generally a child, submits passively to the advances or sexual manipulations of another person – an adult in most instances.**
II. **Theory developed by Freud between 1895 and 1897, and subsequently abandoned, which attributes the determining role in the aetiology of the psycho-neuroses to the memory of real scenes of seduction.**

In the founding period of psycho-analysis, Freud thought that the theory of seduction could account for the repression of sexuality. Before being elaborated theoretically, however, the facts of seduction constituted a *clinical* discovery: in the course of treatment, it transpired that patients would recall experiences of sexual seduction – lived scenes in which the initiative was taken by the other person, who was most often an adult; their content varied from simple advances by word or gesture to more or less typical cases of actual sexual assault, which the subject underwent passively in a state of fright*.

Freud began alluding to seduction as early as 1893. Between 1895 and 1897 he attributed a major theoretical role to it, while being led, as regards chronology, to situate the traumatic scenes of seduction further and further back in childhood.

To speak of a *theory* of seduction is to do more than simply acknowledge that these sexual scenes have an outstanding aetiological function as compared with other traumas: for Freud, this preponderance became the basic assumption of a highly detailed attempt to explain the origins of the mechanism of repression.

Schematically, this theory holds that the trauma* occurs in two stages separated from each other by puberty. The first stage–the moment of the seduction proper–is described by Freud as a 'presexual' sexual event in that it is occasioned by factors external to the subject, who is still incapable of experiencing sexual emotions (the somatic preconditions of excitation are absent, and it is impossible for the experience to be integrated). At the moment of its occurrence, the scene does not undergo a repression. It is only in the second stage that another event, which does not necessarily have an intrinsic sexual meaning, revives the memory of the first one as a result of some associative link: 'Here, indeed, the one possibility is realised of a memory having a greater releasing power subsequently than had been produced by the experience corresponding to it' (1*a*). The memory is repressed because of the flood of endogenous excitation that it has triggered off.

That the scene of seduction is experienced passively means not only that the subject behaves in a passive way during it, but also that he undergoes it without its being able to evoke a response in him, since no corresponding sexual ideas are available: the state of passivity implies an absence of preparation, and the seduction produces 'sexual fright' (*Sexualschreck*).

Such is the importance attached by Freud to seduction in the genesis of repression that he looks systematically for scenes of passive seduction in obsessional neurosis as well as in hysteria, where they first came to light. 'In *all* my cases of obsessional neurosis, at a very early age, years before the experience of pleasure, there had been a *purely passive* experience, and this can hardly be accidental' (1*b*). So although Freud distinguishes obsessional neurosis from hysteria on the grounds that it is determined by precocious sexual experiences which have involved active participation and pleasure, he nevertheless expects to find earlier, passive scenes in obsessional neurosis resembling those that are met with in hysteria.

Freud was of course brought to question the veracity of these seduction scenes, and he abandoned the theory based on them. A letter to Fliess dated September 9, 1897, gives his reasons for this revision. 'I will confide in you at once the great secret that has been dawning on me in the last few months. I no longer believe in my *neurotica*' (1*c*). Freud had discovered that the scenes of seduction are sometimes the product of phantastic reconstruction–a discovery that went hand in hand with the gradual revelation of infantile sexuality.

*   *   *

It is traditional to look upon Freud's dropping of the seduction theory in 1897 as a decisive step in the foundation of psycho-analytic theory, and in the bringing to the fore of such conceptions as unconscious phantasy, psychical reality, spontaneous infantile sexuality and so on. Freud himself asserted the importance of this moment in the history of his thought on several occasions: 'If hysterical subjects trace back their symptoms to traumas that are fictitious, then the new fact which emerges is precisely that they create such scenes in *phantasy*, and this psychical reality requires to be taken into account alongside practical reality. This reflection was soon followed by the discovery that these phantasies were intended to cover up the auto-erotic activity of the first years of childhood, to embellish it and raise it to a higher plane. And now, from behind the phantasies, the whole range of a child's sexual life came to light' (2).

This summary view of the matter calls, however, for some qualification.

I. Right up to the end of his life, Freud continued to assert the existence, prevalence and pathogenic force of scenes of seduction actually experienced by children (3, 4).

As for the chronological position of these scenes, Freud made two observations which are apparently–but only apparently–contradictory:

a. The seduction often takes place at a relatively late stage, in which case the seducer is another child of the same age or a little older. Subsequently, this seduction is transposed, by means of a retrospective phantasy, to an earlier period and attributed to a parental figure (5a).

b. The description of the preoedipal attachment to the mother, especially in the case of the little girl, leads Freud to speak of an actual sexual seduction by the mother, in the form of the bodily attentions bestowed upon the infant at the breast–a real seduction which is taken as the prototype for the subsequent phantasies: 'Here [...] the phantasy touches the ground of reality, for it was really the mother who by her activities over the child's bodily hygiene inevitably stimulated, and perhaps even roused for the first time, pleasurable sensations in her genitals' (6).

II. On the theoretical level, it is doubtful whether it can be said that Freud's explanatory schema, as outlined above, was simply abandoned by him. On the contrary, it would seem that several essential elements from this schema are found once again, after being carried over into the later theoretical constructs of psycho-analysis:

a. The idea that repression cannot be understood without distinguishing between a number of stages in the process, the first stage only acquiring its traumatic significance as a result of the deferred action* of a subsequent stage. This conception is fully developed, for example, in 'From the History of an Infantile Neurosis' (1918b [1914]).

b. The idea that the ego is the victim of an aggression in the second stage of repression, when it has to face a flood of *endogenous* excitation; in the theory of seduction it is the memory, not the event itself, which is traumatic. In this sense, the 'memory' in this theory already has the force of 'psychical reality'*, of a 'foreign body' which subsequently passes over into phantasy*.

c. The idea that, at the same time, this psychical reality of the memory or phantasy must ultimately be based on the 'ground of reality'. Apparently, Freud could never resign himself to treating phantasy as the pure and simple outgrowth of the spontaneous sexual life of the child. He is forever searching, behind the phantasy, for whatever has founded it in its reality: perceived evidence of the primal scene* (in the case-history of the 'Wolf Man'); the seduction of the infant by its mother (see above); and, even more fundamentally, the notion that phantasies are based in the last reckoning on 'primal phantasies'*
–on a mnemic residue transmitted hereditarily from actual experiences in the

history of the human species: '. . . all the things that are told to us today in analysis as phantasy [...] were once real occurrences in the primaeval times of the human family' (5b). Indeed the first schema presented by Freud, with his theory of seduction, seems to us to epitomise this particular dimension of his thought: quite obviously, the first stage–the stage of the scene of seduction– simply must be founded in something more real than the subject's imaginings alone.

d. Lastly, Freud was to acknowledge somewhat belatedly that with the seduction-phantasies he 'had in fact stumbled for the first time upon the Oedipus complex' (7). It was indeed only a short step from the seduction of the little girl by her father to the Oedipal love of the girl for her father.

But the crucial question is to decide whether the seduction-phantasy has to be considered merely as a defensive and projective distortion of the positive component of the Oedipus complex* or whether it is to be treated as the trans-posed expression of a fundamental datum, namely, the fact that the child's sexuality is entirely organised by something which comes to it, as it were, from the outside: the relationship between the parents, and the parents' wishes which pre-date and determine the form of the wishes of the subject. Viewed from this angle, seductions really experienced as well as seduction-phantasies become nothing more than concrete expressions of this basic fact.

Ferenczi was following this same line of thought when he espoused the theory of seduction in 1932 (8); this led him to describe the way in which adult sexuality ('the language of passion') makes a real forcible entry into the infantile world ('the language of tenderness').

There would seem to be a danger in such a revival of the seduction theory– namely, that of re-opening the door to the pre-analytical view of the child as sexually innocent until perverted by adult sexuality. The notion that the child inhabits a private, autonomous world until such time as a violation or perver-sion of this kind occurs is precisely what Freud rejected. It was apparently for this very reason that he placed seduction, in the last analysis, among those 'primal phantasies'* which he traces back to the prehistory of humanity. He does not see seduction, essentially, as a concrete fact which can be assigned its place in the subject's history; instead, he looks upon it as a structural datum whose only possible transposition into historical terms would be in the form of a myth.

(1) FREUD, S. Fliess papers: a) Anf., 157; S.E., I, 221. b) Anf., 160; S.E., I, 223. c) Anf., 229; S.E., I, 259.

(2) FREUD, S. 'On the History of the Psycho-Analytic Movement' (1914d), G.W., X, 56; S.E., XIV, 17–18.

(3) FREUD, S. Three Essays on the Theory of Sexuality (1905d), G.W., V, 91–92; S.E., VII, 191.

(4) FREUD, S. An Outline of Psycho-Analysis (1940a [1938]), G.W., XVII, 113–14; S.E., XIII, 187.

(5) FREUD, S. Introductory Lectures on Psycho-Analysis (1916–17): a) Cf. G.W., XI, 385; S.E., XVI, 370. b) G.W., XI, 386; S.E., XVI, 371.

(6) FREUD, S. New Introductory Lectures on Psycho-Analysis (1933a [1932]), G.W., XV, 129; S.E., XXII, 120.

(7) FREUD, S. An Autobiographical Study (1925d [1924]), G.W., XIV, 60; S.E., XX, 34.

Schizophrenia

(8) Cf. FERENCZI, S. 'Sprachverwirrung zwischen den Erwachsenen und dem Kind' (1932–33). Eng.: 'Confusion of Tongues between Adults and the Child', in *Final Contr.*, 156 *ff. Passim.*

Schizophrenia

= *D.*: Schizophrenie.–*Es.*: esquizofrenia.–*Fr.*: schizophrénie.–*I.*: schizofrenia.– *P.*: esquizofrenia.

Term invented by Eugen Bleuler (1911) to denote a group of psychoses whose unity had already been demonstrated by Kraepelin when he placed them under the general heading of 'dementia praecox' and made what is still the classical distinction between three varieties, namely the hebephrenic, the catatonic and the paranoid types.

Bleuler's aim in introducing the term 'schizophrenia' (from the Greek ςχίζω, meaning to 'split' or 'cleave', and φρήν, 'mind') was to stress what for him constituted the fundamental symptom of these psychoses: *Spaltung* ('dissociation', 'splitting'). The term has been generally accepted in psychiatry and psycho-analysis, in spite of disagreements between different authors about the defining characteristics of schizophrenia and hence about its extension as a nosological category.

From the clinical point of view, schizophrenia takes a variety of apparently very disparate forms. The following characteristics are the ones usually picked out as typical: incoherence of thought, action and affectivity (denoted by the classical terms 'discordance', 'dissociation' and 'disintegration'); detachment from reality accompanied by a turning in upon the self and the predominance of a mental life given over to the production of phantasies (autism); a delusional activity which may be marked in a greater or lesser degree, and which is always badly systematised. Lastly, the disease, which evolves at the most variable of paces towards an intellectual and affective 'deterioration', often ending up by presenting states of apparent dementia, is defined as *chronic* by most psychiatrists, who consider it inadmissible to diagnose schizophrenia in the absence of this major trait.

The outcome of Kraepelin's extension of the name 'dementia praecox' to a large group of illnesses, the kindred nature of which he had demonstrated, was that it became inadequate to cover the clinical pictures envisaged, for neither the noun 'dementia' nor the epithet 'praecox' applied to all of these without exception. It was for this reason that Bleuler proposed a fresh term; he chose 'schizophrenia' out of concern that the denomination itself should evoke what he considered to be a fundamental symptom of the disease, more essential than its 'accessory symptoms'–hallucinations for example–which may be met with elsewhere. This fundamental symptom is *Spaltung*: 'I call dementia praecox "schizophrenia" because [...] the "splitting" of the different psychic functions is one of its most important characteristics' (1*a*).

Although Bleuler drew attention to the influence of Freud's discoveries upon his thinking, and although he took part in Jung's researches while Professor of Psychiatry at Zurich (see 'Association'), he nonetheless employs the term '*Spaltung*' in a very different sense from the one it had for Freud (see 'Splitting of the Ego').

What does Bleuler mean by it? Although the effects of *Spaltung* are to be encountered in different domains of mental life (thought, affectivity, activity), it is first and foremost a disturbance of the associations which govern the train of thought. In schizophrenia, a distinction should be made between 'primary' symptoms, which are the direct expression of the disease process (looked upon by Bleuler as organic) and 'secondary' symptoms which are just the 'reaction of the sick psyche' to the pathogenic process (1*b*).

The primary disturbance of thought might be described as a loosening of associations: '. . . the associations lose their continuity. Of the thousands of associative threads which guide our thinking, this disease seems to interrupt, quite haphazardly, sometimes such simple threads, sometimes a whole group, and sometimes even large segments of them. In this way, thinking becomes illogical and often bizarre' (1*c*).

Other disturbances of thought are secondary, representing the way in which, in the absence of 'purposive ideas' (a term which for Bleuler denotes only conscious or preconscious purposive ideas [q.v.]), ideas are assembled under the sign of affective complexes: 'Everything which opposes the affect is more deeply suppressed than normally, and whatever falls in line with the affect is abnormally facilitated. The result is that an abnormally charged idea cannot even be opposed in thought any more: the ambitious schizophrenic dreams only of his desires; obstacles simply do not exist for him. In this way, complexes which are joined together by a common affect rather than any logical connection are not only formed, but are also more firmly fixed in the patient. Due to the fact that the associational pathways which join such a complex to other ideas are not used, these associational pathways lose their effectiveness in respect of the more adequate associations. In other words, the affectively charged complex of ideas continues to become isolated and *obtains an ever increasing independence* (*splitting of the psychic functions*)' (1*d*).

Bleuler compares schizophrenic splitting in this sense to what Freud described as specific to the unconscious, namely the coexistence of groups of ideas that are independent of one another (1*e*). Bleuler's *Spaltung*, however, in so far as it implies the strengthening of associational groups, takes second place to a primary deficiency that constitutes a true disintegration of the mental process. Thus Bleuler differentiates two moments of the *Spaltung*: a primary *Zerspaltung* (a disintegration, an actual fragmentation) and a *Spaltung* proper (splitting of thought into different groups of ideas): 'The splitting is the prerequisite condition of most of the complicated phenomena of the disease. It is the splitting which gives the peculiar stamp to the entire symptomatology. However, behind this systematic splitting (*Spaltung*) into definite idea-complexes, we have found a previous primary loosening of the associational structure which can lead to an irregular fragmentation (*Zerspaltung*) of such solidly established elements as concrete ideas. The term, schizophrenia, refers to both types of splitting which often fuse in their effects' (1*f*).

409

Screen Memory

The semantic overtones of 'dissociation', often used in English to refer to the schizophrenic *Spaltung*, in fact correspond better to Bleuler's *Zerspaltung*.

* * *

Freud expressed reserves about the choice of the term 'schizophrenia' itself, which 'prejudices the issue, since it is based on a characteristic of the disease which is theoretically postulated–a characteristic, moreover, which does not belong exclusively to that disease, and which, in the light of other considerations, cannot be regarded as the essential one' (2*a*). Although Freud spoke of schizophrenia (while also continuing to use the name of dementia praecox), he had proposed the term 'paraphrenia'*, which he felt could be more easily paired up with 'paranoia'* in order to stress both the unity of the field of the psychoses* and its division into two fundamental types.

Freud acknowledges, in fact, that these two major categories of psychosis may be combined in any number of ways (as the Schreber case illustrates), and that the patient may eventually pass from one of these forms to the other; but at the same time he upholds the specificity of schizophrenia, as compared to paranoia, and he attempts to define this specificity in terms both of *processes* and of *fixations**. At the former level, schizophrenia is characterised by the predominance of the process of repression, or of withdrawal of cathexis from reality, over the tendency towards reconstruction; and, among the reconstruction mechanisms themselves, by the predominance of those which recall hysteria (hallucination) over those which, in paranoia, most resemble obsessional neurosis (projection). As far as fixations are concerned: 'The dispositional fixation must therefore be situated further back than in paranoia, and must lie somewhere at the beginning of the course of development from auto-crotism to object-love' (2*b*).

Even though Freud made numerous other suggestions apropos of schizophrenia–notably on the functioning of schizophrenic thought and language (3) –it is true to say that the task of defining the structure of this illness has fallen to his successors.

(1) BLEULER, E. *Dementia praecox oder Gruppe der Schizophrenien* (Leipzig and Vienna, 1911). English translation: *Dementia Praecox or the Group of Schizophrenias* (New York: International Universities Press, 1950). a) 5; Eng.: 8. b) Cf. 284–85; Eng.: 348–49. c) 10; Eng.: 14. d) 293; Eng.: 359. e) Cf. 296; Eng.: 363. f) 296; Eng.: 362.

(2) FREUD, S. 'Psycho-Analytic Notes on an Autobiographical Account of a Case of Paranoia' (1911*c*): a) G.W., VIII, 312–13; S.E., XII, 75. b) G.W., VIII, 314; S.E., XII, 77.

(3) Cf., in particular, FREUD, S. 'The Unconscious' (1915*e*), G.W., X, Chap. VII; S.E., XIV, Chap. VII.

Screen Memory

= *D.*: Deckerinnerung.–*Es.*: recuerdo encubridor.–*Fr.*: souvenir-écran.– *I.*: ricordo di copertura.–*P.*: recordação encobridora.

A childhood memory characterised both by its unusual sharpness and by the apparent insignificance of its content. The analysis of such memories leads back

to indelible childhood experiences and to unconscious phantasies. Like the symptom, the screen memory is a formation produced by a compromise between repressed elements and defence.

As early as his first psycho-analytic treatments and self-analysis, Freud's attention was caught by a paradox of memory concerning childhood events: whereas important things are not retained (see 'Infantile Amnesia'), apparently insignificant memories sometimes are. Phenomenologically, certain of these memories present themselves with an exceptional clarity and persistence that contrasts strikingly with the banality and innocence of their content – the subject himself is surprised that they should have survived.

Such memories, in so far as they conceal repressed sexual experiences or phantasies, Freud calls screen memories; an article is devoted to them in 1899, the main ideas of which are taken up again in Chapter IV of *The Psychopathology of Everyday Life* (1901*b*).

Screen memories are compromise-formations* like parapraxes* or slips and, more generally, symptoms. The reason for their survival cannot be understood so long as it is sought in the repressed content (1*a*). The predominant mechanism here is displacement*. Freud, coming back to the distinction between screen memories and other childhood memories, goes so far as to raise a more general question: are there memories of which we may truly say that they *emerge from,* or merely memories which are *related to,* our childhood (1*b*)?

Freud distinguishes between different kinds of screen memories: first, between positive and negative ones, according to whether or not their content is contrary to the repressed content; and secondly, between 'retrogressive' screen memories and those which have 'pushed forward', according to whether or not the manifest scene which they evoke precedes or follows those elements with which it is connected. Where it follows, the screen memory's role is obviously restricted to supporting retroactively projected phantasies, and its 'value lies in the fact that it represents in the memory impressions and thoughts of a later date whose content is connected with its own by symbolic or similar links' (1*c*).

Inasmuch as screen memories condense a large number of real and phantasy childhood elements, psycho-analysis ascribes a great deal of importance to them: 'Not only *some* but *all* of what is essential from childhood has been retained in these memories. It is simply a question of knowing how to extract it out of them by analysis. They represent the forgotten years of childhood as adequately as the manifest content of a dream represents the dream-thoughts' (2).

(1) Cf. FREUD, S. 'Screen Memories' (1899*a*): a) G.W., I, 536; S.E., III, 307. b) G.W., I, 553; S.E., III, 321–32. c) G.W., I, 546; S.E., III, 315–16.

(2) FREUD, S. 'Remembering, Repeating and Working-Through' (1914*g*), G.W., X, 128; S.E., XII, 148.

Secondary Revision (or Elaboration)

= *D*.: sekundäre Bearbeitung.–*Es*.: elaboración secundaria.–
Fr.: élaboration secondaire.–*I*.: elaborazione secondaria.–*P*.: elaboração secundária.

Rearrangement of a dream so as to present it in the form of a relatively consistent and comprehensible scenario.

The elimination of the dream's apparent absurdity and incoherence, the filling-in of its gaps, the partial or total reorganisation of its elements by means of selection and addition, the attempt to make it into something like a day-dream (*Tagtraum*)–these, essentially, are what Freud called secondary revision, or, at times, 'considerations of intelligibility' (*Rüchsicht auf Verständlichkeit*).

As the term '*Bearbeitung*' suggests, secondary revision constitutes a second stage of the dream-work* (*Arbeit*); it therefore operates upon the results of a *first* revision by the other mechanisms of the dream-work (condensation*, displacement*, considerations of representability*). At the same time, however, Freud considers that this secondary revision is not brought to bear on ready-made formations that it then proceeds to reorganise: on the contrary, it 'operates simultaneously in a conducive and selective sense upon the mass of material present in the dream-thoughts' (1). It is for this reason that the dream-work can readily make use of reveries that have already been constructed (see 'Phantasy').

Since secondary revision is an effect of the censorship*–which, as Freud emphasises in this connection, does not have a negative role alone but can also be responsible for additions–it is to be seen at work especially when the subject is getting near to a waking state, and *a fortiori* when he comes to recount his dream. All the same, the process does in fact go on at every moment of the dream.

In *Totem and Taboo* (1912–13) Freud compares secondary revision to the formation of certain systems of thought: 'There is an intellectual function in us which demands unity, connection and intelligibility from any material, whether of perception or thought, that comes within its grasp; and if, as a result of special circumstances, it is unable to establish a true connection, it does not hesitate to fabricate a false one. Systems constructed in this way are known to us not only from dreams, but also from phobias, from obsessive thinking and from delusions. The construction of systems is seen most strikingly in delusional disorders (in paranoia), where it dominates the symptomatic picture; but its occurrence in other forms of neuro-psychosis must not be overlooked. In all these cases it can be shown that a rearrangement of the psychical material has been made with a fresh aim in view; and the rearrangement may often have to be a drastic one if the outcome is to be made to appear intelligible from the point of view of the system' (2). In this sense secondary revision may be said to resemble rationalisation*.

(1) FREUD, S. *The Interpretation of Dreams* (1900*a*), G.W., II–III, 503; S.E., V, 499.
(2) FREUD, S., G.W., IX, 117; S.E., XIII, 95.

Self-Analysis

= *D.*: Selbstanalyse.–*Es.*: autoanálisis.–*Fr.*: auto-analyse.–*I.*: autoanalisi.–
P.: auto-análise.

**Investigation of oneself *by* oneself, conducted in a more or less systematic fashion
and utilising certain techniques of the psycho-analytic method, such as free
association*, dream-analysis, the interpretation* of behaviour, etc.**

Freud never devoted a text to the question of self-analysis but he alluded to it
several times, especially with reference to his own experience. 'I soon saw the
necessity of carrying out a self-analysis, and this I did with the help of a series
of my own dreams which led me back through all the events of my childhood;
and I am still of the opinion today that this kind of analysis may suffice for
anyone who is a good dreamer and not too abnormal' (1). Freud states here
that this method is fundamental to psycho-analysis: 'If I am asked how one
can become a psycho-analyst, I reply: "By studying one's own dreams" ' (2).

In many other places, however, he takes a very cautious position on the
efficacy of self-analysis. In the actual course of his own experience he had
written to Fliess: 'My self-analysis is still interrupted and I have realised the
reason. I can only analyse myself with the help of knowledge obtained objectively (like an outsider). Genuine self-analysis is impossible; otherwise there
would be no illness' (3). Later, self-analysis seems to have been definitively
downgraded as compared to analysis proper: 'One learns psycho-analysis on
oneself by studying one's own personality. [...] Nevertheless, there are definite
limits to progress by this method. One advances much further if one is analysed
oneself by a practised analyst' (4).

Freud's reservations regarding self-analysis hold only in so far as self-
analysis pretends to replace a true psycho-analysis. Self-analysis is now generally
thought to be a particular form of resistance to psycho-analysis which flatters
narcissism and bypasses the essential motor force of the treatment–namely the
transference* (5). Even for authors like Karen Horney who recommend self-
analysis, it still only plays the part of a complement to treatment, preparing for
it or prolonging it. As for Freud's own self-analysis, it is clearly unique in that
it had a hand in the discovery of psycho-analysis and did not involve the application of prior knowledge.

As far as analysts themselves are concerned, the continuing elucidation of
the dynamics of their own unconscious is highly desirable. Freud remarked
on this as early as 1910 while discussing the counter-transference*: '. . . no
psycho-analyst goes further than his own complexes and internal resistances
permit; and we consequently require that he shall begin his activity with a self-
analysis and continually carry it deeper while he is making his observations on
his patients. Anyone who fails to produce results in a self-analysis of this kind
may at once give up any idea of being able to treat patients by analysis' (6).
The institution of the training analysis* does not eliminate the need for a self-
analysis: the self-analysis 'indefinitely' prolongs the process set in motion by the
training analysis (α).

413

(α) For a systematic treatment of the question, cf. D. Anzieu, *L'auto-analyse* (Paris: P.U.F., 1959).

(1) FREUD, S. 'On the History of the Psycho-Analytic Movement' (1914*d*), G.W., X, 59; S.E., XIV, 20.

(2) FREUD, S. 'Five Lectures on Psycho-Analysis' (1910*a*), G.W., VIII, 32; S.E., XI, 33.

(3) FREUD, S. *Anf.*, 249; S.E., I, 271.

(4) FREUD, S. *Introductory Lectures on Psycho-Analysis* (1916–17), G.W., XI, 12; S.E., XV, 19.

(5) Cf. ABRAHAM, K. 'A Particular Form of Neurotic Resistance against the Psycho-Analytic Method' (1919), in *Selected Papers* (London: Hogarth Press, 1927; New York: Basic Books, 1953), 303–11.

(6) FREUD, S. 'The Future Prospects of Psycho-Analytic Therapy' (1910*d*), G.W., VIII, 108; S.E., XI, 145.

Sense of Guilt, Guilt Feeling

= *D.*: Schuldgefühl.–*Es.*: sentimiento de culpabilidad.–*Fr.*: sentiment de culpabilité.– *I.*: senso di colpa.–*P.*: sentimento de culpa.

Term applied very broadly by psycho-analysis.

It may designate emotional states (varying from the remorse of the criminal to apparently ridiculous self-reproaches) which follow acts that the subject deems reprehensible, though the reasons he gives for doing so may or may not be adequate ones. Or again, it may refer to a vague sense of personal unworthiness unconnected with any particular act for which the subject blames himself.

At the same time the sense of guilt is postulated by psycho-analysis as a system of unconscious motivations that accounts for 'failure* syndromes', delinquent behaviour, self-inflicted suffering, etc. The words 'feeling' and 'sense' should be employed with caution in this connection, since the subject may not feel guilty at the level of conscious experience.

The sense of guilt was first encountered mainly in obsessional neurosis, in the form of self-reproaches and obsessive ideas against which the subject struggles because they seem reprehensible to him; and also in the form of the shame attached to the subject's precautionary measures themselves.

On this level it is already noticeable that the feeling of guilt is partly unconscious in so far as the real nature of the wishes in play–particularly aggressive ones–is not known to the subject.

A result of the psycho-analytic study of melancholia was a more elaborate theory of the sense of guilt. This trouble, as is well known, is characterised in particular by self-accusations, self-denigration and a tendency towards self-punishment that can end in suicide. Freud shows that we are faced here with an actual splitting of the ego between accuser (the super-ego) and accused–a split which is itself the outcome, through a process of internalisation*, of an inter-subjective relationship: '. . . the self-reproaches are reproaches against a loved

414

object which have been shifted away from it on to the patient's own ego. The melancholic's complaints are really "plaints" in the old sense of the word' (1a).

Once the notion of the super-ego* had thus been formed, Freud was led to assign a more general role in the defensive conflict to the sense of guilt. He had already acknowledged that the 'critical agency which is here split off from the ego might also show its independence in other circumstances' (1b); in Chapter V of *The Ego and the Id* (1923b), devoted to 'The Dependent Relationship of the Ego', he endeavours to distinguish the different modes of the sense of guilt, extending from its normal form to its different manifestations in the whole domain of psychopathological structures (2a).

In fact the differentiation of the super-ego as a critical and punitive agency *vis-à-vis* the ego introduces guilt as an intersystemic relationship within the psychical apparatus: '. . . the sense of guilt is the perception in the ego answering to [the super-ego's] criticism' (2b).

From this standpoint the expression 'unconscious sense of guilt' takes on a more radical sense than the one it had when it meant an unconsciously motivated feeling, for now it is the relationship of the super-ego to the ego that can be unconscious and manifested in subjective effects from which any felt guilt may—in the most extreme instance—be absent. Thus in the case of some delinquents, 'it is possible to detect a very powerful sense of guilt which existed before the crime, and is therefore not its result but its motive. It is as if it was a relief to be able to fasten this unconscious sense of guilt on to something real and immediate' (2c).

Freud was not insensitive to the paradoxical effect produced when he spoke of an *unconscious sense* of guilt; he admitted that, for this reason, the term 'need for punishment'* might be more fitting (3). It will be noted, however, that the latter expression, when taken in its most radical sense, denotes a force tending towards the destruction of the subject, a force that is perhaps irreducible to a tension between systems, whereas the sense of guilt, be it conscious or unconscious, can always be brought down to the same topographical relation—the relation between ego and super-ego, itself a relic of the Oedipus complex: 'One may [...] venture the hypothesis that a great part of the sense of guilt must normally remain unconscious, because the origin of conscience is intimately connected with the Oedipus complex, which belongs to the unconscious' (2d).

(1) FREUD, S. 'Mourning and Melancholia' (1917e): a) G.W., X, 434, S.E., XIV, 248. b) G.W., X, 433, S.E., XIV, 247.

(2) FREUD, S.: a) Cf. G.W., XIII, 276–89; S.E., XIX, 48–59. b) G.W., XIII, 282; S.E., XIX, 53. c) G.W., XIII, 282; S.E., XIX, 52. d) G.W., XIII, 281; S.E., XIX, 52.

(3) Cf. FREUD, S. 'The Economic Problem of Masochism' (1924c), G.W., XIII, 379; S.E., XIX, 166.

Sense (or Feeling) of Inferiority

= *D*.: Mindervertigkeitsgefühl.–*Es*.: sentimiento de inferioridad.–
Fr.: sentiment d'infériorité.–*I*.: senso d'inferiorità.–*P*.: sentimento de inferioridade.

For Adler, a feeling based on an actual organic inferiority. In the inferiority complex, the individual strives with varying degrees of success to compensate for his deficiency. Adler assigns a very general aetiological significance to this kind of mechanism, which is operative in his view in all affections.

According to Freud, a sense of inferiority has no special relation to organic inferiority. Nor is it a fundamental aetiological factor but should instead be understood and interpreted as a symptom.

In psycho-analytic literature the term 'sense of inferiority' has an Adlerian ring to it. Adler's theory sets out to account for neuroses, mental illnesses and, more generally speaking, the formation of the personality, in terms of reactions to inferiorities whose appearance dates from childhood and which may be organic (however minor), morphological or functional in character: 'The constitutional inferiority and similarly effective childhood situations give rise to a feeling of inferiority which demands a compensation in the sense of an enhancement of the self-esteem. Here the fictional, final purpose of the striving for power [...] draws all psychological forces in its direction' (1).

Freud several times demonstrated the onesidedness, inadequacy and poverty of these conceptions: '... whether a man is a homosexual or a necrophilic, a hysteric suffering from anxiety, an obsessional neurotic cut off from society, or a raving lunatic, the "Individual Psychologist" of the Adlerian school will declare that the impelling motive of his condition is that he wishes to assert himself, to overcompensate for his inferiority' (2*a*).

Although a theory such as this is unacceptable as far as aetiology is concerned, this obviously does not mean that psycho-analysis denies the importance of the sense of inferiority, its frequent occurrence or its function in the causal chain of psychological motivation. Freud gives some indications regarding its origin without, however, going into the matter systematically. He considers that the sense of inferiority is a response to the two (real or phantasied) injuries that the child may suffer–namely, loss of love and castration*: 'A child feels inferior if he notices that he is not loved, and so does an adult. The only bodily organ which is really regarded as inferior is the atrophied penis, a girl's clitoris' (2*b*).

From a structural point of view, the sense of inferiority is said to express the tension existing between the ego and the super-ego which passes judgement on it. This explanation underscores the kinship between the sense of inferiority and the sense of guilt*, but it also makes it hard to distinguish between them. Several writers since Freud have tried to clarify the distinction. Daniel Lagache makes the sense of guilt more particularly dependent on his 'Super-Ego/Ego-Ideal system', and the sense of inferiority on the Ideal Ego* (3).

Clinically, the importance of guilt and inferiority feelings in the different forms of depression has often been emphasised. Pasche has sought to isolate

416

a specific form-'inferiority depression'-which in his opinion is particularly common today (4).

(1) ADLER, A. *Über den nervösen Charakter* (1912). Trans.: *The Neurotic Constitution* (New York: Dodd, Mead & Co., 1926). Quoted in H. H. and R. R. Ansbacher (eds.), *The Individual Psychology of Alfred Adler* (New York: Basic Books, 1956), 111.

(2) FREUD, S. *New Introductory Lectures on Psycho-Analysis* (1933a [1932]): a) G.W., XV, 152; S.E., XXII, 141. b) G.W., XV, 71; S.E., XXII, 65.

(3) LAGACHE, D. 'La psychanalyse et la structure de la personnalité', *La Psychanalyse*, 1961, VI, 40–48.

(4) PASCHE, F. 'De la dépression', *R.F.P.*, 1963, No. 2–3, 191.

Sexual Instinct

= *D.*: Sexualtrieb.–*Es.*: instinto sexual.–*Fr.*: pulsion sexuelle.–
I.: istinto *or* pulsione sessuale.–*P.*: impulso *or* pulsão sexual.

Internal pressure which psycho-analysis deems to be at work in a much vaster area than the field of sexual activity as generally conceived. It is the sexual instinct *par excellence* which exemplifies certain characteristics of the Freudian instinct* that distinguish it from instinct in the biological sense. Its *object** is not determined, while its modalities of satisfaction (or *aims**) are variable: though more particularly bound to the functioning of specific bodily areas (erotogenic zones*), this instinct is able to achieve satisfaction through the most varied activities, to which it relates by anaclisis*. This diversity in the somatic *sources** of sexual excitation means that the sexual instinct is not unified from the start but that to begin with it is fragmented into component instincts* obtaining satisfaction locally (organ-pleasure*).

Psycho-analysis shows that the sexual instinct in man is closely bound up with the action of ideas or phantasies which serve to give it specific form. Only at the end of a complex and hazardous evolution is it successfully organised under the primacy of genitality, so taking on the apparently fixed and final aspect of instinct in the traditional sense.

From the economic point of view, Freud postulates the existence of a single energy at work throughout the vicissitudes of the sexual instinct: *libido**.

From the dynamic point of view, he sees the sexual instinct as an invariably present pole of the psychical conflict: it is the special object of repression into the unconscious.

The definition above indicates what an upheaval psycho-analysis wrought in the idea of a 'sexual instinct'–and this as much in the concept's extension as in its comprehension (see 'Sexuality'). This upheaval affects both the notion of instinct and the notion of sexuality. One could even say that his critique of the 'popular' or 'biological' conception of sexuality, which brings Freud to recognise the activity of a sole 'energy'–the libido–in very diverse phenomena, many of them a very far cry from the sexual act, coincides with the uncovering of the

417

thing that creates a fundamental difference in man between instinct in Freud's sense (*Trieb*) and instinct in the traditional sense (*Instinkt*). In this context, it is arguable that the Freudian view of the instinct, worked out on the basis of the study of human sexuality, is only fully validated in the case of the sexual instinct (see 'Instinct', 'Anaclisis', 'Instincts of Self-Preservation').

Freud maintained throughout his work that the action of repression is directed especially against the sexual instinct; consequently he gives this instinct a major role in psychical conflict*, but he leaves the question of the ultimate basis of this special status open. 'Theoretically there is no objection to supposing that any sort of instinctual demand might occasion the same repressions and their consequences; but our observation shows us invariably, so far as we can judge, that the excitations which play this pathogenic part arise from the component instincts of sexual life' (2) (see 'Scene of Seduction', 'Oedipus Complex', 'Deferred Action').

Set in opposition to the self-preservative instincts in Freud's first instinct theory, the sexual instinct is assimilated in his final dualism into the category of the life instincts*, or Eros*. Whereas in the first dualistic scheme it was a force answerable only to the pleasure principle*, hard to 'educate', operating in accordance with the primary process* and forever threatening the equilibrium of the psychical apparatus from within, it is transformed under the denomination of the life instinct into a force seeking to 'bind', to construct and preserve vital unities; conversely, it is its antagonist the death instinct* which now functions according to the principle of absolute discharge.

This metamorphosis cannot be properly understood without taking into account the whole conceptual revision carried through by Freud from 1920 onwards (see 'Death Instincts', 'Ego', 'Binding').

(1) Cf. FREUD, S. *Three Essays on the Theory of Sexuality* (1905*d*), G.W., V, 33; S.E., VII, 135.

(2) FREUD, S. *An Outline of Psycho-Analysis* (1940*a* [1938]), G.W., XVII, 112; S.E., XXIII, 186.

Sexuality

= *D*.: Sexualität.–*Es*.: sexualidad.–*Fr*.: sexualité.–*I*.: sessualità–*P*.: sexualidade.

In psycho-analytic practice and theory, sexuality does not mean only the activities and pleasure which depend on the functioning of the genital apparatus: it also embraces a whole range of excitations and activities which may be observed from infancy onwards and which procure a pleasure that cannot be adequately explained in terms of the satisfaction of a basic physiological need (respiration, hunger, excretory function, etc.); these re-emerge as component factors in the so-called normal form of sexual love.

It is well known that psycho-analysis attributes a very great deal of importance to sexuality in the development and mental life of the human individual. This claim cannot be understood, however, if it is not realised to what extent it assumes a transformation of the concept of sexuality. We do not intend to demarcate the function of sexuality in the psycho-analytic view of mankind here, but merely to clarify the way psycho-analysis uses this *concept* in terms both of its extension and of its comprehension.

If one sets out with the commonly held view that defines sexuality as an instinct*, in the sense of pre-determined behaviour typifying the species and having a relatively fixed *object** (partner of the opposite sex) and *aim** (union of the genital organs in coitus), it soon becomes apparent that this approach can only provide a very inadequate account of the facts that emerge as much from direct observation as from analysis.

I. *Extension*. a. The existence and commonness of the sexual perversions, an inventory of which was undertaken by some psychopathologists at the end of the nineteenth century (Krafft-Ebing, Havelock Ellis), shows that there is a great diversity in the choice of sexual objects and in the types of activity used to obtain satisfaction.

b. Freud establishes the existence of numerous points of overlap between perverse and so-called normal sexuality: the appearance of temporary perversions when the usual form of satisfaction becomes impossible; and the normal presence of types of behaviour – in the form of activity leading up to and accompanying coitus (forepleasure) – which also occur in the perversions either as a substitute for coitus or as an indispensable precondition of satisfaction.

c. Psycho-analysis of the neuroses reveals that symptoms constitute sexual wish-fulfilments realised in a fashion involving their displacement and their modification through compromise with defences, etc. Behind specific symptoms, furthermore, it is often perverse sexual wishes that are to be found.

d. It is the existence of an infantile sexuality, considered by Freud to operate from the start of life, which is responsible above all for the widening of the field which psycho-analysis looks upon as the sexual domain. When we speak of infantile sexuality, our object is not merely to acknowledge the existence of precocious excitations and genital needs, but also the existence of activity resembling perverse behaviour in adults. In the first place, infantile sexuality involves parts of the body – erotogenic zones* – which are not only the genital ones; secondly, such activity – thumbsucking, for instance – is directed towards pleasure quite independently of the carrying out of biological functions (e.g. nutrition). In this sense, psycho-analysts refer to sexuality as anal, oral, etc.

II. *Comprehension*. This broadened extension of the sexual field leads Freud, of necessity, to attempt to lay down the criteria of the specifically sexual nature of these varied activities. Once we have said that the sexual cannot be reduced to the genital* (any more than the psyche can be confined to conscious mental life), the question arises of what justification the psycho-analyst has for attributing a sexual character to processes in which the genital is not concerned. The question applies principally to the case of infantile sexuality, since with adult perversions genital excitation is present as a general rule.

Freud offers a particularly straightforward treatment of this problem in Chapters XX and XXI of the *Introductory Lectures on Psycho-Analysis* (1916–17): ' "Why," ' he has an imaginary critic object, ' "are you so obstinate in describing as being already sexuality what on your own evidence are indefinable manifestations in childhood out of which sexual life will later develop? Why should you not be content instead with giving them a physiological description and simply say that in an infant at the breast we already observe activities, such as sensual sucking or holding back the excreta, which show us that he is striving for 'organ-pleasure'* (*Organlust*)" ' (1*a*).

Although Freud leaves this question open, he does put forward the clinical argument that the analysis of symptoms in the adult leads us back to these pleasurable childhood activities, and this via the intermediary of material that is unquestionably sexual (1*b*). To postulate the sexual nature of the infantile activities themselves is to go a step farther, it is true, but Freud argues that what we find at the end of a process of development which we are able to trace back stage by stage ought to be present – at least *in potentia* – from the beginning of that process. He is forced to acknowledge, however, that 'at the moment we are not in possession of any generally recognized criterion of the sexual nature of a process' (1*c*).

Freud often declares that such a criterion should be sought in the realm of biochemistry. In psycho-analysis, all that can be affirmed is that there exists a sexual energy or libido; clinical experience, while it cannot help us define this energy, does show us its development and transformations.

*   *   *

Thus Freud's thinking seems to come to a dead end both as regards the essence of sexuality (the last word on this being left to a hypothetical biochemical definition) and as regards its genesis, in that he goes no further than postulating that sexuality exists virtually from the beginning.

This difficulty is most apparent where infantile sexuality is concerned, but it is also in this area that we may be able to find pointers towards a solution.

a. In terms of the quasi-physiological description of infantile sexual behaviour, Freud has already shown that the emergence of the sexual instinct is rooted in the functioning of the great mechanisms that are responsible for the preservation of the organism. In a first stage, he argues, the instinct can only be discerned in the guise of that pleasure which is accorded as a marginal result of the achievement of the function (pleasure derived from sucking over and above the appeasement of hunger). Only at a second stage is this marginal pleasure sought for its own sake, irrespective of any alimentary needs, irrespective of any functional pleasure, without any external object and in an entirely localised fashion on the plane of an erotogenic zone.

Anaclisis*, erotogenic zones*, auto-erotism*: these are, for Freud, the three closely interwoven aspects that define infantile sexuality (2). It is clear that when Freud attempts to ascertain the point at which the sexual instinct emerges, this instinct (*Trieb*) appears almost as a perversion of instinct in the traditional sense (*Instinkt*) – a perversion in which the specific object and the organic purpose both vanish.

b. In a rather different temporal perspective, Freud insisted on many occasions upon the notion of deferred action*, according to which comparatively undefined precocious experiences are subsequently invested, as a result of fresh experiences, with a meaning that they did not have originally. May we say then that in the last analysis infantile experiences such as sucking are non-sexual to begin with and that their sexual character is only acquired secondarily, once genital activity has made its appearance? Such a conclusion, in so far as it lays the emphasis on the retroactive element in the consitution of sexuality, would seem to invalidate both what we were saying above about the emergence of the sexual and, *a fortiori*, the genetic approach which holds that the sexual is already present implicitly from the beginning of psychobiological development.

This is in fact a major difficulty of the Freudian sexual theory: in so far as sexuality is not a ready-made mechanism but is established during the course of the individual's history, changing in both its mechanics and its aims, it cannot be understood solely in terms of a biological evolution; on the other hand, however, the facts show that infantile sexuality is not a retroactive illusion.

c. In our view, a way out of this difficulty may be found in the idea of primal phantasies*, an idea which serves in a way as a counterweight to the notion of deferred action. When Freud speaks of primal phantasies, he is appealing to the 'phylogenetic explanation' and referring to specific phantasies (primal scene, castration, seduction) which are encountered in every subject and which inform human sexuality. Sexuality cannot therefore be explained solely in terms of the endogenous maturation of the instinct–it has to be seen as being constituted at the core of intersubjective structures which predate its emergence in the individual.

In its content, as in the somatic meanings that it embraces, the 'primal scene' phantasy can be related to a specific libidinal stage–the anal-sadistic stage–but in its actual structure (representation and solution of the mystery of conception) it cannot be explained, in Freud's view, by the simple conjunction of the observable factors: it constitutes a variant of a 'schema' that is *already given* for the subject. On a different structural plane, the same might be said of the Oedipus complex where this is defined as regulating the triangular relationship between child and parents. It is significant that those psycho-analysts who have been the most concerned to describe the play of phantasies inherent to infantile sexuality–the Kleinian school–also consider that the Oedipal structure exerts an influence from an extremely early stage.

d. Freud's reservations about a purely genetic and endogenous conception of sexuality are further pointed up by the importance that he continued to assign to seduction even after recognising the existence of an infantile sexuality (for further discussion of this point, see our commentary on the 'Scene of Seduction').

e. Thus infantile sexuality is connected–at any rate in its origins–to needs traditionally known as instincts, yet it is also independent of them; it is endogenous inasmuch as it follows a course of development and passes through different stages, and exogenous inasmuch as it invades the subject from the direction of the adult world (since the subject is obliged from the outset to find a place in the phantasy universe of the parents, and since they subject him to more or less veiled sexual incitement). There is another respect too in which infantile sexuality is difficult to comprehend: it cannot be accounted for either by an approach that reduces it to a physiological function or by an interpretation 'from above' that claims that what Freud calls infantile sexuality is the love relationship in its varied embodiments. In fact it is always in the form of *desire** that Freud identifies infantile sexuality in psycho-analysis: as opposed to love, desire is directly dependent on a specific somatic foundation; in contrast to need, it subordinates satisfaction to conditions in the phantasy world which strictly determine object-choice and the orientation of activity.

(1) FREUD, S.: a) G.W., XI, 335; S.E., XVI, 323. b) G.W., XI, 336; S.E., XVI, 324. c) G.W., XI, 331; S.E., XVI, 320.

(2) Cf. FREUD, S. *Three Essays on the Theory of Sexuality* (1905d), G.W., V, 83; S.E., VII, 182.

Signal of Anxiety, Anxiety as Signal

= *D.*: Angstsignal.–*Es.*: señal de angustia.–*Fr.*: signal d'angoisse.– *I.*: segnale d'angoscia.–*P.*: sinal de angústia.

Term introduced by Freud, in the context of his revision of the theory of anxiety (1926), to designate a device activated by the ego, when confronted by a situation of danger, in order to avoid being overwhelmed by the inflowing excitations. The signal of anxiety is a reproduction in attenuated form of the anxiety-reaction originally experienced in a traumatic situation; it makes it possible for defensive operations to be set in motion.

This concept makes its first appearance in *Inhibitions, Symptoms and Anxiety* (1926d) and is the key notion of what is usually referred to as the second theory of anxiety. We do not propose to summarise this revision here, nor to discuss its implications for and functions in the development of Freud's ideas. If only because of its conciseness, however, the term '*Angstsignal*' calls for some comment.

a. In the first place, it embodies the gist of the new theory. Freud's first economic account of anxiety treats this as a *result*–as the subjective manifestation of the fact that a quantity of energy has not been mastered. The expression 'signal of anxiety' points up an additional function of anxiety which makes it a motive of ego-defence.

b. The triggering of the signal of anxiety does not necessarily depend upon economic factors–in fact the signal may operate as the 'mnemic symbol'* or 'affective symbol' (1) of a situation that has not yet arisen and that has to be avoided.

c. The adoption of the idea of anxiety as signal does not, however, exclude an economic explanation. For one thing, the affect–reproduced now in the form of a signal–must have been passively experienced in the past in the form of so-called *automatic anxiety*. And furthermore a certain quantity of energy has to be mobilised before the signal can be set off.

d. Finally, note that Freud associates the signal of anxiety with the ego. This newly discovered function of anxiety may in fact be identified with what Freud had hitherto persistently described in the context of the secondary process*, showing how unpleasurable affects recurring in attenuated form are capable of setting the censorship* in motion.

(1) FREUD, S., G.W., XIV, 120–21; S.E., XX, 93–94.

Somatic Compliance

= *D.*: somatisches Entgegenkommen.–*Es.*: complacencia somática.–
Fr.: complaisance somatique.–*I.*: compiacenza somatica.–*P.*: complacência somática.

Expression introduced by Freud to account for the hysterical 'choice of neurosis', and for the choice of the organ or the somatic apparatus through which conversion* is to operate: the body (especially in the hysteric) or else one particular organ is said to offer a privileged medium for the symbolic expression of the unconscious conflict.

Freud speaks of somatic compliance for the first time apropos of the case of 'Dora'; he takes the view that there is no necessity to choose between a psychical and a somatic origin for hysteria: '. . . every hysterical symptom involves the participation of *both* sides. It cannot occur without the presence of a certain degree of *somatic compliance* offered by some normal or pathological process in or connected with one of the bodily organs' (1*a*). It is this somatic compliance which 'affords the unconscious mental processes a physical outlet' (1*b*); hence it is a determining factor in the 'choice of neurosis'*.

Although it is certainly true that the notion of somatic compliance extends well beyond the field of hysteria and that it raises the general question of the body's expressive powers and particular aptitude for signifying the repressed, it is as well, all the same, to make sure from the start that the different frames of reference within which this matter comes up are not confused. For example:

a. A somatic illness may have an attraction for the expression of the unconcious conflict; thus Freud is able to look upon a rheumatic affection of one of his patients as an 'organic disorder, which was the model copied in her later hysteria' (2).

b. The libidinal cathexis of an erotogenic zone may be displaced in the course of the subject's sexual history on to an area or apparatus of the body which is not intended to serve an erotogenic function (see 'Erotogenic Zone'), and which is thus all the better fitted to operate as a masked expression of a wish provided that it is a repressed one.

c. In so far as the expression 'somatic compliance' is meant to account not only for the choice of a particular bodily organ but also for the choice of the body as such as a means of expression, we find ourselves obliged to pay some attention, notably, to the vicissitudes of the narcissistic cathexis of the subject's own body.

(1) FREUD, S. 'Fragment of an Analysis of a Case of Hysteria (1905*e* [1900]): a) G.W., V, 200; S.E., VII, 40. b) G.W., V, 201; S.E., VII, 41.

(2) FREUD, S. *Studies on Hysteria* (1895*d*), G.W., I, 211; S.E., II, 147.

Source of the Instinct

= *D.*: Triebquelle. – *Es.*: fuente del instinto. – *Fr.*: source de la pulsion. –
I.: fonte dell'istinto *or* della pulsione. – *P.*: fonte do impulso *or* da pulsão.

The specific internal origin of each individual instinct: either the *place* where the excitation appears (erotogenic zone, organ, apparatus) or else the somatic *process* assumed to occur in this part of the body and to be perceived as excitation.

The term 'source' gradually comes in Freud's work to have a sense different from its ordinary metaphorical one. In the *Three Essays on the Theory of Sexuality* (1905*d*), under the heading of 'sources of infantile sexuality', Freud lists phenomena which vary greatly but which may ultimately be subdivided into two groups: first, excitations of the erotogenic zones by a variety of stimuli; and secondly, 'indirect sources' such as 'mechanical excitations', 'muscular activity', 'affective processes' and 'intellectual work' (1*a*). A source of the second type is not the origin of a particular component instinct* but contributes to the increase of 'sexual excitation' in general.

Inasmuch as this chapter of the *Three Essays* presents an exhaustive list of the factors both external and internal responsible for setting off sexual excitation, it would seem that the idea of the instinct's corresponding to a tension of internal origin has lost its force. This was an idea that Freud had previously upheld, beginning with the 'Project for a Scientific Psychology' (1950*a* [1895]) (2): it was the influx of endogenous excitations (*endogene Reize*) that subjected the organism to a tension from which it cannot escape as it does – through flight – from external stimuli.

In 'Instincts and their Vicissitudes' (1915*c*), Freud proceeds to analyse the various aspects of the component instinct more methodically: he breaks it down into its source, pressure*, aim* and object*. These distinctions are valid for all the instincts but apply more especially to the sexual ones.

The sense of 'source' here is once more that of Freud's first metapsychological work of 1895, and it is a precise one: it means the source which lies within the organism, the 'organic source' (*Organquelle*) or 'somatic source' (*somatische Quelle*) (3*a*). The term is now sometimes used to designate the actual organ which is the seat of the excitation. In a more exact sense, however, Freud uses it for the organic, physico-chemical process from which the excitation derives. The source is thus the somatic, as opposed to the psychical, process 'whose stimulus (*Reiz*) is represented in mental life by an instinct' (3*b*). This somatic process is outside the province of psychology, and usually unknown, but it is assumed to be specific in the case of each component instinct, and to determine that instinct's particular aim.

Freud proposes assigning a specific source to each instinct: aside from the erotogenic zones, which are the sources of well-defined instincts, the musculature is said to be the source of the instinct to master*, and the eye that of the 'scopophilic instinct' (*Schautrieb*) (3*c*).

*   *   *

424

By the end of this development the notion of source is so clear-cut that it contains no ambiguity at all: the specificity of the sexual instincts has been brought down, in the final analysis, to the specificity of an organic process. A thorough-going systematisation would further name distinct sources for each of the instincts of self-preservation. It might be argued, however, that this terminological rigour is only got at the price of a one-sided solution to the theoretical problem of the origin of the instincts. For instance, the inventory of 'sources of infantile sexuality' in the *Three Essays* had led up to the conclusion that the sexual instinct makes its appearance as the concomitant effect or marginal product (*Nebenwirkung, Nebenprodukt*) (1b) of various non-sexual activities: this holds not only for the so-called 'indirect' sources but also for the operation of the erotogenic zones (save for the genital one), where the sexual instinct depends anaclitically upon a type of functioning tied to self-preservation (see 'Anaclisis'). The common trait of all these 'sources', therefore, is that they do not give birth to the sexual instinct as to their natural, specific product–like organs producing their secretions; instead, they engender it as a side-effect of a vital function. The origin or–in the broad sense–the 'source' of the sexual instinct would on this view be constituted by such a vital function *as a whole* (itself comprising a source, a pressure, an aim and an object).

Libido is thus specified here as oral, anal, etc., on the basis of the mode of relationship laid down for it by a particular vital activity (during the oral stage, for example, love is constituted in the mode of eating/being eaten).

(1) FREUD, S.: a) G.W., V, 101–7; S.E., VII, 201–6. b) Cf. G.W., V, 106; S.E., VII, 204.

(2) Cf. FREUD, S., *Anf.*, 402; S.E., I, 317–18.

(3) FREUD, S.: a) G.W., X, 216, 225; S.E., XIV, 123, 132. c) G.W., X, 215; S.E., XIV, 123. c) G.W., X, 225; S.E., XIV, 132.

Specific Action

= *D.*: spezifische Aktion.–*Es.*: accíon específica.–*Fr.*: action spécifique.– *I.*: azione specifica.–*P.*: ação específica.

Term used by Freud in some of his early works to denote the entire process necessary for the resolution of the internal tension created by need; the specific action embraces both the adequate external intervention and the whole of the organism's predetermined responses which allow for the successful carrying out of the action.

It is mainly in his 'Project for a Scientific Psychology' (1950*a* [1895]) that Freud makes use of the concept of specific action. The *principle of inertia**, which he postulates in this work as the regulator of the functioning of the neuronal apparatus, is jeopardised as soon as endogenous stimuli make themselves felt. These are stimuli, in fact, which the organism has no means of evading. The tension they occasion may be discharged in two ways:

a. In an *immediate* way, by means of non-specific reactions such as expressions of emotion, cries, etc. This type of response, however, is inadequate, being unable to stem the continuing flow of excitations.

Specific Action

b. In a *specific* way – alone capable of achieving a lasting release from the tension. Freud outlines this kind of action – making notable use of the idea of a threshold – in his paper 'On the Grounds for Detaching a Particular Syndrome from Neurasthenia under the Description "Anxiety Neurosis" ' (1895b) (1a).

If the specific or adequate action is to be carried through, a specific object and a particular set of external conditions (e.g. a supply of food in the case of hunger) are indispensable prerequisites. For the suckling, since it exists in a state of primal helplessness (q.v.), aid from outside is the absolute precondition of the satisfaction of its needs. Freud is thus able to use the term 'specific action' to mean either the group of reflex-actions whereby the necessary operation is carried out, or else the adequate external intervention, or again the two combined.

Such specific action is implicit in the notion of the *experience of satisfaction**.

*   *   *

It is tempting to look upon Freud's conception of specific action as a first sketch of the theory of the instincts* (α). How far is this conception indeed consistent with the notion of the sexual instinct* as it emerges from Freud's later work? Freud's way of posing the problem was somewhat modified between 1895 and 1905:

a. In the 'Project' sexuality is classed as one of the 'major needs' (2), calling, as does hunger, for a specific action (see 'Instincts of Self-Preservation').

b. In 1895, it should be remembered, Freud had not yet discovered infantile sexuality. The use of the concept of specific action at this point implies an analogy between the adult sexual act and the satisfaction of hunger.

c. In the paper we have already cited, which is contemporary with the 'Project', the specific action required for sexual satisfaction is definitely described in terms appropriate to the adult. But in addition to the behavioural components which together make up a sort of organic pattern Freud introduces 'psychical' conditions, historical in their origin, under the heading of what he calls the working over of psychical libido (1b).

d. With the discovery of infantile sexuality there comes a change in perspective (see 'Sexuality'): Freud now criticises any attempt to define human sexuality on the basis of the adult act and to treat this act as invariable in its enactment, its object and its aim. 'Popular opinion has quite definite ideas about the nature and characteristics of this sexual instinct. It is generally understood to be absent in childhood, to set in at the time of puberty in connection with the process of coming to maturity and to be revealed in the manifestations of an irresistible attraction exercised by one sex upon the other; while its aim is presumed to be sexual union, or at all events actions leading in that direction' (3).

In the *Three Essays on the Theory of Sexuality* (1905d), Freud shows how unspecific are the organic conditions placed upon the obtaining of sexual pleasure in the mechanism of infantile sexuality. In so far as such conditions may be said to become specific rapidly, this is ascribed to historical rather than organic factors. Certainly the preconditions of adult sexual satisfaction can be highly determinate in the case of a given individual: it is as though man finds his way via the history of each individual to a form of behaviour which has

426

all the appearances of an instinctual pattern. This impression is, of course, the basis of what Freud, in the above-quoted lines, refers to as the ideas of 'popular opinion'.

(α) From this point of view a parallel could be drawn between the Freudian theory of specific action and the analysis of the instinctual process offered by modern animal psychology (the ethological school).

(1) FREUD, S.: a) Cf. G.W., I, 334–35; S.E., III, 108. b) Cf. G.W., I, 333–39; S.E., III, 106–12.

(2) Cf. FREUD, S., *Anf.*, 381; S.E., I, 297.

(3) FREUD, S. *Three Essays on the Theory of Sexuality* (1905d), G.W., V, 33; S.E., VII, 135.

Splitting of the Ego

= *D.*: Ichspaltung.–*Es.* escisión del yo.–*Fr.*: clivage du moi.–*I.*: scissione dell'io.– *P.*: clivagem do ego.

Term used by Freud to denote a very specific phenomenon which he deems to be at work above all in fetishism and in the psychoses: the coexistence at the heart of the ego of two psychical attitudes towards external reality in so far as this stands in the way of an instinctual demand. The first of these attitudes takes reality into consideration, while the second disavows it and replaces it by a product of desire. The two attitudes persist side by side without influencing each other.

I. The term '*Spaltung*'–splitting–has very old and very varied uses in psychoanalysis and psychiatry. Many authors, including Freud, have used it to evoke the fact that man, in one respect or another, is divided within himself. Psychopathological works dating from the end of the nineteenth century, especially those dealing with hysteria and hypnosis, are full of such notions as 'split personality', '*double conscience*', 'dissociation of psychological phenomena', etc.

For Breuer and Freud, the expressions 'splitting of consciousness' (*Bewusstseinsspaltung*), 'splitting of the content of consciousness', 'psychical splitting', etc., connote identical realities: on the basis of cases displaying those alternating states of dual personality or consciousness which appear in certain hysterical patients, or as a consequence of hypnosis, Janet, Breuer and Freud arrived at the idea of a coexistence within the psyche of two groups of phenomena –or even of two distinct personalities each of which may know absolutely nothing of the other. 'Since the fine work done by Pierre Janet, Josef Breuer and others, it may be taken as generally recognised that the syndrome of hysteria, so far as it is as yet intelligible, justifies the assumption of there being a splitting of consciousness, accompanied by the formation of separate psychical groups. Opinions are less settled, however, about the origins of this splitting of consciousness and about the part played by this characteristic in the structure of the hysterical neurosis' (1). Such a divergence of view is indeed the starting-point for the development of the Freudian view of the unconscious as separated off from

427

the field of consciousness by the action of repression – a conception which stands opposed to Janet's ideas on the 'weakness of psychological synthesis' and which is quickly to part company with Breuer's notions of 'hypnoid states'* and 'hypnoid hysteria'.

For Freud, splitting is the result of the conflict; thus in his view the notion has a descriptive value but no intrinsic explanatory one. On the contrary, it gives rise to the question of why and how the conscious subject has become separated in this way from a segment of his ideas.

When Freud retraces the history of the years during which the discovery of the unconscious was made, he does not hesitate to use the term '*Spaltung*' and kindred terms denoting the same fundamental datum of a division within the psyche. In the actual development of his work, however, '*Spaltung*' is only used from time to time, and it never becomes a conceptual tool. When Freud does employ it, it is primarily in order to evoke the fact that the psychical apparatus is separated into systems (Unconscious, Preconscious-Conscious) or agencies (id, ego, super-ego); or else the fact that the ego comprises a part that observes and a part that is observed.

*   *   *

At the same time, it is well known that Bleuler used '*Spaltung*' to denote what he considered to be the fundamental symptom of the group of disturbances to which he had given the name 'schizophrenia'. For Bleuler '*Spaltung*' does more than connote an observable fact: it implies a particular hypothesis concerning mental functioning (see 'Schizophrenia').

It is impossible not to be struck here by the analogy between the type of explanation proposed by Bleuler to account for schizophrenic *Spaltung* and Janet's: in both cases the splitting of the psyche into distinct associative groups is conceived of as a secondary regrouping within a mental world already broken up by reason of a primary associative weakness.

Freud does not adopt Bleuler's hypothesis, he criticises the term 'schizophrenia' which presupposes this hypothesis, and when, at the end of his life, he takes up the notion of splitting once more, it is from quite a different standpoint.

II. Freud worked out the notion of splitting of the ego chiefly in 'Fetishism' (1927e), 'Splitting of the Ego in the Process of Defence' (1940e [1938]) and *An Outline of Psycho-Analysis* (1904a [1938]); the context is a discussion of the psychoses and fetishism. According to Freud these disturbances mainly affect the relations between the ego and 'reality'. Study of them enabled him to establish with increasing certainty the existence of a specific mechanism, disavowal* (*Verleugnung*), whose prototypical form is the disavowal of castration*.

Disavowal by itself, however, does not account adequately for the data provided by the clinical observation of the psychoses and fetishism. Indeed, as Freud remarks: 'The problem of psychoses would be simple and perspicuous if the ego's detachment from reality could be carried through completely. But that seems to happen only rarely or perhaps never' (2a). In all psychoses – even in the most extreme cases – two mental attitudes are to be found: '. . . one, the normal one, which takes account of reality, and another which under the influence of the instincts detaches the ego from reality' (2b). It is this second attitude which finds expression in the production of a new, delusional reality. In the case of fetishism, Freud again discovers the coexistence of two contradictory attitudes within the ego—in connection, here, with the 'reality' of castration. 'On the one hand, [fetishists] are disavowing the fact of their perception —the fact that they saw no penis in the female genitals'. This disavowal is expressed by the formation of the fetish, which stands for the woman's penis. Yet 'on the other hand they are recognizing the fact that females have no penis and are drawing the correct conclusions from it. The two attitudes persist side by side throughout their lives without influencing each other. Here is what may rightly be called a splitting of the ego' (2c).

This splitting, as can be seen, is not properly speaking a defence of the ego, but rather a means of having two procedures of defence exist side by side, one directed towards reality (disavowal) and the other towards the instinct; this second procedure may lead to the formation of neurotic symptoms (e.g. phobic symptoms).

When he introduced the expression 'splitting of the ego', Freud asked himself whether this idea 'should be regarded as something long familiar and obvious or as something entirely new and puzzling' (3). And it is true that the coexistence within a single subject of 'two contrary and independent attitudes' (2d) is actually a characteristic tenet of the psycho-analytic theory of the individual. But Freud's intention in speaking of a splitting *of the ego* (intrasystemic) rather than a splitting *between agencies* (between ego and id) is to bring out a process that *is* new in comparison with the model of repression* and of the return of the repressed*. In fact one of the specific traits of this process is that it does not result in the formation of a compromise* between the two attitudes present but that it maintains them simultaneously instead, with no dialectical relationship being established.

It is of some interest to note that it was in the field of psychosis—the very area where Bleuler too, from his different theoretical standpoint, speaks of *Spaltung* —that Freud felt the need to develop a certain conception of the splitting of the ego. It seemed to us worth outlining this conception here, even though few psycho-analysts have adopted it: it has the merit of emphasising a typical phenomenon despite the fact that it does not provide an entirely satisfactory explanation of it.

(1) FREUD, S. 'The Neuro-Psychoses of Defence' (1894a), G.W., I, 60; S.E., III, 45–46.

(2) FREUD, S. *An Outline of Psycho-Analysis* (1940a [1938]); a) G.W., XVII, 132; S.E., XXIII, 201. b) G.W., XVII, 133; S.E., XXIII, 202. c) G.W., XVII, 134; S.E., XXIII, 203. d) XVII, 134; S.E., XXIII, 204.

(3) FREUD, S. 'Splitting of the Ego in the Process of Defence' (1940e [1938]), G.W., XVII, 59; S.E., XXIII, 275.

Splitting of the Object

= *D.*: Objektspaltung.–*Es.*: escisión del objeto.–*Fr.*: clivage de l'objet.–
I.: scissione dell' oggetto.–*P.*: clivagem do objeto.

Mechanism described by Melanie Klein and considered by her to be the most primitive kind of defence against anxiety: the object, with both erotic and destructive instincts directed towards it, splits into a 'good' and a 'bad' object; these two parts will have relatively distinct parts in the interplay of introjections and projections. Splitting of the object comes about especially in the paranoid-schizoid position, where it affects part-objects*. It is found also in the depressive position, affecting the whole object.

The splitting of objects is accompanied by a parallel splitting of the ego into a 'good' ego and a 'bad' one, the ego being constituted for Kleinians essentially through the introjection of objects.

For the term 'splitting' (*Spaltung*), see our commentary on 'Splitting of the Ego'. Melanie Klein's conceptions claim to be based on certain remarks made by Freud concerning the subject-object relationship (see 'Object', 'Pleasure-Ego/Reality-Ego'). For the Kleinian contribution to this theme, see under ' "Good" Object/"Bad" Object', 'Paranoid Position', 'Depressive Position'.

Subconscious, Subconsciousness

= *D.*: Unterbewusste, Unterbewusstsein.–*Es.*: subconsciente, subconciencia.–
Fr.: subconscient, subconscience.–*I.*: subconscio.–*P.*: subconsciente, subconsciência.

Term used in psychology as a designation for what is scarcely conscious or else for what is below the threshold of immediate consciousness or even inaccessible to it. Used by Freud in his earliest writings as a synonym for 'unconscious', it was very quickly discarded because of the confusion it tends to foster.

The texts in which the 'young Freud' adopts this term–which was in fairly common use in the late nineteenth century, particularly in connection with the phenomenon known as 'dual personality' (α)–are few and far between. It occurs in an article of Freud's first published in French, 'Some Points for a Comparative Study of Hysterical and Motor Paralyses' (1893c), and in a passage of the *Studies on Hysteria* (1895d) (1, β). To judge from the context there does not seem to be any difference for Freud at this period between what is described as 'subconscious' and the concept that is emerging under the name 'unconscious'.

Before long, however, the term 'subconscious' is abandoned and its use criticised. Freud writes in *The Interpretation of Dreams* (1900a): 'We must avoid the distinction between "supraconscious" and "subconscious", which has become so popular in the more recent literature of the psychoneuroses, for such a distinction seems precisely calculated to stress the equivalence of what is psychical to what is conscious' (2).

This sort of criticism recurs several times, the most explicit passage being this one from *The Question of Lay Analysis* (1926e): 'If someone talks of sub-consciousness, I cannot tell whether he means the term topographically–to indicate something lying in the mind beneath consciousness–or qualitatively–to indicate another consciousness, a subterranean one, as it were' (3, γ).

If Freud refuses to speak of a 'subconscious' it is because this seems to him to imply the idea of a 'second consciousness' which, however feeble it is taken to be, remains qualitatively coextensive with the phenomena of consciousness. In his view only the term 'unconscious', by virtue of the negation that it contains, is able to express the topographical split between two psychical domains and the qualitative distinction between the processes that occur therein (δ). The strongest argument against the notion of a second consciousness derives from 'the fact that analytic investigation reveals some of these latent processes as having characteristics and peculiarities which seem alien to us, or even incredible, and which run directly counter to the attributes of consciousness with which we are familiar' (4).

(α) In particular, the notion of a subconscious level, as is well known, is one of the basic concepts of the thought of Pierre Janet. Even though Freud's criticisms regarding the term 'subconscious' appear to be directed at Janet they can hardly be said to constitute a valid refutation of Janet's views. The difference between Janet's 'subconscious' and Freud's un-conscious resides not so much in the relationship with consciousness as in the nature of the process that brings about the 'splitting'* of the psyche.

(β) The term appears more often in Breuer's contributions.

(γ) The lack of specificity that the term 'subconscious' owes in part to its prefix is found also in the definition proposed by Lalande's *Vocabulaire technique et critique de la philsophie*: the connotation of 'feebly conscious' is indicated alongside the notion of a 'personality more or less distinct from the conscious personality'.

(δ) It may be noted in this connection that some authors claiming allegiance to psycho-analysis only accept the concept of the unconscious under the designation 'subconscious'.

(1) Cf. FREUD, S., G.W., I, 54 and 122*n*.; S.E., I, 171, 172 and II, 69*n*.

(2) FREUD, S., G.W., II–III, 620; S.E., V, 615.

(3) FREUD, S., G.W., XIV, 225; S.E., XX, 198.

(4) FREUD, S. 'The Unconscious' (1915e), G.W., X, 269; S.E., XIV, 170.

Sublimation

= *D*.: Sublimierung.–*Es*.: sublimación.–*Fr*.: sublimation.–*I*.: sublimazione.–
P.: sublimação.

Process postulated by Freud to account for human activities which have no apparent connection with sexuality but which are assumed to be motivated by the force of the sexual instinct. The main types of activity described by Freud as sublimated are artistic creation and intellectual inquiry.

The instinct is said to be sublimated in so far as it is diverted towards a new, non-sexual aim and in so far as its objects are socially valued ones.

Sublimation

Introduced into psycho-analysis by Freud, this term evokes the sense 'sublime' has when it is used, particularly in the fine arts, to qualify works that are grand or uplifting. It also evokes the sense 'sublimation' has for chemistry: the procedure whereby a body is caused to pass directly from a solid to a gaseous state.

Freud calls upon the notion of sublimation throughout his work when seeking to account in economic and dynamic terms for certain kinds of activity governed by a desire not visibly directed towards a sexual end; examples would be artistic creation, intellectual pursuits and in a general way those activities to which a particular society assigns great value. Freud looks for the ultimate motor force of these types of behaviour in a transformation of the sexual instincts*: the sexual instinct 'places extraordinarily large amounts of force at the disposal of civilised activity, and it does this in virtue of its especially marked characteristic of being able to displace its aim without materially diminishing its intensity. This capacity to exchange its originally sexual aim for another one, which is no longer sexual but which is psychically related to the first aim, is called the capacity for *sublimation*' (1*a*).

Even on the purely *descriptive* plane Freud's formulations regarding sublimation were never very far-reaching. The domain of sublimated activities is badly demarcated: for example, does it include all work involving thought or merely certain types of intellectual production? Should the fact that the activities described as sublimated in a given culture are accorded particularly high social esteem be taken as a defining characteristic of sublimation? Or does sublimation also cover the whole of the so-called adaptative activities–work, leisure, etc.? As for the change that is supposed to affect the instinctual process, the question arises whether it concerns the *aim** alone, as Freud long maintained, or both the *aim* and the *object** of the instinct, as he states in the *New Introductory Lectures on Psycho-Analysis* (1933*a*): 'A certain kind of modification of the aim and change of the object, in which our social valuation is taken into account, is described by us as "sublimation"' (2).

When matters are viewed from the *metapsychological** point of view this uncertainty persists, as Freud noted himself (3). And this is true even in a work centred on the theme of intellectual and artistic production such as *Leonardo da Vinci and a Memory of his Childhood* (1910*c*).

*   *   *

No comprehensive theory of sublimation will be put forward here; none is implicit in the somewhat undeveloped discussion of the topic found in Freud's writings. Without attempting any synthesis, we shall merely indicate a number of trends in Freudian thinking.

a. Sublimation especially affects the component instincts*, above all those which do not achieve a successful integration into the definitive form of genitality: 'The forces that can be employed for cultural activities are thus to a great extent obtained through the suppression of what are known as the *perverse* elements of sexual excitation' (1*b*).

b. As for the *mechanism* of sublimation, Freud proposed two successive hypotheses. The first is based on the theory of the anaclitic* relationship of the sexual instincts to the self-preservative* ones. Just as the non-sexual functions can be contaminated by sexuality (as they are, for instance, in psychogenic disturbances of eating, vision, etc.), so 'the same pathways [...] along which sexual disturbances trench upon the other somatic functions must also perform another important function in normal health. They must serve as paths for the attraction of sexual instinctual forces to aims that are other than sexual, that is to say, for the sublimation of sexuality' (4). A hypothesis of this type underpins Freud's study of Leonardo da Vinci.

With the introduction of the idea of narcissism* and the advent of the final theory of the psychical apparatus Freud adopts a new approach. The transformation of a sexual activity into a sublimated one (assuming both are directed towards external, independent objects) is now said to require an intermediate period during which the libido is withdrawn on to the ego so that desexualisation may become possible. It is in this sense that Freud speaks in *The Ego and the Id* (1923b) of the ego's energy as a 'desexualised and sublimated' one capable of being displaced on to non-sexual activities. 'If this displaceable energy is desexualised libido, it may also be described as *sublimated* energy; for it would still retain the main purpose of Eros–that of uniting and binding –in so far as it helps towards establishing the unity, or tendency to unity, which is particularly characteristic of the ego' (5).

One might interpret this as confirmation of the idea that sublimation depends to a high degree on the narcissistic dimension of the ego, and that consequently the object of sublimated activity may be expected to display the same appearance of a beautiful whole which Freud here assigns to the ego. Melanie Klein could be said to be pursuing the same line of thought when she describes sublimation as a tendency to repair* and restore the 'good' object* that has been shattered by the destructive instincts (6).

c. Because Freud left the theory of sublimation in such a primitive state we have only the vaguest hints as to the dividing-lines between sublimation and processes akin to it (reaction-formation*, aim-inhibition*, idealisation*, repression*). Similarly, although Freud held the capacity to sublimate to be an essential factor in successful treatment, he never described its operation in concrete terms.

d. The hypothesis of sublimation was brought forward in connection with the sexual instincts, but Freud did also mention the possibility of a sublimation of the aggressive instincts* (7); this question has since been taken up by others.

*   *   *

In the psycho-analytic literature the concept of sublimation is frequently called upon; the idea indeed answers a basic need of the Freudian doctrine and it is hard to see how it could be dispensed with. The lack of a coherent theory of sublimation remains one of the lacunae in psycho-analytic thought.

(1) FREUD, S. ' "Civilized" Sexual Morality and Modern Nervous Illness' (1908d): a) G.W., VII, 150; S.E., IX, 187. b) G.W., VII, 151; S.E., IX, 189.

(2) FREUD, S., G.W., XV, 103; S.E., XXII, 97.

(3) Cf. FREUD, S. *Civilization and its Discontents* (1930a), G.W., XIV, 438; S.E., XXI, 79.

(4) FREUD, S. *Three Essays on the Theory of Sexuality* (1905d), G.W., V, 107; S.E., VII, 206.

(5) FREUD, S., G.W., XIII, 274; S.E., XIX, 45.

(6) Cf., for example, KLEIN, M. 'Infantile Anxiety-Situations Reflected in a Work or Art and in the Creative Impulse' (1929), in *Contributions*, 227–35.

(7) Cf. JONES, E. *Sigmund Freud*, III, 493–94.

Substitute-Formation (or Substitutive Formation)

= *D*.: Ersatzbildung.–*Es*.: formación sustituta.–*Fr*.: formation substitutive.–
I.: formazione sostitutiva.–*P*.: formação substitutiva.

Designates symptoms–or equivalent formations such as parapraxes*, jokes, etc.–in so far as they stand for unconscious contents.

This substitution is to be understood in two senses: *economically*, the symptom furnishes the unconscious wish with a replacement satisfaction; *symbolically*, one content of the unconscious is supplanted by another according to certain chains of association.

When Freud takes up the whole question of the formation of neurotic symptoms in *Inhibitions, Symptoms and Anxiety* (1926*d*) he identifies them with substitutive formations 'created in place of the instinctual process that has been affected by defence' (1). This is a longstanding notion of Freud's–we find it in his earliest writings, where it is also expressed by the term '*Surrogat*' (cf. for example 'The Neuro-Psychoses of Defence' (1894*a*) (2)).

What exactly does the substitution consist in? To begin with, it may be understood in the context of the economic theory of libido as the replacement of one satisfaction which is bound to a reduction of tensions by another one. It cannot be completely explained in quantitative terms, however, for psycho-analysis shows that associative links exist between the symptom and what it replaces. So '*Ersatz*' takes on the meaning of a symbolic substitution–the product of the displacement and condensation which determine the symptom in its specificity.

The term 'substitute-formation' should be seen in conjunction with 'compromise-formation'* and 'reaction-formation'*. Every symptom, inasmuch as it is the product of the defensive conflict, is a compromise-formation. In so far as it is principally the wish which seeks satisfaction by means of the symptom, this symptom appears above all as a substitute-formation; in reaction-formations, by contrast, the defensive process predominates.

(1) FREUD, S., G.W., XVI, 176; S.E., XX, 145.
(2) Cf. FREUD, S., G.W., I, 68; S.E., III, 54.

Sum of Excitation

= *D*.: Erregungssumme.–*Es*.: suma de excitación.–*Fr*.: somme d'excitation.–
I.: somma di eccitazione.–*P*.: soma de excitação.

**One of the terms used by Freud to designate the quantitative factor whose trans-
formations the economic* hypothesis seeks to explain. The term lays emphasis
on the *origin* of this factor, i.e. stimuli both external and internal but especially
the latter (instincts).**

At the end of his article on 'The Neuro-Psychoses of Defence' (1894*a*), Freud
writes that 'in mental functions something is to be distinguished–a quota of
affect or sum of excitation–which possesses all the characteristics of a quantity
(though we have no means of measuring it), which is capable of increase,
diminution, displacement and discharge, and which is spread over the memory-
traces of ideas somewhat as an electric charge is spread over the surface of a
body' (1).

It will be noticed that the term 'sum of excitation' appears in this context
as synonymous with 'quota of affect'; in fact, however, each of these two
expressions lays the stress on a different aspect of the quantitative factor. The
use of 'sum of excitation' draws attention to two ideas:

a. The origin of the quantity. Psychical energy is conceived of as derived
from stimuli–mainly internal ones–whose action is continuous and which
cannot be evaded by flight.

b. The idea that the psychical apparatus is subjected to stimulations which
are constantly threatening the aims of the principle which governs it–the principle of constancy*.

This term should be set alongside that of 'summation' (*Summation*) of
excitation which Freud used in his 'Project for a Scientific Psychology' (1950*a*
[1895]), and which was borrowed by him from the physiologist Sigmund
Exner (2); psychical excitations only circulate within the apparatus when an
accumulation or summation has come about such as to enable them to pass
across a threshold of permeability (3).

(1) Freud, S., G.W., I, 74; S.E., III, 60.
(2) Cf. Jones, E. *Sigmund Freud*, I, 417.
(3) Cf. Freud, S. *Anf.*, 400; S.E., I, 316.

Super-Ego

= *D*.: Über-Ich.–*Es*.: superyó.–*Fr*.: surmoi *or* sur-moi.–*I*.: super-io.–*P*.: superego.

**One of the agencies of the personality as described by Freud in the framework
of his second theory of the psychical apparatus: the super-ego's role in relation
to the ego may be compared to that of a judge or a censor. Freud sees conscience,
self-observation and the formation of ideals as functions of the super-ego.**

Super-Ego

In classical theory, the super-ego is described as the heir of the Oedipus complex in that it is constituted through the internalisation of parental prohibitions and demands.

Some psycho-analysts hold that the super-ego is formed at an earlier period, on the grounds that its action may be observed as from the preoedipal stages (Melanie Klein); or, at any rate, that very early psychological mechanisms may be found which constitute forerunners of the super-ego (e.g. Glover, Spitz).

The term 'super-ego' was introduced by Freud in *The Ego and The Id* (1923*b*). He brings forward the fact that the critical function thus named constitutes an agency* which has become separated from the ego and which seems to dominate it, as is shown by pathological states of mourning or melancholia where the subject feels that he is the brunt of criticism and denigration: 'We see how [...] one part of the ego sets itself over against the other, judges it critically, and, as it were, takes it as its object' (1).

The notion of the super-ego belongs to Freud's second topography*. Even before it was given this name and differentiated in this way, however, psycho-analytic clinical practice and theory had already acknowledged the part played in psychical conflict by that function whose aim is to prohibit wishes being fulfilled or becoming conscious–the concept of the dream-censorship* is a case in point. What is more, Freud recognised (and this is what distinguishes Freud's conceptions, from the start, from classical notions of conscience) that this censorship could work in an unconscious way. Similarly, he noted that the self-reproaches of the obsessional neurotic need not necessarily be conscious: '. . . the sufferer from compulsions and prohibitions behaves as if he were dominated by a sense of guilt*, of which, however, he knows nothing, so that we must call it an unconscious sense of guilt, in spite of the apparent contradiction in terms' (2).

It was when he came to consider delusions of being watched, melancholia and pathological mourning, however, that Freud was led to differentiate a *super-ego* within the personality: one part of the ego set against the other, so to speak, which comes for the subject to have the value of a model and the function of a judge. Freud first identifies such an agency in 1914–15, as a system itself comprising two partial structures: the ego-ideal proper and a critical agency (see 'Ego-Ideal').

If the notion of the super-ego is taken in a broad and rather undifferentiated sense–as is the case in *The Ego and The Id*, where, as we have said, the *term* appears for the first time–then it embraces the functions of prohibition and of the ideal. On the other hand, if the ego-ideal is postulated, even if only as a specific substructure, then the super-ego appears mainly as an agency embodying a law and prohibiting its transgression.

*   *   *

According to Freud, the *formation* of the super-ego is a corollary of the decline of the Oedipus complex*: when the child stops trying to satisfy his Oedipal wishes, which have become prohibited, he transforms his cathexis of his parents into an identification with them–he internalises the prohibition.

436

Freud points to the difference which exists here between the development of the boy and that of the little girl. In the case of the boy the Oedipus complex clashes inevitably with the threat of castration: '. . . a severe super-ego is set up as its heir' (3a). For girls, on the contrary, 'The castration complex prepares for the Oedipus complex instead of destroying it [...]. Girls remain in the Oedipus complex for an indeterminate length of time; they demolish it late and, even so, incompletely. In these circumstances the formation of the super-ego must suffer; it cannot attain the strength and independence which give it its cultural significance' (3b).

Although the formation of the super-ego is grounded on the renunciation of loving and hostile Oedipal wishes, it is subsequently refined, according to Freud, by the contributions of social and cultural requirements (education, religion, morality). On the other hand it has been claimed that either a premature super-ego or else stages prefiguring the super-ego exist prior to the moment to which super-ego formation is ascribed by classical theory. Thus several authors emphasise the fact that the internalisation of prohibitions definitely precedes the decline of the Oedipus complex: the precepts of education are adopted very early on, particularly, as Ferenczi noted in 1925, those relating to sphincter-control (cf. 'Psycho-Analysis of Sexual Habits'). For Melanie Klein's followers a super-ego exists from the oral stage, formed through the introjection of 'good' and 'bad' objects* and rendered especially cruel by infantile sadism, at its height at this point. Other authors, without going so far as to speak of a preoedipal super-ego, show how super-ego formation is a process which begins at a very early stage. René Spitz, for example, recognises three primordia of the super-ego: imposed physical actions, the attempt at mastery of gestures by means of identification, and identification with the aggressor* – this last mechanism playing the most important part (5).

*   *   *

If we consider the different forms of identification, it is difficult to decide which specific ones among them play a part in the formation of the super-ego, of the ego-ideal*, of the ideal ego* and even of the ego* itself.

'The installation of the super-ego can be described as a successful instance of identification with the parental agency,' writes Freud in the *New Introductory Lectures on Psycho-Analysis* (1933a) (3c). That he should use the expression 'identification with the parental agency' is enough in itself to indicate that the identification which founds the super-ego is not to be understood as an identification with other people. In an unusually explicit passage, Freud clarifies this idea as follows: 'Thus a child's super-ego is in fact constructed on the model not of its parents but of its parents' super-ego; the contents which fill it are the same and it becomes the vehicle of tradition and of all the time-resisting judgements of value which have propagated themselves in this manner from generation to generation' (3d).

It is generally apropos of the super-ego that criticism is levelled at the concepts of the second Freudian topography on the grounds of their anthropomorphism. As Daniel Lagache has pointed out, however, one definite contribution of psycho-analysis is to have brought out the role of anthropomorphism in the functioning and genesis of the psychical apparatus, and to have exposed the existence of 'animistic enclaves' in this apparatus (6). Similarly, the clinical experience of psycho-analysis reveals that the super-ego operates in a 'realist' mode and as an autonomous agency (internal 'bad object', *'grosse voix'* (α) etc.). Several authors, following in Freud's footsteps, have stressed that the character of the super-ego is very far removed from the prohibitions and precepts actually enunciated by parents and teachers–so much so, in fact, that the 'severity' of the super-ego may even be in inverse proportion to theirs.

(α) Freud insisted on the idea that the super-ego is essentially composed of word-presenta-tions* and that these contents are derived from aural perceptions, from instruction and from reading (7).

(1) FREUD, S. 'Mourning and Melancholia' (1917e). G.W., X, 433; S.E., XIV, 247.

(2) FREUD, S. 'Obsessive Actions and Religious Practices' (1907b), G.W., VII, 135; S.E., IX, 123.

(3) FREUD, S. *New Introductory Lectures on Psycho-Analysis* (1933a [1932]): a) G.W., XV, 138; S.E., XXII, 129. b) G.W., XV, 138; S.E., XXII, 129. c) Cf. G.W., XV, 70; S.E., XXII, 63–64. d) G.W., XV, 73; S.E., XXII, 67.

(4) Cf. KLEIN, M. 'The Early Development of Conscience in the Child' (1933), in *Contri-butions, passim.*

(5) Cf. SPITZ, R. 'On the Genesis of Super-ego Components', *Psa. Study of the Child*, 1958, XIII, 375–404.

(6) Cf. LAGACHE, D. 'La psychanalyse et la structure de la personnalité', *La Psychanalyse* (Paris: P.U.F., 1961), VI, 12–13.

(7) Cf. FREUD, S. *The Ego and the Id* (1923b), G.W., XIII, 282; S.E., XIX, 52–53.

Suppression

= *D.*: Unterdrückung.–*Es.*: supresión.–*Fr.*: répression.–*I.*: repressione.–*P.*: supressão.

I. In a broad sense: mental operation tending to eliminate distressing or un-welcome contents (ideas, affects, etc.) from consciousness. When suppression is understood in this way, repression is seen as a specific mode of suppression.

II. In a narrower sense, the term denotes certain types of suppression in sense I which differ from repression either (a) in that the procedure is of a conscious nature, while the suppressed content passes only into the preconscious, not into the unconscious; or (b) because, in the case of the suppression of an affect, this is not transposed into the unconscious but instead inhibited, or even abolished.

Although the term is often used in psycho-analysis, the denotation of 'suppres-sion' has not been clearly defined.

Our sense I is found occasionally–as, for example, in Freud's *Three Essays on the Theory of Sexuality* (1905d) (1)–but on the whole it is not often used. It should be noticed that suppression in this sense does not embrace all the 'defence mechanisms'*, since a number of these do not involve the exclusion of a content from the field of consciousness (e.g. undoing what has been done*).

The most usual meaning, encountered in *The Interpretation of Dreams* (1900*a*) (2), is our sense II, especially IIa. Here suppression stands in opposition to repression*, especially from the topographical point of view. In repression, the repressing agency (the ego), the operation itself and its outcome are all unconscious. Suppression, on the other hand, is seen as a conscious mechanism working on the level of that 'second censorship' which Freud places between the conscious and the preconscious; suppression involves an exclusion from the field of consciousness, not a translation from one system (the preconscious-conscious) to another (the unconscious). From the dynamic standpoint, ethical motives play a leading part in suppression.

A further distinction should be drawn between suppression and the judgement of condemnation* (*Verurteilung*), which may be the motive for an expulsion from consciousness, but which does not necessarily presuppose this.

Lastly, it may be remarked that suppression in our sense IIb is met with above all in Freud's theory of repression, where it is intended to denote the fate reserved for the affect*. For Freud, the ideational representative* of the instinct is alone repressed, while the affect, for its part, cannot become unconscious: it is either transformed into another affect or else suppressed 'so that no trace of it is to be found' (3), or so that 'all that corresponds [to it in the unconscious system] is a potential beginning which is prevented from developing' (4).

(1) Cf. FREUD, S., G.W., V, 71 and 77; S.E., VII, 61–62 and 69.
(2) FREUD, S., G.W., II–III, 611–12*n*.; S.E., V, 606*n*.
(3) FREUD, S. 'Repression' (1915*d*), G.W., X, 255–6; S.E., XIV, 153.
(4) FREUD, S. 'The Unconscious' (1915*e*), G.W., X, 277; S.E., XIV, 178.

Symbolic (sb.)

= *D*.: Symbolische.–*Es*.: simbólico.–*Fr*.: symbolique.–*I*.: simbolico.–*P*.: simbólico.

Term introduced (in its masculine, substantival form) by Jacques Lacan, who distinguishes three essential orders of the psycho-analytic field–the Symbolic, the Imaginary* and the Real (α). The Symbolic covers those phenomena with which psycho-analysis deals in so far as they are structured like a language. The term also refers to the idea that the effectiveness of the cure is based on the constitutive nature of the Word (*le caractère fondateur de la parole*).

I. A substantival use of 'symbolic' can be found in Freud's work: in *The Interpretation of Dreams* (1900*a*), for example, he speaks of '*die Symbolik*', by which he understands all the symbols having a constant meaning that are to be met with in various products of the unconscious.

There is an obvious difference between Freud's '*die Symbolik*' and Lacan's '*le symbolique*'. Freud stresses the relation which, however complex the connections may be, unites the symbol and what it represents. For Lacan, on the other hand, it is the structure of the symbolic system which is the main consideration, while the links with what is being symbolised – the element of resemblance or isomorphism, for example – are secondary and impregnated by the Imaginary.

Freud's notion of the symbolic does, however, imply a requirement which might serve to link these two conceptions: behind the particularity of images and symptoms Freud discerns a sort of universal 'fundamental language', although it is true that he is more concerned with what this says than with the way it is structured.

II. The idea of a symbolic order which structures interhuman reality was introduced into the social sciences above all by Claude Lévi-Strauss (1), who took as his model the structural linguistics developed from the teaching of Ferdinand de Saussure. The thesis of Saussure's *Cours de linguistique générale* (1955) is that the linguistic signifier, taken in isolation, has no intrinsic link with the signified: it only refers to a meaning inasmuch as it forms part of a system of signification characterised by differential opposition (β).

Lévi-Strauss extends and transposes structuralist conceptions to the study of cultural data, an area where it is not only the transmission of signs that is at work, and he describes the structures envisaged as a *symbolic system*: 'Any culture may be looked upon as an ensemble of symbolic systems, in the front rank of which are to be found language, marriage laws, economic relations, art, science and religion' (2).

III. Lacan's use of the notion of the Symbolic in psycho-analysis seems to us to have two aims:

a. To compare the structure of the unconscious with that of language, and to apply to the former a method which has borne fruit in its application to linguistics.

b. To show how the human subject is inserted into a pre-established order which is itself symbolic in nature in Lacan's sense.

To attempt to contain the meaning of 'Symbolic' within strict boundaries – to define it – would amount to a contradiction of Lacan's thought, since he refuses to acknowledge that the signifier can be permanently bound to the signified. We shall therefore confine ourselves to pointing out that Lacan's use of this term takes two different yet complementary paths. First, he uses it to designate a *structure* whose discrete elements operate as signifiers (linguistic model) or, more generally, the order to which such structures belong (the symbolic order). Secondly, he uses it to refer to the *law* on which this order is based; thus when Lacan speaks of the *symbolic father*, or of the Name-of-the-Father, he has an agency in mind which cannot be reduced to whatever forms may be taken by the 'real' or the 'imaginary' father – an agency which promulgates the law.

(α) [In capitalising these terms, I have followed the suggestion of Lacan's translator, Anthony Wilden; cf. *The Language of the Self* (Baltimore: Johns Hopkins Press, 1968), xv. I have also followed Wilden in using 'the Word' for '*la parole*', but the reader is referred to Wilden's discussion of the difficulties of translation here, *ibid.*, xvi-xvii. – *tr.*]

(β) It is worth noting that for Saussure the term 'symbol', in so far as it implies a 'natural' or 'rational' relation with what is symbolised, cannot be taken as a synonym of 'linguistic sign' (3).

(1) Cf. LÉVI-STRAUSS, C. *Les structures élémentaires des la parenté* (Paris: P.U.F., 1949); English translation: *The Elementary Structures of Kinship* (London: Eyre and Spottiswoode, 1969; Boston: Beacon Press, 1969). And *Anthropologie structurale* (Paris: Plon, 1958): English translation: *Structural Anthropology* (New York: Basic Books, 1963; London: Allen Lane, 1968).

(2) Cf. LÉVI-STRAUSS, C. Introduction to MAUSS, M. *Sociologie et Anthropologie* (Paris: P.U.F., 1950).

(3) Cf. SAUSSURE, F. de (Paris: Payot, 1955), 101. Trans.: *Course in General Linguistics* (New York, 1959).

Symbolic Realisation

= *D.*: symbolische Wunscherfüllung.–*Es.*: realización simbólica.–
Fr.: réalisation symbolique.–*I.*: realizzazione simbolica.–*P.*: realização simbólica.

Term employed by Marguerite Sechehaye to designate her method of analytic psychotherapy of schizophrenics: this consists in an attempt to make up for the privations the subject has suffered in his earliest years by meeting his needs on a symbolic level and thus giving him access to reality.

The method known as symbolic realisation is associated with Marguerite Sechehaye, who discovered it during the analytic psychotherapy of a young schizophrenic girl (α). The reader will find an account of the 'case of Renée'– which is the basis of Sechehaye's views–in *A New Psychotherapy in Schizophrenia* (1954) (1*a*); the patient's own version has been published as *Autobiography of a Schizophrenic Girl* (1950) (2*a*).

In this context 'realisation' connotes the idea that the schizophrenic's basic needs must be effectively met during the treatment; 'symbolic' means that this must be done in the same mode as that in which these needs are expressed– namely, a 'magico-symbolic' one in which a unity exists between the satisfying object (e.g. the mother's breast) and its symbol (in the Renée case, apples).

This technique may be defined as a form of *mothering** where the psychotherapist plays the role of the 'good mother' who is able to understand and satisfy frustrated oral needs. 'Far from demanding of the schizophrenic an impossible adjustment to the situation of conflict which he cannot overcome, this method seeks to arrange, to modify harsh reality and to replace it with another, more gentle and more tolerable one' (1*b*).

Symbolic realisations of basic needs, according to Sechehaye, must meet the subject at the level of his deepest regression; they must be effected in an order which tends to reflect the sequence of genetic stages*, so facilitating the reconstruction of the schizophrenic ego and a corresponding mastery of the real world (2*b*).

(α) Sechehaye first expounded her method in 'La réalisation symbolique (Nouvelle méthode de psychothérapie appliquée a un cas de schizophrénie)', suppl. to the *Revue suisse de psychologie et de psychologie appliquée*, No. 12 (Berne: Éd. Medicales, Hans Huber, 1947). Translation: *Symbolic Realization: A New Method of Psychotherapy Applied in a Case of Schizophrenia* (New York: I.U.P., 1951).

Symbolism

(1) SECHEHAYE, M.-A. *Introduction à une psychothérapie des schizophrènes*: a) 22. b) 9. Translation (New York: Grune & Stratton, 1956): a) 16. b) 8.

(2) SECHEHAYE, M.-A. *Journal d'une schizophrène*: a) Chap. XI. b) Cf. especially Part II. Translation: New York: Grune & Stratton, 1951.

Symbolism

= *D.*: Symbolik.–*Es.*: simbolismo.–*Fr.*: symbolisme.–*I.*: simbolismo.–*P.*: simbolismo.

I. Speaking broadly: mode of indirect and figurative representation of an unconscious idea, conflict or wish. In this sense, one may in psycho-analysis hold any substitutive formation* to be symbolic.

II. In a more restricted sense: mode of representation distinguished chiefly by the constancy of the relationship between the symbol and what it symbolises in the unconscious. This constancy is found not only in the same individual and from one individual to the next, but also in the most varied spheres (myth, religion, folklore, language, etc.), and in the most widely separated cultures.

The notion of symbolism is nowadays so closely tied to psycho-analysis, the words 'symbolic', 'symbolise' and 'symbolisation' are used so often–and so variously–and the problems surrounding symbolic thought and the creation and utilisation of symbols fall within the scope of so many disciplines (psychology, linguistics, epistemology, history of religions, anthropology, etc.), that it is particularly hard in this case to mark off a specifically psycho-analytic use of these terms and to distinguish their various senses. The following remarks aim to do no more than help the reader get his bearings in the psycho-analytic literature.

I. There is general agreement that symbols fall within the category of *signs*. But several objections can be raised as soon as symbols are characterised as 'evoking, through a natural relationship, something absent or impossible to perceive' (1):

a. To speak of *mathematical symbols* or *linguistic symbols* (α) is to exclude any 'natural relationship' or any correspondence based on analogy. Moreover, what psychology calls *symbolic behaviour* is a type of behaviour revealing the subject's aptitude for discerning an order of reality within the perceived that cannot be accounted for in terms of 'things': in fact this aptitude is precisely what permits the subject's generalised handling of 'things'.

Linguistic usage thus attests a very wide variation in the employment of 'symbol'. The word does not necessarily imply the idea of an internal relation between the symbol and the thing symbolised (β)–witness the sense 'symbolic'* has for Claude Lévi-Strauss in anthroplogy and for Jacques Lacan in psycho-analysis.

b. To say that the symbol 'evokes something impossible to perceive' (e.g. the sceptre as symbolic of royalty) must not be taken as implying that the symbol forms a bridge between abstract and concrete. The thing symbolised can indeed be every whit as substantial or material as the symbol itself (e.g. the sun as symbolic of Louis XIV).

II. In differentiating a broad and a narrow sense of the term 'symbolism' we are merely adopting a distinction which Freud proposed and on which Jones based his theory of symbolism. Today this contrast would appear to have lost some of its clarity in common psycho-analytical usage.

It is the broad meaning that we have in mind when we say, for instance, that dreams or symptoms are the *symbolic* expression of the defensive conflict–in other words, they express it in a way that is indirect, figurative and more or less hard to decipher (children's dreams being considered less symbolic than those of adults in so far as the child's wish is expressed in a form that is veiled lightly or not at all, and is consequently easy to make out).

In a more general way, the term 'symbolic' is used to describe the relation which links the manifest content of behaviour, thought or speech to their latent meaning; it is applicable *a fortiori* where the manifest meaning is most lacking (as, for example, in the case of symptomatic acts that are obviously inexplicable in terms of any of the conscious motives which the subject might adduce). A number of authors–Rank and Sachs, Ferenczi, Jones–hold the view that we should only speak of symbolism in psycho-analysis in cases where what is symbolised is unconscious: 'Not all similes [...] are symbols, but only those in which the one member of the equation is repressed into the unconscious' (2).

It will be noticed that in this sense symbolism embraces all forms of indirect representation, implying no further discrimination between particular mechanisms: it covers displacement*, condensation*, over-determination* and considerations of representability*. In fact just as soon as we see that a piece of behaviour, say, has at least two meanings, one of which is standing for the other, both concealing and expressing it, then we may describe the relationship between them as a symbolic one (γ).

III. For Freud, however–more so no doubt than for present-day psycho-analytical writers–symbolism also has a narrower sense. This usage was introduced by him at a rather late date, a fact he confirms himself, acknowledging in particular the influence of Stekel (3).

Indeed, the most significant of Freud's late additions to the text of *The Interpretation of Dreams* (1900a) concern symbolism in dreams. In the chapter on the dream-work* the section devoted to representation by symbols was inserted only in 1914.

Careful inspection, however, suggests some qualification of Freud's testimony on this point: the fact is that the narrow sense of symbolism is not really foreign to early psycho-analysis.

Thus as early as the *Studies on Hysteria* (1895d) Freud had distinguished in several passages between an *associative* determination of symptoms and a *symbolic* one: the paralysis of Elisabeth von R., for example, is determined in the first place by its being bound–in accordance with associative pathways (4)–to various traumatic events; at the same time, it symbolises certain traits of the patient's moral situation (the mediation being provided by specific turns of phrase which can be taken either in a moral or in a literal sense–e.g. 'It won't work', 'I won't swallow that', etc.).

Symbolism

Note that, as from the first edition of *The Interpretation of Dreams*:

a. Although Freud criticises the ancient methods of dream-interpretation, which he describes as symbolic, he nonetheless takes pains to point out a kinship between them and his own technique.

b. He gives an important place to figurative representations that are comprehensible without the dreamer bringing out any associations; he stresses the mediating role played here by ordinary linguistic expressions (5*a*).

c. He maintains that the existence of 'typical dreams', where a particular wish or conflict is expressed in a similar fashion regardless of the individual dreamer, shows that there are elements of the language of dreams that are independent of the subject's personal discourse.

It is arguable, therefore, that Freud had recognised the existence of symbols from the first. Consider the following lines, for instance: '. . . dreams make use of any symbolisations which are already present in unconscious thinking, because they fit in better with the requirements of dream-construction on account of their representability and also because as a rule they escape censorship' (5*b*). This said, however, the fact remains that it was only gradually that Freud came to accord increased significance to symbols, a course urged upon him, in particular, by the bringing to light of a great variety of typical dreams (δ), as also by anthropological work revealing the presence of symbolism in areas beyond the realm of dreams (Rank). It should be pointed out in addition that precisely in so far as the Freudian theory resisted the 'scientific' approach and returned to 'popular' views which attribute meaning to dreams, it was obliged to mark itself off clearly from the dream-book type of reading, which presupposes a universal symbolic code and is liable to lead to virtually automatic interpretation.

Bringing all Freud's indications together (6, 5*c*, 7*a*), we can define symbols schematically—and in the strict sense of the word implied by Freud's use of '*die Symbolik*' (the symbolic)—by the following traits:

a. Symbols emerge in dream-interpretation as 'mute elements' (7*b*): the subject is unable to furnish associations in connection with them. For Freud this is a characteristic that cannot be accounted for by resistance* to the treatment; rather, it is typical of the symbolic mode of expression.

b. The essence of symbolism consists in a 'constant relation' between a manifest element and its equivalent or equivalents. This constancy is found not only in dreams but also in very diverse forms of expression (symptoms and other products of the unconscious: myths, folklore, religion, etc.) as well as in highly disparate cultural spheres. It is relatively impervious (just as a fixed vocabulary is) to individual initiative: an individual may choose among the senses of a symbol but he cannot create new ones.

c. The constant relation is based essentially on *analogy* (of form, size, function, rhythm, etc.). Freud points out, however, that certain symbols may have something in common with *allusion*: nudity, for instance, may be symbolised by clothes, the relation here being one of contiguity and contrast (7*c*). It may be noted further that many symbols crystallise a variety of relations holding between the symbol and the thing symbolised: Jones has demonstrated, for example, that Punch stands for the phallus seen under the most varied aspects (8*a*).

d. Whereas the symbols discovered by psycho-analysis are very numerous, the range of the things they symbolise is very narrow: the body, parents

444

and blood-relations, birth, death, nudity and above all sexuality (sexual organs, the sexual act).

With the extension of the theory of symbolism Freud is led to reserve a special place for it in his *theory* of dreams and of the products of the unconscious, and also in the *practice* of interpretation*. 'Even if the dream-censorship was out of action we should still not be in a position to understand dreams' (7*d*). The meaning of symbols eludes consciousness, yet their unconscious nature cannot be explained by the mechanisms of the dream-work. Freud indicates that the unconscious comparisons underlying symbolism 'are not freshly made on each occasion; they lie ready to hand and are complete, once and for all' (7*e*). One gets the impression, therefore, that regardless of diversity in culture or language individuals have access to a 'basic language' (to use the expression borrowed from Schreber) (7*f*). Thus Freud holds that there are two kinds of dream-interpretation: one is based on the dreamer's associations, while the other (independent) one is the interpretation of the symbols (5*d*).

f. The existence of a mode of expression having these characteristics raises genetic problems: how did humanity forge symbols in the first place? And how does the individual make them his own? Note that it was questions of this kind which led Jung to his theory of the 'collective unconscious' (8*b*). Freud never committed himself completely here, though he did put forward the hypothesis of a phylogenetic inheritance (9)–a hypothesis which benefits, in our opinion, by being viewed in the light of the notion of *primal phantasies* (q.v.).

(α) It is worth pointing out that Ferdinand de Saussure criticises the use of the expression 'linguistic symbol' (10).

(β) The etymological sense of 'symbol' is well known: for the Greeks the ὁύμβολον was a means of identification (between two members of the same sect, for example) consisting of the two halves of a broken object that can be fitted back together. The notion that it is the *link* that creates the meaning is thus already present in the original conception.

(γ) This is the frame of reference intended when the term 'mnemic symbol'* is used.

(δ) The section on 'typical dreams' underwent a series of expansions between 1900 and 1911; a large portion of the material contained in it was transferred in 1914 into the section which appeared at this date on 'representation by symbols' (11).

(1) LALANDE, A. *Vocabulaire technique et critique de la philosophie* (Paris: P.U.F., 1951).

(2) FERENCZI, S. 'The Ontogenesis of Symbols' (1913), in *First Contributions*, 277–78.

(3) Cf. FREUD, S. 'On the History of the Psycho-Analytic Movement' (1914*d*), G.W., X, 58; S.E., XIV, 19.

(4) Cf. FREUD, S., G.W., I, 216–17; S.E., II, 152.

(5) FREUD, S. *The Interpretation of Dreams* (1900*a*): a) Cf. G.W., II–III, 347; S.E., V, 341–42. b) G.W., II–III, 354; S.E., V, 349. c) Cf. 4th edn., revised and enlarged (1914), S.E., V, chap. 6, section E. d) Cf. G.W., II–III, 365; S.E., V, 359.

(6) Cf. FREUD, S. 'On Dreams' (1901*a*), 2nd edn.

(7) FREUD, S. *Introductory Lectures on Psycho-Analysis* (1916–17): a) Cf. *passim*. b) G.W., XI, 151; S.E., XV, 150. c) G.W., XI, 154–55; S.E., XV, 153. d) Cf. G.W., XI, 150 & 171; S.E., XV, 149 & 168. e) G.W., XI, 168; S.E., XV, 165. f) G.W., XI, 169; S.E., XV, 166.

(8) Cf. JONES, E. 'The Theory of Symbolism', in *Papers on Psycho-Analysis*, 5th edn. (London: Baillière, Tindall & Cox, 1950): a) 93 *ff*. b) 93–104.

(9) Cf. FREUD, S. *Moses and Monotheism* (1939*a*), G.W., XVI, 205–6; S.E., XXIII, 99–100.

(10) SAUSSURE, F. DE, *Cours de linguistique générale* (1916; Paris: Payot, 1955). Trans.: *Course in General Linguistics* (New York, 1959).

(11) Cf. S.E., IV, Preface.

Symptom-Formation

= *D*.: Symtombildung.–*Es*.: formación de síntoma.–*Fr*.: formation de symptôme.–
I.: formazione di sintoma.–*P*.: formação de sintoma.

Term used to denote the fact that the psychoneurotic symptom is the result of a specific process, of a psychical working out.

This term, which recurs all the way through Freud's work, underscores the fact that the formation of psychoneurotic symptoms should be looked upon as a specific moment in the genesis of neurosis. Freud appears to have had some initial hesitation before deeming it a moment essentially distinct from the moment of defence, but he eventually assimilates symptom-formation to the return of the repressed and makes the latter into a separate process, since the factors which lend the symptom its characteristic form are comparatively independent of those which operate in the defensive conflict: '. . . is the mechanism of forming symptoms the same as that of repression? The general probability would seem to be that the two are widely different, and that it is not the repression itself which produces substitutive formations and symptoms but that these latter are indications of a *return of the repressed* and owe their existence to quite other processes' (1) (see 'Return of the Repressed', 'Choice of Neurosis').

In a broad sense symptom-formation embraces not only the return of the repressed in the form of 'substitutive formations'* or 'compromise-formations'*, but also 'reaction-formations'* (2).

It may be noted, apropos of these different terms, that the German word '*Bildung*', like 'formation', means the process itself as well as the result of that process.

(1) FREUD, S. 'Repression' (1915*d*), G.W., X, 256–57; S.E., XIV, 154.
(2) Cf., for example, FREUD, S. 'On Psycho-Analysis' (1911), S.E., XII, 208.

T

Thanatos

= *D.*: Thanatos.–*Es.*: Tánatos.–*Fr.*: Thanatos.–*I.*: Thanatos.–*P.*: Tânatos.

Greek term (= Death) sometimes used by analogy with 'Eros' to designate the death instincts; its use underscores the fundamental nature of the instinctual dualism by lending it a quasi-mythical sense.

This name is not to be found in Freud's writings, but according to Jones he occasionally used it in conversation. Seemingly Federn introduced it into the psycho-analytical literature (1).

As we know, Freud employed the term 'Eros'* in the context of his theory of the life* and death* instincts. He appeals to metaphysics and Classical mythology in order to embody his psychological and biological speculations in a dualistic conception of broader scope. The chief references here are Chapter VI of *Beyond the Pleasure Principle* (1920g) (2) and the seventh section of 'Analysis Terminable and Interminable' (1937c), where Freud identifies his own theory with the antithesis set up by Empedocles between φιλία (love) and νεῖχος (discord): 'The two fundamental principles of Empedocles–φιλία and νεῖχος –are, both in name and function, the same as our own two primal instincts, *Eros* and *destructiveness*' (3).

The use of the term 'Thanatos' serves to emphasise the status of universal principles achieved by the two great classes of instincts in the final Freudian theory.

(1) Cf. JONES, E. *Sigmund Freud*, III, 295.
(2) Cf. FREUD, S., G.W., XIII, 23–34; S.E., XVIII, 22–33.
(3) Cf. FREUD, S., G.W., XVI, 93–96; S.E., XXIII, 247–50.

Thing-Presentation/Word-Presentation

= *D.*: Sachvorstellung (*or* Dingvorstellung)/Wortvorstellung.–
  Es.: representación de cosa/representación de palabra.–
  Fr.: représentation de chose/représentatión de mot.–
  I.: rappresentazione di cosa/rappresentazione di parola.–
  P.: representação de coisa/ representação de palavra.

Terms used by Freud in his metapsychological works in order to distinguish between two types of 'presentation'–between the (essentially visual) type which is derived from things and the (essentially auditory) one derived from words. This distinction has metapsychological implications for Freud because the preconscious-

447

conscious system is characterised by the fact that thing-presentations therein are bound to the corresponding word-presentations – a situation which does not exist, by contrast, in the unconscious system, where only thing-presentations are found.

As regards the term 'presentation' and the way it may be distinguished from the term 'memory-trace', although the two are occasionally used synonymously, the reader is referred to the articles 'Idea' and 'Memory-Trace'.

The distinction between thing- and word-presentations has its origin in Freud's early researches on aphasia.

The idea of thing-presentations makes its appearance very early, as does the very closely related notion of 'memory-traces' left in the different mnemic systems. In *On Aphasia* (1891*b*) we find the term '*Objektvorstellung*' and, in *The Interpretation of Dreams* (1900*a*), '*Dingvorstellung*' (1). One of the most exact definitions of the concept given by Freud runs as follows: the thing-presentation 'consists in the cathexis, if not of the direct memory-images of the thing, at least of remoter memory-traces derived from these' (2*a*). This definition calls for two remarks:

a. The presentation is here clearly distinguished from the memory-trace: the presentation recathects and revives the memory-trace which, in itself, is nothing more than the registration of the event.

b. The thing-presentation is not to be understood as a mental correlate of the thing in its entirety. The thing has a place in different systems or associative complexes, but only in one or another of its aspects.

Word-presentations are introduced as part of an approach which links verbalisation with the bringing of anything to consciousness. Thus, as early as the 'Project for a Scientific Psychology' (1950*a* [1895]), we encounter the idea that the memory-image, by becoming associated with a verbal image, can acquire that 'indication of quality' which is the specific mark of consciousness. Freud never abandoned this conception, which is fundamental to any understanding of the transition from the primary to the secondary process*, from perceptual identity* to thought-identity. It recurs in 'The Unconscious' (1915*e*), this time expressed in a way that accentuates its topographical* significance: 'The conscious presentation comprises the presentation of the thing plus the presentation of the word belonging to it, while the unconscious presentation is the presentation of the thing alone' (2*b*).

The special status of the word-presentation cannot be reduced to a dominance of the aural over the visual. More is involved here than a difference between sensory apparatuses. Freud showed that in schizophrenia word-presentations are themselves treated like thing-presentations, that is, according to the laws of the primary process. This also happens in dreams, when certain sentences uttered while the subject was in the waking state undergo condensation and displacement just as thing-presentations do: '... where the word-presentations occurring in the day's residues are recent and current residues of *perceptions*, and not the expression of thoughts, they are themselves treated like thing-presentations' (3). It is, therefore, clear that 'thing-presentation' and 'word-presentation' are not simply names for two varieties of memory-trace, and that the distinction between them has an essential topographical importance for Freud.

What is the structure of the relationship between word-presentations and those pre-verbal signifiers which thing-presentations constitute from the outset? How does each of them relate to perception? What are the conditions of their being produced in a hallucinatory form? And upon what, in the last analysis, is the special status of verbal linguistic symbols grounded? To such questions as these Freud attempted on several occasions to give an answer (4).

(1) Cf. FREUD, S., G.W., II–III, 302; S.E., IV, 296.

(2) FREUD, S. 'The Unconscious' (1915e): a) G.W., X, 300; S.E., XIV, 201. b) G.W., X, 300; S.E., XIV, 201.

(3) FREUD, S. 'A Metapsychological Supplement to the Theory of Dreams' (1917d [1915]), G.W., X, 418–19; S.E., XIV, 228.

(4) Cf. particularly: FREUD, S. 'Project for a Scientific Psychology' (1950a [1895]), Anf., 443; S.E., I, 364. The Interpretation of Dreams (1900a), chap. on 'Regression' (VII B). 'A Metapsychological Supplement to the Theory of Dreams' (1917d [1915]), passim. The Ego and the Id (1923b), G.W., XII, 247 et sqq.; S.E., XIX, 20 et sqq.

Topography; Topographical

= D.: Topik; topisch. – Es.: tópica; topográfico. – Fr.: topique. – I.: punta di vista topico; topico. – P.: tópica; tópico.

Theory or point of view which implies a differentiation of the psychical apparatus into a number of subsystems. Each of these has distinct characteristics or functions and a specific position vis-à-vis the others, so that they may be treated, metaphorically speaking, as points in a psychical space which is susceptible of figurative representation.

Two topographies are commonly identified in Freud's work: in the first, the major distinction is that between Unconscious, Preconscious and Conscious, while the second differentiates the three agencies of id, ego and super-ego.

The term 'topography', meaning theory of 'places' (Greek: τόποι), has had a role in philosophical language since Greek antiquity. For the Ancients, particularly for Aristotle, τόποι were rubrics with a logical or rhetorical value from which the premises of the argument derive. It is noteworthy that in German philosophy Kant had recourse to this term.

He describes his 'transcendental topic' as 'the decision as to the place which belongs to every concept', as a 'doctrine which distinguishes the cognitive faculty to which in each case the concepts properly belong' (1, α).

*   *   *

I. The Freudian hypothesis of a psychical topography has its roots in a whole scientific context embracing neurology, physiology, psychopathology. Only the most directly influential factors in this context can be indicated here:

a. The anatomico-physiological theory of cerebral localisations which predominated during the second half of the nineteenth century sought to anchor highly specialised functions or specific types of ideas or images to strictly localised neurological foundations. Such functions or ideas were thus seen as stored up, as it were, in a particular region of the cerebral cortex. In the short book which he devoted to the then topical question of aphasia (1891*b*), Freud subjected this type of theory to criticism, describing it as topographical: he showed up the limitations and contradictions of the complicated anatomical schemas being put forward at that time by such authors as Wernicke and Lichtheim, and upheld the necessity of supplementing consideration of the topographical data of localisation with an explanation of a functional type.

b. In the domain of pathological psychology, a whole series of observations imposed the conclusion that forms of behaviour, ideas and memories that are not always nor as a whole at the subject's disposition, but that are nevertheless capable of demonstrating their force, can be assigned in a quasi-realistic fashion to different psychical groups: hypnotic phenomena, cases of 'dual personality', etc. (see 'Splitting of the Ego').

This is the terrain on which the Freudian discovery of the unconscious originates, yet this discovery is not limited to the recognition of the *existence* of distinct psychical locations: it further assigns to each of them a separate character and operational mode. From the *Studies on Hysteria* (1895*d*) on, the conception of the unconscious implies a topographical differentiation of the psychical apparatus: the unconscious itself is organised in strata, and analytic investigation proceeds of necessity via specific paths which presuppose a specific order among the groups of ideas. The organisation of memories, which are arranged in veritable 'files' around a 'pathogenic nucleus', is not only chronological in nature: it also has a logical dimension, since the associations between the various ideas are made in diverse ways. Moreover, the bringing to consciousness and reintegration into the ego of unconscious memories is described in terms of a spatial model, with consciousness defined as a 'defile' which only allows one memory at a time to pass through into the 'breadth of the ego' (2).

c. It is well known that Freud always acknowledged his debt to Breuer for a hypothesis which is indispensable to a topographical theory of the psyche— namely, the hypothesis that in so far as the psychical apparatus comprises different systems this differentiation must have a functional significance. Consistent with this, in particular, is the idea that a single part of the apparatus cannot carry out both of two contradictory functions: receiving excitations and preserving traces of them (3).

d. Lastly, the study of dreams strengthened the hypothesis of a separation between psychical systems by irrefutably imposing the idea of an unconscious domain functioning according to its own laws. On this point Freud drew attention to the value of Fechner's intuitive recognition that the scene of the action in dreams was not an extension, in attenuated form, of waking ideational activity, but rather a genuinely 'other scene' (*eine andere Schauplatz*) (4*a*).

II. The first topographical conceptualisation of the psychical apparatus is proposed in Chapter VII of *The Interpretation of Dreams* (1900*a*), but the notion's evolution can be traced in the 'Project for a Scientific Psychology' (1950*a* [1895]), where it is still embedded in the neurological framework of a neuronal apparatus, and thence through the letters to Fliess, particularly those of January 1 and December 6, 1896 (*β*). Thisfirst topography (further developed in the metapsychological papers of 1915) distinguishes between three systems—

unconscious*, preconscious* and conscious*–each of which has its own function, type of process*, cathectic energy and specific ideational contents. Between each of these systems Freud places censorships* which inhibit and control transposition from one to another. The term 'censorship', like other images of Freud's ('anterooms', 'frontiers' between systems), points up the spatial aspect of the theory of the psychical apparatus.

The topographical perspective goes beyond this basic differentiation. To begin with, in the schemas of Chapter VII of *The Interpretation of Dreams* and in the letter to Fliess of December 6, 1896, Freud posits the existence of a succession of mnemic systems constituted by groups of ideas obeying distinct laws of association. Further, the difference between systems correlates with a prescribed organisation according to which energy passing from one point to another must follow an order already laid down: the systems may be traversed either in a normal–or 'progressive'–direction, or else in a regressive one. What Freud means by the term 'topographical regression' is illustrated by the phenomenon of dreams, where thoughts can take on a visual character to the point of hallucination, a regression* thus occurring to the kinds of images closest to *perception*, which is located at the point of departure of the excitation.

How are we to understand the notion of psychical locations that Freud's theory implies? It would be a mistake, as Freud himself emphasised, to look upon it as merely another attempt at anatomical localisation of functions: 'I shall entirely disregard the fact that the mental apparatus with which we are here concerned is also known to us in the form of an anatomical preparation, and I shall carefully avoid the temptation to determine psychical locality in any anatomical fashion' (4b). It will be noted, all the same, that the anatomical reference is far from absent; in *The Interpretation of Dreams*, the whole of the psychical process is situated between a perceptual and a motor extremity of the apparatus: the schema of the reflex arc, to which Freud has recourse here, retains its literal meaning even though it functions at the same time as a 'model' (γ). Subsequently Freud was to return on more than one occasion to his search, if not for precise correspondences, then at least for analogies–or metaphors, perhaps–in the spatial structure of the nervous system. He continues, for example, to assert the existence of a relationship between the fact that the Perception-Consciousness system is the recipient of the external excitation and the actual peripheral position of the cerebral cortex.

Freud shows himself to be firmly committed, however, to his attempt–in his view an original one–'to make the complications of mental functioning intelligible by dissecting the function and assigning its different constituents to different component parts of the apparatus' (4c). As can be seen, the notion of 'psychical locality' implies the mutual exclusion of the different parts and a specialisation of each one of them. The idea also allows us to apply a fixed order of succession to a process evolving along a temporal scale (δ).

Lastly, light is thrown on what Freud understands by psychical locality by his comparison between the psychical apparatus and an optical apparatus such as a complex microscope: in this analogy, the psychical systems would correspond to the ideal points between lenses rather than to the tangible component parts of the optical instrument (4d).

III. The major thesis of a distinction between systems–and, basically, of the separation of Unconscious from Preconscious-Conscious (ε)–cannot be isolated from the *dynamic* view, equally essential for psycho-analysis, according to which the systems are in conflict with one another (see 'Dynamic', 'Psychical Conflict'). The reconciliation of the two standpoints raises the problem of the origin of the topographical distinction. Schematically speaking, it is possible to indicate two very different sorts of solution to this problem in Freud. The first one, coloured by geneticism, which the advent of the second theory of the psychical apparatus serves to strengthen (see especially 'Id'), consists in assuming that the agencies of the mind emerge and are gradually differentiated from an unconscious system whose own roots are sunk deep in the biological realm ('everything which is conscious has first been unconscious'). The second solution attempts to account for the constitution of an unconscious in terms of the process of repression, and it leads Freud to posit the existence, at a first stage, of a *primal repression**.

IV. From 1920 onwards Freud worked out another conception of the personality–often given the concise title of 'the second topography'. According to the classical account, the principal reason for this was the ever-greater consideration demanded by the unconscious defences–a consideration which supposedly made it impossible to go on identifying the poles of the defensive conflict with the systems we have been describing above–i.e. the repressed with the Unconscious and the ego with the Preconscious-Conscious.

In reality the motives for the revision in question cannot be reduced to this idea, which had in any case long been more or less explicitly present in Freud's work (see 'Ego'). One of the chief discoveries that made it necessary was that of the role played by the various identifications in the formation of the personality and of the permanent structures which they leave within it (ideals, critical agencies, self-images). In its schematic form, this second theory involves three 'agencies'*: the *id*, instinctual pole of the personality; the *ego*, which puts itself forward as representative of the whole person, and which, as such, is cathected by narcissistic libido; and the *super-ego* or agency of judgement and criticism, constituted by the internalisation of parental demands and prohibitions. This approach does not merely set up an interplay between the three agencies: for one thing, more specific formations are isolated within these (e.g. ideal ego*, ego-ideal*), so that 'intrasystemic' relations are brought into play as well as 'intersystemic' ones; further, special importance comes to be assigned to the 'relations of dependence' obtaining between the various systems, particularly in the case of the ego, where the satisfaction of instinctual demands is found to occur–even within the sphere of the ego's so-called adaptative activities.

What becomes of the idea of psychical locality in this new 'topography'? It is clear even from the choice of names for the agencies that the model here is no longer one borrowed from the physical sciences but is instead shot through with anthropomorphism: the intrasubjective field tends to be conceived of after the fashion of intersubjective relations, and the systems are pictured as relatively autonomous persons-within-the-person (the super-ego, for instance, is said to behave in a sadistic way towards the ego). To this extent then, the scientific theory of the psychical apparatus tends to resemble the way the subject comprehends and perhaps even constructs himself in his phantasy-life.

Freud did not give up any attempt to reconcile his two topographies. On a number of occasions he presents spatially pictured conceptions of the whole psychical apparatus, including both the ego/id/super-ego and the unconscious/ preconscious/conscious subdivisions (5, 6). The most precise version is to be found in Chapter IV of *An Outline of Psycho-Analysis* (1940*a* [1938]).

(α) It is tempting to place the Kantian use of the notion of topography midway between the logical or rhetorical sense it has for the Ancients and the conception of mental localities that was to be Freud's. For Kant, the good logical use of concepts depends on our ability to relate representations of things correctly to one or other of our faculties (sensuousness or understanding).

(β) In the second of these letters, at the very time when Freud is working out the theory of the psychical apparatus which will become that of *The Interpretation of Dreams*, the word 'topography' is still so overladen with anatomical resonances that he makes a point of insisting that the distinction between the psychical systems is 'not necessarily topographical'.

(γ) It should also be stressed that this so-called schema of a reflex arc restoring in motor form the same energy that has been taken in at the sensory extremity does not take into account facts already established by the neurophysiology of the time–facts with which Freud, as an accomplished neurologist, was perfectly well acquainted. This 'negligence' on Freud's part is perhaps due to the fact that he was attempting to have a single schema account for the circulation of both instinctual energy–described as 'internal excitation'–and 'external excitations'. From this viewpoint the model proposed should be looked upon as a model of desire* generalised by Freud, who claims that even the energy of external excitations circulates *within* the system, into an overall model of the psychophysiological system. Yet there is probably a deeper truth behind this pseudo-physiology, and the metaphors it furnishes, in so far as it brings us to picture desire as a 'foreign body' mounting an attack upon the subject from within.

(δ) This extended character of the psychical apparatus is such a basic fact for Freud that he goes so far as to reverse the Kantian perspective by seeing it as the origin of the *a priori* form of space: 'Space may be the projection of the extension of the psychical apparatus. No other derivation is probable. Instead of Kant's a priori determinants of our psychical apparatus. Psyche is extended; knows nothing about it' (7).

(ε) It will be recalled that Freud usually links consciousness to the preconscious under the heading of the Preconscious-Conscious system (see 'Consciousness').

(1) KANT *Critique of Pure Reason*, Kemp Smith translation (New York: St. Martins Press, 1965), 281.

(2) FREUD, S. *Studies on Hysteria* (1895*d*), G.W., I, 295–96; S.E., II, 291.

(3) BREUER, J. 'Theoretical' chapter of *ibid.*, 1st German edition, 164*n*.; S.E., II, 188–89*n*.

(4) FREUD, S. *The Interpretation of Dreams* (1900*a*): a) G.W., II–III, 51 and 541; S.E., IV, 48 and V, 536. b) G.W., II–III, 541; S.E., V, 536. c) G.W., II–III, 541; S.E., V, 536. d) Cf. G.W., II–III, 541; S.E., 536.

(5) Cf. FREUD, S. *The Ego and the Id* (1923*b*), G.W., XIII, 252; S.E., XIX, 24.

(6) Cf. FREUD, S. *New Introductory Lectures on Psycho-Analysis* (1933*a* [1932]), G.W., XV, 85; S.E., XXII, 78.

(7) FREUD, S. MS. note, G.W., XVII, 152; S.E., XXIII, 300.

Training Analysis

= *D.*: Lehranalyse, didaktische Analyse.–*Es.*: análisis didáctico.–*Fr.*: analyse didactique.– *I.*: analisi didattica.–*P.*: análise didática.

Course of psycho-analysis undergone by candidates to the profession of psycho-analyst; the training analysis is the cornerstone of the student's psycho-analytical training.

Training Analysis

The discovery of psycho-analysis is intimately bound up with the personal exploration that Freud undertook of himself (see 'Self-Analysis'). It seemed to Freud right from the start that to practise analysis successfully one must be armed with a knowledge of one's own unconscious. At the 1910 Nuremberg Congress he maintained that what he called a 'self-analysis' was an indispensable requirement if the physician was to 'recognise [the] counter-transference in himself and overcome it' (1). It is not possible, however, to be sure from the term Freud used on this occasion–'*Selbstanalyse*'–whether he meant a true self-analysis or an analysis conducted by another person. The context would seem to suggest the former meaning, but according to Otto Rank's report of the Congress (2) Freud was certainly also envisaging the institution of the training analysis. At all events, it would seem that at this date the nature of the training analysis as distinct from a self-analysis was not yet clear to Freud.

The formative value of a personal analysis is more clearly acknowledged in Freud's 'Recommendations to Physicians Practising Psycho-Analysis' (1912*e*). Such an analysis is here brought into relation with the theory that the analyst 'must turn his own unconscious like a receptive organ towards the transmitting unconscious of the patient' (3*a*). In order to do this, the analyst must be able to communicate more freely with his own unconscious (see 'Attention'), and this is precisely what the training analysis aims to facilitate. Freud praises the Zurich school for their stress on 'the demand that everyone who wishes to carry out analyses on other people shall first himself undergo an analysis by someone with expert knowledge' (3*b*).

It was in 1922, at the Congress of the International Psycho-Analytical Association, two years after the foundation of the Berlin Institute of Psycho-Analysis, that a training analysis was made obligatory for every would-be analyst.

Ferenczi apparently contributed the most to bringing out the value of the training analysis, which in his eyes constitutes the 'second fundamental rule of psycho-analysis' (4). For Ferenczi the training analysis is no less thoroughgoing, no less profound than therapeutic analysis: 'To stand firm against this general assault by the patient the analyst requires to have been fully and completely analysed himself. I mention this because it is often held to be sufficient if a candidate spends, say, a year gaining acquaintance with the principal mechanisms in his so-called training analysis. His further development is left to what he learns in the course of his own experience. I have often stated on previous occasions that in principle I can admit no difference between a therapeutic and a training analysis, and I now wish to supplement this by suggesting that, while every case undertaken for therapeutic reasons need not be carried to the depth we mean when we talk of a complete ending of the analysis, the analyst himself, on whom the fate of so many other people depends, must know and be in control of even the most recondite weaknesses of his own character; and this is impossible without a fully completed analysis' (5).

The requirements formulated by Ferenczi are very generally accepted today (α); they tend to make the personal analysis of the future psycho-analyst into a procedure in which the acquisition of knowledge through experience takes second place–in fact to speak of 'training' is to lay unjustified emphasis on this aspect.

A problem at once theoretical and practical is inherent to the notion itself and to the institutionalisation of the training analysis: how can an analysis be directed from the outset towards a specific goal, towards such a preconceived 'purposive idea' as the derivation, from an instituted procedure in which the training analyst's assessment plays an important part, of the capacity to exercise the profession? This question is the subject of ongoing debate within the psychoanalytical movement (β).

(α) Freud himself adopted a rather reserved position on the possibilities held out by the training analysis: In 'Analysis Terminable and Interminable' (1937c), he holds to the view that 'for practical reasons' such an analysis 'can only be short and incomplete. Its main object is to enable the teacher to make a judgement as to whether the candidate can be accepted for further training. It has accomplished its purpose if it gives the learner a firm conviction of the existence of the unconscious, if it enables him, when repressed material emerges, to perceive in himself things which would otherwise be incredible to him, and if it shows him a first sampling of the technique which has proved to be the only effective one in psycho-analytic work' (6).

(β) For the problems posed by analytic training and their history in the movement, see especially Balint, 'On the Psycho-Analytic Training System' (7).

(1) FREUD, S. 'The Future Prospects of Psycho-Analytic Therapy' (1910d), G.W., VIII, 108; S.E., XI, 144–45.

(2) Cited by KOVACS, B. 'Training and Control Analysis', I.J.P., 1936, XVII, 346–54.

(3) FREUD, S.: a) G.W., VIII, 381; S.E., XII, 115. b) G.W., VIII, 382; S.E., XII, 116.

(4) FERENCZI, S. 'Die Elastizität der psychoanalytischen Technik', Intern. Zeit. für Psychoanalyse, 1928, XIV. In Final Contributions, 88–89.

(5) FERENCZI, S. 'Das Problem der Beeindigung der Analyse' (1928). In Final Contributions, 83–84.

(6) FREUD, S., G.W., XVI, 94–95; S.E., XXIII, 248.

(7) BALINT, M., I.J.P., 1948, 29, 163–73.

Transference

= D.: Übertragung.–Es.: transferencia.–Fr.: transfert.–I.: traslazione or transfert.–P.: transferência.

For psycho-analysis, a process of actualisation of unconscious wishes. Transference uses specific objects and operates in the framework of a specific relationship established with these objects. Its context *par excellence* is the analytic situation.

In the transference, infantile prototypes re-emerge and are experienced with a strong sensation of immediacy.

As a rule what psycho-analysts mean by the unqualified use of the term 'transference' is *transference during treatment*.

Classically, the transference is acknowledged to be the terrain on which all the basic problems of a given analysis play themselves out: the establishment, modalities, interpretation and resolution of the transference are in fact what define the cure.

The use of the term 'transference' has on the whole been confined to psychoanalysis, and it should not be confused with the various psychological uses of 'transfer' (1).

*   *   *

Transference

The reason it is so difficult to propose a definition of transference is that for many authors the notion has taken on a very broad extension, even coming to connote all the phenomena which constitute the patient's relationship with the psycho-analyst. As a result the concept is burdened down more than any other with each analyst's particular views on the treatment – on its objective, dynamics, tactics, scope, etc. The question of the transference is thus beset by a whole series of difficulties which have been the subject of debate in classical psycho-analysis:

a. As regards the specificity of the transference to the analysis: does not the analytic situation, given the strictness and constancy of its conditions, merely offer an especially favourable ground for the emergence and the observation of phenomena that are actually present elsewhere?

b. As regards the relations between the transference and reality: when we have to decide whether a particular phenomenon occurring during the treatment is adapted to reality or not, whether it indicates transference or not, what help can we get from so controversial a notion as 'dereistic' or 'unrealistic', or from an idea as hard to tie down as the reality of the analytic situation?

c. As regards the *function* of the transference in treatment: what is the therapeutic value of remembering and lived-out repetition, respectively?

d. As regards the nature of *what is transferred*: are we concerned with behaviour patterns, with types of object-relation, with positive or negative feelings, with affects, with libidinal cathexis, with phantasies, with a whole imago or with a specific trait of an imago – or even with 'agencies'* in the sense this term has in the final theory of the psychical apparatus*?

*　　*　　*

The encounter with the signs of transference in psycho-analysis – an event whose strangeness Freud never tired of emphasising (2) – was what cleared the way for the recognition of the operation of this process in *other* situations, whether as the actual foundation of the type of relationship concerned (hypnosis, suggestion), or as a factor in the relationship with an importance to be evaluated in each case (primarily the relation between doctor and patient, but also those between teacher and pupil, confessor and penitent, etc.). Similarly, among the developments immediately preceding the invention of analysis, transference had displayed its far-reaching effects in the case of Anna O., whom Breuer treated by the 'cathartic method'*, long before the therapist could either identify the process or – most importantly – make use of it (α). Furthermore, there is a discrepancy in the development of the concept of transference in Freud's work between his stated views and his actual experience – an inconsistency whose unfortunate consequences he himself suffered, as he noted apropos of the case of 'Dora'. So anyone wishing to trace the evolution of this concept must be ready to extrapolate – to recognise the action of the transference in those case-histories left to us by Freud by reading between the lines.

*　　*　　*

When Freud speaks of 'transference' or 'transference thoughts' in connection with dreams, he is referring to a mode of *displacement** in which the unconscious wish is expressed in masked form through the material furnished by the pre-

456

conscious residues* of the day before (3a). All the same, it would be mistaken to treat the process described here as distinct from the mechanism Freud postulated to account for his experiences in treatment: '... an unconscious idea is as such quite incapable of entering the preconscious and [...] it can only exercise any effect there by establishing a connection with an idea which already belongs to the preconscious, by transferring its intensity on to it and by getting itself "covered" by it. Here we have the fact of "transference", which provides an explanation of so many striking phenomena of the mental life of neurotics' (3b). In the *Studies on Hysteria* (1895d), Freud had described in similar terms cases where the patient transfers unconscious ideas on to the person of his physician: 'The content of the wish had appeared first of all in the patient's consciousness without any memories of the surrounding circumstances which would have assigned it to a past time. The wish which was present was then, owing to the compulsion to associate which was dominant in her consciousness, linked to my person, with which the patient was legitimately concerned; and as the result of this *mésalliance*–which I describe as a "false connection"–the same affect was provoked which had forced the patient long before to repudiate this forbidden wish' (4a).

To begin with, Freud looks upon transference theoretically at any rate as just a particular instance of displacement of affect from one idea to another. If the idea of the analyst enjoys a special status this is, first, because it constitutes a type of 'day's residue' that is always available to the subject; and secondly, because this kind of transference aids resistance* in that it is particularly hard to admit the repressed wish when this acknowledgement has to be made to the very person the wish concerns (4b, 5a). It is clear too that at this period Freud considers transference to be a highly localised phenomenon. Each transference is to be treated like any other symptom (4c), the aim being to keep up or restore a therapeutic relationship based on a trusting cooperation. Among other factors contributing to such a relationship, Freud names the personal influence of the doctor (4d) without in any way relating this to transference.

It would therefore seem that transference as initially described by Freud is not an essential part of the therapeutic relationship. This view is confirmed even by Freud's account of the case of 'Dora', notwithstanding the clearly major part played in it by the transference: in the critical commentary added to the *résumé* of his clinical notes, Freud goes so far as to blame the premature curtailment of Dora's treatment on a faulty interpretation of the transference. Numerous turns of phrase reveal that Freud does not look upon the treatment as a whole, in its structure and dynamics, as a transference relationship: 'What are transferences? They are new editions or facsimiles of the impulses and phantasies which are aroused and made conscious during the progress of the analysis; but they have this peculiarity, which is characteristic for their species, that they replace some earlier person by the person of the physician' (6). Freud remarks that these transferences (note the plural) do not differ in nature whether they are directed towards the analyst or towards some other person, and further that they do not constitute aids to cure except in so far as they are explicated and 'destroyed' one by one.

The gradual incorporation of the discovery of the Oedipus complex* was bound to affect the way Freud viewed the transference. As early as 1909 Ferenczi

Transference

had shown how in analysis–as also in the earlier techniques of suggestion and hypnosis–the patient unconsciously made the doctor play the role of loved or feared parental figures (7). In his first general exposition of transference (1912*b*), Freud stresses that it is connected with 'prototypes' or imagos* (chiefly the imago of the father, but also of the mother, brother, etc.): the doctor is inserted 'into one of the psychical "series" which the patient has already formed' (5*b*).

Freud reveals how it is the subject's relationship to parental figures that is once again lived out in the transference–a relationship still characterised, notably, by instinctual ambivalence*; '. . . it was only along the painful road of transference that [the Rat Man] was able to reach a conviction that his relation to his father really necessitated the postulation of this unconscious complement' (8). In this context Freud distinguishes between two kinds of transference–one positive, the other negative: a transference of affectionate feelings and a transference of hostile ones (β). The kinship between these terms and the 'positive' and 'negative' components of the Oedipus complex should be noted.

This extension of the notion of transference so that it becomes a process structuring the whole treatment around prototypical infantile conflicts culminates with Freud's introduction of a new concept–that of transference neurosis*: '. . . we regularly succeed in giving all the symptoms of the illness a new transference meaning and in replacing the patient's ordinary neurosis by a "transference-neurosis" of which he can be cured by the therapeutic work' (9).

*   *   *

As for its *function in the treatment*, Freud at first classes transference, in the most explicit fashion, among the 'obstacles' which impede the remembering of the repressed material (4*e*). But–also from the outset–he indicates that its occurrence is frequent if not general: 'We can [...] reckon on meeting it in every comparatively serious analysis' (4*f*). Similarly, Freud establishes at this point in his thinking that the mechanism of transference on to the person of the physician is triggered off precisely at the moment when particularly important repressed contents are in danger of being revealed. Seen in this light, transference appears as a form of resistance, while at the same time testifying to the proximity of the unconscious conflict. Thus, right from the start, Freud ran up against the essential contradiction of transference–the reason for the great divergence in his formulations regarding its function: transference in one sense–seen in relation to verbalised recollection–is 'transference-resistance' (*Übertragungswiderstand*). Yet in another sense, inasmuch as it offers a superlative way for the subject as for the analyst to grasp the elements of the infantile conflict *in vitro* and *in statu nascendi*, the transference becomes the terrain upon which the patient's unique set of problems is played out with an ineluctable immediacy, the area where the subject finds himself face to face with the existence, the permanence and the force of his unconscious wishes and phantasies: 'It is on that field that the victory must be won [...]. It cannot be disputed that controlling the phenomena of transference presents the psycho-analyst with the greatest difficulties. But it should not be forgotten that it is precisely they that do us the inestimable service of making the patient's hidden and forgotten erotic impulses immediate and manifest. For when all is said and done, it is impossible to destroy anyone *in absentia* or *in effigie*' (5*c*).

458

Irresistibly, this second aspect of transference takes on more and more importance for Freud: 'This *transference* alike in its positive and negative form is used
as a weapon by the resistance; but in the hands of the physician it becomes the
most powerful therapeutic instrument and it plays a part scarcely to be over-
estimated in the dynamics of the process of cure' (10).

But on the other hand it must be borne in mind that even where Freud goes
farthest in acknowledging the special status of transference repetition–even
when he writes: 'The patient cannot remember the whole of what is repressed
in him, and what he cannot remember may be precisely the essential part of it.
[...] He is obliged to *repeat* the repressed material as a contemporary experience'
(11*a*)–he nevertheless immediately stresses the need for the analyst 'to keep this
transference neurosis within the narrowest limits: to force as much as possible
into the channel of memory and to allow as little as possible to emerge as
repetition' (11*b*).

Thus Freud never abandons the view that the ideal of the treatment is complete *recollection*, and in cases where this turns out to be unattainable he falls
back on 'constructions'* to fill in the gaps in the infantile history. Furthermore,
he never esteems the transference relationship for its own sake, either from the
point of view of the abreaction* of childhood experiences or from that of the
rectification of unrealistic modes of object-relationship.

*   *   *

In the *Studies on Hysteria*, Freud writes apropos of the manifestations of transference that 'this new symptom that has been produced on the old model must
be treated in the same way as the old symptoms' (4*g*). Again, when he later
describes transference neurosis as an 'artificial illness', he is surely making the
assumption that transference reactions are both economically and structurally
equivalent to ordinary symptoms.

And indeed Freud does sometimes explain the emergence of the transference
in terms of 'a compromise between [the] demands [of the resistance] and those
of the work of investigation' (5*d*). But he is aware from the beginning that the
signs of the transference become more and more insistent the closer one gets to
the 'pathogenic complex', and when he relates these manifestations to a repetition compulsion* he states that such a compulsion can only express itself in the
transference 'after the work of treatment has gone halfway to meet it and has
loosened the repression' (11*c*). All the way from the case-history of 'Dora', where
Freud likens transferences to actual 'new impressions', often quite undistorted
by comparison with the corresponding unconscious phantasies, to *Beyond the
Pleasure Principle* (1920*g*), where he says of reproductions in the transference
that they 'emerge with unwished-for exactitude, always have as their subject
some portion of infantile sexual life–of the Oedipus complex, that is, and its
derivatives' (11*d*)–all the way, the idea that transference actualises the essence
of the childhood conflict is constantly gaining ground.

As we know, transference repetition is one of the facts invoked by Freud in
Beyond the Pleasure Principle to justify bringing the repetition compulsion to the
fore: situations and emotions are repeated in the treatment which ultimately
express the indestructibility of unconscious phantasies.

It may therefore be asked what sense we ought to give to what Freud calls *transference-resistance*. In *Inhibitions, Symptoms and Anxiety* (1926*d*), he ascribes it to the ego-resistances in that it reactivates the mechanism of a past repression, which mere recollection does not do. It is worth pointing out, however, that in this same work the repetition compulsion is described as basically id-resistance (see 'Repetition Compulsion').

Finally, when Freud speaks of the transference repetition of past experiences, of attitudes towards parents, etc., this repetition should not be understood in the literal sense that restricts such actualisation to really lived relationships. For one thing, what is transferred, essentially, is psychical reality*–that is to say, at the deepest level, unconscious wishes and the phantasies associated with them. And further, manifestations of transference are not verbatim repetitions but rather symbolic equivalents of what is being transferred.

*   *   *

One of the classical criticisms directed at self-analysis* as regards its therapeutic efficacity is that by definition it prevents any interpersonal relationship from coming into being or playing a part.

Freud himself pointed out the limited character of self-analysis; he stressed further that an interpretation* is often only accepted in so far as the transference, operating like suggestion, has conferred a special authority upon the analyst. All the same, it is true to say that the task of thoroughly clarifying the role played in the treatment by the analyst *qua* other has fallen to Freud's successors. In so doing they have followed several paths:

a. As an expansion of the second Freudian theory of the psychical apparatus, the analytic treatment may be deemed to provide the ground on which intra-subjective conflicts–themselves the relics of the real or phantasied intersubjective relationships of childhood–can once more find expression in a relationship where communication is possible. As Freud noted, the analyst may for example find himself placed in the position of the super-ego; more generally, the whole interplay of identifications* is given free rein to develop and to become 'unbound'.

b. Following the line of thought that has brought the idea of object-relation-ships* to the fore, there has been an attempt to treat the transference *relationship* (γ) as an expression of the particular modalities of the subject's relations with his different types of (partial or whole) object. As Michael Balint has remarked, such an approach ends by 'interpreting every detail of the patient's transference *in terms of object-relations*' (12). This orientation may even encourage an attempt to recognise the successive genetic stages in the development of the treatment.

c. Another orientation lays the emphasis upon the special importance of the spoken word in the analysis–and hence in the transference relationship. This approach can trace its ancestry to the very origins of psycho-analysis, for the cathartic method* holds the verbalisation of repressed (talking cure) to be at least as important as the abreaction of affects. But it is a surprising fact that when Freud describes the most incontestable signs of transference he places them under the heading of 'acting out'* (*Agieren*), contrasting recollection with repetition on the grounds that the latter alone is lived-out experience. It may legitimately be asked whether such a contrast really helps us get a clearer picture of the transference in its two dimensions—actualisation of the past and displacement on to the person of the analyst.

Indeed it is hard to see why the analyst should be any less implicated when the subject is *recounting* some event of his past to him, or *telling* him some dream (δ), than he is when the patient involves him in his *actions*.

The patient's words express a relational mode just as his acts do: their aim, for example, may be to please the analyst, to keep him at arm's length, etc.; and, just like words, acts carry messages (e.g. parapraxes*).

d. Lastly, reacting against an extreme thesis which looks upon transference as a purely spontaneous phenomenon—a projection on to the screen constituted by the analyst—some authors have sought to pursue to its logical conclusion the theory which has transference depend essentially upon a factor specific to the subject, namely the *predisposition to transference*. These authors highlight whatever in the analytic situation tends to facilitate the emergence of such a predisposition.

Some, like Ida Macalpine (13), have accentuated the concrete elements of the analytic environment (constancy of conditions, frustration, the patient's infantile position). Others have looked to the relationship of *demand* that analysis institutes from the outset, and by virtue of which 'the whole past opens up, back to the farthest reaches of earliest infancy. The subject has never done anything but make demands, only by doing so has been able to live, and we carry on this pattern. [...] Regression indicates nothing more than the re-emergence, in the present, of signifiers used in demands that can be filled' (14).

Freud did not ignore the existence of a correlation between the analytic situation as such and the transference. He even pointed out that, although various types of transference can be identified (maternal, fraternal, etc.), 'the real relations of the subject to his doctor' mean that 'the "father-imago" [...] is the decisive factor' (5e).

(α) For the consequences of this episode, see Ernest Jones's *Sigmund Freud*, I.

(β) It will be noted that 'positive' and 'negative' here refer to the nature of the affects transferred, not to the favourable or unfavourable long-term effects of the transference on the treatment. According to Daniel Lagache, 'it would be more comprehensive and more precise to speak of the positive or negative effects of the transference. We know that the transference of positive feelings may have negative effects; on the other hand, the expression of negative feelings may constitute a decisive advance' (15).

(γ) The use of this term by Freud is worth noting (16).

(δ) Cf. what are called 'dreams of compliance'—meaning dreams whose analysis reveals that the wish they fulfil is that of satisfying the analyst, confirming his interpretations, etc.

(1) Cf. ENGLISH, H. B. and ENGLISH, A. C. *A Comprehensive Dictionary of Psychological and Psychoanalytical Terms* (1958), articles on 'Transfer' and 'Transference'.

(2) Cf. FREUD, S. *An Outline of Psycho-Analysis* (1940a [1938]), G.W., XVII, 100; S.E., XXIII, 174-75.

(3) FREUD, S. *The Interpretation of Dreams* (1900a): a) Cf. G.W., II–III, 568; S.E., V, 562. b) G.W., II–III, 568; S.E., V, 562.

(4) FREUD, S. 'The Psychotherapy of Hysteria', in *Studies on Hysteria* (1895d): a) G.W., I, 309; S.E., II, 303. b) Cf. G.W., I, 308–9; S.E., II, 303. c) Cf. G.W., I, 308–9; S.E., II, 303.

Transference Neurosis

d) Cf. G.W., I, 285–86; S.E., II, 282–83. e) Cf. G.W., I, 308–9; S.E., II, 303. f) G.W., I, 307; S.E., II, 301. g) G.W., I, 309; S.E., II, 303.

(5) FREUD, S. 'The Dynamics of Transference' (1912*b*): a) Cf. G.W., VIII, 370; S.E., XII, 104. b) G.W., VIII, 365; S.E., XII, 100. c) G.W., VIII, 374; S.E., XII, 108. d) G.W., VIII, 369; S.E., XII, 103. e) G.W., VIII, 365–66; S.E., XII, 100.

(6) FREUD, S. 'Fragment of an Analysis of a Case of Hysteria' (1905*e* [1901]), G.W., V, 279; S.E., VII, 116.

(7) Cf. FERENCZI, S. 'Introjection and Transference' (1909), in *First Contributions*, 35–93.

(8) FREUD, S. 'Notes upon a Case of Obsessional Neurosis' (1909*d*), G.W., VII, 429; S.E., X, 209.

(9) FREUD, S. 'Remembering, Repeating and Working-Through' (1914*g*), G.W., X, 134–35; S.E., XII, 154.

(10) FREUD, S. 'Two Encyclopaedia Articles' (1923*a*), G.W., XIII, 223; S.E., XVIII, 247.

(11) FREUD, S. *Beyond the Pleasure Principle* (1920*g*): a) G.W., XII, 16; S.E., XVIII, 18. b) G.W., XIII, 17; S.E., XVIII, 19. c) G.W., XIII, 18; S.E., XVIII, 20. d) G.W., XIII, 16–17 S.E., XVIII, 18.

(12) BALINT, M. *Primary Love and Psycho-Analytic Technique* (London: Hogarth Press, 1952), 225; 2nd edition (London: Tavistock, 1965), 212.

(13) Cf. MACALPINE, I. 'The Development of the Transference', *P.Q.*, 1950, XIX, 4.

(14) LACAN, J. 'La direction de la cure et les principes de son pouvoir', *La Psychanalyse*, 1961, VI, 180. Reprinted in *Écrits* (Paris: Seuil, 1967), 617–18.

(15) LAGACHE, D. 'Le problème du transfert', *R.F.P.*, 1952, XVI, 102.

(16) Cf., for example, FREUD, S. 'Constructions in Analysis' (1937*d*), G.W., XVI, 44; S.E., XXIII, 258.

Transference Neurosis

= *D*.: Übertragungsneurose. – *Es*.: neurosis de transferencia. – *Fr*.: névrose de transfert. – *I*.: nevrosi di transfert. – *P*.: neurose de transferência.

I. Nosographically, a category of neuroses – comprising anxiety hysteria*, conversion hysteria* and obsessional neurosis* – which Freud distinguishes from the narcissistic neuroses* within the group of psychoneuroses*. In contrast to the narcissistic neuroses, the transference neuroses are characterised by the libido's always being displaced on to real or imaginary objects instead of being withdrawn from these and directed on to the ego. They are consequently more amenable to psycho-analytic treatment, for they lend themselves to the constitution, during the treatment, of a transference neurosis in sense II.

II. In the theory of the psycho-analytic cure, this term refers to an artificial neurosis into which the manifestations of the transference tend to become organised. It is built around the relationship with the analyst and it is a new edition of the clinical neurosis; its elucidation leads to the uncovering of the infantile neurosis.

I. In sense I, the term 'transference neurosis' was introduced by Jung as the opposite of 'psychosis' (1). In psychosis, libido was said to be 'introverted' (Jung) or to cathect the ego (Abraham (2) and Freud (3)). This reduces the patient's capacity to transfer his libido on to objects, and he is consequently not

462

very amenable to a form of treatment founded on transference. The upshot was that those neuroses to which psycho-analytic treatment was first applied were defined as conditions in which this transference capacity exists, and they were called 'transference neuroses'.

Freud's system of classification–as set out, for example, in the *Introductory Lectures on Psycho-Analysis* (1916–17)–can be summarised as follows: transference and narcissistic neuroses stand in opposition to one another within the group of psychoneuroses. This group as a whole is in turn contrasted with the group of actual neuroses* (whose mechanism is deemed to be essentially somatic) in that psychoneurotic symptoms are the symbolic expression of a psychical conflict.

It may be remarked that, although the distinction between the two categories of the psychoneuroses still retains its validity, it is no longer accepted that this distinction can be drawn purely and simply on the grounds of the presence or absence of transference. On the contrary, the accepted view today is that the apparent absence of transference in psychoneurotic conditions is in most cases merely one trait (which may be very pronounced) of that mode of transference peculiar to psychotics.

II. Freud introduces the notion of transference neurosis in sense II in 'Remembering, Repeating and Working-Through' (1914g), where it is related to the idea that the patient *repeats* his infantile conflicts within the transference. 'Provided only that the patient shows compliance enough to respect the necessary conditions of the analysis, we regularly succeed in giving all the symptoms of the illness a new transference meaning and in replacing his ordinary neurosis by a "transference-neurosis" of which he can be cured by the therapeutic work' (4a).

The lesson of this passage would seem to be that the difference between transference reactions and transference neurosis proper is that in such a neurosis the whole of the patient's pathological behaviour comes to be re-orientated around his relationship to the analyst. The transference neurosis could be said to do two jobs: first, it coordinates formerly disparate transference reactions (Glover's 'floating transference'), and, secondly, it allows the whole of the symptoms and pathological behaviour of the patient to take on a new function by becoming related to the analytic situation.

Freud sees the establishment of a transference neurosis as a positive factor in the dynamics of the cure: 'The new condition has taken over all the features of the illness; but it represents an artificial illness which is at every point accessible to our intervention' (4b).

From this standpoint, the following pattern of development constitutes the ideal model of the course of the cure: the clinical neurosis is transformed into a transference neurosis, whose elucidation leads to the uncovering of the infantile neurosis (α).

It must nevertheless be noted that Freud later put forward a less one-sided view of the transference neurosis when, in stressing the sway of the compulsion to repeat, he draws attention to the risks run if its development is allowed to get out of hand: 'It has been the physician's endeavour to keep this transference neurosis within the narrowest limits: to force as much as possible into the channel of memory and to allow as little as possible to emerge as repetition. [...] The physician cannot as a rule spare his patient this phase of the treatment.

463

Transitional Object

He must get him to re-experience some portion of his forgotten life, but must see to it, on the other hand, that the patient retains some degree of aloofness, which will enable him, in spite of everything, to recognise that what appears to be reality is in fact only a reflection of a forgotten past' (5).

(α) S. Rado, in his communication to the Salzburg Congress of 1924 on the theory of the cure, 'The Economic Principle in Psycho-Analytic Technique' (6), described the 'therapeutic neurosis' in preanalytic techniques (hypnosis and catharsis), as distinct from the neurosis which arises in psycho-analytic treatment: only in psycho-analysis can the transference neurosis be analysed and resolved.

(1) Cf. JUNG, C. G. *Über die Psychologie der Dementia praecox* (Halle, 1907); 'Wandlungen und Symbole der Libido', *Jahrbuch Psa.-Forsch.*, 1911, 1912.

(2) Cf. ABRAHAM, K. 'The Psycho-Sexual Differences between Hysteria and Dementia Praecox', *Selected Papers* (London: Hogarth, 1927; New York: Basic Books, 1953).

(3) Cf. FREUD, S. 'On Narcissism: An Introduction' (1914c).

(4) FREUD, S.: a) G.W., X, 134–35; S.E., XII, 154. b) G.W., X, 135; S.E., XII, 154.

(5) FREUD, S. *Beyond the Pleasure Principle* (1920g), G.W., XIII, 17; S.E., XVIII, 18–19.

(6) Cf. RADO, S., in *I.J.P.*, 1925, VI, 35–44.

Transitional Object

= *D.*: Übergangsobjekt.–*Es.*: objeto transicional.–*Fr.*: objet transitionnel.–
I.: oggetto transizionale.–*P.*: objeto transicional.

Term introduced by D. W. Winnicott to designate a material object with a special value for the suckling and young child, particularly when it is on the point of falling asleep (e.g. the corner of a blanket or napkin that is sucked).

Reliance on such objects, according to Winnicott, is a normal phenomenon which allows the child to make the transition from the first oral relationship with the mother to the 'true object-relationship'.

The gist of Winnicott's ideas on the transitional object will be found in an article entitled 'Transitional Objects and Transitional Phenomena' (1953).

a. On the level of clinical description, Winnicott brings out a type of behaviour often observed in the infant which he calls the relationship with the transitional object.

Between the ages of four and twelve months, the infant is frequently seen to form an attachment to a specific object such as a bundle of wool or the corner of a blanket or eiderdown, etc., which it sucks and holds close to itself and which becomes especially vital to it at the time of going to sleep. This 'transitional object' retains its significance for a long time before gradually losing it; it may re-emerge later, notably with the approach of a period of depression.

Winnicott subsumes certain gestures and various oral activities (e.g. babbling) under one heading–the heading of *transitional phenomena*.

b. Genetically speaking, the transitional object lies 'between the thumb and the teddy bear' (1a). For while this object is 'an almost inseparable part of the infant' (1*b*), distinct in this sense from the future toy, it is also 'the first not-me possession'.

From the libidinal point of view, the activity we are concerned with here is still oral in character. What has changed is the status of the object. In the very earliest oral activity (relationship to the breast) we find what Winnicott calls a 'primary creativity': '. . . the breast is created by the infant over and over again out of the infant's capacity to love or (one can say) out of need. [...] The mother places the actual breast just where the infant is ready to create, and at the right moment' (1*c*). Later on, reality-testing* will come into opertaion. Between these two phases lies the relationship to the transitional object–a halfway house between subjective and objective in which the object 'comes from without from one point of view, but not so from the point of view of the baby. Neither does it come from within; it is not an hallucination' (1*d*).

c. The transitional object, although it constitutes an intermediate step towards the perception of an object clearly differentiated from the subject–towards a 'true object-relationship'–is not for all that destined to see its function abolished by the subject's later development: 'The transitional object and the transitional phenomena start each human being off with what will always be important for them, i.e. a neutral area of experience which will not be challenged' (1*e*). According to Winnicott, they belong to the sphere of *illusion*: 'This intermediate area of experience, unchallenged in respect of its belonging to inner or external (shared) reality, constitutes the greater part of the infant's experience and throughout life is retained in the intense experiencing that belongs to the arts and to religion and to imaginative living, and to creative scientific work' (1 *f*).

(1) WINNICOTT, D. W. 'Transitional Objects and Transitional Phenomena', *I.J.P.*, 1953, XXXIV, 2: a) 89. b) 92. c) 95. d) 91. e) 95. f) 97.

Trauma (Psychical)

= *D*.: Trauma.–*Es*.: trauma, traumatismo.–*Fr*.: trauma, traumatisme.–*I*.: trauma.– *P*.: trauma, traumatismo.

An event in the subject's life defined by its intensity, by the subject's incapacity to respond adequately to it, and by the upheaval and long-lasting effects that it brings about in the psychical organisation.

In economic terms, the trauma is characterised by an influx of excitations that is excessive by the standard of the subject's tolerance and capacity to master such excitations and work them out psychically.

'Trauma' is a term that has long been used in medicine and surgery. It comes from the Greek τραῦμα, meaning wound, which in turn derives from τιτρώσκω, to pierce. It generally means any injury where the skin is broken as a consequence of external violence, and the effects of such an injury upon the organism as a whole; the implication of the skin being broken is not always present, however– we may speak, for example, of 'closed head and brain traumas'.

Trauma (Psychical)

In adopting the term, psycho-analysis carries the three ideas implicit in it over on to the psychical level: the idea of a violent shock, the idea of a wound and the idea of consequences affecting the whole organisation.

* * *

The notion of the trauma fits primarily–as Freud points out himself–into an economic* perspective: 'We apply it to an experience which within a short period of time presents the mind with an increase of stimulus too powerful to be dealt with or worked off in the normal way, and this must result in permanent disturbances of the manner in which the energy operates' (1a). The influx of excitations is excessive in relation to the tolerance of the psychical apparatus, whether it is a case of a single very violent event (strong emotion) or of an accumulation of excitations each of which would be tolerable by itself; at first, the operation of the principle of constancy* is held in check, since the apparatus is incapable of discharging the excitation.

Freud suggested a figurative conceptualisation of this state of affairs in *Beyond the Pleasure Principle* (1920g), envisaging it in terms of an elementary relationship between an organism and its surroundings: the 'living vesicle' is sheltered from external stimuli by a protective shield* or layer which allows only tolerable quantities of excitation through. Should this barrier suffer any breach, we have a trauma: the task of the apparatus at this juncture is to muster all its available forces so as to establish anticathexes, to immobilise the inflowing quantities of excitation and thus to permit the restoration of the necessary conditions for the functioning of the pleasure principle*.

* * *

A classic description of the beginnings of psycho-analysis (from 1890 to 1897) runs as follows: *theoretically*, the aetiology of neurosis is related to past traumatic experiences whose occurrence is assigned to a constantly receding date according as the analytic investigation penetrates more deeply, proceeding step by step from adulthood back to infancy; *technically*, effective cure is sought by means of an abreaction* and a psychical working out* of the traumatic experiences. This traditional account adds that such an approach has gradually receded into the background.

In this period, the founding period of psycho-analysis, the term 'trauma' is applied in the first place to an event in the subject's personal history that can be dated and that has subjective importance owing to the unpleasurable affects it can trigger off. No complete view of traumatic events is possible without taking into account the subject's particular 'predisposition' (*Empfänglichkeit*). For there to be a trauma in the strict sense of the word–that is, non-abreaction of the experience, which remains in the psyche as a 'foreign body'–certain objective conditions have to be met. Granted, the 'very nature' of the event may preclude the possibility of a complete abreaction (e.g. 'the apparently irreparable loss of a loved person'), but aside from this extreme instance the event in question derives its traumatic force from specific circumstances: the particular psychological state of the subject at the time of the occurrence (Breuer's 'hypnoid state'*); the concrete situation–social circumstances, demands of the task in hand, etc.–which prohibits or hinders an adequate

466

reaction ('retention'*); lastly–and most importantly in Freud's view–psychical conflict preventing the subject from integrating the experience into his conscious personality (defence*). Breuer and Freud note further that a series of events, none of which on its own would have a traumatic effect, may, in concert, produce just such a consequence ('summation') (2*a*).

It will be observed that the factor common to the various conditions enumerated in the *Studies on Hysteria* (1895*d*) is the economic one; the outcome of the trauma is always the incapacity of the psychical apparatus to eliminate the excitations in accordance with the principle of constancy. It is also easy to see that a gamut of traumatic events might be described, ranging from the type which derives its pathogenic force from its violence and unexpectedness (e.g. accidents), to the type which owes its importance merely to its intervention in a psychical organisation already characterised by its own specific points of rupture.

*   *   *

Freud's highlighting of the defensive conflict in the genesis of hysteria and, more generally, in that of the 'neuro-psychoses of defence', does not imply that the function of the trauma is weakened, but it does complicate the theory of the trauma. We may note first of all that the thesis of the trauma's essentially sexual nature matures in the years 1895–97, and that the same period sees the discovery of the original trauma in prepubertal life.

There can be no question of our giving any systematic presentation here of Freud's approach of that time to the relations between the notion of trauma and that of defence, since his views on the aetiology of the psychoneuroses were in constant evolution. All the same, several texts of the period (3) expose or presuppose a well-defined thesis tending to explain how the traumatic event triggers the setting up by the ego of a 'pathological defence' (of which repression constituted the model for Freud at this point) operating in accordance with the primary process, instead of the normal defences generally used against an unpleasurable event (e.g. diversion of attention).

The trauma's action is broken down into several elements, while it now presupposes at least two events. In a first scene–the so-called scene of seduction–the child is the object of sexual advances from the adult which fail to arouse any sexual excitement in him. A second scene, occurring after puberty, often of a seemingly innocent nature, evokes the first one through some association. It is the memory of the first scene that occasions an influx of sexual stimuli which overwhelm the ego's defences. Although Freud calls the first scene traumatic, it is plain that, from the strict economic point of view, this quality is only ascribed to it after the fact (*nachträglich**); or to put it another way: it is only *as a memory* that the first scene becomes pathogenic by deferred action, in so far as it sparks off an influx of internal excitation. Such a theory brings out the full meaning of the celebrated formulation of the *Studies on Hysteria* according to which 'hysterics suffer mainly from reminiscences' ('*der Hysterische leide[t] grösstenteils an Reminiszenzen*') (2*b*).

At the same time we see a change of emphasis in the evaluation of the part played by the external event. The idea of the psychical trauma modelled on that of the physical one fades, for the second scene does not have its effect by virtue of its own energy but only in so far as it arouses an excitation of endogenous origin. In this sense the Freudian view that we are describing here already clears the way for the idea that external events derive their effectiveness from the phantasies they activate and from the influx of instinctual excitation they provoke. It is also clear, however, that Freud is not satisfied at this period with a description of the trauma as the arousal of an internal excitation by an external event that is thus nothing more than a trigger mechanism: he feels the need to relate this event in its turn to a previous one, which he places at the source of the whole process (see 'Scene of Seduction').

*　　*　　*

In later years the aetiological significance of traumas tends to give way in Freud's work to that of phantasy-life and fixations at the various libidinal stages. The 'traumatic line of approach', though it is not 'abandoned' (as Freud suggests (1*b*)), is integrated with a conception bringing in other factors such as constitution and childhood history. In conjunction with disposition, the trauma which precipitates neurosis in the adult constitutes a complemental series*, while disposition itself comprises two complemental factors–endogenous and exogenous:

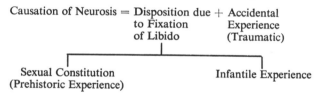

It will be noted that in this schema–given by Freud in his *Introductory Lectures on Psycho-Analysis* (1916–17) (1*c*)–the term 'trauma' denotes an event occurring during a second period, not the childhood experience that is found at the origin of a fixation. The trauma's import is reduced and at the same time its singularity diminishes–in fact it tends to become synonymous, in the context of the causation of neurosis, with what Freud elsewhere calls *Versagung*, frustration*.

But while the *traumatic theory of neurosis* is thus scaled down, the existence of accident neuroses, especially war neuroses, brings the problem of traumas–in the clinical form of the *traumatic neuroses**–back to the forefront of Freud's concerns.

From a theoretical point of view, *Beyond the Pleasure Principle* (1920*g*) attests to this interest of Freud's. He readopts the economic definition of the trauma as a breach, and this even leads him to frame the hypothesis that an excessive influx of excitation immediately halts the operation of the pleasure principle, obliging the psychical apparatus to carry out a more urgent task 'beyond the pleasure principle' which consists in binding the excitations in such a way as to allow for their subsequent discharge. The repetition of dreams in which the subject relives the accident intensely, placing himself once more in the traumatic situation as if attempting to dominate it, is attributed to a repetition compulsion*. More generally, the whole group of clinical phenomena in which Freud sees this compulsion at work displays the fact that the pleasure principle, if it is to function, requires that certain conditions be met; these conditions are destroyed by the occurrence of the trauma inasmuch as this is not just a disturbance of the libidinal economy but constitutes a more radical threat to the integrity of the subject (see 'Binding').

$$* \quad * \quad *$$

Finally, in the revised theory of anxiety as expounded in *Inhibitions, Symptoms and Anxiety* (1926*d*), and in a more general way in the second topography, the notion of the trauma assumes renewed significance aside from any reference to traumatic neurosis proper. The ego, by releasing the signal of anxiety*, seeks to avoid being overwhelmed by the surge of automatic anxiety* which defines that traumatic situation where the ego is defenceless (see 'Helplessness'). This account in effect postulates a kind of diametrical opposition between the external danger and the internal one: the ego is attacked from within–that is to say, by instinctual excitations–*just as* it is from without. The simplified model of the vesicle as Freud had presented it in *Beyond the Pleasure Principle* (see above) no longer holds good.

It may be noted, lastly, that when Freud looks for the kernel of the danger, he finds it in an intolerable increase in tension resulting from an influx of internal excitations that have to be eliminated. According to Freud, it is this which accounts, in the last analysis, for the 'birth trauma'.

(1) FREUD, S. *Introductory Lectures on Psycho-Analysis* (1916–17): a) G.W., XI, 284; S.E., XVI, 275. b) Cf. G.W., XI, 285; S.E., XVI, 276. c) Cf. G.W., XI, 376; S.E., XVI, 362.

(2) Cf. BREUER, J. and FREUD, S. 'On the Psychical Mechanism of Hysterical Phenomena: Preliminary Communication' (1893*a*): a) G.W., I, 86–90; S.E., II, 8–11. b) G.W., I, 86; S.E., II, 7.

(3) Cf. especially FREUD, S., *Anf.*, 156–66 and 432–36; S.E., I, 220–29 and 352–57.

Traumatic Hysteria

= *D.*: traumatische Hysterie.–*Es.*: histeria traumática.–*Fr.*: hystérie traumatique.– *I.*: isteria traumatica.–*P.*: histeria traumática.

Type of hysteria described by Charcot. It is characterised by somatic symptoms, particularly paralyses, which appear following a physical trauma–though often after a phase of latency; the trauma, however, does not provide a satisfactory mechanical explanation of the symptoms in question.

In his work on hysteria between 1880 and 1890, Charcot studied certain hysterical paralyses which follow physical traumas of sufficient seriousness for the subject to feel his life to be in danger, though they do not cause loss of consciousness. From a neurological point of view, such traumas can not account for the paralysis; and Charcot observed that this established itself only after a period of 'incubation' or psychical 'working over'*.

Charcot had the idea of reproducing paralyses of the same type experimentally, under hypnosis, by using a minimal trauma or simply suggestion. In this way he proved that the symptoms in question are brought about not by the physical shock but by the ideas which are associated with it and which only make their appearance during a specific psychical state.

Freud acknowledged the continuity between this kind of explanation and the first accounts that he and Breuer gave of hysteria: ' *"There is a complete analogy between traumatic paralysis and common, non-traumatic hysteria."* The only difference is that in the former a major trauma has been operative, whereas in the latter there is seldom a *single* major event to be signalised, but rather a *series* of affective impressions [...]. Even in the case of the major mechanical trauma in traumatic hysteria what produces the result is not the mechanical factor but the affect of fright, the *psychical* trauma' (1).

It will be recalled that the schema of hypnoid hysteria* embraces the two aetiological factors which Charcot had already identified, namely, the psychical trauma* and the particular psychical state (hypnoid state*, affect of fright*) during which it occurs.

(1) FREUD, S. Lecture 'On the Psychical Mechanism of Hysterical Phenomena' (1893*h*), *Wien. med. Presse.* XXXIV, 4, 121–26; S.E., III, 30–31.

Traumatic Neurosis

= *D.*: traumatische Neurose.–*Es.*: neurosis traumática.–*Fr.*: névrose traumatique.– *I.*: nevrose traumatica.–*P.*: neurose traumática.

Type of neurosis in which the appearance of symptoms follows upon an emotional shock generally associated with a situation where the subject has felt his life to be in danger. Such a neurosis manifests itself, at the moment of the shock, in the form of a paroxystic anxiety attack which may provoke states of agitation, stupor or mental confusion. Its later development, usually occurring after a period of remission, seems to justify a schematic distinction between two subtypes:

a. Cases where the trauma acts as a precipitating factor, revealing a pre-existing neurotic structure.

b. Cases where the trauma is a decisive factor in the actual content of the symptom (rumination over the traumatic event, recurring nightmares, insomnia, etc.): the symptom appears as a repeated attempt to 'bind' and abreact the trauma; such 'fixations to the trauma' are accompanied by a more or less general inhibition of the subject's activity.

It is to this second clinical picture that Freud and the psycho-analysts are generally referring to when they speak of traumatic neurosis.

The term 'traumatic neurosis' predates psycho-analysis (α) and it is still used in psychiatry in a way that varies in consequence of the ambiguities of the notion of trauma, and of the diversity of theoretical options to which these have given rise.

The notion of trauma has a primary somatic application, when it refers to 'the lesions produced accidentally, in an immediate fashion, by mechanical agents whose injurious force is superior to the resistance of the tissues or organs that they encounter' (1). Traumas in this sense are subdivided into wounds and contusions (or closed traumas) according to whether or not the skin is broken.

In neuropsychiatry traumas are spoken of in two very different senses. In the first, the surgical notion of trauma is applied to the particular case of the central nervous system, with its possible consequences ranging from manifest lesions of the nervous tissue to hypothesised microscopic lesions (cf. the idea of 'commotional shock'). In its second sense, the notion is metaphorically transposed to the mental sphere, where it is applied to any event that makes a sudden incursion into the individual's psychical organisation. Most situations that give rise to traumatic neuroses (accidents, fights, explosions, etc.) present psychiatrists with a practical diagnostic problem: is there a neurological lesion or not? And, theoretically speaking, they leave a wide margin of freedom for the exponents of the various orientations to point to what each considers to be the ultimate source of the trouble. Some writers, going to the extreme, would place the clinical picture of the traumatic neuroses in the category of 'head and brain injuries' (2) (see 'Trauma').

* * *

Limiting ourselves to the area covered by the idea of the trauma in psychoanalysis, we may view the term 'traumatic neurosis' from two rather different angles.

I. With reference to what Freud calls a 'complemental series'* in the causation of neurosis, two factors have to be taken into consideration which vary in inverse ratio to each other: predisposition and trauma. We may thus expect to find a whole range of cases–extending from those where an event of minimal importance has causative force by virtue of the subject's low level of tolerance to any (or to some particular) excitation, to those cases where an event that is objectively of exceptional intensity suddenly shatters the subject's equilibrium.

A number of comments are called for in this connection:

a. The notion of the trauma has become quite relative here.

b. The trauma-predisposition problem tends to become identical with the problem of the respective roles of 'actual' factors and of a pre-existing conflict (see 'Actual Neurosis').

c. In cases where an important trauma is clearly evident at the point of emergence of the symptoms, the psycho-analyst sets out to find neurotic conflicts in the subject's history that the event might merely have served to activate. It should be noted that this approach is lent support by the fact that the disturbances precipitated by a trauma (war, accident, etc.) often resemble those met with in the classical transference neuroses*.

d. Of particular interest from this point of view are those cases where an external event comes as a realisation of a repressed wish of the subject's, so bringing to light an unconscious phantasy. In such cases the resulting neurosis has characteristics giving it a resemblance to a traumatic neurosis: rumination, recurrent dreams, etc. (3).

e. Following the same train of thought, some authors have sought to relate the actual occurrence of the traumatic event to a specific neurotic predisposition. Certain subjects appear to seek out the traumatic situation unconsciously–

although they dread it at the same time. According to Fenichel, these subjects want to repeat a childhood trauma as a means of abreacting it: 'The repetition is desired [by the ego] to relieve a painful tension; but [...] the repetition itself is also painful. [...] The patient has entered a vicious circle. The "belated mastery", which the repetitions strive for, is never obtained because every attempt to reach it brings about a new traumatic experience' (4a). Fenichel looks upon these subjects, whom he calls 'traumatophilic', as an exemplification of a typical case of the 'combination of traumatic neuroses and psychoneuroses' (4b). It may be further noted in this context that Karl Abraham, who introduced the term 'traumatophilia', related even the sexual traumas of childhood to a pre-existent traumatophilic disposition (5).

II. It may thus be seen how psycho-analytic investigation throws the concept of traumatic neurosis into question: it contests the decisive function of the traumatic event–first by stressing its relativity *vis-à-vis* the subject's tolerance, and secondly by inserting the traumatic experience into the context of the subject's particular history and organisation. Seen in this light, the notion of traumatic neurosis appears as nothing more than an initial, purely descriptive approximation which cannot survive any deeper analysis of the factors in question.

All the same, should we not set aside a special place, from the nosographical and aetiological points of view, for neuroses where a trauma, by virtue of its very nature and of its intensity, is by far the most important causative factor, and where the mechanisms at work and the symptomatology are relatively specific as compared with those of the psychoneuroses?

This would indeed appear to be Freud's position as developed chiefly in *Beyond the Pleasure Principle* (1920g): 'The symptomatic picture presented by traumatic neurosis approaches that of hysteria in the wealth of its similar motor symptoms, but surpasses it as a rule in its strongly marked signs of subjective ailment (in which it resembles hypochondria and melancholia) as well as in the evidence it gives of a far more comprehensive general enfeeblement and disturbance of the mental capacities' (6a). When Freud speaks of traumatic neurosis, he stresses the fact that the character of the trauma is at once somatic– the disruption (*Erschütterung*) of the organism causes an influx of excitation– and psychical (fright*: *Schreck*) (7). This fright–defined as 'the state a person gets into when he has run into a danger without being prepared for it' (6b)– is what Freud acknowledges to be the determining factor in traumatic neurosis.

Neither by an adequate discharge nor by psychical working out* is the subject able to respond to the influx of excitation which breaks through and threatens his cohesion. With his binding functions overwhelmed, he can only repeat the traumatic situation in compulsive fashion, particularly in the form of dreams (β), as a way of trying to bind it (see 'Repetition Compulsion', 'Binding').

Nevertheless, Freud did point out that common ground may exist between traumatic and transference neuroses–witness the following lines from the *Outline of Psycho-Analysis* (1940a [1938]): 'It is possible that what are known as traumatic neuroses (due to excessive fright or severe somatic shocks, such as railway collisions, burials under falls of earth, and so on) are an exception to this: their relations to determinants in childhood have hitherto eluded investigation' (9).

472

(α) It was apparently introduced by Oppenheim (cf. H. Ey, *Encyclopédie médico-chirurgicale: Psychiatrie*, 37520 C 10, 6).

(β) 'Now dreams occurring in traumatic neuroses have the characteristic of repeatedly bringing the patient back into the situation of his accident, a situation from which he wakes up in another fright' (6c).

(1) FORGUE, E. *Précis de pathologie externe*, 11th edn. (Paris: Masson, 1948), I, 220.

(2) Cf. on this point EY, H. *Encyclopédie médico-chirurgicale: Neurologie* (1955), article on 'Traumatismes cranio-cérébraux', 17585.

(3) Cf., for example, LAGACHE, D. 'Deuil pathologique', in *La Psychanalyse* (Paris: P.U.F., 1957), II, 45–74.

(4) FENICHEL, O. *The Psychoanalytic Theory of Neurosis* (New York: Norton, 1945): a) 543–44. b) Chapter XXI.

(5) Cf. ABRAHAM, K. 'The Experience of Sexual Traumas as a Form of Sexual Activity', in *Selected Papers* (London: Hogarth Press, 1927; New York: Basic Books, 1953).

(6) FREUD, S.: a) G.W., XIII, 9; S.E., XVIII, 12. b) G.W., XIII, 10; S.E., XVIII, 12. c) G.W., XIII, 10; S.E., XVIII, 13.

(7) Cf. FREUD, S. *Three Essays on the Theory of Sexuality* (1905d), G.W., V, 103; S.E., VII, 202.

(8) Cf. FREUD, S. Introduction to *Psycho-Analysis and War Neuroses* (1919d), G.W., XII, 321 *ff.*; S.E., XVII, 207 *ff.*

(9) FREUD, S., G.W., XVII, 111; S.E., XXIII, 184.

Turning Round upon the Subject's Own Self

= *D.*: Wendung gegen die eigene Person.–*Es.*: vuelta en contra del sujeto.–
Fr.: retournement sur la personne propre.–*I.*: riflessione sulla propria persona.–
P.: volta contra si mesmo.

Process whereby the instinct replaces an independent object* by the subject's own self.

See 'Reversal into the Opposite'.

U

Unconscious (sb. & adj.)

= *D*.: das Unbewusste; unbewusste. – *Es*.: inconsciente. – *Fr*.: inconscient. – *I*.: inconscio. – *P*.: inconsciente.

I. The adjective 'unconscious' is at times used to connote all those contents that are not present in the field of consciousness at a given moment; this is a 'descriptive', not a 'topographical', sense of the word, for no distinction is being made here between the respective contents of the preconscious and unconscious systems.

II. In its 'topographical' sense, the term 'unconscious' describes one of the systems defined by Freud in the context of his first theory of the psychical apparatus: this system comprises the repressed contents which have been denied access to the preconscious-conscious* system by the operation of repression* (primal repression* plus repression proper or 'after-pressure').

The essential characteristics of the unconscious as a system (*Ucs.*) may be enumerated as follows:

a. Its 'contents' are 'representatives'* of the instincts.

b. These contents are governed by the mechanisms specific to the primary process, especially by condensation* and displacement*.

c. Strongly cathected by instinctual energy, they seek to re-enter consciousness and resume activity (the return of the repressed*), but they can only gain access to the system *Pcs.-Cs.* in compromise-formations* after having undergone the distortions of the censorship*.

d. It is more especially childhood wishes that become fixated* in the unconscious.

The abbreviation *Ucs.* (German *Ubw.* for *Unbewusst*) designates the unconscious in its substantival form as a system; *ucs.* (*ubw.*) is the shortened form of the adjectival 'unconscious' (*unbewusst*) wherever it is applied in the strict sense to qualify the contents of this system.

III. Within the framework of the second Freudian topography the term 'unconscious' is used above all in its adjectival form; indeed, no single agency can now hold a monopoly on its application, since not only the id but also parts of the ego and super-ego are described as unconscious. But it should be noted:

a. That the characteristics attributed to the system *Ucs.* in the first topography fall *grosso modo* to the id in the second.

b. That the difference between preconscious and unconscious, even though no longer based on a distinction *between* systems, nevertheless survives *within* systems, since the ego and super-ego are partly preconscious and partly unconscious.

If Freud's discovery had to be summed up in a single word, that word would without doubt have to be 'unconscious'. Consequently, given the limitations of the present work, we do not intend here to trace this discovery from its pre-

474

Freudian origins through its genesis and successive refinements in Freud. We shall instead restrict ourselves to underlining, in the interests of clarity, a few essential aspects which have often become obscure as a result of the term's wide currency.

I. The Freudian unconscious is primarily–and indissolubly–a topographical* and dynamic* notion formed on the basis of the experience of treatment. This experience showed that the psyche cannot be reduced to the conscious domain and that certain 'contents' only become accessible to consciousness once resistances have been overcome; it revealed that mental life is 'full of active yet unconscious ideas' and that 'symptoms proceed from such ideas' (1); and it led to the postulation of the existence of 'separate psychical groups', and more generally to the recognition of the unconscious as a particular 'psychical locality' that must be pictured not as a second consciousness but as a system with its own contents, mechanisms and–perhaps–a specific 'energy'.

II. What are these *contents*?

a. In his article on 'The Unconscious' (1915*e*), Freud calls them 'instinctual representatives'*. The fact is that the instinct, lying as it does on the border between somatic and mental, precedes the opposition between conscious and unconscious. In the first place, it can never become an object of consciousness and, secondly, it is only present in the unconscious through its representatives (chiefly the 'ideational representative'*). We may add that one of Freud's very first theoretical models defines the psychical apparatus as a succession of inscriptions (*Niederschriften*) of signs (2)–a notion that is taken up and discussed in his later writings. The unconscious ideas are organised into phantasies or imaginary scenarios to which the instinct becomes fixated and which may be conceived of as true *mises en scène* of desire* (see 'Phantasy').

b. Most Freudian texts prior to the second topography assimilate the unconscious and the repressed. This assimilation is not made without reservations, however: on more than one occasion Freud sets aside a place for contents not acquired by the individual himself–phylogenetic contents which are held to constitute the 'nucleus of the unconscious' (3*a*).

This idea finds a finished form in the notion of primal phantasies*, understood as pre-individual schemata that inform the subject's infantile sexual experiences (α).

c. Another traditionally recognised equation is that between the unconscious and the *infantile* in us, but here too a rider is needed. Not all infantile experiences are destined to become identical with the subject's unconscious life just because they are lived through naturally in the mode described by phenomenology as unreflective consciousness. For Freud, the first split between the unconscious and the system *Pcs.-Cs.* comes about through the action of infantile *repression*. The Freudian unconscious is *constituted*–even if the first stage of repression (primal repression) may be considered mythical; it is not an undifferentiated form of experience.

III. It is well known that dreams provided Freud with his 'royal road' to the unconscious. The mechanisms which Freud showed to be at work in dreams (*The Interpretation of Dreams* [1900a]) and which constitute the *primary process** –namely, displacement, condensation and symbolism*–are again encountered in other formations of the unconscious (parapraxes, etc.), which are equivalent

475

to symptoms by virtue of their structure of compromise and their function of 'wish-fulfilment'*.

Seeking to define the unconscious as a system, Freud lists its specific characteristics as follows (3b): primary process (mobility of cathexes typical of free energy*); absence of negation, of doubt, of degrees of certitude; indifference to reality and exclusive subordination to the principle of pleasure and unpleasure (whose aim is the restitution, by the shortest available route, of perceptual identity*).

IV. Finally, Freud sought to anchor the specific cohesion of the system Ucs. and its fundamental distinction from the system Pcs. by introducing the economic notion of a 'cathectic energy'* peculiar to each system. The unconscious energy is supposed to apply to ideas that it cathects or decathects, while the transposition of an element from one system to another is effected by a withdrawal of cathexis on the part of the first and a recathexis on the part of the second system.

But this unconscious energy – and herein lies a difficulty of the Freudian view – appears at times as a force attracting the ideas and resisting their coming to consciousness (this situation obtains in the theory of repression, where the attraction exerted by the elements already repressed works hand in hand with repression by the higher system) (4); at other times, however, the unconscious appears instead as a force trying to make its 'derivatives'* emerge into consciousness – a force only contained thanks to the vigilance of the censorship (3c).

V. Topographical considerations must not blind us to that *dynamic* force of the unconscious so often stressed by Freud: on the contrary, topographical distinctions should be seen as the means of accounting for the conflict, for repetition and for resistances.

*　　*　　*

As we know, from 1920 onwards the Freudian theory of the psychical apparatus is subjected to a thoroughgoing revision: new topographical distinctions are introduced that no longer coincide with those between unconscious, preconscious and conscious. In fact, although the chief properties of the system Ucs. reappear in the agency of the id, the other agencies of ego and super-ego also have an unconscious origin and an unconscious portion ascribed to them (see 'Id', 'Ego', 'Super-Ego', 'Topography').

(α) Although Freud himself never connected primal phantasies (*Urphantasien*) with the hypothesis of primal repression (*Urverdrängung*), it is impossible to avoid noticing that they fulfil almost identical functions relative to the ultimate origin of the unconscious.

(1) FREUD, S. 'A Note on the Unconscious in Psycho-Analysis' (1912g), G.W., VIII, 433; S.E., XII, 262.

(2) Cf. FREUD, S., letter to Fliess dated December 6, 1896, Anf., 185–86; S.E., I, 233.

(3) Cf. FREUD, S. 'The Unconscious' (1915e): a) G.W., X, 294; S.E., XIV, 195. b) G.W., X, 285–88; S.E., XIV, 186–89. c) G.W., X, 280; S.E., XIV, 181.

(4) Cf. FREUD, S. 'Repression' (1915d), G.W., X, 250–51; S.E., XIV, 148.

Undoing (what has been done)

D.: Ungeschehenmachen.–*Es.*: anulación retroactiva.–*Fr.*: annulation rétroactive.–
I.: rendere non accaduto *or* annullamento retroattivo.–*P.*: anulação retroativa.

Psychological mechanism whereby the subject makes an attempt to cause past thoughts, words, gestures or actions not to have occurred; to this end he makes use of thought or behaviour having the opposite meaning.

We are concerned here with a compulsion of 'magical' aspect which is especially characteristic of obsessional neurosis.

Freud gives a cursory description of 'undoing' in the case-history of the 'Rat Man' (1909*d*), where he analyses 'compulsive acts […], in two successive stages, of which the second neutralises the first'. The 'true significance' of such acts 'lies in their being a representation of a conflict between two opposing impulses of approximately equal strength: and hitherto I have invariably found that this opposition has been one between love and hate' (1*a*).

In *Inhibitions, Symptoms and Anxiety* (1926*d*) Freud again spotlights this process, now giving it the name of '*Ungeschehenmachen*': to make null and void. He looks upon it, along with isolation*, as the typical form of defence in obsessional neurosis, and he describes it as a magical procedure. He shows in particular how it is at work in the rituals of obsessional patients (2*a*).

Anna Freud lists undoing in her inventory of the ego's defence mechanisms (3), and it is generally so categorised in the psycho-analytic literature (4*a*).

It should be pointed out that the mechanism in question takes various forms. Sometimes an act is 'undone' by an opposite one (as when the Rat Man replaces a stone in the middle of the road after having earlier moved it to the side lest the carriage of his lady friend should run into it). At other times the same act is repeated but the meaning attached to it–whether conscious or unconscious–is the opposite one. Or again, the act of undoing may be contaminated by the act it is supposed to annul. These last two modes of undoing are illustrated by an example given by Fenichel (4*b*): a subject reproaches himself for having wasted money by buying a newspaper; he would like to undo his purchase by asking for his money back, but he dare not do so; he feels that to buy another paper would relieve him, but by this time the newsstand has closed, so finally he takes out a coin to the value of the paper and throws it to the ground. Freud refers to such sequences in terms of 'diphasic' symptoms: 'An action which carries out a certain injunction is immediately succeeded by another action which stops or undoes the first one even if it does not go quite so far as to carry out its opposite' (2*b*).

The classification of undoing among the ego's defence mechanisms also raises the question whether the 'second stage' involved is to be treated merely as a product of the defence. The variety of clinical instances of undoing rules out such a simple answer. Indeed instinctual motives are generally in evidence at both stages, particularly in the shape of the ambivalence* between love and hate; in some cases, in fact, it is the second stage that best displays the triumph of the instinct. In Fenichel's example the subject's entire behaviour indubitably constitutes a symptomatic whole.

477

Urethral Erotism (or Urinary Erotism)

We may further note in this connection that Freud–at a time when emphasis has not yet been laid upon the ego's defence mechanisms–appears to limit the operation of defence here to a secondary rationalisation* serving to mask the set of factors actually in play (1*b*).

Finally, one might distinguish two approaches here–although they are admittedly only distinct as two levels of interpretation, or as two levels of the psychical conflict. The first puts the accent on the conflict between instincts, where, in the last analysis, we rediscover the ambivalence between love and hate. The second view locates the conflict between the instincts and the ego–the ego being able to enlist the support of an instinct opposed to the one against which it is protecting itself.

*　　*　　*

It may be asked whether the mechanism of undoing ought not to be compared to a very common form of *normal* behaviour: we withdraw statements, make up for injuries, rehabilitate convicted criminals; we attenuate the import of a thought, word or action by a negation, sometimes even in an anticipatory way (e.g. 'Don't go thinking that . . .'), and so on.

Note, however, that in all these cases it is a matter of limiting or negating the meaning, force or consequences of an act. Undoing in the pathological sense is directed at the act's very reality, and the aim is to suppress it absolutely, as though time were reversible.

No doubt this might seem a fine distinction: surely the subject proceeds by bringing opposite *meanings* into play even when he is seeking to annul his act itself? Clinical experience shows, however, that the obsessional patient is not content with withdrawals of cathexis* or with anticathexes*: his goal is the impossible one of undoing the past event (*Geschehen*) as such.

(1) FREUD, S. 'Notes upon a Case of Obsessional Neurosis' (1909*d*): a) G.W., VII, 414; S.E., X, 192. b) Cf. G.W., VII, 414; S.E., X, 192.

(2) FREUD, S.: a) Cf. G.W., XIV, 149–50; S.E., XX, 119–20. b) G.W., XIV, 142; S.E., XX, 113.

(3) Cf. FREUD, A. *The Ego and the Mechanisms of Defence* (London: Hogarth Press, 1937; New York: I.U.P., 1946), 36.

(4) Cf., for example, FENICHEL, O. *The Psychoanalytic Theory of Neurosis* (New York: Norton, 1945): a) 153–55. b) 154.

Urethral Erotism (or Urinary Erotism)

= *D*.: Urethralerotik *or* Harnerotik.–*Es*.: erotismo uretral *or* urinario.–
Fr.: érotisme urétral *or* urinaire.–*I*.: erotismo uretrale.– *P*.: erotismo uretral *or* urinário.

Mode of libidinal satisfaction associated with micturition.

The pleasure derived from the function of urination and its erotic meaning were first brought out by Freud in the *Three Essays on the Theory of Sexuality*

(1905*d*), and (in a manner closer to actual experience) in the case-history of 'Dora' (1905*e* [1901]). In the first place Freud interprets infantile enuresis as equivalent to masturbation (1). Secondly, he points out the symbolic links that can exist between micturition and fire–links which he later elaborated on in 'The Acquisition and Control of Fire' (1932*a*).

A third contribution of Freud's is to suggest the existence of a relationship between certain character-traits and urethral erotism. Thus he writes at the end of the article on 'Character and Anal Erotism' (1908*b*): 'We ought in general to consider whether other character-complexes, too, do not exhibit a connection with the excitations of particular erotogenic zones. At present I only know of the intense "burning" ambition of people who earlier suffered from enuresis' (2). Following the same train of thought, Karl Abraham draws attention to the childhood phantasies of omnipotence that may accompany the act of urinating –the feeling of 'possessing great and even unlimited power to create or destroy every object' (3).

Melanie Klein has stressed the importance of such phantasies, particularly those of aggression and destruction by urine. She points up the role, 'hitherto little recognised, of urethral sadism in the development of the child', and adds: 'In analysing both grown-up patients and children I have constantly come across phantasies in which urine was imagined as a burning, dissolving and corrupting liquid and as a secret and insidious poison. These urethral-sadistic phantasies have no small share in giving the penis the unconscious significance of an instrument of cruelty and in bringing about disturbances of sexual potency in the male' (4).

It is also worth pointing out that several authors (Fenichel is one) have distinguished between various modes of pleasure associated with the urinary function: 'passively letting it flow', 'holding back', etc.

*   *   *

It should be noted that while Freud speaks of urinary *erotism*, and other authors (starting with Sadger: *Über Urethralerotik*, 1910) of urethral *erotism*, no urethral *stage* has been evoked–not even by those who, with Melanie Klein, assign an important part to urethral sadism.

Notice, in this connection, that Freud situates urethral erotism more especially in the 'second phase of infantile masturbation' (around the fourth year). 'The symptoms of these sexual manifestations are scanty; they are mostly displayed on behalf of the still undeveloped sexual apparatus by the *urinary* apparatus, which thus acts, as it were, as the former's trustee. Most of the so-called bladder disorders of this period are sexual disturbances: nocturnal enuresis [...] corresponds to a nocturnal emission' (5). It would seem that this period is the same as what Freud later called the phallic phase*. The relations between urethral erotism and phallic erotism are therefore too closely knit for a specifically urethral phase to be marked off.

Freud noted the different relations holding between the two functions in the adult on the one hand and the child on the other. According to an infantile belief, 'babies are made by the man urinating into the woman's body. But the adult knows that in reality the acts are incompatible–as incompatible as fire and water' (6).

Wild Psycho-Analysis

(1) Cf. FREUD, S. 'Fragment of an Analysis of a Case of Hysteria' (1905e [1901]), G.W., V, 236–37; S.E., VII, 74.

(2) FREUD, S., G.W., VIII, 209; S.E., IX, 175.

(3) ABRAHAM, K. 'The Narcissistic Evaluation of Excretory Processes in Dreams and Neurosis' (1920), in *Selected Papers* (London: Hogarth, 1927; New York: Basic Books, 1953), 322.

(4) KLEIN, M. *The Psycho-Analysis of Childen* (London: Hogarth, 1932), 186.

(5) FREUD, S. *Three Essays on the Theory of Sexuality* (1905d), G.W., V, 90; S.E., VII, 190.

(6) FREUD, S. 'The Acquisition and Control of Fire' (1932a), G.W., XVI, 9; S.E., XXII, 192.

W

Wild Psycho-Analysis

= *D*.: wilde Psychoanalyse. – *Es*.: psicoanálisis silvestre. – *Fr*.: psychanalyse sauvage. – *I*.: psicoanalisi selvaggia. – *P*.: psicanálise selvagem *or* inculta.

Broadly understood, this expression refers to the procedure of amateur or inexperienced 'analysts' who attempt to interpret symptoms, dreams, utterances, actions, etc., on the basis of psycho-analytic notions which they have as often as not misunderstood. In a more technical sense, an interpretation is deemed 'wild' if a specific analytic situation is misapprehended in its current dynamics and its particularity – and especially if the repressed content is simply imparted to the patient with no heed paid to the resistances* and to the transference*.

In the article which Freud devoted to ' "Wild" Psycho-Analysis' (1910*k*), he defined it first of all in terms of ignorance. The doctor whose intervention he criticises here has committed errors both *scientific* (regarding the nature of sexuality, repression, anxiety) and *technical*: 'Attempts to "rush" [the patient] at first consultation, by brusquely telling him the secrets which have been discovered by the physician, are technically objectionable' (1*a*). Thus anyone who 'knows a few of the findings of psycho-analysis' but has not undergone the required theoretical and technical training (α) can be said to be a practitioner of wild analysis.

Freud's criticism does not halt there, however – it extends to cases where the diagnosis made is the correct one, and the interpretation of the unconscious content exact: 'It is a long superseded idea [...] that the patient suffers from a sort of ignorance, and that if one removes this ignorance by giving him information (about the causal connection of his illness with his life, about his experiences in childhood, and so on) he is bound to recover. The pathological factor is not his ignorance in itself, but the root of this ignorance in his *inner resistances*;

480

it was they that first called this ignorance into being, and they still maintain it now. [...] informing the patient of his unconscious regularly results in an intensification of the conflict in him and an exacerbation of his troubles' (1b). For this reason such revelations must not be made until the transference is well established and the repressed contents have come close to consciousness. Otherwise, they give rise to an anxiety-situation that is out of the analyst's control. In this sense one might retrospectively describe psycho-analysis at its beginnings, when as Freud often stressed it was still unclearly marked off from hypnotic and cathartic* techniques, as 'wild analysis'.

It would be presumptuous, however, to make wild analysis the prerogative of unqualified psychotherapists and of an era now passed for psycho-analysis itself: such claims are merely expressions of the desire to be immune from this type of error oneself. Indeed, what Freud castigates in wild analysis is less ignorance than a certain attitude adopted by analysts who justify their power by appealing to their 'superior knowledge'. In an article where Freud raises the question of wild analysis without naming it specifically, he quotes Hamlet: '. . . do you think I am easier to be played on than a pipe?' (2). Seen in this light, analysis of defences or of the transference may obviously be every bit as *wild* as analysis of unconscious contents.

Ferenczi defined wild analysis as a kind of 'compulsive analysing' which may appear as easily within the analytic situation as outside it; he contrasts it with the *elasticity* that every analysis must have if it is not to be treated as structured according to a preordained plan (3). Glover notes that the analyst who jumps on a slip or isolates a dream or a dream-fragment from its context is merely 'seeking to enjoy a gossamer omnipotence' (4).

Pursuing these ideas a little further, one might describe wild analysis, be it of the 'expert' or the ignorant variety, as a resistance of the analyst to the particular analysis in which he is involved—a resistance that incites him to misunderstand his patient's statements and to impose ready-made interpretations.

(α) The year this article was published–1910–was also the date of the foundation of the International Psycho-Analytical Association.

(1) FREUD, S.: a) G.W., VIII, 124; S.E., XI, 226. b) G.W., VIII, 123; S.E., XI, 225.

(2) FREUD, S. 'On Psychotherapy' (1905a), G.W., V, 19; S.E., VII, 262.

(3) FERENCZI, S. 'The Elasticity of Psycho-Analytic Technique' (1928), in *Final Contributions*, 98–99.

(4) GLOVER, E. *The Technique of Psycho-Analysis* (London: Baillière, Tindall & Cox, 1955; New York: I.U.P., 1955), 8.

Wish (Desire)

= *D*.: Wunsch (*sometimes* Begierde *or* Lust).–*Es*.: deseo.–*Fr*.: désir.–*I*.: desiderio.–*P*.: desejo.

One of the poles of the defensive conflict in Freud's dynamic perspective: unconscious wishes tend to be fulfilled through the restoration of signs which are bound to the earliest experiences of satisfaction; this restoration operates

according to the laws of the primary process. Psycho-analysis, taking dreams as its model, has shown how wishes, in the form of compromises, may be identified in symptoms.

Any general theory of man is bound to contain ideas too fundamental to be circumscribed; this is no doubt true of desire in the Freudian doctrine. We shall confine our remarks here to terminology.

I. It should be noted first of all that the word 'desire' does not have the same connotations as the German '*Wunsch*', which corresponds to 'wish'; German evokes the notion of desire by using '*Begierde*' or '*Lust*'. [*Translator's note:* French psycho-analysis uses '*désir*' for all these words, though its connotations are similar to those of its English cognate. I have rendered it by 'desire' wherever this seemed more appropriate than 'wish]'.

II. Freud's sense of '*Wunsch*' receives its clearest elucidation in the theory of dreams, where it is possible to distinguish it from a certain number of closely related concepts.

His most thorough definition refers to the experience of satisfaction (q.v.), after which the mnemic image of a particular perception 'remains associated [...] with the memory-trace of the excitation produced by the need. As a result of the link that has thus been established, next time this need arises a psychical impulse will at once emerge which will seek to re-cathect the mnemic image of the perception and to re-evoke the perception itself, that is to say, to re-establish the situation of the original satisfaction. An impulse of this kind is what we call a wish; the reappearance of the perception is the fulfilment of the wish' (1*a*). Such a definition invites the following comments:

a. Freud does not identify need with desire: need, which derives from a state of internal tension, achieves satisfaction (*Befriedigung*) through the specific action* which procures the adequate object (e.g. food). Wishes, on the other hand, are indissolubly bound to 'memory-traces', and they are fulfilled (*Erfüllung*) through the hallucinatory reproduction of the perceptions which have become the signs of this satisfaction (see 'Perceptual Identity/Thought-Identity'). This distinction is not always reflected so clearly in Freud's use of terms, however: the compound '*Wunschbefriedigung*' is met with in some texts.

b. The search for the object in the real world is entirely governed by this relationship with signs. It is the organisation of these signs which constitutes phantasy*–that correlate of desire.

c. The Freudian conception of desire refers above all to unconscious wishes, bound to indestructible infantile signs. It is notable, however, that Freud does not always use the word 'wish' in as strict a sense as that laid down in the definition quoted above: he talks of the wish to sleep, of preconscious wishes, and he even goes so far, on occasion, as to express the outcome of the conflict as a compromise between 'two opposing wishes, arising each from a different psychical system' (1*b*).

*   *   *

Jacques Lacan has attempted to re-orientate Freud's doctrine around the notion of desire, and to replace this notion in the forefront of analytic theory.

This perspective has led Lacan to distinguish desire from concepts with which it is often confused, such as need and demand. Need is directed towards a specific object and is satisfied by it. Demands are formulated and addressed to others; where they are still aimed at an object, this is not essential to them, since the articulated demand is essentially a demand for love.

Desire appears in the rift which separates need and demand; it cannot be reduced to need since, by definition, it is not a relation to a real object independent of the subject but a relation to phantasy; nor can it be reduced to demand, in that it seeks to impose itself without taking the language or the unconscious of the other into account, and insists upon absolute recognition from him.

(1) FREUD, S. *The Interpretation of Dreams* (1900*a*): a) G.W., II–III, 571; S.E., V, 565–66. b) G.W., II–III, 575; S.E., V, 569.

(2) Cf. LACAN, J. 'Les formations de l'inconscient', *comptes-rendus* of seminars, 1957–58, by PONTALIS, J.-B., in *Bulletin de Psychologie*, 1958, XI, 4/5; XII, 2/3; XII, 4.

Wish-Fulfilment

= *D*.: Wunscherfüllung.–*Es*.: realización de deseo.–*Fr*.: accomplissement de désir.– *I*.: appagamento di desiderio.–*P*.: realização de desejo.

A psychological formation in which the wish seems to the imagination to have been realised. The products of the unconscious–dreams, symptoms, and above all phantasies–are all wish-fulfilments wherein the wish is to be found expressed in a more or less disguised form.

This is not the place to set forth the psycho-analytic theory of dreams, but it will be recalled that the fundamental postulate of this theory, when it first became clear to Freud, was the earliest intimation of the discovery that he was on the point of making (α); this postulate is that *dreams are the fulfilments of wishes*. Freud's purpose in *The Interpretation of Dreams* (1900*a*) is to establish the universal applicability of this hypothesis and to demonstrate its validity in all those cases, such as anxiety-dreams and punishment-dreams, which appear on first inspection to constitute exceptions to the rule. Note that in *Beyond the Pleasure Principle* (1920*g*) the problem of the dream-repetition of the original accident in traumatic neurosis* was to lead Freud to question the dream's wish-fulfilling function and to assign it a more primitive role (1) (see 'Repetition Compulsion' and 'Binding').

Freud had no hesitation in recognising the analogy between dreams and symptoms: he refers to it as early as 1895 (2*a*), and after *The Interpretation of Dreams* he realised its full implications. Consider for instance the following remarks addressed to Fliess: 'My last generalisation has held good and seems inclined to grow to an unpredictable extent. It is not only dreams which are wish-fulfilments but hysterical attacks as well. This is true of hysterical symptoms but probably of every neurotic event too, for I recognised it long ago (β) of delusional insanity' (2b).

It will be noticed that Freud uses a substantival form to express the idea of dreams fulfilling wishes. The reader is liable, for example, to come across formulations where mention is made of *two wish-fulfilments which are to be found in the latent content of a particular dream*, etc. As a result the term 'wish-fulfilment' takes on an extra connotation, appearing as it does to designate not just a *function* of dreams but also an actual internal dream-*structure*. Used in this sense, 'wish-fulfilment' becomes virtually synonymous with 'phantasy'*.

It should be stressed in this connection that no product of the unconscious can strictly speaking be said to fulfil *one* wish, for each such product is the outcome of a conflict and a compromise*. 'A hysterical symptom develops only where the fulfilments of two opposing wishes, arising each from a different psychical system, are able to converge in a single expression' (3).

*   *   *

The English expression 'wishful thinking', as commonly used, bears some relation to the psycho-analytic conception of wish-fulfilment, but it would certainly be a mistake to equate the two. When we speak of wishful thinking, what is uppermost in our minds is the reality which the subject is misjudging – whether because he is overlooking the preconditions of his actually putting his wish into practice, or because his apprehension of reality is distorted, etc. To speak of wish-fulfilment, by contrast, is to stress the wish itself, and its phantasied actualisation; there is as a rule no possibility here of a misapprehension of reality, for reality is a dimension which is simply not in play (cf. dreams). Moreover, the term 'wishful thinking' tends rather to be used when there is some question of longings, projects or wishes to understand which we do not necessarily have to refer to the unconscious.

(α) Cf., for example, Freud's letter to Fliess dated June 12, 1900: 'Do you suppose that some day a marble tablet will be placed on the house, inscribed with these words: "In this House, on July 24th, 1895, the Secret of Dreams was Revealed by Dr. Sigm. Freud"?'

(β) Freud alludes here to an idea put forward in 'The Neuro-psychoses of Defence' (1894a).

(1) Cf. FREUD, S., G.W., XIII, 31 *ff.*; S.E., XVIII, 31 *ff.*

(2) FREUD, S.: a) Cf. *Anf.*, 419–20; S.E., I, 335–36. b) *Anf.*, 295–96; S.E., I, 278.

(3) FREUD, S. *The Interpretation of Dreams* (1900a), G.W., II–III, 575; S.E., V, 569.

Withdrawal of Cathexis (or Decathexis)

= *D.*: Entziehung (*or* Abziehung) der Besetzung; Unbesetztheit. –
Es.: retiro *or* ausencia de carga psíquica. – *Fr.*: désinvestissement. –
I.: sottrazione di carica; disinvestimento. –
P.: retraimento de carga psíquica; desinvestimento.

Cathexis* is said to be withdrawn from previously cathected ideas, groups of ideas, objects, agencies, etc.

Psycho-analysis postulates the withdrawal of cathexis as the economic sub-stratum of various psychical processes, and of repression* in particular. From the first, Freud had recognised that the detachment of the quota of affect* from the idea* was the decisive factor in repression. When he came to give a systematic account of this process he showed how the existence of 'after-pressure' implies that ideas formerly admitted into the preconscious-conscious system–and therefore cathected by it–must lose their charge of energy. The energy liberated in this way may possibly be the same as that used for investing a defensive formation (reaction-formation*) when it becomes the object of an anticathexis* (1).

Similarly, in narcissistic states, the cathexis of the ego increases in proportion to the withdrawal of cathexis from objects (2).

(1) Cf. FREUD, S. 'The Unconscious' (1915e), G.W., X, 279–80; S.E., XIV, 180–81.

(2) Cf. FREUD, S. 'On Narcissism: An Introduction' (1914c), passim.

Work of Mourning

= D.: Trauerarbeit.–Es.: trabajo del duelo.–Fr.: travail du deuil.–
I.: lavoro del lutto (or del cordoglio).–P.: trabalho or labor do luto.

Intrapsychic process, occurring after the loss of a loved object, whereby the subject gradually manages to detach himself from this object.

This now classical expression was introduced by Freud in 'Mourning and Melancholia' (1917e). The term itself is eloquent testimony to the fresh view which psycho-analysis afforded in our understanding of a psychical phenomenon treated traditionally as a gradual and apparently automatic attenuation of the suffering caused by the death of a loved one. For Freud, this end result is the terminal point of a whole internal process implying an activity on the part of the subject–an activity which may indeed turn out to be ineffectual, as is illustrated by clinical experience of pathological cases of mourning.

The concept of the work of mourning should be seen in its kinship with the more general one of *psychical working out**, understood as a necessity for the psychical apparatus to bind* traumatic impressions. As early as the *Studies on Hysteria* (1895d) Freud had noted the specific form taken by such working out in the case of mourning; referring to an hysterical woman whom he had observed, he writes: 'Shortly after her patient's death [...] there would begin in her a work of reproduction which once more brought up before her eyes the scenes of the illness and death. Every day she would go through each impression once more, would weep over it and console herself–at her leisure, one might say' (1).

The existence of a work of mourning is borne out, according to Freud, by the lack of interest in the outside world which sets in with the loss of the object: all the subject's energy seems to be monopolised by his pain and his memories, until at last 'the ego, confronted as it were with the question whether it shall share [the] fate [of the lost object], is persuaded by the sum of the narcissistic satisfactions it derives from being alive to sever its attachment to the object that has been abolished' (2a). Before this detachment can be brought about, so finally making new cathexes possible, a psychical task has to be carried out: 'Each single one of the memories and expectations in which the libido is bound to the object is brought up and hypercathected, and detachment of the libido is accomplished in respect of it' (2b). In this sense it has been said that the work of mourning consists in 'killing death' (3a).

Freud showed that there is a gradation between *normal mourning, pathological forms of mourning* (where the subject holds himself responsible for the death that has occurred, denies it, believes that he is influenced or possessed by the dead person, or that he is himself a victim of the illness that has caused the death, etc.) and, lastly, *melancholia*. Very schematically, we may say that, on Freud's view, in pathological mourning the conflict of ambivalence has come to the fore; with melancholia, a further step has been taken: the ego identifies with the lost object.

In Freud's wake, the psycho-analysts have sought to clarify the phenomenon of normal mourning on the basis of its pathological variants – primarily the depressive and melancholic ones, but also the maniacal; they have laid especial stress on the role of ambivalence* and on the function of aggressiveness towards the dead person in so far as this is thought to facilitate detachment from him.

These psychopathological data have been fruitfully brought into conjunction with the findings of cultural anthropology on mourning in certain primitive societies, and on the collective beliefs and rites which accompany it (3b, 4).

(1) FREUD, S., G.W., I, 229; S.E., II, 162.

(2) FREUD, S. 'Mourning and Melancholia' (1917e): a) G.W., X, 442–43; S.E., XIV, 255. b) G.W., X, 430; S.E., XIV, 245.

(3) LAGACHE, D. 'Le travail du deuil', R.F.P., 1938, X, 4: a) 695. b) Cf. 695.

(4) Cf. HERTZ, R. 'Contribution à une étude de la représentation collective de la mort', in *Mélanges de sociologie religieuse et de folklore* (Paris: Alcan, 1928).

Working-off Mechanisms

= *D*.: Abarbeitungsmechanismen. – *Es*.: mecanismos de deprendimiento. – *Fr*.: mécanismes de dégagement. – *I*.: meccanismi di disimpegno. – *P*.: mecanismos de desimpedimento.

Notion introduced by Edward Bibring (1943) and taken up later by Daniel Lagache (1956), in his development of the psycho-analytic theory of the ego, to account for the resolution of defensive conflict, especially in the cure. Lagache contrasts working-off mechanisms with defence mechanisms: whereas the latter have as their only aim the urgent reduction of internal tensions, in conformity with the pleasure-pain principle, the former tend towards the realisation of possibilities, even if the price paid for this is an increase in tension. This contrast is based on the fact that the defence mechanisms (or defensive compulsions) are automatic

and unconscious, that they remain under the domination of the primary processes*
and that they tend towards perceptual identity*. The working-off mechanisms,
on the other hand, obey the principle of thought-identity and gradually allow the
subject to free himself from repetition and from his alienating identifications.

It was Edward Bibring who proposed describing certain mechanisms of the
ego, which might appropriately be distinguished from the defence mechanisms,
as 'working-off' mechanisms; this suggestion was related to his conception of
the repetition compulsion*. According to Bibring, the repetition of painful
experiences under the control of the ego may permit a progressive reduction
or assimilation of tensions: 'Working-off mechanisms of the ego are directed
neither toward discharge [abreaction] nor toward rendering the tension harmless [defence mechanisms]; their function is to dissolve the tension gradually
by changing the internal conditions which give rise to it' (1). Bibring further
describes different methods of working-off, such as detachment of libido (in
the work of mourning*), familiarisation with the anxiety-producing situation,
and so on.

Daniel Lagache, following up this line of thought, has drawn attention to
the unjustified extension of the concept of the defence mechanism, which is
invoked to account for automatic and unconscious compulsions which psycho-
analysis aims to destroy and, at the same time, in the case of 'successful defence',
for operations which themselves have the object of abolishing these compulsions.

Lagache inserts the notion of the working-off mechanism in the context of
an opposition between consciousness and the Ego: consciousness (the Ego-
subject) may identify itself with the Ego-object, alienating itself in it (narcissism);
alternatively, it may objectify the Ego and thus disengage itself from it
(working off) (2).

In his comprehensive exposition of the structure of the personality, Lagache
comes back to this concept and elaborates upon it. He enumerates the modes
of the working-off process in the context of the therapeutic experience: the
transition from the action of repetition to recollection by thought and word
[...]; the transition from identification, where the subject fails to distinguish
himself from his lived experience, to objectivation, where he stands back from
this experience; the transition from dissociation to integration; the detachment
from the imaginary object, brought to completion with the change of object;
that familiarisation with phobic situations which replaces the anxious expectation of the traumatic and phantasy-dominated situation; the substitution of
control for inhibition, of experience for obedience–in all these examples, the
defensive operation is only neutralised in so far as a working-off operation is
substituted for it' (3a).

There is thus a defensive activity of the Ego for dealing with the instincts
of the Id, to be distinguished from a working-off activity of the Ego for dealing
with its own defensive operations. If there is a justification for assigning such
discrepant functions to the Ego, it lies in the fact that they have in common a
capacity for selection and rejection.

(1) BIBRING, E. 'The Conception of the Repetition Compulsion', *Psychoanalytic Quarterly*,
1943, XII, 4, 502.

(2) Cf. LAGACHE, D. 'Fascination de la Conscience par le Moi', *La Psychanalyse*, 1957, III, 33–46.

(3) LAGACHE, D. 'La Psychanalyse et la structure de la personnalité', *La Psychanalyse*, 1958, VI: a) 34. b) Cf. 34.

Working-Through

= *D.*: Durcharbeitung *or* Durcharbeiten.–*Es.*: trabajo elaborativo.–
Fr.: perlaboration.–*I.*: elaborazione.–*P.*: perlaboração.

Process by means of which analysis implants an interpretation and overcomes the resistances to which it has given rise. Working-through is taken to be a sort of psychical work which allows the subject to accept certain repressed elements and to free himself from the grip of mechanisms of repetition. It is a constant factor in treatment, but it operates more especially during certain phases where progress seems to have come to a halt and where a resistance persists despite its having been interpreted.

From the technical point of view, by the same token, working-through is expedited by interpretations from the analyst which consist chiefly in showing how the meanings in question may be recognised in different contexts.

The idea that the analysand carries out certain work during the treatment is met with as early as the *Studies on Hysteria* (1895d); Freud even uses the words '*durcharbeiten*' and '*Durcharbeitung*' in this work, though not in any strictly defined sense (1).

They were assigned such a strict sense only in the article on 'Remembering, Repeating and Working-Through' (1914g), the title of which seems to suggest that working-through constitutes as fundamental an aspect of the treatment as do the recollection of repressed memories and the repetition that occurs in the transference*. In point of fact the article in question leaves us in considerable doubt as to what Freud means exactly by working-through. Some points, however, are made clear:

a. Working-through applies to resistances.

b. It generally follows the interpretation* of a resistance that has apparently had no effect; in this sense a period of relative stagnation may in fact conceal that eminently positive work which Freud looks upon as the principal factor in therapeutic efficacy.

c. Working-through permits the subject to pass from rejection or merely intellectual acceptance to a conviction based on lived experience (*Erleben*) of the repressed instincts which 'are feeding the resistance' (2a). In this sense, it is by 'becoming more conversant with this resistance' (2b) that the patient is enabled to carry out the working-through.

Freud makes scarcely any attempt to correlate the concept of working-through with those of remembering and repeating. All the same, it would seem that in his opinion working-through is a third term in which the other two are combined. And it is true that working-through is undoubtedly a repetition, albeit one modified by interpretation and–for this reason–liable to facilitate the subject's freeing himself from repetition mechanisms. It is no doubt because Freud has in mind its character as lived experience and its importance for resolution that he considers working-through to play a role analogous to that of abreaction* in hypnotic therapy.

The topographical distinction that Freud introduces in *Inhibitions, Symptoms and Anxiety* (1926*d*) between the id's resistance and the ego's allows him to get rid of a number of the ambiguities of the earlier text: repression is not removed once the resistance of the ego has been overcome, for 'the power of the compulsion to repeat–the attraction exerted by the unconscious prototypes upon the repressed instinctual process–has still to be overcome' (3). Here is the basis of the necessity for working-through. Seen in this light, working-through might be defined as that process which is liable to halt the repetitive insistence characteristic of unconscious formations by bringing these into relation with the subject's personality as a whole.

*   *   *

In the Freudian texts considered above, working-through is unquestionably treated as a form of work accomplished by the *analysand*. Those authors since Freud who have insisted on the necessity for working-through have also emphasised the part invariably played in this process by the *analyst*. Witness, for example, this passage from Melanie Klein: 'The necessity to work through is again and again proved in our day-to-day experience: for instance, we see that patients, who at some time have gained insight, repudiate this very insight in the following sessions and sometimes even seem to have forgotten that they had ever accepted it. It is only by drawing our conclusions from the material as it reappears in different contexts, and is interpreted accordingly, that we gradually help the patient to acquire insight in a more lasting way' (4).

(1) Cf. FREUD, S., G.W., I, 292, 295; S.E., II, 288, 291.
(2) FREUD, S.: a) G.W., X, 136; S.E., XII, 155. b) G.W., X, 135; S.E., XII, 155.
(3) FREUD, S., G.W., XIV, 192; S.E., XX, 159.
(4) KLEIN, M. *Narrative of a Child Analysis* (London: Hogarth Press, 1961; New York: Basic Books, 1961), 12.

Bibliography

Works by authors other than Freud are usually cited in full at the foot of each article. Some short titles and abbreviations have been used, however, and these are listed below.

Works by Freud are referred to throughout by their English title in the *Standard Edition*. Page-references are to both English and German texts (*Standard Edition* and *Gesammelte Werke* wherever possible). Also given in each case is the date of first publication and—when this is different—the date of composition. The letters attached to the publication dates refer to the corresponding entries in the complete bibliography of Freud's works in Volume XXIV of the *Standard Edition*. Listed here are all works by Freud mentioned or cited in this book. This list follows the *Standard Edition* bibliography, to which acknowledgement is therefore due.

Works by Freud Cited

Short Titles and Abbreviations Used

Anf. = *Aus den Anfängen der Psychoanalyse* (1950*a*).

C.P. = *Collected Papers* (5 vols.), London, 1924–50.

G.S. = *Gesammelte Schriften* (12 vols.), Vienna, 1924–34.

G.W. = *Gesammelte Werke* (18 vols.), Vols. I–XVII, London, 1940–52; Vol. XVIII, Frankfurt am Main, 1968.

Origins = *The Origins of Psycho-Analysis* (1950*a*).

S.E. = *The Standard Edition of the Complete Psychological Works of Sigmund Freud* (24 vols.), London, 1953–73.

(1888–89) Translation with Preface and Notes of H. Bernheim's *De la suggestion et de ses applications à la thérapeutique*, Paris, 1886, under the title *Die Suggestion und ihre Heilwirkung*, Vienna. (2nd edn., revised M. Kahane, Vienna, 1896.)
    TRANS.: Preface to the Translation of Bernheim's *Suggestion*, C.P., V, 11; S.E., I, 73.

(1891*b*) *Zur Auffassung der Aphasien*, Vienna.
    TRANS.: *On Aphasia*, London and New York, 1953.

(1892–93) 'Ein Fall von hypnotischer Heilung nebst Bemerkungen über die Enstehung hysterischer Symptome durch den "Gegenwillen"', G.S., 258; G.W., I, 3.
    TRANS.: 'A Case of Successful Treatment by Hypnotism', C.P., V, 33; S.E., I, 117.

(1893*a*) With Breuer, J., 'Über den psychischen Mechanismus hysterischer Phänomene: Vorläufige Mitteilung', G.S., I, 7; G.W., I, 81.
    TRANS.: 'On the Psychical Mechanism of Hysterical Phenomena: Preliminary Communication', C.P., I, 24; S.E., II, 3.

(1893*c*) 'Quelques considérations pour une étude comparative des paralysies motrices organiques et hystériques', G.S., I, 273; G.W., I, 39.
    TRANS.: 'Some Points for a Comparative Study of Organic and Hysterical Motor Paralyses', C.P., I, 42; S.E., I, 157.

(1893*h*) Vortrag 'Über den psychischen Mechanismus hysterischer Phänomene', *Wien. med. Pr.*, XXXIV, No. 4, 121 & 5, 165.
    TRANS.: Lecture 'On the Psychical Mechanism of Hysterical Phenomena', *I.J.P.*, XXXVII, 8; S.E., III, 27.

Bibliography

(1894*a*) 'Die Abwehr-Neuropsychosen', G.S., I, 290; G.W., I, 59.
TRANS.: 'The Neuro-Psychoses of Defence', C.P., I, 59; S.E., III, 43.

(1895*b* [1894]) 'Über die Berechtigung, von der Neurasthenie einen bestimmten Symptomenkomplex als "Angstneurose" abzutrennen', G.S., I, 306; G.W., I, 315.
TRANS.: 'On the Grounds for Detaching a Particular Syndrome from Neurasthenia under the Description "Anxiety Neurosis"', C.P., I, 76; S.E., I, 315.

(1895*c* [1894]) 'Obsessions et Phobies', G.S., I, 334; G.W., I, 345.
TRANS.: 'Obsessions and Phobias', C.P., I, 128; S.E., III, 71.

(1895*d*) With Breuer, J., *Studien über Hysterie*, Vienna; reprinted, Frankfurt am Main, 1970. (Omitting Breuer's contributions): G.S., I, 3; G.W., I, 77.
TRANS.: *Studies on Hysteria*, S.E., XX (including Breuer's contributions).

(1896*a*) 'L'hérédité et l'étiologie des névroses', G.S., I, 388; G.W., I, 407.
TRANS.: 'Heredity and the Aetiology of the Neuroses', C.P., I, 138; S.E., III, 143.

(1896*b*) 'Weitere Bemerkungen über die Abwehr-Neuropsychosen', G.S., I, 363; G.W., I, 379.
TRANS.: 'Further Remarks on the Neuro-Psychoses of Defence', C.P., I, 155; S.E., III, 159.

(1898*a*) 'Die Sexualität in der Ätiologie der Neurosen', G.S., I, 439; G.W., I, 491.
TRANS.: 'Sexuality in the Aetiology of the Neuroses', C.P., I, 220; S.E., III, 261.

(1899*a*) 'Über Deckerinnerungen', G.S., I, 465; G.W., I, 531.
TRANS.: 'Screen Memories', C.P., V, 47; S.E., III, 301.

(1900*a*) *Die Traumdeutung*, Vienna. G.S., II–III; G.W., II–III.
TRANS.: *The Interpretation of Dreams*, London and New York, 1955; S.E., IV–V.

(1901*a*) *Über den Traum*, Wiesbaden. G.S., III, 189; G.W., II–III, 643.
TRANS.: *On Dreams*, London and New York, 1951; S.E., V, 633.

(1901*b*) *Zur Psychopathologie des Alltagslebens*, Berlin, 1904. G.S., IV, 3; G.W., IV.
TRANS.: *The Psychopathology of Everyday Life*, London, 1966; S.E., VI.

(1905*a*) 'Über Psychotherapie', G.S., VI, 11; G.W., V, 13.
TRANS.: 'On Psychotherapy', C.P., I, 249; S.E., VII, 257.

(1905*c*) *Der Witz und seine Beziehung zum Unbewussten*, Vienna. G.S., IX, 5; G.W., VI.
TRANS.: *Jokes and their Relation to the Unconscious*, S.E., VIII.

(1905*d*) *Drei Abhandlungen zur Sexualtheorie*, Vienna. G.S., V, 3; G.W., V, 29.
TRANS.: *Three Essays on the Theory of Sexuality*, London, 1949; S.E., VII, 125.

(1905*e* [1901]) 'Bruchstück einer Hysterie-Analyse', G.S., VIII, 3; G.W., V, 163.
TRANS.: 'Fragment of an Analysis of a Case of Hysteria', C.P., III, 13; S.E., VII, 3.

(1906*a*) 'Meine Ansichten über die Rolle der Sexualität in der Ätiologie der Neurosen', G.S. V, 123; G.W., V, 149.
TRANS.: 'My Views on the Part Played by Sexuality in the Aetiology of the Neuroses', C.P., I, 272; S.E., VII, 271.

(1906*c*) 'Tatbestandsdiagnostik und Psychoanalyse', G.S., X, 197; G.W., VII, 3.
TRANS.: 'Psycho-Analysis and the Establishment of the Facts in Legal Proceedings', C.P., II, 13; S.E., IX, 99.

(1907*a*) *Der Wahn und die Träume in W. Jensens 'Gradiva'*, Vienna. G.S., IX, 273; G.W., VIII, 31.
TRANS.: *Delusions and Dreams in Jensen's 'Gradiva'*, S.E., IX, 3.

(1907*b*) 'Zwangshandlungen und Religionsübung', G.S., X, 210; G.W., VII, 129.
TRANS.: 'Obsessive Actions and Religious Practices', C.P., II, 25; S.E., IX, 116.

(1908*a*) 'Hysterische Phantasien und ihre Beziehung zur Bisexualität', G.S., V, 246; G.W., VII, 291.
TRANS.: 'Hysterical Phantasies and their Relation to Bisexuality', C.P., II, 51; S.E. IX, 157.

(1908*b*) 'Charakter und Analerotik', G.S., V, 261; G.W., VII, 203.
TRANS.: 'Character and Anal Erotism', C.P., II, 45; S.E., IX, 169.

(1908*c*) 'Über infantile Sexualtheorien', G.S., V, 168; G.W., VIII, 171.
TRANS.: 'On the Sexual Theories of Children', C.P., II, 59; S.E., IX, 207.

(1908d) 'Die "kulturelle" Sexualmoral und die moderne Nervosität', G.S., V, 143; G.W., VII, 143.
    TRANS.: ' "Civilized" Sexual Morality and Modern Nervous Illness', C.P., II, 76; S.E., IX, 179.

(1909a [1908]) 'Allgemeines über den hysterischen Anfall', G.S., V, 255; G.W., VII, 235.
    TRANS.: 'Some General Remarks on Hysterical Attacks', C.P., II, 100; S.E., IX, 229.

(1909b) 'Analyse der Phobie eines fünfjährigen Knaben', G.S., VIII, 129; G.W., VII, 235.
    TRANS.: 'Analysis of a Phobia in a Five-Year-Old Boy', C.P., III, 149; S.E., X, 3.

(1909c) 'Der Familienroman der Neurotiker', G.S., XII, 367; G.W., VII, 227.
    TRANS.: 'Family Romances', C.P., V, 74; S.E., IX, 237.

(1909d) 'Bemerkungen über einen Fall von Zwangsneurose', G.S., VIII, 269; G.W., VII, 381.
    TRANS.: 'Notes upon a Case of Obsessional Neurosis', C.P., III, 293; S.E., X, 155.

(1910a [1909]) *Über Psychoanalyse*, Vienna. G.S., IV, 349; G.W., VIII, 3.
    TRANS.: 'Five Lectures on Psycho-Analysis', *Amer. J. Psychol.*, XXI (1910), 181; S.E., XI, 3.

(1910c) *Eine Kindheitserinnerung des Leonardo da Vinci*, Vienna. G.S., IX, 371; G.W., VIII, 128.
    TRANS.: *Leonardo da Vinci and a Memory of his Childhood*, S.E., IX, 252.

(1910d) 'Die zukünftigen Chancen der psychoanalytischen Therapie', G.S., VI, 25; G.W., VIII, 104.
    TRANS.: 'The Future Prospects of Psycho-Analytic Therapy', C.P., II, 285; S.E., XI, 141.

(1910h) 'Über einen besonderen Typus der Objektwahl beim Manne', G.S., V, 186; G.W., VIII, 66.
    TRANS.: 'A Special Type of Choice of Object made by Men', C.P., IV, 192; S.E., XI, 165.

(1910i) 'Die psychogene Sehstörung in psychoanalytischer Auffassung', G.S., V, 310; G.W., VIII, 94.
    TRANS.: 'The Psycho-Analytic View of Psychogenic Disturbance of Vision', C.P., II, 105; S.E., XI, 211.

(1910k) 'Über "wilde" Psychoanalyse', G.S., VI, 37; G.W., VIII, 118.
    TRANS.: ' "Wild" Psycho-Analysis', C.P., II, 297; S.E., XI, 221.

(1911b) 'Formulierungen über die zwei Prinzipien des psychischen Geschehens', G.S., V, 409; G.W., VIII, 230.
    TRANS.: 'Formulations on the Two Principles of Mental Functioning', C.P., IV, 13; S.E., XII, 215.

(1911c) 'Psychoanalytische Bemerkungen über einen autobiographisch beschriebenen Fall von Paranoia (Dementia Paranoides)', G.S., VIII, 355; G.W., VIII, 240.
    TRANS.: 'Psycho-Analytic Notes on an Autobiographical Account of a Case of Paranoia (Dementia Paranoides)', C.P., III, 387; S.E., XII, 3.

(1911e) 'Die Handhabung der Traumdeutung in der Psychoanalyse', G.S., VI, 45; G.W., VIII, 350.
    TRANS.: 'The Handling of Dream-Interpretation in Psycho-Analysis', C.P., II, 305; S.E., XII, 91.

(1912b) 'Zur Dynamik der Übertragung', G.S., VI, 53; G.W., VIII, 364.
    TRANS.: 'The Dynamics of Transference', C.P., II, 312; S.E., XII, 99.

(1912c) 'Über neurotische Erkrankungstypen', G.S., V, 400; G.W., VIII, 322.
    TRANS.: 'Types of Onset of Neurosis', C.P., II, 113; S.E., XII, 229.

(1912d) 'Über die allgemeinste Erniedrigung des Liebeslebens', G.S., V, 198; G.W., VIII, 78.
    TRANS.: 'On the Universal Tendency to Debasement in the Sphere of Love', C.P., IV, 203; S.E., XI, 179.

(1912e) 'Ratschläge für den Arzt bei der psychoanalytischen Behandlung', G.S., VI, 64; G.W., VIII, 376.
    TRANS.: 'Recommendations to Physicians Practising Psycho-Analysis', C.P., II, 323; S.E., XII, 111.

Bibliography

(1912*f*) 'Zur Onanie-Diskussion', G.S., III, 324; G.W., VIII, 332.
TRANS.: 'Contributions to a Discussion on Masturbation', S.E., XII, 243.

(1912*g*) 'A Note on the Unconscious in Psycho-Analysis', C.P., IV, 22; S.E., XII, 257.
GERMAN TRANS. (by Hanns Sachs): 'Einige Bermerkungen über den Begriff des Unbewussten in der Psychoanalyse', G.S., V, 433; G.W., VIII, 430.

(1912–13) *Totem und Tabu*, Vienna, 1913. G.S., X, 3; G.W., IX.
TRANS.: *Totem and Taboo*, London, 1950; New York, 1952; S.E., XIII, 1.

(1913*i*) 'Die Disposition zur Zwangsneurose', G.S., V, 277; G.W., VIII, 442.
TRANS.: 'The Disposition to Obsessional Neurosis', C.P., II, 122; S.E., XII, 313.

(1914*c*) 'Zur Einführung des Narzissmus', G.S., VI, 155; G.W., X, 138.
TRANS.: 'On Narcissism: An Introduction', C.P., IV, 30; S.E., XIV, 69.

(1914*d*) 'Zur Geschichte der psychoanalytischen Bewegung', G.S., IV, 411; G.W., X, 44.
TRANS.: 'On the History of the Psycho-Analytic Movement', C.P., I, 287; S.E., XIV, 3.

(1914*g*) 'Weitere Ratschläge zur Technik der Psychoanalyse: II. Erinnern, Wiederholen und Durcharbeiten', G.S., VI, 109; G.W., X, 126.
TRANS.: 'Remembering, Repeating and Working-Through (Further Recommendations on the Technique of Psycho-Analysis, II)', C.P., II, 366; S.E., XII, 147.

(1915*b*) 'Zeitgemässes über Krieg und Tod', G.S., X, 315; G.W., X, 324.
TRANS.: 'Thoughts for the Times on War and Death', C.P., IV, 288; S.E., XIV, 275.

(1915*c*) 'Triebe und Triebschicksale', G.S., V, 443; G.W., X, 210.
TRANS.: 'Instincts and their Vicissitudes', C.P., IV, 60; S.E., XIV, 111.

(1915*d*) 'Die Verdrängung', G.S., V, 466; G.W., X, 248.
TRANS.: 'Repression', C.P., IV, 84; S.E., XIV, 143.

(1915*e*) 'Das Unbewusste', G.S., V, 480; G.W., X, 264.
TRANS.: 'The Unconscious', C.P., IV, 98; S.E., XIV, 161.

(1915*f*) 'Mitteilung eines der psychoanalytischen Theorie, widersprechenden Falles von Paranoia', G.S., V, 288; G.W., X, 234.
TRANS.: 'A Case of Paranoia Running Counter to the Psycho-Analytic Theory of the Disease', C.P., II, 150; S.E., XIV, 263.

(1916*d*) 'Einige Charaktertypen aus der psychoanalytischen Arbeit', G.S., X, 287; G.W., X, 364.
TRANS.: 'Some Character-Types Met with in Psycho-Analytic Work', C.P., IV, 318; S.E., XIV, 311.

(1916–17) *Vorlesungen zur Einführung in die Psychoanalyse*, Vienna. G.S., VII; G.W., XI.
TRANS.: *Introductory Lectures on Psycho-Analysis*, London, 1929; revised edn., New York, 1966; S.E., XV–XVI.

(1917*a*) 'Eine Schwierigkeit der Psychoanalyse', G.S., X, 347; G.W., XII, 3.
TRANS.: 'A Difficulty in the Path of Psycho-Analysis', C.P., IV, 347; S.E., XVII, 137.

(1917*c*) 'Über Triebumsetzungen insbesondere der Analerotik', G.S., V, 268; G.W., X, 402.
TRANS.: 'On the Transformations of Instinct, as Exemplified in Anal Erotism', C.P., II, 164; S.E., XVII, 127.

(1917*d* [1915]) 'Metapsychologische Ergänzung zur Traumlehre', G.S., V, 520; G.W., X, 412.
TRANS.: 'A Metapsychological Supplement to the Theory of Dreams', C.P., IV, 137; S.E., XIV, 219.

(1917*e* [1915]) 'Trauer und Melancholie', G.S., V, 535; G.W., X, 428.
TRANS.: 'Mourning and Melancholia', C.P., IV, 152; S.E., XIV, 239.

(1918*b* [1914]) 'Aus der Geschichte einer Infantile Neurose', G.S., VIII, 439; G.W., XII, 29.
TRANS.: 'From the History of an Infantile Neurosis', C.P., III, 473; S.E., XVII, 3.

(1919*a* [1918]) 'Wege der psychoanalytischen Therapie', G.S., VI, 136; G.W., XII, 183.
TRANS.: 'Lines of Advance in Psycho-Analytic Therapy', C.P., II, 392; S.E., XVII, 159.

(1919*d*) Einleitung zu *Zur Psychoanalyse der Kriegsneurosen*, Vienna. G.S., XI, 252; G.W., XII, 321.
TRANS.: Introduction to *Psycho-Analysis and the War Neuroses*, London and New York, 1921. C.P., V, 83; S.E., XVII, 207.

494

(1919e) ' "Ein Kind wird geschlagen" ', G.S., V, 344; G.W., XII, 197.
TRANS.: ' "A Child is Being Beaten" ', C.P., II, 172; S.E., XVII, 177.

(1919h) 'Das Unheimliche', G.S., X, 369; G.W., XII, 229.
TRANS.: 'The "Uncanny" ', C.P., IV, 368; S.E., XVII, 219.

(1920a) 'Über die Psychogenese eines Falles von weiblicher Homosexualität', G.S., V, 312; G.W., XII, 271.
TRANS.: 'The Psychogenesis of a Case of Female Homosexuality', C.P., II, 202; S.E., XVIII, 147.

(1920b) 'Zur Vorgeschichte der analytischen Technik', G.S., VI, 148; G.W., XII, 309.
TRANS.: 'A Note on the Prehistory of the Technique of Analysis', C.P., V, 101; S.E., XVIII, 263.

(1920g) Jenseits des Lustprinzips, Vienna. G.S., VI, 191; G.W., XIII, 3.
TRANS.: Beyond the Pleasure Principle, London, 1950; S.E., XVIII, 7.

(1921c) Massenpsychologie und Ich-Analyse, Vienna. G.S., VI, 261; G.W., XIII, 73.
TRANS.: Group Psychology and the Analysis of the Ego, London and New York, 1959; S.E., XVIII, 69.

(1922a) 'Traum und Telepathie', G.S., III, 78; G.W., XIII, 165.
TRANS.: 'Dreams and Telepathy', C.P., IV, 408; S.E., XVIII, 197.

(1922b) 'Über einige neurotische Mechanismen bei Eifersucht, Paranoia und Homosexualität', G.S., V, 387; G.W., XIII, 195.
TRANS.: 'Some Neurotic Mechanisms in Jealousy, Paranoia and Homosexuality', C.P., II, 232; S.E., XVIII, 223.

(1923a [1922]) ' "Psychoanalyse" und "Libido Theorie" ', G.S., XI, 201; G.W., XIII, 211.
TRANS.: 'Two Encyclopaedia Articles', C.P., V, 107; S.E., XVIII, 235.

(1923b) Das Ich und das Es, Vienna. G.S., VI, 353; G.W., XIII, 237.
TRANS.: The Ego and the Id, London, 1927; S.E., XIX, 3.

(1923c [1922]) 'Bemerkungen zur Theorie und Praxis der Traumdeutung', G.S., III, 305; G.W., XIII, 301.
TRANS.: 'Remarks on the Theory and Practice of Dream-Interpretation', C.P., V, 136; S.E., XIX, 109.

(1923d [1922]) 'Eine Teufelsneurose im siebzehnten Jahrhundert', G.S., X, 409; G.W., XIII, 317.
TRANS.: 'A Seventeenth Century Demonological Neurosis', C.P., IV, 436; S.E., XIX, 69.

(1923e) 'Die infantile Genitalorganisation', G.S., V, 232; G.W., XIII, 293.
TRANS.: 'The Infantile Genital Organization', C.P., II, 244; S.E., XIX, 141.

(1924b [1923]) 'Neurose und Psychose', G.S., V, 418; G.W., XIII, 387.
TRANS.: 'Neurosis and Psychosis', C.P., II, 250; S.E., XIX, 149.

(1924c) 'Das ökonomische Problem des Masochismus', G.S., V, 374; G.W., XIII, 371.
TRANS.: 'The Economic Problem of Masochism', C.P., II, 255; S.E., XIX, 157.

(1924d) 'Der Untergang des Ödipuskomplexes', G.S., V, 423; G.W., XIII, 395.
TRANS.: 'The Dissolution of the Oedipus Complex', C.P., II, 269; S.E., XIX, 173.

(1924e) 'Die Realitätsverlust bei Neurose und Psychose', G.S., VI, 409; G.W., XIII, 363.
TRANS.: 'The Loss of Reality in Neurosis and Psychosis', C.P., II, 277; S.E., XIX, 183.

(1925a [1924]) 'Notiz über den "Wunderblock" ', G.S., VI, 415; G.W., XIV, 3.
TRANS.: 'A Note upon the "Mystic Writing-Pad" ', C.P., V, 175; S.E., XIX, 227.

(1925d [1924]) Selbstdarstellung, Vienna, 1934. G.S., XI, 119; G.W., XIV, 33.
TRANS.: An Autobiographical Study, London, 1935 (Autobiography, New York, 1935); S.E., XX, 3.

(1925h) 'Die Verneinung', G.S., XI, 3; G.W., XIV, 11.
TRANS.: 'Negation', C.P., V, 181; S.E., XIX, 235.

(1925j) 'Einige psychische Folgen des anatomischen Geschlechtsunterschieds', G.S., XI, 8; G.W., XIV, 19.
TRANS.: 'Some Psychical Consequences of the Anatomical Distinction between the Sexes', C.P., V, 186; S.E., XIX, 243.

Bibliography

(1926*d* [1925]) *Hemmung, Symptom und Angst*, Vienna. G.S., XI, 23; G.W., XIV, 113.
TRANS.: *Inhibitions, Symptoms and Anxiety*, London, 1936 (*The Problem of Anxiety*, New York, 1936); S.E., XX, 77.

(1926*e*) *Die Frage der Laienanalyse*, Vienna. G.S., XI, 307; G.W., XIV, 209.
TRANS.: *The Question of Lay Analysis*, London, 1947; S.E., XX, 179.

(1926*f*) 'Psycho-Analysis: Freudian School', *Enclopædia Britannica*, 13th edn., New Vol. III, 253; S.E., XX, 261.
GERMAN TEXT: 'Psycho-Analysis', G.S., XII, 372; G.W., XIV, 299.

(1927*e*) 'Fetischismus', G.S., XI, 395; G.W., XIV, 311.
TRANS.: 'Fetishism', C.P., V, 198; S.E., XXI, 149.

(1930*a*) *Das Unbehagen in der Kultur*, Vienna. G.S., XII, 29; G.W., XIV, 421.
TRANS.: *Civilization and its Discontents*, London and New York, 1930; S.E., XXI, 59.

(1931*a*) 'Über libidinöse Typen', G.S., XII, 115; G.W., XIV, 509.
TRANS.: 'Libidinal Types', C.P., V, 247; S.E., XXI, 215.

(1931*b*) 'Über die weibliche Sexualität', G.S., XII, 120; G.W., XIV, 517.
TRANS.: 'Female Sexuality', C.P., V, 252; S.E., XXI, 223.

(1932*a*) 'Zur Gewinnung des Feuers', G.S., XII, 141; G.W., XVI, 3.
TRANS.: 'The Acquisition and Control of Fire', C.P., V, 288; S.E., XXII, 185.

(1933*a*) *Neue Folge der Vorlesungen zur Einführung in die Psychoanalyse*, Vienna. G.S., XII, 151; G.W., XV, 207.
TRANS.: *New Introductory Lectures on Psycho-Analysis*, London, 1933; New York, 1966; S.E. XXII, 3.

(1937*c*) 'Die endliche und die unendliche Analyse', G.W., XVI, 59.
TRANS.: 'Analysis Terminable and Interminable', C.P., V, 316; S.E., XXIII, 211.

(1937*d*) 'Konstruktionen in der Analyse', G.W., XVI, 43.
TRANS.: 'Constructions in Analysis', C.P., V, 358; S.E., XXIII, 257.

(1939*a* [1937–39]) *Der Mann Moses und die monotheistische Religion*, G.W., XVI, 103.
TRANS.: *Moses and Monotheism*, London and New York, 1939; S.E., XXIII, 3.

(1940*a* [1938]) *Abriss der Psychoanalyse*, G.W., XVII, 67.
TRANS.: *An Outline of Psycho-Analysis*, London and New York, 1949; S.E., XXIII, 141.

(1940*d* [1892]) With Breuer, J., 'Zur Theorie des hysterischen Anfalls', G.W., XVII, 9.
TRANS.: 'On the Theory of Hysterical Attacks', C.P., V, 27; S.E., I, 151.

(1940*e* [1938]) 'Die Ichspaltung im Abwehrvorgang', G.W., XVII, 59.
TRANS.: 'Splitting of the Ego in the Process of Defence', C.P., V, 372; S.E., XXIII, 273.

(1950*a* [1887–1902]) *Aus den Anfängen der Psychoanalyse*, London. Includes 'Entwurf einer Psychologie' (1895).
TRANS.: *The Origins of Psycho-Analysis*, London and New York, 1954. (Partly, including 'A Project for a Scientific Psychology', in S.E., I.)

Other authors

Ferenczi, S., *First Contributions* = *First Contributions to Psycho-Analysis* (London: Hogarth Press, 1952). Published in the U.S.A. as *Sex in Psycho-Analysis*. Original title: *Contributions to Psycho-Analysis*.

Ferenczi, S., *Further Contributions* = *Further Contributions to the Theory and Technique of Psycho-Analysis* (London: Hogarth Press, 1926; second edn., 1950). Published in the U.S.A. as *The Selected Papers of Sandor Ferenczi, M.D., II* (New York: Basic Books, 1952).

Ferenczi, S., *Final Contributions* = *Final Contributions to the Problems and Methods of Psycho-Analysis* (London: Hogarth Press, 1955; New York: Basic Books, 1955).

Jones, E., *Sigmund Freud* = *Sigmund Freud: Life and Work*, 3 vols. (London: Hogarth Press, 1953, 1955, 1957). Published in the U.S.A. as *The Life and Work of Sigmund Freud* (New York: Basic Books, 1953, 1955, 1957). Page-references are to the British edition.

Klein, M., *Contributions* = *Contributions to Psycho-Analysis* (London: Hogarth Press, 1950).

Klein *et al.*, *Developments* = Klein, M., Heimann, P., Isaacs, S., and Riviere, J., *Developments in Psycho-Analysis* (London: Hogarth Press, 1952).

Psa. Read. = Fliess, R. (ed.) *The Psycho-Analytic Reader* (London: Hogarth Press, 1950).

Journals

Bul. Psycho. = *Bulletin de Psychologie*, published by the Groupe d'Études de Psychologie, University of Paris.

I.J.P. = *International Journal of Psycho-Analysis.*

P.Q. = *Psycho-Analytic Quarterly.*

R.F.P. = *Revue française de psychanalyse.*

Index of German Terms

Compiled by Mme. E. Rosenblum

Abarbeitungsmechanismen, 486
Abfuhr, 121
Abkömmling des Unbewussten, 116
Abreagieren (das), 1
Abstinenz (Grundsatz der —,
  Prinzip der —), 2
Abwehr, 103
Abwehrhysterie, 107
Abwehrmechanismen, 109
Abwehr-Neuropsychose, 266
Acting out, 4
Affekt, 13
Affektbetrag, 374
Aggression, 17
Aggressionstrieb, 16
Aggressivität, 17
Agieren (das), 4
Aktion (spezifische —), 425
aktive Technik, 6
Aktivität–Passivität, 8
Alloerotismus, 25
alloplastisch, 48
ambivalent, prä-ambivalent, post-
  ambivalent, 29
Ambivalenz, 26
Amnesie (Infantile —), 212
anagogische Deutung, 34
Analyse (didaktische or Lehr-), 453
Analyse (direkte —), 117
Analyse (Kontroll-), 89
Analysenkontrolle, cf, 89
Angreifer (Identifizierung mit
  dem —), 208
Angst (automatische —), 48
Angstentwicklung, 184
Angsthysterie, 37
Angstneurose, 38
Angst (Real-), 379
Angstsignal, 422
Anlehnung, 29
Anlehnungsdepression, 32

Anlehnungstypus der Objektwahl,
  33
Aphanisis, 40
Apparat (psychischer or seelischer
  —), 358
Arbeit (Trauer-), 485
Arbeit (Traum-), 125
Assoziation, 41
Assoziation (Methode or Regel der
  freien —), 169
Aufmerksamkeit (gleichschwebende
  —), 43
Aufschubsperiode, 234
Autoerotismus, 45
automatische Angst, 48
autoplastisch–alloplastisch, 48

Bahnung, 157
Bearbeitung (sekundäre —), 412
Befriedigungserlebnis, 156
Begierde, 481
Bemächtigungstrieb, 217
Bemuttern (das), 253
Besetzung, 62
Besetzung (Entziehung or
  Abziehung der —), 484
Besetzung (Gegen-), 36
Besetzungsenergie, 62
Betreuen (Mütterliches —), 253
Bewusstheit, 84
Bewusstsein, 84
Bindung, 50
Bisexualität, 52
'böses' Objekt, 187

Charakterneurose, 67

Darstellbarkeit (Rücksicht auf —),
  389
Deckerinnerung, 410
Denkidentität, 305

Index of German Terms

Depression (Anlehnungs-), 32
depressive Einstellung, 114
Destruktionstrieb, 116
Deutung, 227
Deutung (anagogische —), 34
didaktische Analyse, 453
direkte Analyse, 117
Drang, 330
Durcharbeitung (or Durcharbeiten), 488
dynamisch, 126

Egoismus, 149
Einstellung (depressive —), 114
Einstellung (paranoide —), 298
Elektrakomplex, 152
Eltern-Imago (vereinigte —), 70
Energie (Besetzungs-), 62
Energie (freie — gebundene —), 171
Entmischung (der Triebe), 180
Entstellung, 124
Entziehung (or Abziehung) der Besetzung, 484
Ergänzungsreihe, 71
Erinnerung (Deck-), 410
Erinnerungsspur (or Erinnerungsrest), 247
Erinnerungssymbol, 253
erogen, 154
Erogeneität, 155
erogene Zone, 154
Eros, 153
Erotik (urethral —), 478
Erregungssumme, 435
Ersatzbildung, 434
Es, 197

Familienneurose, 159
Fehlleistung, 300
Fixierung, 162
Flucht in die Krankheit, 165
Frau (phallische —), 311
freie Assoziation (Methode or Regel der—), 169
freie Energie –gebundene Energie, 171
funktionales Phänomen, 176

Gegenbesetzung, 36
Gegensatzpaar, 295
Gegenübertragung, 92
gemischte Neurose, 252
genitale Liebe, 185
genitale Stufe (or Genitalorganisation), 186
gleichschwebende Aufmerksamkeit, 43
Grenzfall, 54
Grundregel, 178
Grundsatz or Prinzip der Abstinenz, 2
'gutes' Objekt, 'böses' Objekt, 187

Harnerotik, 478
Hilflosigkeit, 189
Hintergrund (Traum-), 124
Hospitalismus, 190
hypnoider Zustand, 192
Hypnoidhysterie, 192
Hysterie, 194
Hysterie (Abwehr-), 107
Hysterie (Angst-), 37
Hysterie (Hypnoid-), 192
Hysterie (Konversions-), 92
Hysterie (Retentions-), 397
Hysterie (traumatische —), 469
hysterogene Zone, 196

Ich, 130
ichgerecht, 151
Ichideal, 144
Ich (Ideal-), 201
Ichinteresse, 226
Ichlibido–Objektlibido, 150
Ich (Lust-, Real-), 320
Ichspaltung, 427
Ichtriebe, 146
Ichveränderung, 25
Idealich, 201
Ideal (Ich-), 144
Idealisierung, 202
Identifizierung, 205
Identifizierung mit dem Angreifer, 208
Identifizierung (primäre —), 336
Identifizierung (Projektions-), 356

Identität (Wahrnehmungs-, Denk-), 305
Imaginäre (das), 210
Imago, 211
Imago (vereinigte Eltern-), 70
infantile Amnesie, 212
Inhalt (latenter —), 235
Inhalt (manifester —), 243
Innervation, 213
Instanz, 15
Instinkt, 214
Intellektualisierung, 224
Interesse (*or* Ich-), 226
Introjektion, 229
Introversion, 231
Isolieren (das) (*or* Isolierung), 232

kannibalisch, 55
Kastrationskomplex, 56
kathartisches Heilverfahren (*or* kathartische Methode), 60
Klebrigkeit der Libido, 12
Kloakentheorie, 69
Komplex, 72
Komplex (Elektra-), 152
Komplex (Kastrations-), 56
Komplex (Minderwertigkeits-), 213
Komplex (Ödipus-), 282
Komplex (Vater-), 162
Kompromissbildung, 76
Konflikt (psychischer-), 359
Konstanzprinzip, 341
Konstruktion, 88
Kontrollanalyse, 89
Konversion, 90
Konversionshysterie, 92
Krankheitsgewinn (primärer und sekundärer —), 182

latenter Inhalt, 235
latente Traumgedanken, 235
Latenzperiode *or* Latenzzeit, 234
Lebenstriebe, 241
Lehranalyse, 453
Libido, 239
Libido (Ich-, Objekt-), 150
Libido (Klebrigkeit der —), 12
Libido (narzisstische —), 257

Libido (Organisation der —), 289
Libido (Plastizität der —), 319
Libidostauung, 94
Libidostufe, 236
Liebe (genitale —), 185
Lust, 481
Lust-ich–Real-Ich, 320
Lust (Organ-), 290
Lustprinzip, 322

Männlichkeit–Weiblichkeit, 243
manifester Inhalt, 243
Masochismus, 244
Masochismus (Sado-), 401
Material, 246
Mechanismen (Abarbeitungs-), 486
Mechanismen (Abwehr-), 109
Metapsychologie, 249
Methode (kathartische —), 60
Minderwertigkeitsgefühl, 416
Minderwertigkeitskomplex, 213
Mischung–Entmischung (der Triebe), 180
Misserfolgsneurose, 158
mütterliches Betreuen, 253
Mutter (phallische —), 311

Nachträglichkeit, nachträglich, 111
Narzissmus, 255
Narzissmus (primärer —, sekundärer —), 337
narzisstische Libido, 257
narzisstische Neurose, 258
narzisstische Objektwahl, 258
negative therapeutische Reaktion, 263
Neid (Penis-), 302
Neurasthenie, 265
Neuronenträgheit (Prinzip der —), 347
Neuropsychose (Abwehr-), 266
Neurose, 266
Neurose (Aktual-), 10
Neurose (Angst-), 38
Neurose (Charakter-), 67
Neurose (Familien-), 159
Neurose (gemischte —), 252
Neurose (Misserfolgs-), 158

Index of German Terms

Neurose (narzisstische —), 258
Neurosenwahl, 69
Neurose (phobische —), 319
Neurose (Schicksals-), 161
Neurose (traumatische —), 470
Neurose (Übertragungs-), 462
Neurose (Verlassenheits-), 270
Neurose (Zwangs-), 281
Neutralität, 271
Nirwanaprinzip, 272

Objekt, 273
Objektbeziehung, 277
Objekt ('gutes'—'böses' —), 187
Objektlibido, 150
Objekt (Partial-), 301
Objektspaltung, 430
Objekt (Übergangs-), 464
Objektwahl, 277
Objektwahl (Anlehnungstypus der —), 33
Objektwahl (narzisstische —), 258
Ödipuskomplex, 282
ökonomisch, 127
orale Stufe (or Phase), 287
oral-sadistische Stufe (or Phase), 288
Organisation der Libido, 289
Organisation (Genital-), 186
Organlust, 290

Paranoia, 296
paranoide Einstellung, 298
Paraphrenie, 299
Partialobjekt, 301
Partialtrieb, 74
Passivität, 8
Penisneid, 302
Periode (Aufschubs-), 234
Periode (Latenz-), 234
Perversion, 306
phallische Frau, 311
phallische Mutter, 311
phallische Stufe (or Phase), 309
Phallus, 312
Phantasie, 314
Phantasien (Ur-), 331
Phobische Neurose, 319

Plastizität der Libido, 319
post-ambivalent, 29
prä-ambivalent, 29
prägenital, 328
präödipal, 328
primäre Identifizierung, 336
primärer und sekundärer Krankheitsgewinn, 182
Primärvorgang, Sekundärvorgang, 339
Prinzip der Neuronenträgheit, 347
Prinzip (Konstanz-), 341
Prinzip (Lust-), 322
Prinzip (Nirwana-) 272
Projektion, 349
Projektionsidentifizierung, 356
psychische Realität, 363
psychische Repräsentanz (or psychischer Repräsentant), 364
psychischer Konflikt, 359
psychischer (or seelischer) Apparat, 358
psychische Verarbeitung (or Bearbeitung, or Ausarbeitung, or Aufarbeitung), 365
Psychoanalyse, 367
Psychoanalyse (wilde —), 480
Psychose, 369
Psychotherapie, 373

Rationalisierung, 375
Reaktionsbildung, 376
Realangst, 379
Real-Ich, 320
Realität (psychische —), 363
Realitätsprüfung, 382
Regression, 386
Reizschutz, 357
Repräsentanz or Repräsentant (Vorstellungs-), 203
Repräsentanz (psychische —), or Repräsentant (psychischer —), 364
Retentionshysterie, 397
Rückkehr des Verdrängten, 398
Rücksicht auf Darstellbarkeit, 389

Sach- or Dingvorstellung, 447

Sadismus-Masochismus, Sadomaso-
chismus, 401
sadistisch-anale Stufe (or Phase), 35
Schicksalsneurose, 161
Schizophrenie, 408
Schreck, 174
Schuldgefühl, 414
sekundäre Bearbeitung, 412
Sekundärvorgang, 339
Selbstanalyse, 413
Selbsterhaltungstriebe, 220
Sexualität, 418
Sexualität (Bi-), 52
Sexualtrieb, 417
somatisches Entgegenkommen, 423
Spaltung (Ich-), 427
Spaltung (Objekt-), 430
spezifische Aktion, 425
Spiegelstufe, 250
Stauung (Libido-), 94
Strafbedürfnis, 260
Stufe (genitale —), 186
Stufe (Libido-), 236
Stufe or Phase (orale —), 287
Stufe (orale-sadistische —), 288
Stufe (phallische —), 309
Stufe (sadistisch-anale —), 35
Stufe (Spiegel-), 250
Sublimierung, 431
Symbol (Erinnerungs-), 253
Symbolik, 442
Symbolische (das), 439
symbolische Wunscherfüllung, 441
Symptombildung, 446
System (see Instanz)

Tagesreste, 96
Tagtraum, 95
Technik (aktive —), 6
Thanatos, 447
Topik, topisch, 449
Trägheitsprinzip, 347
Trauerarbeit, 485
Trauma, 465
Traumarbeit, 125
traumatische Hysterie, 469
traumatische Neurose, 470
Traumgedanken (latente —), 235

Traumhintergrund, 124
Trauminhalt (latenter —), 235
Trauminhalt (manifester —), 243
Traum (Tag-), 95
Trieb, 214
Trieb (Aggressions-), 16
Trieb (Bemächtigungs-), 217
Trieb (Destruktions-), 116
Triebe (Entmischung der —), 180
Triebe (Ich-), 146
Triebe (Lebens-), 241
Triebe (Selbsterhaltungs-), 220
Triebkomponente, 222
Triebmischung – Triebentmischung,
180
Trieb (Objekt des —es), 273
Trieb (Partial-), 74
Triebquelle, 424
Triebregung, 222
Triebrepräsentanz (or Triebreprä-
sentant), 223
Trieb (Sexual-), 417
Trieb (Verkehrung eines —es ins
Gegenteil), 399
Triebziel, 21

Überbesetzung, 191
Überdeterminierung (or mehrfache
Determinierung), 292
Überdeutung, 293
Übergangsobjekt, 464
Über-Ich, 435
Übertragung, 455
Übertragung (Gegen-), 92
Übertragungsneurose, 462
Unbesetztheit, 484
Unbewusste (Abkömmling des —n),
116
Unbewusste (das), unbewusst, 474
Ungeschehenmachen (das), 477
Unterbewusste (das), Unterbewusst-
sein, 430
Unterdrückung, 438
Urethralerotik, 478
Urphantasien, 331
Urszene, 334
Urteilsverwerfung, 81
Urverdrängung, 333

Index of German Terms

Vaterkomplex, 162
Veränderung (Ich-), 25
Verarbeitung (psychische), (*or*
    Bearbeitung, *or* Ausarbeitung,
    or Aufarbeitung), 365
Verdichtung, 82
Verdrängte (Wiederkehr *or* Rück-
    kehr des —n), 398
Verdrängung, 390
Verdrängung (Ur-), 333
vereinigte Eltern, vereinigte Eltern-
    Imago, 70
Verführung (Verführungsszene,
    Verführungstheorie), 404
Verinnerlichung, 226
Verkehrung (eines Triebes) ins
    Gegenteil, 399
Verlassenheitsneurose, 270
Verleugnung, 118
Verneinung, 261
Versagung, 175
Verschiebung, 121
Verurteilung, 81
Verwerfung, 166
Verwerfung (Urteils-), 81, cf. 166
Vorbewusste (das), vorbewusst, 325
Vorstellung, 200
Vorstellung (Sach- *or* Ding-),
    (Wort-), 447
Vorstellungsrepräsentanz (*or*
    Vorstellungsrepräsentant), 203

Vorstellung (Ziel-), 373

Wahl (Neurosen-), 69
Wahl (Objekt-), 277
Wahrnehmungsidentität – Denk-
    identität, 305
Weiblichkeit, 243
Wendung gegen die eigene Person,
    473
Widerstand, 394
Wiederholungszwang, 78
Wiederkehr des Verdrängten, 398
wilde Psychoanalyse, 480
Wortvorstellung, 447
Wunsch, 481
Wunscherfüllung, 483
Wunscherfüllung (symbolische —),
    441
Wunschphantasie, cf. 317

Zärtlichkeit, 15
Zensur, 65
zielgehemmt, 24
Ziel (Trieb-), 21
Zielvorstellung, 373
Zone (erogene —), 154
Zone (hysterogene —), 196
Zwang, Zwangs-, 77
Zwangsneurose, 281
Zwang (Wiederholungs-), 78

Index of English Terms

Abandonment neurosis, 270
Abreaction, 1
Abstinence, rule of, 2
Acting out, 4
Action, specific, 425
Active technique, 6
Activity/passivity, 8
Actual neurosis, 10
Adhesiveness of the libido, 12
Affect, 13
   quota of, 374
Affection, 15
Agency, 15
Aggressive instinct, 16
Aggressiveness (aggression, aggressivity), 17
Aim of the instinct, 21
Aim-inhibited, 24
Allo-erotism, 25
Alloplastic, 48
Alteration of the ego, 25
Ambivalence, 26
Ambivalent, 29
Amnesia, infantile, 212
Anaclisis; anaclitic, 29
Anaclitic depression, 32
Anaclitic object-choice, 33
Anagogic interpretation, 34
Anal-sadistic stage, 35
Analysis
   control, 89
   direct, 117
   self-, 413
   supervised or supervisory, 89
   training, 453
Anticathexis, 36
Anxiety
   automatic, 48
   generation of, 184
   realistic, 379
   as signal; signal of, 422
Anxiety hysteria, 37
Anxiety neurosis, 38

Aphanisis, 40
Association, 41
   free, 169
Attachment, 29
   see also Anaclitic depression;
     Anaclitic type of object-choice
Attention, (evenly) suspended, 43
Auto-erotism, 45
Automatic anxiety, 48
Autoplastic/alloplastic, 48

'Bad' object, 187
Binding, 50
Bisexuality, 52
Borderline case, 54
Bound energy, 171

Cannibalistic, 55
Castration complex, 56
Cathartic method, 60
Cathectic energy, 62
Cathexis, 62
   anticathexis, 36
   countercathexis, 36
   decathexis, 484
   hypercathexis, 191
   withdrawal of, 484
Censorship, 65
Character neurosis, 67
Choice of neurosis, 69
Cloaca(1) theory, 69
Combined parent-figure, 70
Complemental series, 71
Complex, 72
   castration, 56
   Electra, 152
   father, 162
   inferiority, 213
   Oedipus, 282
Compliance, somatic, 423
Component instinct, 74
Compromise-formation, 76
Compulsion; compulsive, 77

Index of English Terms

Compulsion to repeat, 78
Condemnation, 81
Condensation, 82
Conflict, psychical, 359
Consciousness, 84
Considerations of representability, 389
Constancy, principle of, 341
Construction, 88
Content
  latent, 235
  manifest, 243
Control analysis, 89
Conversion, 90
Conversion hysteria, 91
Countercathexis, 36
Counter-transference, 92

Daily residue, 96
Damming up of libido, 94
Day-dream, 95
Day's residues, 96
Death instincts, 97
Decathexis, 484
Defence, 103
Defence hysteria, 107
Defence mechanisms, 109
Defence neuro-psychosis (or psychoneurosis), 266
Deferred action, 111
Defusion of instincts, 180
Denial, see Disavowal; Negation
Depression, anaclitic, 32
Depressive position, 114
Derivative of the unconscious, 116
Desire, 481
Destructive instinct, 116
Direct analysis, 117
Disavowal, 118
Discharge, 121
Displacement, 121
Distortion, 124
Dream screen, 124
Dream-thoughts, see Latent content
Dream-work, 125
Drive, see Instinct
Dynamic, 126

Economic, 127
Ego, 130
  alteration of, 25
  ideal, 201
  pleasure-, 320
  reality-, 320
  splitting of, 427
Ego-ideal, 144
Ego-instincts, 146
Ego-interest, 226
Egoism, 149
Ego-libido/object-libido, 150
Ego-syntonic, 151
Elaboration, secondary, 412
Electra complex, 152
Envy, penis, 302
Erogenicity, 155
Erogenous zone, 154
Eros, 153
Erotism
  allo-, 27
  auto-, 45
  urethral or urinary, 478
Erotogenic, 154
Erotogenic zone, 154
Erotogenicity, 155
Evenly suspended attention, 43
Excitation, sum of, 435
Experience of satisfaction, 156

Facilitation, 157
Failure neurosis, 158
Family neurosis, 159
Family romance, 160
Fantasy, see Phantasy
Fate neurosis, 161
Father complex, 162
Feeling(s) of guilt, 414
Feeling(s) of inferiority, 416
Femininity, 243
Fixation, 162
Flight into illness, 165
Foreclosure, 166
Free association, 169
Free energy/bound energy, 171
Fright, 174
Frustration, 175
Functional phenomenon, 176

Fundamental rule, 178
Fusion/defusion of instincts, 180

Gain from illness, 182
Generation of anxiety, 184
Genital love, 185
Genital stage or organisation, 186
'Good' object/'bad' object, 187
Guilt feeling(s), 414

Helplessness, 189
Hospitalism, 190
Hypercathexis, 191
Hypnoid hysteria, 192
Hypnoid state, 192
Hysteria, 194
    anxiety, 37
    conversion, 91
    defence, 107
    hypnoid, 192
    retention, 397
    traumatic, 469
Hysterogenic zone, 196

Id, 197
Idea, 200
    purposive, 373
Ideal ego, 201
Idealisation, 202
Ideational representative, 203
Identification, 205
    primary, 336
    projective, 356
Identification with the aggressor,
    208
Identity, perceptual or thought,
    305
Illness
    flight into, 165
    gain from, 182
Imaginary, 210
Imago, 211
Incorporation, 211
Inertia, principle of, 347
Infantile amnesia, 212
Inferiority complex, 213
Inferiority feeling(s), 416
Innervation, 213

Instinct, 214
    aggressive, 16
    component, 74
    death, 97
    destructive, 116
    ego-, 146
    fushion/defusion of, 180
    life, 241
    object of, 273
    partial, 74
    pressure of, 330
    reversal of, into the opposite,
        399
    sexual, 417
    source of, 424
Instinct to master (or for mastery),
    217
Instincts of self-preservation, 220
Instinctual aim, 21
Instinctual component, 222
Instinctual impulse, 222
Instinctual representative, 223
Instinctual source, 424
Intellectualisation, 224
Interest, 226
Internalisation, 226
Interpretation, 227
    anagogic, 34
    over-, 293
Introjection, 229
Introversion, 231
Isolation, 232

Judgement of condemnation, 81

Latency period, 234
Latent content, 235
Libidinal stage, 236
Libido, 239
    adhesiveness of, 12
    damming up of, 94
    ego-, 150
    narcissistic, 257
    object-, 150
    organisation of, 289
    plasticity of, 319
Life instincts, 241
Love, genital, 185

Index of English Terms

Manifest content, 243
Masculinity/femininity, 243
Masochism, 244
Mastery, instinct for, 217
Material, 246
Mechanisms of defence, 109
Memory, screen, 410
Memory-trace, 247
Mental, *see* Psychical
Metapsychology, 249
Mirror phase, 250
Mixed neurosis, 252
Mnemic symbol, 253
Mnemic trace, 247
Mother, phallic, 311
Mothering, 253
Mourning, work of, 485

Narcissism, 255
   primary and secondary, 337
Narcissistic libido, 257
Narcissistic neurosis, 258
Narcissistic object-choice, 258
Need for punishment, 260
Negation, 261
Negative therapeutic reaction, 263
Neurasthenia, 265
Neuronal inertia, principle of, 347
Neuro-psychosis, *see* Psychoneurosis
Neuro-psychosis of defence, 266
Neurosis, 266
   abandonment, 270
   actual, 10
   anxiety, 38
   character, 67
   choice of, 69
   failure, 158
   family, 159
   fate, 161
   mixed, 252
   narcissistic, 258
   obsessional, 281
   phobic, 319
   transference, 462
   traumatic, 470
Neurosis of abandonment, 270
Neutrality, 271
Nirvana principle, 272

Object, 273
   'good' and 'bad', 187
   part-, 301
   splitting of, 430
   transitional, 464
Object-choice, 277
   anaclitic, 33
   narcissistic, 258
Object-libido, 150
Object-relation(ship), 277
Obsessional neurosis, 281
Oedipus complex, 282
Opposites, pair of, 295
Oral stage, 287
Oral-sadistic stage, 288
Organisation, genital, 186
Organisation of the libido, 289
Organ-pleasure, 290
Over-determination, 292
Over-interpretation, 293

Pair of opposites, 295
Paranoia, 296
Paranoid position, 298
Paraphrenia, 299
Parapraxis, 300
Parent-figure, combined, 70
Partial instinct, 74
Part-object, 301
Passivity, 8
Penis envy, 302
Perceptual identity/thought-
   identity, 305
Perversion, 306
Phallic stage, 309
Phallic woman or mother, 311
Phallus, 312
Phantasies, primal, 331
Phantasy, 314
Phase, *see* Stage,
Phobic neurosis, 319
Plasticity of the libido, 319
Pleasure-ego/reality-ego, 320
Pleasure principle, 322
Poised attention, 43
Position
   depressive, 114
   paranoid, 298

Post-ambivalent, 29
Pre-ambivalent, 29
Preconscious, 325
Pregenital, 328
Preoedipal, 328
Presentation, 200
   thing- and word-, 447
Pressure of the instinct, 330
Primal phantasies, 331
Primal repression, 333
Primal scene, 334
Primary gain from illness, 182
Primary identification, 336
Primary narcissism, 337
Primary process, 339
Principle
   Nirvana, 272
   pleasure, 322
   reality, 379
Principle of constancy, 341
Principle of neuronal inertia, 347
Projection, 349
Projective identification, 356
Protective shield, 357
Psychical apparatus, 358
Psychical conflict, 359
Psychical reality, 363
Psychical representative, 364
Psychical trauma, 465
Psychical working out, 365
Psycho-analysis, 367
   wild, 480
Psychoneurosis, 369
Psychoneurosis of defence, 266
Psychosis, 369
Psychotherapy, 373
Punishment, need for, 260
Purposive idea, 373

Quota of affect, 374

Rationalisation, 375
Reaction-formation, 376
Realisation, symbolic, 441
Realistic anxiety, 379
Reality principle, 379
Reality, psychical, 363
Reality-ego, 320

Reality-testing, 382
Regression, 386
Reparation, 388
Repetition compulsion, 78
Representability, considerations of,
   389
Representation, 200
Representative
   ideational, 203
   instinctual, 223
   psychical, 364
Repressed, return of the, 398
Repression, 390
   primal, 333
Repudiation, 166
Resistance, 394
Retention hysteria, 397
Return of the repressed, 398
Reversal into the opposite, 399
Revision, secondary, 412
Rule, fundamental, 178
Rule of abstinence, 2
Rule of free association, 169

Sadism, 400
Sadism/masochism, 401
Sadistic-anal stage, 35
Sadistic-oral stage, 288
Sado-masochism, 401
Satisfaction, experience of, 156
Scene, primal, 334
Scene of seduction, 404
Schizophrenia, 408
Screen memory, 410
Secondary elaboration, 412
Secondary gain from illness, 182
Secondary narcissism, 337
Secondary process, 339
Secondary revision, 412
Seduction, 404
Self-analysis, 413
Self-preservation, instincts of, 220
Sense of guilt, 414
Sense of inferiority, 416
Sexual instinct, 417
Sexuality, 418
Shield against stimuli, 357
Signal of anxiety, 422

Index of English Terms

Somatic compliance, 423
Source of the instinct, 424
Specific action, 425
Splitting of the ego, 427
Splitting of the object, 430
Stage (or phase)
  anal-sadistic, 35
  genital, 186
  libidinal, 236
  mirror, 250
  oral, 287
  oral-sadistic, 288
  phallic, 309
Subconscious(ness), 430
Sublimation, 431
Substitute-formation, substitutive
  formation, 434
Sum of excitation, 435
Super-ego, 435
Suppression, 438
Suspended attention, 43
Symbolic, 439
Symbolic realisation, 441
Symbolism, 442
Symptom-formation, 446
System, *see* Agency

Technique, active, 6
Tenderness, 15
Thanatos, 447
Theory of seduction, 404
Therapeutic reaction, negative, 263
Thing-presentation/word-presenta-
  tion, 447

Thought-identity, 305
Topography; topographical, 449
Training analysis, 453
Transference, 455
  counter-, 92
Transference neurosis, 462
Transitional object, 464
Trauma, 465
Traumatic hysteria, 469
Traumatic neurosis, 470
Turning round upon the subject's
  own self, 473

Unconscious, 474
  derivative of the, 116
Undoing what has been done,
  477
Urethral erotism, 478
Urinary erotism, 478

Wild psycho-analysis, 480
Wish, 481
Wish-fulfilment, 483
Withdrawal of cathexis, 484
Word-presentation, 447
Work of mourning, 485
Working-off mechanisms, 486
Working out (or over), 365
Working-through, 488

Zone
  erotogenic, 154
  hysterogenic, 196